Hamid Sulaiman

FREEDOM
HOSPITAL

Translated by Francesca Barrie

Interlink Books

An imprint of Interlink Publishing Group, Inc.
Northampton, Massachusetts

First American edition published in 2018 by

INTERLINK BOOKS
An imprint of Interlink Publishing Group, Inc.
46 Crosby Street, Northampton, Massachusetts 01060
www.interlinkbooks.com

First published in France by Arte Editions et Editions ca et la in 2016

Published in the United Kingdom by Jonathan Cape, an imprint of Vintage in 2017.
Vintage is part of the Penguin Random House group of companies.

Library of Congress Cataloging-in-Publication Data available
ISBN 978-1-62371-995-1 • paperback
ISBN 978-1-62371-994-4 • hardback

Printed and bound in the United States of America

INSTITUT FRANÇAIS
ROYAUME-UNI

This book is supported by the Institut français (Royaume-Uni) as part of the Burgess programme

WINNER ENGLISH PEN AWARD

ENGLISH PEN

ARTS COUNCIL ENGLAND

Supported using public funding by
ARTS COUNCIL ENGLAND

This book has been selected to receive financial assistance from English PEN's "PEN Translates" programme, supported by Arts Council England. English PEN exists to promote literature and our understanding of it, to uphold writers' freedoms around the world, to campaign against the persecution and imprisonment of writers for stating their views, and to promote the friendly co-operation of writers and the free exchange of ideas. www.englishpen.org

المورد الثقافي
Culture Resource

The author received a grant to create this book from the Culture Resource (Al Mawred Al Thaqafi)

With thanks to Coline Houssias, Khalil Bendib, Nizar Toulaimat, Anne Clerc, Ammar Abd Rabbo, Aurélie Ruby, Mariam Al-Awani, Pauline Amelin, Élodie Remy, Henriette Souk and to the publishers, Serge and Isabelle.

This book is dedicated to my friend Hussam Khayat (1989-2013) who walked beside me at the Damascus demonstrations, and who was tortured to death in prison by the Syrian secret police.

YASMIN

Born in Damascus in April 1984, Yasmin grew up in a moderate Sunni family. She lived with her family in the United Arab Emirates for ten years, before returning to study Pharmacy at Aleppo University, completing her Master's in Damascus. She is due to start a PhD in the U.S. Like many young people, Yasmin threw herself into the revolution. She runs an underground hospital, Freedom Hospital, in Houria, a town in northern Syria.

SOPHIE

Born in Damascus in 1980, Sophie and her family left Syria to live in France when she was eight years old and she became a journalist following her studies at Sciences Po in Paris. She and Yasmin were childhood friends; they spent their holidays together in Damascus. When the revolution breaks out, only journalists working for pro-Assad organisations are allowed to enter the country. Sophie decides to smuggle herself back in to make a documentary about Freedom Hospital and its occupants.

ABU TAYSIR

Born in Hama in 1953, Abu Taysir survived the massacres that took place in the city in 1982, but he witnessed the execution of his brother and cousins. Accused by the regime of being a member of the Muslim Brotherhood (when he was in fact a communist at the time), in total he has spent eleven years behind bars. He took part in the very early demonstrations and following the regime's massacre of tens of thousands of civilians, he joins forces with the Muslim Brotherhood, eventually taking charge of the local branch of the Free Syrian Army.

ABU AZAB

Born in Aleppo in 1982, Azab is working as a mechanic when the revolution begins. Initially pro-Bashar, he sees the revolution as a conspiracy against the wise rule of Assad, until his pregnant wife and two children are killed by Syrian army bombing. It is then that he joins the Free Syrian Army.

'ONE EYED' ELIAS/JAMAL

Born in 1981 in Qamishli, Elias is Assyrian and a practising Christian. He moves to Qatar for work at the beginning of the revolution. Shortly afterwards, he quits his job and returns to Syria to take part in demonstrations going on in his hometown. He is arrested during one of these demonstrations and tortured by the secret police, who suspect him of being sent by Prince Hamad of Qatar to bring down the regime. He loses an eye under torture in prison.

HAVAL

Born in 1988 in the Kurdish district of Zor Ava in Damascus, Haval has a Master's degree in Philosophy. He is doing his military service when the revolution breaks out and deserts his post when he is ordered to open fire on protesters. Wounded by army gunfire in the course of a demonstration, he is awaiting a kidney transplant. He is being treated at Freedom Hospital, but doesn't strictly need to be there every day – he stays to be near Zahabiah as much as possible.

DR YAZAN

Born in 1972 in Daraa, the birthplace of the revolution in Southern Syria in 2011, Yazan comes from a Sunni family and is close to the Muslim Brotherhood. He is married with two young daughters, having gained his medical degree in Damascus in 1996. At the beginning of the revolution, Yazan treats rebels in secret, which gets him thrown in prison. Having escaped from Damascus, he sends his family to a refugee camp in Turkey, and sets off for Northern Syria to run Freedom Hospital with Yasmin.

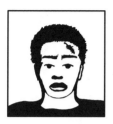

SALEM

An inpatient in Freedom Hospital, Salem suffers memory loss having survived a battle between the regular army and the rebels. No one knows his background. He seems to be around twenty-six or twenty-seven years old and his accent indicates he might come from a coastal town, maybe Latakia or Tartus.

WALID ABU QATADA

Born in 1972 in Homs. A former taxi driver, he stays out of the early peaceful demonstrations but joins the rebels when they take up arms. Seriously injured in combat, he has been an inpatient at the hospital for some time. He claims to be pro-Muslim Brotherhood, but his true beliefs are in fact closer to the Salafist jihadi.

ZAHABIAH

Born in 1992 in Ma'arrat al-Numan near Idlib, Zahabiah comes from a conservative Sunni family that refuses to allow her to study in the co-educational environment of a university. When the civil war breaks out she flees her hometown with her five brothers, who join the Free Syrian Army. To help Zahabiah's family, Yasmin hires her as the cook at Freedom Hospital. Zahabiah is Haval's girlfriend.

DR FAWAZ AL-FAWAZ

Born in 1979 in Latakia, Fawaz is from an Alawite family but is a self-professed agnostic. He meets Yasmin for the first time at a demonstration in Duma, near Damascus. He and Yasmin go on to provide medical assistance in several Syrian towns. When Yasmin announces that she's going to open an underground hospital, Fawaz decides to volunteer as one of the doctors.

THE COLONEL

Born in 1951 in the suburbs of Homs, the Colonel comes from a traditional Alawite family with close ties to the Assad family. He studied engineering in Russia and was high up in the Syrian communist party that ran against Hafez al-Assad in the late 1970s. He then left the party to join the army, where he has spent his career. He was one of the first officials to authorise the use of firearms against civilians at peaceful demonstrations.

Chapter 1

SPRING

TURKEY. NEAR THE SYRIAN BORDER.

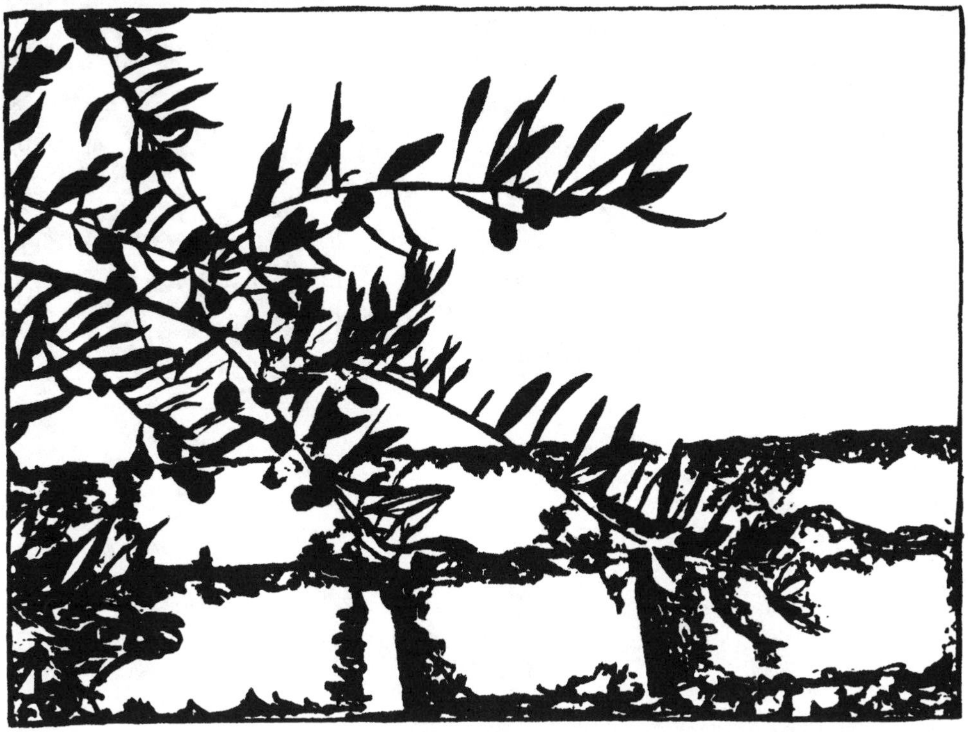

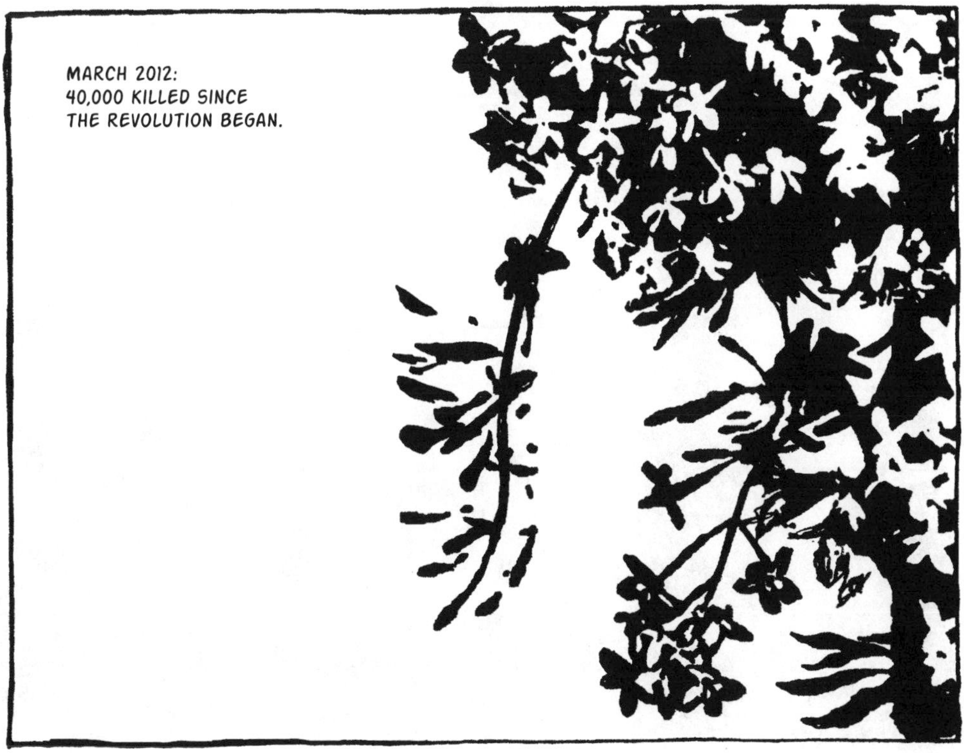
MARCH 2012:
40,000 KILLED SINCE
THE REVOLUTION BEGAN.

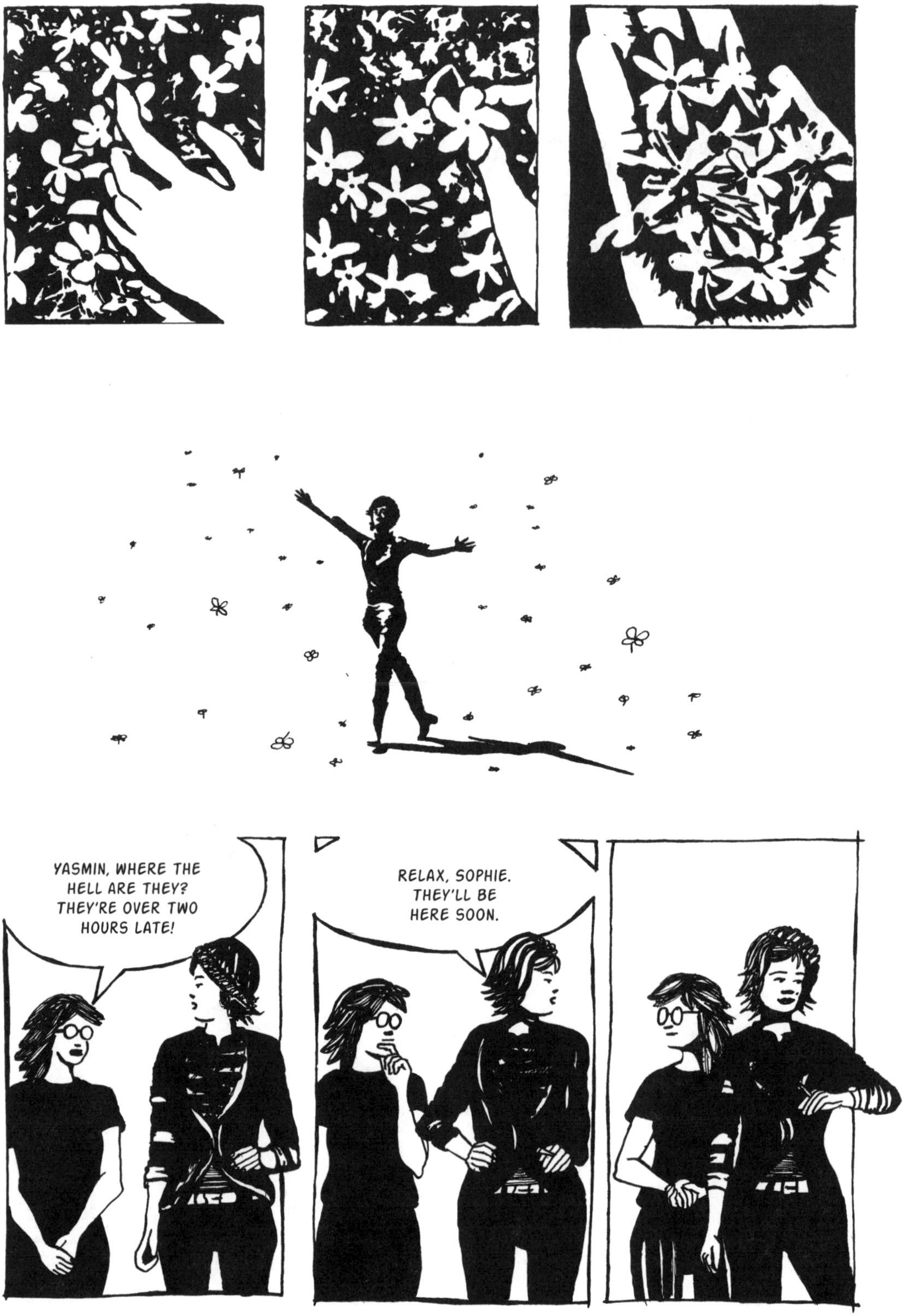
YASMIN, WHERE THE HELL ARE THEY? THEY'RE OVER TWO HOURS LATE!
RELAX, SOPHIE. THEY'LL BE HERE SOON.

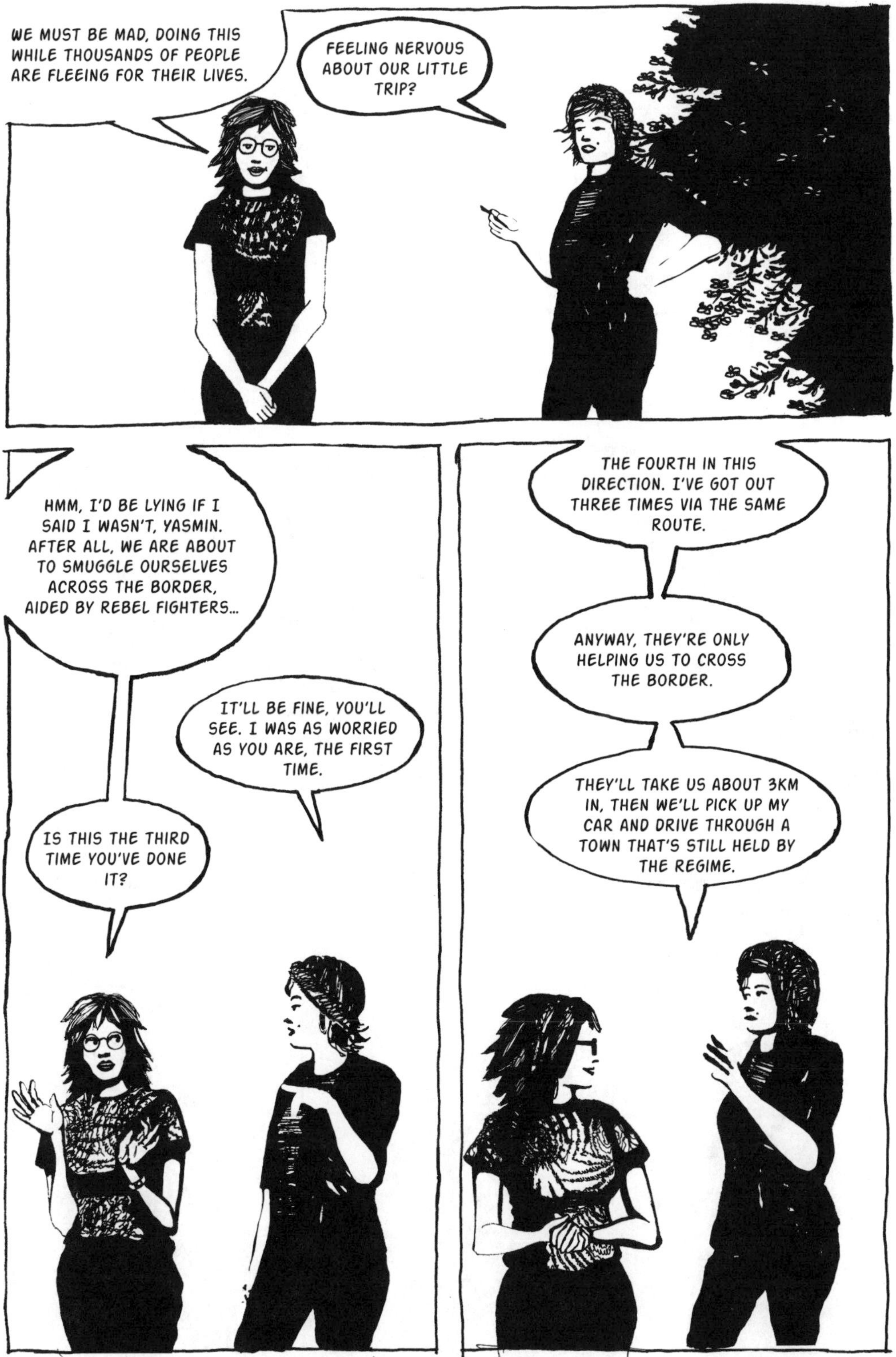
WE MUST BE MAD, DOING THIS WHILE THOUSANDS OF PEOPLE ARE FLEEING FOR THEIR LIVES.
FEELING NERVOUS ABOUT OUR LITTLE TRIP?
HMM, I'D BE LYING IF I SAID I WASN'T, YASMIN. AFTER ALL, WE ARE ABOUT TO SMUGGLE OURSELVES ACROSS THE BORDER, AIDED BY REBEL FIGHTERS...
IT'LL BE FINE, YOU'LL SEE. I WAS AS WORRIED AS YOU ARE, THE FIRST TIME.
IS THIS THE THIRD TIME YOU'VE DONE IT?
THE FOURTH IN THIS DIRECTION. I'VE GOT OUT THREE TIMES VIA THE SAME ROUTE.
ANYWAY, THEY'RE ONLY HELPING US TO CROSS THE BORDER.
THEY'LL TAKE US ABOUT 3KM IN, THEN WE'LL PICK UP MY CAR AND DRIVE THROUGH A TOWN THAT'S STILL HELD BY THE REGIME.

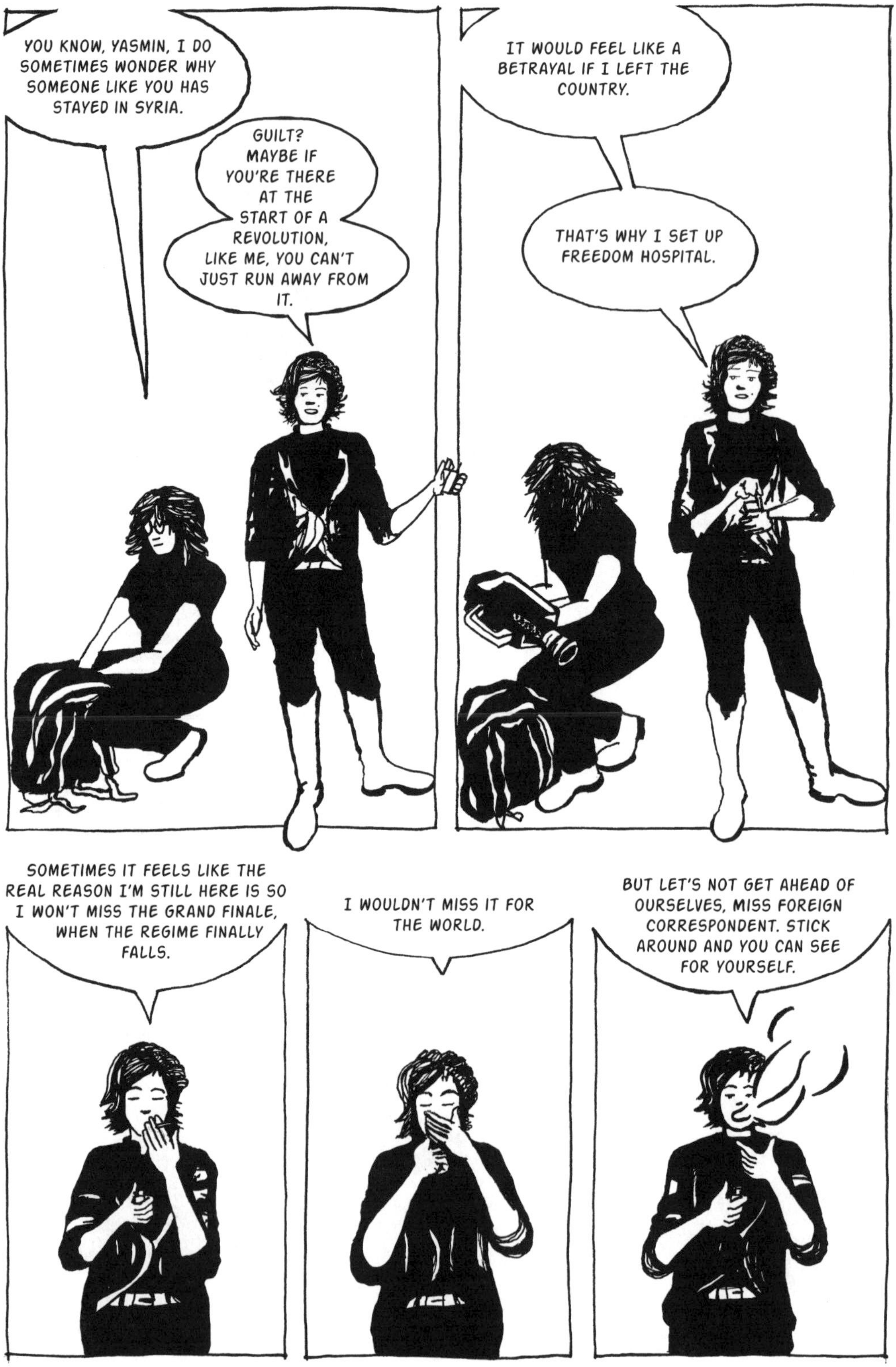

YOU KNOW, YASMIN, I DO SOMETIMES WONDER WHY SOMEONE LIKE YOU HAS STAYED IN SYRIA.
GUILT? MAYBE IF YOU'RE THERE AT THE START OF A REVOLUTION, LIKE ME, YOU CAN'T JUST RUN AWAY FROM IT.
IT WOULD FEEL LIKE A BETRAYAL IF I LEFT THE COUNTRY.
THAT'S WHY I SET UP FREEDOM HOSPITAL.
SOMETIMES IT FEELS LIKE THE REAL REASON I'M STILL HERE IS SO I WON'T MISS THE GRAND FINALE, WHEN THE REGIME FINALLY FALLS.
I WOULDN'T MISS IT FOR THE WORLD.
BUT LET'S NOT GET AHEAD OF OURSELVES, MISS FOREIGN CORRESPONDENT. STICK AROUND AND YOU CAN SEE FOR YOURSELF.

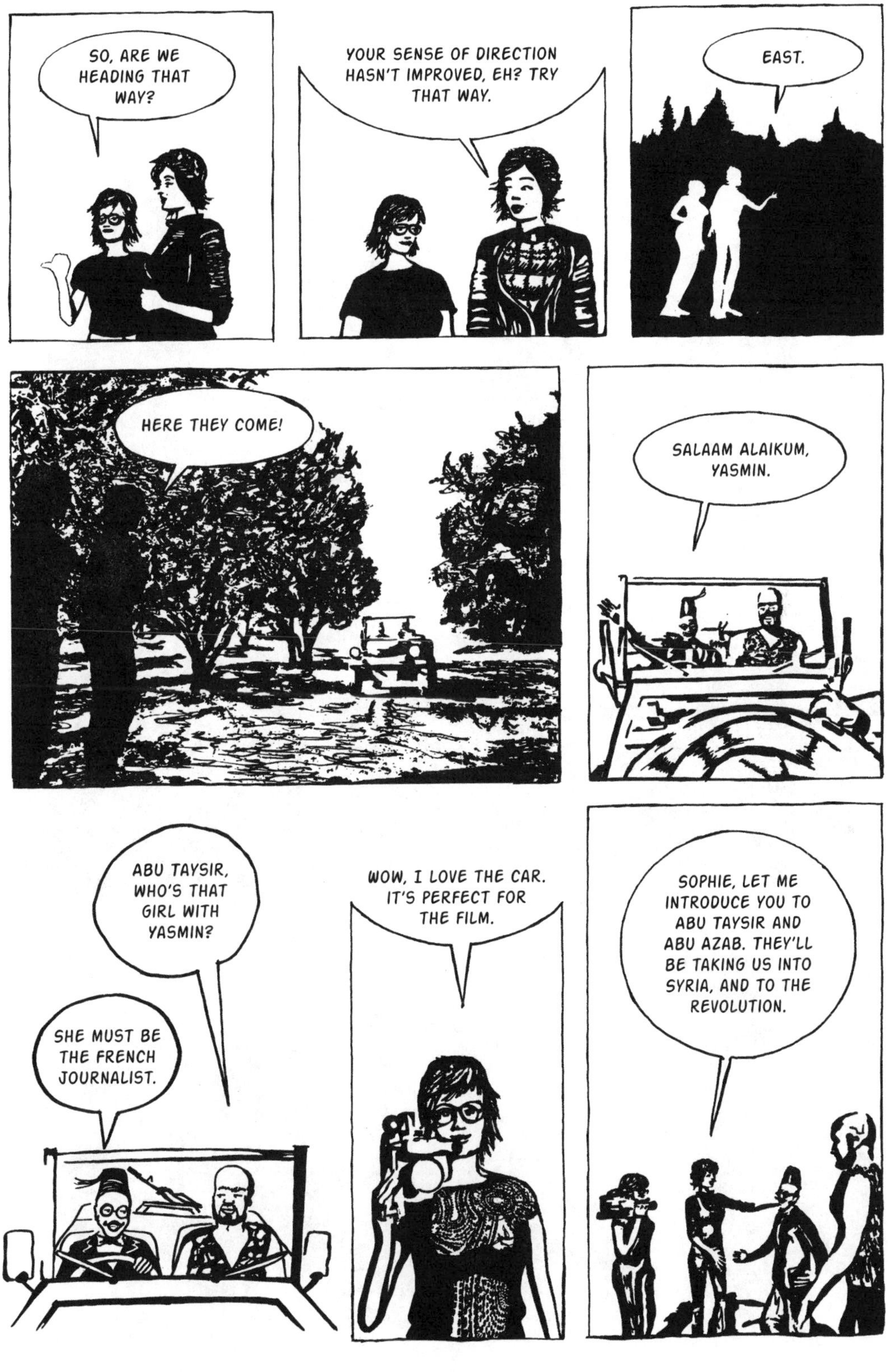
SO, ARE WE HEADING THAT WAY?
YOUR SENSE OF DIRECTION HASN'T IMPROVED, EH? TRY THAT WAY.
EAST.
HERE THEY COME!
SALAAM ALAIKUM, YASMIN.
ABU TAYSIR, WHO'S THAT GIRL WITH YASMIN?
SHE MUST BE THE FRENCH JOURNALIST.
WOW, I LOVE THE CAR. IT'S PERFECT FOR THE FILM.
SOPHIE, LET ME INTRODUCE YOU TO ABU TAYSIR AND ABU AZAB. THEY'LL BE TAKING US INTO SYRIA, AND TO THE REVOLUTION.

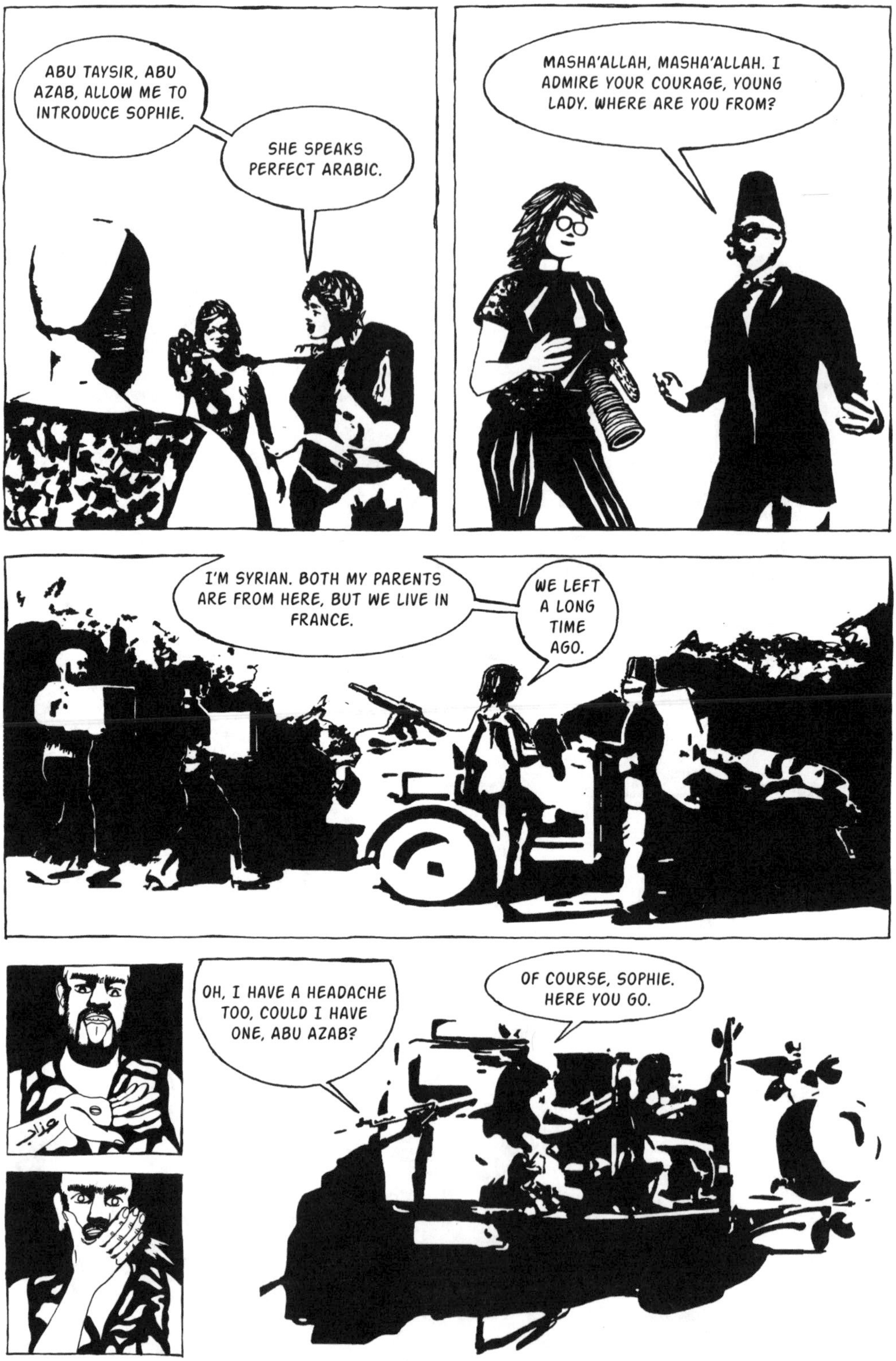
ABU TAYSIR, ABU AZAB, ALLOW ME TO INTRODUCE SOPHIE.
SHE SPEAKS PERFECT ARABIC.
MASHA'ALLAH, MASHA'ALLAH. I ADMIRE YOUR COURAGE, YOUNG LADY. WHERE ARE YOU FROM?
I'M SYRIAN. BOTH MY PARENTS ARE FROM HERE, BUT WE LIVE IN FRANCE.
WE LEFT A LONG TIME AGO.
OH, I HAVE A HEADACHE TOO, COULD I HAVE ONE, ABU AZAB?
OF COURSE, SOPHIE. HERE YOU GO.

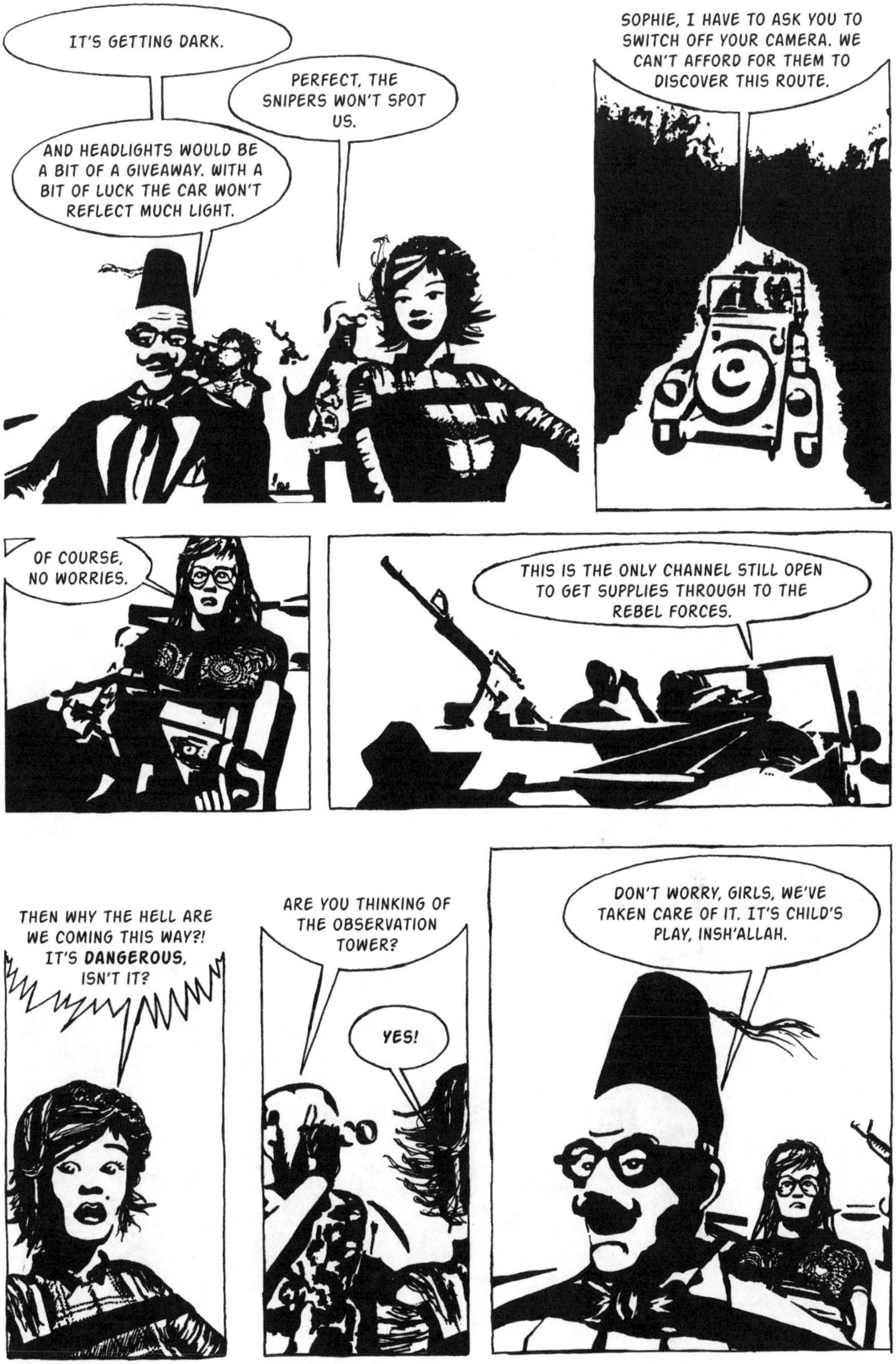
IT'S GETTING DARK.
AND HEADLIGHTS WOULD BE A BIT OF A GIVEAWAY. WITH A BIT OF LUCK THE CAR WON'T REFLECT MUCH LIGHT.
PERFECT, THE SNIPERS WON'T SPOT US.
SOPHIE, I HAVE TO ASK YOU TO SWITCH OFF YOUR CAMERA. WE CAN'T AFFORD FOR THEM TO DISCOVER THIS ROUTE.
OF COURSE, NO WORRIES.
THIS IS THE ONLY CHANNEL STILL OPEN TO GET SUPPLIES THROUGH TO THE REBEL FORCES.
THEN WHY THE HELL ARE WE COMING THIS WAY?! IT'S **DANGEROUS**, ISN'T IT?
ARE YOU THINKING OF THE OBSERVATION TOWER?
YES!
DON'T WORRY, GIRLS, WE'VE TAKEN CARE OF IT. IT'S CHILD'S PLAY, INSH'ALLAH.

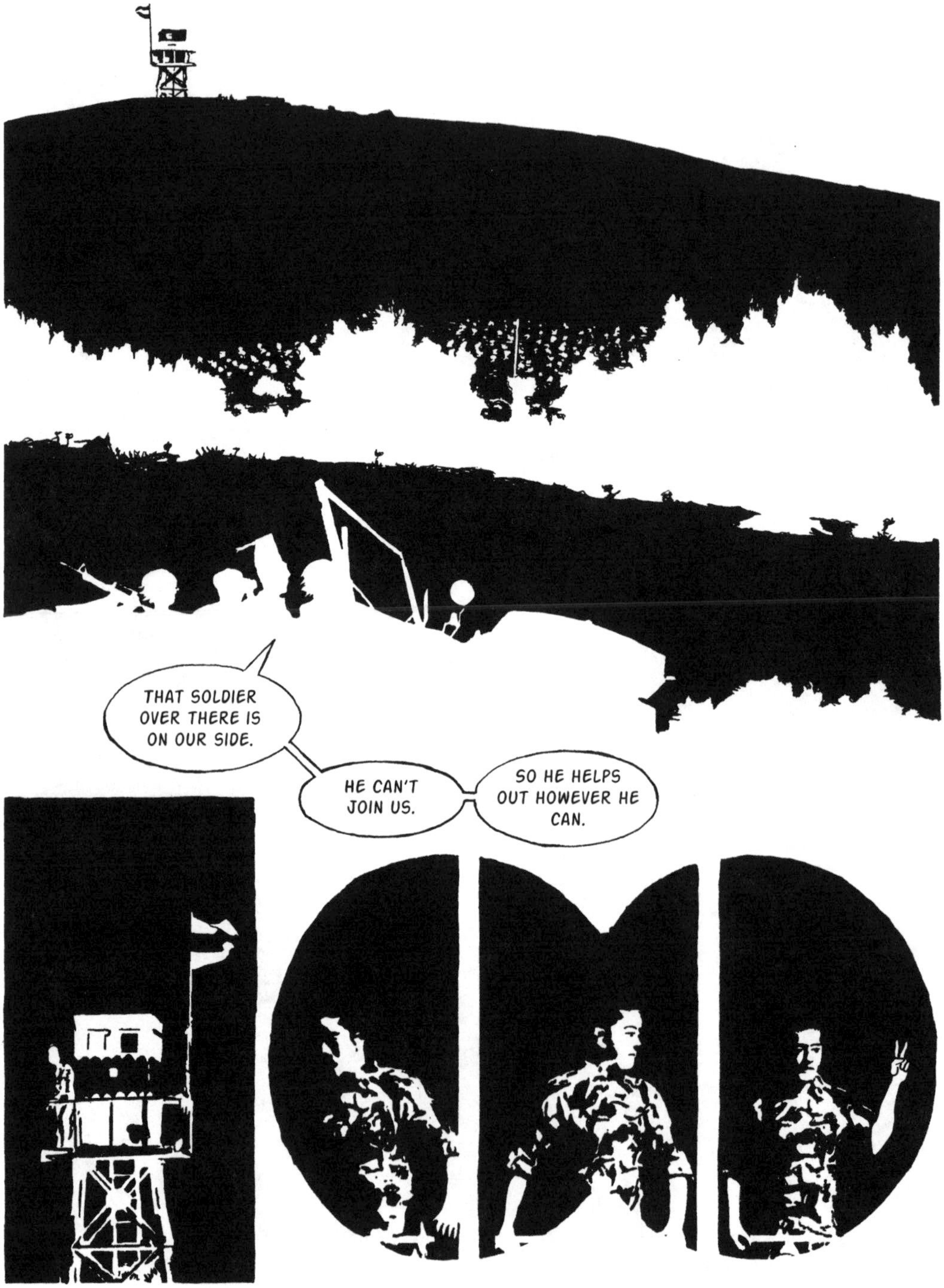
THAT SOLDIER OVER THERE IS ON OUR SIDE.
HE CAN'T JOIN US.
SO HE HELPS OUT HOWEVER HE CAN.

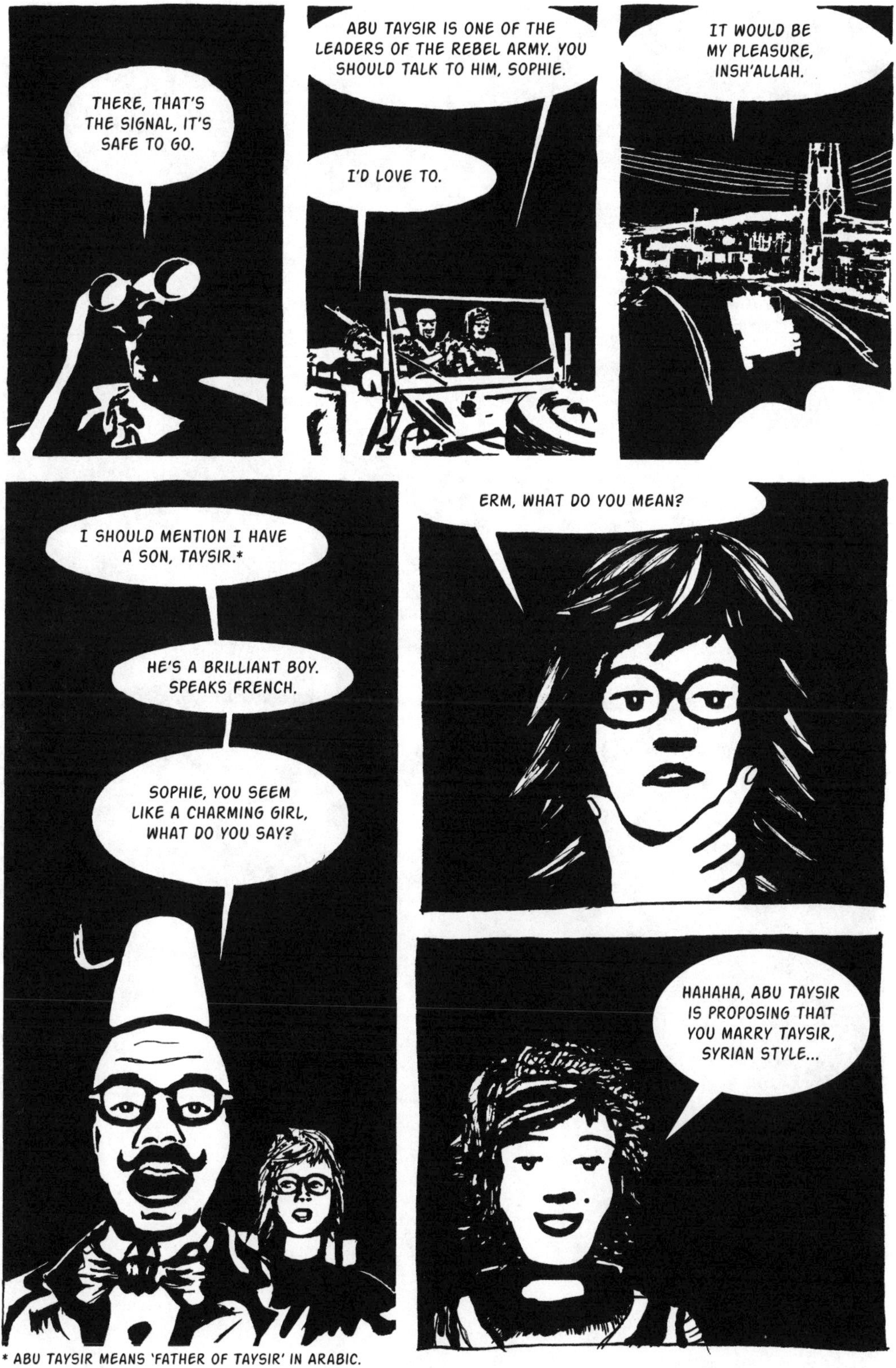
THERE, THAT'S THE SIGNAL, IT'S SAFE TO GO.
ABU TAYSIR IS ONE OF THE LEADERS OF THE REBEL ARMY. YOU SHOULD TALK TO HIM, SOPHIE.
I'D LOVE TO.
IT WOULD BE MY PLEASURE, INSH'ALLAH.
I SHOULD MENTION I HAVE A SON, TAYSIR.*
HE'S A BRILLIANT BOY. SPEAKS FRENCH.
SOPHIE, YOU SEEM LIKE A CHARMING GIRL, WHAT DO YOU SAY?
ERM, WHAT DO YOU MEAN?
HAHAHA, ABU TAYSIR IS PROPOSING THAT YOU MARRY TAYSIR, SYRIAN STYLE...

* ABU TAYSIR MEANS 'FATHER OF TAYSIR' IN ARABIC.

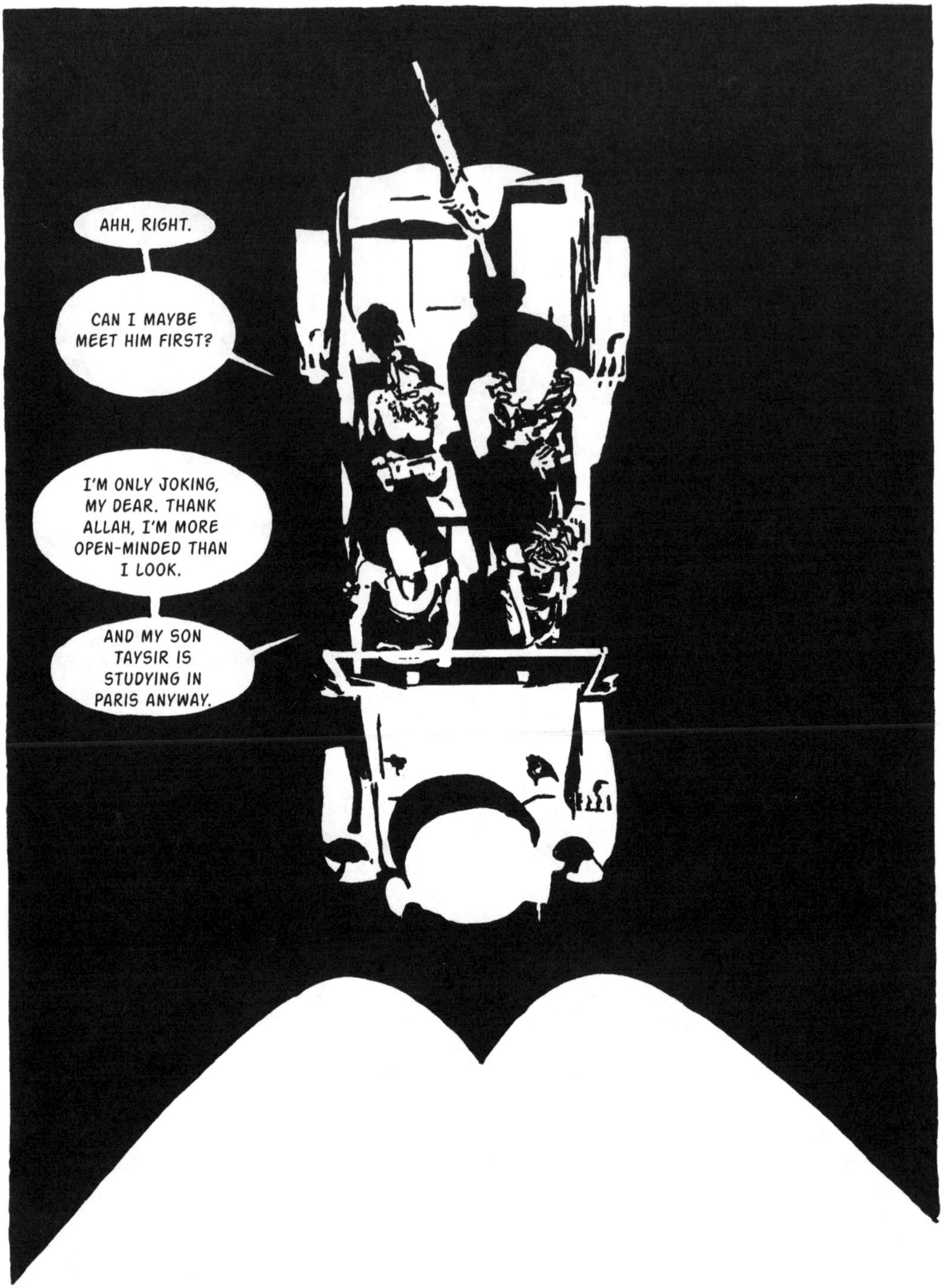
AHH, RIGHT.
CAN I MAYBE MEET HIM FIRST?
I'M ONLY JOKING, MY DEAR. THANK ALLAH, I'M MORE OPEN-MINDED THAN I LOOK.
AND MY SON TAYSIR IS STUDYING IN PARIS ANYWAY.

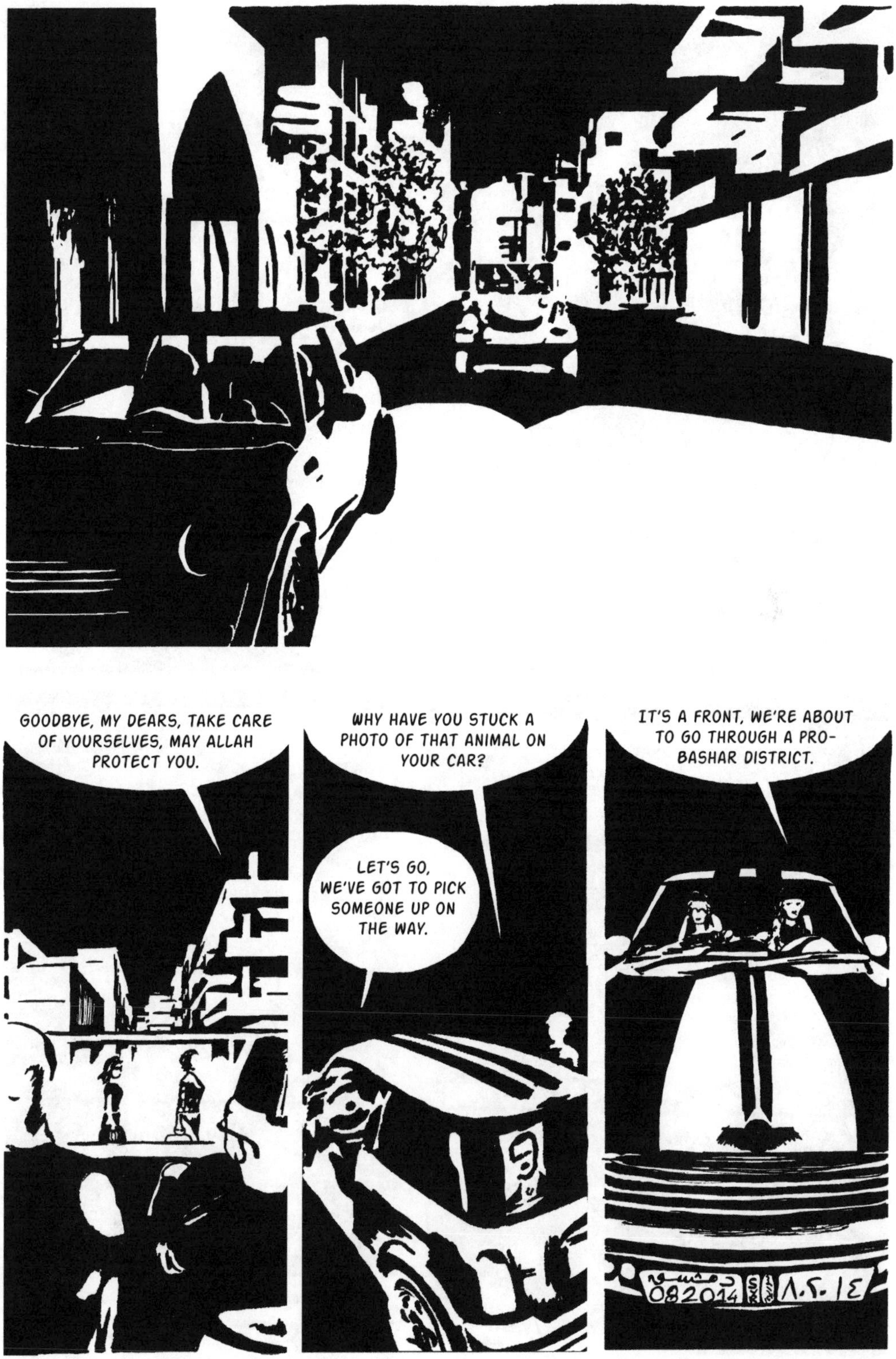
GOODBYE, MY DEARS, TAKE CARE OF YOURSELVES, MAY ALLAH PROTECT YOU.
WHY HAVE YOU STUCK A PHOTO OF THAT ANIMAL ON YOUR CAR?
LET'S GO, WE'VE GOT TO PICK SOMEONE UP ON THE WAY.
IT'S A FRONT, WE'RE ABOUT TO GO THROUGH A PRO-BASHAR DISTRICT.

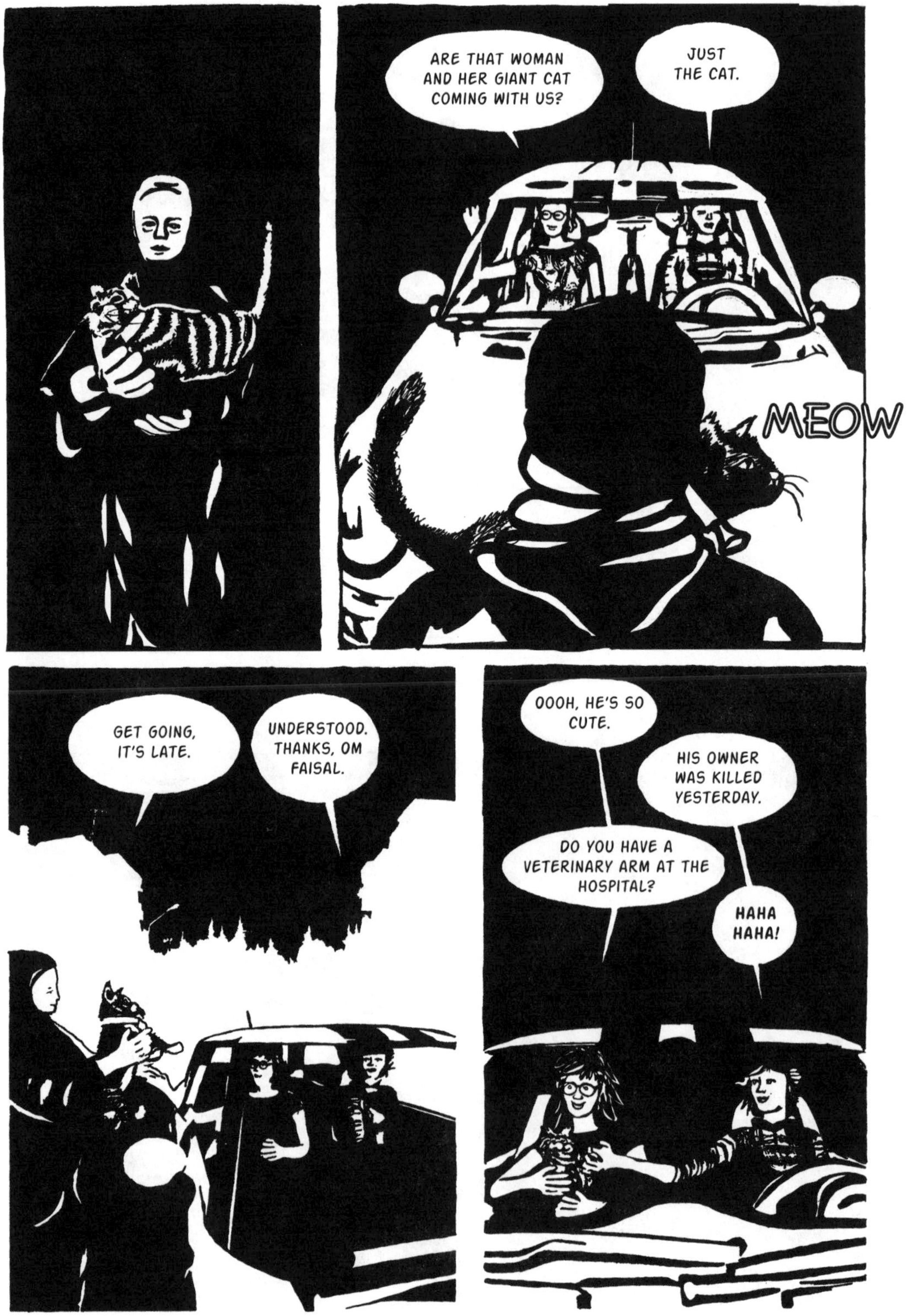
ARE THAT WOMAN AND HER GIANT CAT COMING WITH US?
JUST THE CAT.
MEOW
GET GOING, IT'S LATE.
UNDERSTOOD. THANKS, OM FAISAL.
OOOH, HE'S SO CUTE.
HIS OWNER WAS KILLED YESTERDAY.
DO YOU HAVE A VETERINARY ARM AT THE HOSPITAL?
HAHA HAHA!

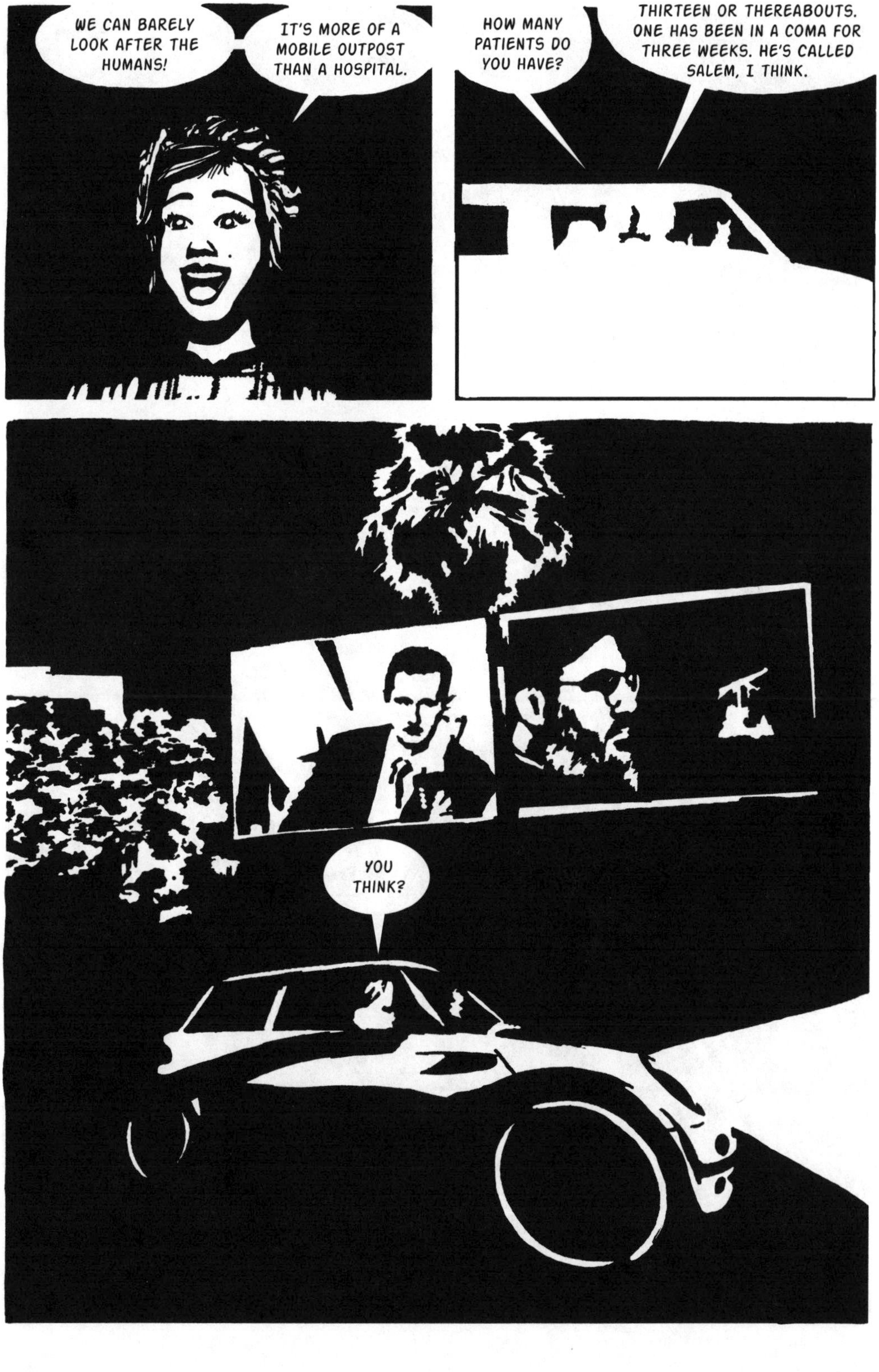
WE CAN BARELY LOOK AFTER THE HUMANS!
IT'S MORE OF A MOBILE OUTPOST THAN A HOSPITAL.
HOW MANY PATIENTS DO YOU HAVE?
THIRTEEN OR THEREABOUTS. ONE HAS BEEN IN A COMA FOR THREE WEEKS. HE'S CALLED SALEM, I THINK.
YOU THINK?

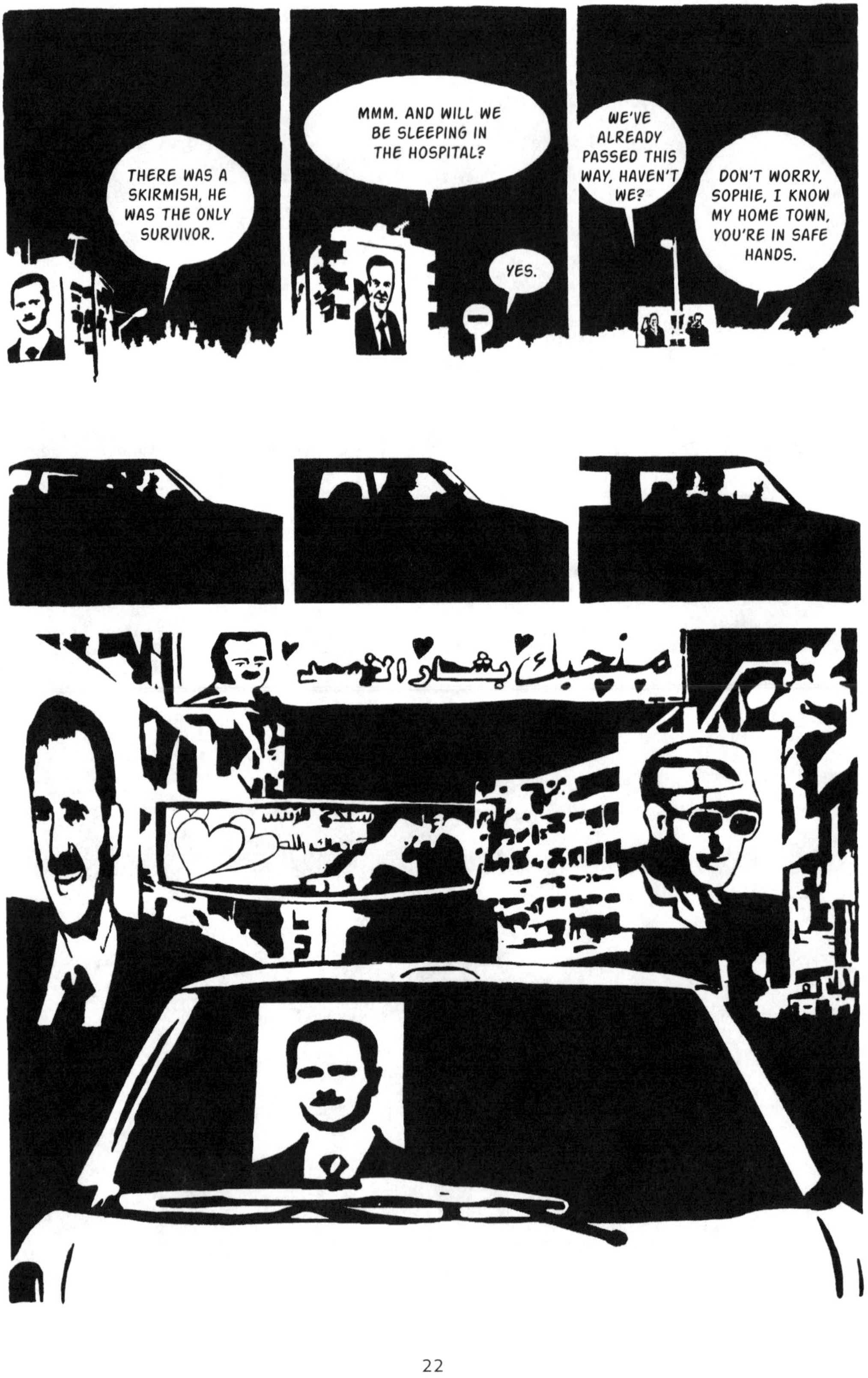
THERE WAS A SKIRMISH, HE WAS THE ONLY SURVIVOR.
MMM. AND WILL WE BE SLEEPING IN THE HOSPITAL?
YES.
WE'VE ALREADY PASSED THIS WAY, HAVEN'T WE?
DON'T WORRY, SOPHIE, I KNOW MY HOME TOWN, YOU'RE IN SAFE HANDS.
منحبك بشار الأسد

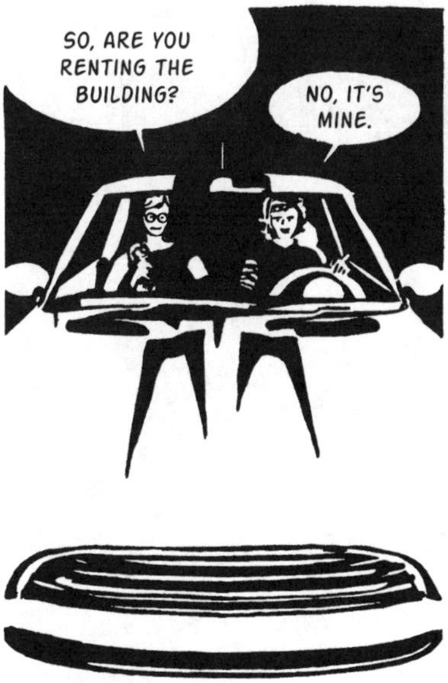
SO, ARE YOU RENTING THE BUILDING?
NO, IT'S MINE.

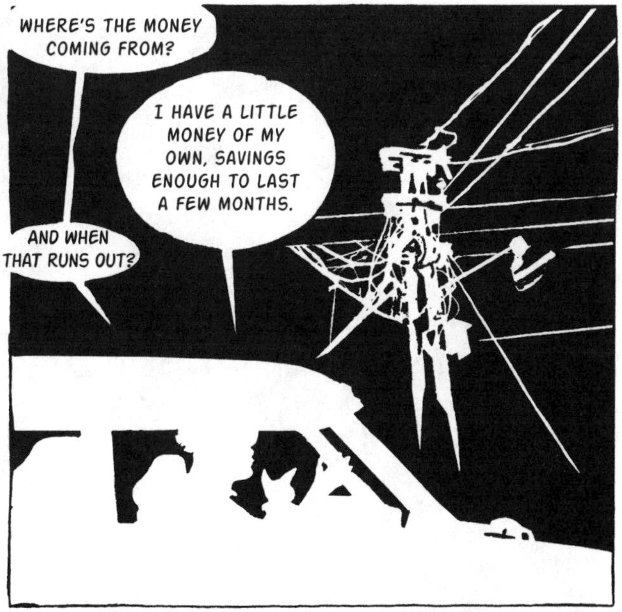
WHERE'S THE MONEY COMING FROM?
I HAVE A LITTLE MONEY OF MY OWN, SAVINGS ENOUGH TO LAST A FEW MONTHS.
AND WHEN THAT RUNS OUT?

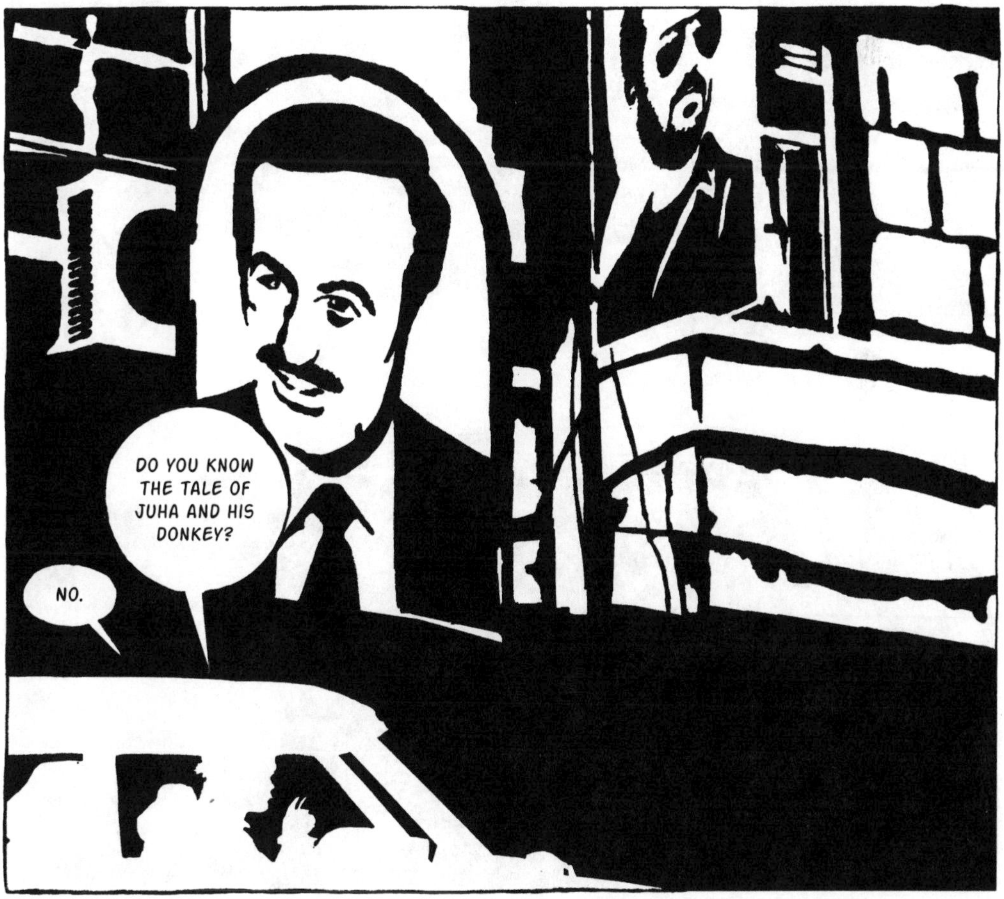
DO YOU KNOW THE TALE OF JUHA AND HIS DONKEY?
NO.

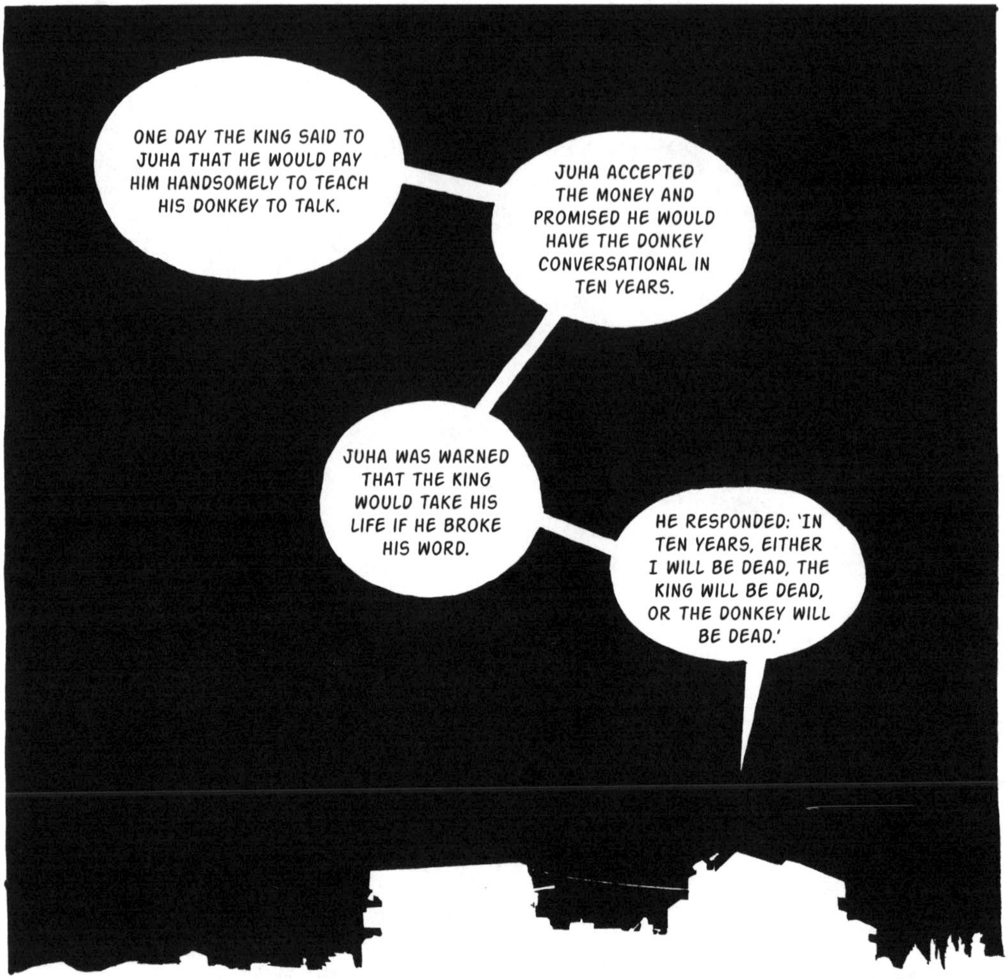
ONE DAY THE KING SAID TO JUHA THAT HE WOULD PAY HIM HANDSOMELY TO TEACH HIS DONKEY TO TALK.
JUHA ACCEPTED THE MONEY AND PROMISED HE WOULD HAVE THE DONKEY CONVERSATIONAL IN TEN YEARS.
JUHA WAS WARNED THAT THE KING WOULD TAKE HIS LIFE IF HE BROKE HIS WORD.
HE RESPONDED: 'IN TEN YEARS, EITHER I WILL BE DEAD, THE KING WILL BE DEAD, OR THE DONKEY WILL BE DEAD.'

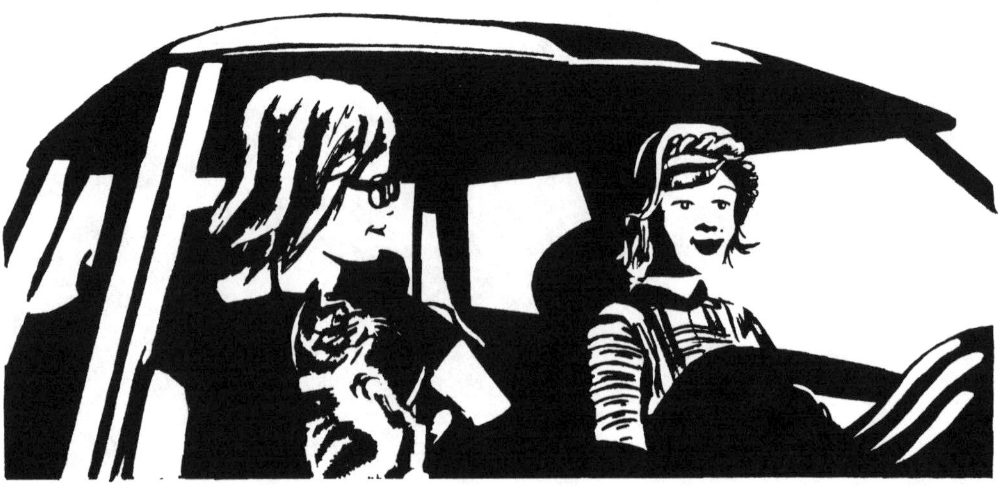

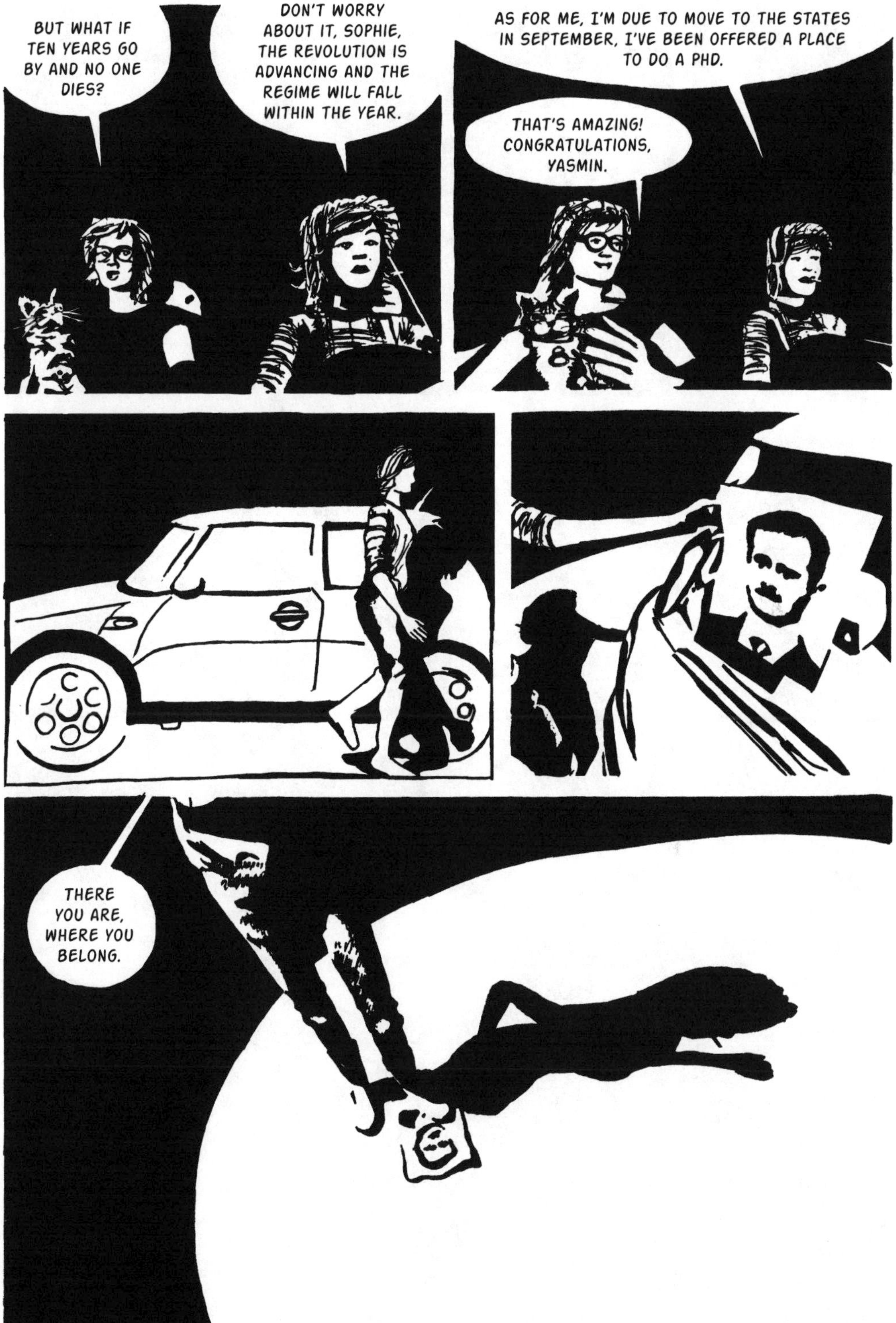
BUT WHAT IF TEN YEARS GO BY AND NO ONE DIES?
DON'T WORRY ABOUT IT, SOPHIE, THE REVOLUTION IS ADVANCING AND THE REGIME WILL FALL WITHIN THE YEAR.
AS FOR ME, I'M DUE TO MOVE TO THE STATES IN SEPTEMBER, I'VE BEEN OFFERED A PLACE TO DO A PHD.
THAT'S AMAZING! CONGRATULATIONS, YASMIN.
THERE YOU ARE, WHERE YOU BELONG.

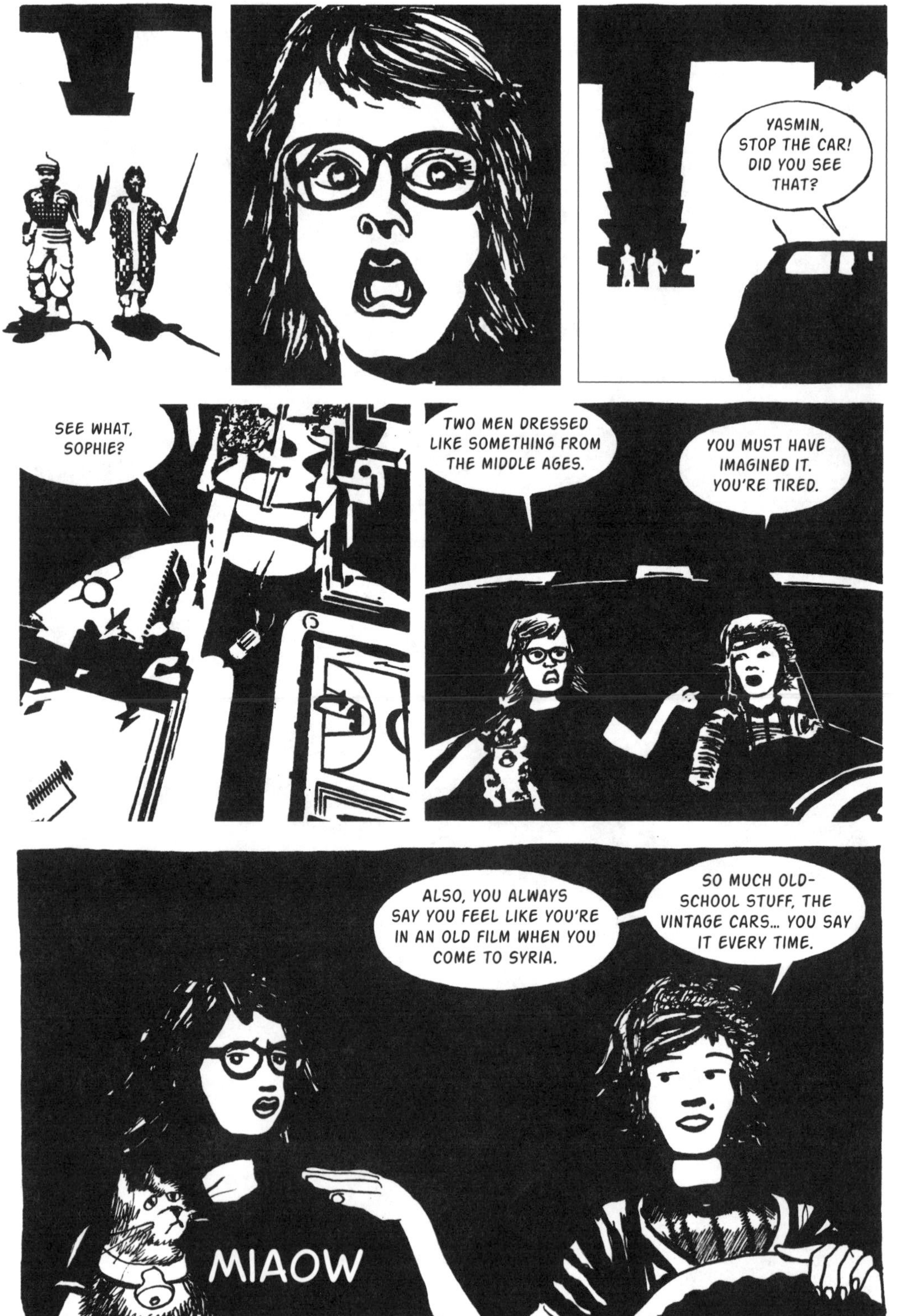
YASMIN, STOP THE CAR! DID YOU SEE THAT?
SEE WHAT, SOPHIE?
TWO MEN DRESSED LIKE SOMETHING FROM THE MIDDLE AGES.
YOU MUST HAVE IMAGINED IT. YOU'RE TIRED.
ALSO, YOU ALWAYS SAY YOU FEEL LIKE YOU'RE IN AN OLD FILM WHEN YOU COME TO SYRIA.
SO MUCH OLD-SCHOOL STUFF, THE VINTAGE CARS... YOU SAY IT EVERY TIME.
MIAOW

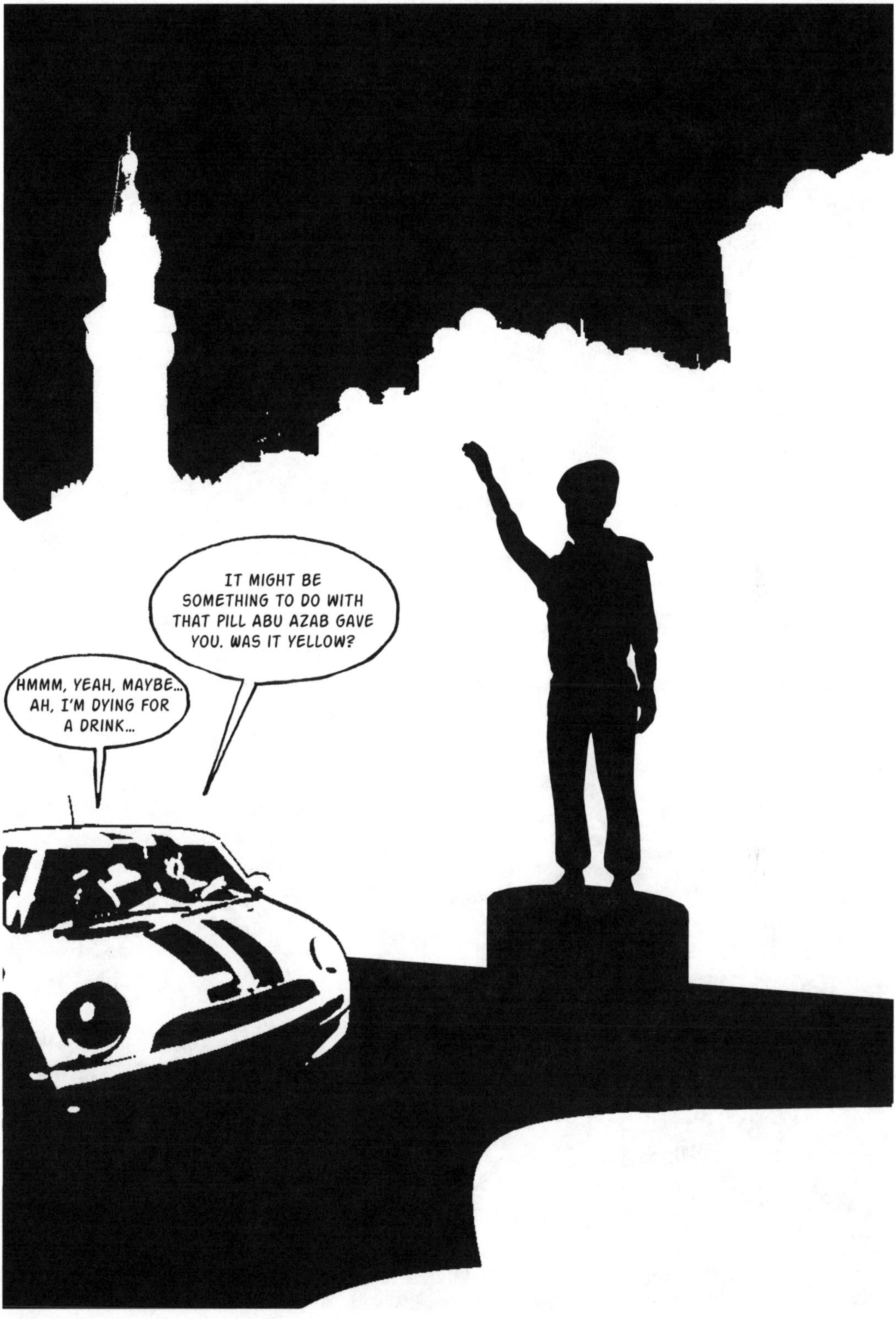
HMMM, YEAH, MAYBE... AH, I'M DYING FOR A DRINK...
IT MIGHT BE SOMETHING TO DO WITH THAT PILL ABU AZAB GAVE YOU. WAS IT YELLOW?

MEANWHILE, AT THE HOSPITAL.

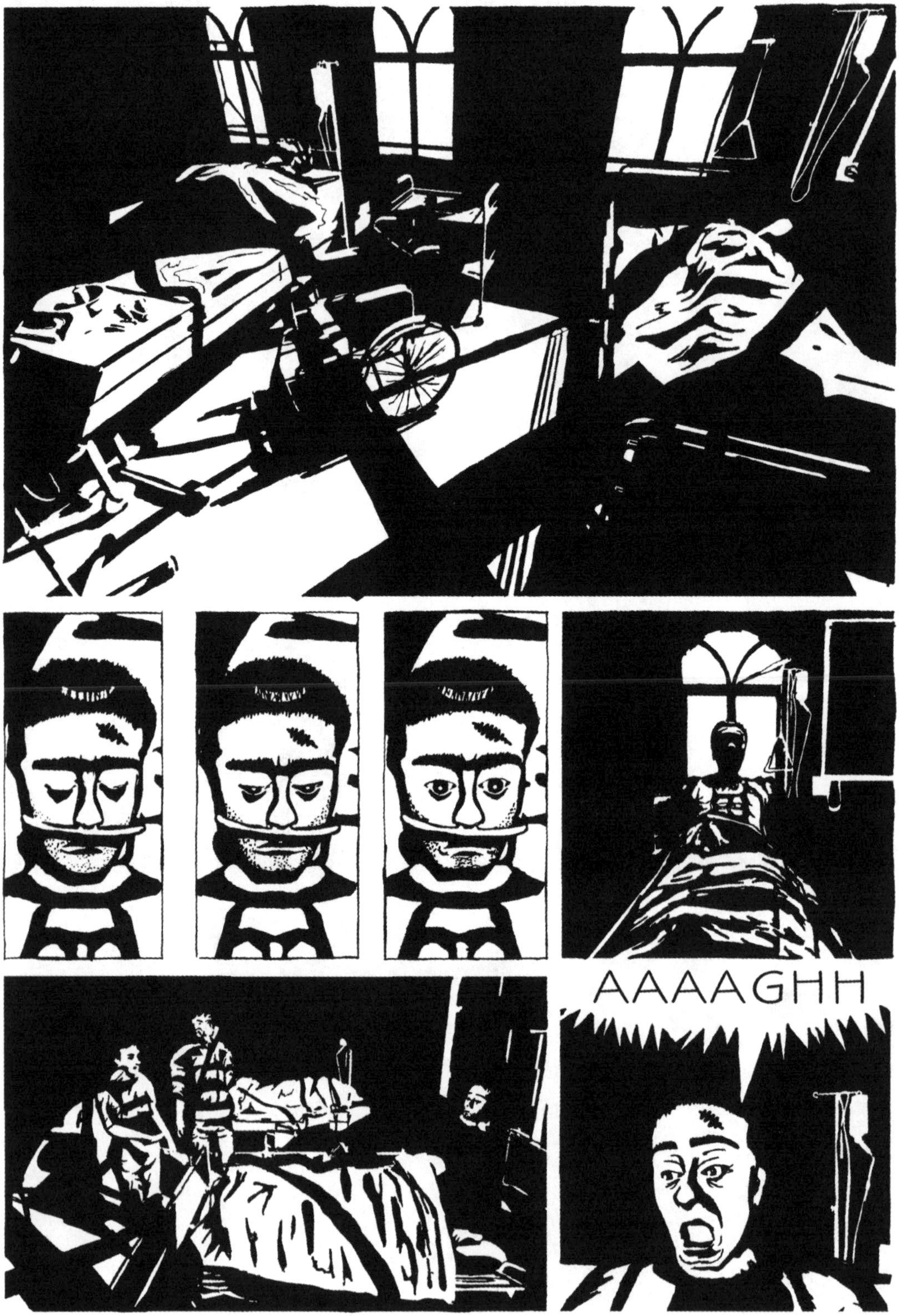
AAAAGHH

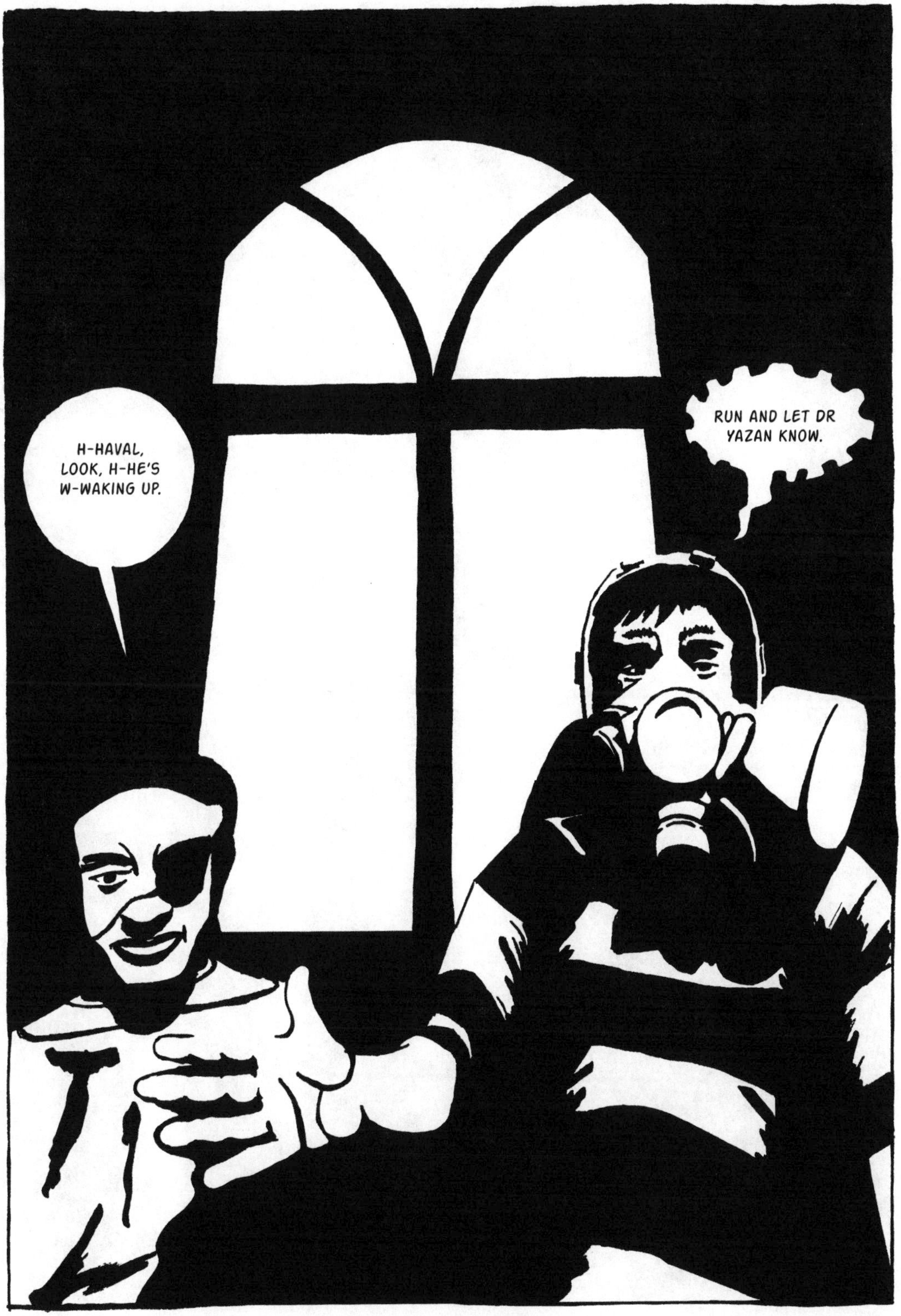
H-HAVAL, LOOK, H-HE'S W-WAKING UP.
RUN AND LET DR YAZAN KNOW.

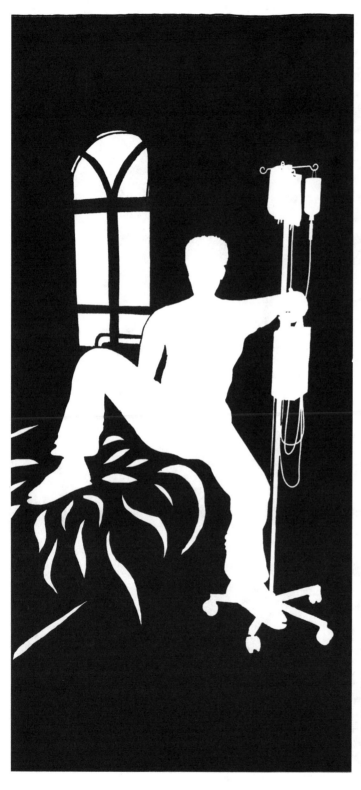
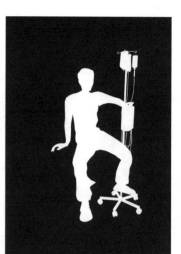
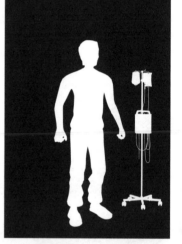
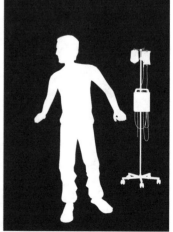

30

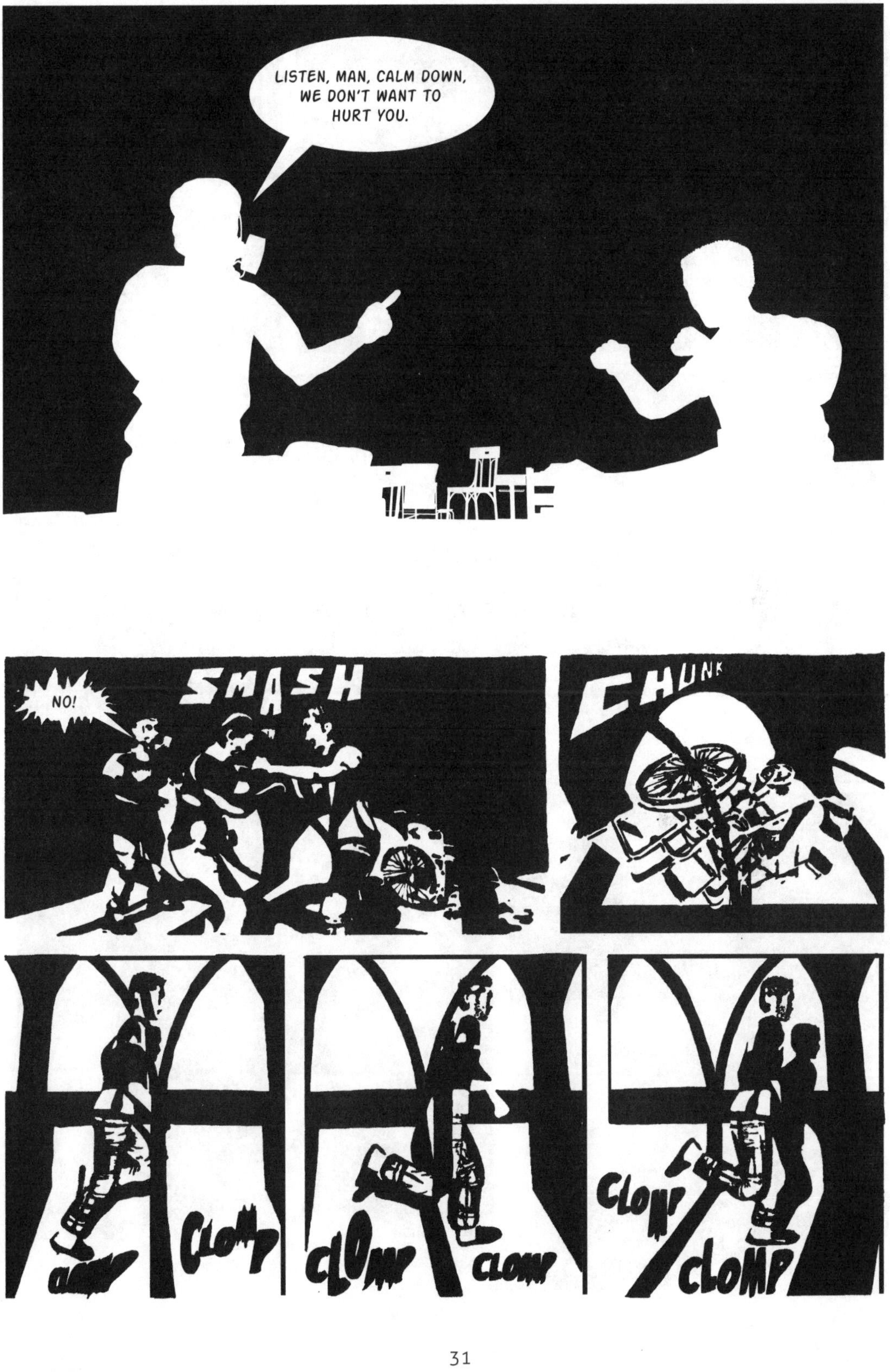
LISTEN, MAN, CALM DOWN, WE DON'T WANT TO HURT YOU.
NO!
SMASH
CHUN
CLOMP
CLOMP
CLOMP
CLOMP
CLOMP
CLOMP

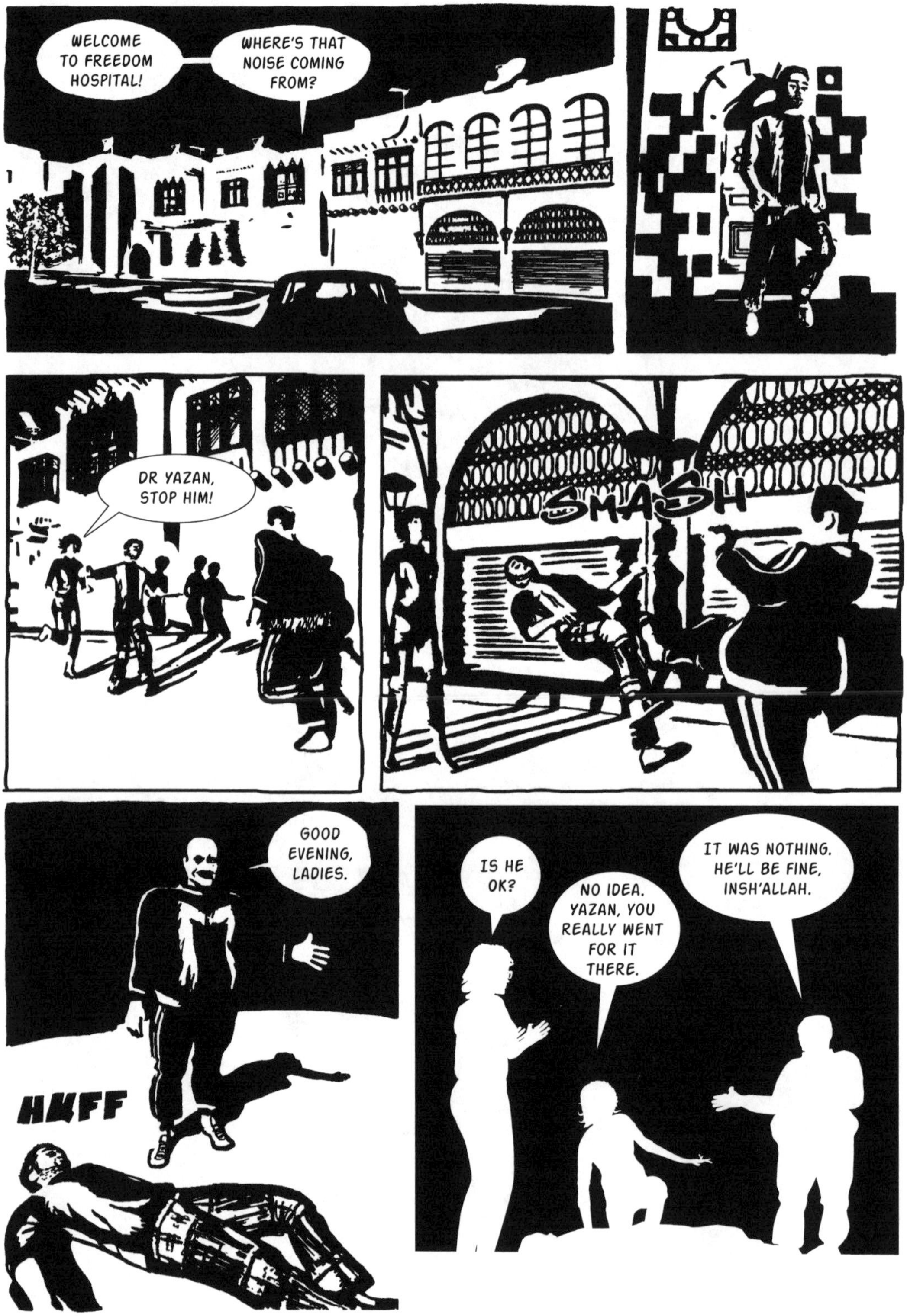
WELCOME TO FREEDOM HOSPITAL!
WHERE'S THAT NOISE COMING FROM?
DR YAZAN, STOP HIM!
SMASH
GOOD EVENING, LADIES.
HUFF
IS HE OK?
NO IDEA. YAZAN, YOU REALLY WENT FOR IT THERE.
IT WAS NOTHING. HE'LL BE FINE, INSH'ALLAH.

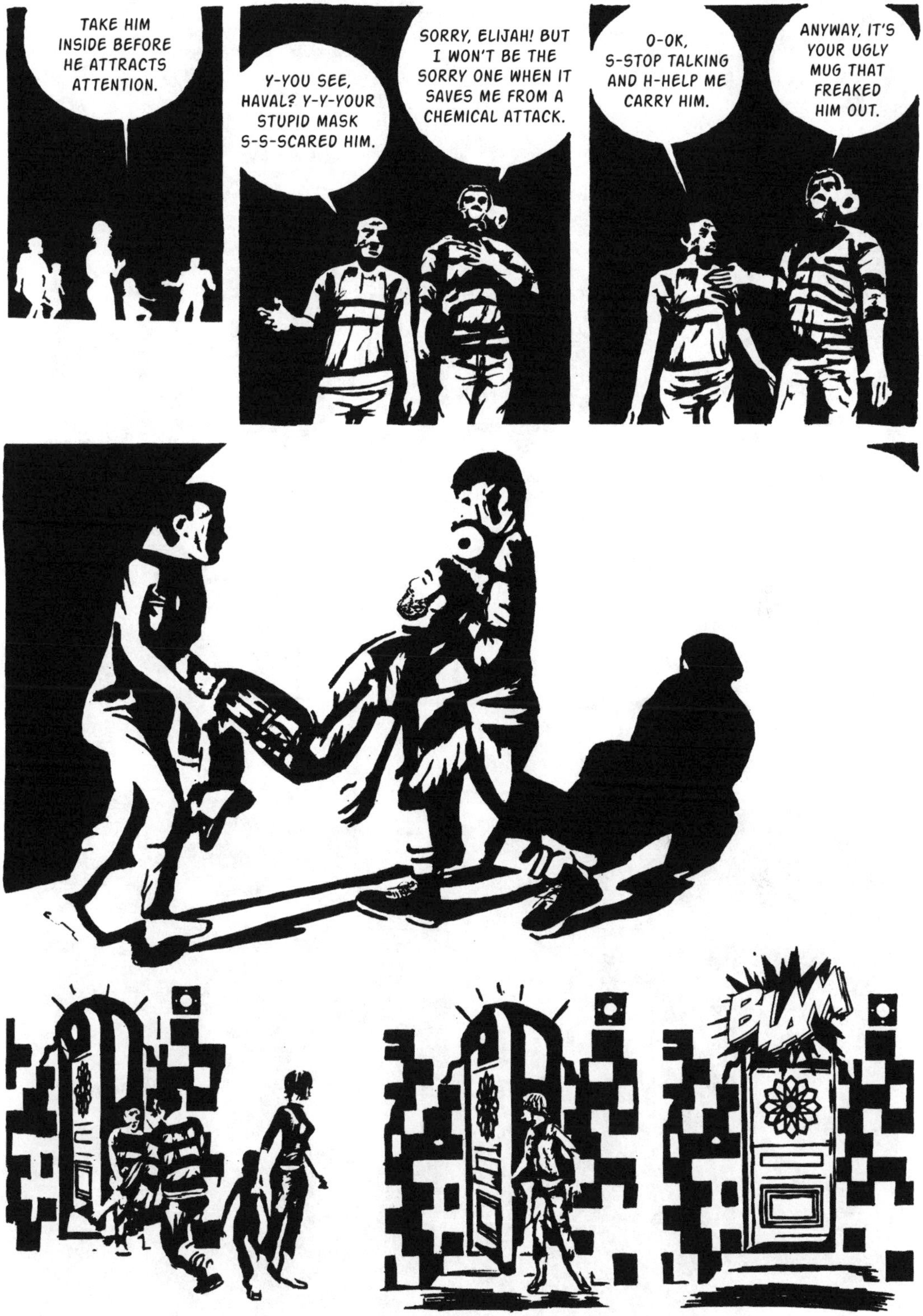
TAKE HIM INSIDE BEFORE HE ATTRACTS ATTENTION.
Y-YOU SEE, HAVAL? Y-Y-YOUR STUPID MASK S-S-SCARED HIM.
SORRY, ELIJAH! BUT I WON'T BE THE SORRY ONE WHEN IT SAVES ME FROM A CHEMICAL ATTACK.
O-OK, S-STOP TALKING AND H-HELP ME CARRY HIM.
ANYWAY, IT'S YOUR UGLY MUG THAT FREAKED HIM OUT.
BLAM

A FEW DAYS LATER: ANOTHER 150 KILLED.

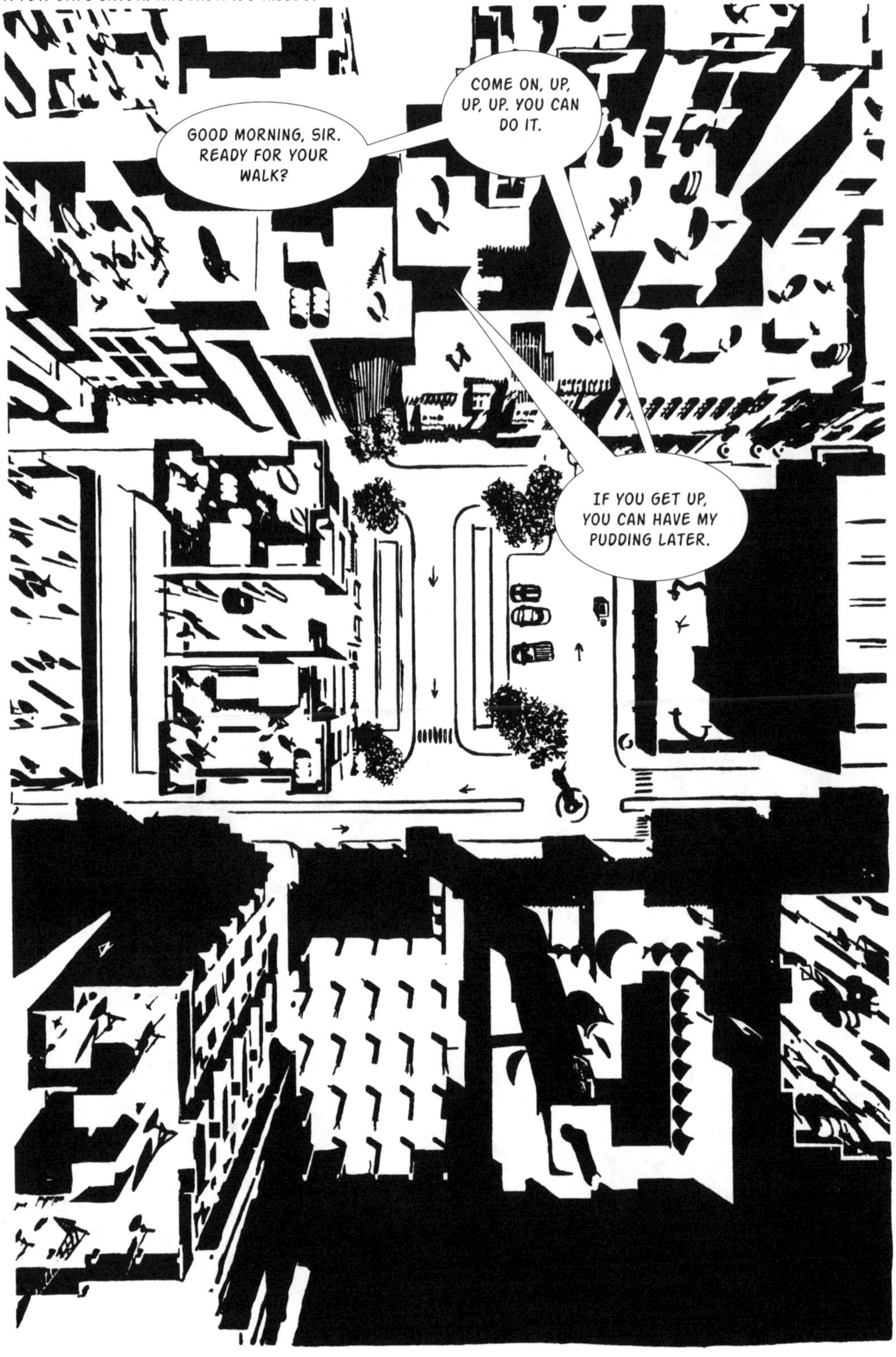
GOOD MORNING, SIR. READY FOR YOUR WALK?
COME ON, UP, UP, UP. YOU CAN DO IT.
IF YOU GET UP, YOU CAN HAVE MY PUDDING LATER.

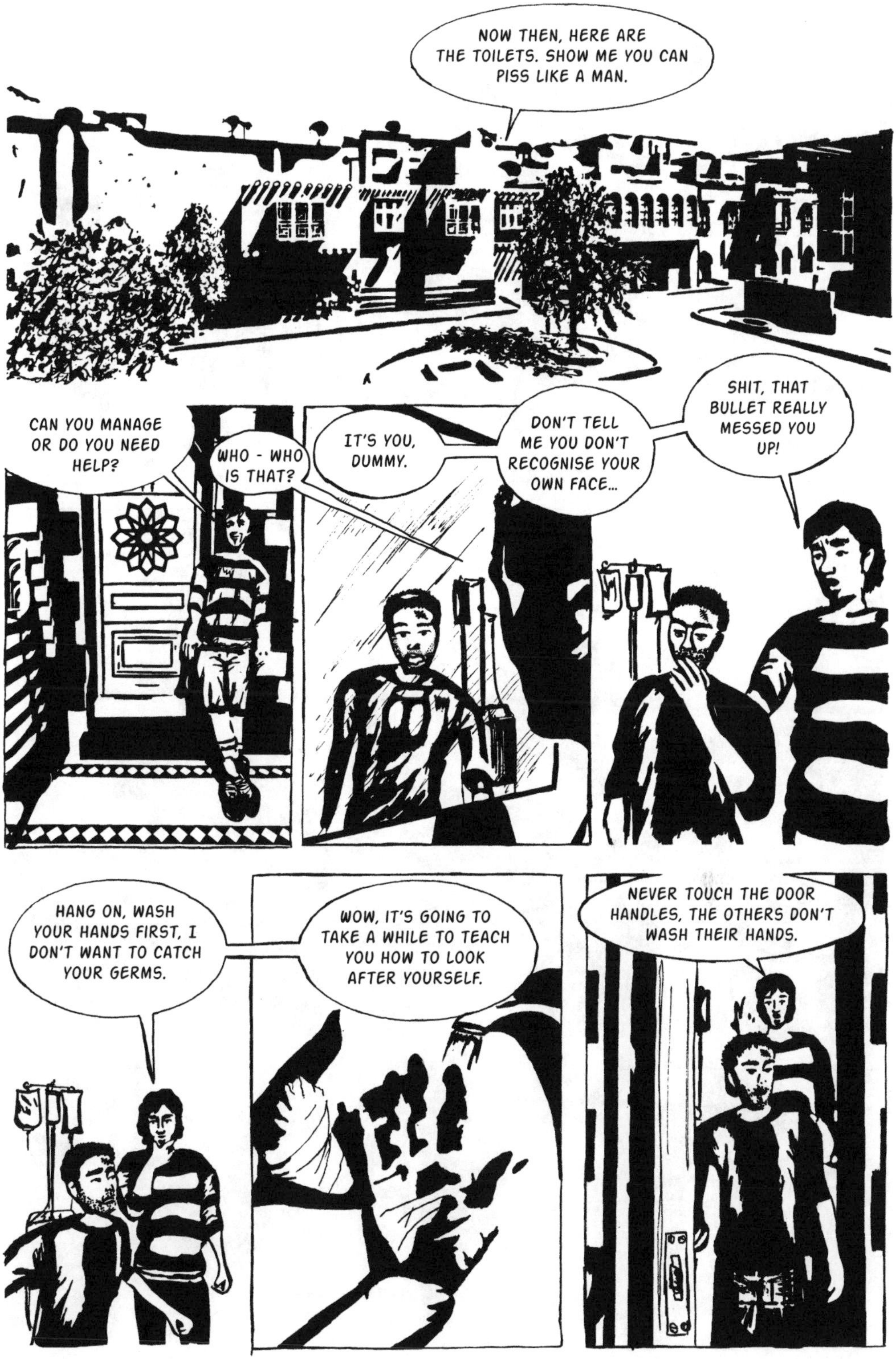
NOW THEN, HERE ARE THE TOILETS. SHOW ME YOU CAN PISS LIKE A MAN.
CAN YOU MANAGE OR DO YOU NEED HELP?
WHO - WHO IS THAT?
IT'S YOU, DUMMY.
DON'T TELL ME YOU DON'T RECOGNISE YOUR OWN FACE...
SHIT, THAT BULLET REALLY MESSED YOU UP!
HANG ON, WASH YOUR HANDS FIRST, I DON'T WANT TO CATCH YOUR GERMS.
WOW, IT'S GOING TO TAKE A WHILE TO TEACH YOU HOW TO LOOK AFTER YOURSELF.
NEVER TOUCH THE DOOR HANDLES, THE OTHERS DON'T WASH THEIR HANDS.

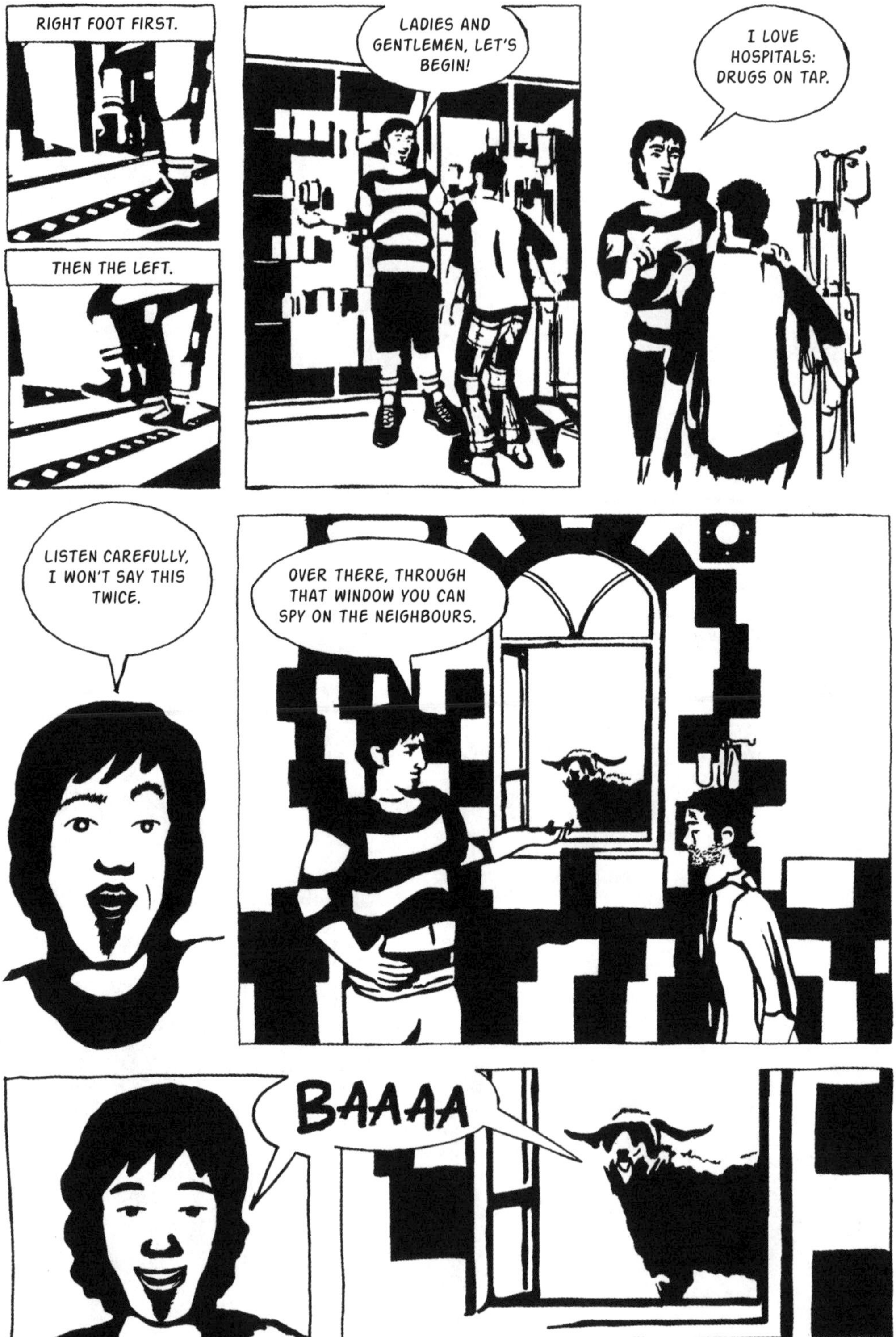
RIGHT FOOT FIRST.
THEN THE LEFT.
LADIES AND GENTLEMEN, LET'S BEGIN!
I LOVE HOSPITALS: DRUGS ON TAP.
LISTEN CAREFULLY, I WON'T SAY THIS TWICE.
OVER THERE, THROUGH THAT WINDOW YOU CAN SPY ON THE NEIGHBOURS.
BAAAA

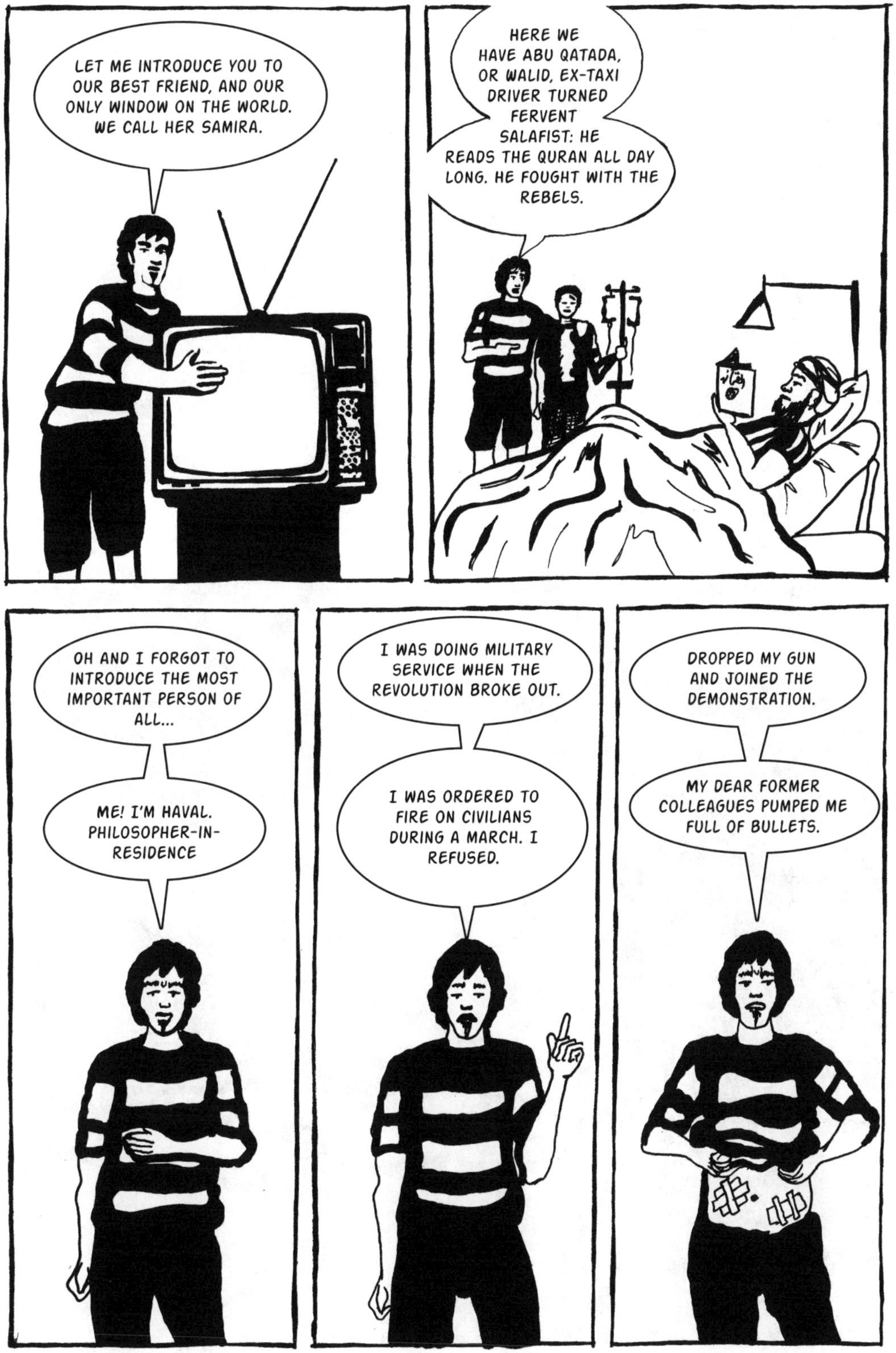
LET ME INTRODUCE YOU TO OUR BEST FRIEND, AND OUR ONLY WINDOW ON THE WORLD. WE CALL HER SAMIRA.
HERE WE HAVE ABU QATADA, OR WALID, EX-TAXI DRIVER TURNED FERVENT SALAFIST: HE READS THE QURAN ALL DAY LONG. HE FOUGHT WITH THE REBELS.
OH AND I FORGOT TO INTRODUCE THE MOST IMPORTANT PERSON OF ALL...
ME! I'M HAVAL. PHILOSOPHER-IN-RESIDENCE
I WAS DOING MILITARY SERVICE WHEN THE REVOLUTION BROKE OUT.
I WAS ORDERED TO FIRE ON CIVILIANS DURING A MARCH. I REFUSED.
DROPPED MY GUN AND JOINED THE DEMONSTRATION.
MY DEAR FORMER COLLEAGUES PUMPED ME FULL OF BULLETS.

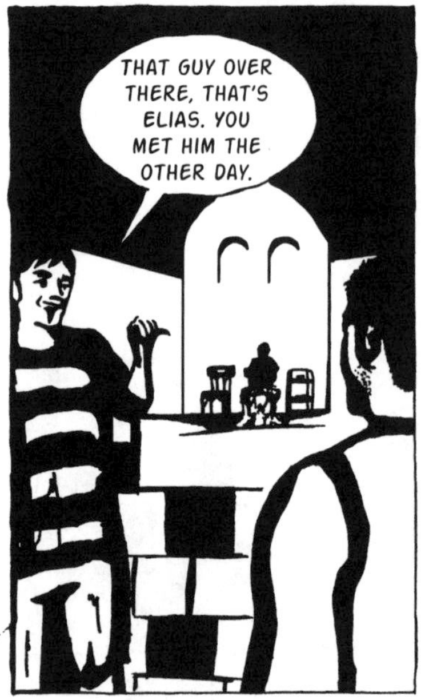
THAT GUY OVER THERE, THAT'S ELIAS. YOU MET HIM THE OTHER DAY.

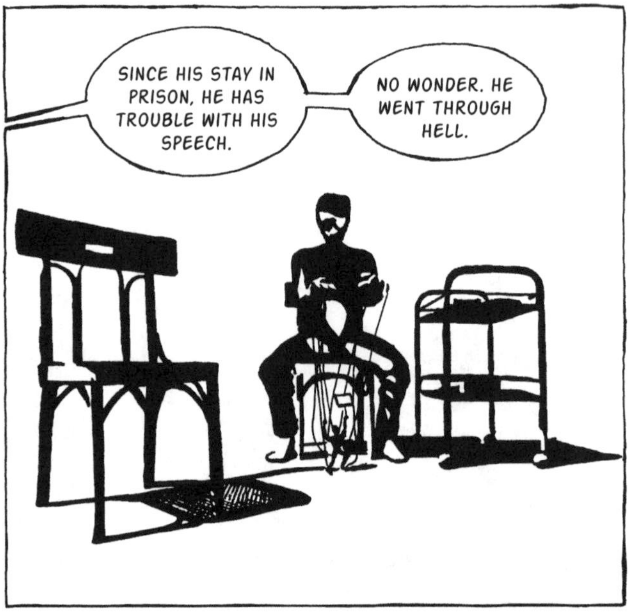
SINCE HIS STAY IN PRISON, HE HAS TROUBLE WITH HIS SPEECH.
NO WONDER. HE WENT THROUGH HELL.

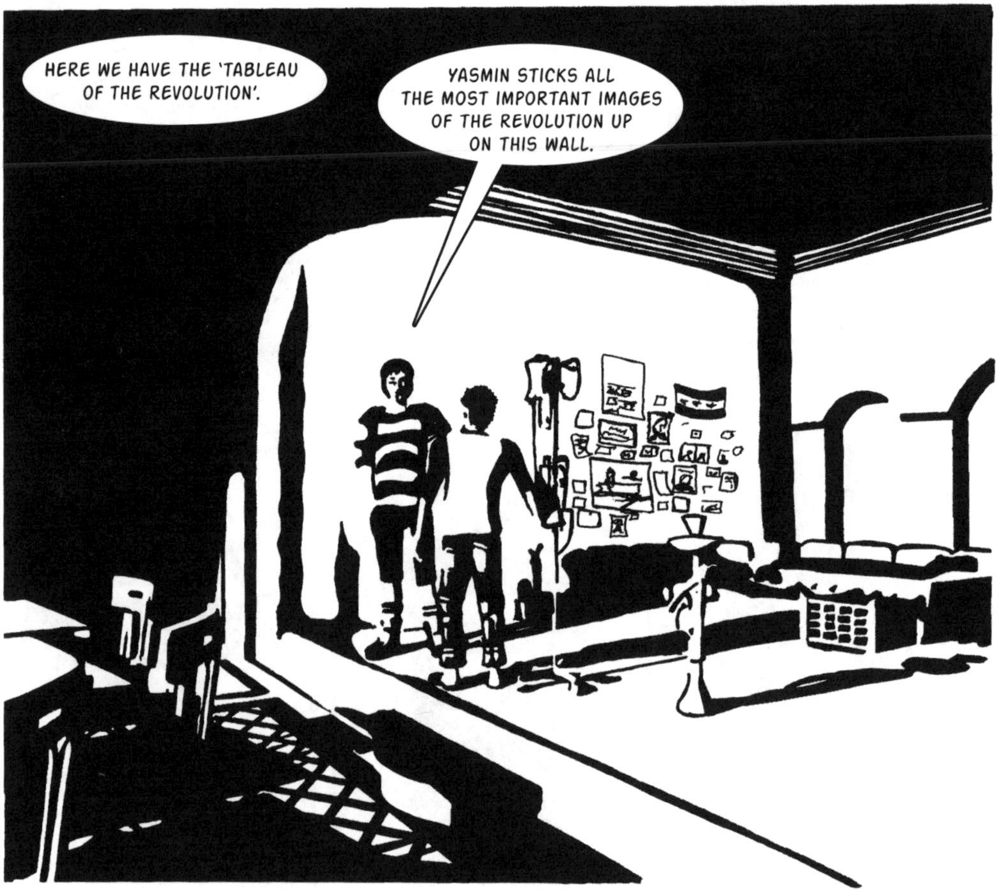
HERE WE HAVE THE 'TABLEAU OF THE REVOLUTION'.
YASMIN STICKS ALL THE MOST IMPORTANT IMAGES OF THE REVOLUTION UP ON THIS WALL.

YALLA, I'M STARVING. GET READY FOR THE BEST BREAKFAST OF YOUR LIFE.

LEFT.

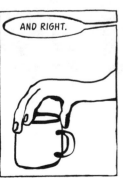

AND RIGHT.

THE ONLY GOOD THING IN THIS DUMP ARE THE DELICACIES COOKED UP BY OUR CHEF, ZAHABIAH.

MORNING, GUYS.

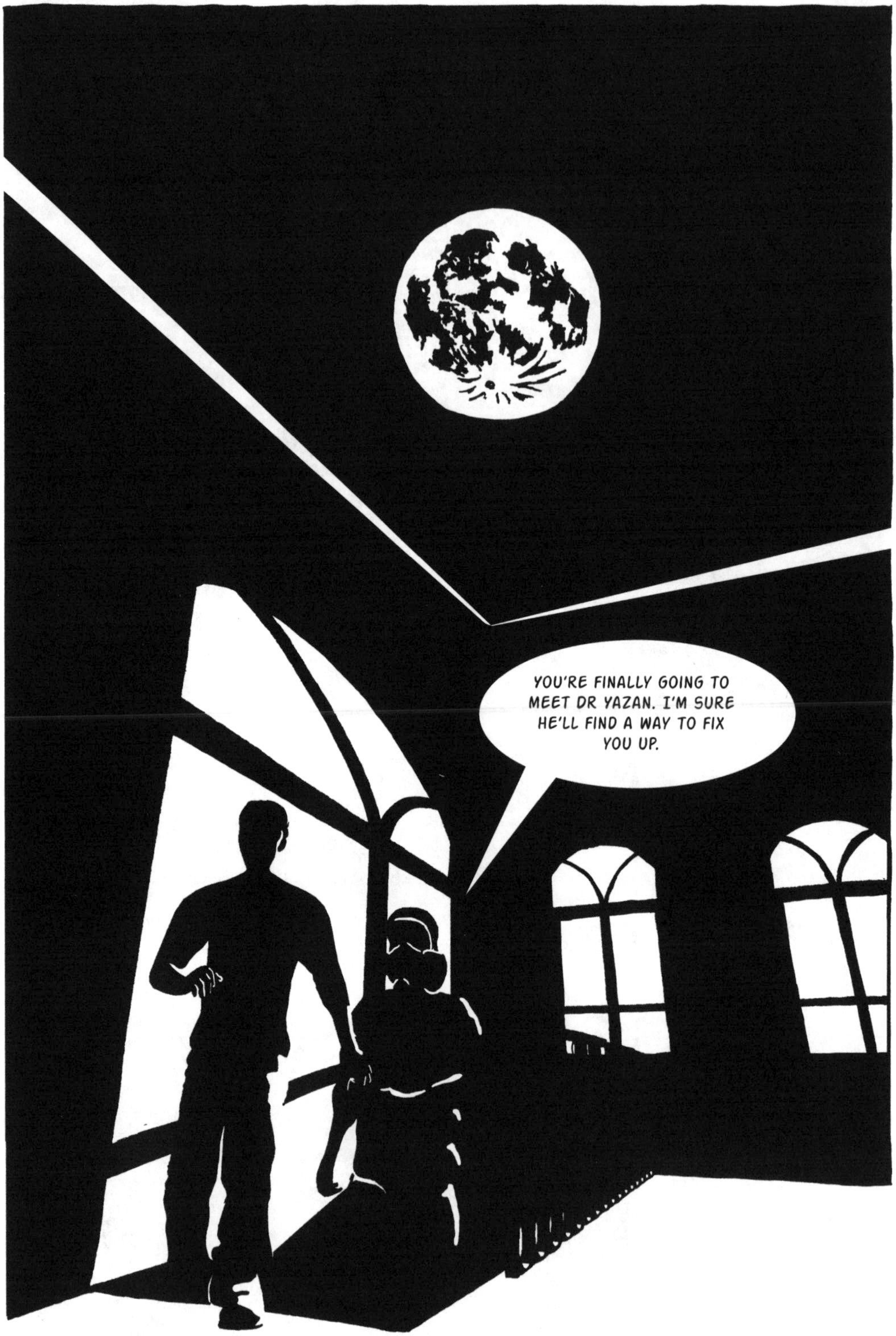
YOU'RE FINALLY GOING TO MEET DR YAZAN. I'M SURE HE'LL FIND A WAY TO FIX YOU UP.

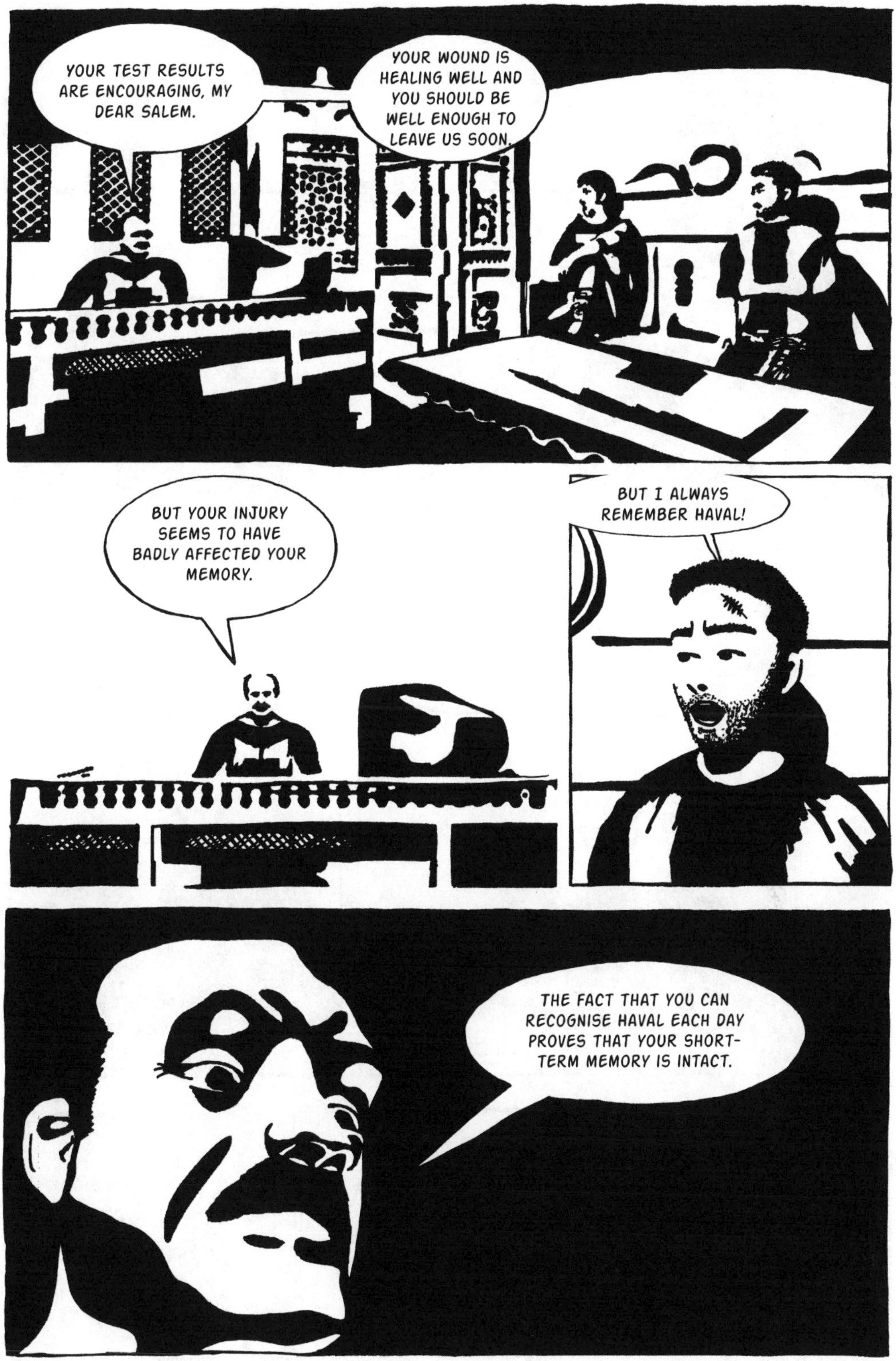
YOUR TEST RESULTS ARE ENCOURAGING, MY DEAR SALEM.
YOUR WOUND IS HEALING WELL AND YOU SHOULD BE WELL ENOUGH TO LEAVE US SOON.
BUT YOUR INJURY SEEMS TO HAVE BADLY AFFECTED YOUR MEMORY.
BUT I ALWAYS REMEMBER HAVAL!
THE FACT THAT YOU CAN RECOGNISE HAVAL EACH DAY PROVES THAT YOUR SHORT-TERM MEMORY IS INTACT.

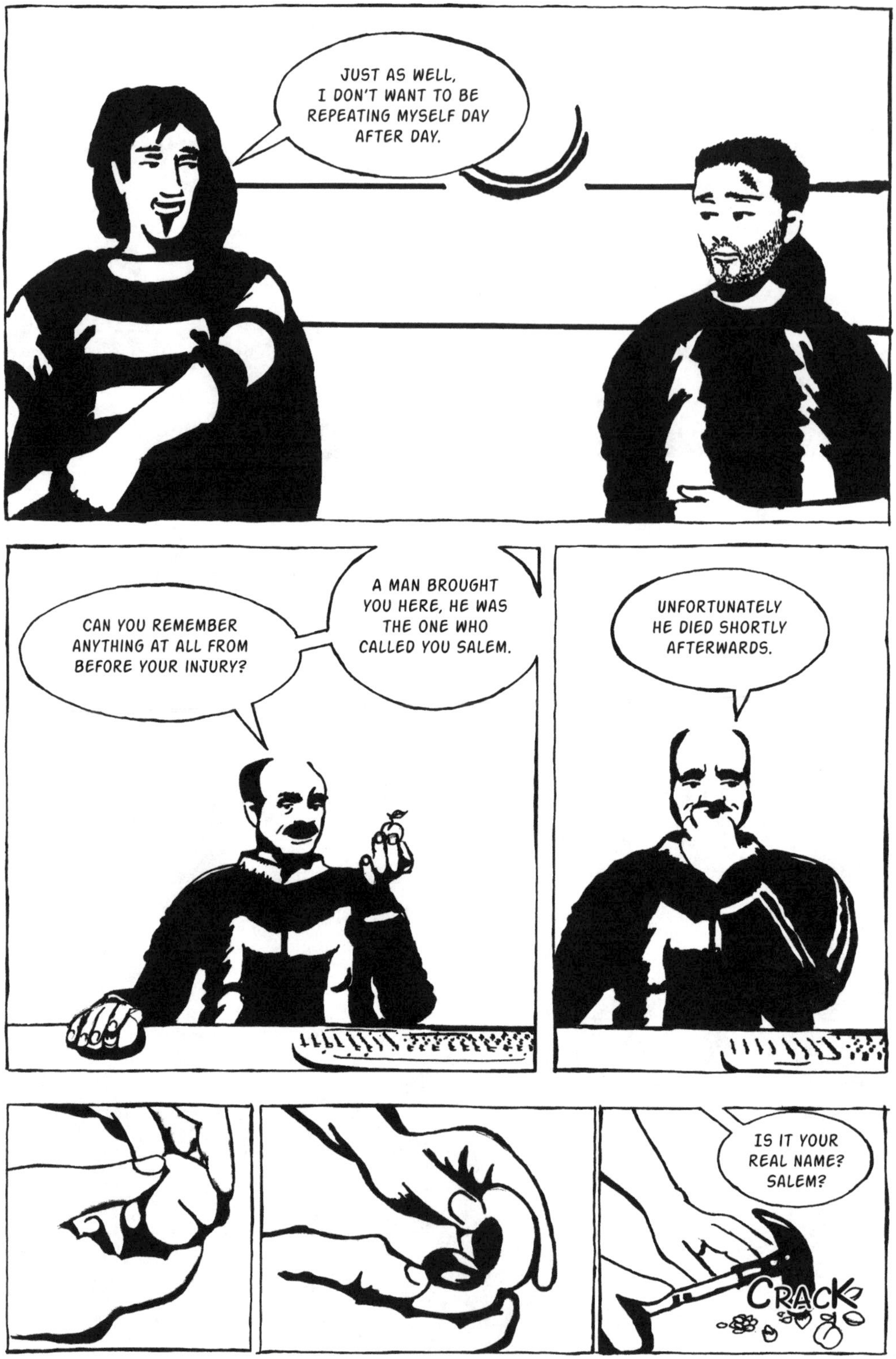
JUST AS WELL, I DON'T WANT TO BE REPEATING MYSELF DAY AFTER DAY.
CAN YOU REMEMBER ANYTHING AT ALL FROM BEFORE YOUR INJURY?
A MAN BROUGHT YOU HERE, HE WAS THE ONE WHO CALLED YOU SALEM.
UNFORTUNATELY HE DIED SHORTLY AFTERWARDS.
IS IT YOUR REAL NAME? SALEM?
CRACK

I DON'T KNOW. THE LAST THING I REMEMBER IS LOOKING DOWN THE BARREL OF A GUN.

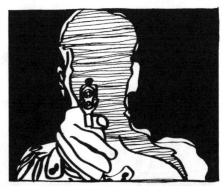

BY THE WAY, SORRY FOR BEING ROUGH WITH YOU THE OTHER DAY.

BUT THIS IS AN UNDERGROUND HOSPITAL. WE HAD TO STOP YOU BEFORE SOMEONE SPOTTED YOU IN THE STREET.

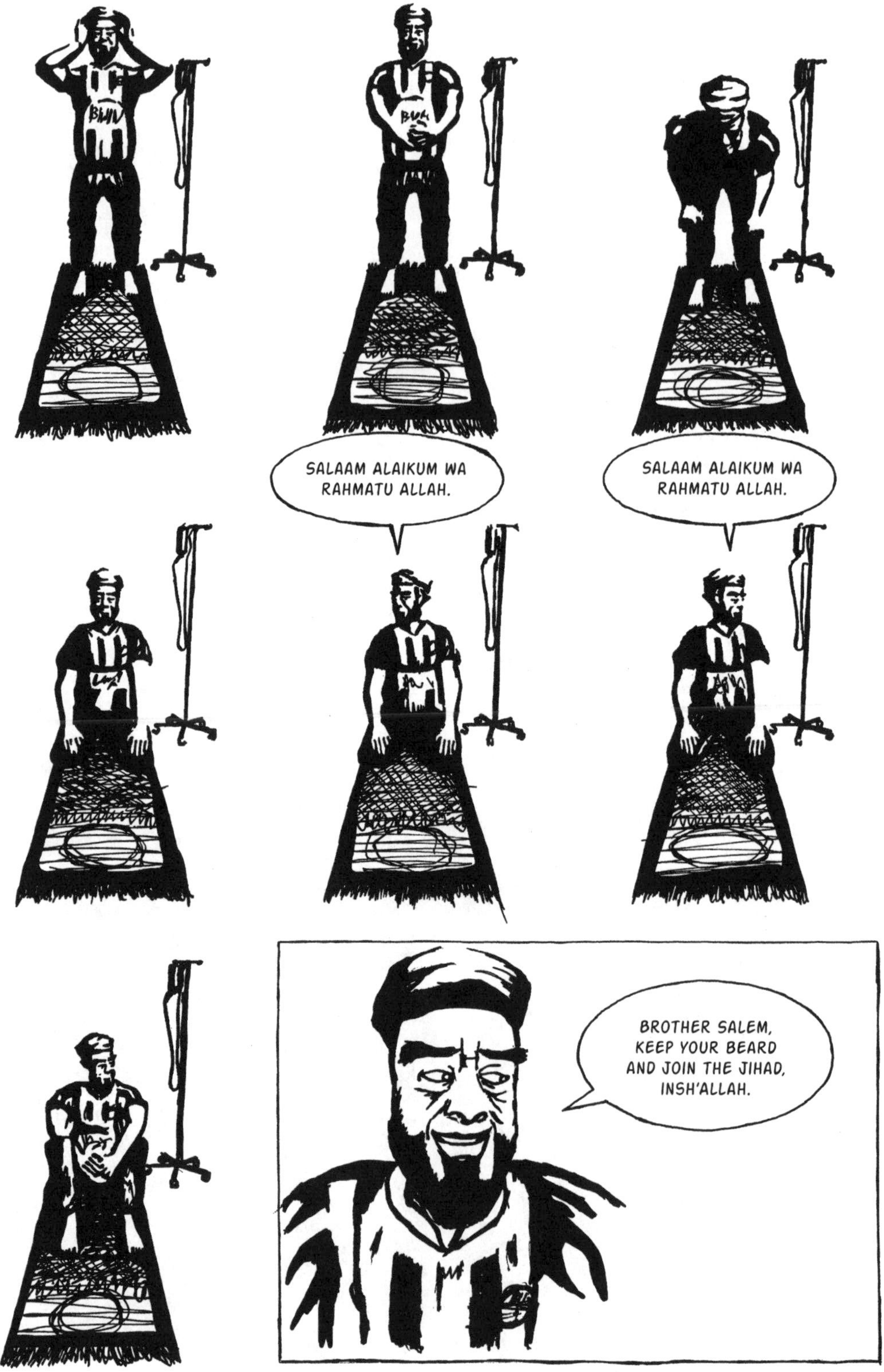
SALAAM ALAIKUM WA RAHMATU ALLAH.
SALAAM ALAIKUM WA RAHMATU ALLAH.
BROTHER SALEM, KEEP YOUR BEARD AND JOIN THE JIHAD, INSH'ALLAH.

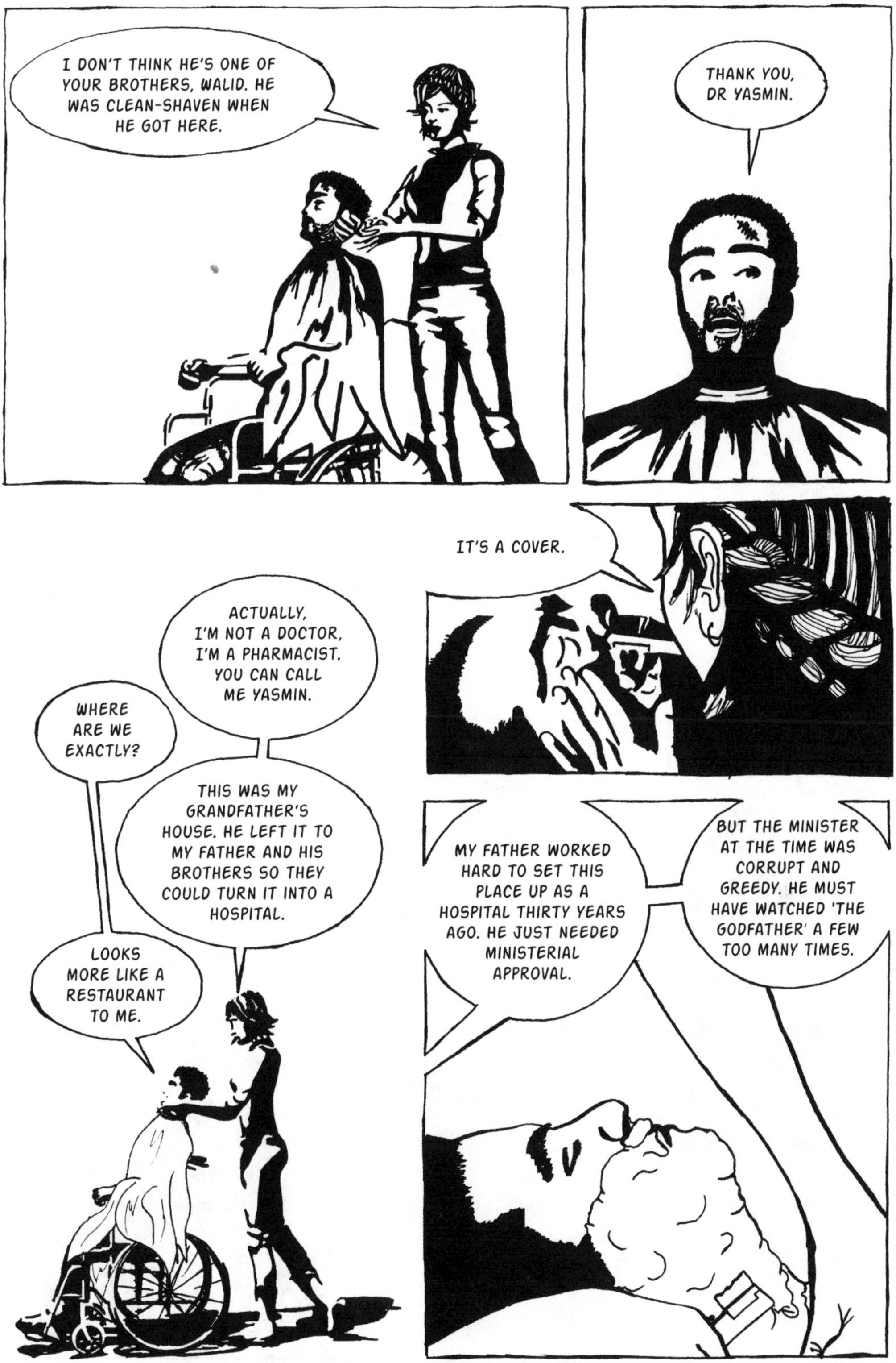
I DON'T THINK HE'S ONE OF YOUR BROTHERS, WALID. HE WAS CLEAN-SHAVEN WHEN HE GOT HERE.
THANK YOU, DR YASMIN.
IT'S A COVER.
WHERE ARE WE EXACTLY?
ACTUALLY, I'M NOT A DOCTOR, I'M A PHARMACIST. YOU CAN CALL ME YASMIN.
THIS WAS MY GRANDFATHER'S HOUSE. HE LEFT IT TO MY FATHER AND HIS BROTHERS SO THEY COULD TURN IT INTO A HOSPITAL.
LOOKS MORE LIKE A RESTAURANT TO ME.
MY FATHER WORKED HARD TO SET THIS PLACE UP AS A HOSPITAL THIRTY YEARS AGO. HE JUST NEEDED MINISTERIAL APPROVAL.
BUT THE MINISTER AT THE TIME WAS CORRUPT AND GREEDY. HE MUST HAVE WATCHED 'THE GODFATHER' A FEW TOO MANY TIMES.

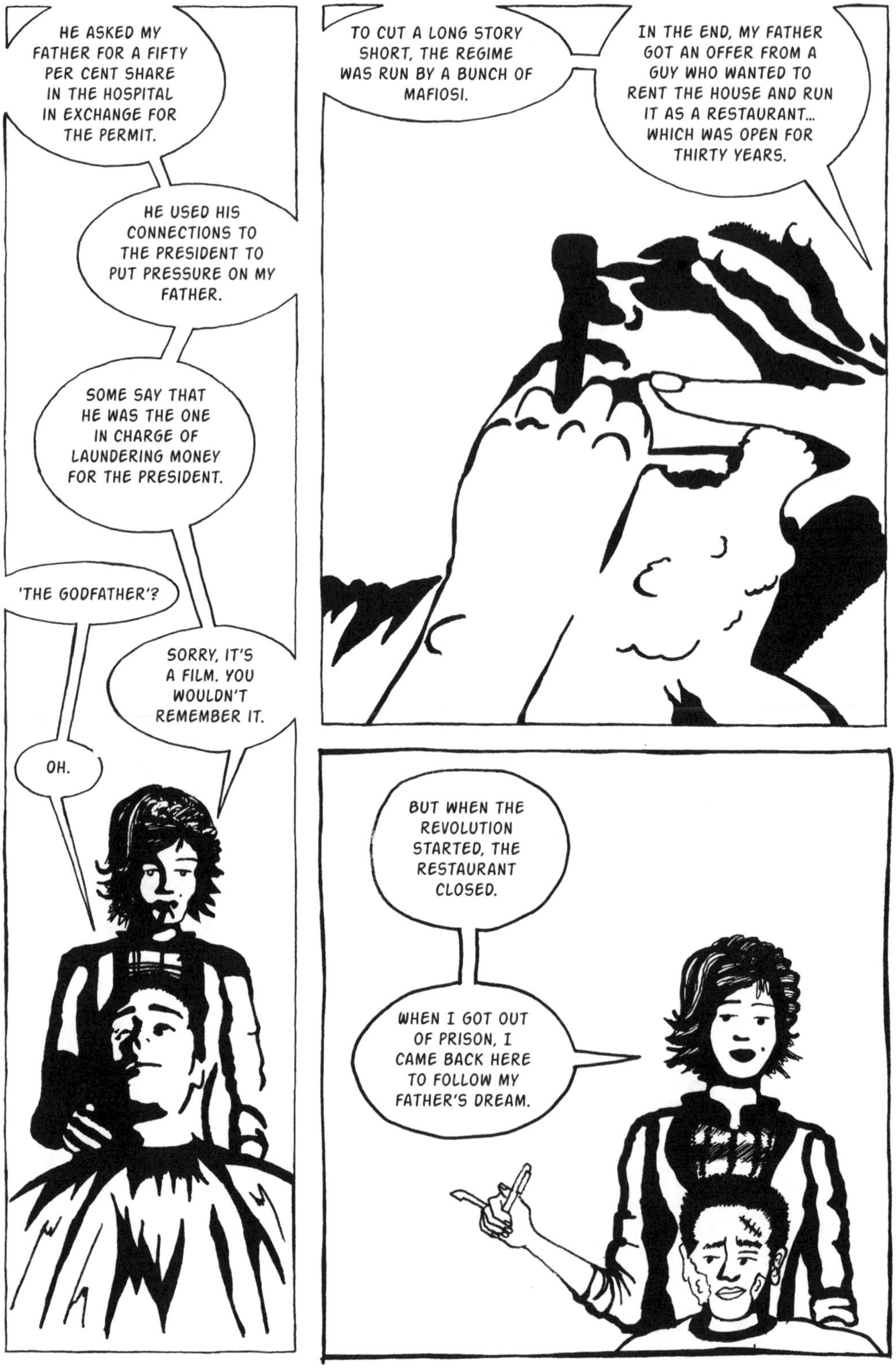
HE ASKED MY FATHER FOR A FIFTY PER CENT SHARE IN THE HOSPITAL IN EXCHANGE FOR THE PERMIT.
HE USED HIS CONNECTIONS TO THE PRESIDENT TO PUT PRESSURE ON MY FATHER.
SOME SAY THAT HE WAS THE ONE IN CHARGE OF LAUNDERING MONEY FOR THE PRESIDENT.
'THE GODFATHER'?
SORRY, IT'S A FILM. YOU WOULDN'T REMEMBER IT.
OH.
TO CUT A LONG STORY SHORT, THE REGIME WAS RUN BY A BUNCH OF MAFIOSI.
IN THE END, MY FATHER GOT AN OFFER FROM A GUY WHO WANTED TO RENT THE HOUSE AND RUN IT AS A RESTAURANT... WHICH WAS OPEN FOR THIRTY YEARS.
BUT WHEN THE REVOLUTION STARTED, THE RESTAURANT CLOSED.
WHEN I GOT OUT OF PRISON, I CAME BACK HERE TO FOLLOW MY FATHER'S DREAM.

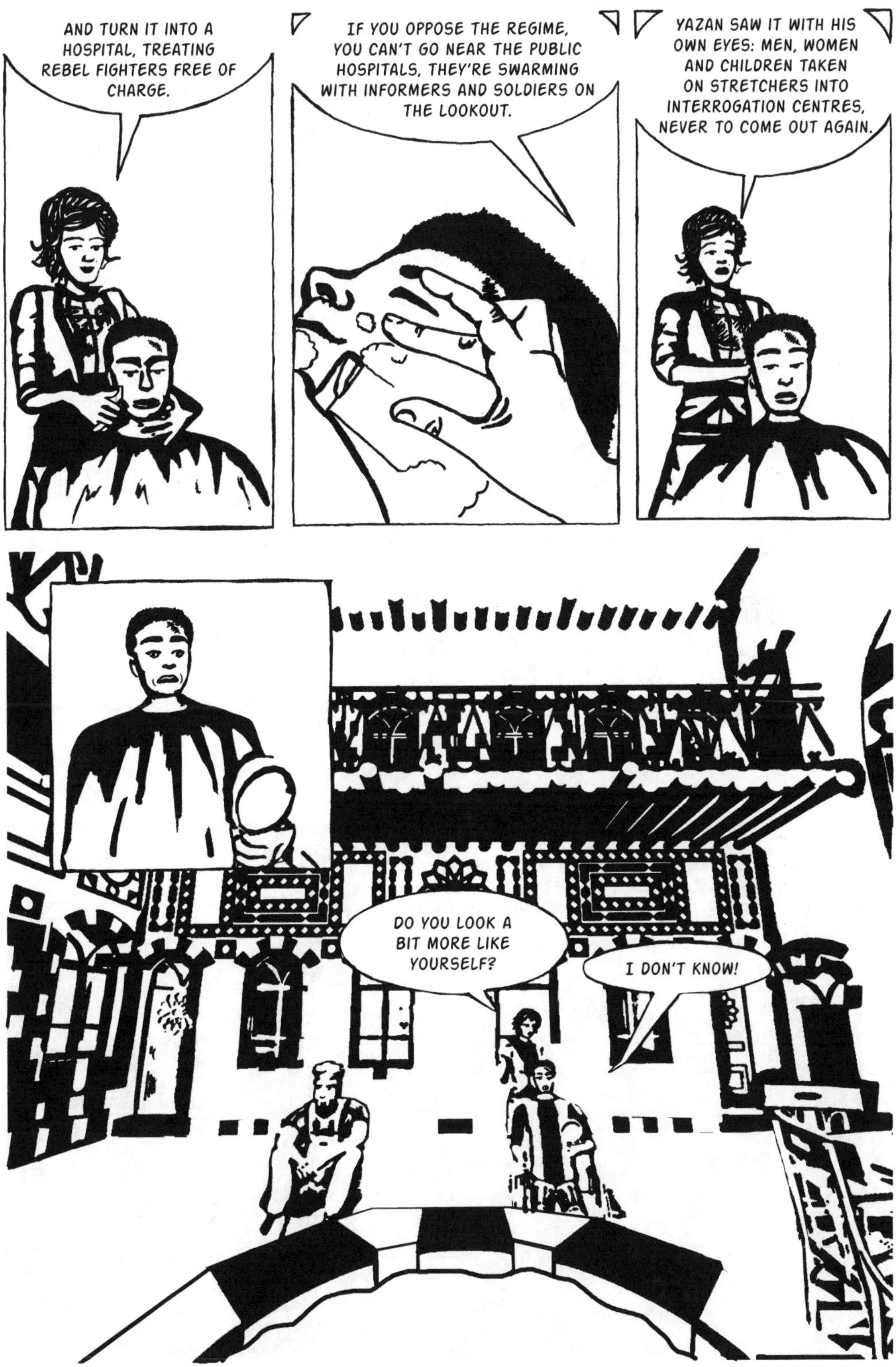
AND TURN IT INTO A HOSPITAL, TREATING REBEL FIGHTERS FREE OF CHARGE.
IF YOU OPPOSE THE REGIME, YOU CAN'T GO NEAR THE PUBLIC HOSPITALS, THEY'RE SWARMING WITH INFORMERS AND SOLDIERS ON THE LOOKOUT.
YAZAN SAW IT WITH HIS OWN EYES: MEN, WOMEN AND CHILDREN TAKEN ON STRETCHERS INTO INTERROGATION CENTRES, NEVER TO COME OUT AGAIN.
DO YOU LOOK A BIT MORE LIKE YOURSELF?
I DON'T KNOW!

TWO DAYS LATER: ANOTHER 472 KILLED.

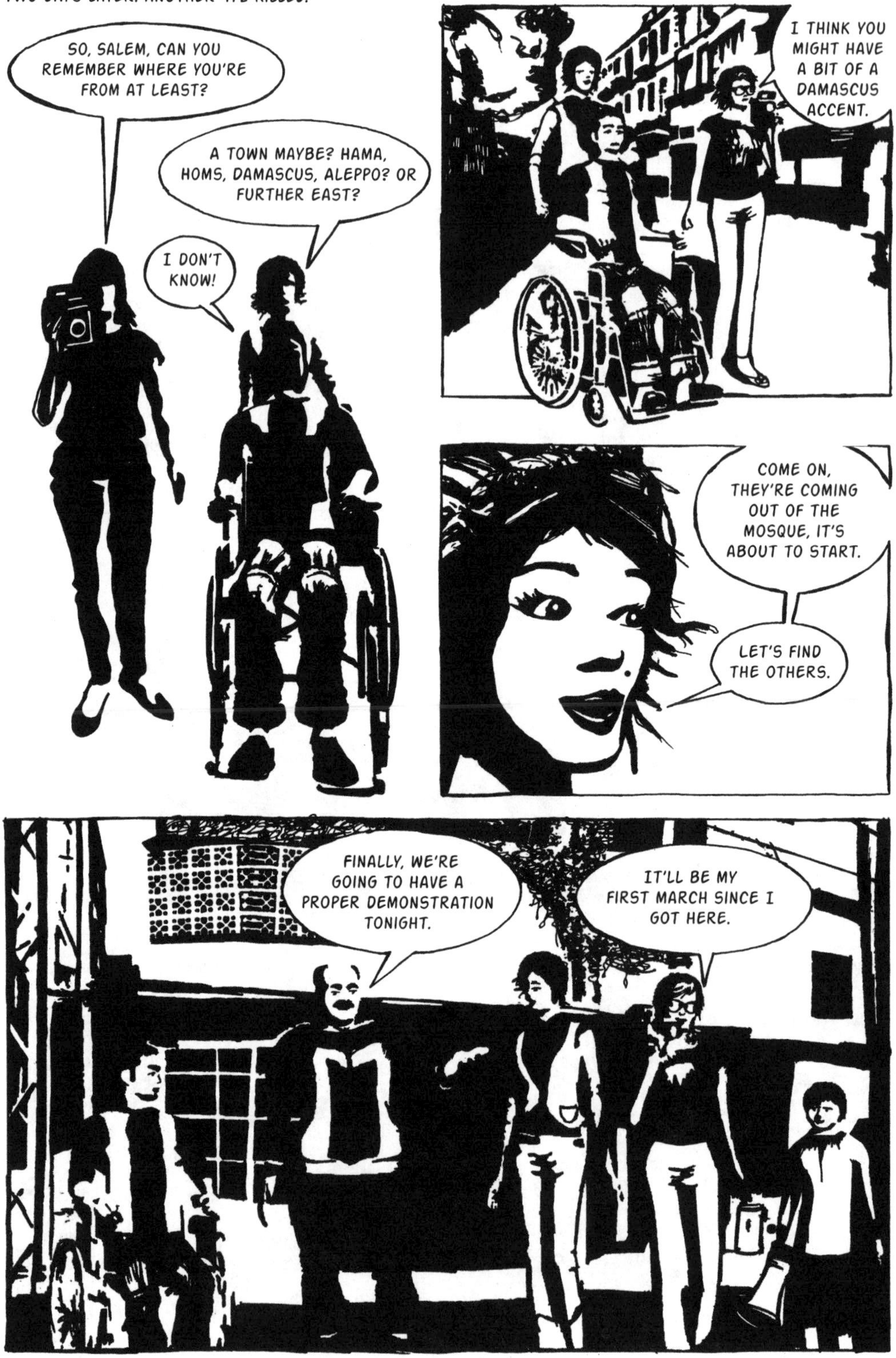
SO, SALEM, CAN YOU REMEMBER WHERE YOU'RE FROM AT LEAST?
A TOWN MAYBE? HAMA, HOMS, DAMASCUS, ALEPPO? OR FURTHER EAST?
I DON'T KNOW!
I THINK YOU MIGHT HAVE A BIT OF A DAMASCUS ACCENT.
COME ON, THEY'RE COMING OUT OF THE MOSQUE, IT'S ABOUT TO START.
LET'S FIND THE OTHERS.
FINALLY, WE'RE GOING TO HAVE A PROPER DEMONSTRATION TONIGHT.
IT'LL BE MY FIRST MARCH SINCE I GOT HERE.

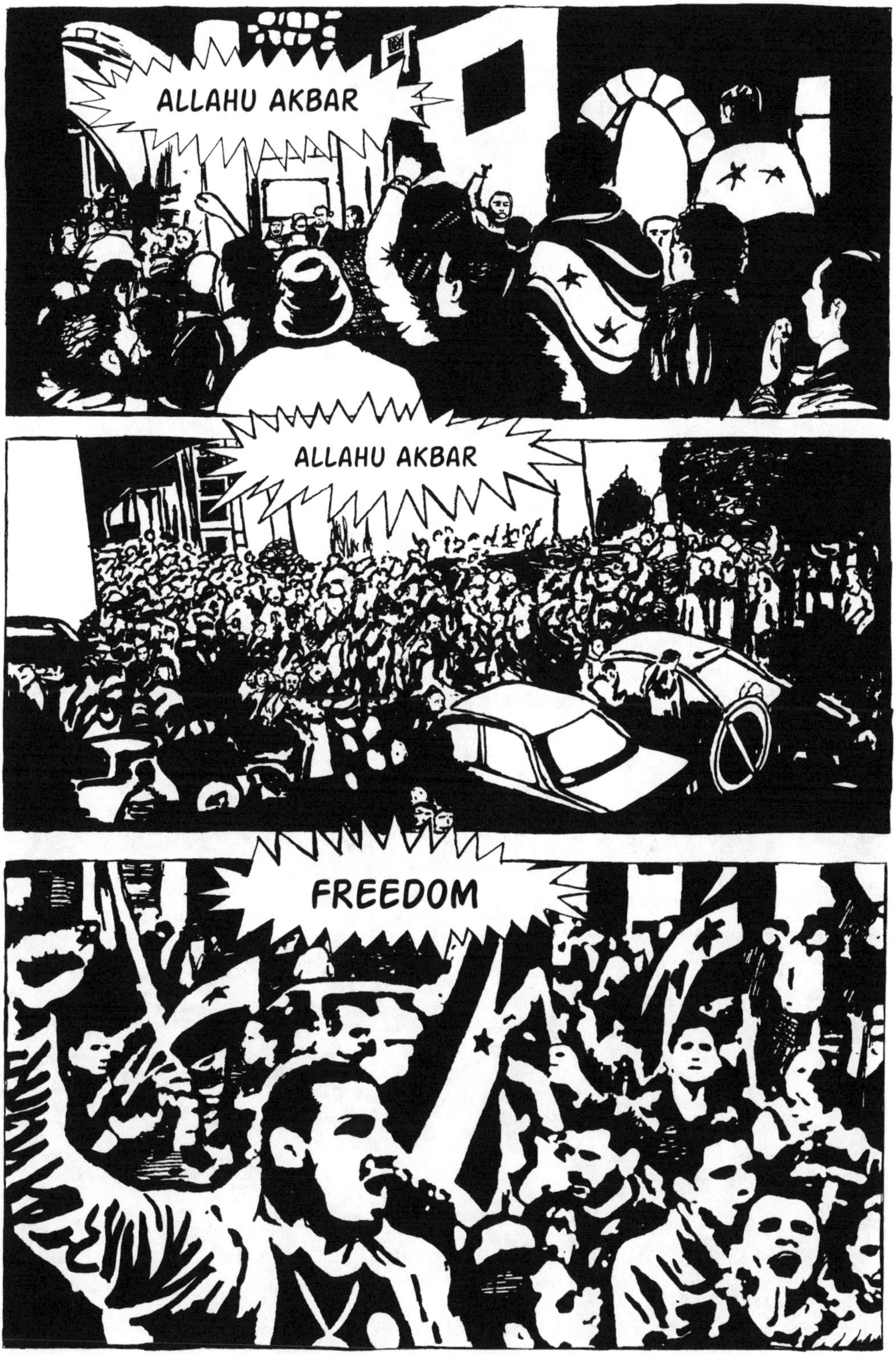
ALLAHU AKBAR
ALLAHU AKBAR
FREEDOM

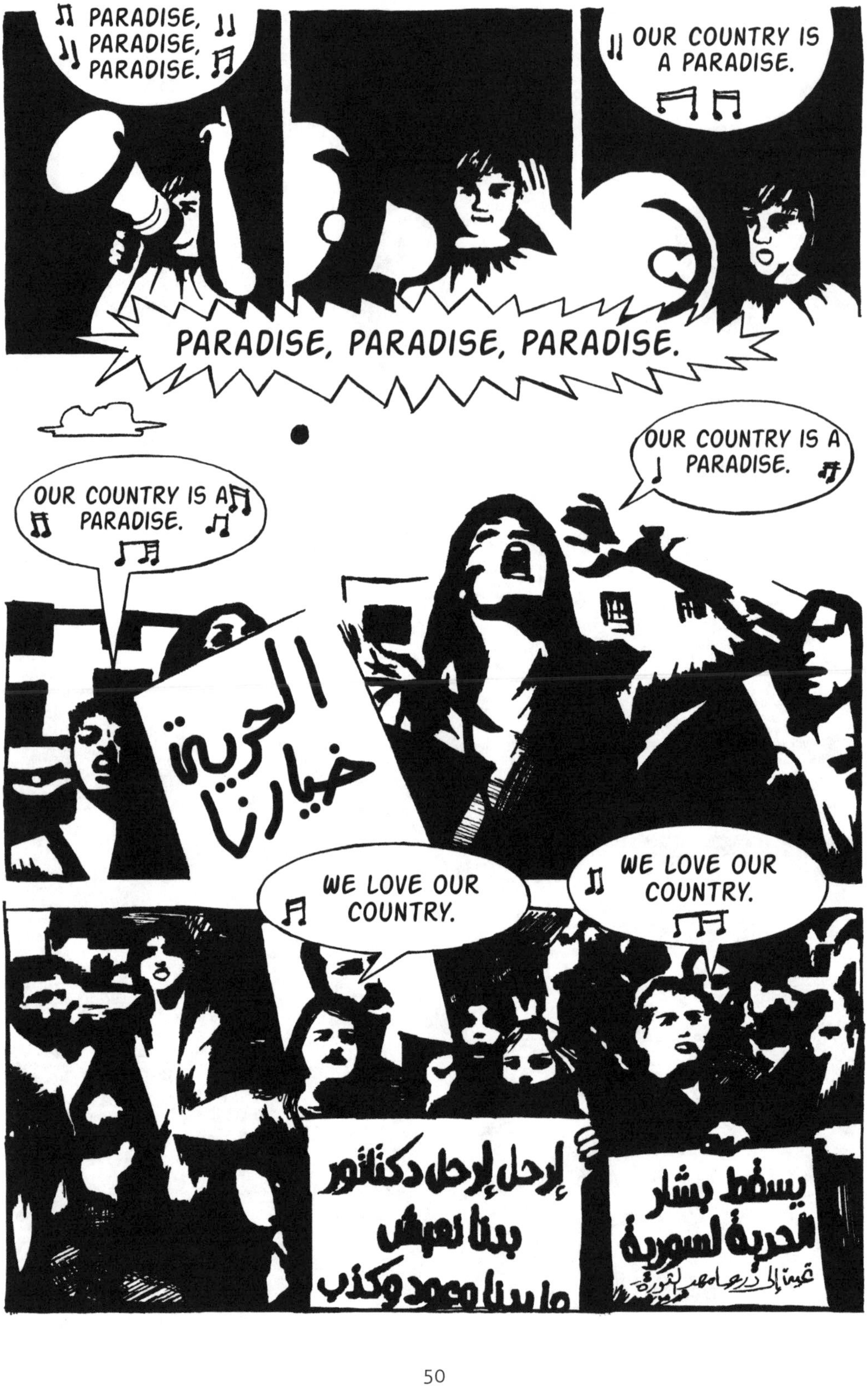
PARADISE, PARADISE, PARADISE.
OUR COUNTRY IS A PARADISE.
PARADISE, PARADISE, PARADISE.
OUR COUNTRY IS A PARADISE.
OUR COUNTRY IS A PARADISE.
الحرية خيارنا
WE LOVE OUR COUNTRY.
WE LOVE OUR COUNTRY.
إرحل إرحل دكتاتور
بدنا نعيش
يسقط بشار
الحرية لسورية

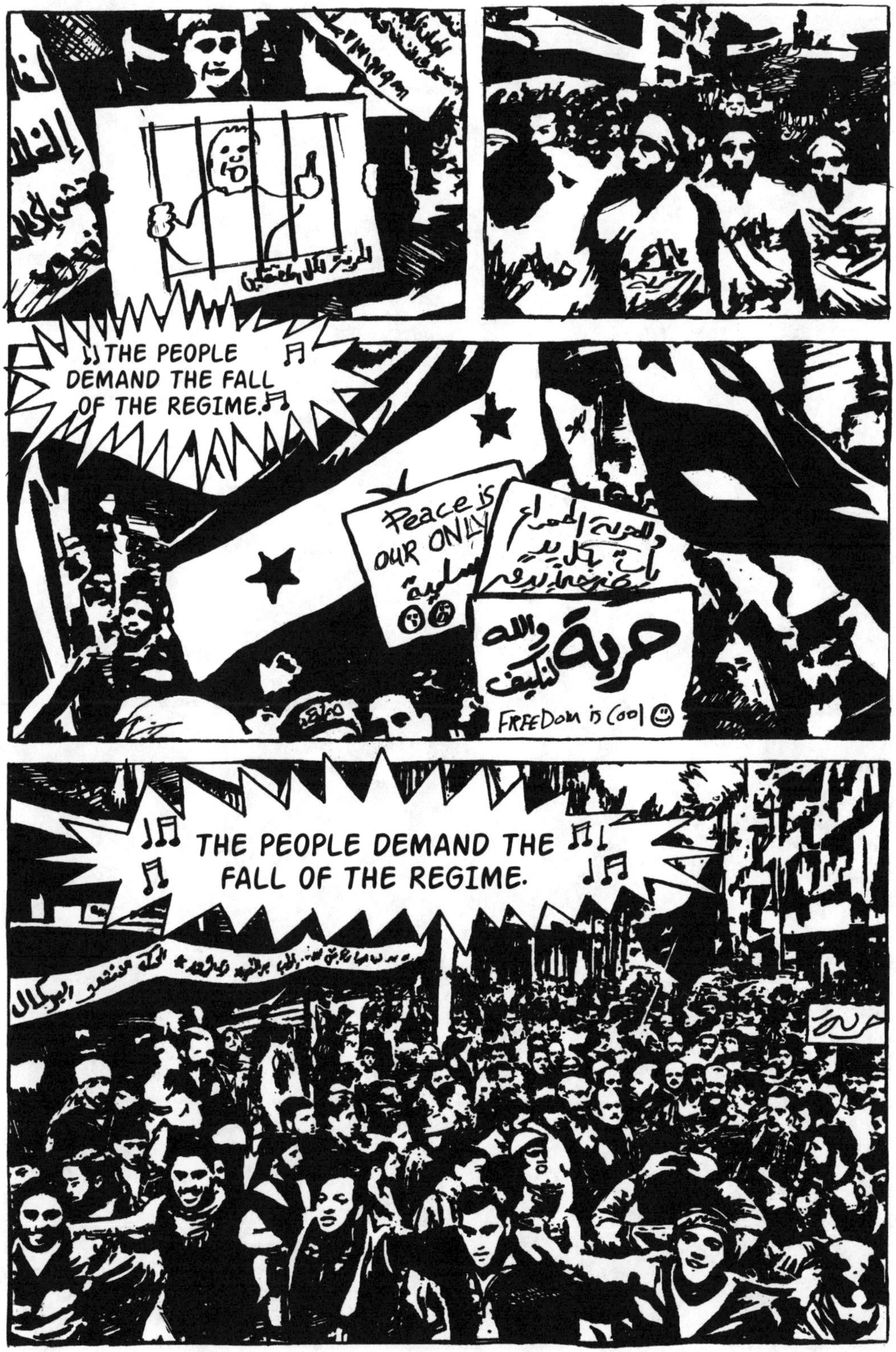
THE PEOPLE DEMAND THE FALL OF THE REGIME.
Peace is OUR ONLY
FREEDOM is Cool
THE PEOPLE DEMAND THE FALL OF THE REGIME.

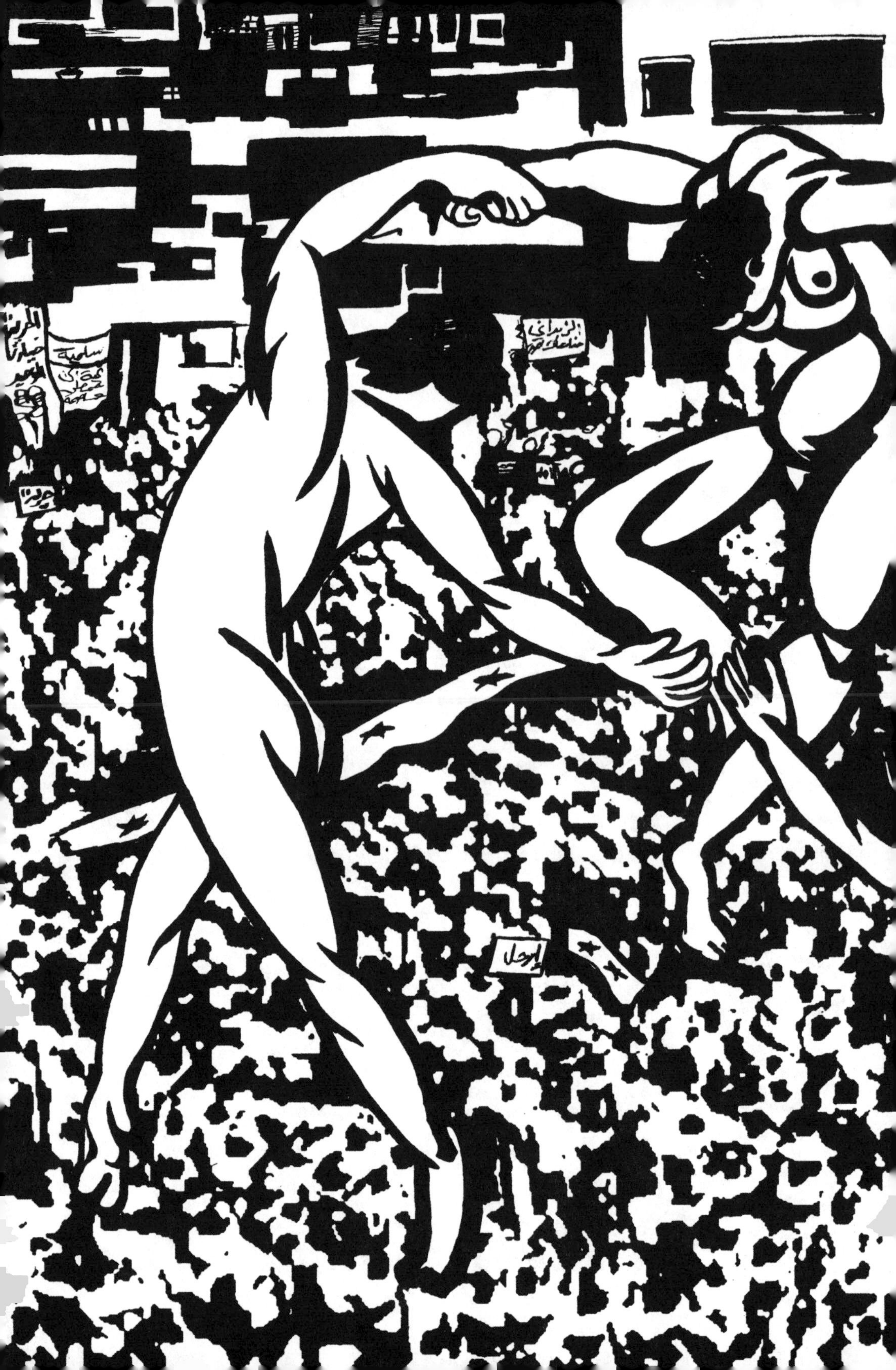
ارحل

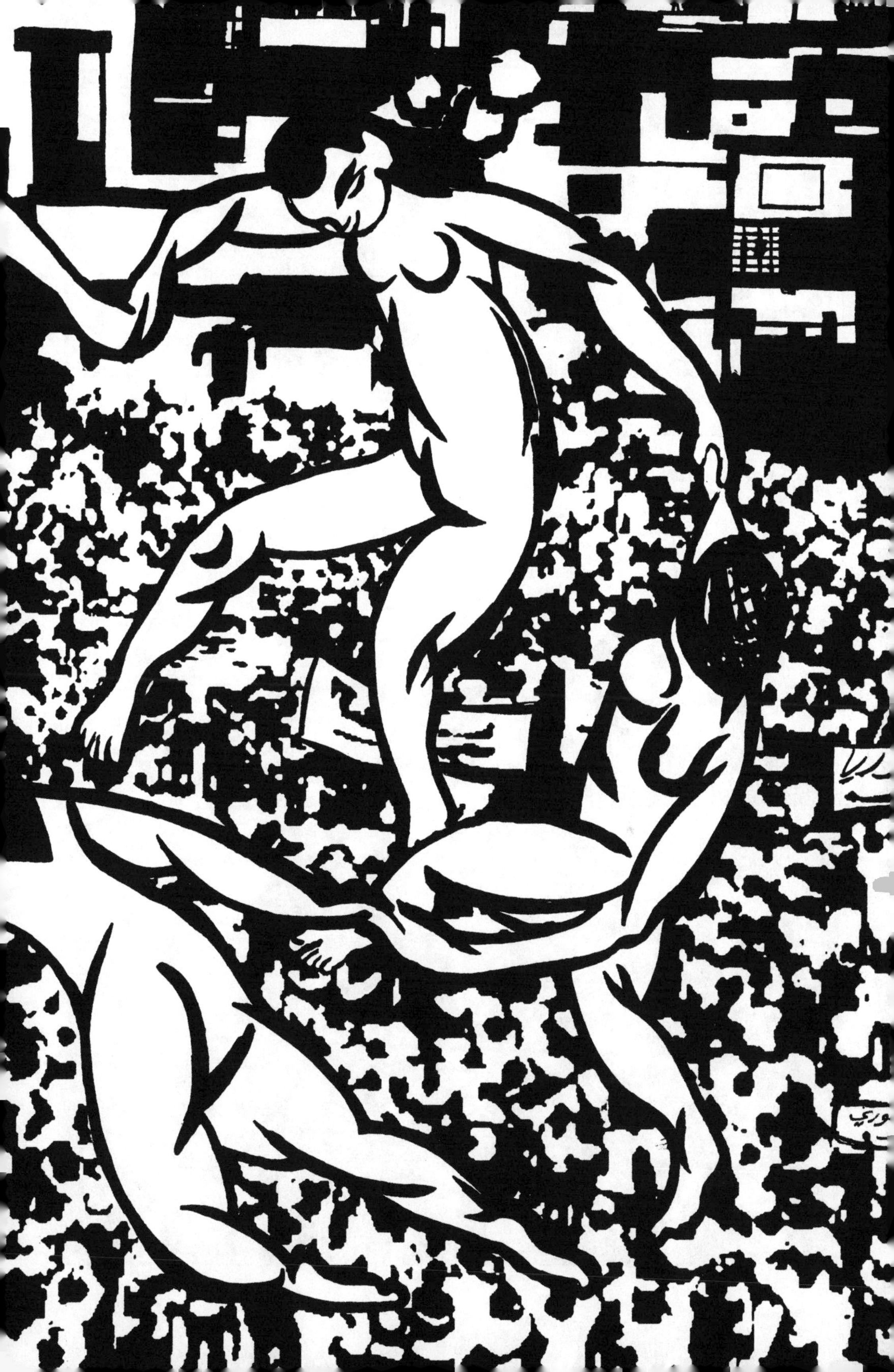

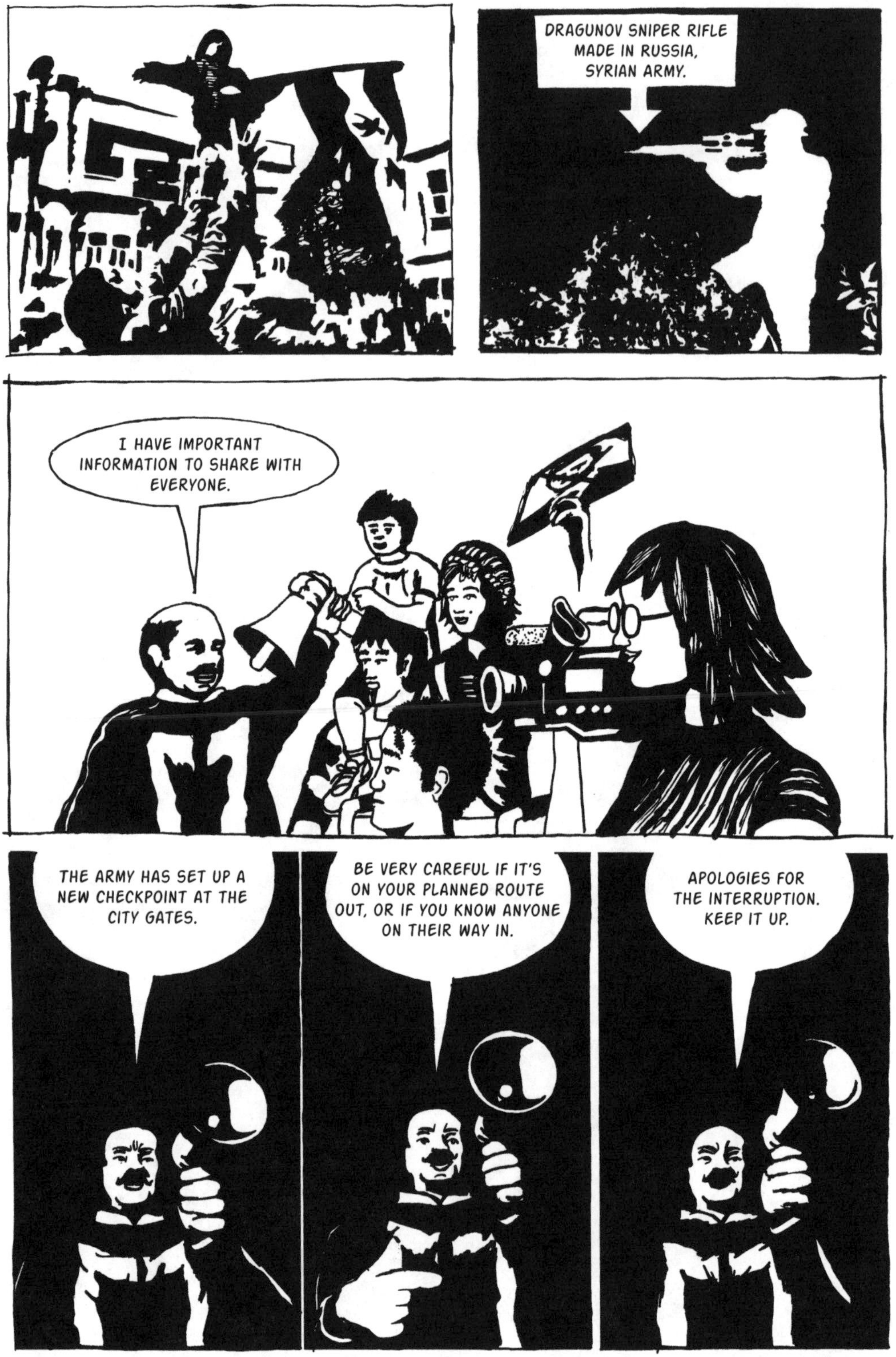
DRAGUNOV SNIPER RIFLE MADE IN RUSSIA, SYRIAN ARMY.
I HAVE IMPORTANT INFORMATION TO SHARE WITH EVERYONE.
THE ARMY HAS SET UP A NEW CHECKPOINT AT THE CITY GATES.
BE VERY CAREFUL IF IT'S ON YOUR PLANNED ROUTE OUT, OR IF YOU KNOW ANYONE ON THEIR WAY IN.
APOLOGIES FOR THE INTERRUPTION. KEEP IT UP.

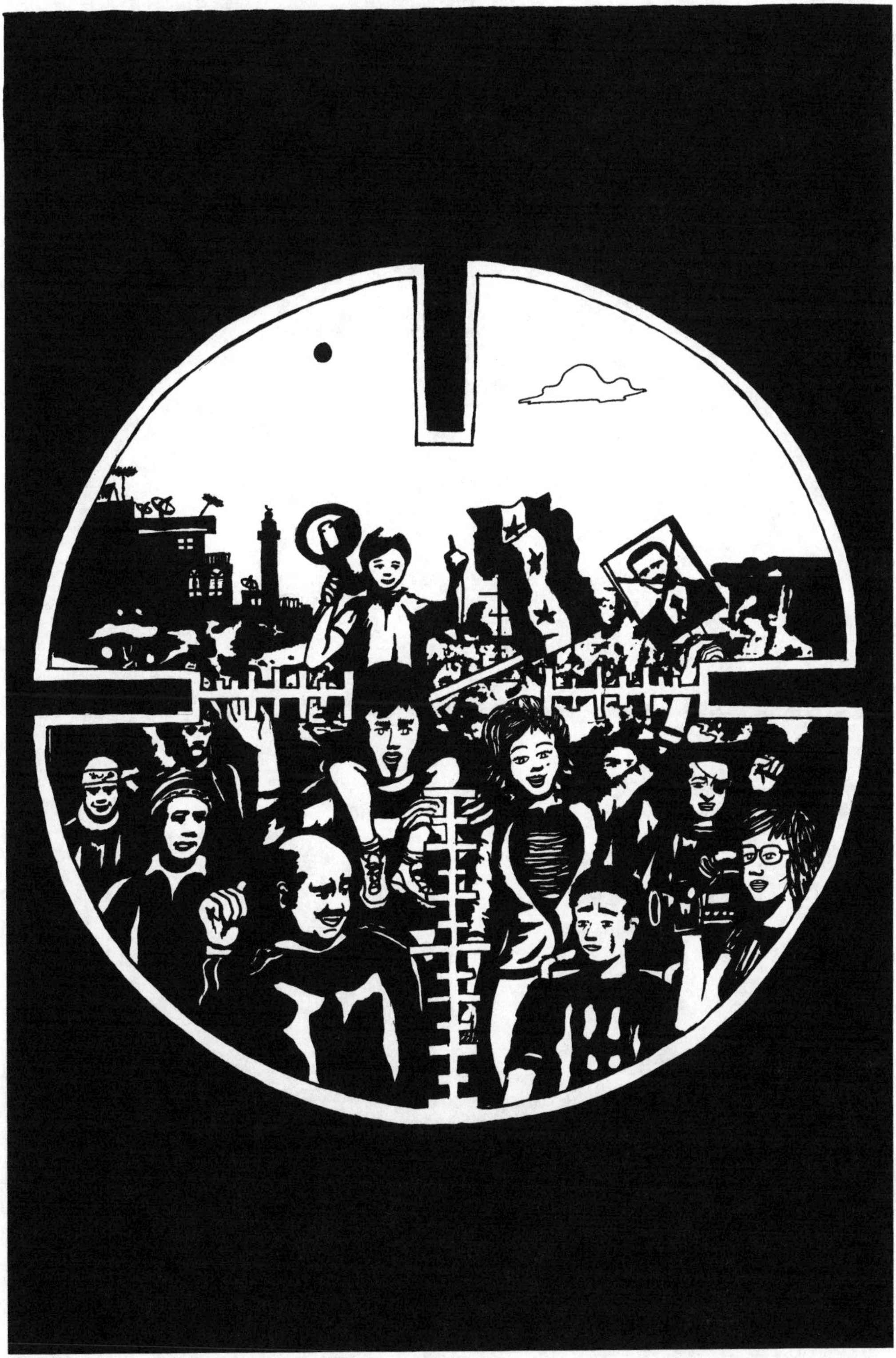

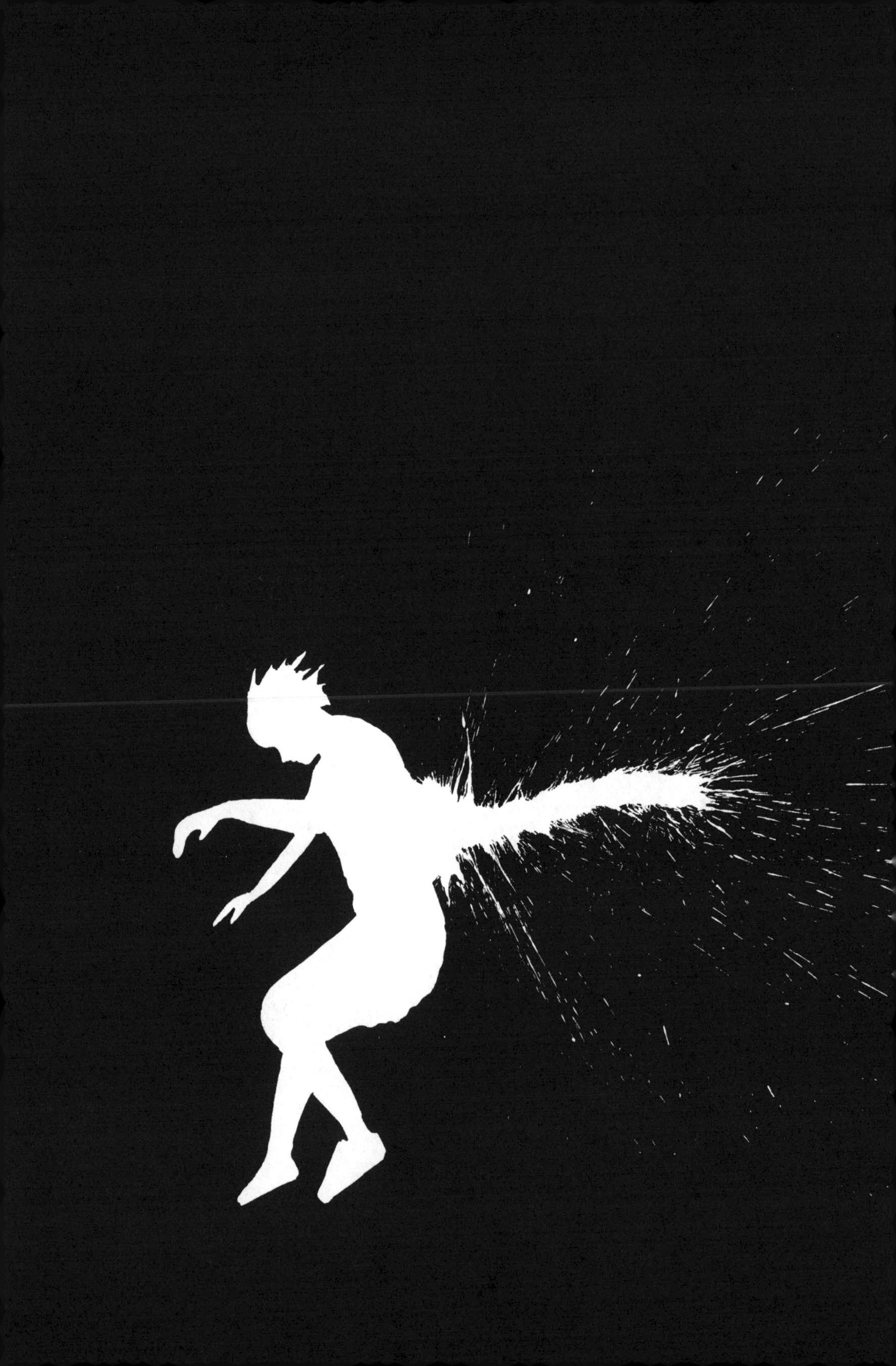

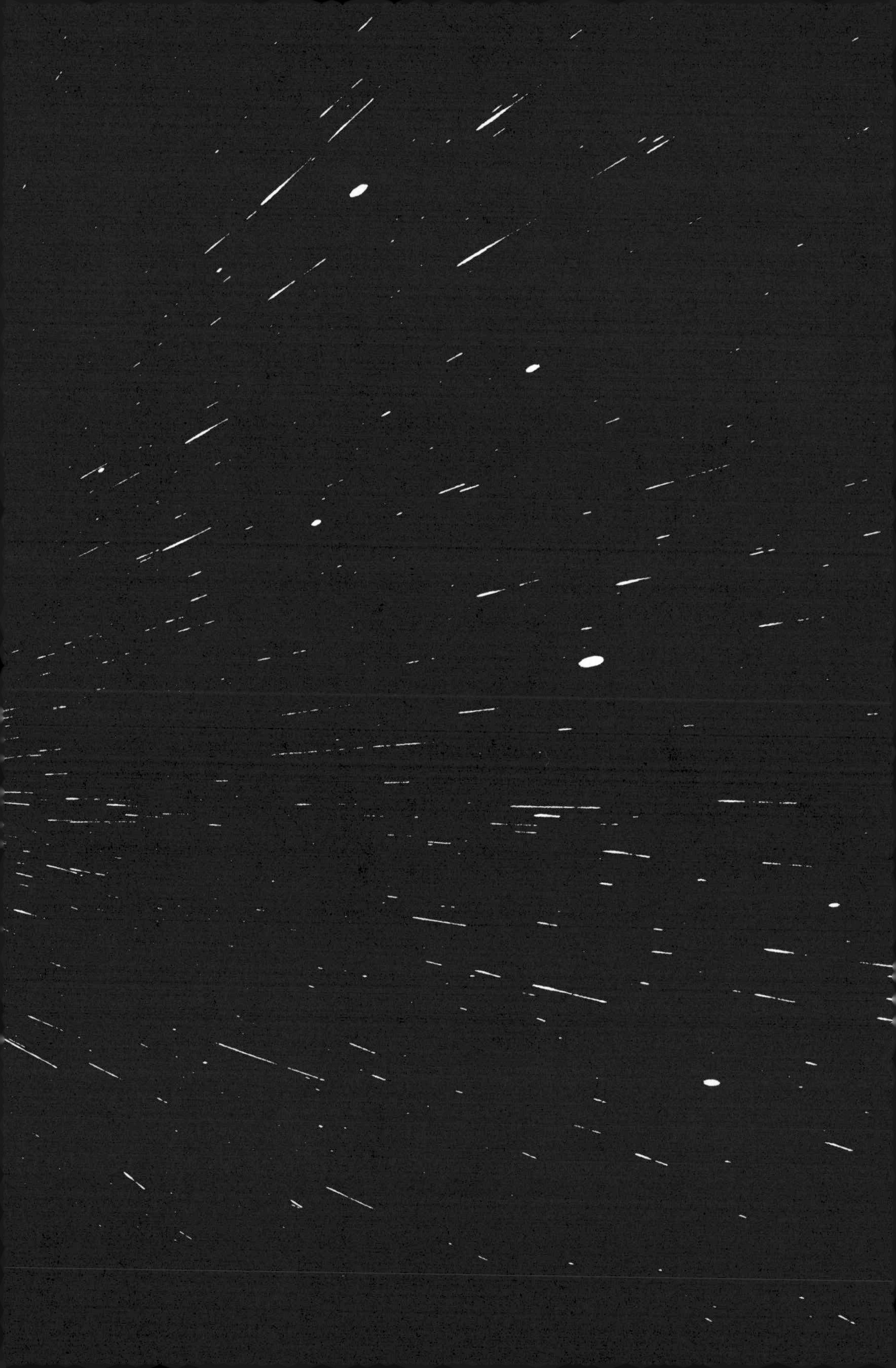

MEANWHILE, ON THE ROUTE INTO TOWN.

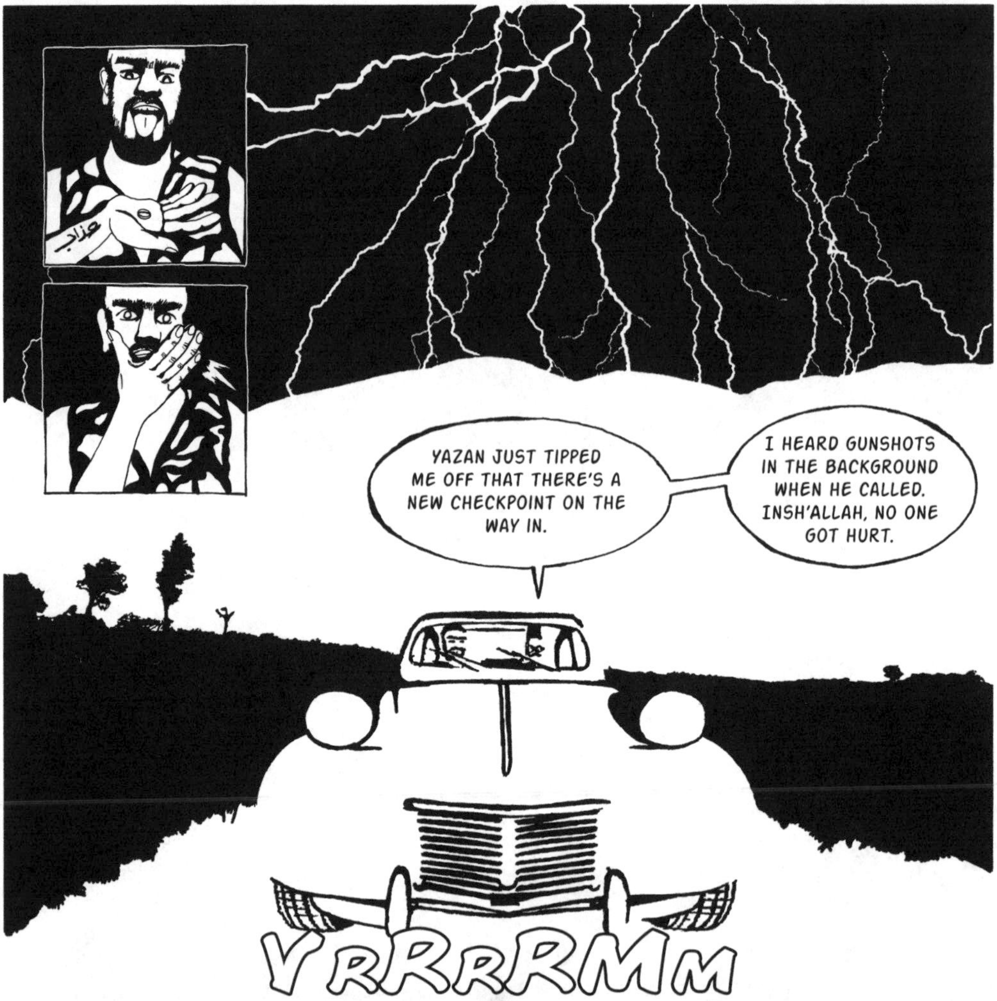

عذاب
YAZAN JUST TIPPED ME OFF THAT THERE'S A NEW CHECKPOINT ON THE WAY IN.
I HEARD GUNSHOTS IN THE BACKGROUND WHEN HE CALLED. INSH'ALLAH, NO ONE GOT HURT.
VRRRRMM

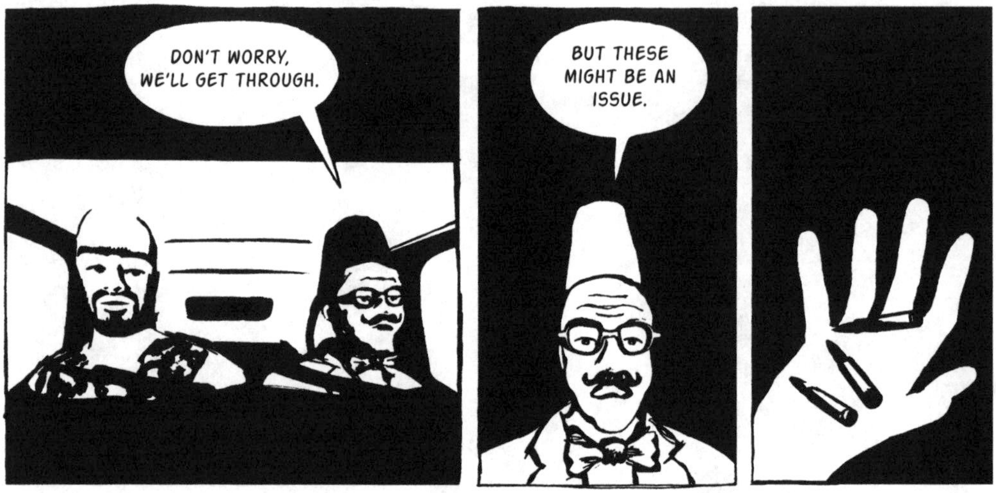

DON'T WORRY, WE'LL GET THROUGH.
BUT THESE MIGHT BE AN ISSUE.

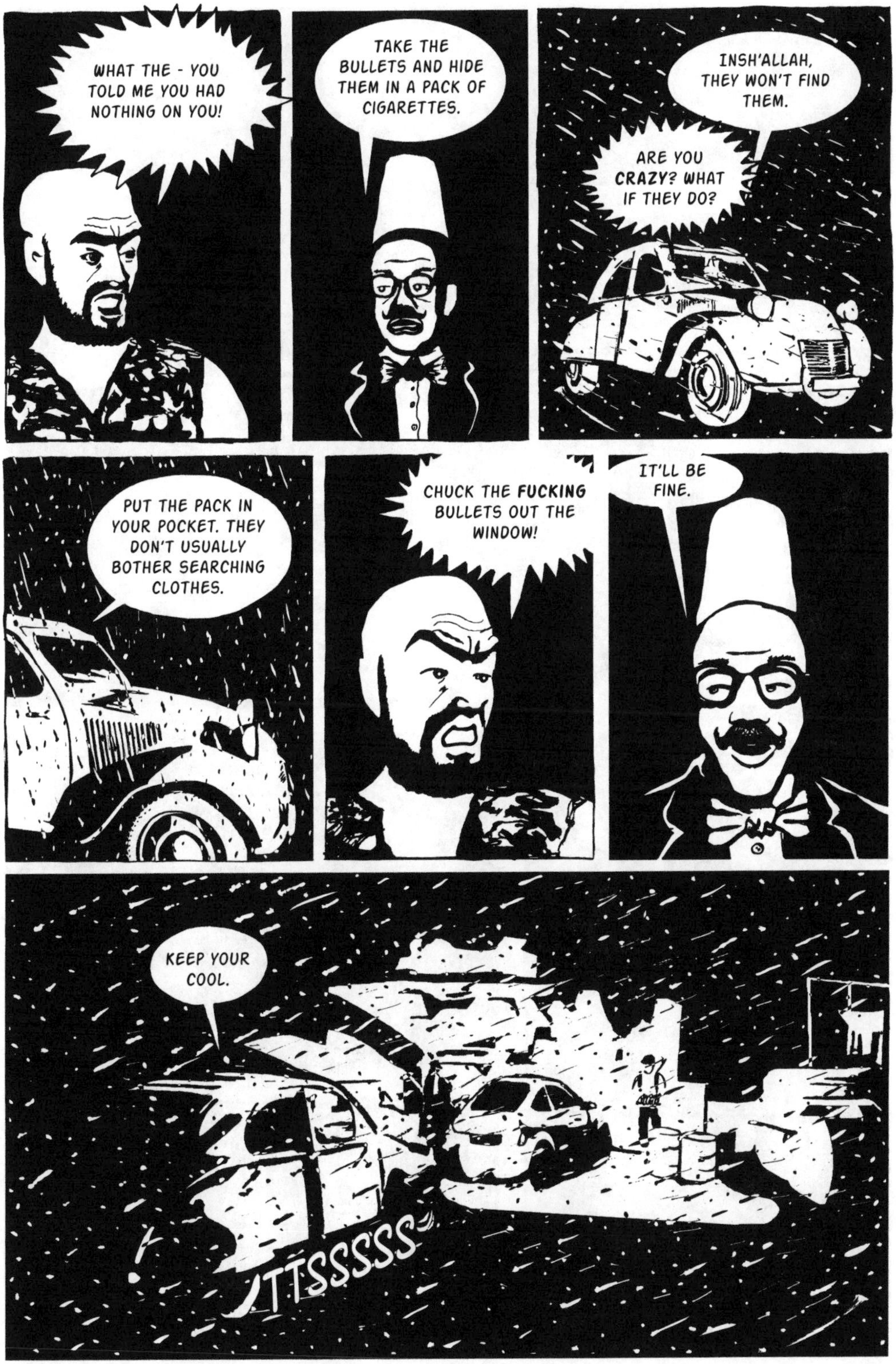
WHAT THE - YOU TOLD ME YOU HAD NOTHING ON YOU!
TAKE THE BULLETS AND HIDE THEM IN A PACK OF CIGARETTES.
ARE YOU **CRAZY**? WHAT IF THEY DO?
INSH'ALLAH, THEY WON'T FIND THEM.
PUT THE PACK IN YOUR POCKET. THEY DON'T USUALLY BOTHER SEARCHING CLOTHES.
CHUCK THE **FUCKING** BULLETS OUT THE WINDOW!
IT'LL BE FINE.
KEEP YOUR COOL.
TTSSSSS

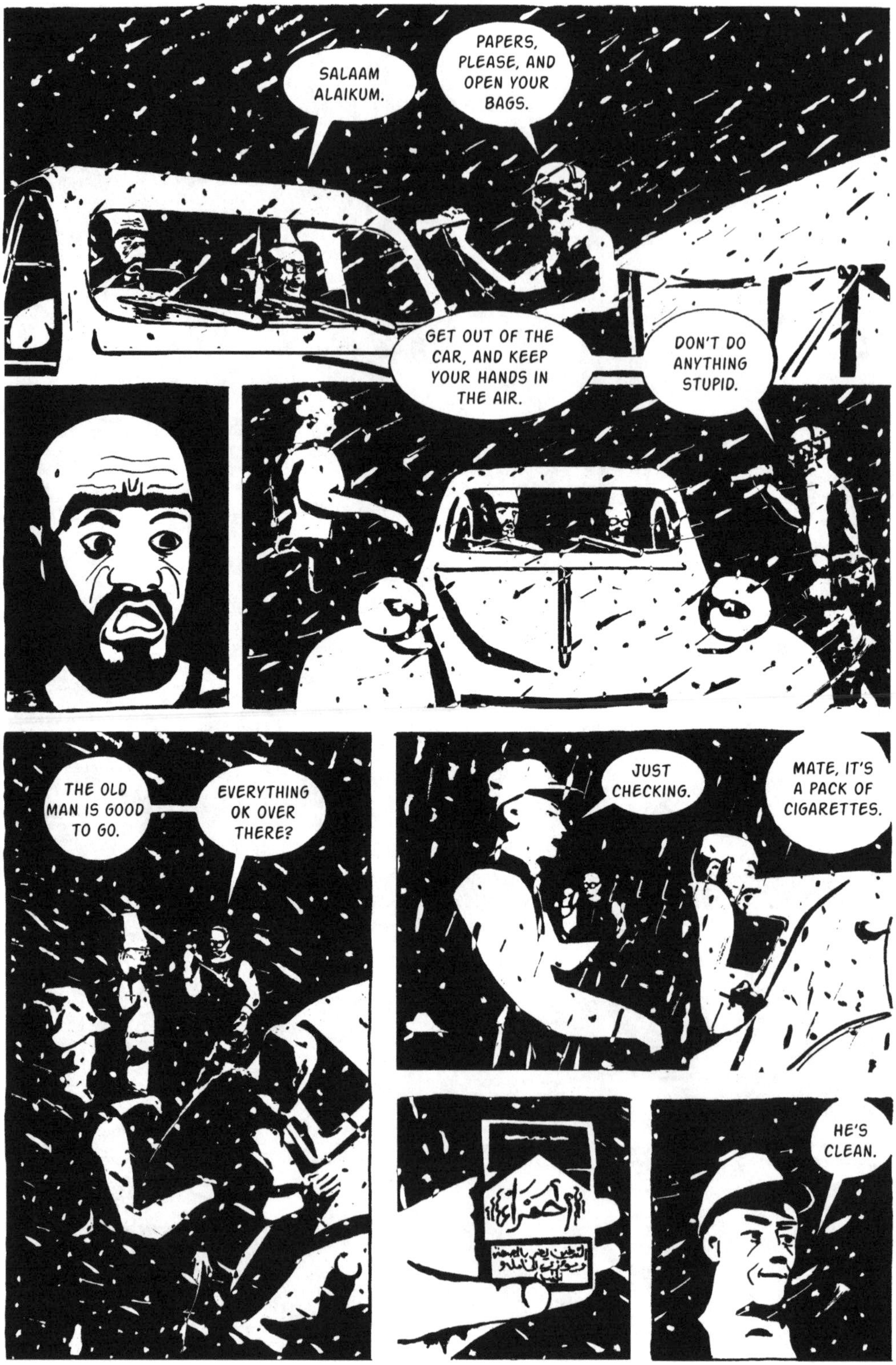
SALAAM ALAIKUM.
PAPERS, PLEASE, AND OPEN YOUR BAGS.
GET OUT OF THE CAR, AND KEEP YOUR HANDS IN THE AIR.
DON'T DO ANYTHING STUPID.
THE OLD MAN IS GOOD TO GO.
EVERYTHING OK OVER THERE?
JUST CHECKING.
MATE, IT'S A PACK OF CIGARETTES.
HE'S CLEAN.

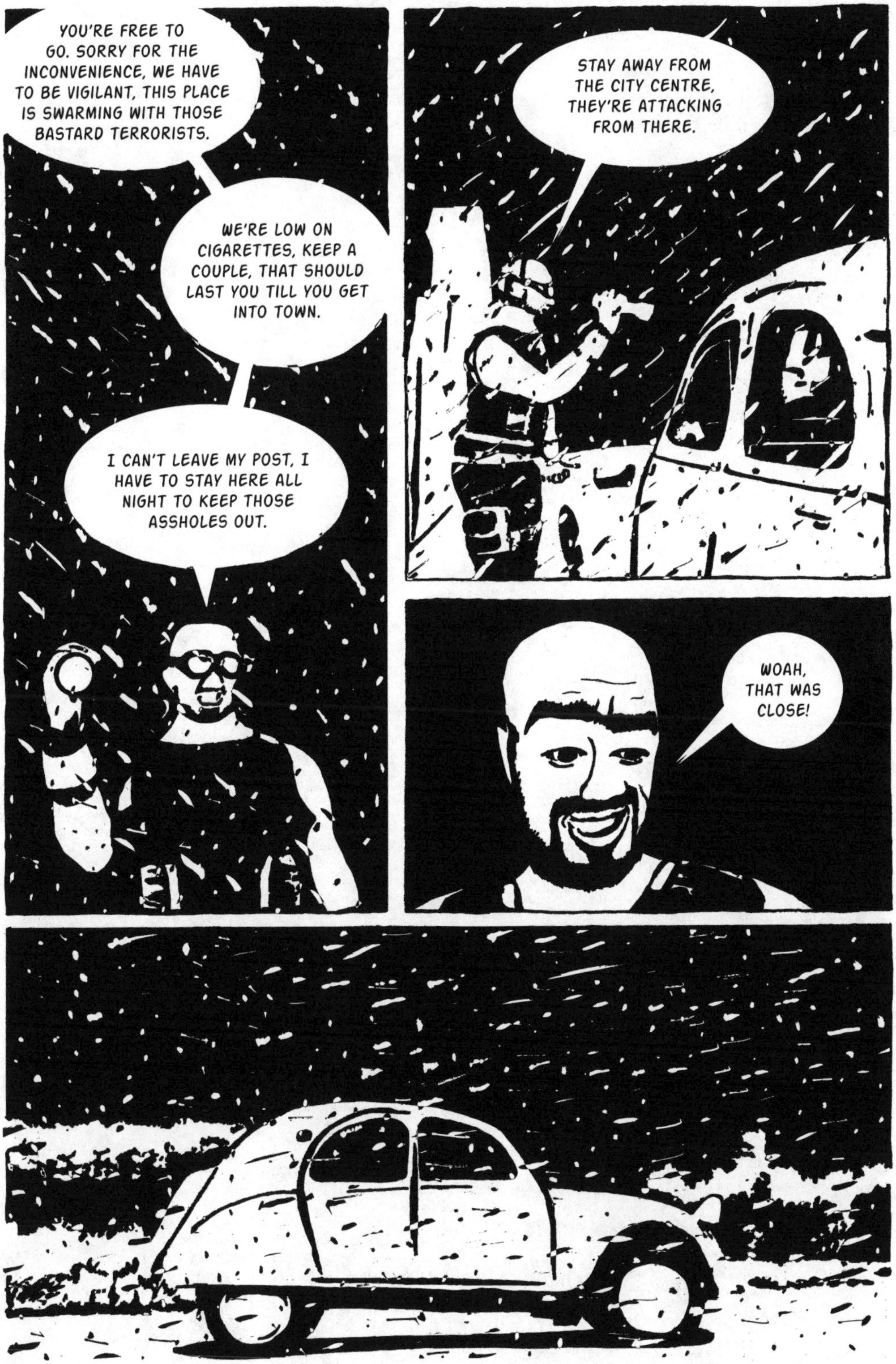
YOU'RE FREE TO GO. SORRY FOR THE INCONVENIENCE, WE HAVE TO BE VIGILANT, THIS PLACE IS SWARMING WITH THOSE BASTARD TERRORISTS.
WE'RE LOW ON CIGARETTES, KEEP A COUPLE, THAT SHOULD LAST YOU TILL YOU GET INTO TOWN.
I CAN'T LEAVE MY POST, I HAVE TO STAY HERE ALL NIGHT TO KEEP THOSE ASSHOLES OUT.
STAY AWAY FROM THE CITY CENTRE, THEY'RE ATTACKING FROM THERE.
WOAH, THAT WAS CLOSE!

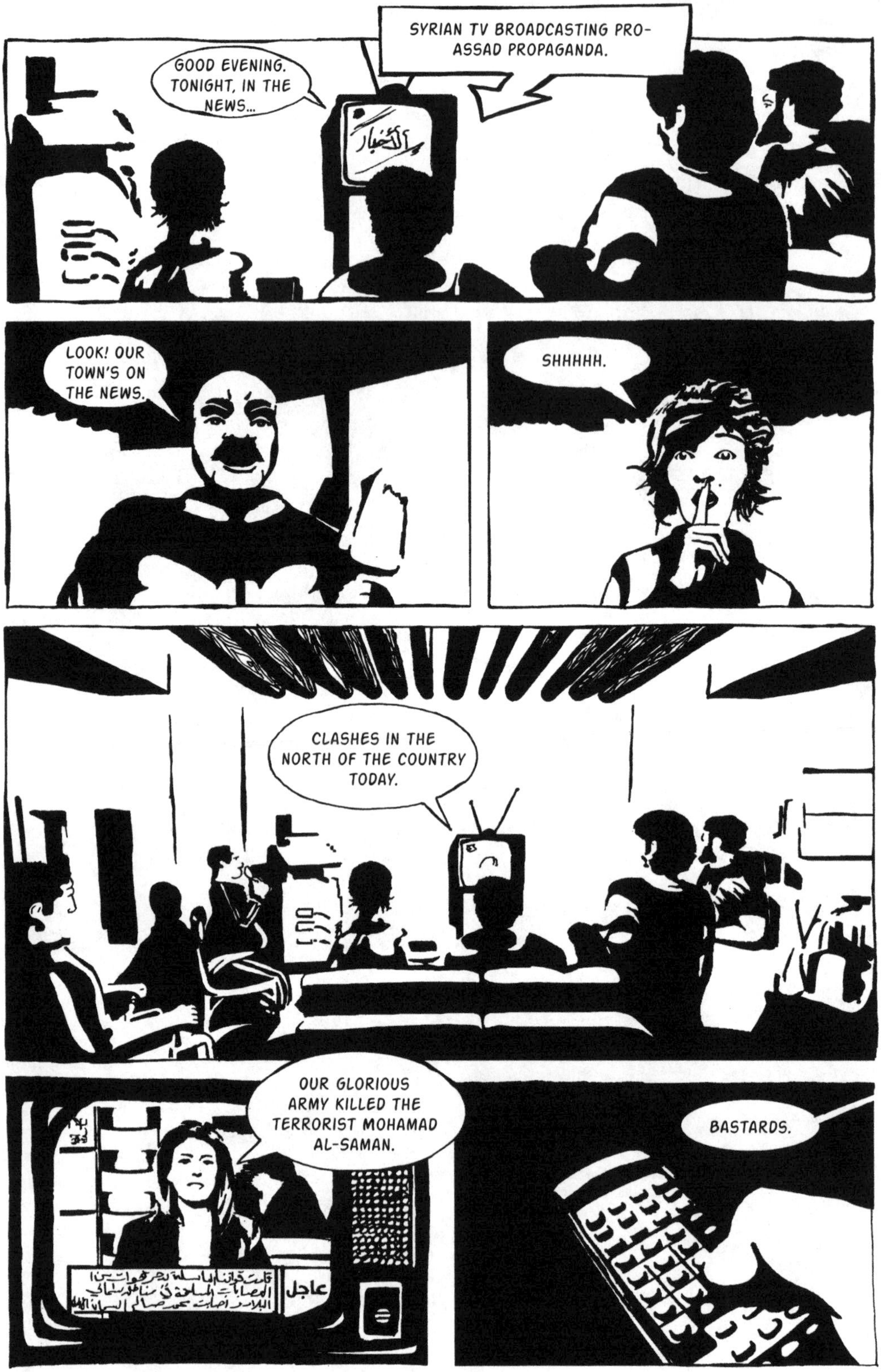
SYRIAN TV BROADCASTING PRO-ASSAD PROPAGANDA.
GOOD EVENING. TONIGHT, IN THE NEWS...
الأخبار
LOOK! OUR TOWN'S ON THE NEWS.
SHHHHH.
CLASHES IN THE NORTH OF THE COUNTRY TODAY.
OUR GLORIOUS ARMY KILLED THE TERRORIST MOHAMAD AL-SAMAN.
عاجل
BASTARDS.

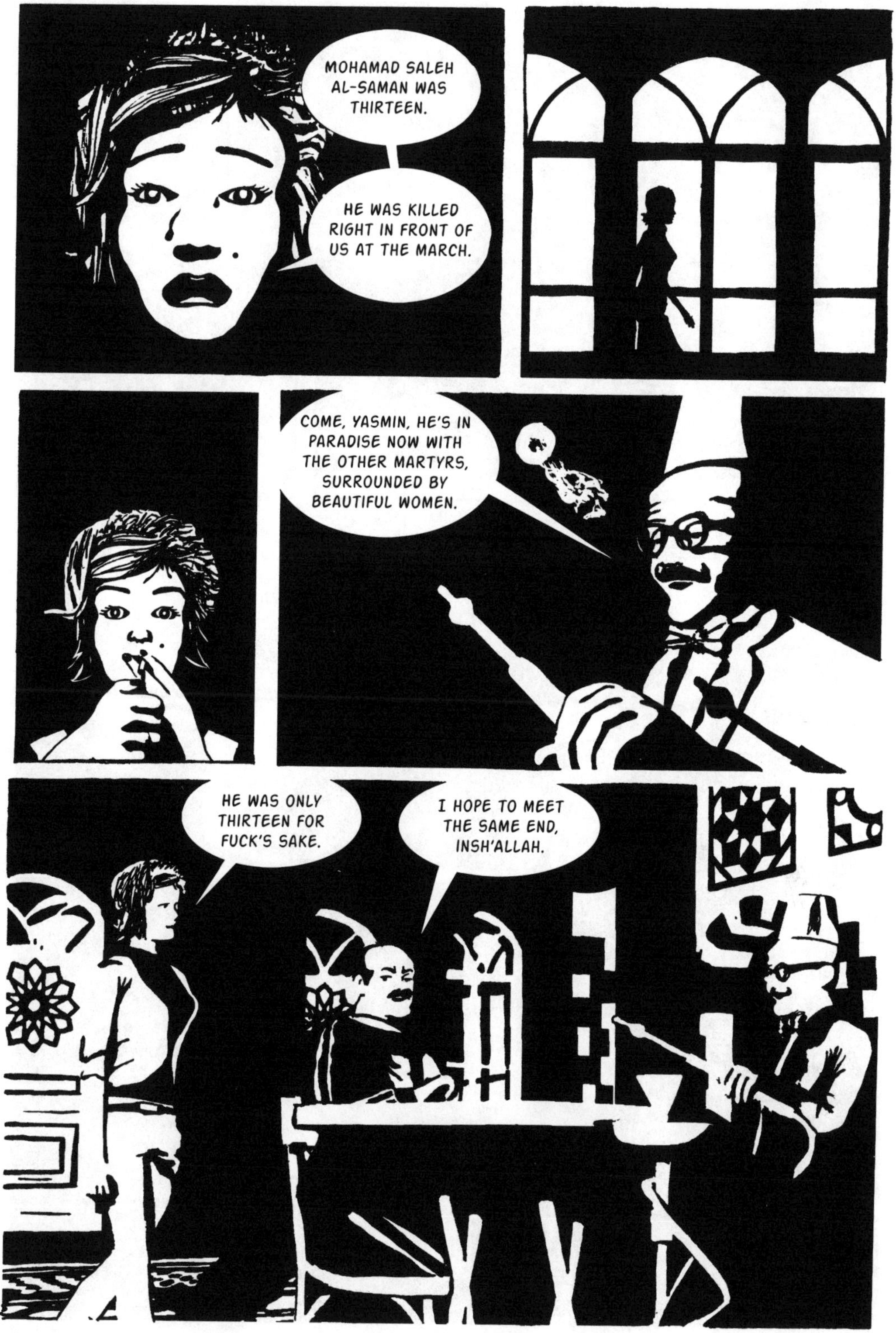
MOHAMAD SALEH AL-SAMAN WAS THIRTEEN.
HE WAS KILLED RIGHT IN FRONT OF US AT THE MARCH.
COME, YASMIN, HE'S IN PARADISE NOW WITH THE OTHER MARTYRS, SURROUNDED BY BEAUTIFUL WOMEN.
HE WAS ONLY THIRTEEN FOR FUCK'S SAKE.
I HOPE TO MEET THE SAME END, INSH'ALLAH.

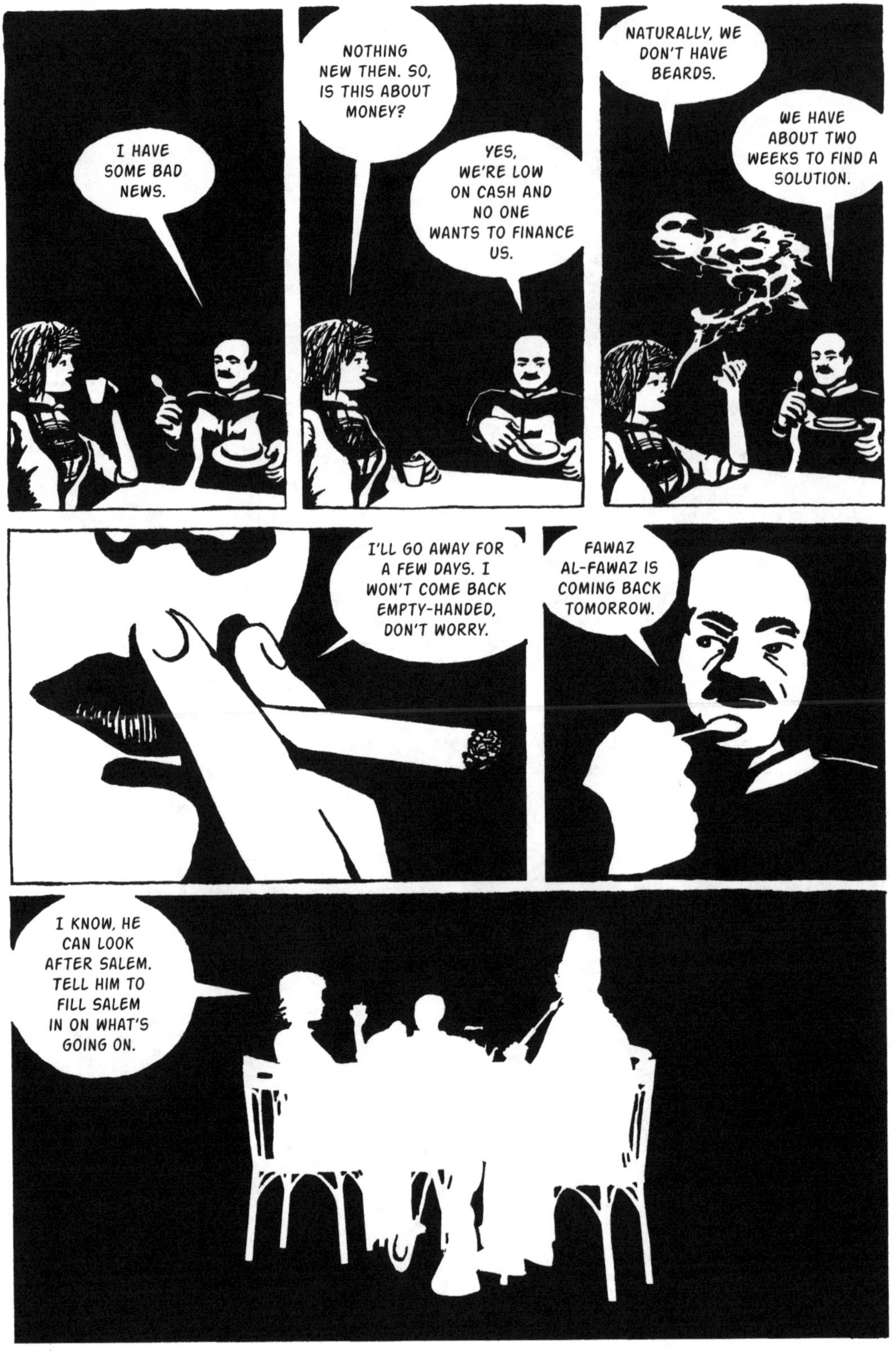
I HAVE SOME BAD NEWS.
NOTHING NEW THEN. SO, IS THIS ABOUT MONEY?
YES, WE'RE LOW ON CASH AND NO ONE WANTS TO FINANCE US.
NATURALLY, WE DON'T HAVE BEARDS.
WE HAVE ABOUT TWO WEEKS TO FIND A SOLUTION.
I'LL GO AWAY FOR A FEW DAYS. I WON'T COME BACK EMPTY-HANDED, DON'T WORRY.
FAWAZ AL-FAWAZ IS COMING BACK TOMORROW.
I KNOW, HE CAN LOOK AFTER SALEM. TELL HIM TO FILL SALEM IN ON WHAT'S GOING ON.

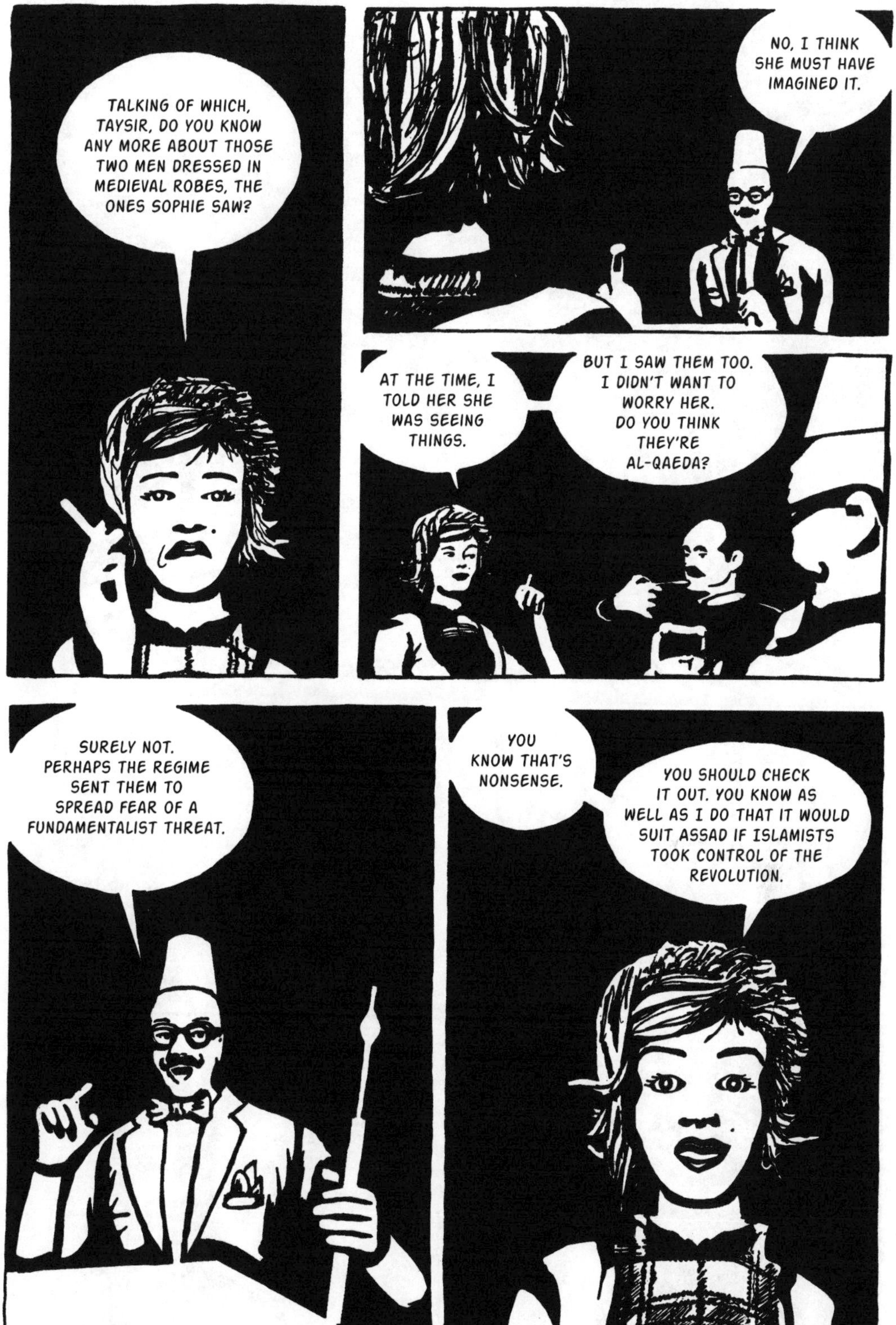
TALKING OF WHICH, TAYSIR, DO YOU KNOW ANY MORE ABOUT THOSE TWO MEN DRESSED IN MEDIEVAL ROBES, THE ONES SOPHIE SAW?
NO, I THINK SHE MUST HAVE IMAGINED IT.
AT THE TIME, I TOLD HER SHE WAS SEEING THINGS.
BUT I SAW THEM TOO. I DIDN'T WANT TO WORRY HER. DO YOU THINK THEY'RE AL-QAEDA?
SURELY NOT. PERHAPS THE REGIME SENT THEM TO SPREAD FEAR OF A FUNDAMENTALIST THREAT.
YOU KNOW THAT'S NONSENSE.
YOU SHOULD CHECK IT OUT. YOU KNOW AS WELL AS I DO THAT IT WOULD SUIT ASSAD IF ISLAMISTS TOOK CONTROL OF THE REVOLUTION.

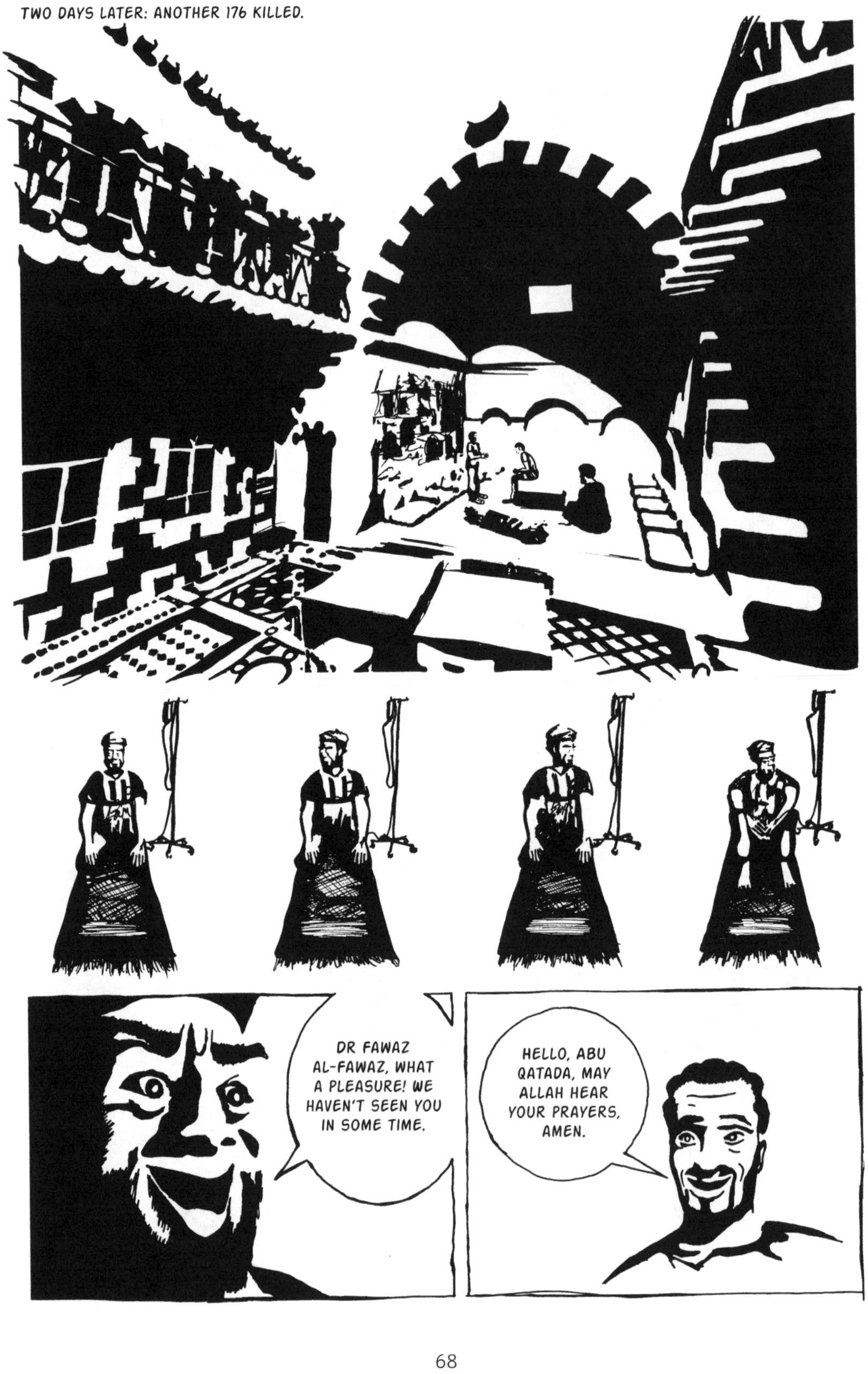
TWO DAYS LATER: ANOTHER 176 KILLED.
DR FAWAZ AL-FAWAZ, WHAT A PLEASURE! WE HAVEN'T SEEN YOU IN SOME TIME.
HELLO, ABU QATADA, MAY ALLAH HEAR YOUR PRAYERS, AMEN.

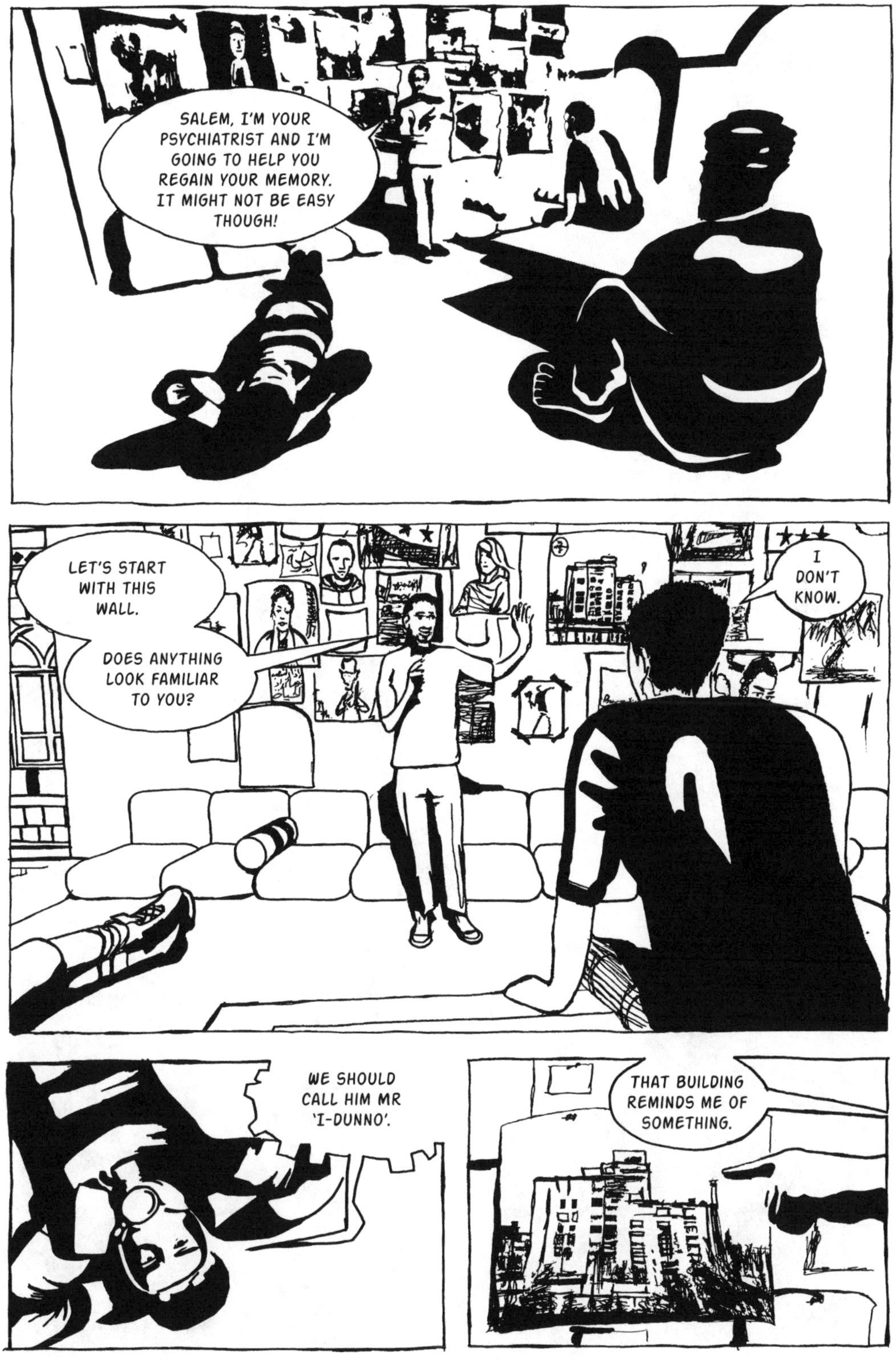
SALEM, I'M YOUR PSYCHIATRIST AND I'M GOING TO HELP YOU REGAIN YOUR MEMORY. IT MIGHT NOT BE EASY THOUGH!
LET'S START WITH THIS WALL.
DOES ANYTHING LOOK FAMILIAR TO YOU?
I DON'T KNOW.
WE SHOULD CALL HIM MR 'I-DUNNO'.
THAT BUILDING REMINDS ME OF SOMETHING.

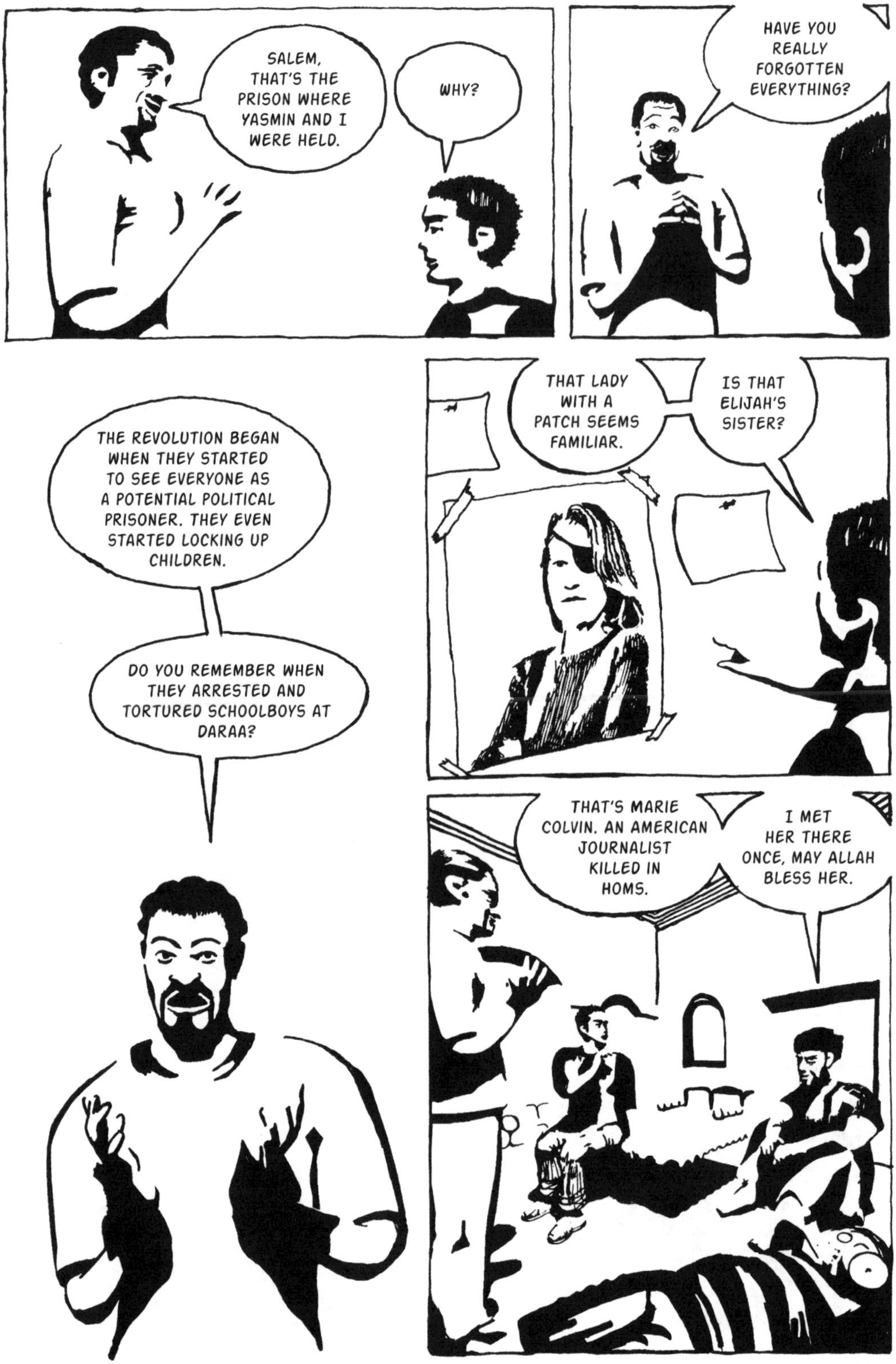
SALEM, THAT'S THE PRISON WHERE YASMIN AND I WERE HELD.
WHY?
HAVE YOU REALLY FORGOTTEN EVERYTHING?
THE REVOLUTION BEGAN WHEN THEY STARTED TO SEE EVERYONE AS A POTENTIAL POLITICAL PRISONER. THEY EVEN STARTED LOCKING UP CHILDREN.
DO YOU REMEMBER WHEN THEY ARRESTED AND TORTURED SCHOOLBOYS AT DARAA?
THAT LADY WITH A PATCH SEEMS FAMILIAR.
IS THAT ELIJAH'S SISTER?
THAT'S MARIE COLVIN. AN AMERICAN JOURNALIST KILLED IN HOMS.
I MET HER THERE ONCE, MAY ALLAH BLESS HER.

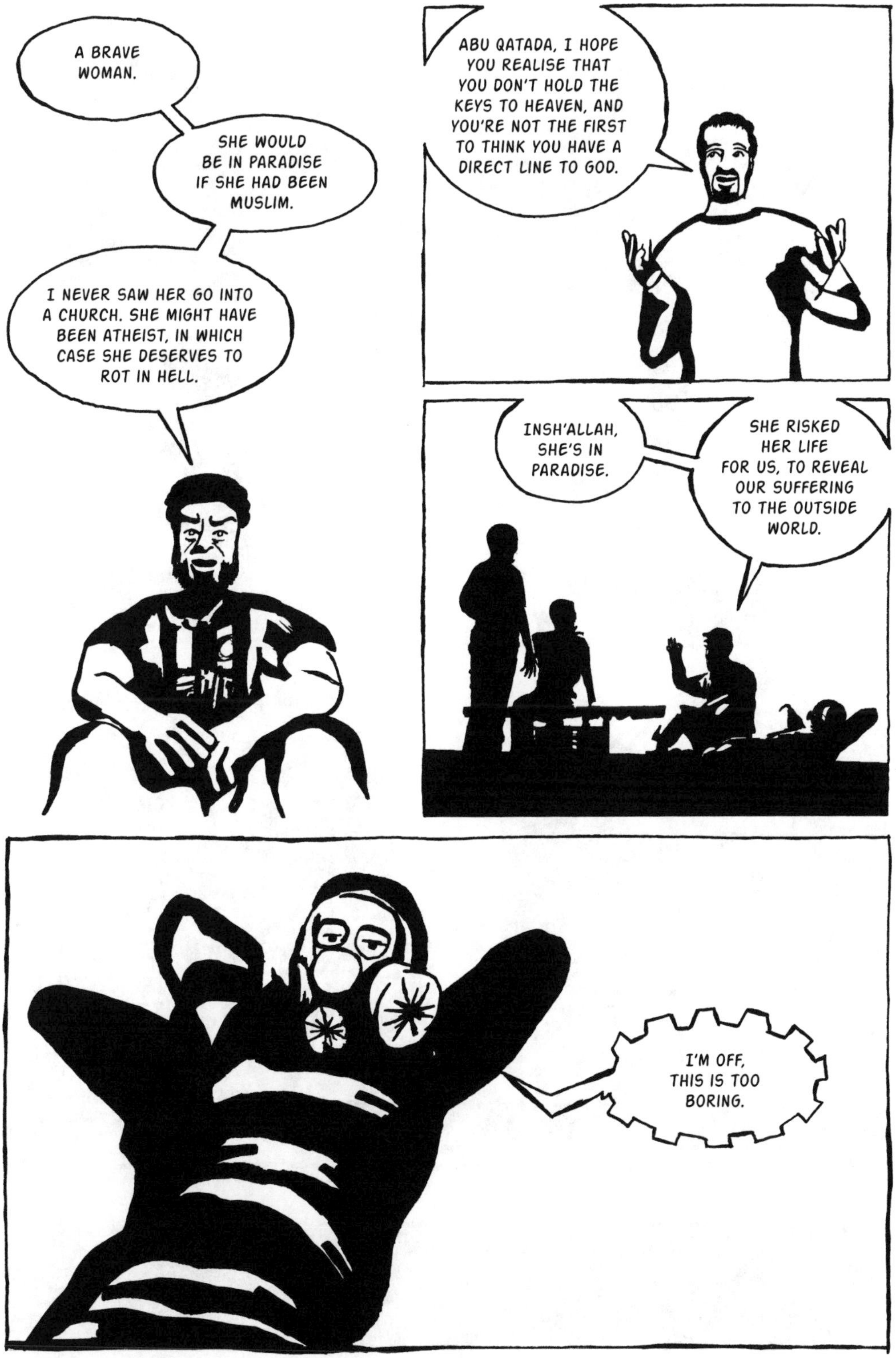
A BRAVE WOMAN.
SHE WOULD BE IN PARADISE IF SHE HAD BEEN MUSLIM.
I NEVER SAW HER GO INTO A CHURCH. SHE MIGHT HAVE BEEN ATHEIST, IN WHICH CASE SHE DESERVES TO ROT IN HELL.
ABU QATADA, I HOPE YOU REALISE THAT YOU DON'T HOLD THE KEYS TO HEAVEN, AND YOU'RE NOT THE FIRST TO THINK YOU HAVE A DIRECT LINE TO GOD.
INSH'ALLAH, SHE'S IN PARADISE.
SHE RISKED HER LIFE FOR US, TO REVEAL OUR SUFFERING TO THE OUTSIDE WORLD.
I'M OFF, THIS IS TOO BORING.

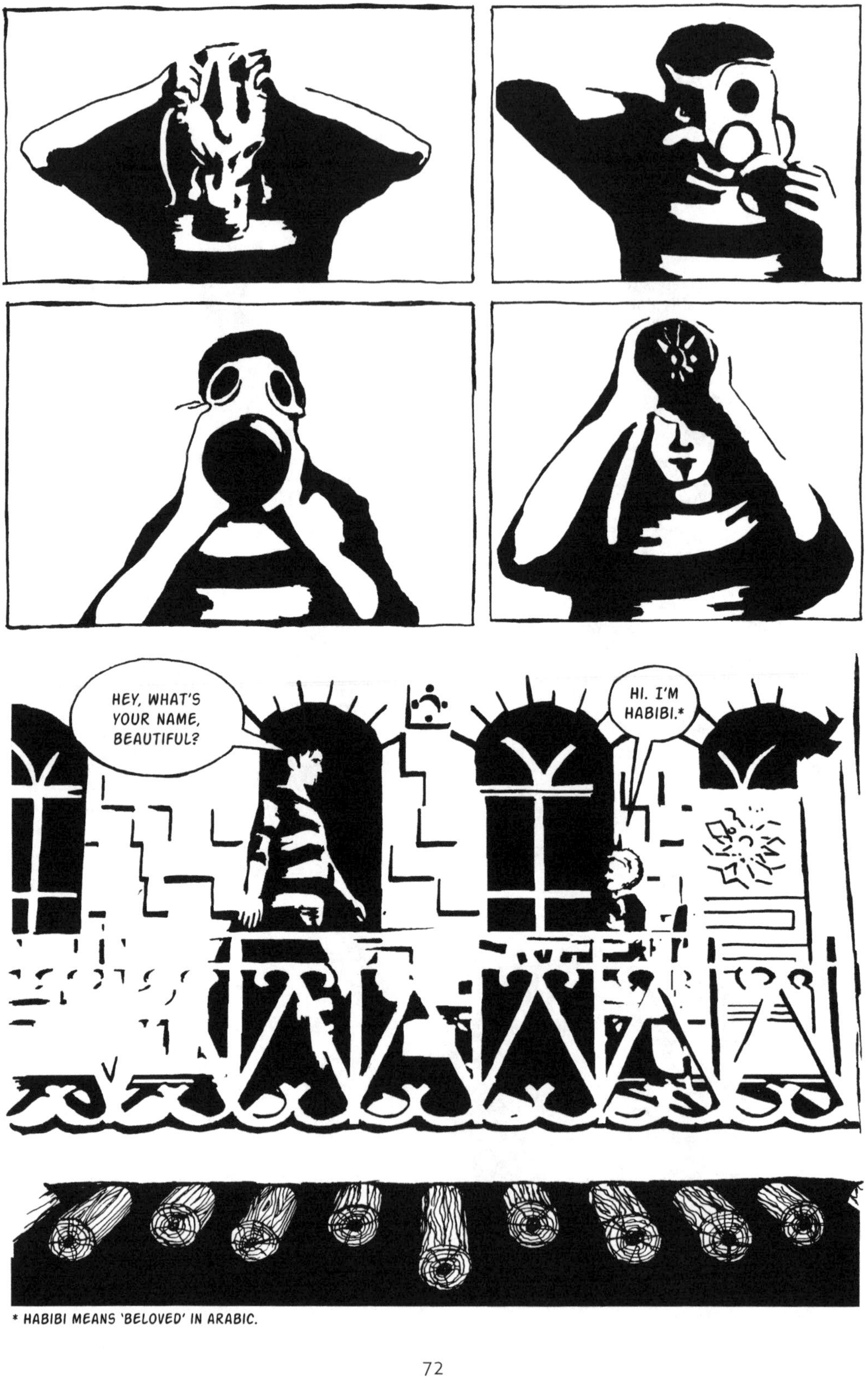
HEY, WHAT'S YOUR NAME, BEAUTIFUL?
HI. I'M HABIBI.*

* HABIBI MEANS 'BELOVED' IN ARABIC.

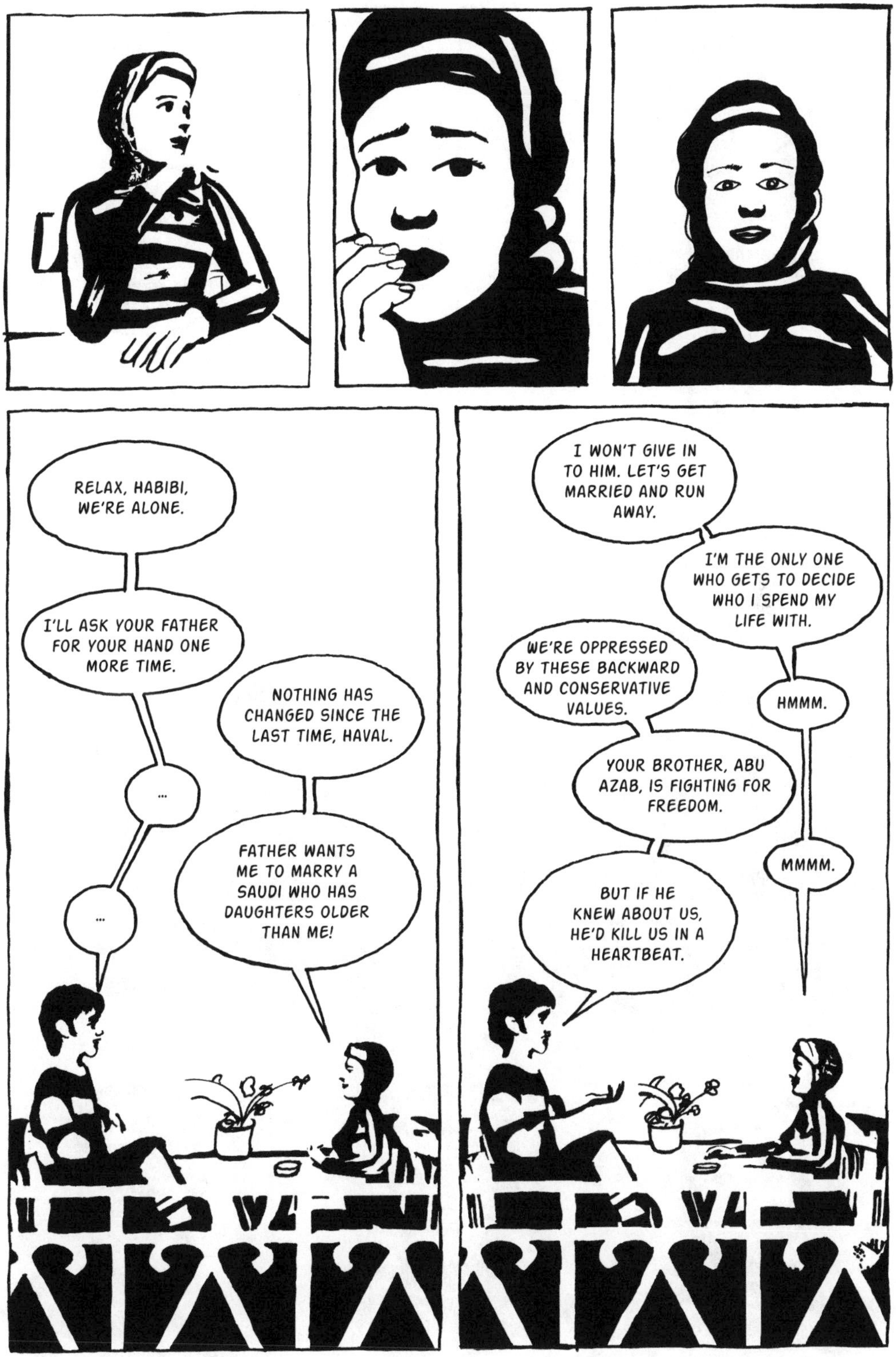
RELAX, HABIBI, WE'RE ALONE.
I'LL ASK YOUR FATHER FOR YOUR HAND ONE MORE TIME.
NOTHING HAS CHANGED SINCE THE LAST TIME, HAVAL.
...
FATHER WANTS ME TO MARRY A SAUDI WHO HAS DAUGHTERS OLDER THAN ME!
...
I WON'T GIVE IN TO HIM. LET'S GET MARRIED AND RUN AWAY.
I'M THE ONLY ONE WHO GETS TO DECIDE WHO I SPEND MY LIFE WITH.
WE'RE OPPRESSED BY THESE BACKWARD AND CONSERVATIVE VALUES.
HMMM.
YOUR BROTHER, ABU AZAB, IS FIGHTING FOR FREEDOM.
MMMM.
BUT IF HE KNEW ABOUT US, HE'D KILL US IN A HEARTBEAT.

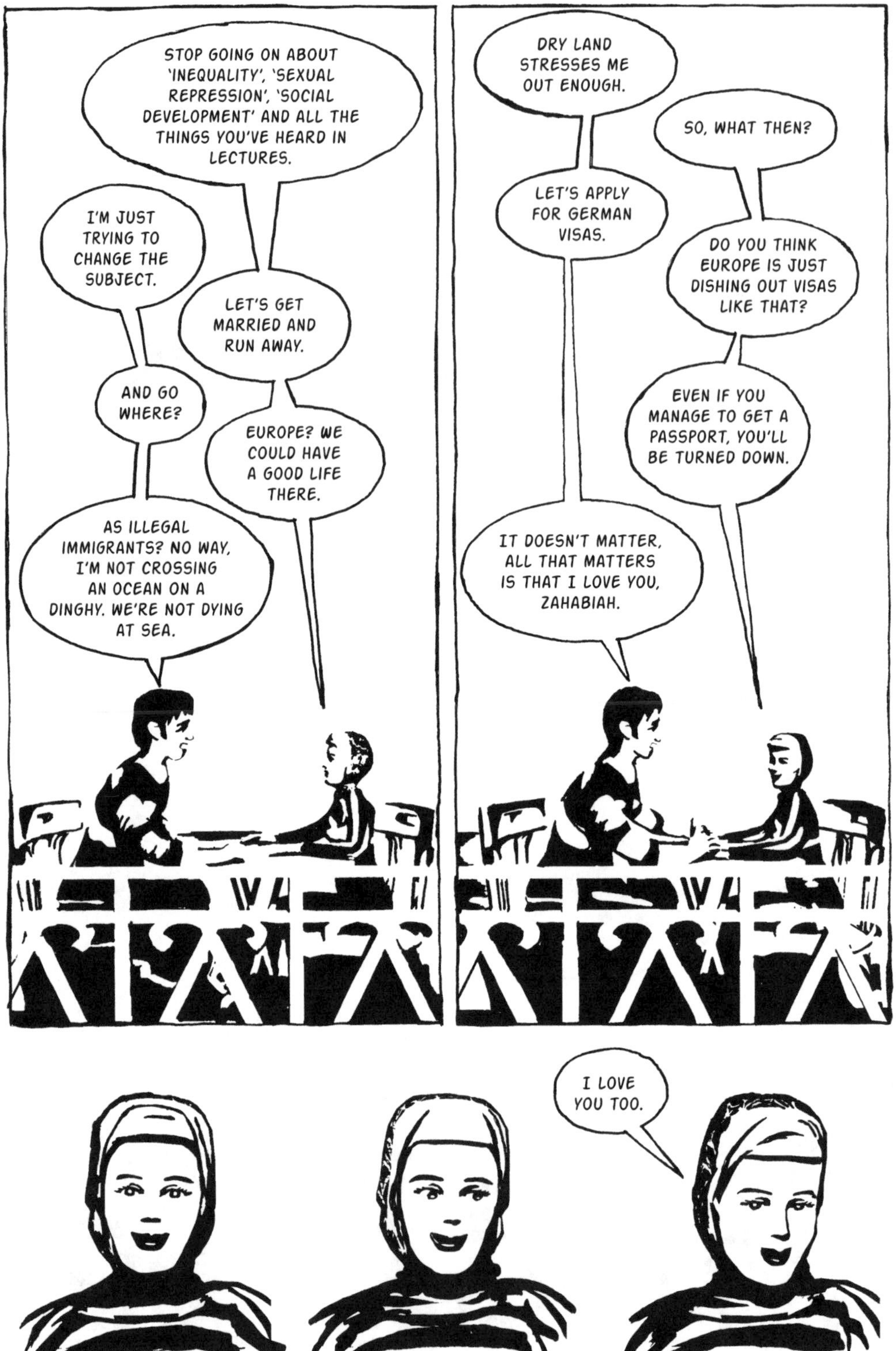
STOP GOING ON ABOUT 'INEQUALITY', 'SEXUAL REPRESSION', 'SOCIAL DEVELOPMENT' AND ALL THE THINGS YOU'VE HEARD IN LECTURES.
I'M JUST TRYING TO CHANGE THE SUBJECT.
LET'S GET MARRIED AND RUN AWAY.
AND GO WHERE?
EUROPE? WE COULD HAVE A GOOD LIFE THERE.
AS ILLEGAL IMMIGRANTS? NO WAY, I'M NOT CROSSING AN OCEAN ON A DINGHY. WE'RE NOT DYING AT SEA.
DRY LAND STRESSES ME OUT ENOUGH.
SO, WHAT THEN?
LET'S APPLY FOR GERMAN VISAS.
DO YOU THINK EUROPE IS JUST DISHING OUT VISAS LIKE THAT?
EVEN IF YOU MANAGE TO GET A PASSPORT, YOU'LL BE TURNED DOWN.
IT DOESN'T MATTER, ALL THAT MATTERS IS THAT I LOVE YOU, ZAHABIAH.
I LOVE YOU TOO.

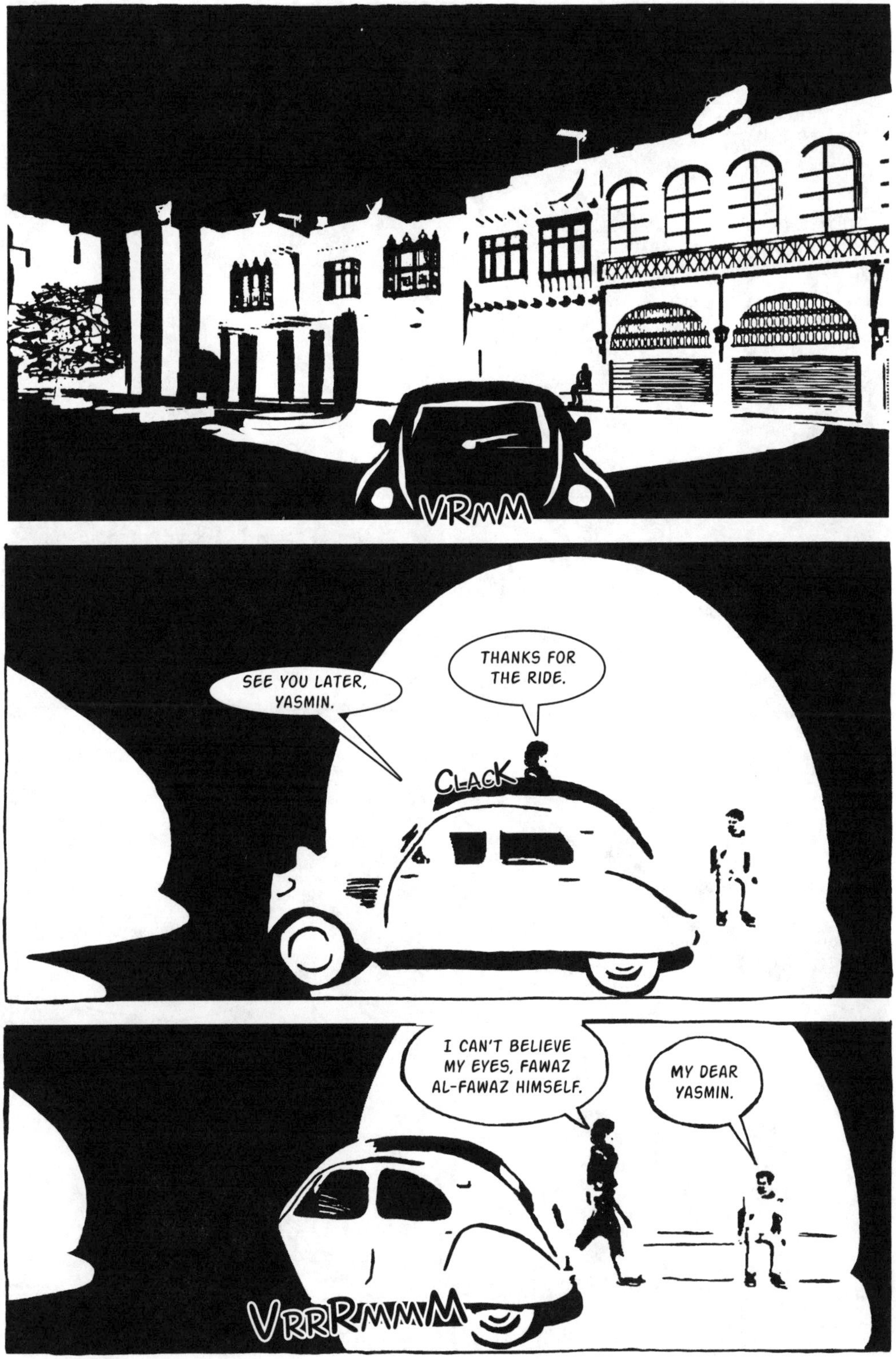
VRMM
SEE YOU LATER, YASMIN.
THANKS FOR THE RIDE.
CLACK
I CAN'T BELIEVE MY EYES, FAWAZ AL-FAWAZ HIMSELF.
MY DEAR YASMIN.
VRRRMMMM

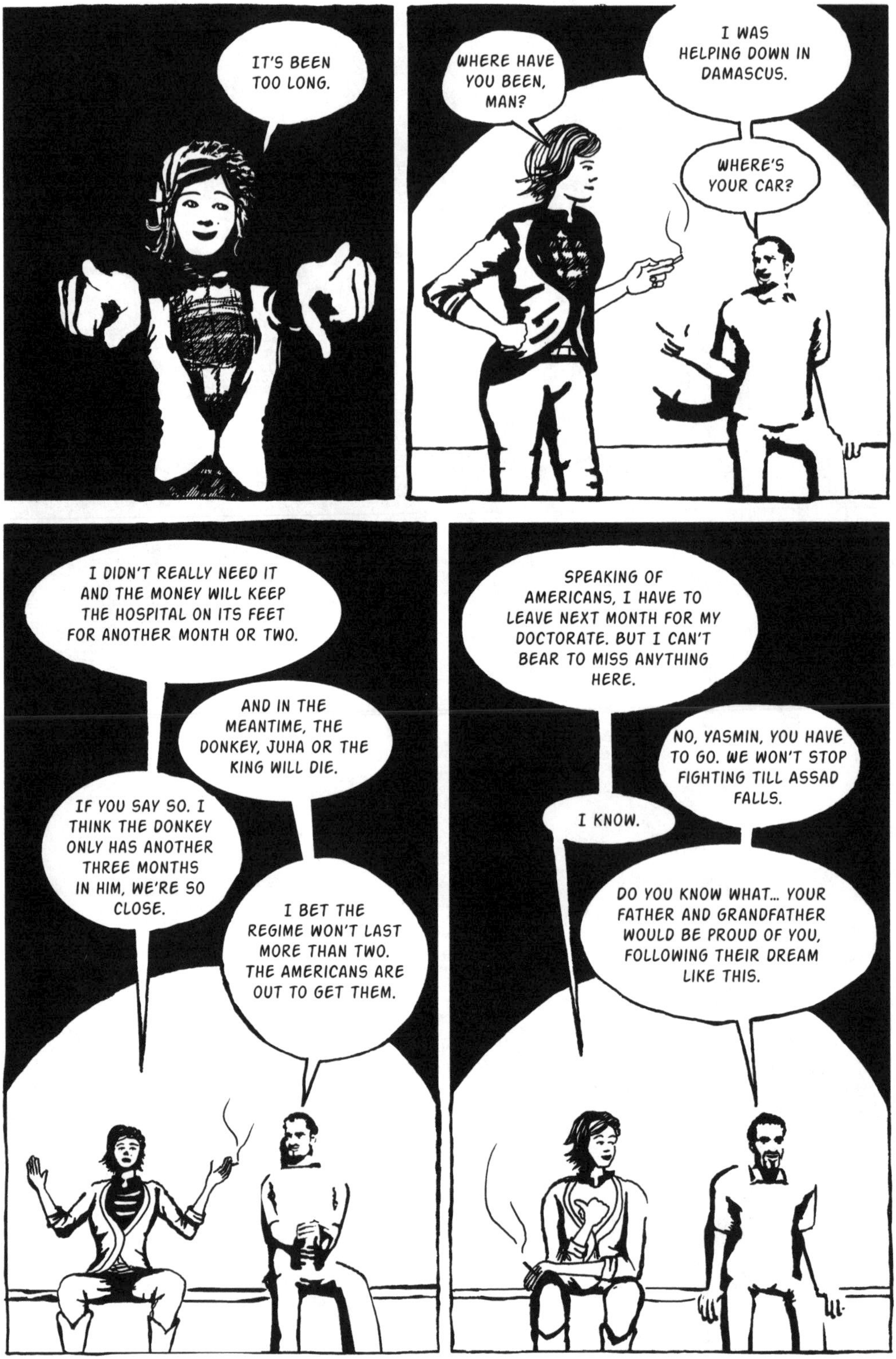
IT'S BEEN TOO LONG.
WHERE HAVE YOU BEEN, MAN?
I WAS HELPING DOWN IN DAMASCUS.
WHERE'S YOUR CAR?
I DIDN'T REALLY NEED IT AND THE MONEY WILL KEEP THE HOSPITAL ON ITS FEET FOR ANOTHER MONTH OR TWO.
AND IN THE MEANTIME, THE DONKEY, JUHA OR THE KING WILL DIE.
IF YOU SAY SO. I THINK THE DONKEY ONLY HAS ANOTHER THREE MONTHS IN HIM, WE'RE SO CLOSE.
I BET THE REGIME WON'T LAST MORE THAN TWO. THE AMERICANS ARE OUT TO GET THEM.
SPEAKING OF AMERICANS, I HAVE TO LEAVE NEXT MONTH FOR MY DOCTORATE. BUT I CAN'T BEAR TO MISS ANYTHING HERE.
NO, YASMIN, YOU HAVE TO GO. WE WON'T STOP FIGHTING TILL ASSAD FALLS.
I KNOW.
DO YOU KNOW WHAT... YOUR FATHER AND GRANDFATHER WOULD BE PROUD OF YOU, FOLLOWING THEIR DREAM LIKE THIS.

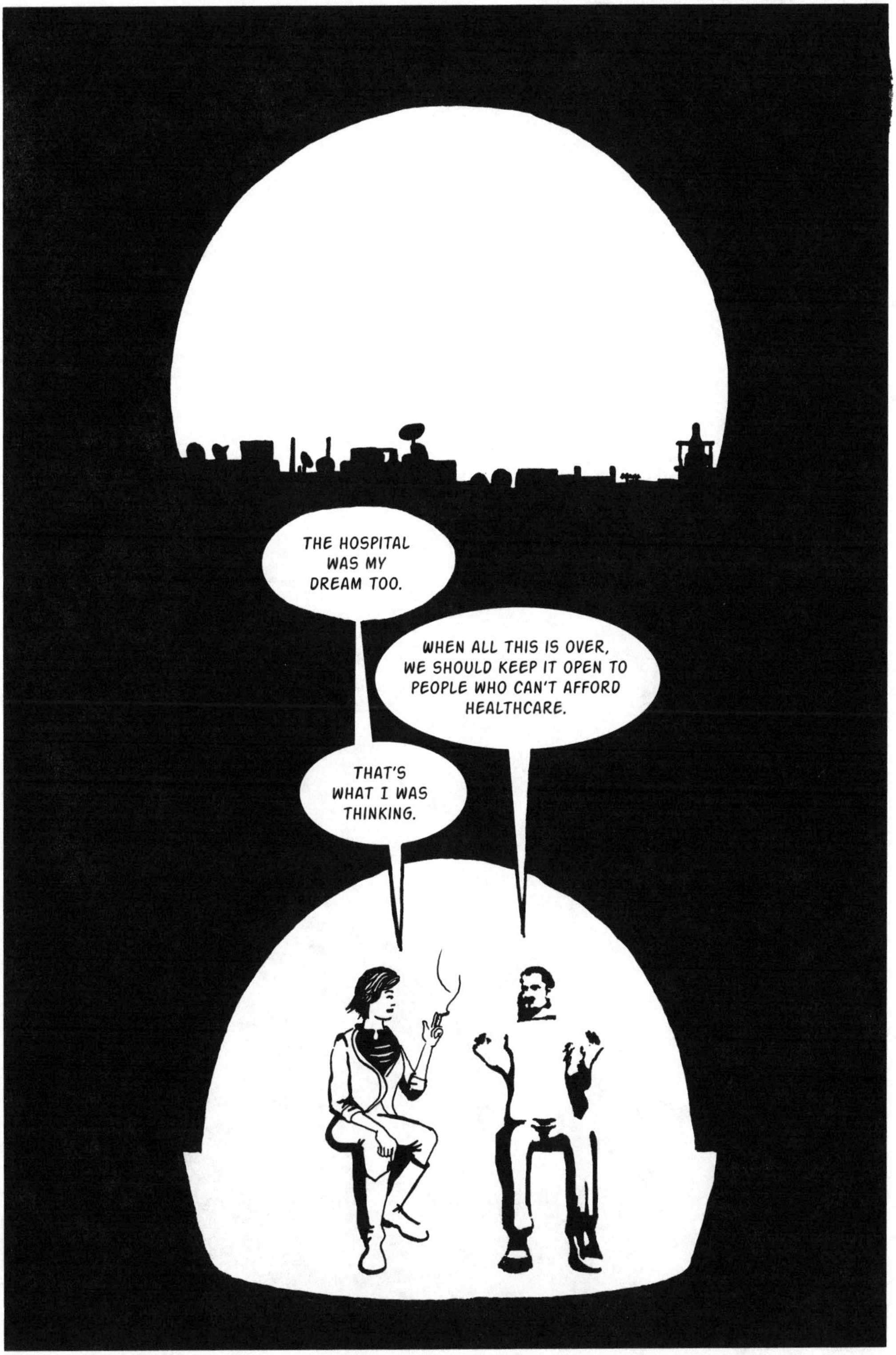
THE HOSPITAL WAS MY DREAM TOO.
WHEN ALL THIS IS OVER, WE SHOULD KEEP IT OPEN TO PEOPLE WHO CAN'T AFFORD HEALTHCARE.
THAT'S WHAT I WAS THINKING.

ONE WEEK LATER: ANOTHER 450 KILLED.

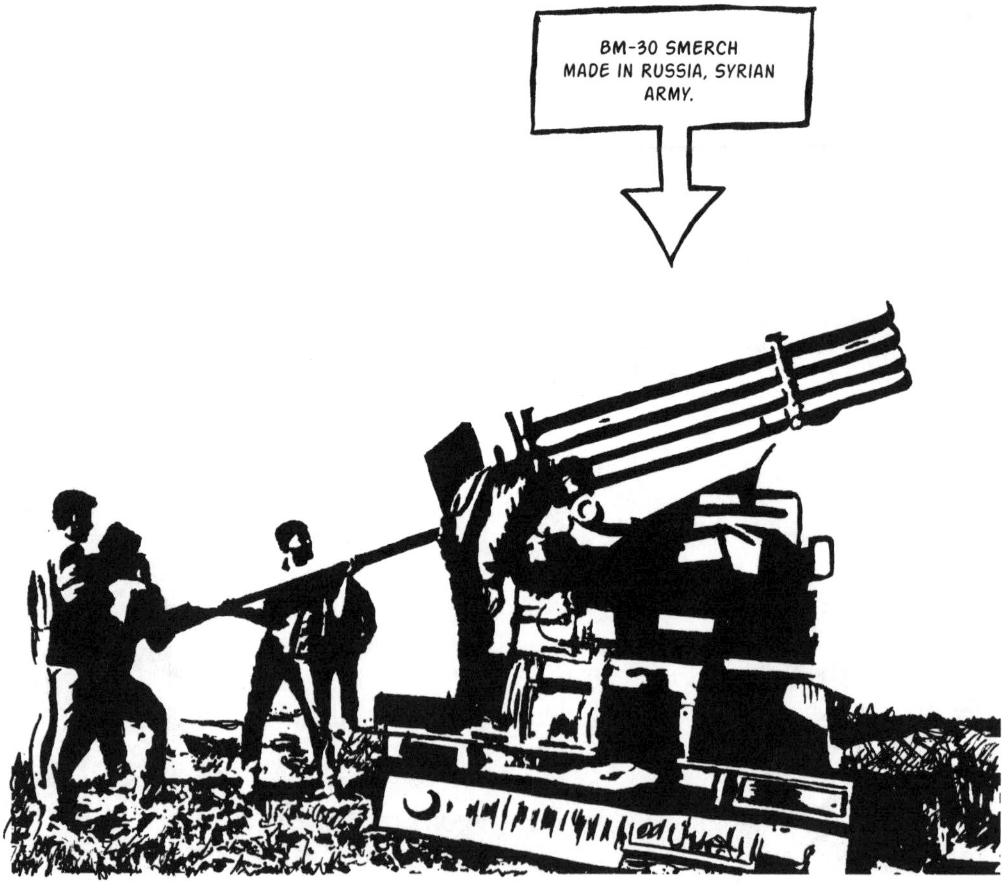
BM-30 SMERCH
MADE IN RUSSIA, SYRIAN ARMY.

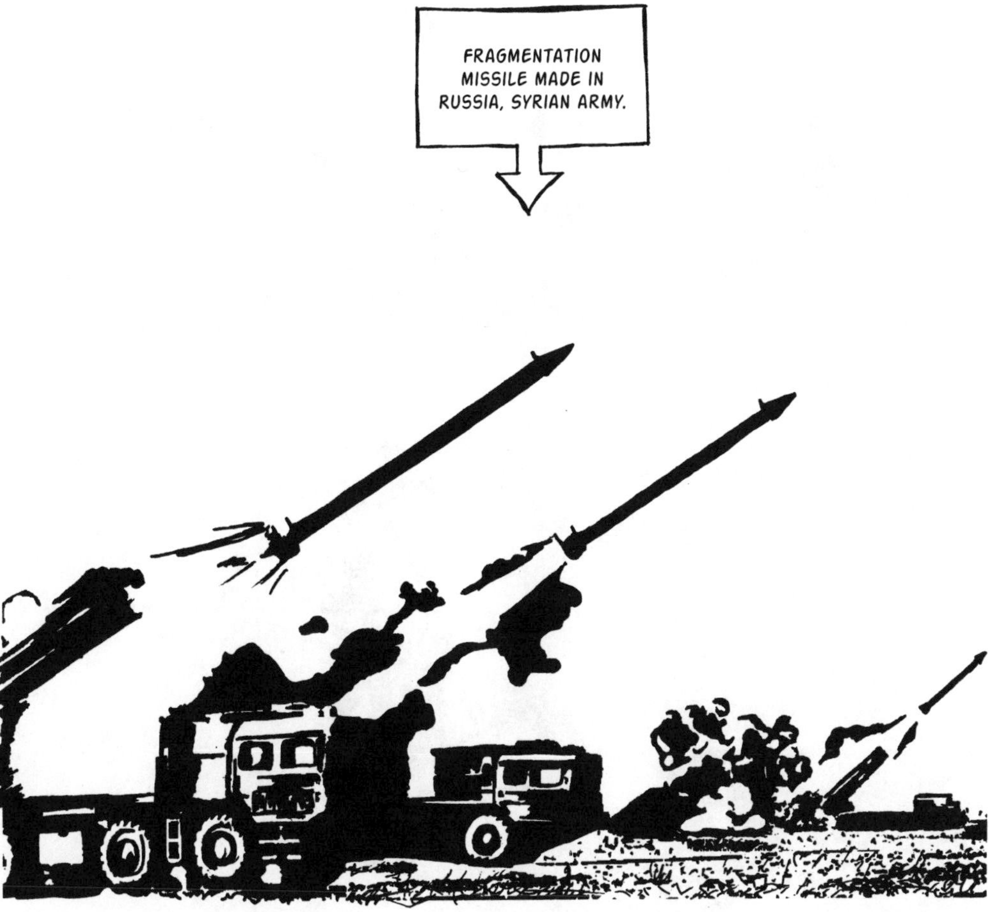
FRAGMENTATION MISSILE MADE IN RUSSIA, SYRIAN ARMY.

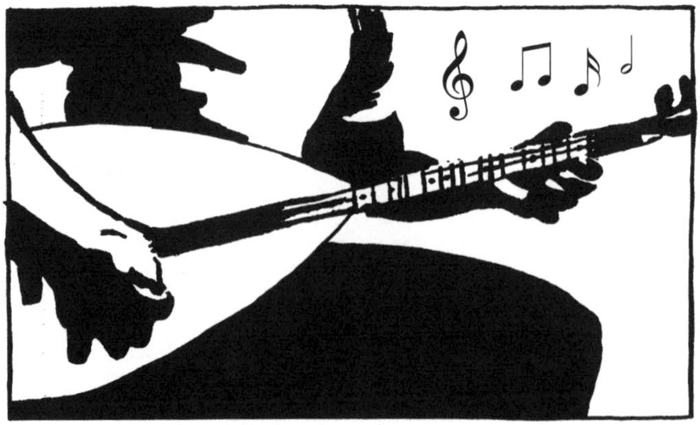

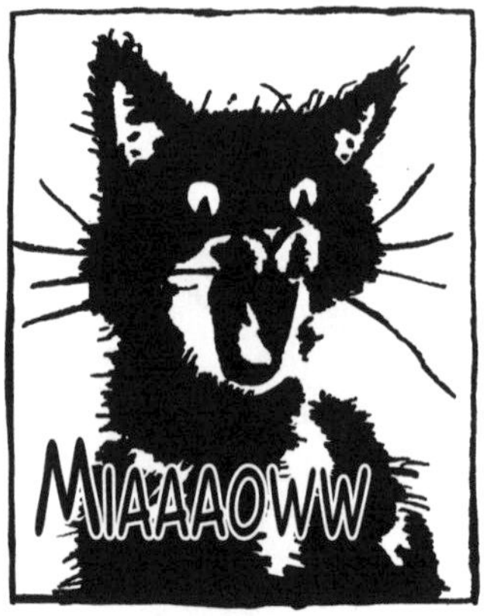
MIAAAOWW

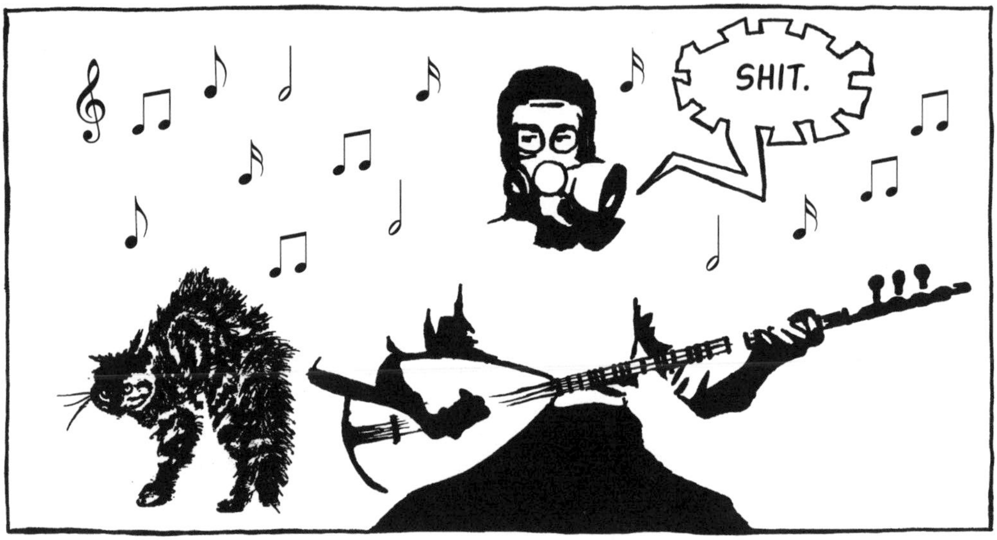
SHIT.

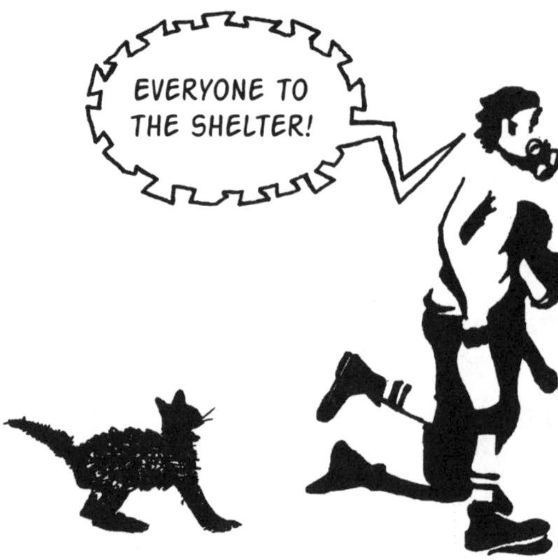
EVERYONE TO THE SHELTER!

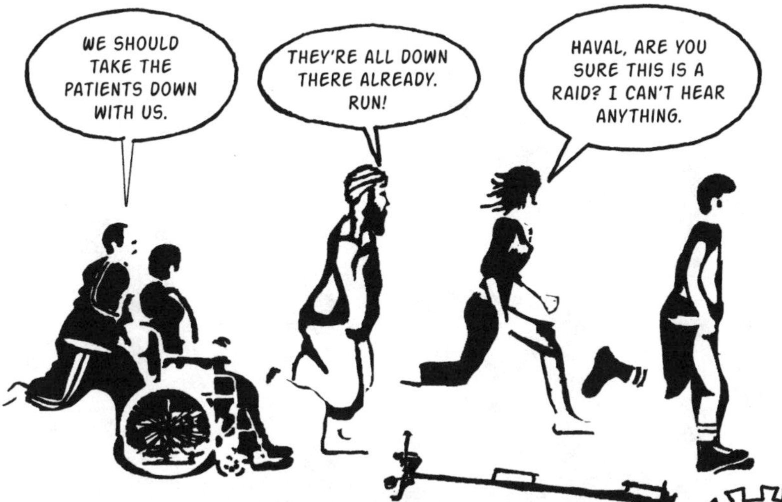
WE SHOULD TAKE THE PATIENTS DOWN WITH US.
THEY'RE ALL DOWN THERE ALREADY. RUN!
HAVAL, ARE YOU SURE THIS IS A RAID? I CAN'T HEAR ANYTHING.

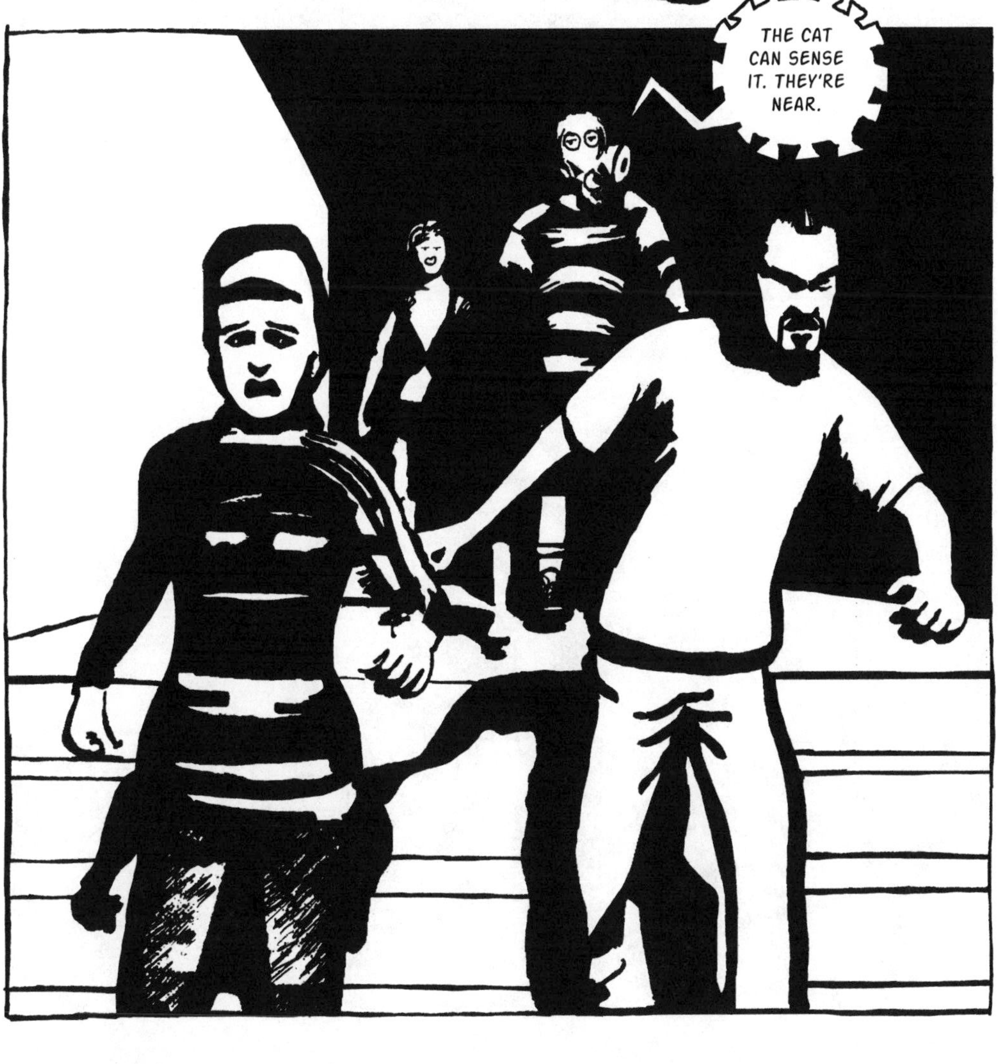
THE CAT CAN SENSE IT. THEY'RE NEAR.

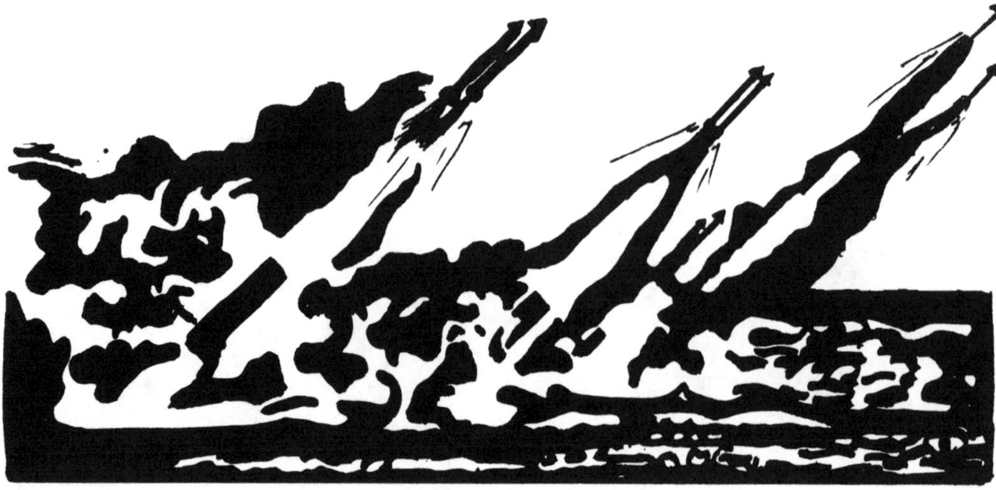

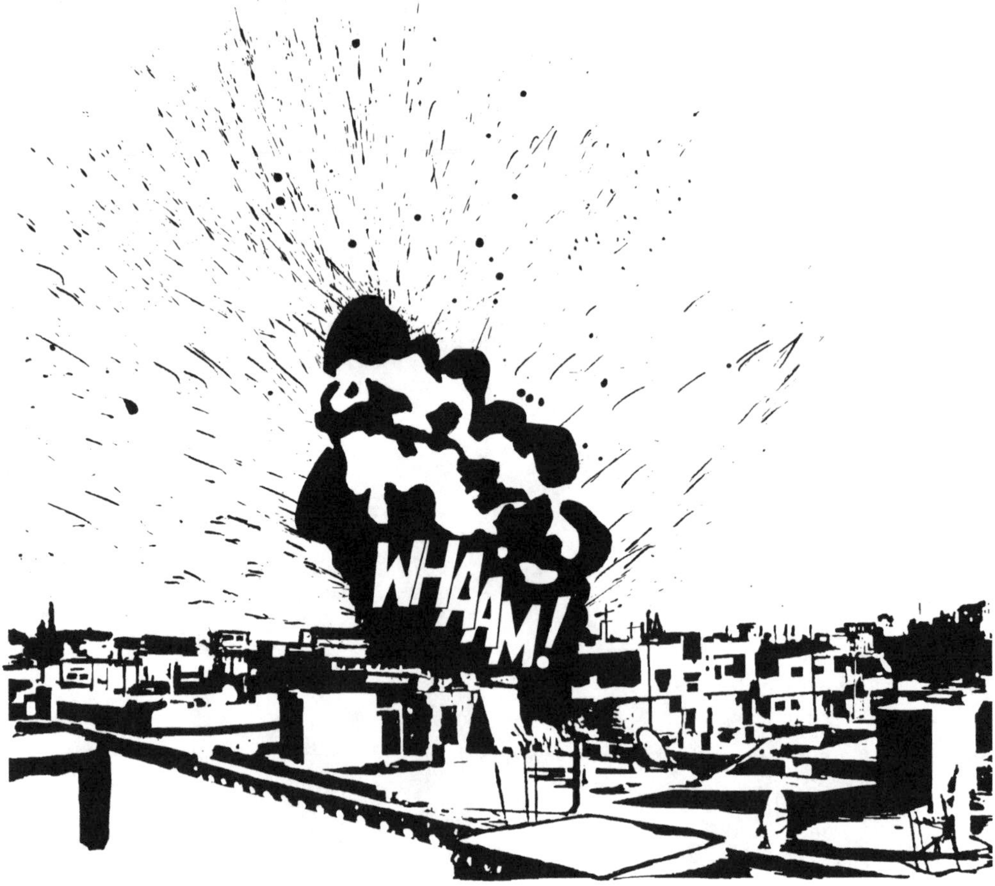
WHAAM!

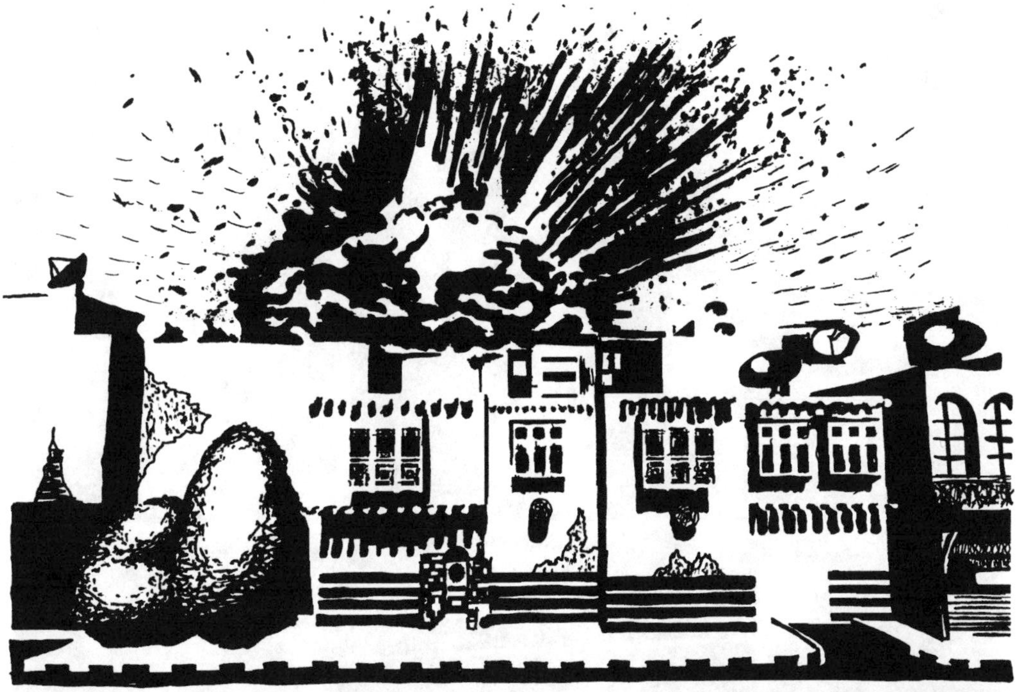

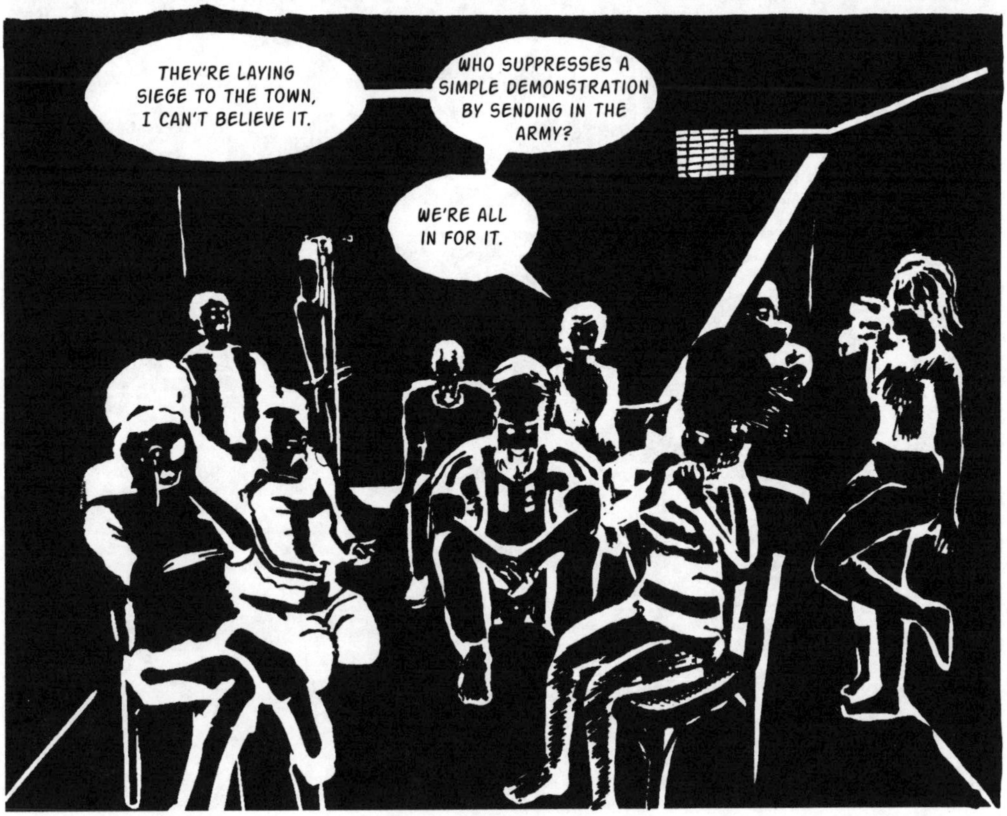
THEY'RE LAYING SIEGE TO THE TOWN, I CAN'T BELIEVE IT.
WHO SUPPRESSES A SIMPLE DEMONSTRATION BY SENDING IN THE ARMY?
WE'RE ALL IN FOR IT.

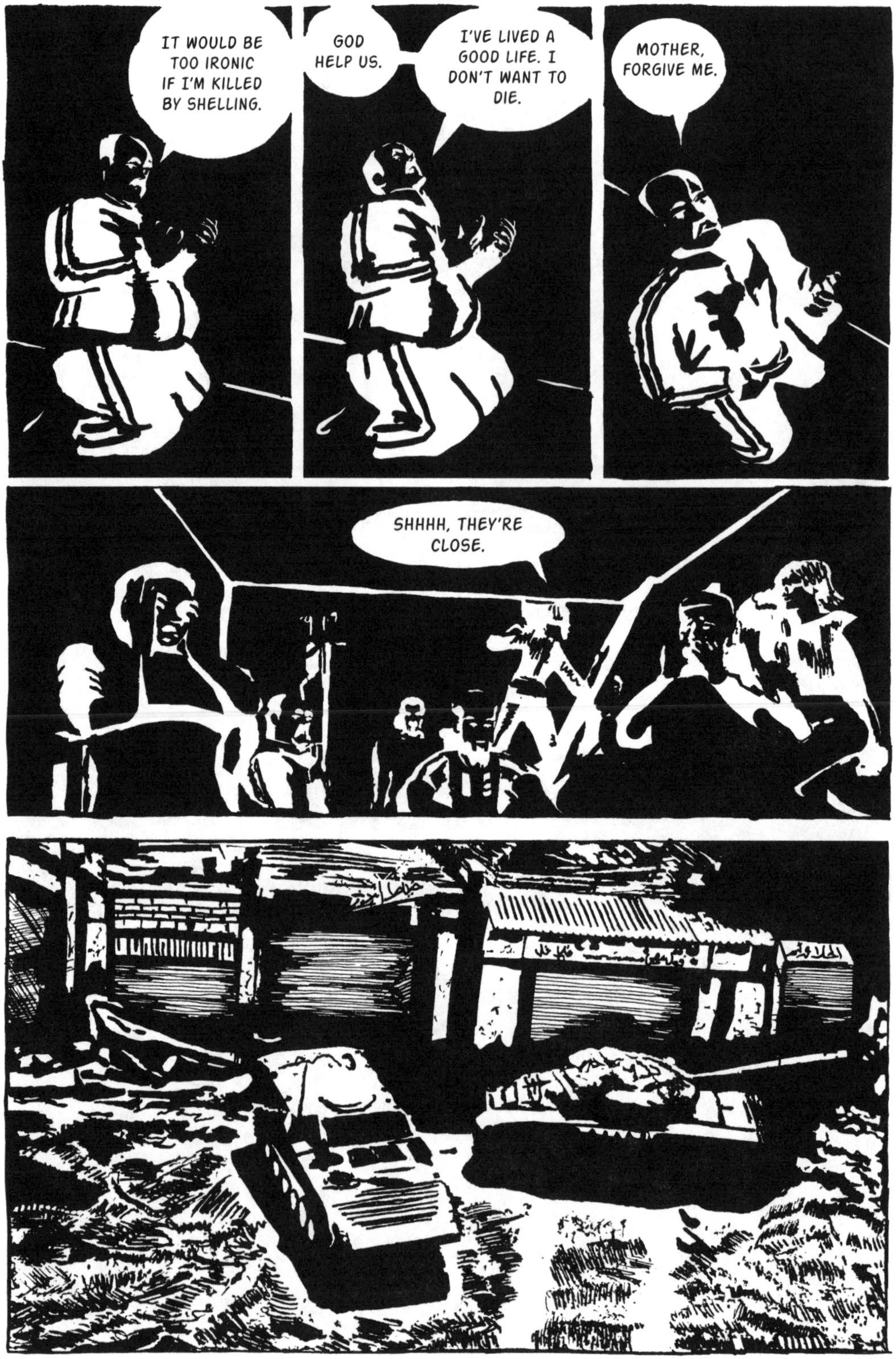
IT WOULD BE TOO IRONIC IF I'M KILLED BY SHELLING.
GOD HELP US.
I'VE LIVED A GOOD LIFE. I DON'T WANT TO DIE.
MOTHER, FORGIVE ME.
SHHHH, THEY'RE CLOSE.

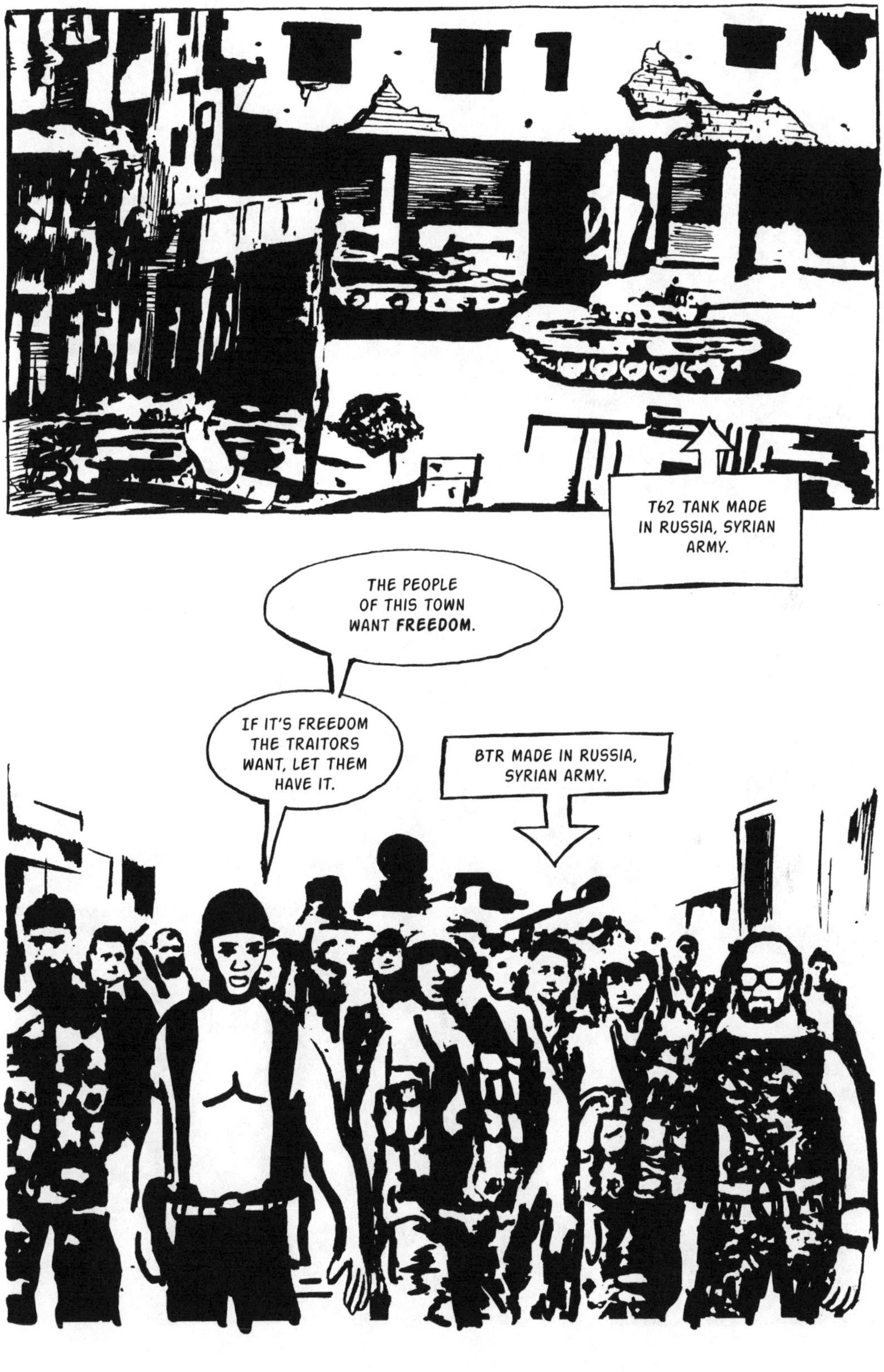
T62 TANK MADE IN RUSSIA, SYRIAN ARMY.
THE PEOPLE OF THIS TOWN WANT **FREEDOM**.
IF IT'S FREEDOM THE TRAITORS WANT, LET THEM HAVE IT.
BTR MADE IN RUSSIA, SYRIAN ARMY.

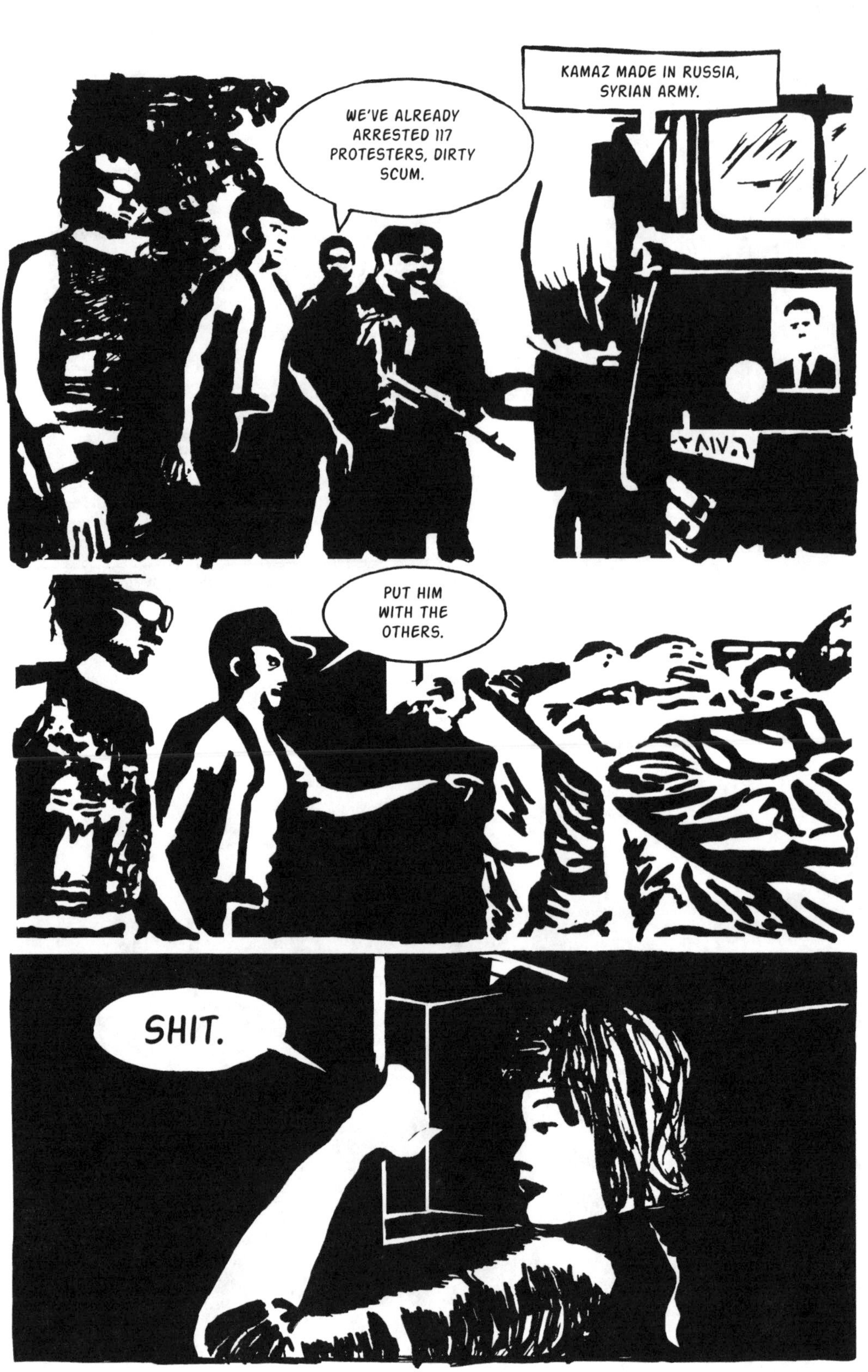
WE'VE ALREADY ARRESTED 117 PROTESTERS, DIRTY SCUM.
KAMAZ MADE IN RUSSIA, SYRIAN ARMY.
PUT HIM WITH THE OTHERS.
SHIT.

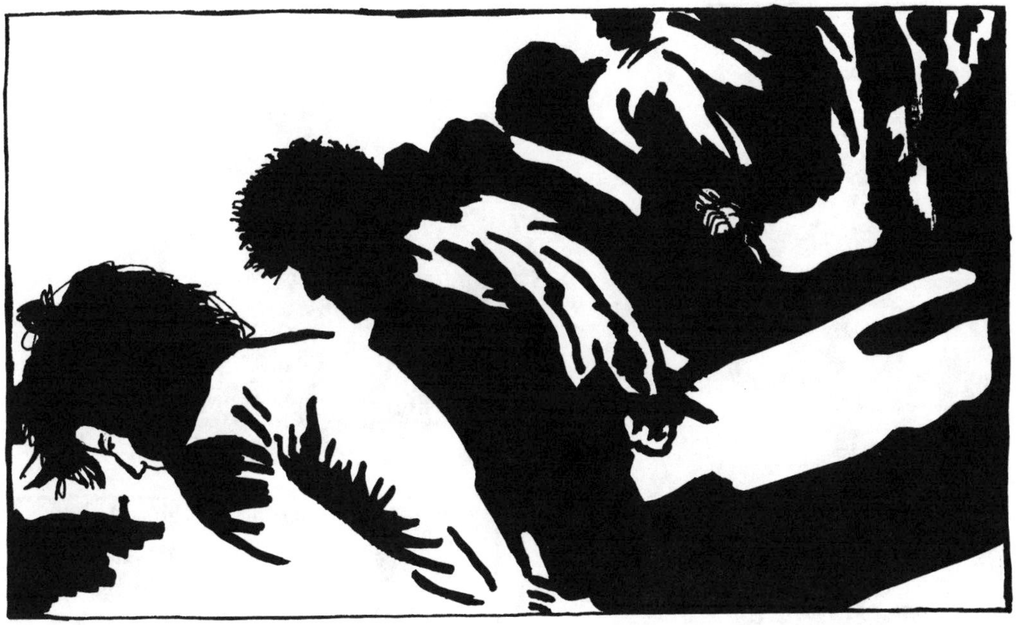

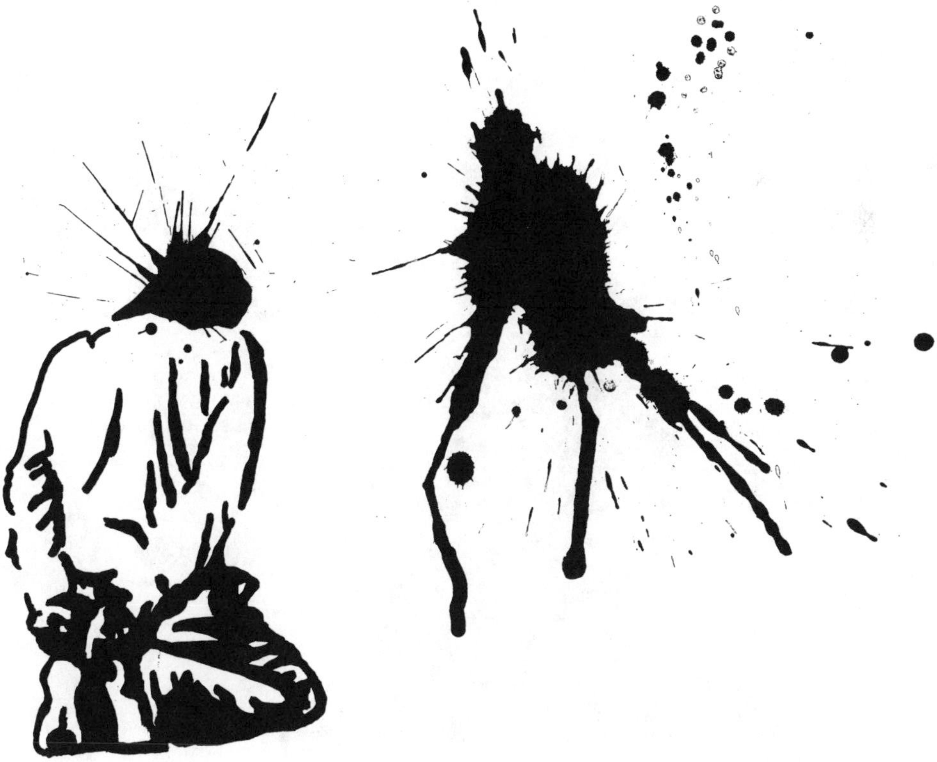

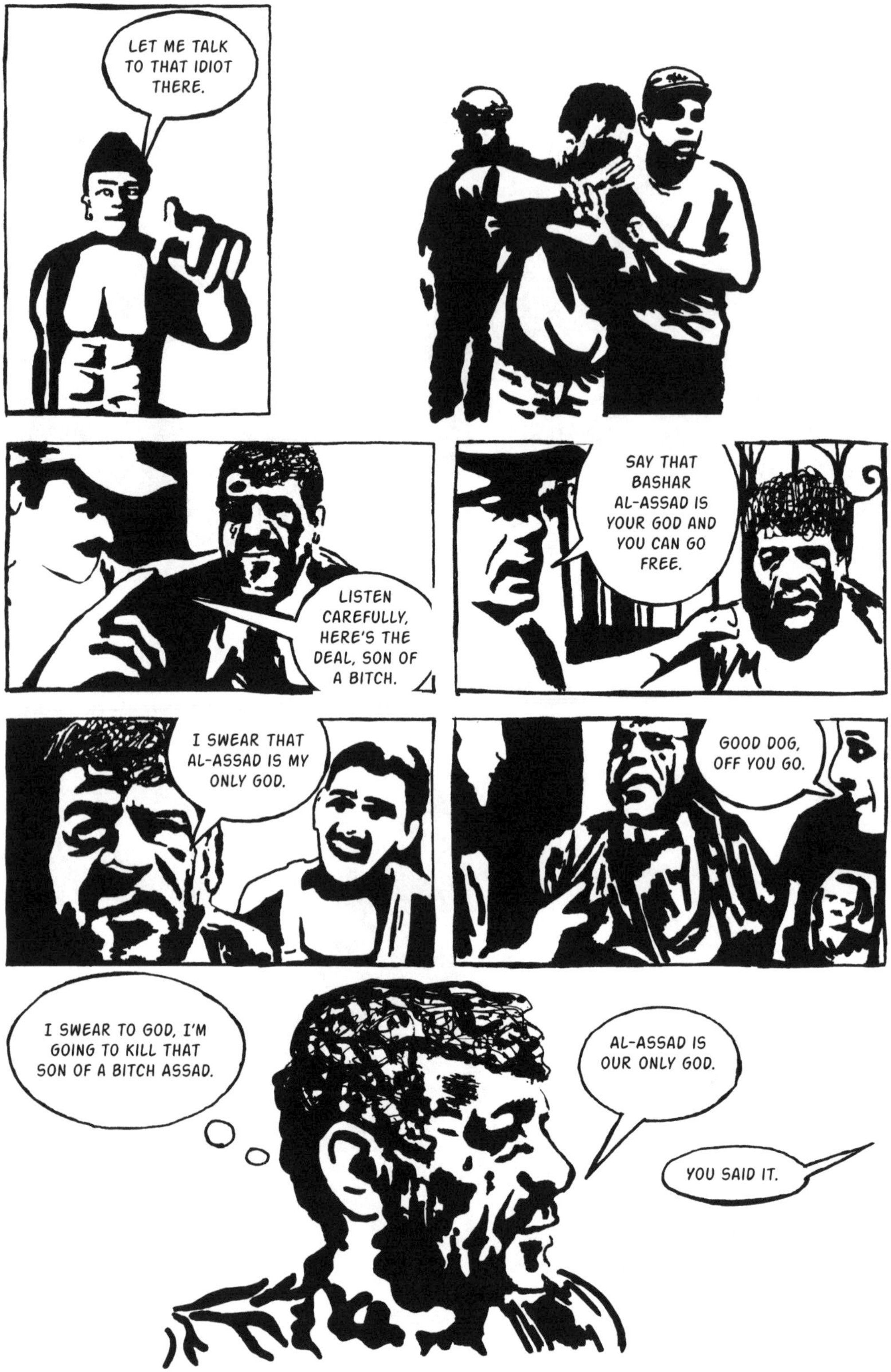
LET ME TALK TO THAT IDIOT THERE.
LISTEN CAREFULLY, HERE'S THE DEAL, SON OF A BITCH.
SAY THAT BASHAR AL-ASSAD IS YOUR GOD AND YOU CAN GO FREE.
I SWEAR THAT AL-ASSAD IS MY ONLY GOD.
GOOD DOG, OFF YOU GO.
I SWEAR TO GOD, I'M GOING TO KILL THAT SON OF A BITCH ASSAD.
AL-ASSAD IS OUR ONLY GOD.
YOU SAID IT.

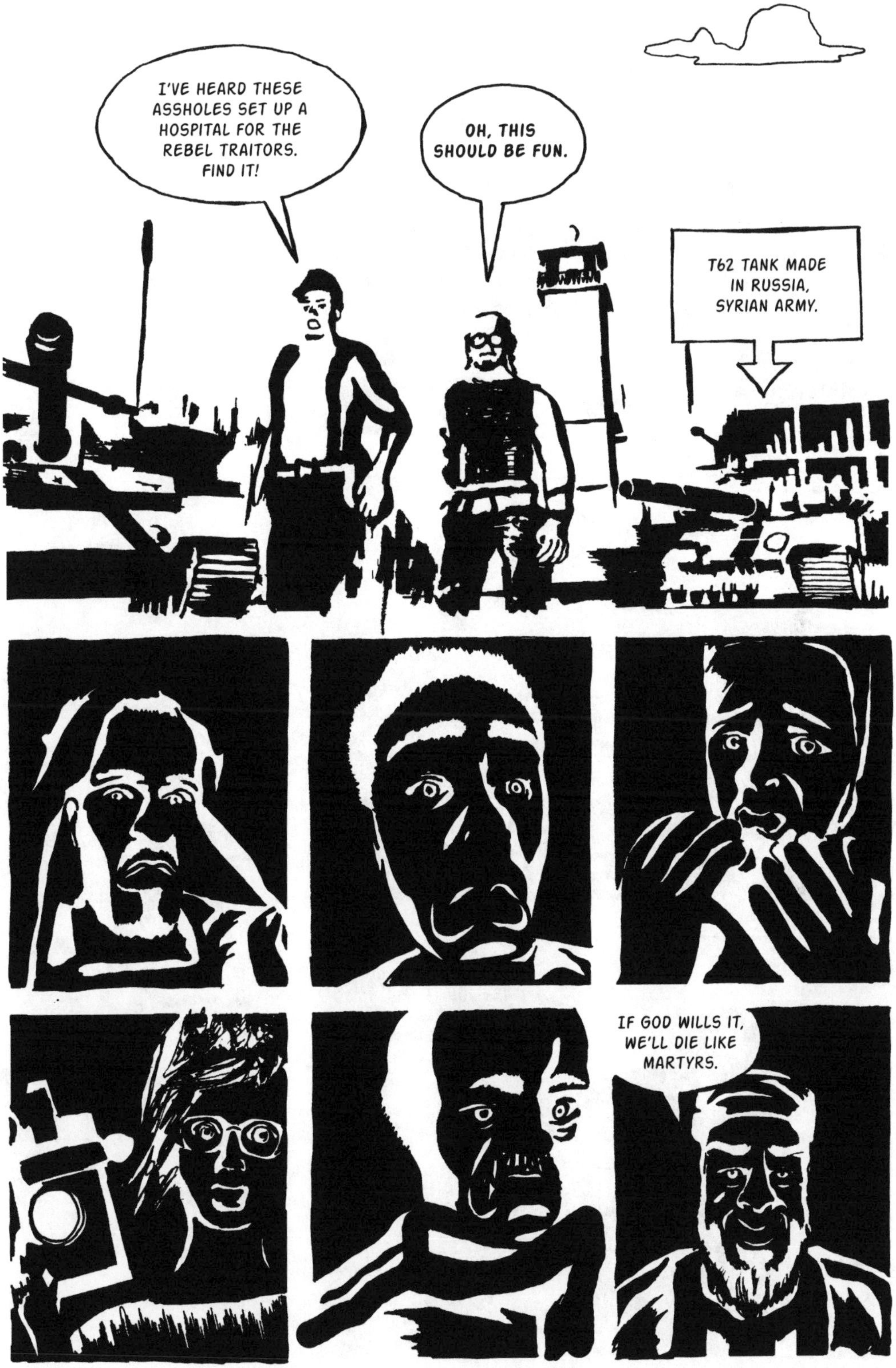
I'VE HEARD THESE ASSHOLES SET UP A HOSPITAL FOR THE REBEL TRAITORS. FIND IT!
OH, THIS SHOULD BE FUN.
T62 TANK MADE IN RUSSIA, SYRIAN ARMY.
IF GOD WILLS IT, WE'LL DIE LIKE MARTYRS.

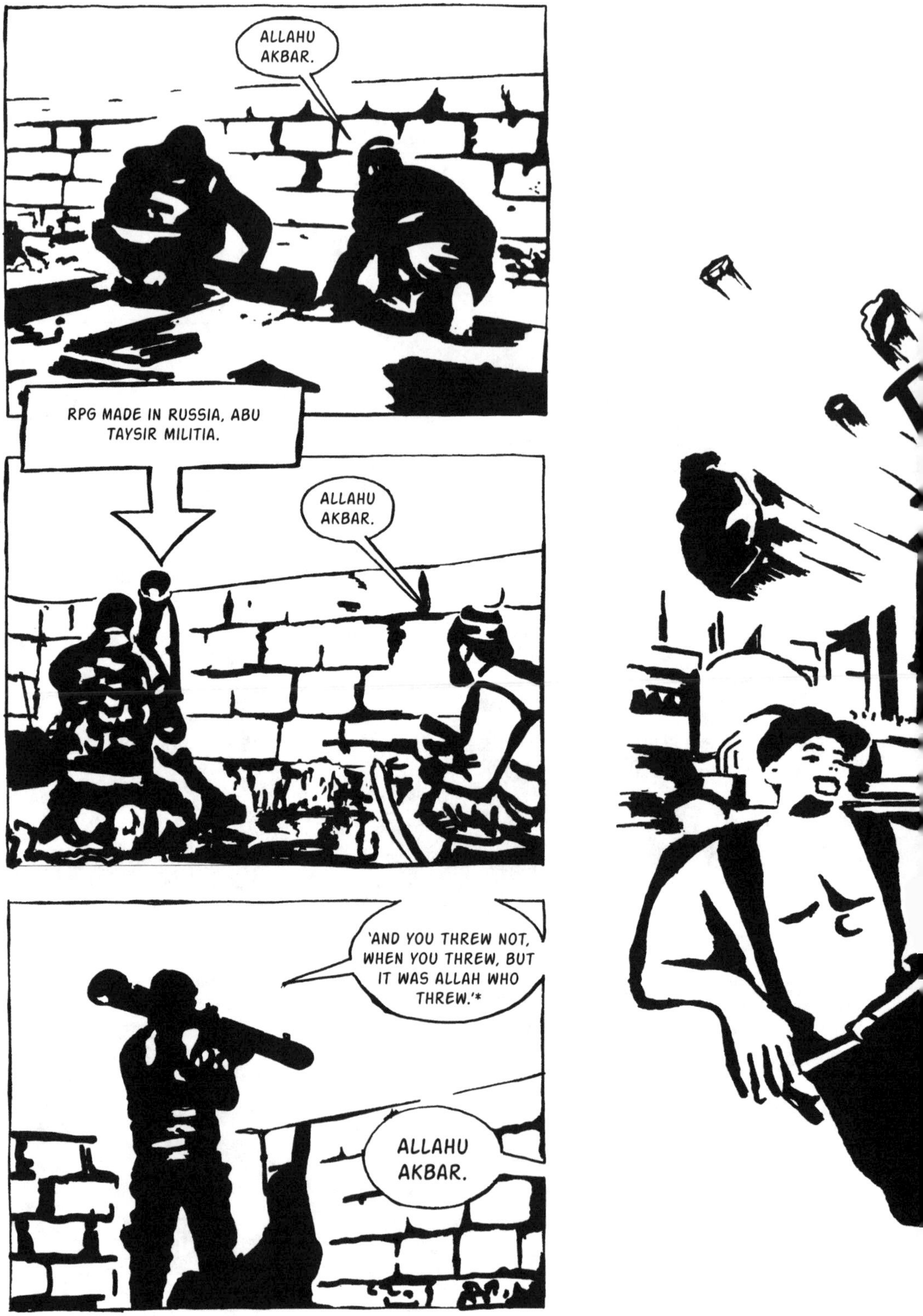
ALLAHU AKBAR.
RPG MADE IN RUSSIA, ABU TAYSIR MILITIA.
ALLAHU AKBAR.
'AND YOU THREW NOT, WHEN YOU THREW, BUT IT WAS ALLAH WHO THREW.'*
ALLAHU AKBAR.

* QURAN AL-ANFAL SURAH 8, VERSE 17.

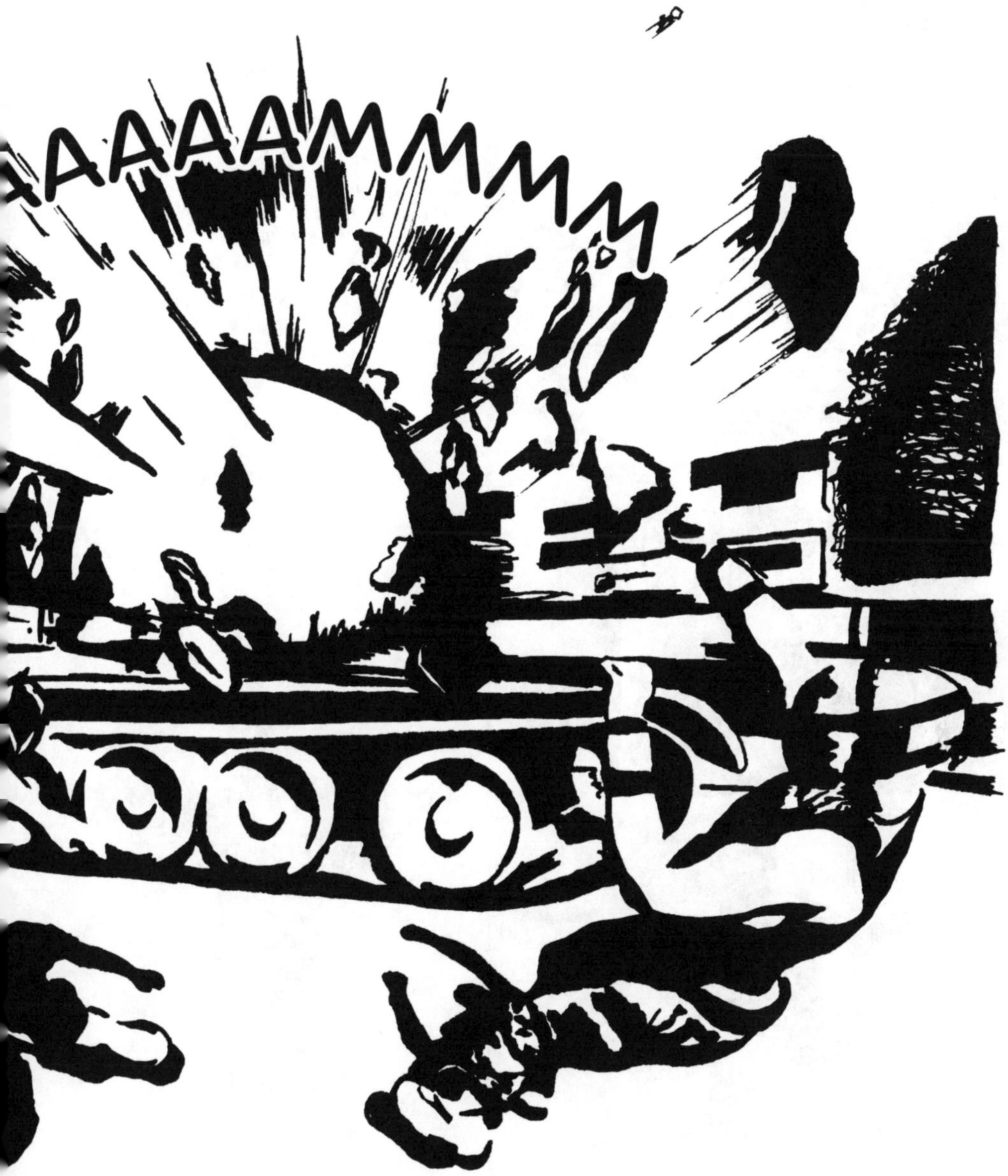
AAAAAMMMM

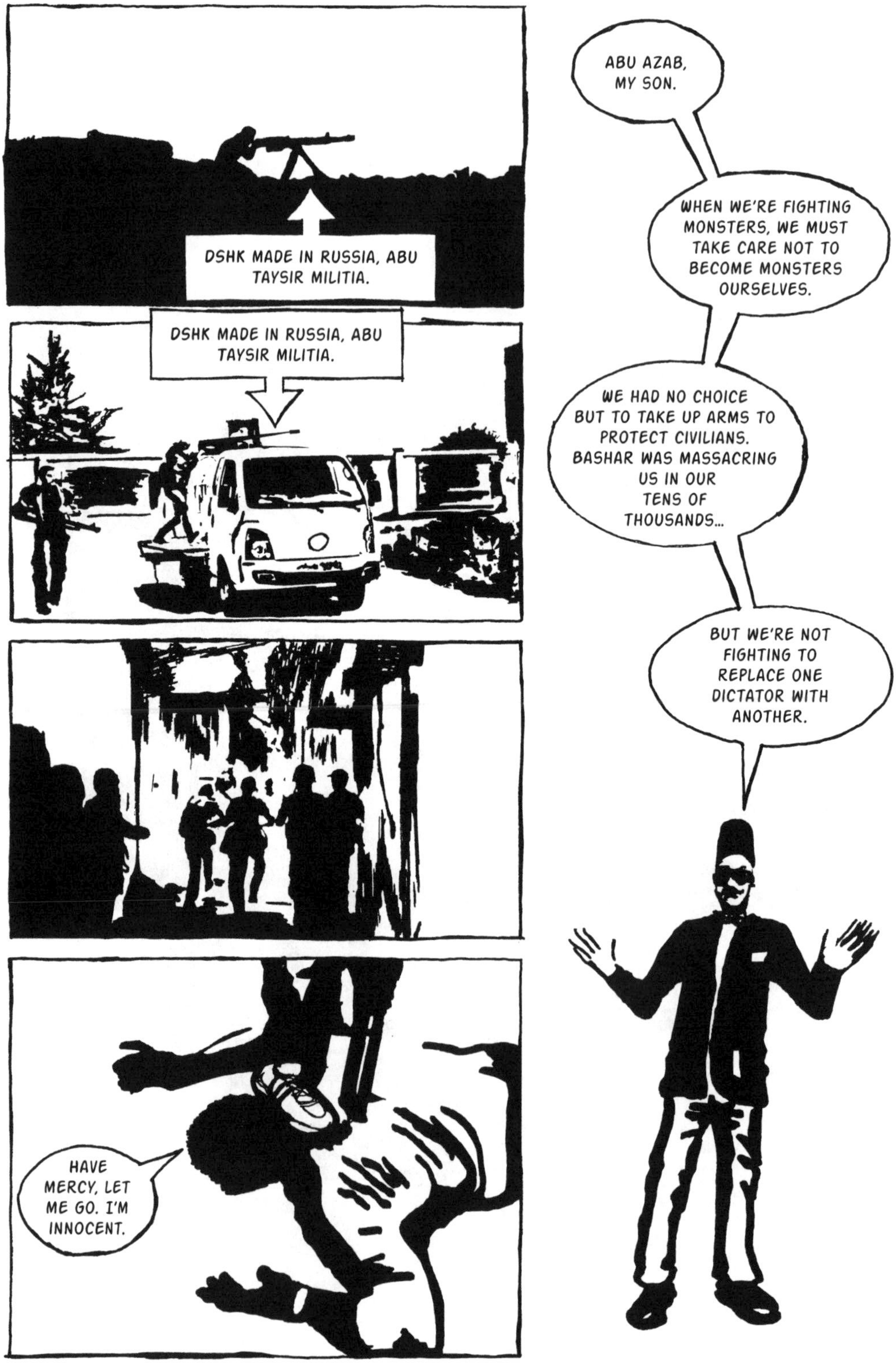
DSHK MADE IN RUSSIA, ABU TAYSIR MILITIA.
DSHK MADE IN RUSSIA, ABU TAYSIR MILITIA.
HAVE MERCY, LET ME GO. I'M INNOCENT.
ABU AZAB, MY SON.
WHEN WE'RE FIGHTING MONSTERS, WE MUST TAKE CARE NOT TO BECOME MONSTERS OURSELVES.
WE HAD NO CHOICE BUT TO TAKE UP ARMS TO PROTECT CIVILIANS. BASHAR WAS MASSACRING US IN OUR TENS OF THOUSANDS...
BUT WE'RE NOT FIGHTING TO REPLACE ONE DICTATOR WITH ANOTHER.

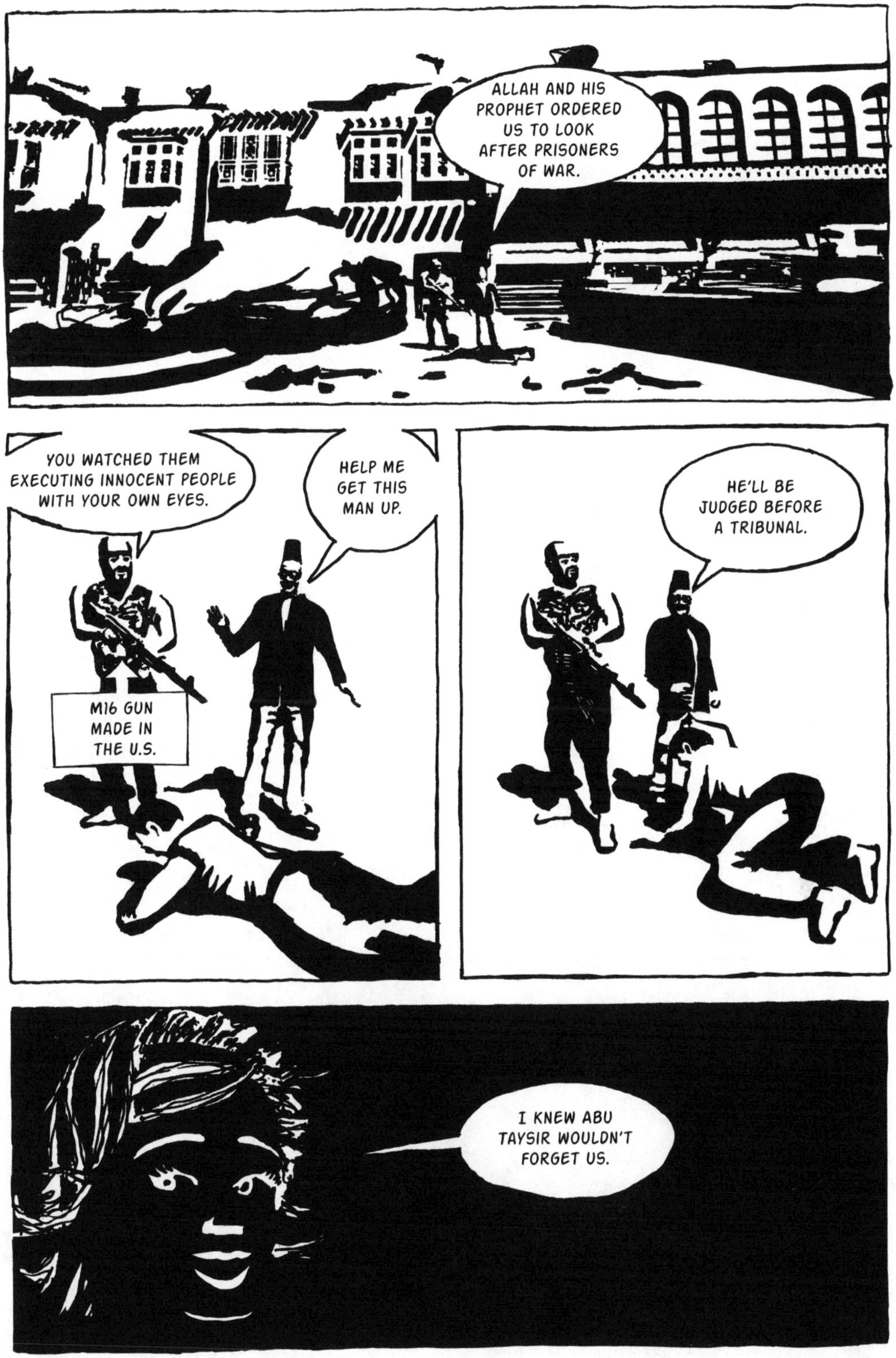
ALLAH AND HIS PROPHET ORDERED US TO LOOK AFTER PRISONERS OF WAR.
YOU WATCHED THEM EXECUTING INNOCENT PEOPLE WITH YOUR OWN EYES.
HELP ME GET THIS MAN UP.
M16 GUN MADE IN THE U.S.
HE'LL BE JUDGED BEFORE A TRIBUNAL.
I KNEW ABU TAYSIR WOULDN'T FORGET US.

Chapter 2

SUMMER

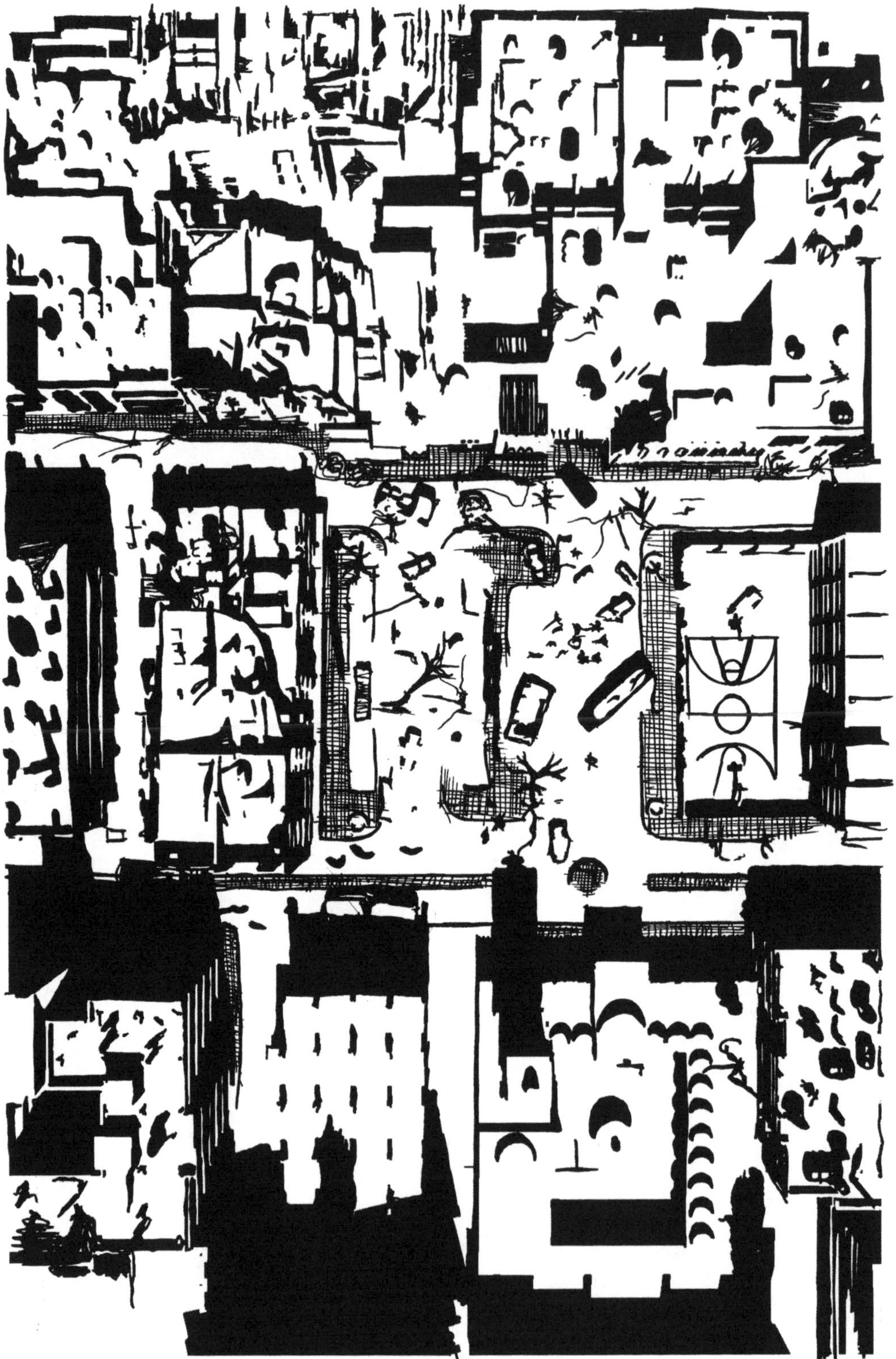

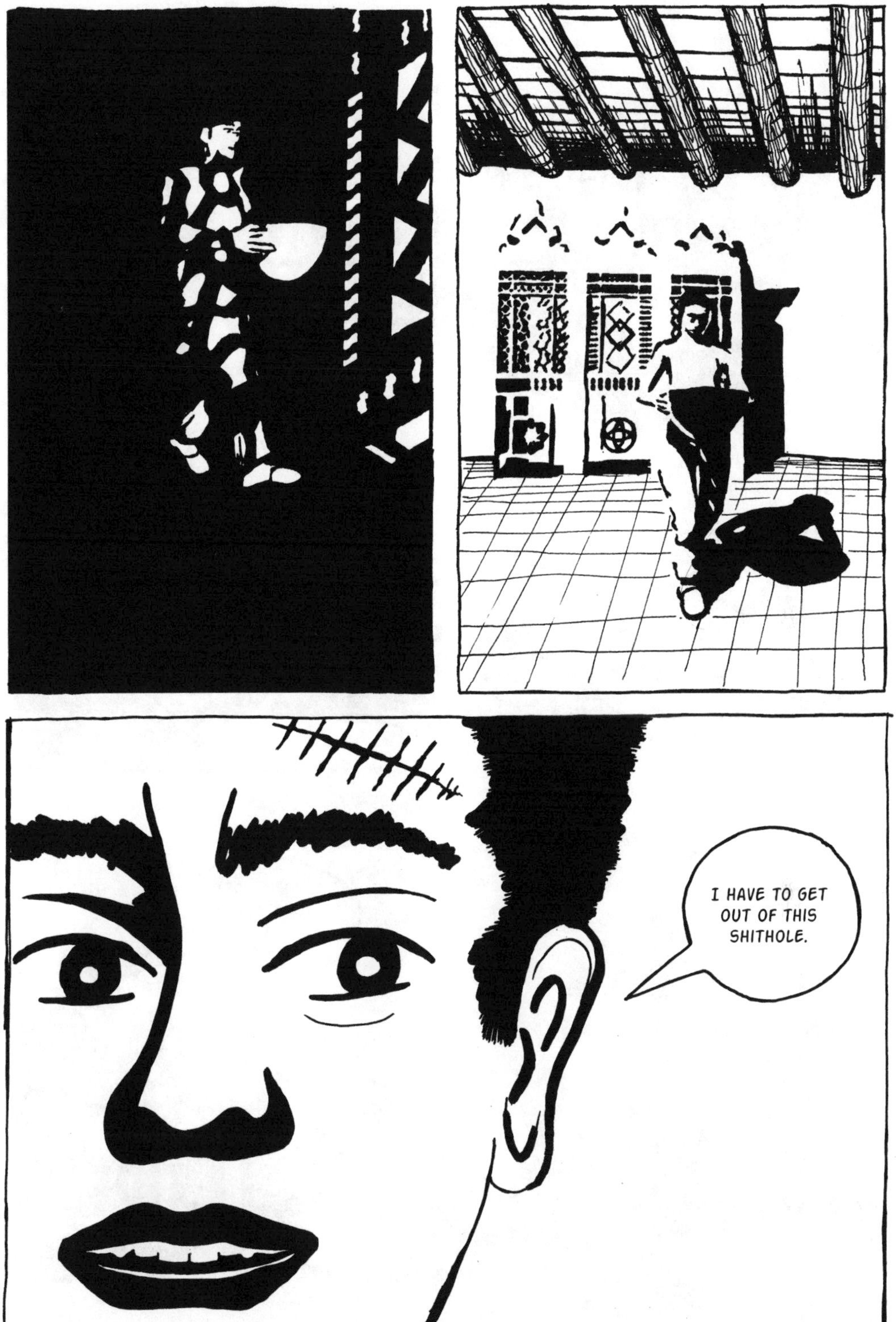
I HAVE TO GET OUT OF THIS SHITHOLE.

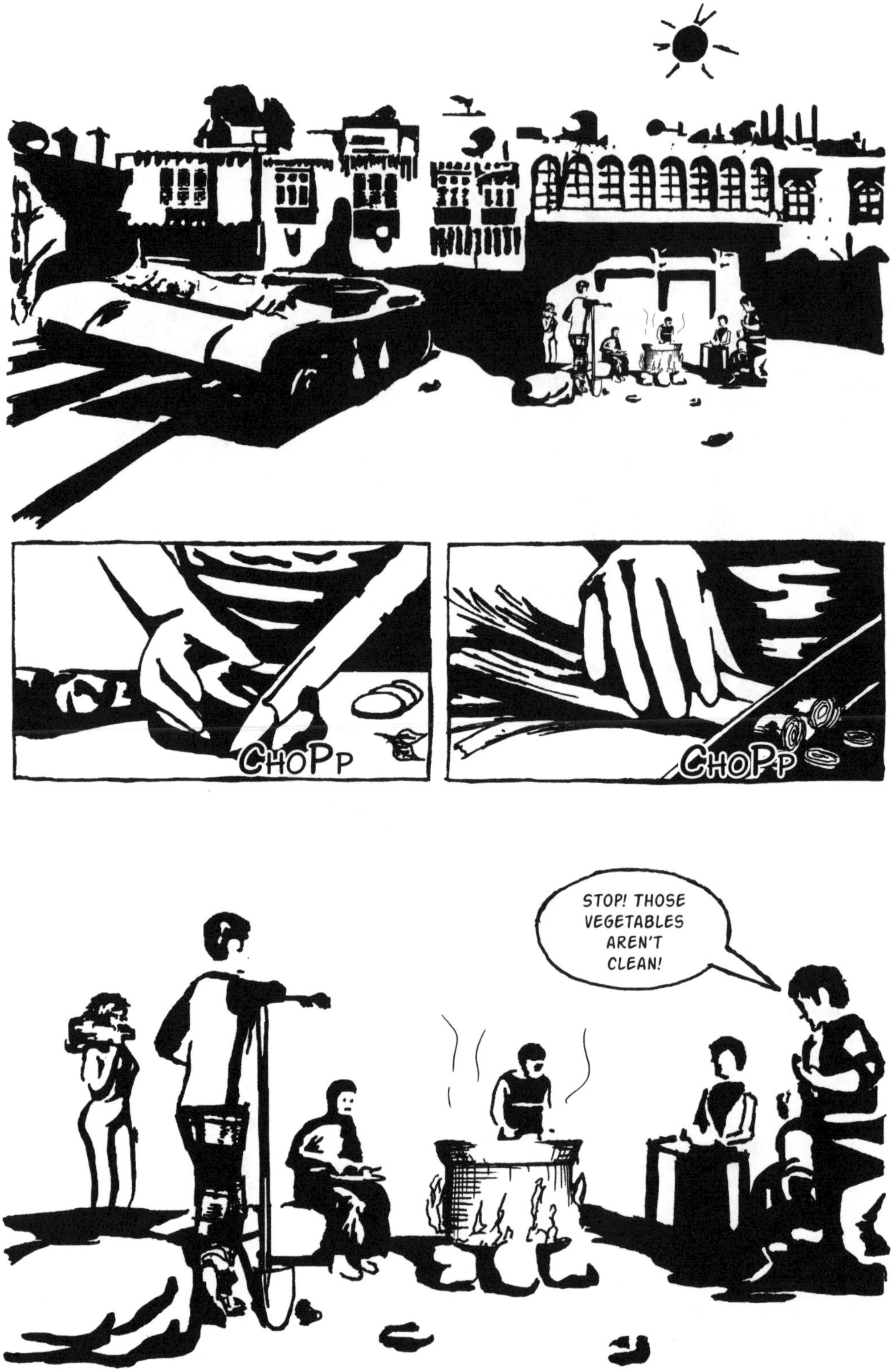
CHOPP
CHOPP
STOP! THOSE VEGETABLES AREN'T CLEAN!

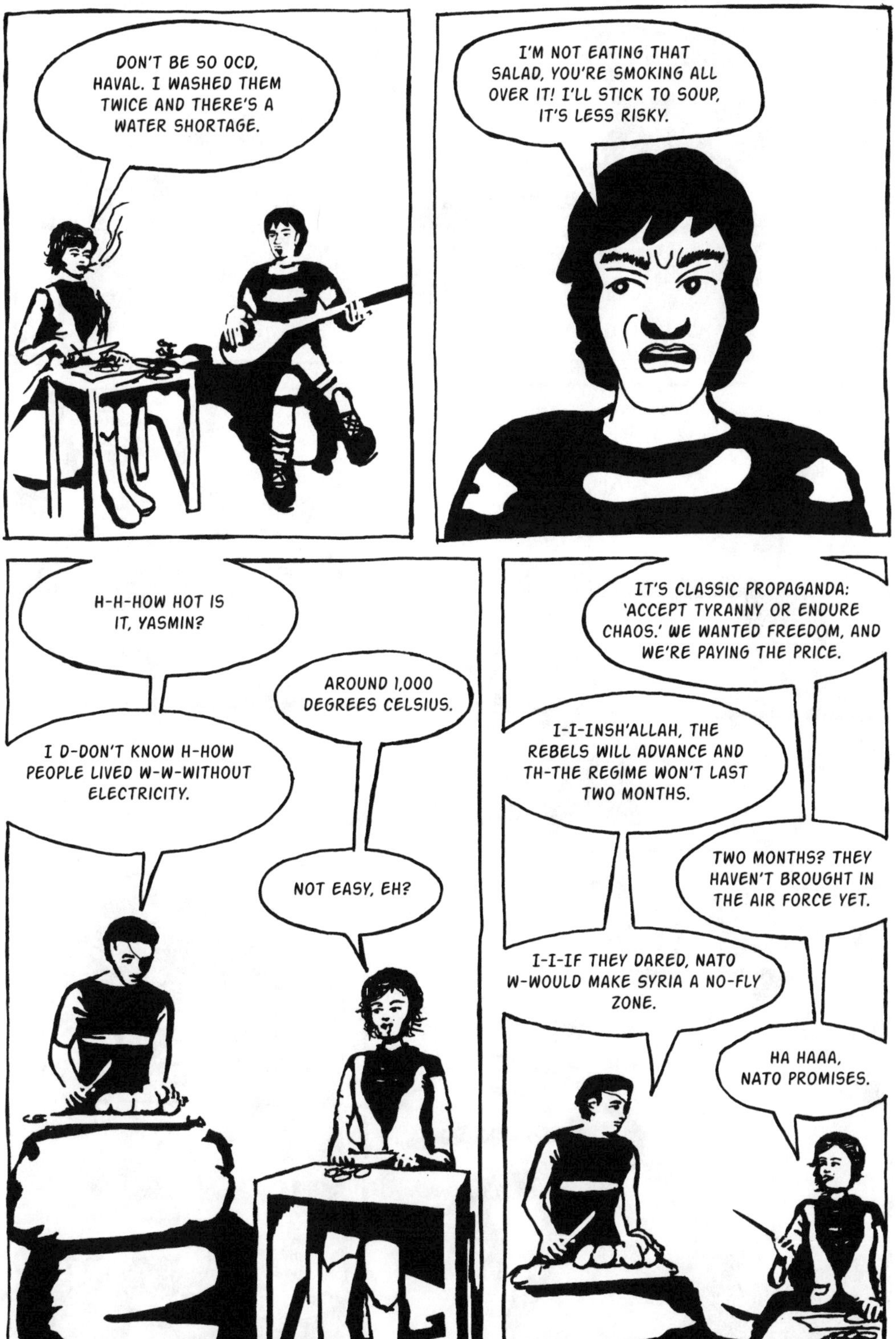
DON'T BE SO OCD, HAVAL. I WASHED THEM TWICE AND THERE'S A WATER SHORTAGE.
I'M NOT EATING THAT SALAD, YOU'RE SMOKING ALL OVER IT! I'LL STICK TO SOUP, IT'S LESS RISKY.
H-H-HOW HOT IS IT, YASMIN?
AROUND 1,000 DEGREES CELSIUS.
I D-DON'T KNOW H-HOW PEOPLE LIVED W-W-WITHOUT ELECTRICITY.
NOT EASY, EH?
IT'S CLASSIC PROPAGANDA: 'ACCEPT TYRANNY OR ENDURE CHAOS.' WE WANTED FREEDOM, AND WE'RE PAYING THE PRICE.
I-I-INSH'ALLAH, THE REBELS WILL ADVANCE AND TH-THE REGIME WON'T LAST TWO MONTHS.
TWO MONTHS? THEY HAVEN'T BROUGHT IN THE AIR FORCE YET.
I-I-IF THEY DARED, NATO W-WOULD MAKE SYRIA A NO-FLY ZONE.
HA HAAA, NATO PROMISES.

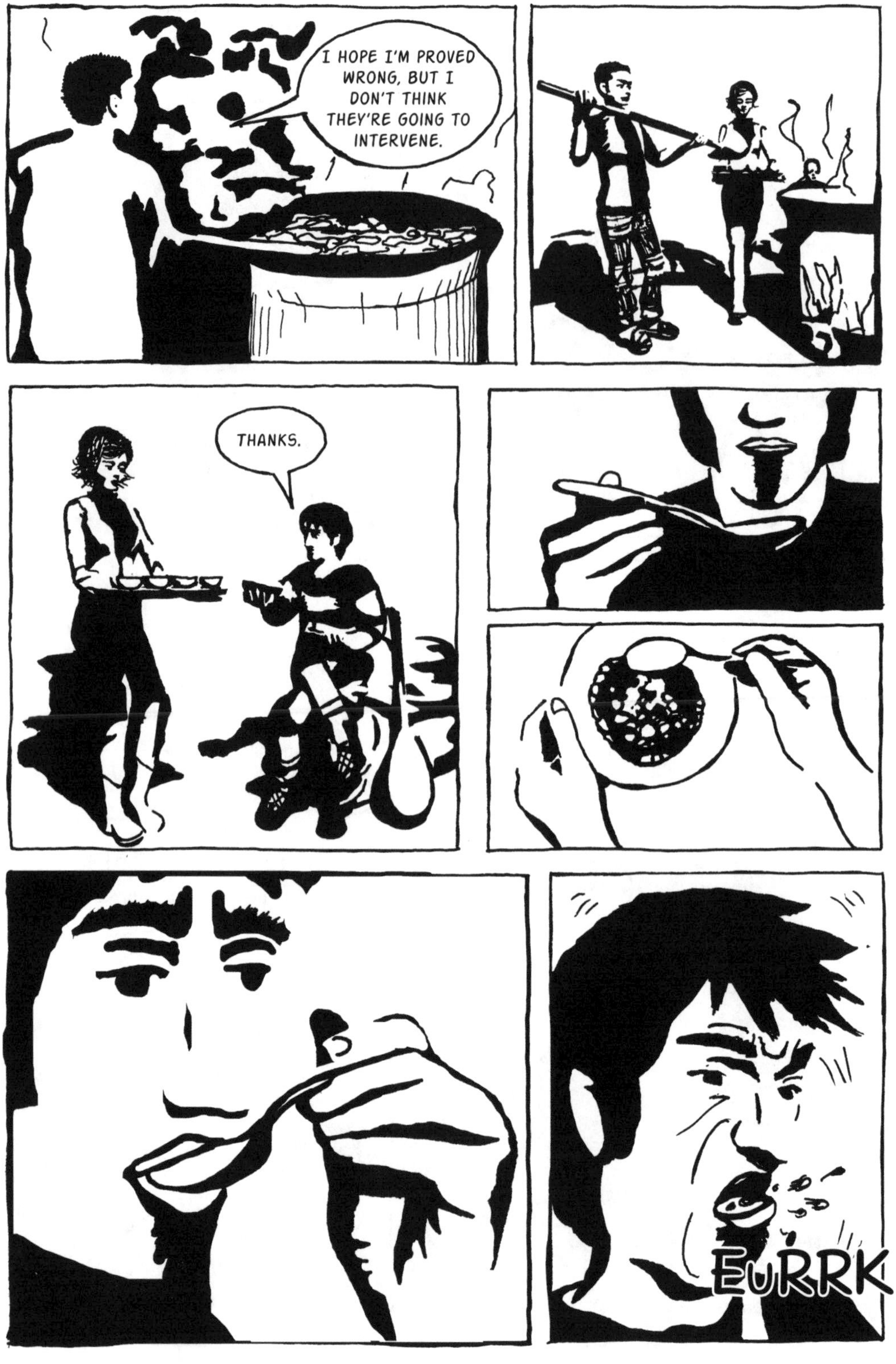
I HOPE I'M PROVED WRONG, BUT I DON'T THINK THEY'RE GOING TO INTERVENE.
THANKS.
EURRK

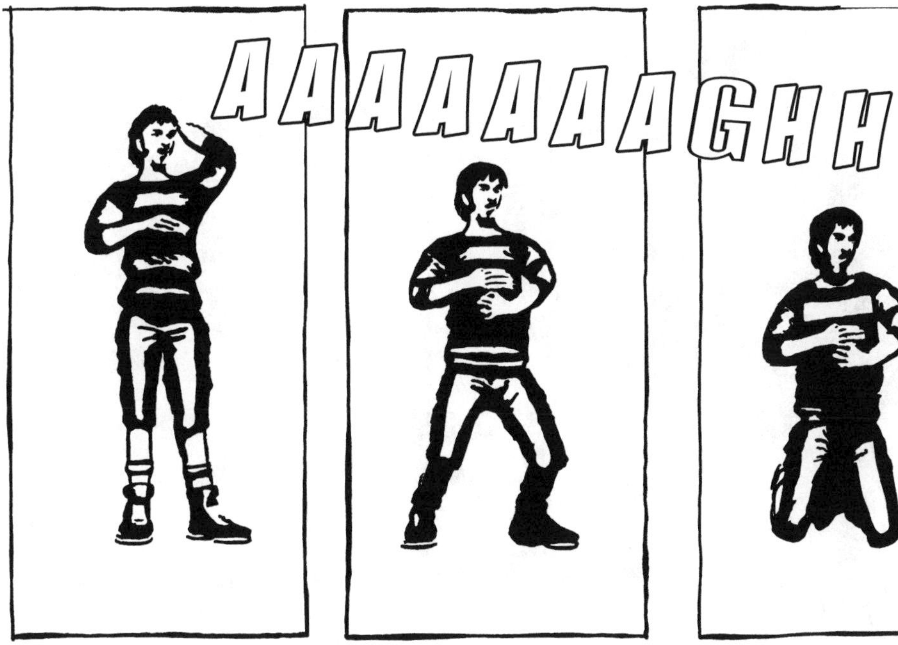
AAAAAAAAGHH

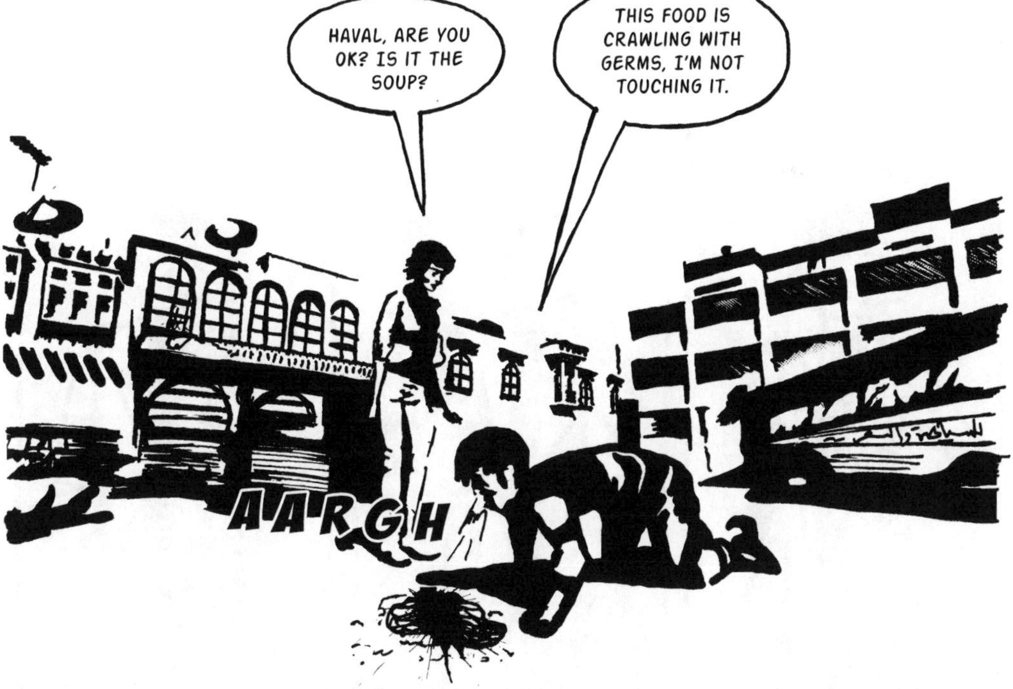
HAVAL, ARE YOU OK? IS IT THE SOUP?
THIS FOOD IS CRAWLING WITH GERMS, I'M NOT TOUCHING IT.
AARGH

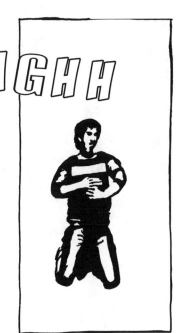

SIX DAYS LATER: ANOTHER 731 KILLED.

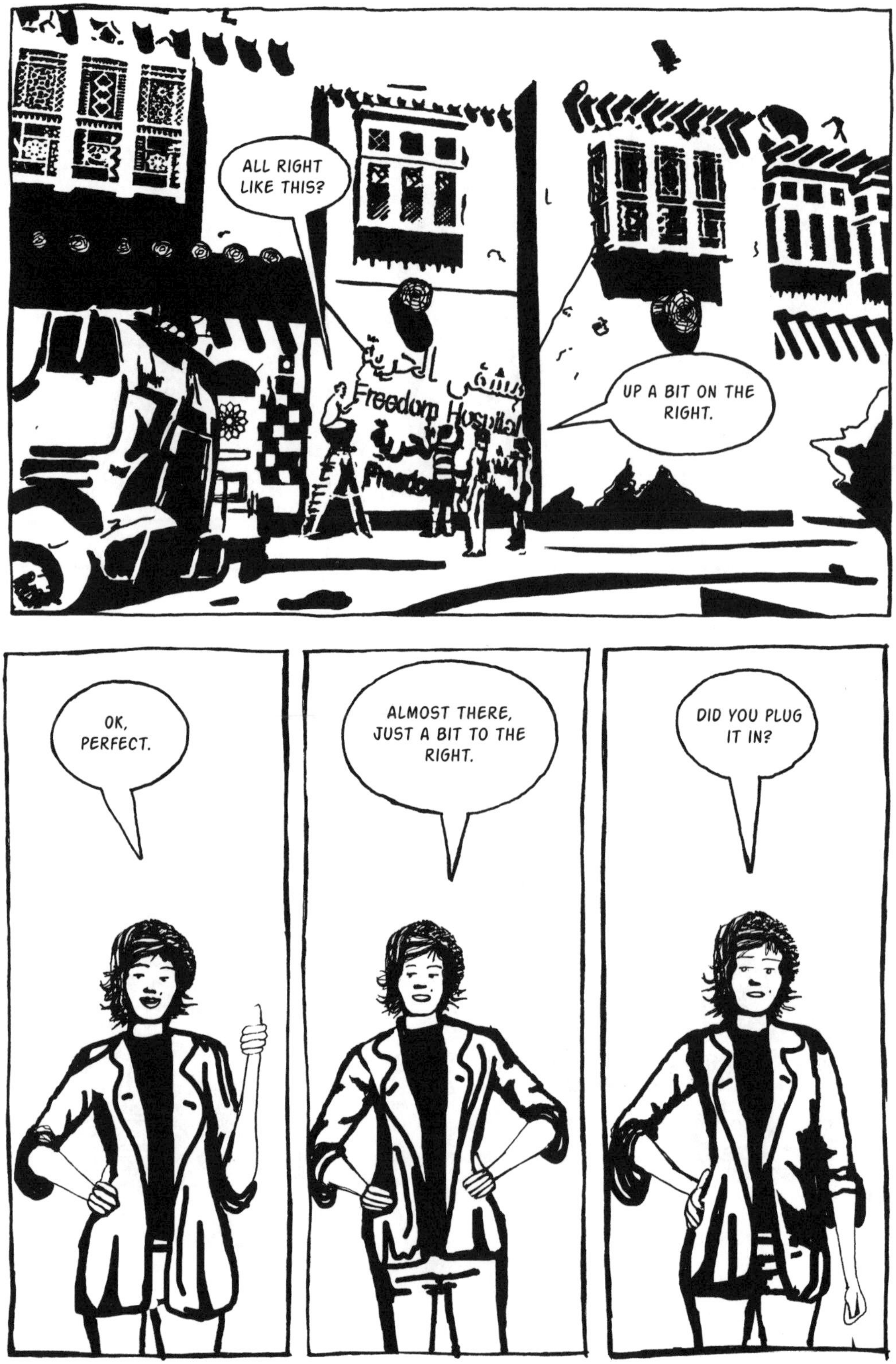
ALL RIGHT LIKE THIS?
Freedom Hospital
UP A BIT ON THE RIGHT.
OK, PERFECT.
ALMOST THERE, JUST A BIT TO THE RIGHT.
DID YOU PLUG IT IN?

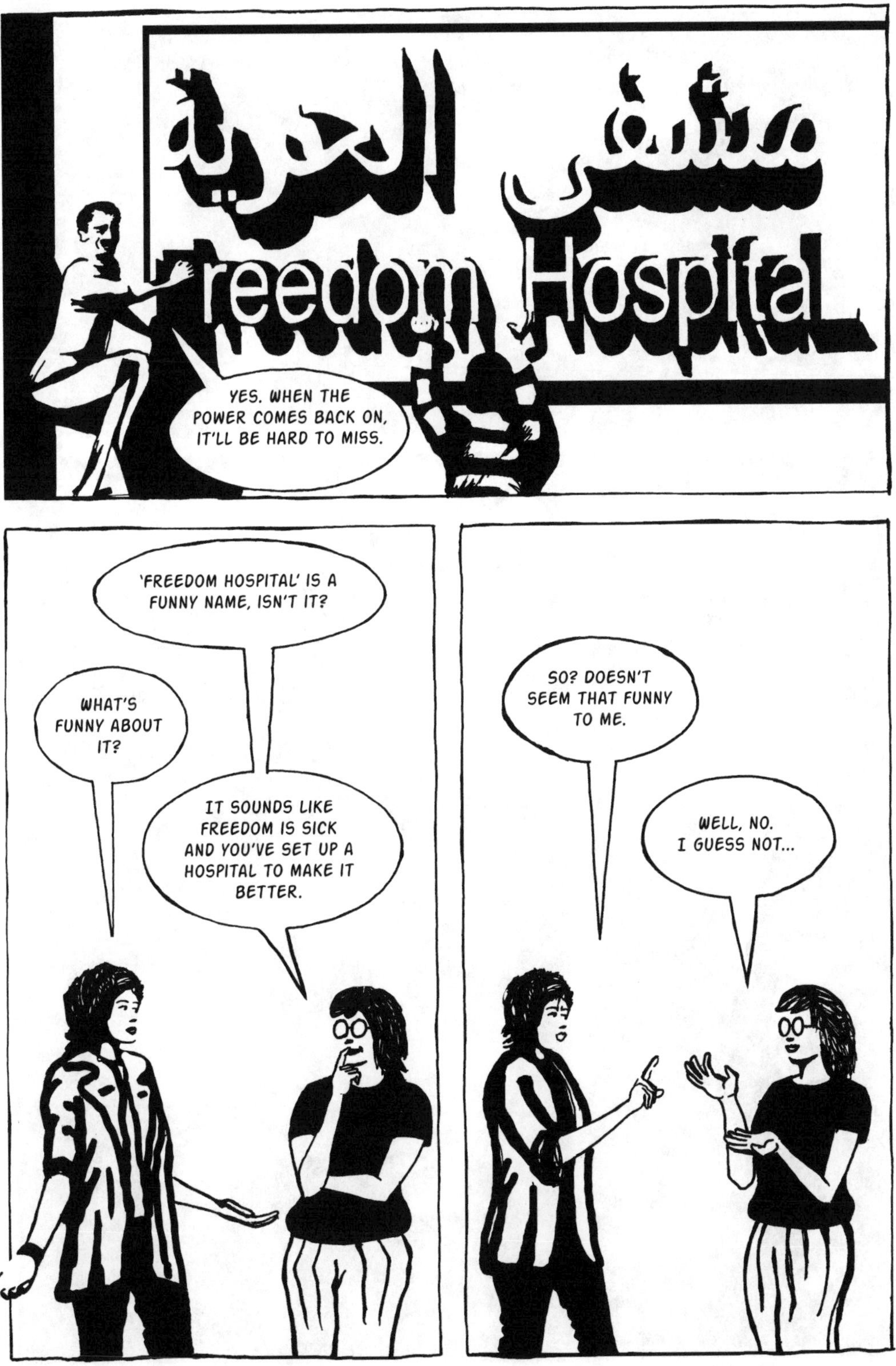
مستشفى الحرية
reedom Hospital
YES. WHEN THE POWER COMES BACK ON, IT'LL BE HARD TO MISS.
'FREEDOM HOSPITAL' IS A FUNNY NAME, ISN'T IT?
WHAT'S FUNNY ABOUT IT?
IT SOUNDS LIKE FREEDOM IS SICK AND YOU'VE SET UP A HOSPITAL TO MAKE IT BETTER.
SO? DOESN'T SEEM THAT FUNNY TO ME.
WELL, NO. I GUESS NOT...

TEN HOURS LATER: ANOTHER 69 KILLED.

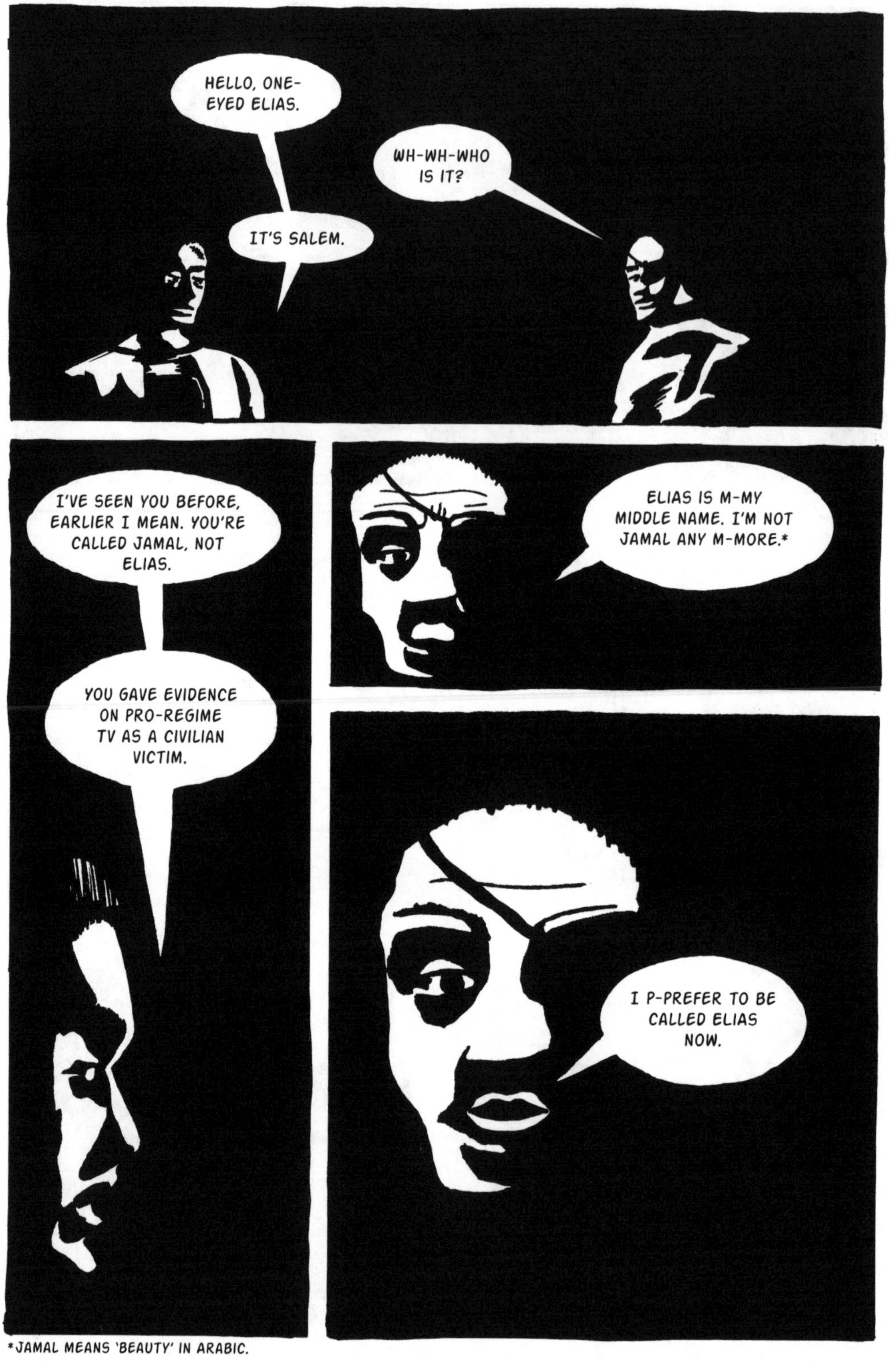
HELLO, ONE-EYED ELIAS.
WH-WH-WHO IS IT?
IT'S SALEM.
I'VE SEEN YOU BEFORE, EARLIER I MEAN. YOU'RE CALLED JAMAL, NOT ELIAS.
ELIAS IS M-MY MIDDLE NAME. I'M NOT JAMAL ANY M-MORE.*
YOU GAVE EVIDENCE ON PRO-REGIME TV AS A CIVILIAN VICTIM.
I P-PREFER TO BE CALLED ELIAS NOW.

*JAMAL MEANS 'BEAUTY' IN ARABIC.

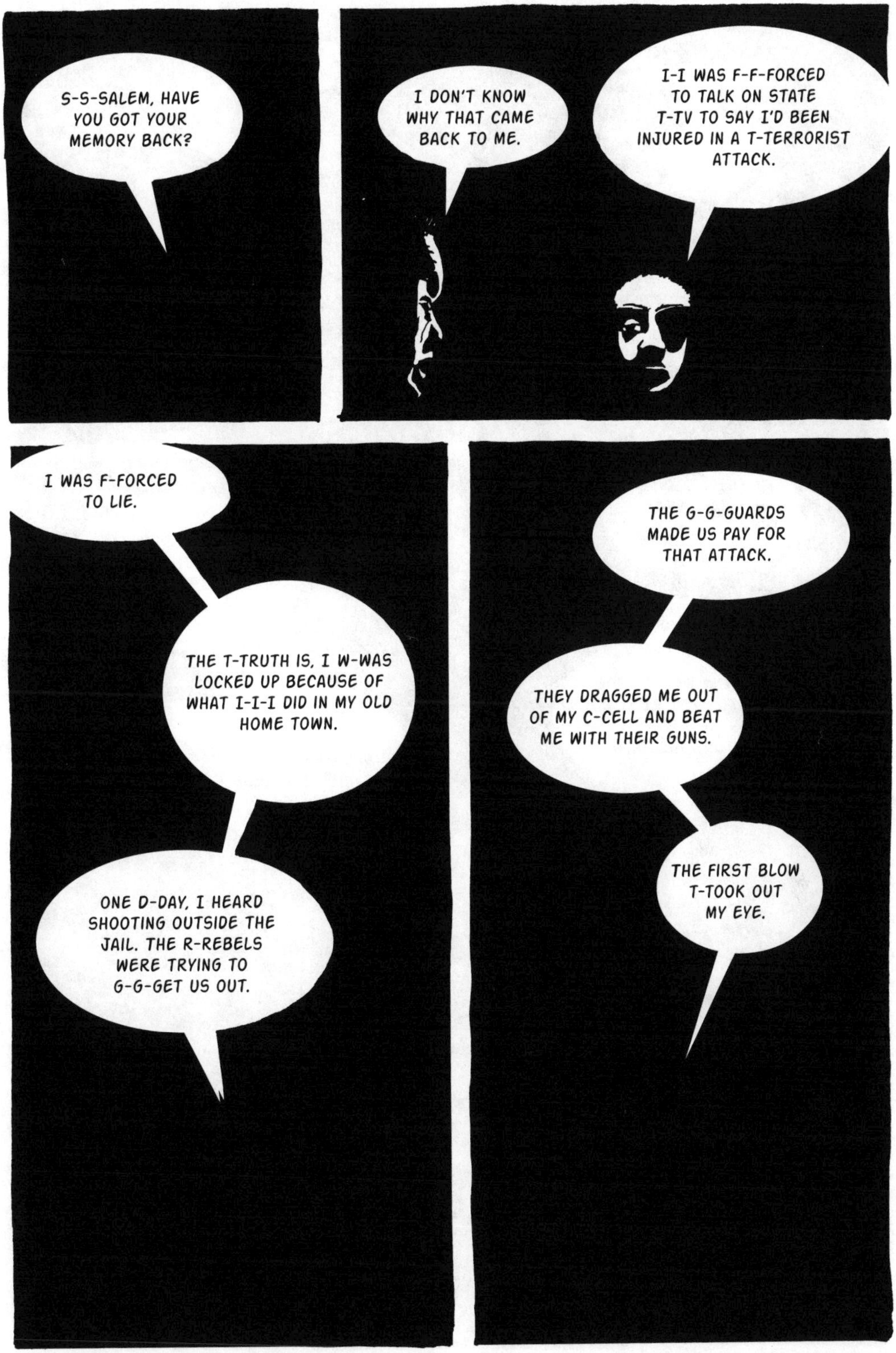
S-S-SALEM, HAVE YOU GOT YOUR MEMORY BACK?
I DON'T KNOW WHY THAT CAME BACK TO ME.
I-I WAS F-F-FORCED TO TALK ON STATE T-TV TO SAY I'D BEEN INJURED IN A T-TERRORIST ATTACK.
I WAS F-FORCED TO LIE.
THE T-TRUTH IS, I W-WAS LOCKED UP BECAUSE OF WHAT I-I-I DID IN MY OLD HOME TOWN.
ONE D-DAY, I HEARD SHOOTING OUTSIDE THE JAIL. THE R-REBELS WERE TRYING TO G-G-GET US OUT.
THE G-G-GUARDS MADE US PAY FOR THAT ATTACK.
THEY DRAGGED ME OUT OF MY C-CELL AND BEAT ME WITH THEIR GUNS.
THE FIRST BLOW T-TOOK OUT MY EYE.

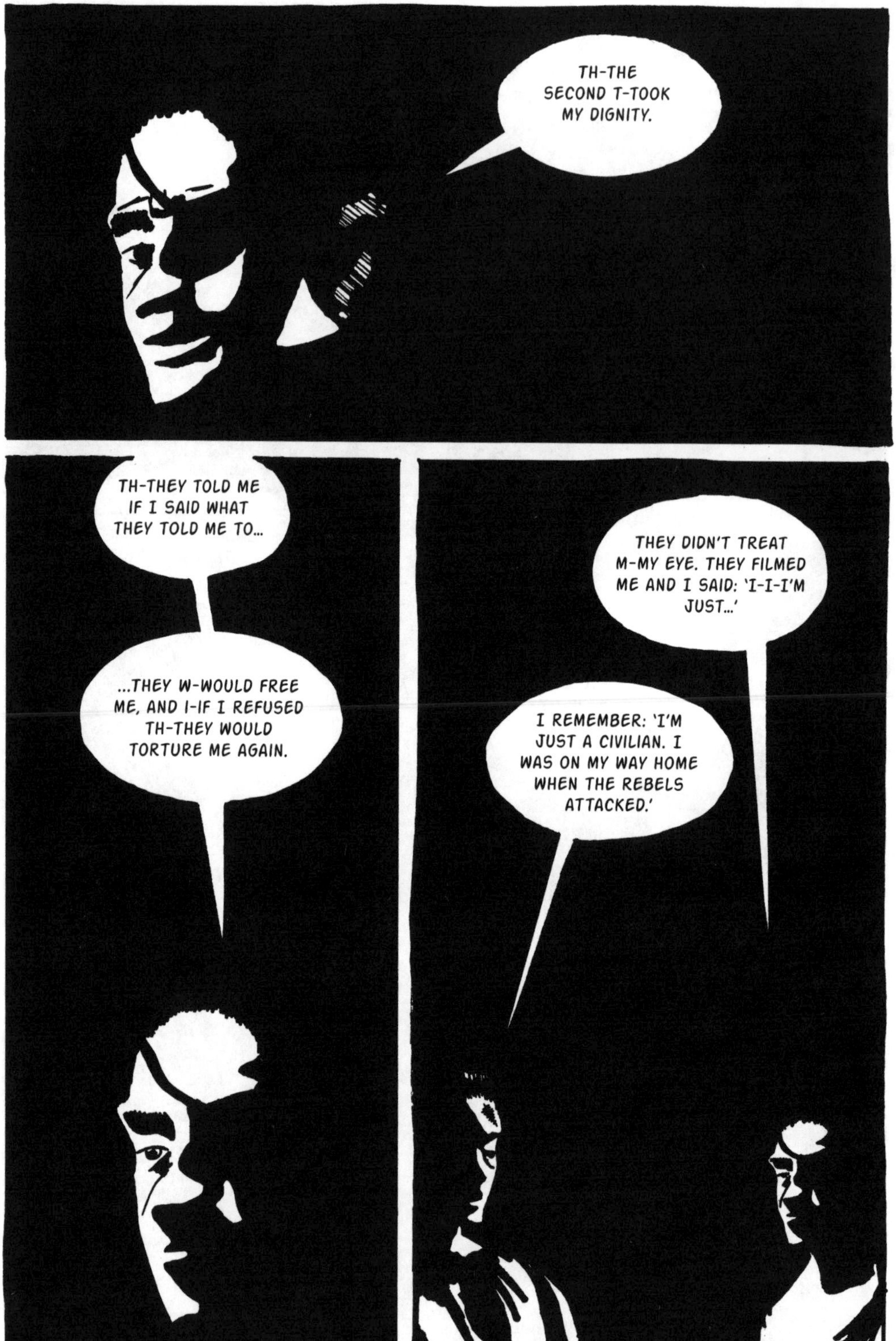
TH-THE SECOND T-TOOK MY DIGNITY.
TH-THEY TOLD ME IF I SAID WHAT THEY TOLD ME TO...
...THEY W-WOULD FREE ME, AND I-IF I REFUSED TH-THEY WOULD TORTURE ME AGAIN.
THEY DIDN'T TREAT M-MY EYE. THEY FILMED ME AND I SAID: 'I-I-I'M JUST...'
I REMEMBER: 'I'M JUST A CIVILIAN. I WAS ON MY WAY HOME WHEN THE REBELS ATTACKED.'

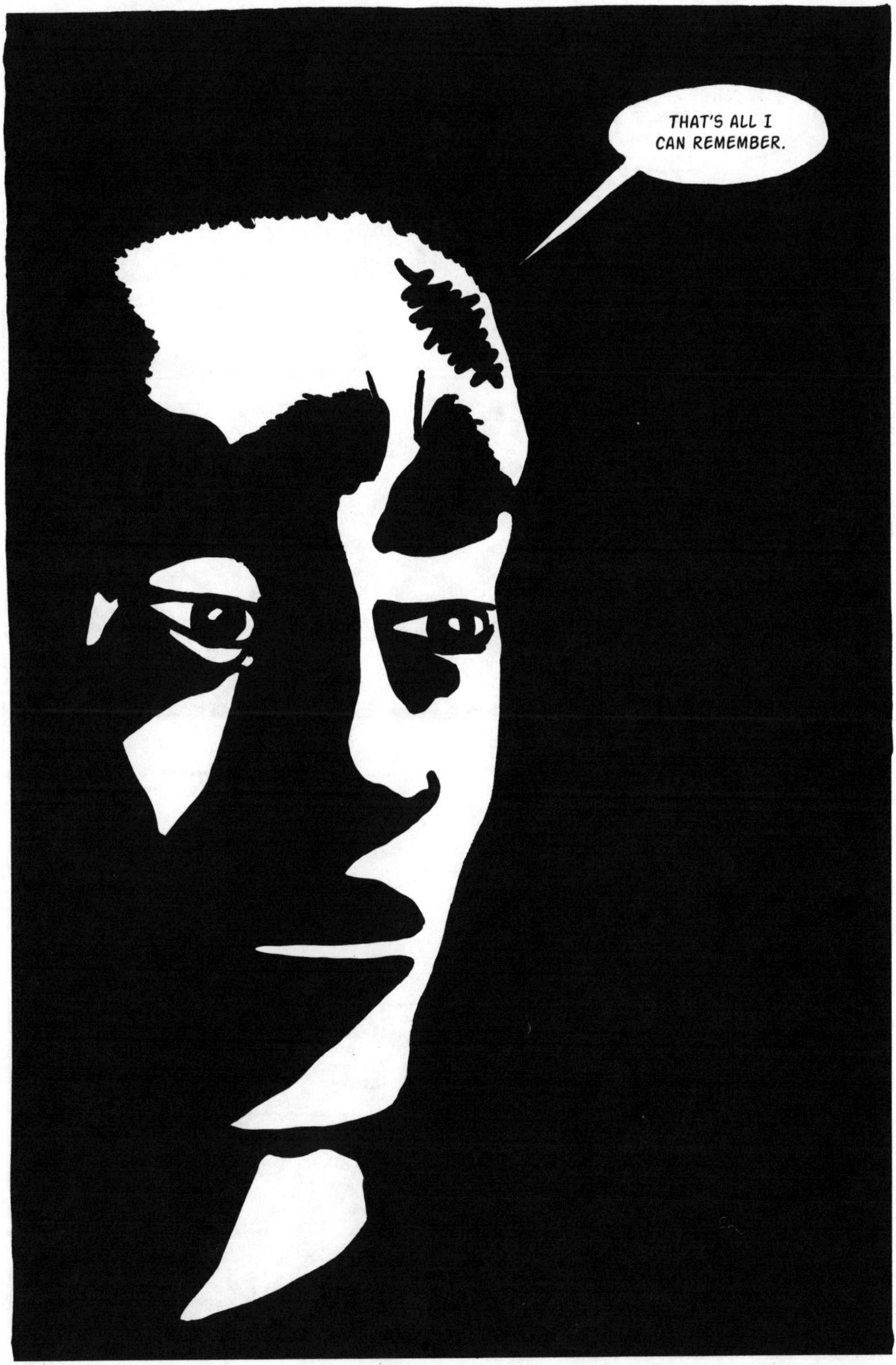
THAT'S ALL I CAN REMEMBER.

TWO WEEKS LATER: ANOTHER 2,157 KILLED.

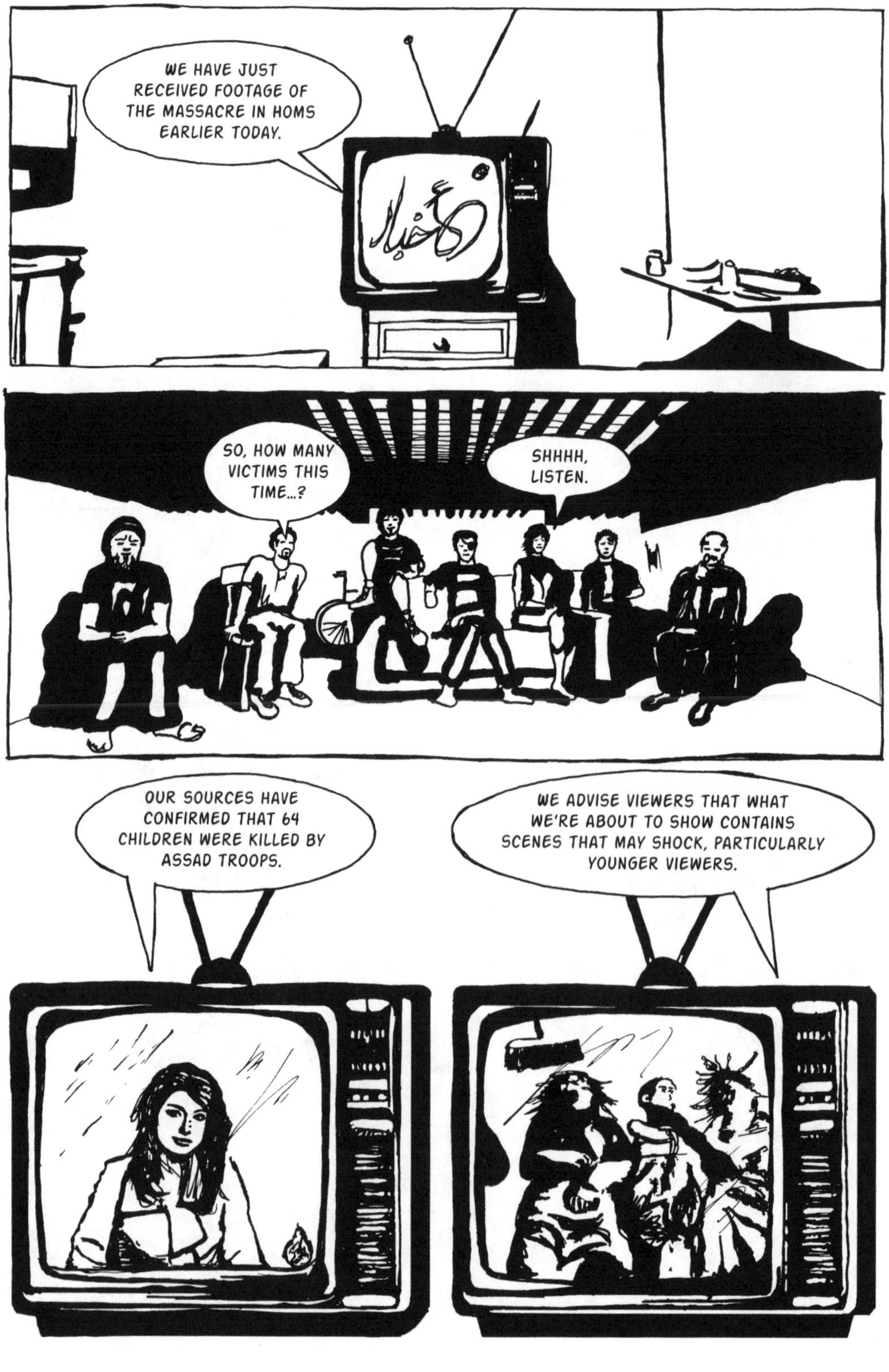
WE HAVE JUST RECEIVED FOOTAGE OF THE MASSACRE IN HOMS EARLIER TODAY.
SO, HOW MANY VICTIMS THIS TIME...?
SHHHH, LISTEN.
OUR SOURCES HAVE CONFIRMED THAT 64 CHILDREN WERE KILLED BY ASSAD TROOPS.
WE ADVISE VIEWERS THAT WHAT WE'RE ABOUT TO SHOW CONTAINS SCENES THAT MAY SHOCK, PARTICULARLY YOUNGER VIEWERS.

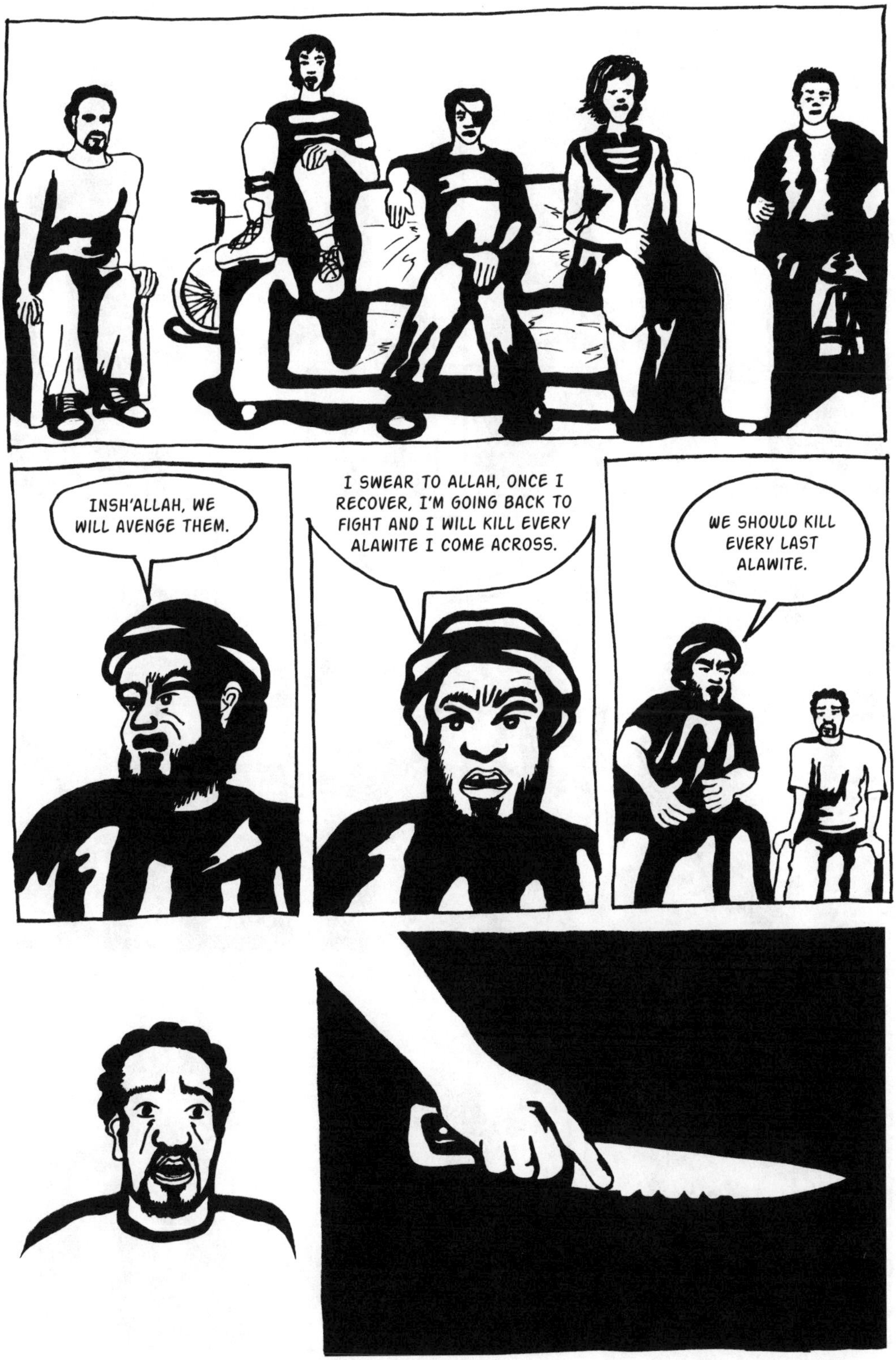
INSH'ALLAH, WE WILL AVENGE THEM.
I SWEAR TO ALLAH, ONCE I RECOVER, I'M GOING BACK TO FIGHT AND I WILL KILL EVERY ALAWITE I COME ACROSS.
WE SHOULD KILL EVERY LAST ALAWITE.

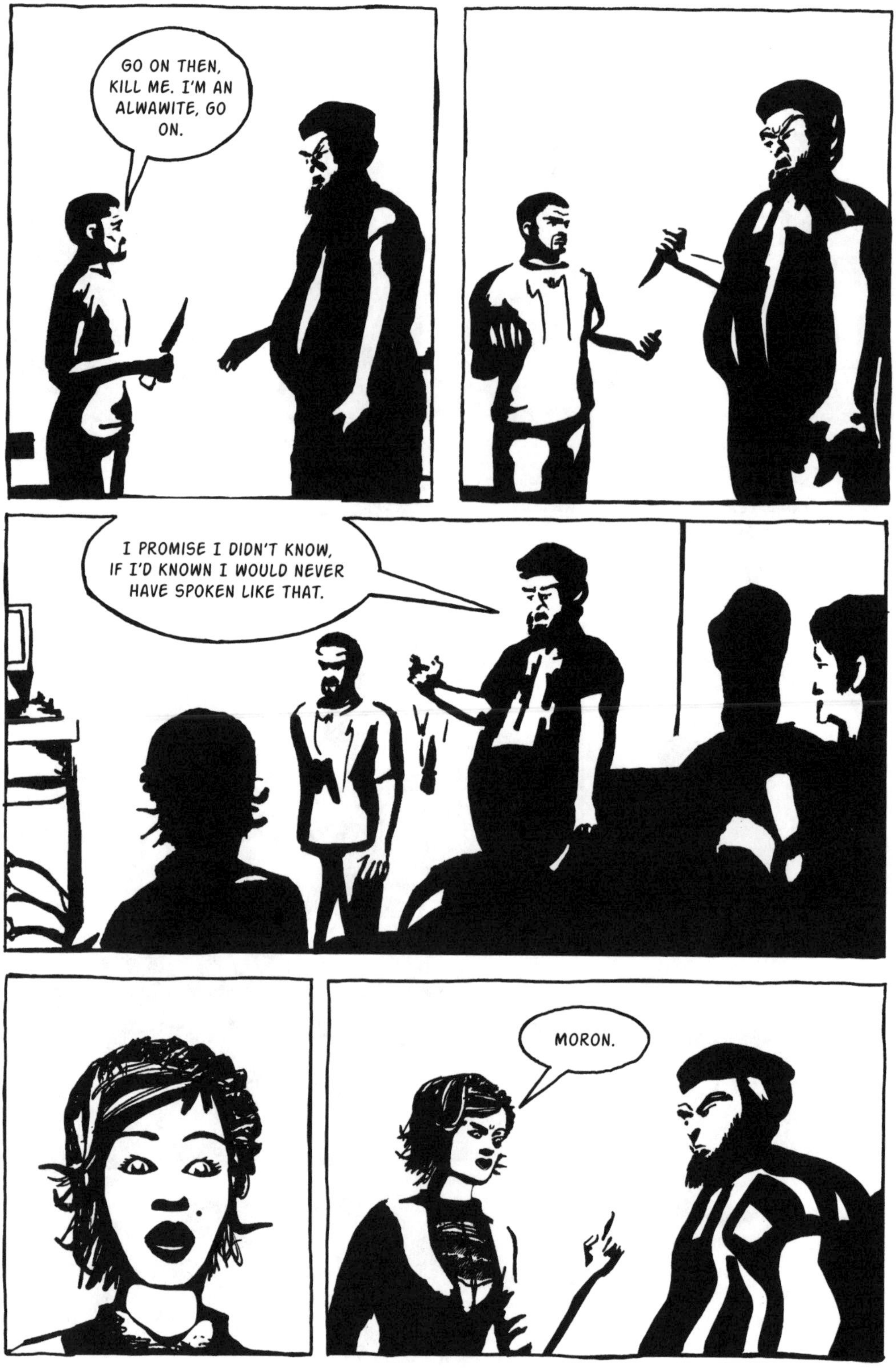
GO ON THEN, KILL ME. I'M AN ALWAWITE, GO ON.
I PROMISE I DIDN'T KNOW, IF I'D KNOWN I WOULD NEVER HAVE SPOKEN LIKE THAT.
MORON.

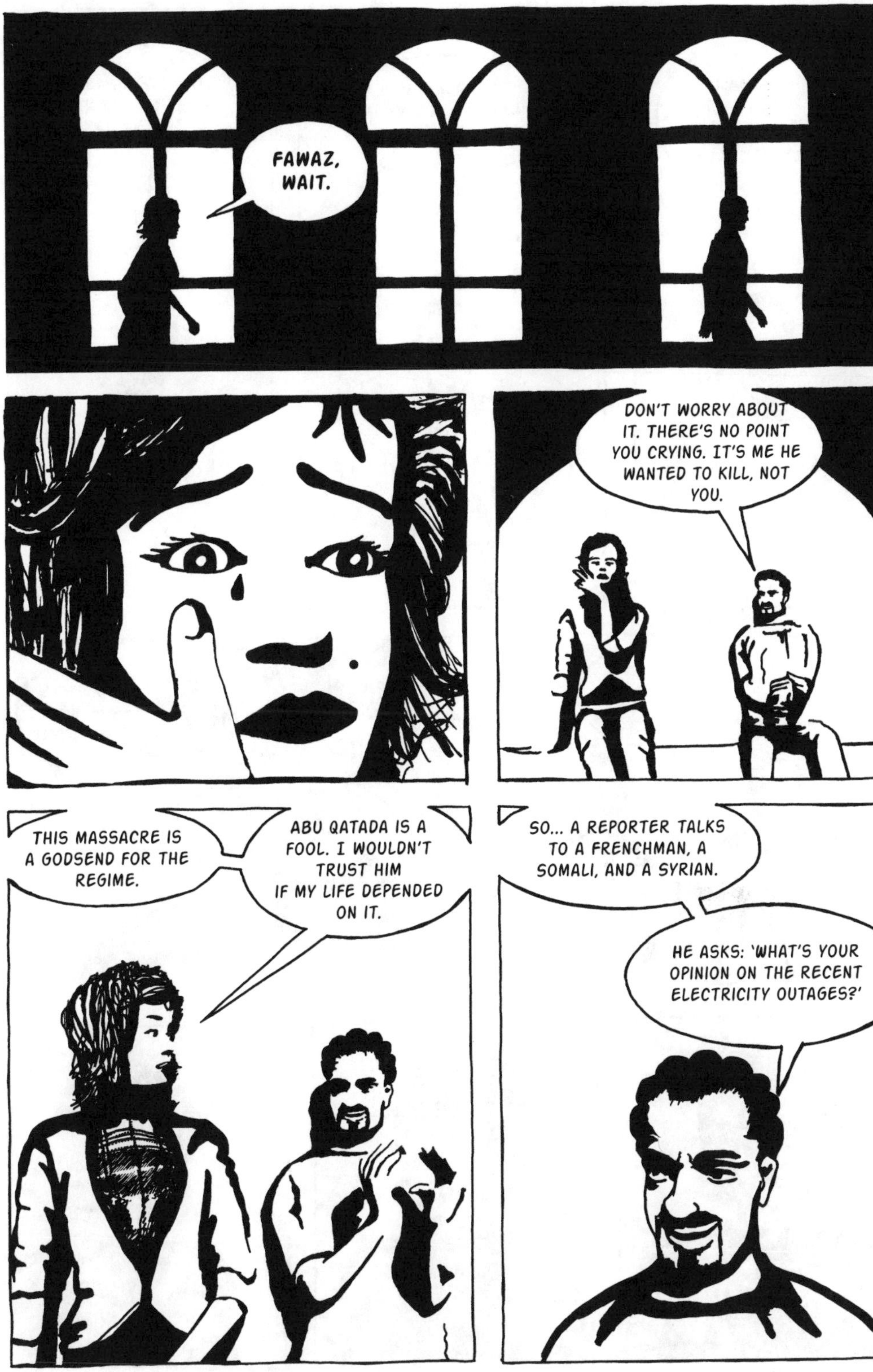
FAWAZ, WAIT.
DON'T WORRY ABOUT IT. THERE'S NO POINT YOU CRYING. IT'S ME HE WANTED TO KILL, NOT YOU.
THIS MASSACRE IS A GODSEND FOR THE REGIME.
ABU QATADA IS A FOOL. I WOULDN'T TRUST HIM IF MY LIFE DEPENDED ON IT.
SO... A REPORTER TALKS TO A FRENCHMAN, A SOMALI, AND A SYRIAN.
HE ASKS: 'WHAT'S YOUR OPINION ON THE RECENT ELECTRICITY OUTAGES?'

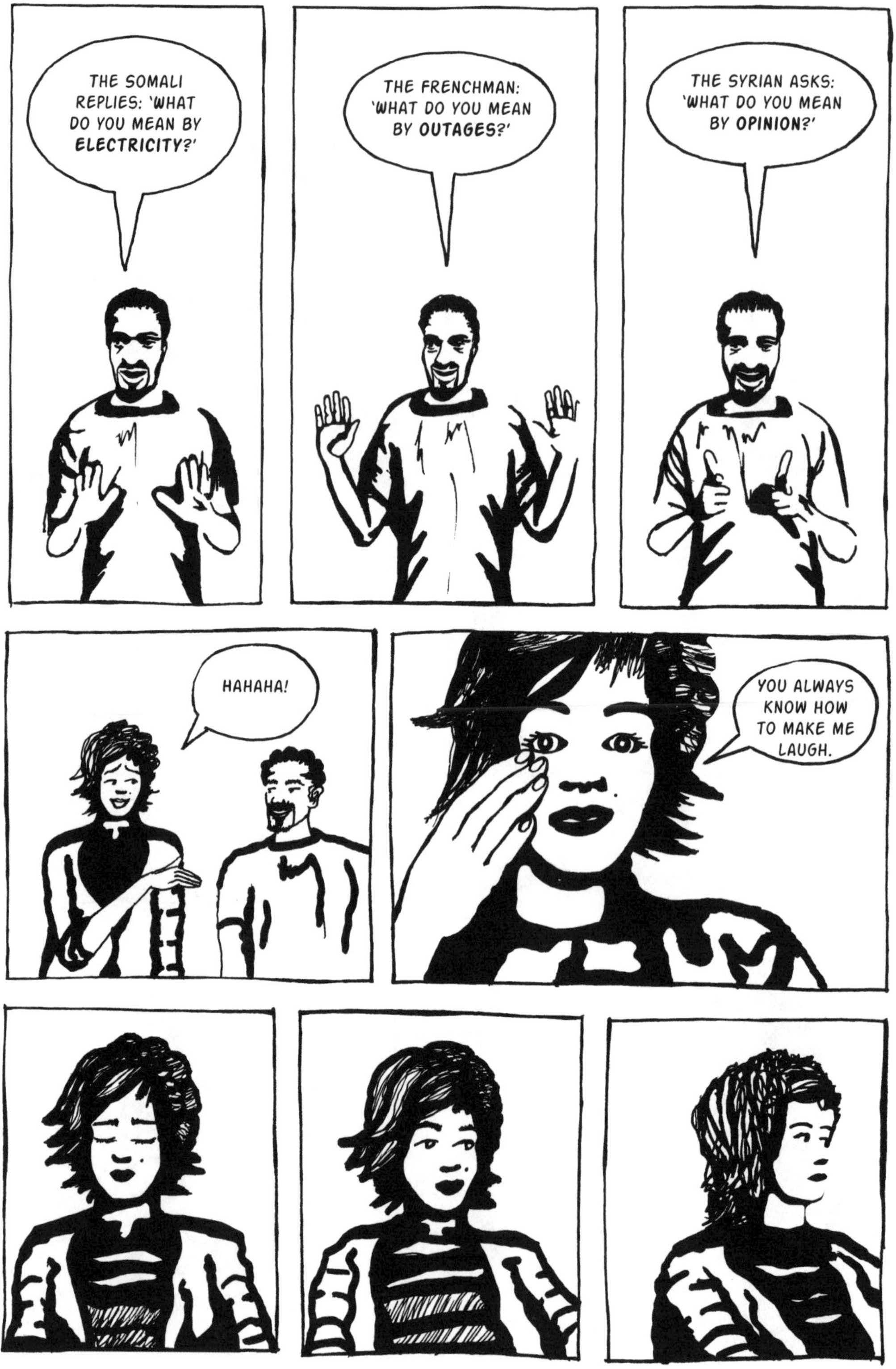
THE SOMALI REPLIES: 'WHAT DO YOU MEAN BY **ELECTRICITY**?'
THE FRENCHMAN: 'WHAT DO YOU MEAN BY **OUTAGES**?'
THE SYRIAN ASKS: 'WHAT DO YOU MEAN BY **OPINION**?'
HAHAHA!
YOU ALWAYS KNOW HOW TO MAKE ME LAUGH.

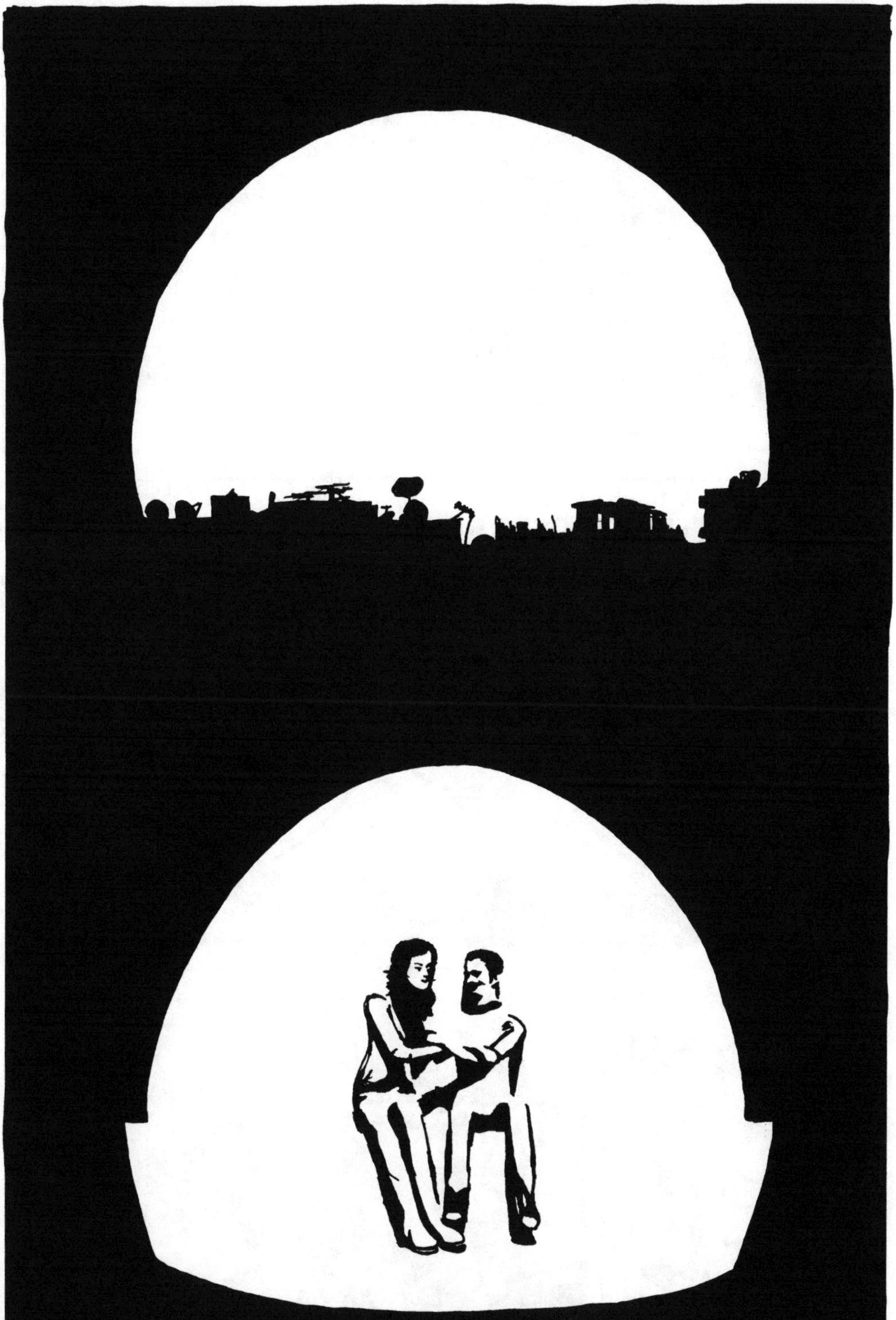

TWELVE DAYS LATER: ANOTHER 793 KILLED.

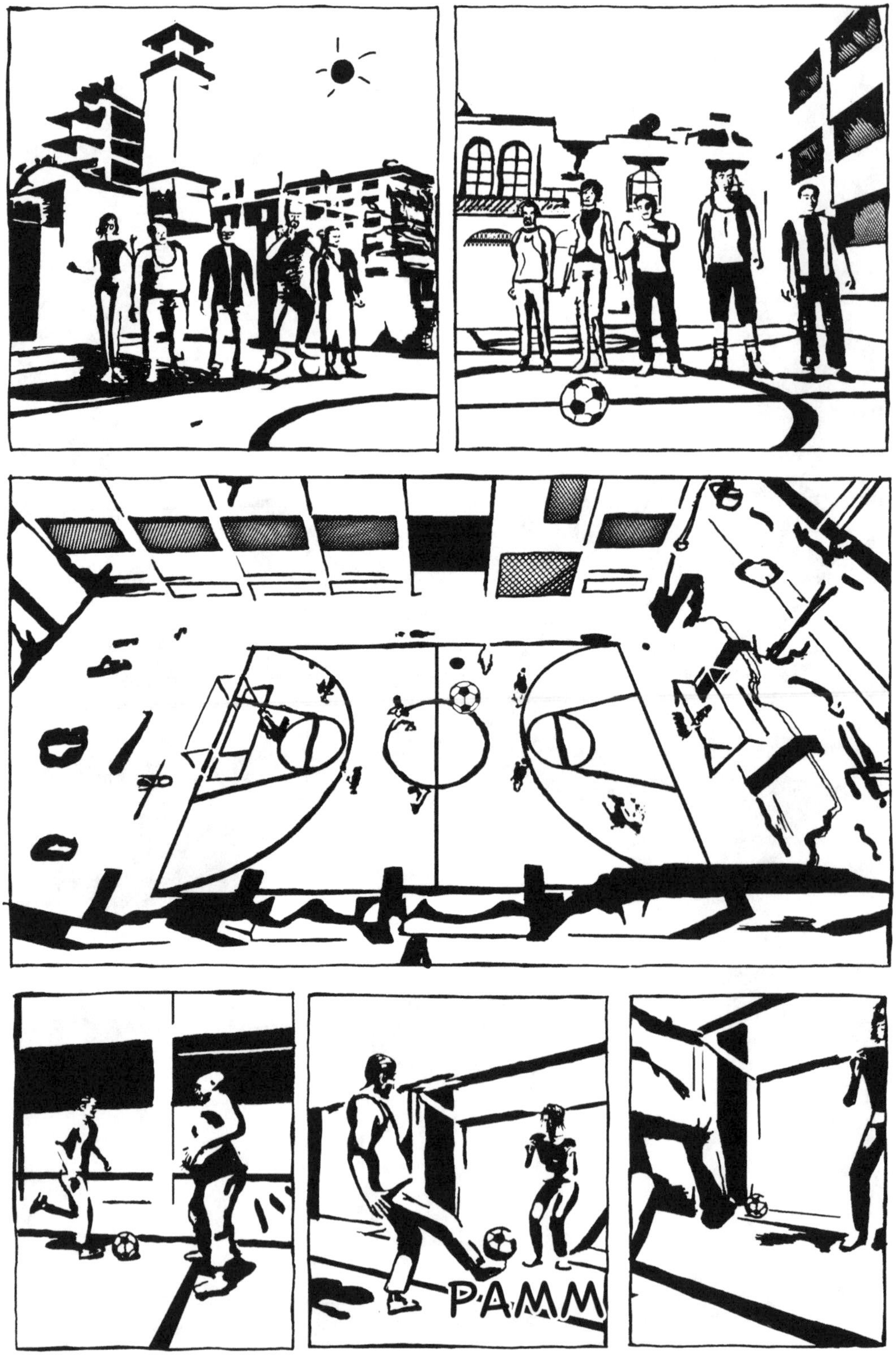
PAMM

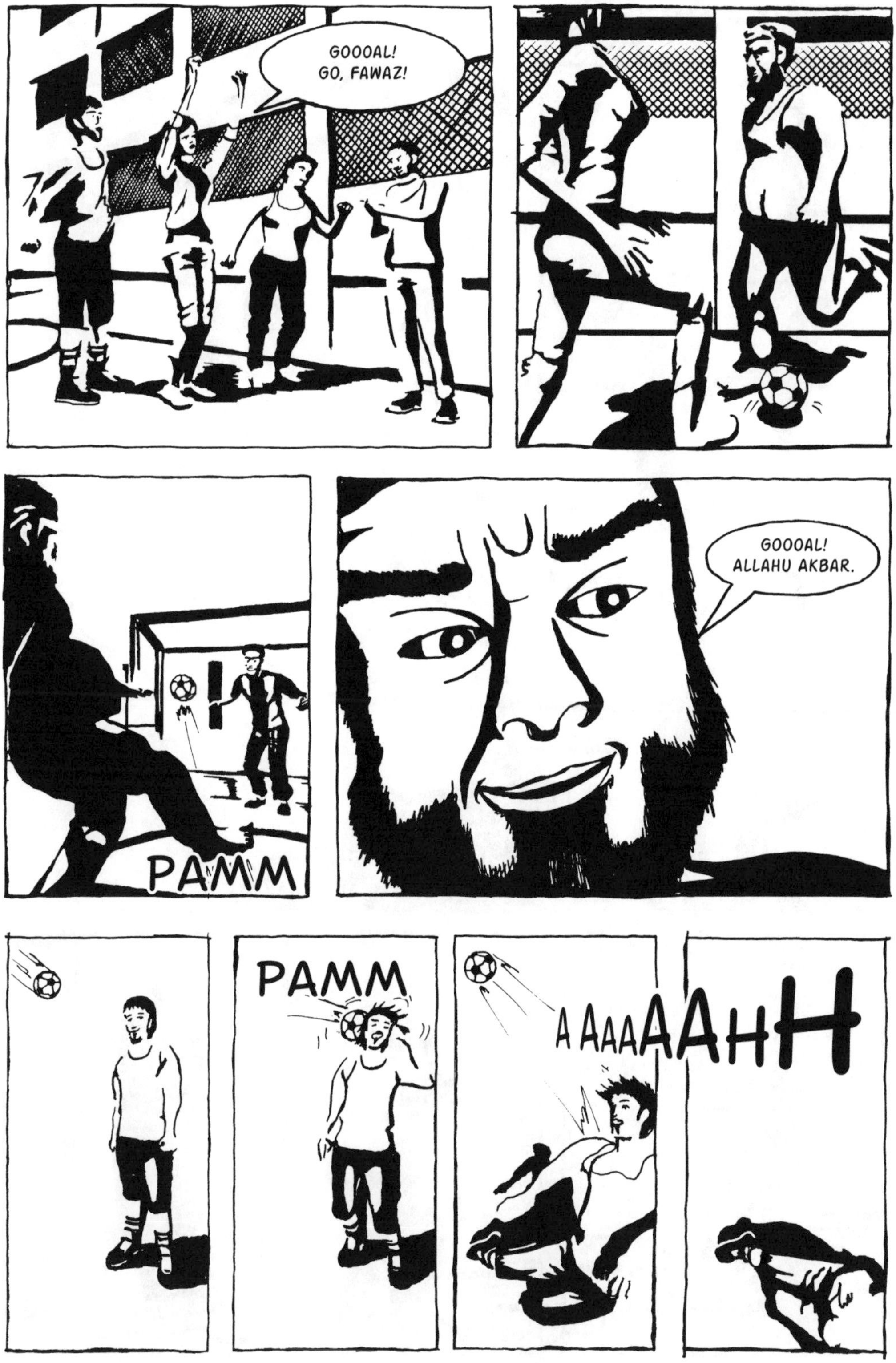
GOOOAL!
GO, FAWAZ!
PAMM
GOOOAL!
ALLAHU AKBAR.
PAMM
A AAAAAHH

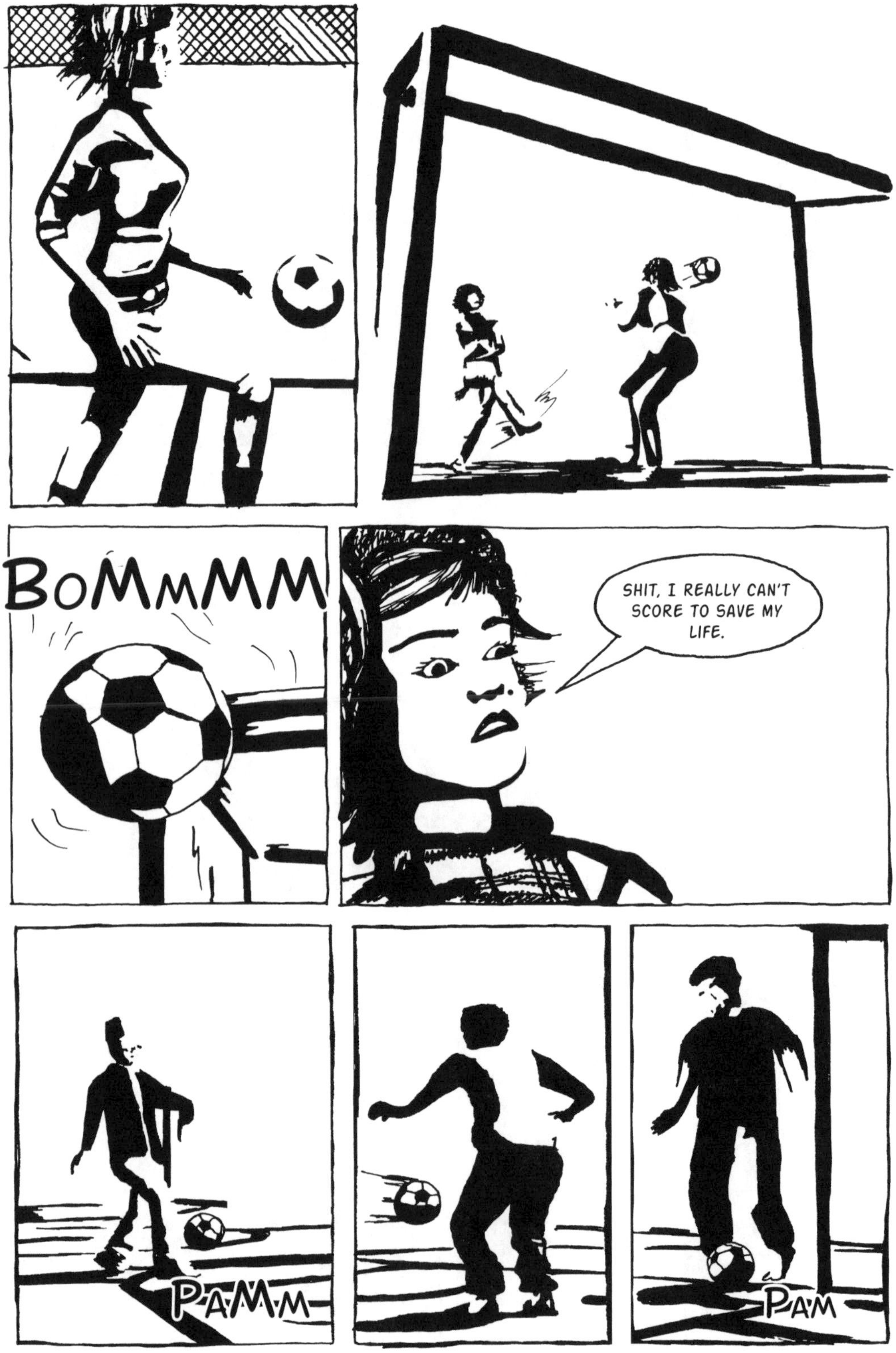
BOMMMM
SHIT, I REALLY CAN'T SCORE TO SAVE MY LIFE.
PAMM
PAM

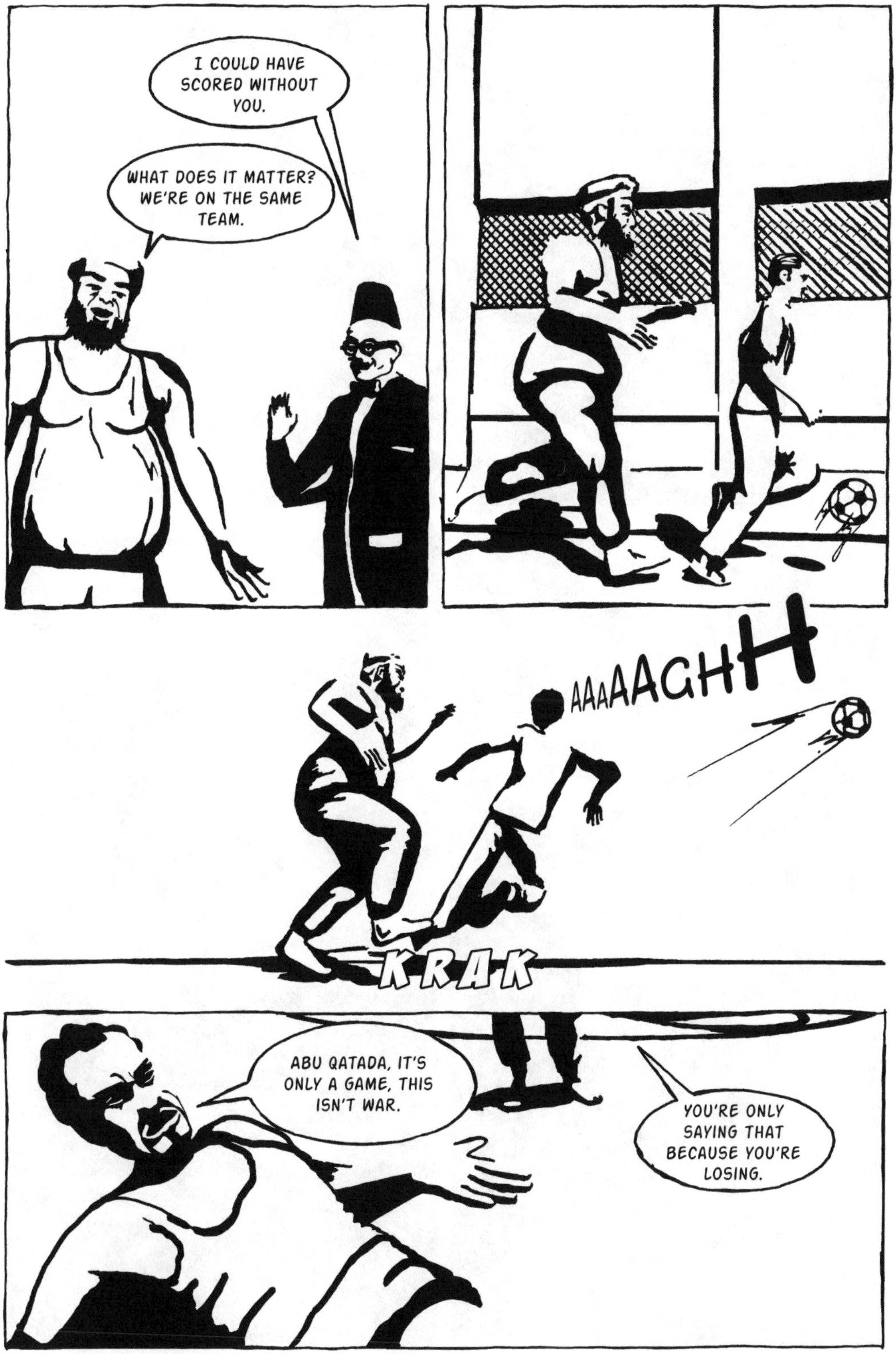
I COULD HAVE SCORED WITHOUT YOU.
WHAT DOES IT MATTER? WE'RE ON THE SAME TEAM.
AAAAAGHHH
KRAK
ABU QATADA, IT'S ONLY A GAME, THIS ISN'T WAR.
YOU'RE ONLY SAYING THAT BECAUSE YOU'RE LOSING.

THAT NIGHT: ANOTHER 34 KILLED.

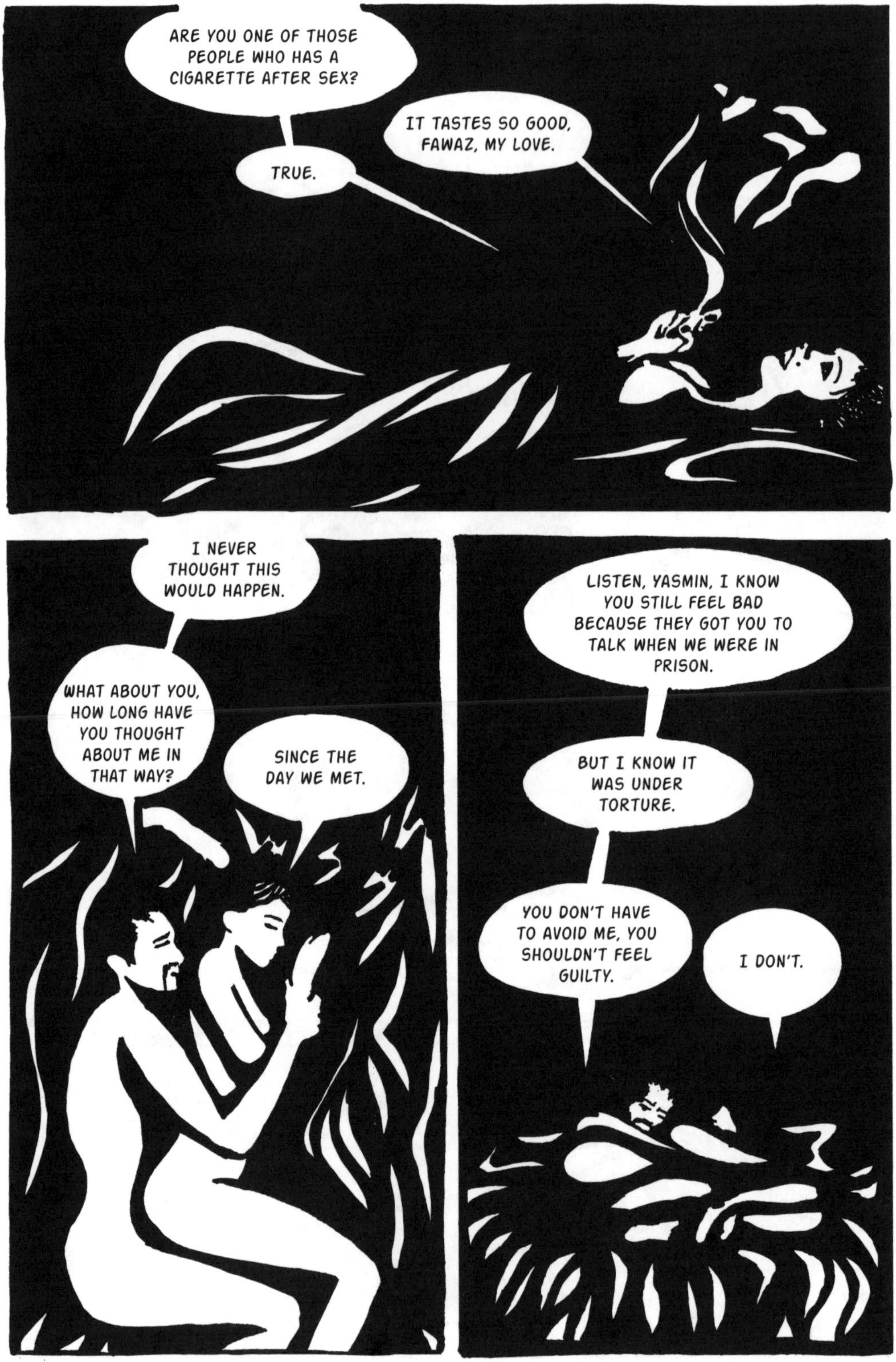
ARE YOU ONE OF THOSE PEOPLE WHO HAS A CIGARETTE AFTER SEX?
TRUE.
IT TASTES SO GOOD, FAWAZ, MY LOVE.
I NEVER THOUGHT THIS WOULD HAPPEN.
WHAT ABOUT YOU, HOW LONG HAVE YOU THOUGHT ABOUT ME IN THAT WAY?
SINCE THE DAY WE MET.
LISTEN, YASMIN, I KNOW YOU STILL FEEL BAD BECAUSE THEY GOT YOU TO TALK WHEN WE WERE IN PRISON.
BUT I KNOW IT WAS UNDER TORTURE.
YOU DON'T HAVE TO AVOID ME, YOU SHOULDN'T FEEL GUILTY.
I DON'T.

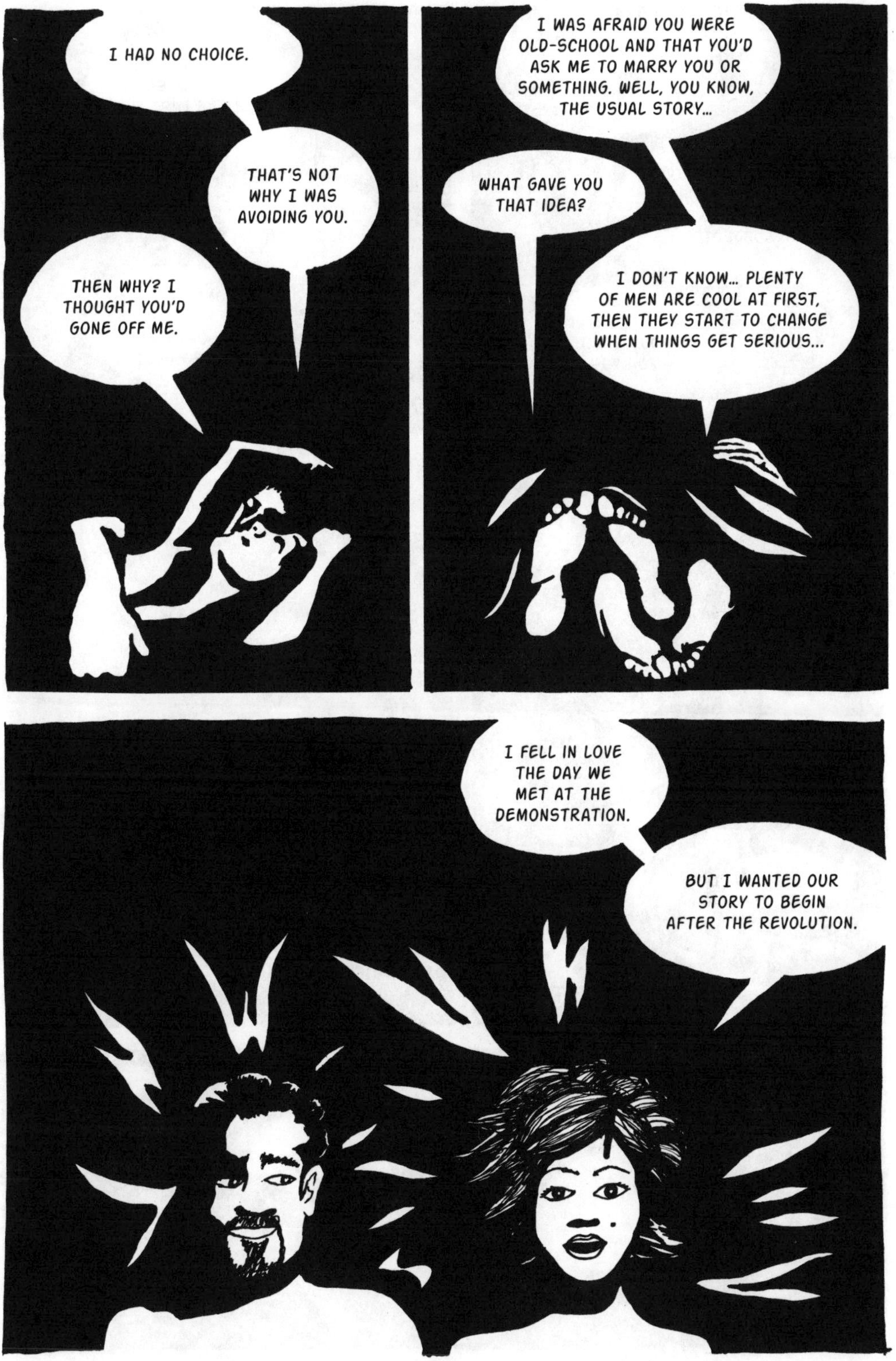
I HAD NO CHOICE.
THAT'S NOT WHY I WAS AVOIDING YOU.
THEN WHY? I THOUGHT YOU'D GONE OFF ME.
I WAS AFRAID YOU WERE OLD-SCHOOL AND THAT YOU'D ASK ME TO MARRY YOU OR SOMETHING. WELL, YOU KNOW, THE USUAL STORY...
WHAT GAVE YOU THAT IDEA?
I DON'T KNOW... PLENTY OF MEN ARE COOL AT FIRST, THEN THEY START TO CHANGE WHEN THINGS GET SERIOUS...
I FELL IN LOVE THE DAY WE MET AT THE DEMONSTRATION.
BUT I WANTED OUR STORY TO BEGIN AFTER THE REVOLUTION.

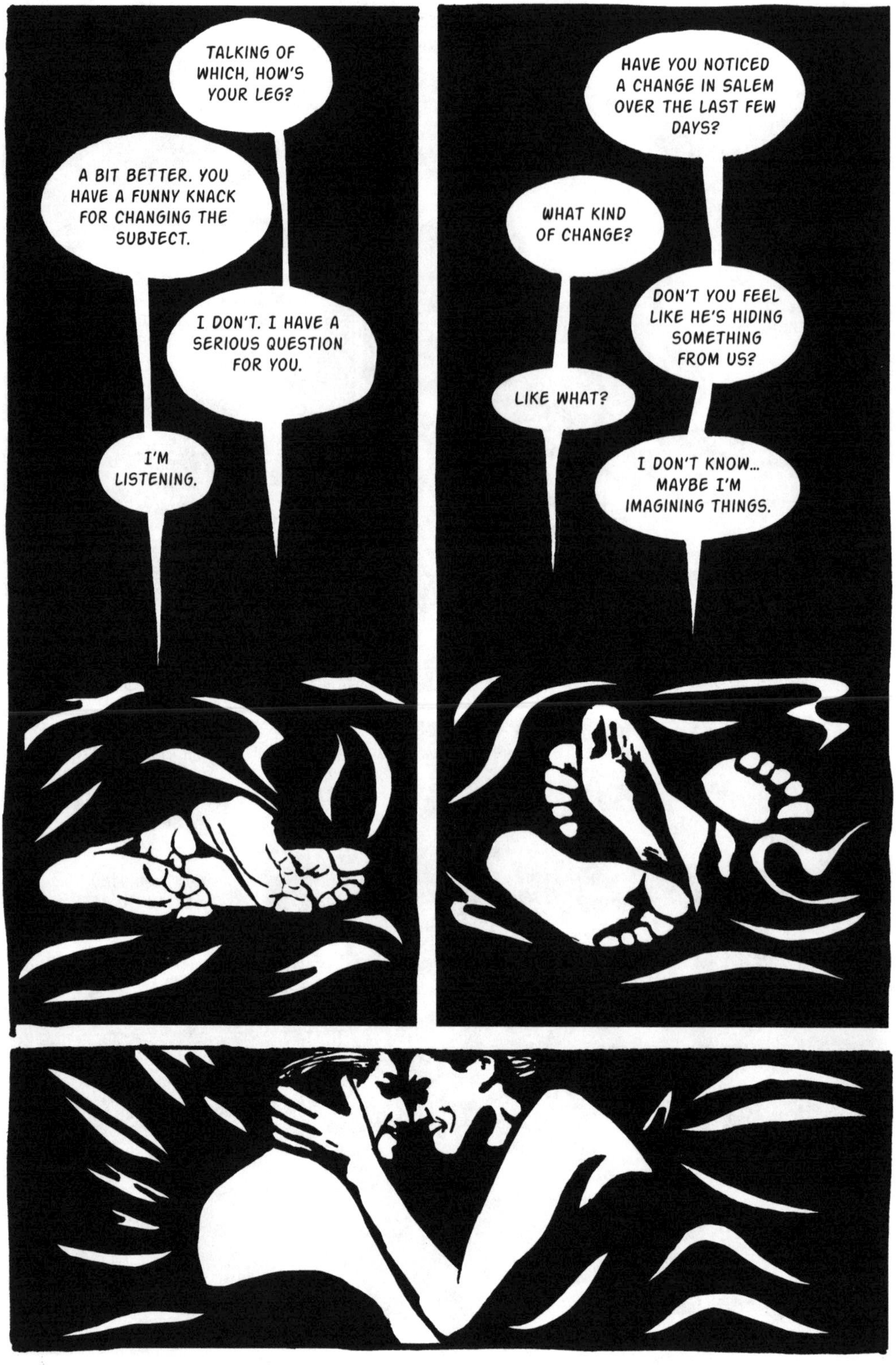
TALKING OF WHICH, HOW'S YOUR LEG?
A BIT BETTER. YOU HAVE A FUNNY KNACK FOR CHANGING THE SUBJECT.
I DON'T. I HAVE A SERIOUS QUESTION FOR YOU.
I'M LISTENING.
HAVE YOU NOTICED A CHANGE IN SALEM OVER THE LAST FEW DAYS?
WHAT KIND OF CHANGE?
DON'T YOU FEEL LIKE HE'S HIDING SOMETHING FROM US?
LIKE WHAT?
I DON'T KNOW... MAYBE I'M IMAGINING THINGS.

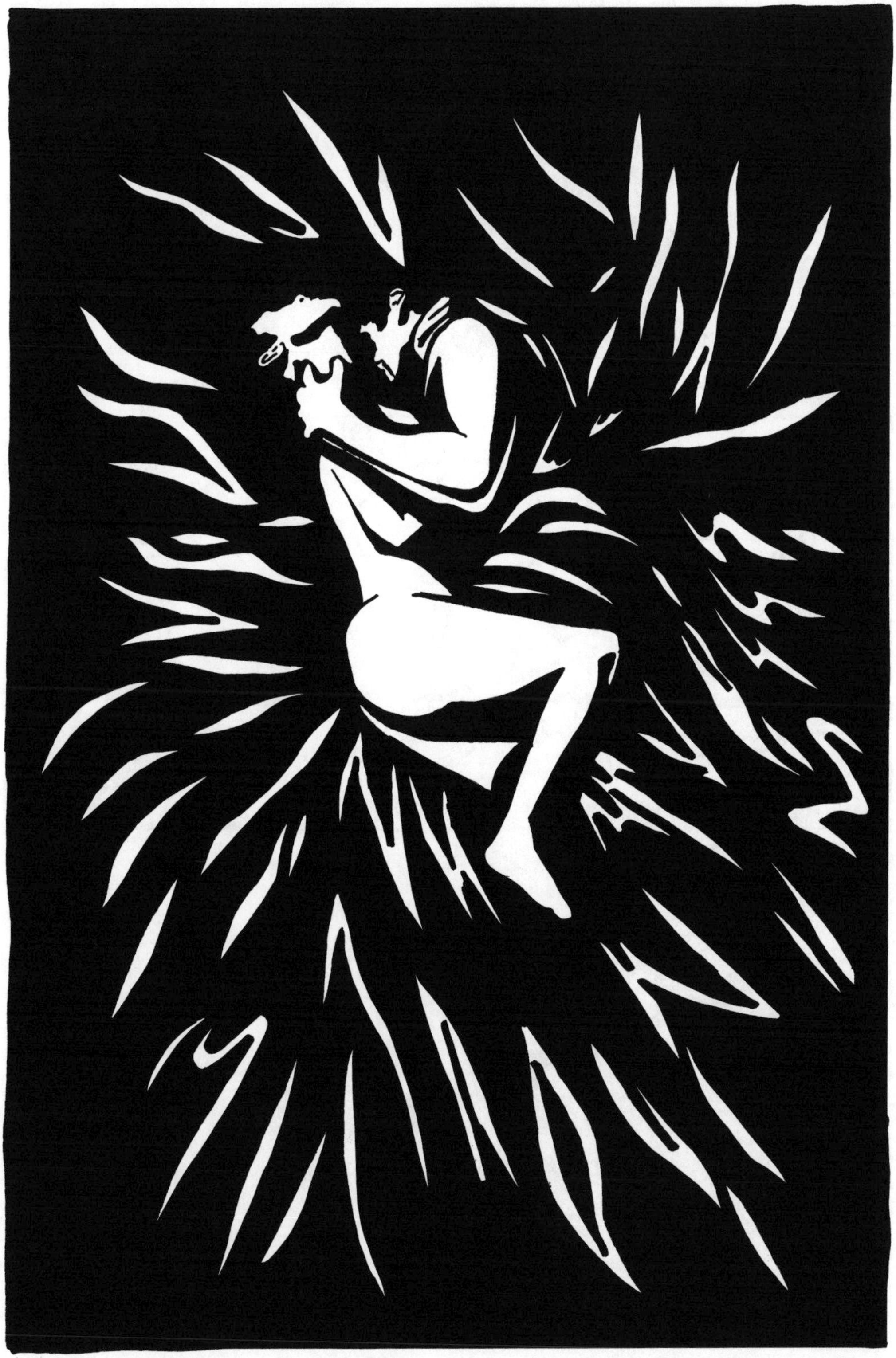

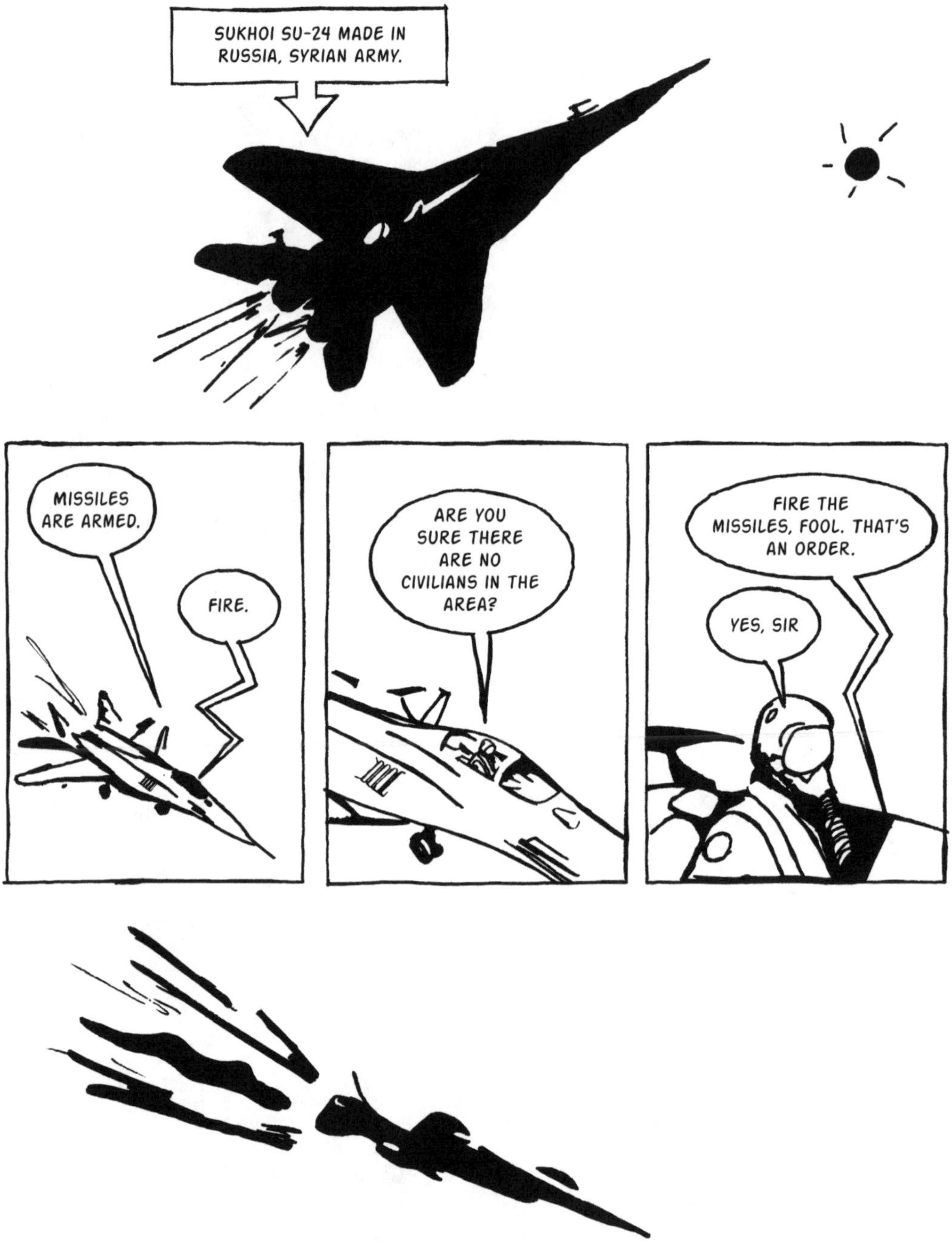
SUKHOI SU-24 MADE IN RUSSIA, SYRIAN ARMY.
MISSILES ARE ARMED.
FIRE.
ARE YOU SURE THERE ARE NO CIVILIANS IN THE AREA?
FIRE THE MISSILES, FOOL. THAT'S AN ORDER.
YES, SIR

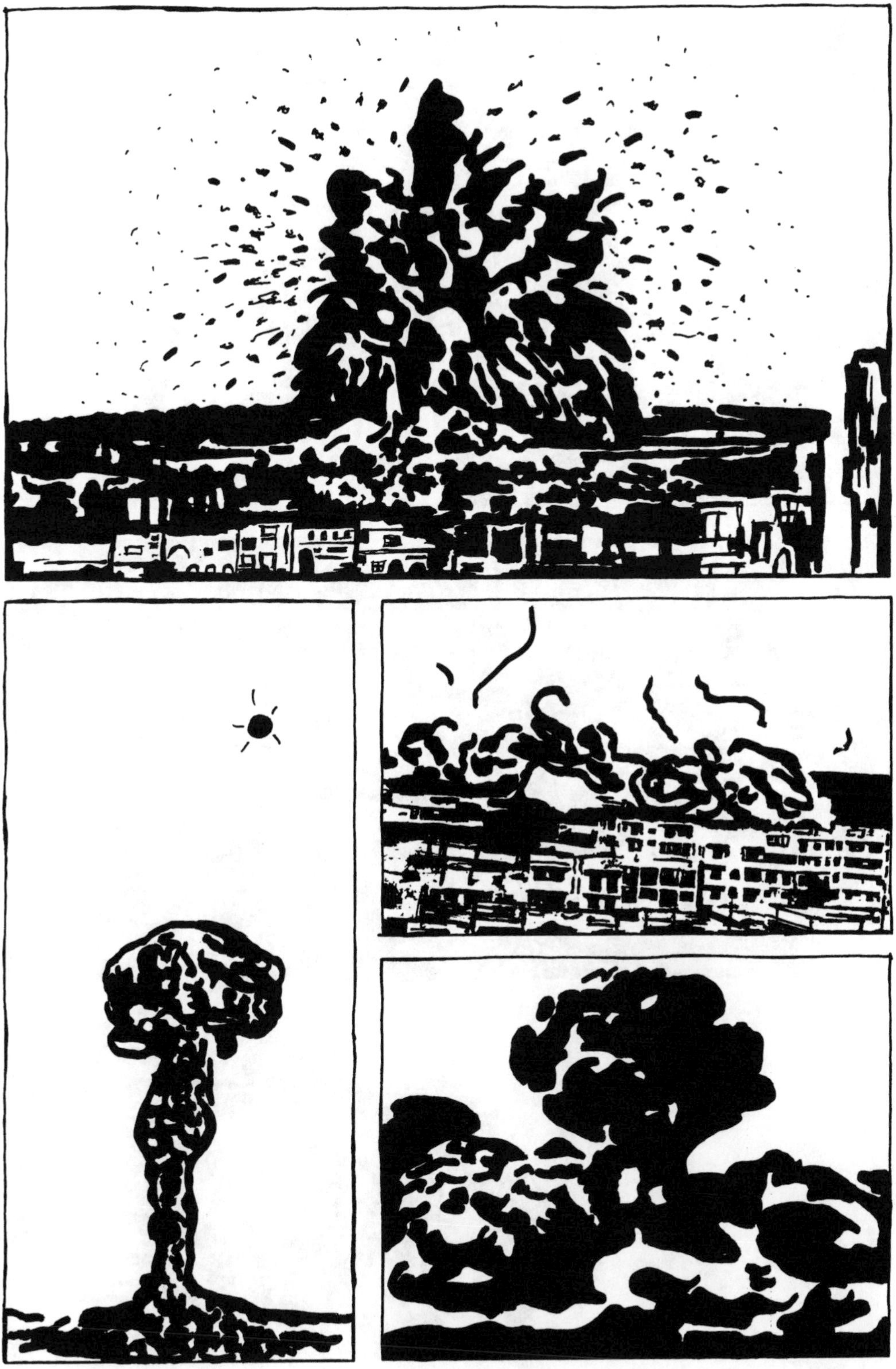

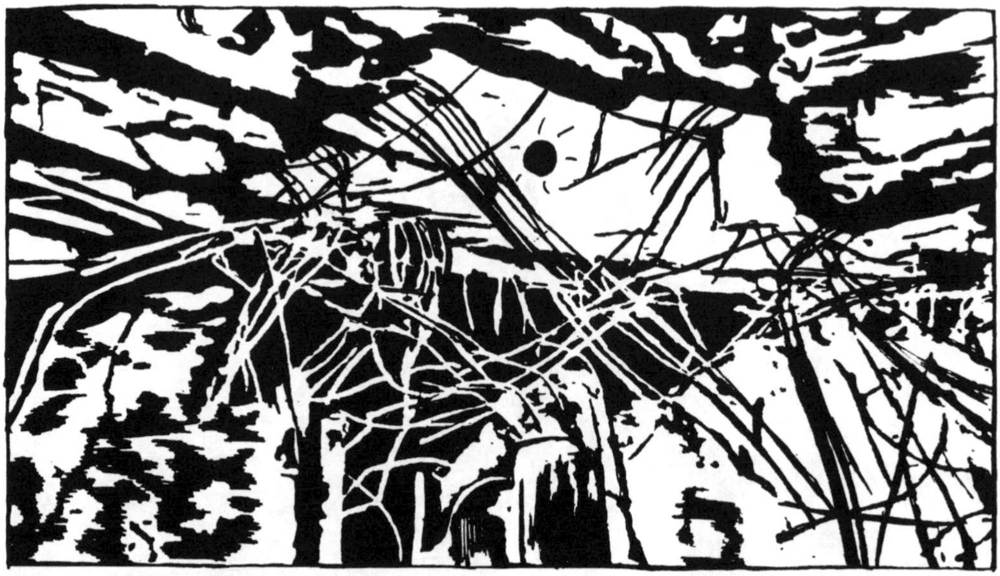

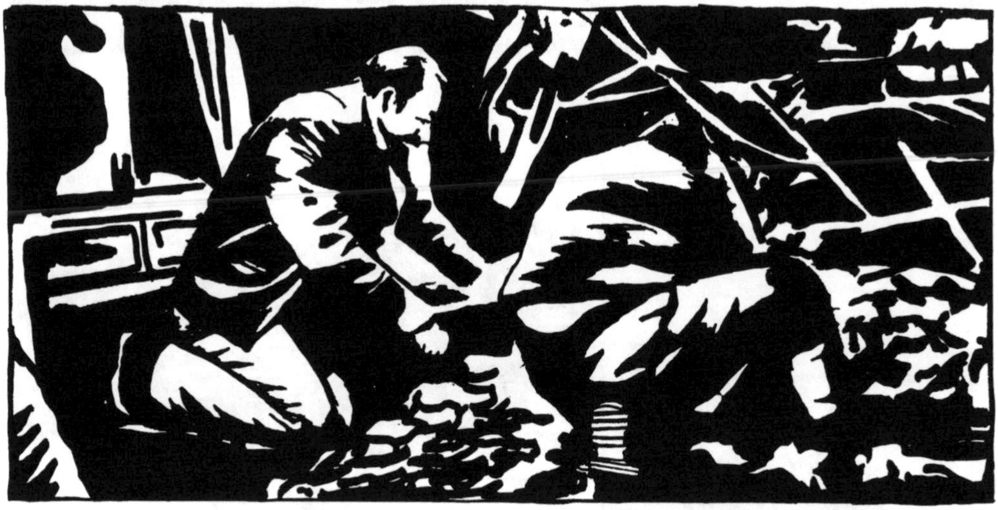

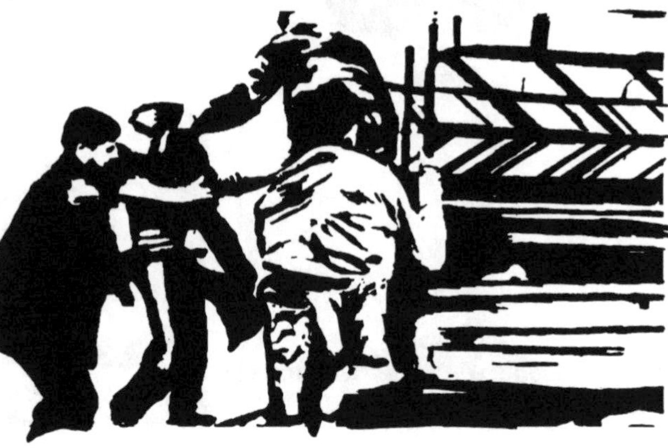

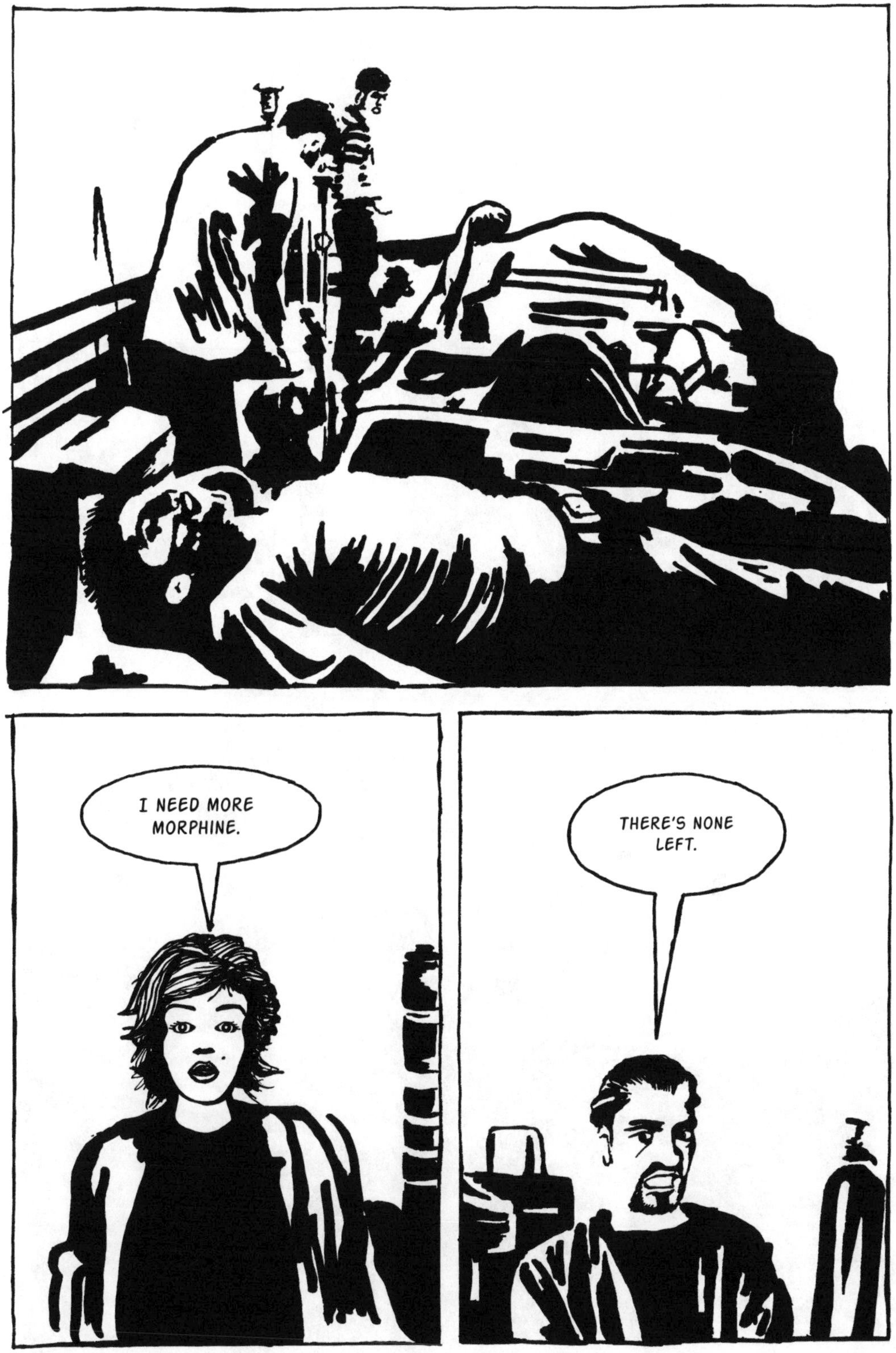
I NEED MORE MORPHINE.
THERE'S NONE LEFT.

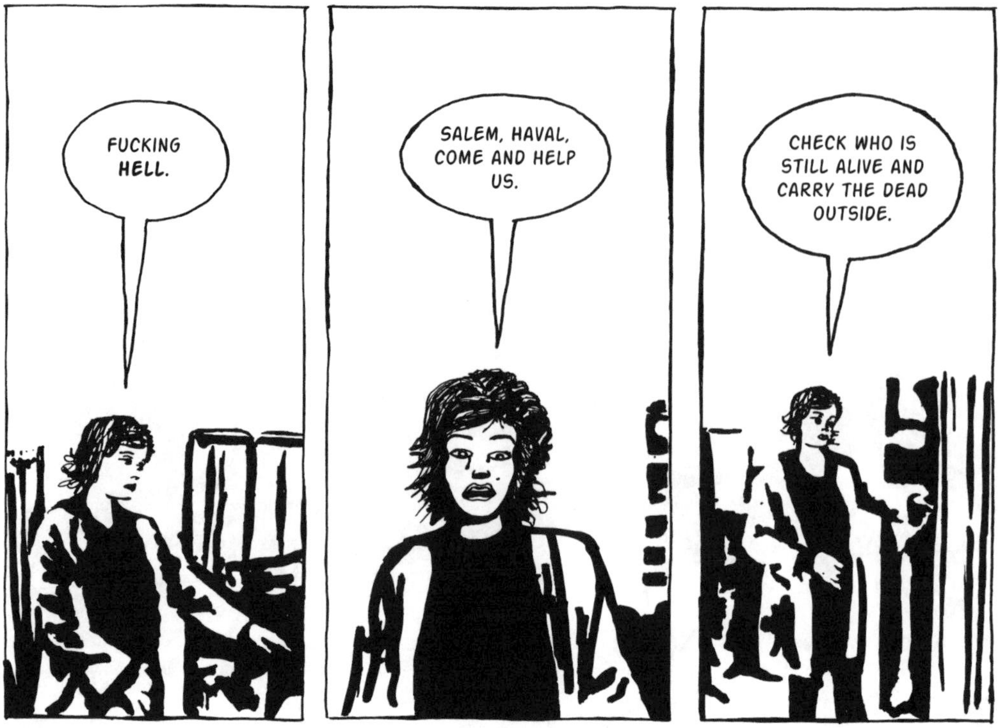
FUCKING HELL.
SALEM, HAVAL, COME AND HELP US.
CHECK WHO IS STILL ALIVE AND CARRY THE DEAD OUTSIDE.

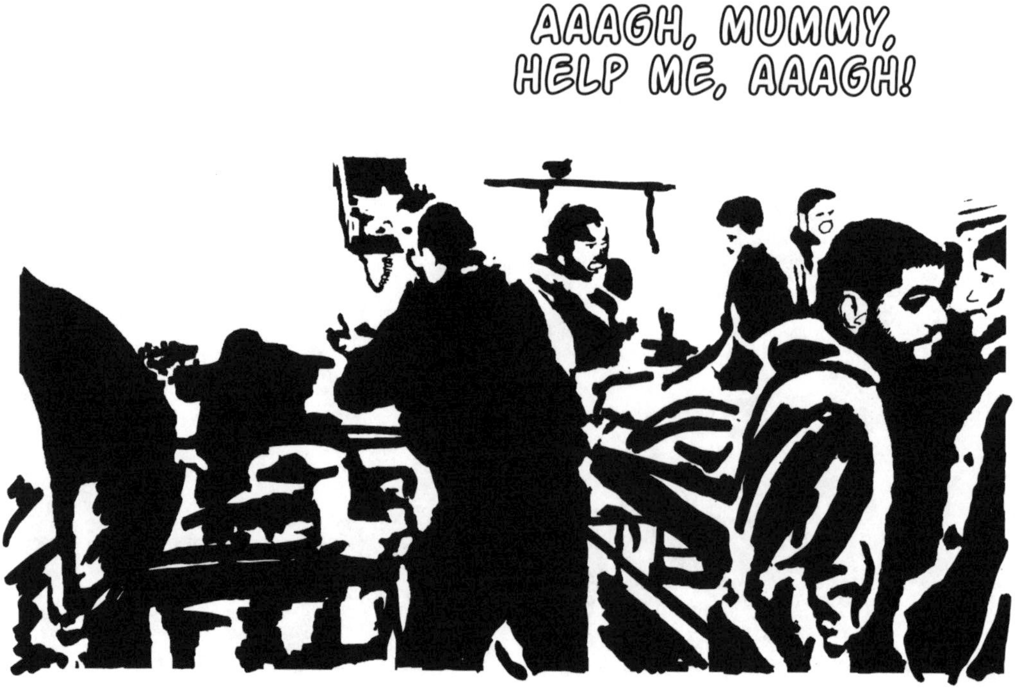
AAAGH, MUMMY, HELP ME, AAAGH!

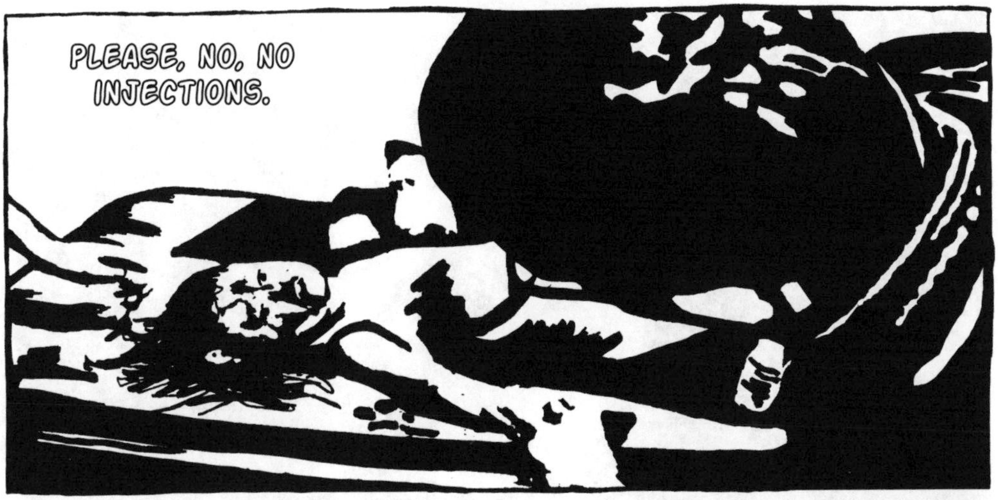
PLEASE, NO, NO
INJECTIONS.

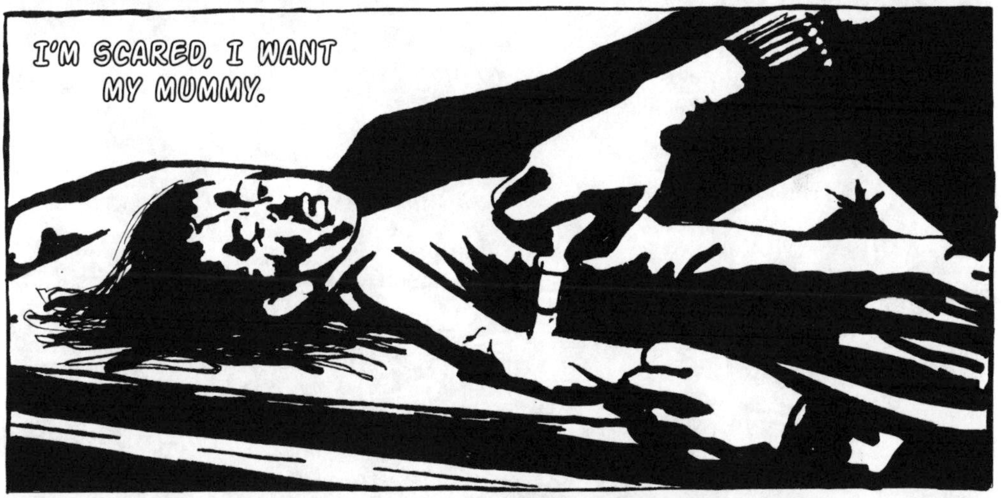
I'M SCARED, I WANT
MY MUMMY.

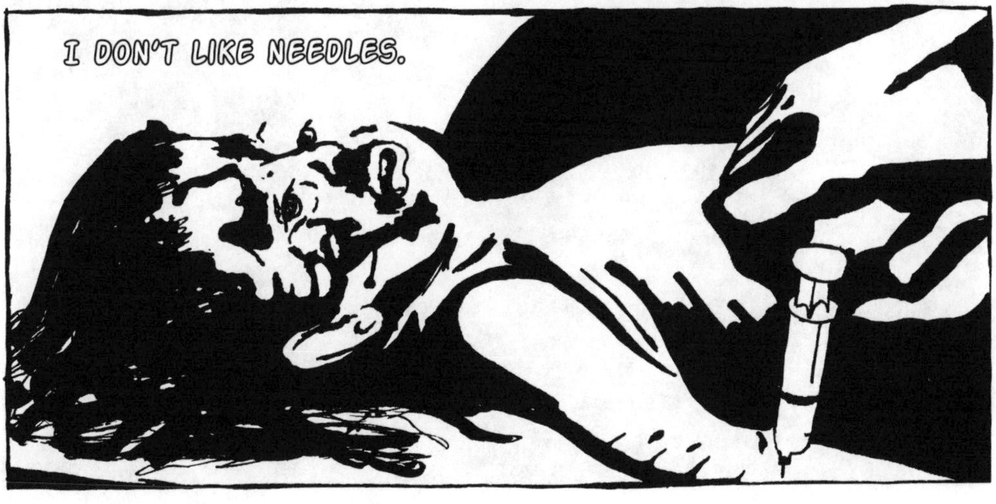
I DON'T LIKE NEEDLES.

THREE DAYS LATER: ANOTHER 893 KILLED.

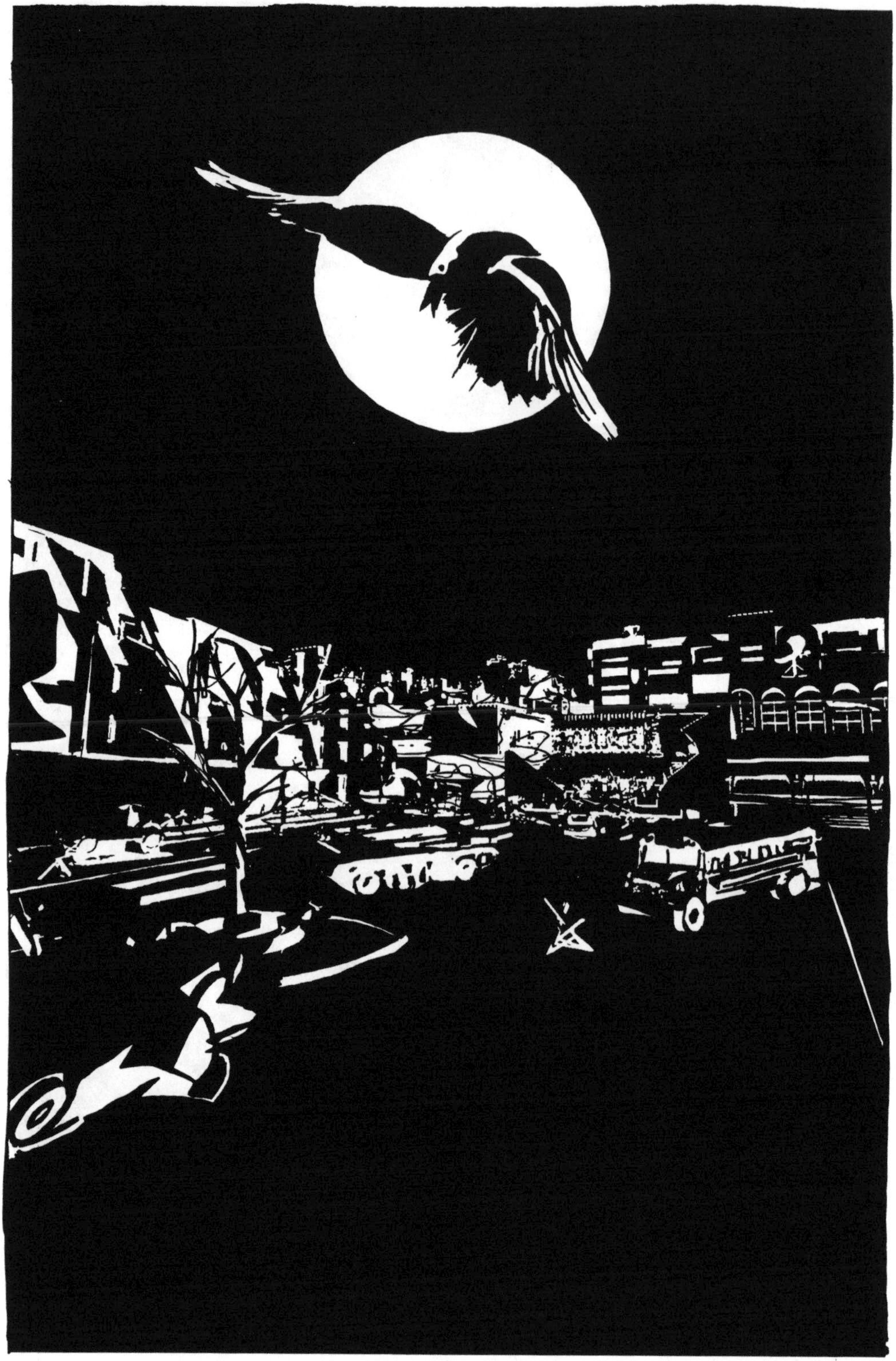

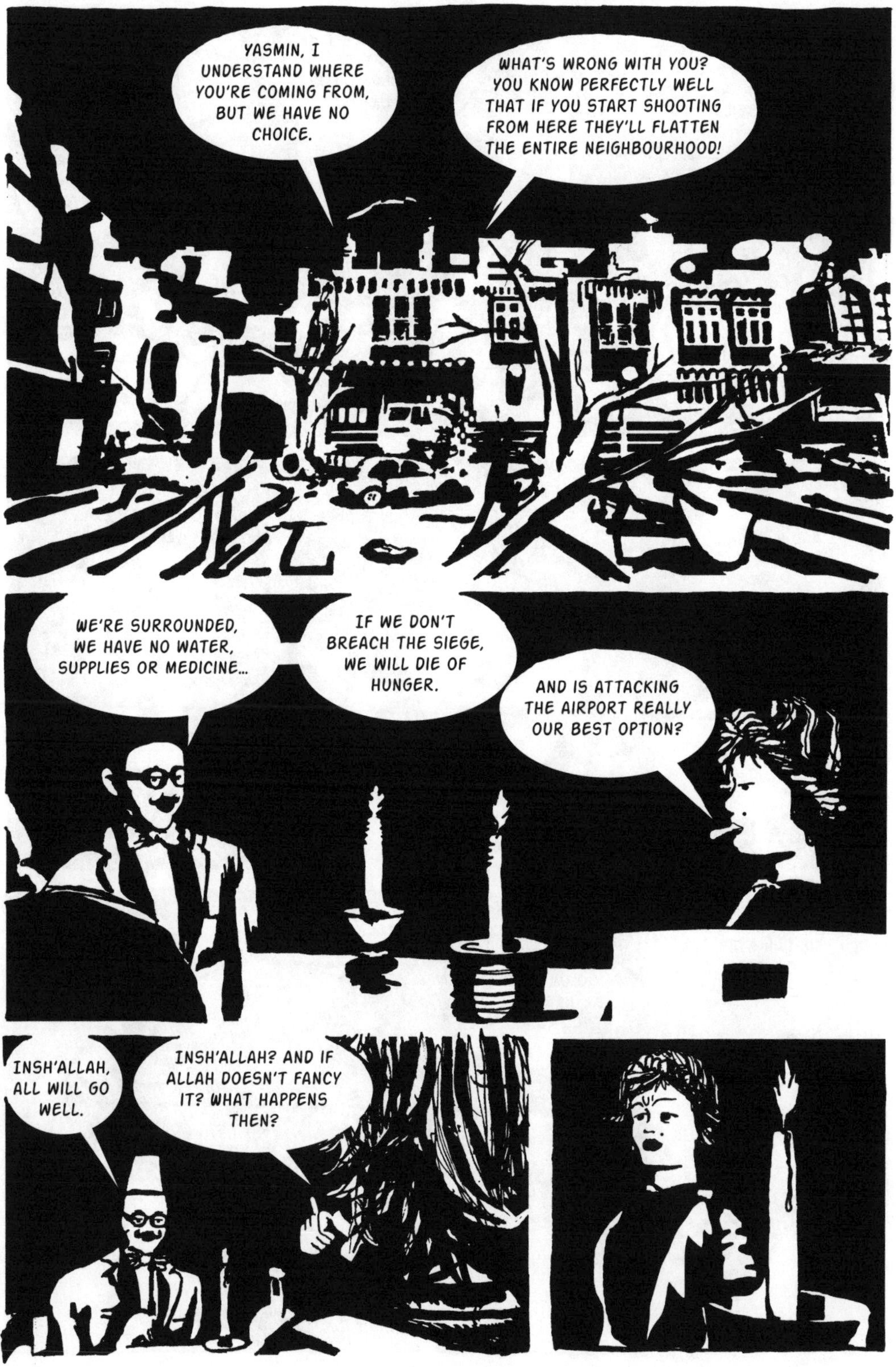
YASMIN, I UNDERSTAND WHERE YOU'RE COMING FROM, BUT WE HAVE NO CHOICE.
WHAT'S WRONG WITH YOU? YOU KNOW PERFECTLY WELL THAT IF YOU START SHOOTING FROM HERE THEY'LL FLATTEN THE ENTIRE NEIGHBOURHOOD!
WE'RE SURROUNDED, WE HAVE NO WATER, SUPPLIES OR MEDICINE...
IF WE DON'T BREACH THE SIEGE, WE WILL DIE OF HUNGER.
AND IS ATTACKING THE AIRPORT REALLY OUR BEST OPTION?
INSH'ALLAH, ALL WILL GO WELL.
INSH'ALLAH? AND IF ALLAH DOESN'T FANCY IT? WHAT HAPPENS THEN?

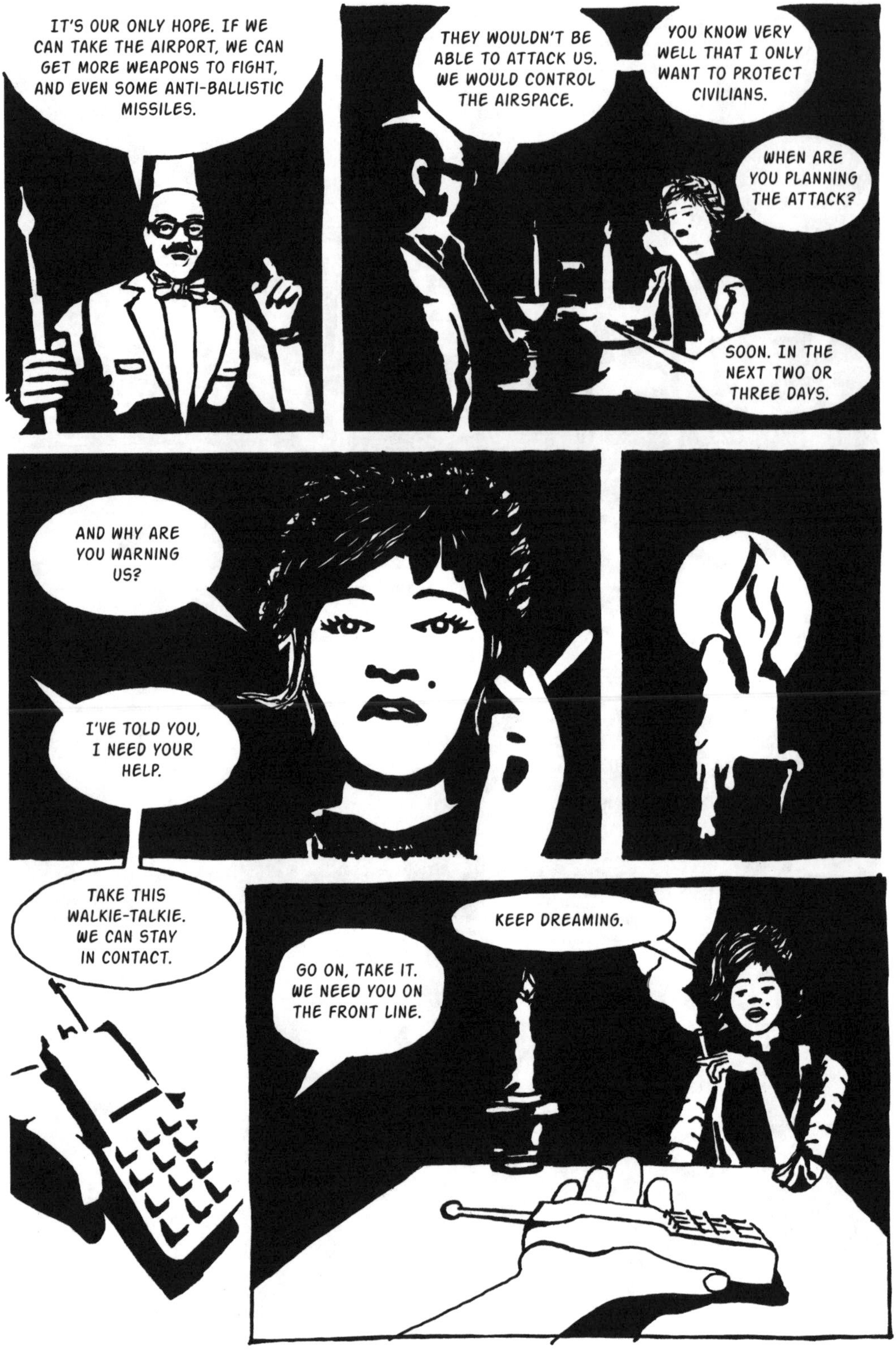
IT'S OUR ONLY HOPE. IF WE CAN TAKE THE AIRPORT, WE CAN GET MORE WEAPONS TO FIGHT, AND EVEN SOME ANTI-BALLISTIC MISSILES.
THEY WOULDN'T BE ABLE TO ATTACK US. WE WOULD CONTROL THE AIRSPACE.
YOU KNOW VERY WELL THAT I ONLY WANT TO PROTECT CIVILIANS.
WHEN ARE YOU PLANNING THE ATTACK?
SOON. IN THE NEXT TWO OR THREE DAYS.
AND WHY ARE YOU WARNING US?
I'VE TOLD YOU, I NEED YOUR HELP.
TAKE THIS WALKIE-TALKIE. WE CAN STAY IN CONTACT.
KEEP DREAMING.
GO ON, TAKE IT. WE NEED YOU ON THE FRONT LINE.

TWO DAYS LATER: ANOTHER 392 PEOPLE KILLED.

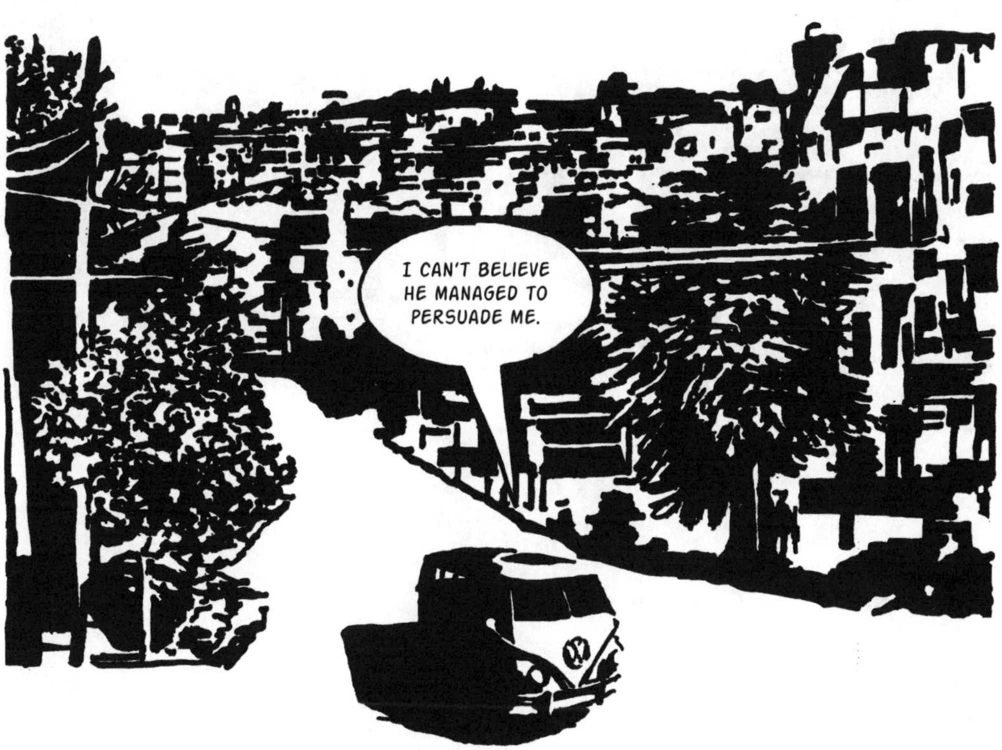
I CAN'T BELIEVE HE MANAGED TO PERSUADE ME.

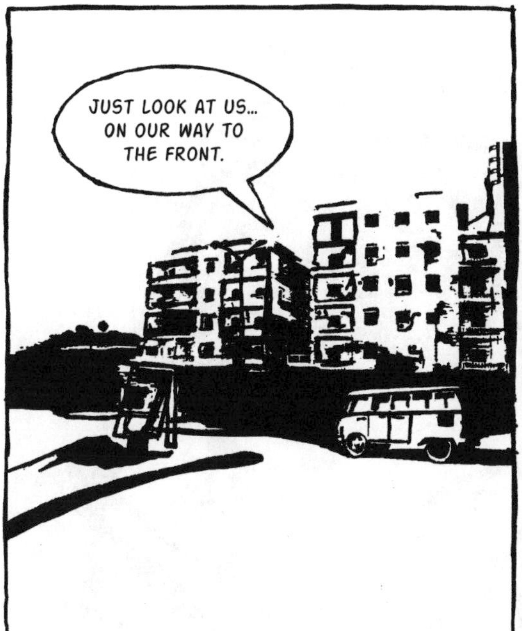
JUST LOOK AT US... ON OUR WAY TO THE FRONT.

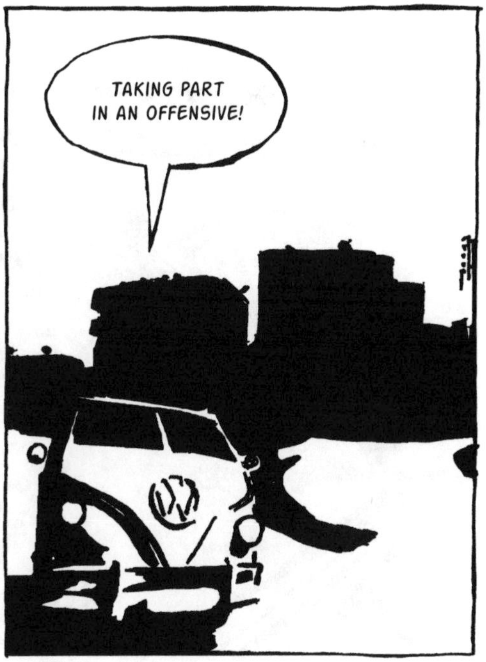
TAKING PART IN AN OFFENSIVE!

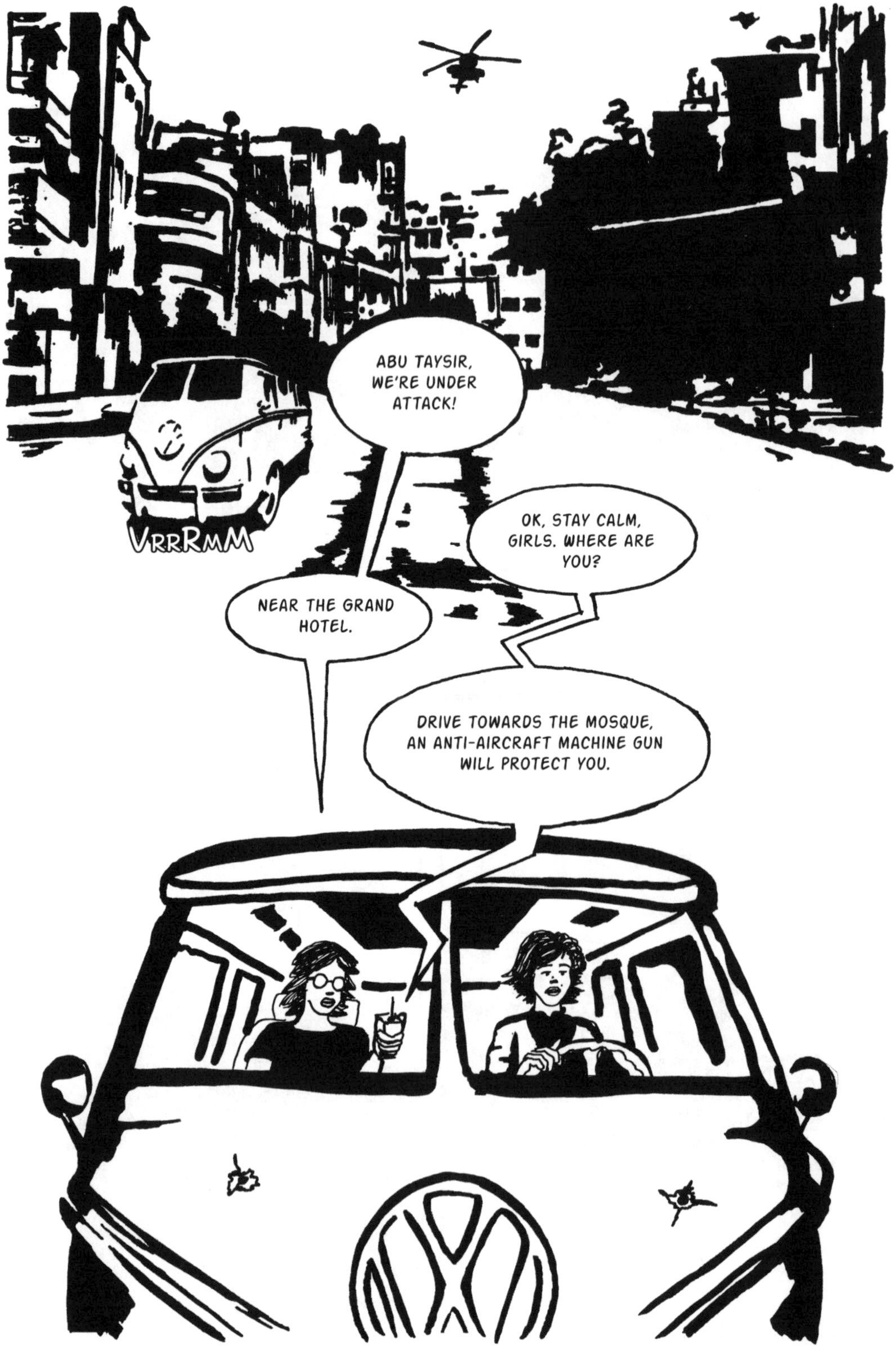
ABU TAYSIR, WE'RE UNDER ATTACK!
VRRRMM
OK, STAY CALM, GIRLS. WHERE ARE YOU?
NEAR THE GRAND HOTEL.
DRIVE TOWARDS THE MOSQUE, AN ANTI-AIRCRAFT MACHINE GUN WILL PROTECT YOU.

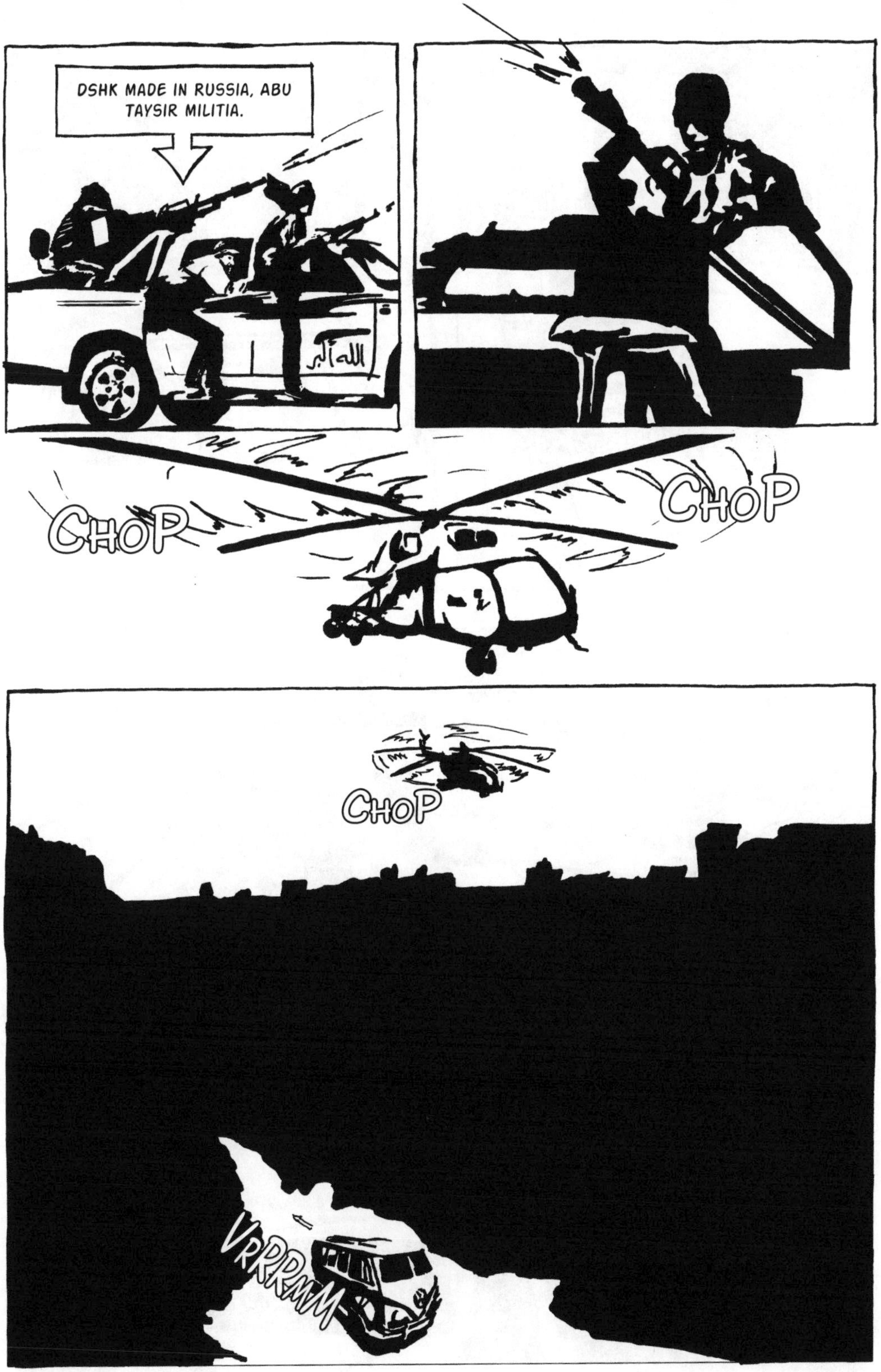
DSHK MADE IN RUSSIA, ABU TAYSIR MILITIA.
الله أكبر
CHOP
CHOP
CHOP
VRRRMM

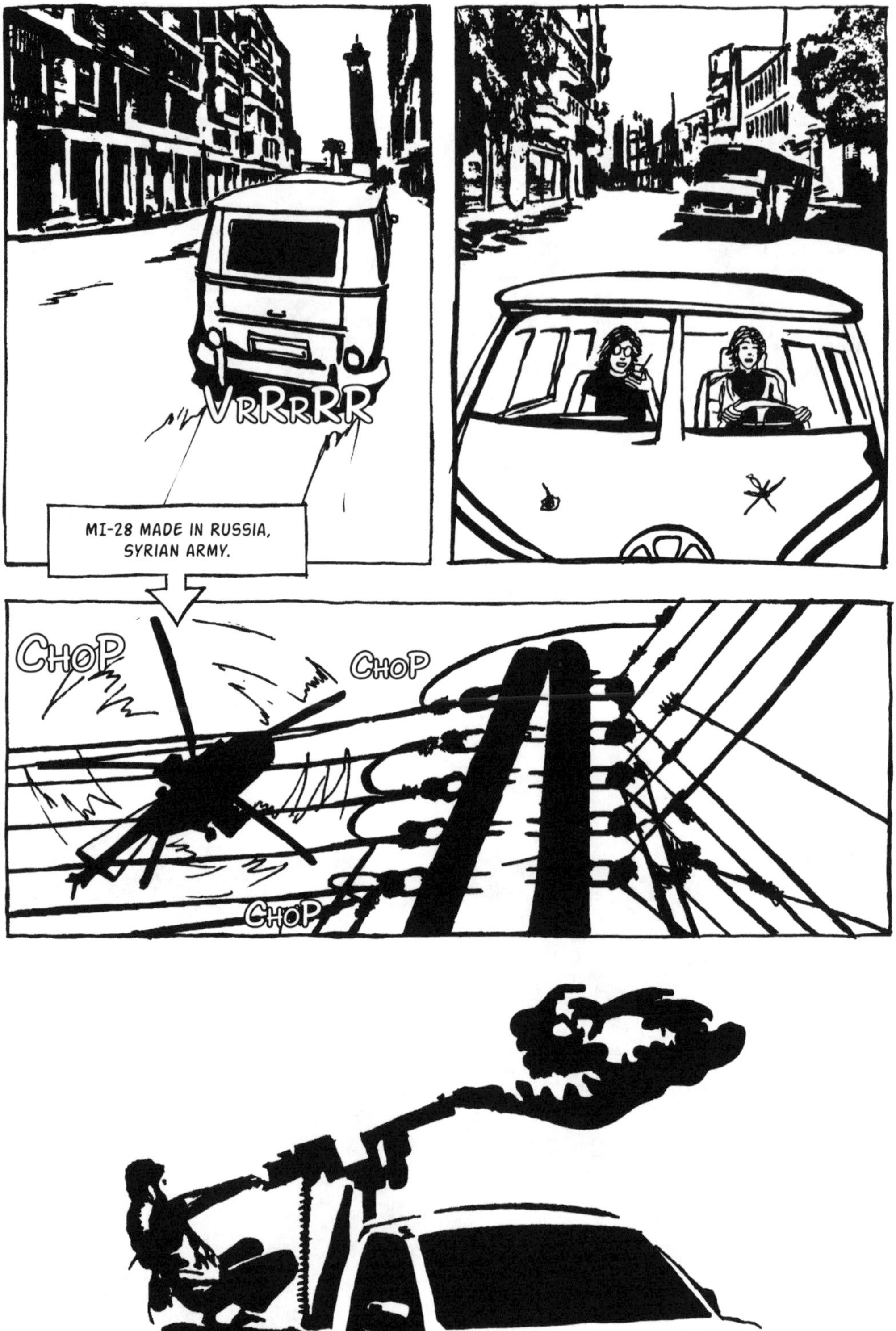
VRRRRR
MI-28 MADE IN RUSSIA, SYRIAN ARMY.
CHOP
CHOP
CHOP

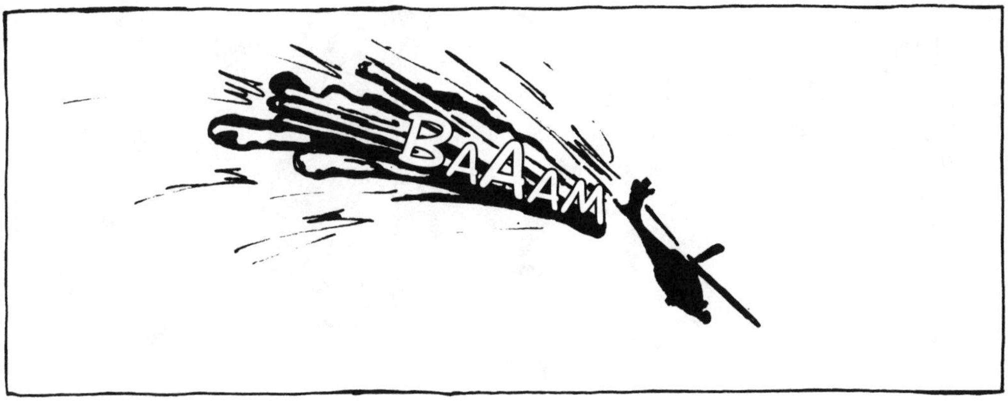
BAAAAM

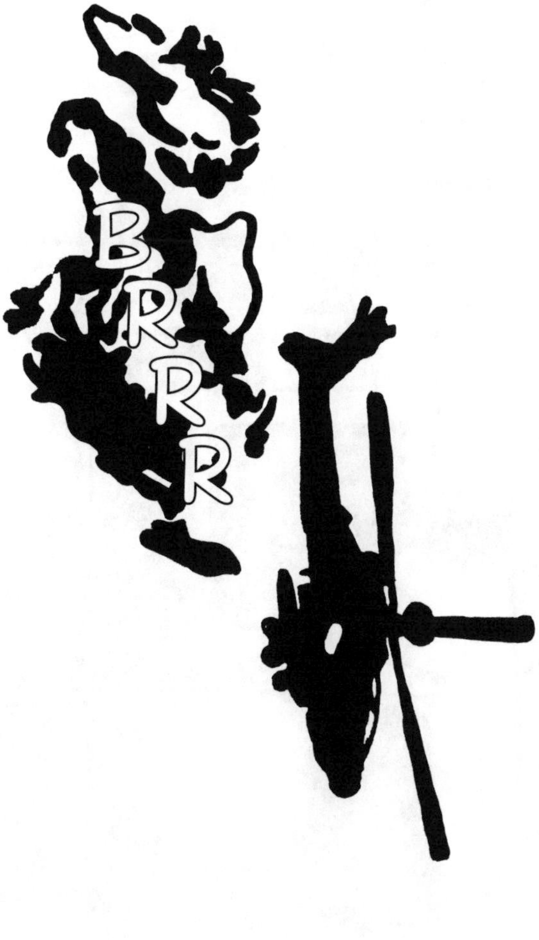
BRRRR

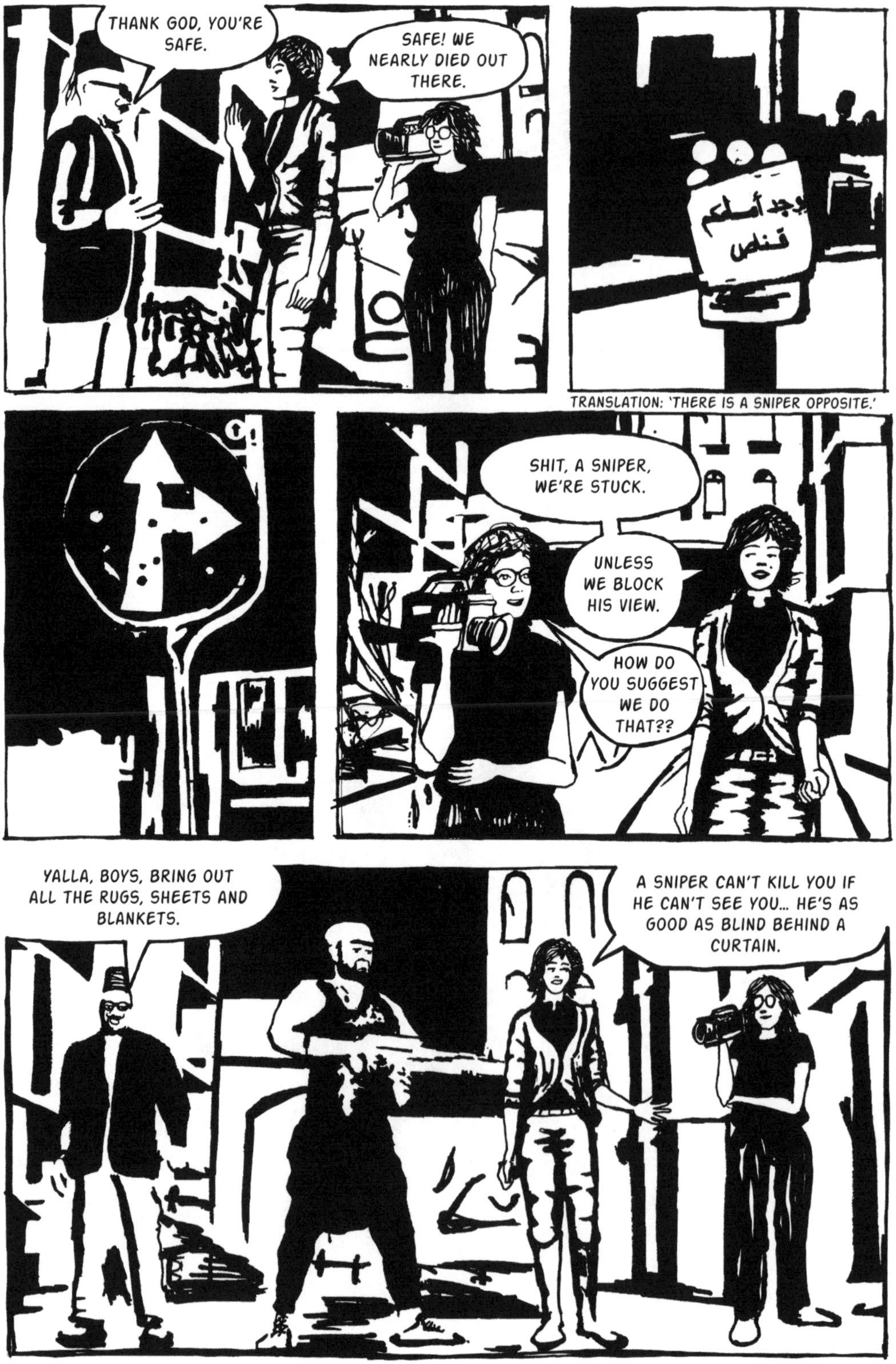
THANK GOD, YOU'RE SAFE.
SAFE! WE NEARLY DIED OUT THERE.
وجد أمامكم
قناص
TRANSLATION: 'THERE IS A SNIPER OPPOSITE.'
SHIT, A SNIPER, WE'RE STUCK.
UNLESS WE BLOCK HIS VIEW.
HOW DO YOU SUGGEST WE DO THAT??
YALLA, BOYS, BRING OUT ALL THE RUGS, SHEETS AND BLANKETS.
A SNIPER CAN'T KILL YOU IF HE CAN'T SEE YOU... HE'S AS GOOD AS BLIND BEHIND A CURTAIN.

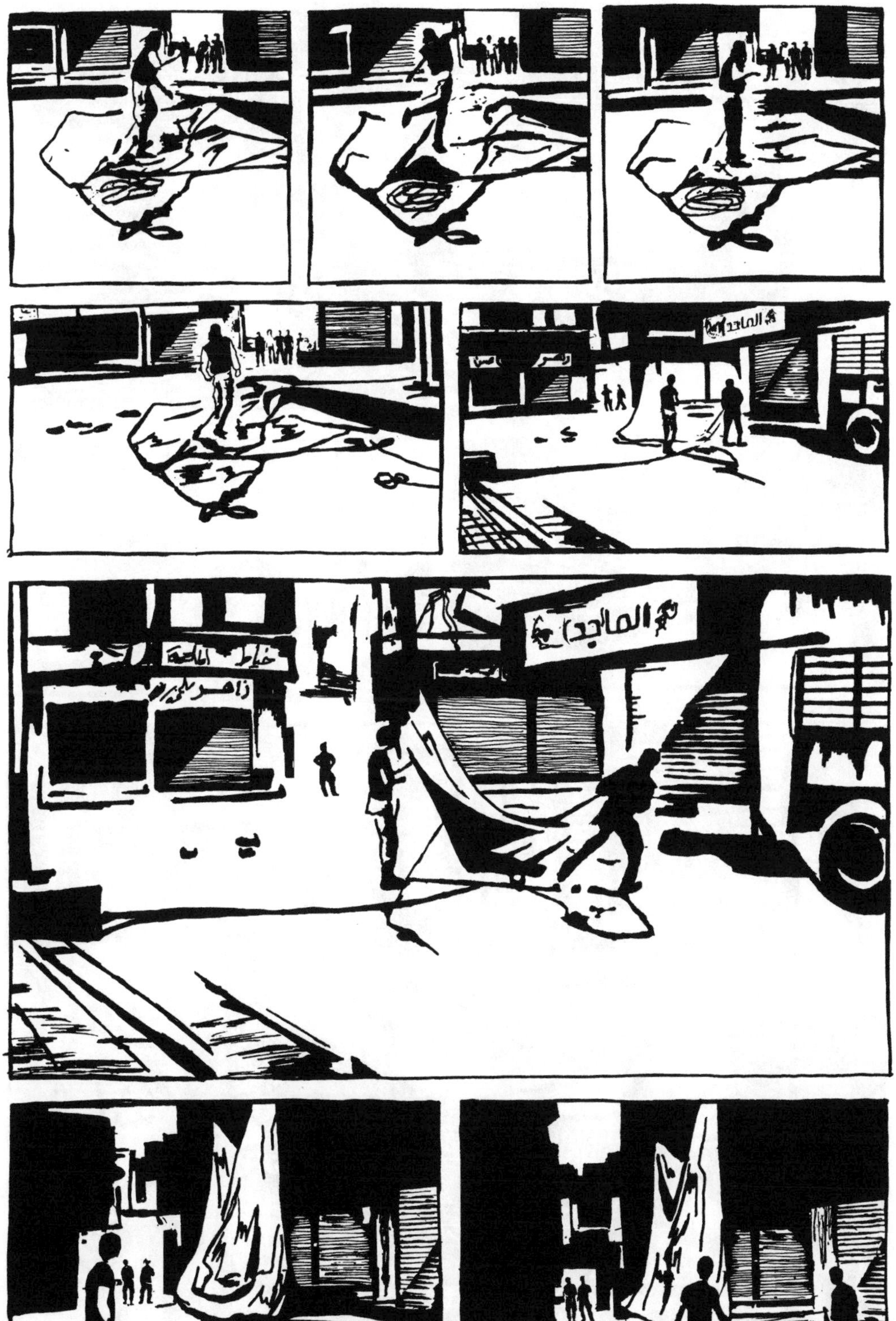
الماجد

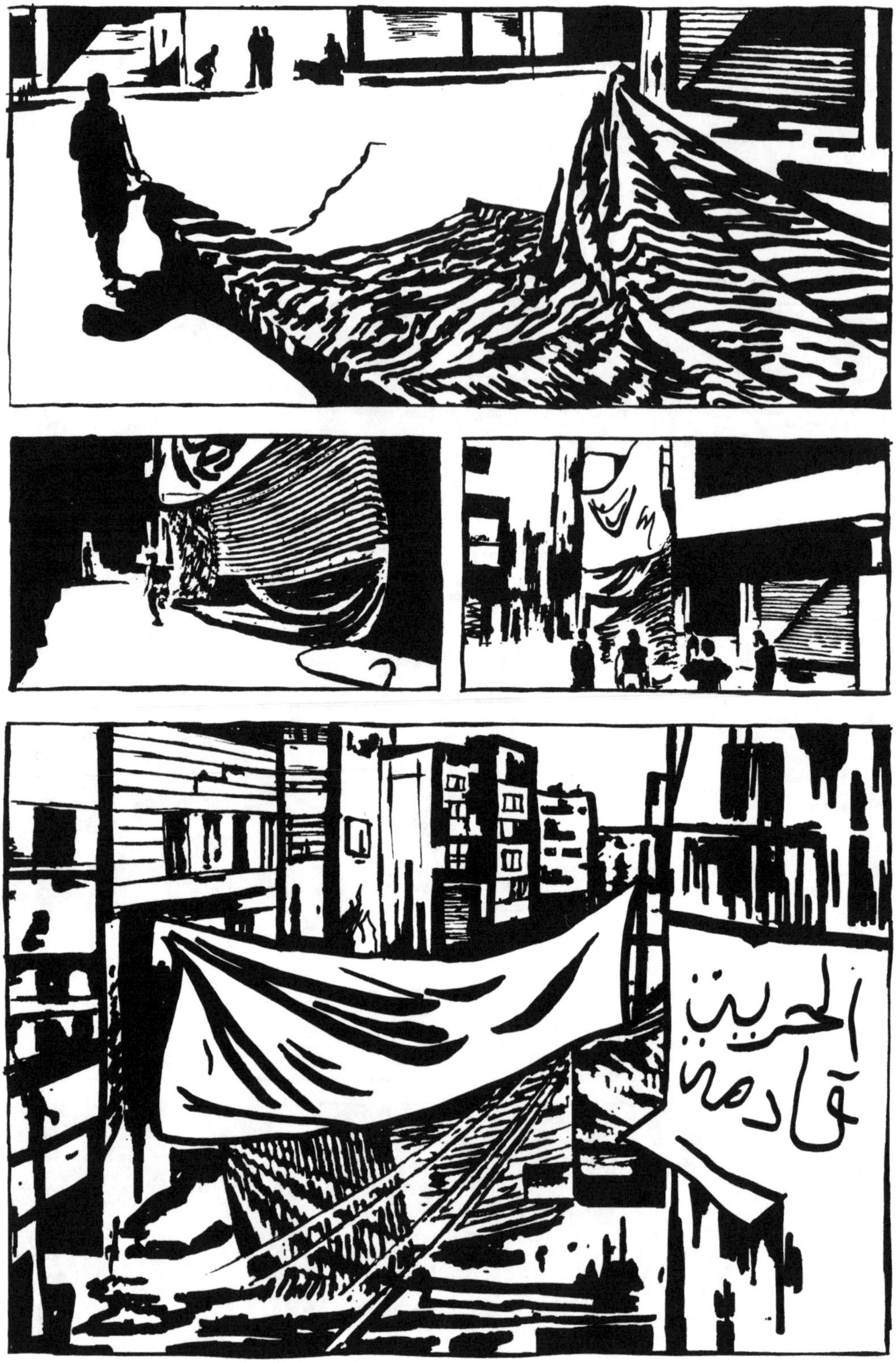
الحرية
قادمة

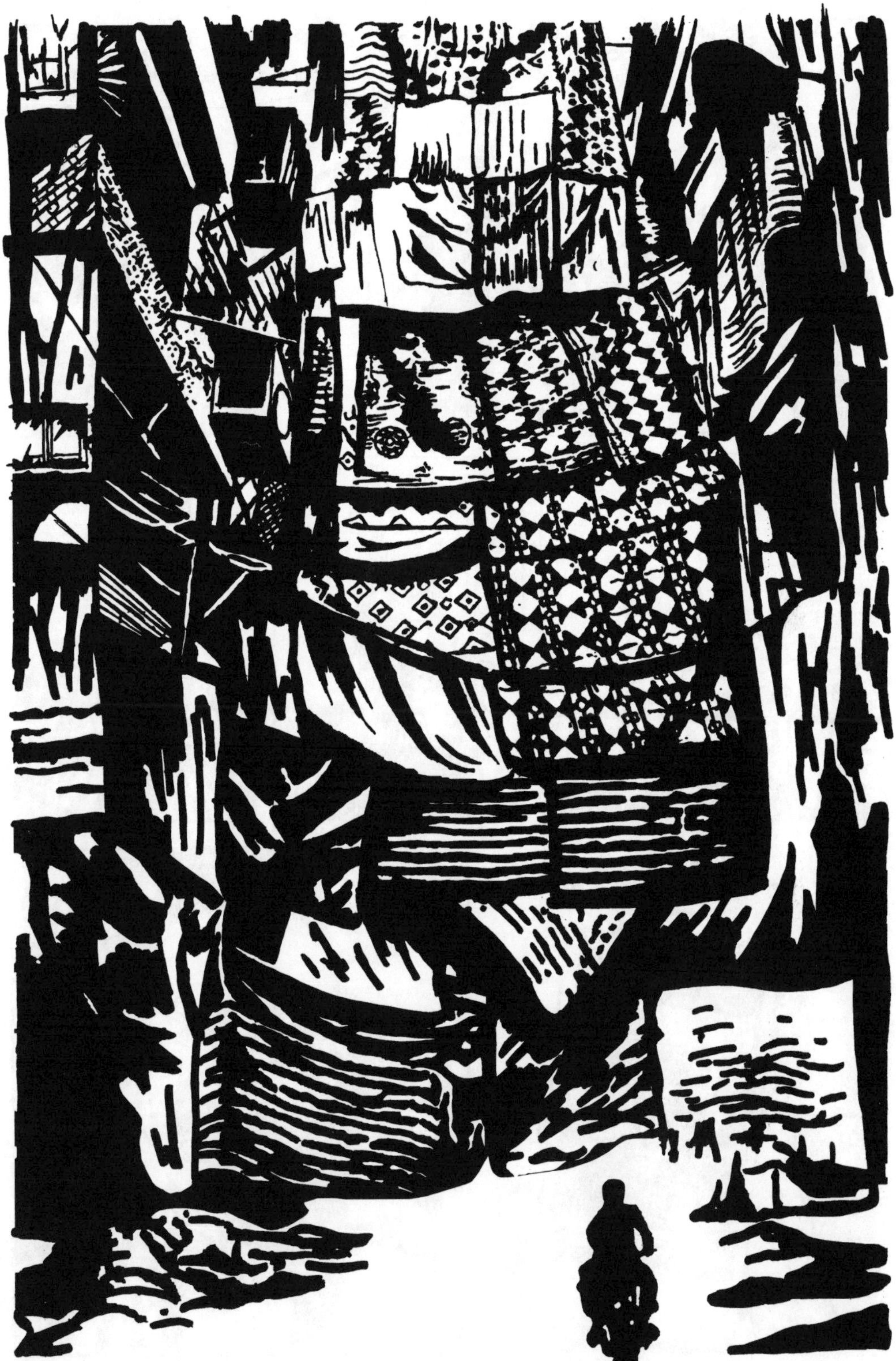

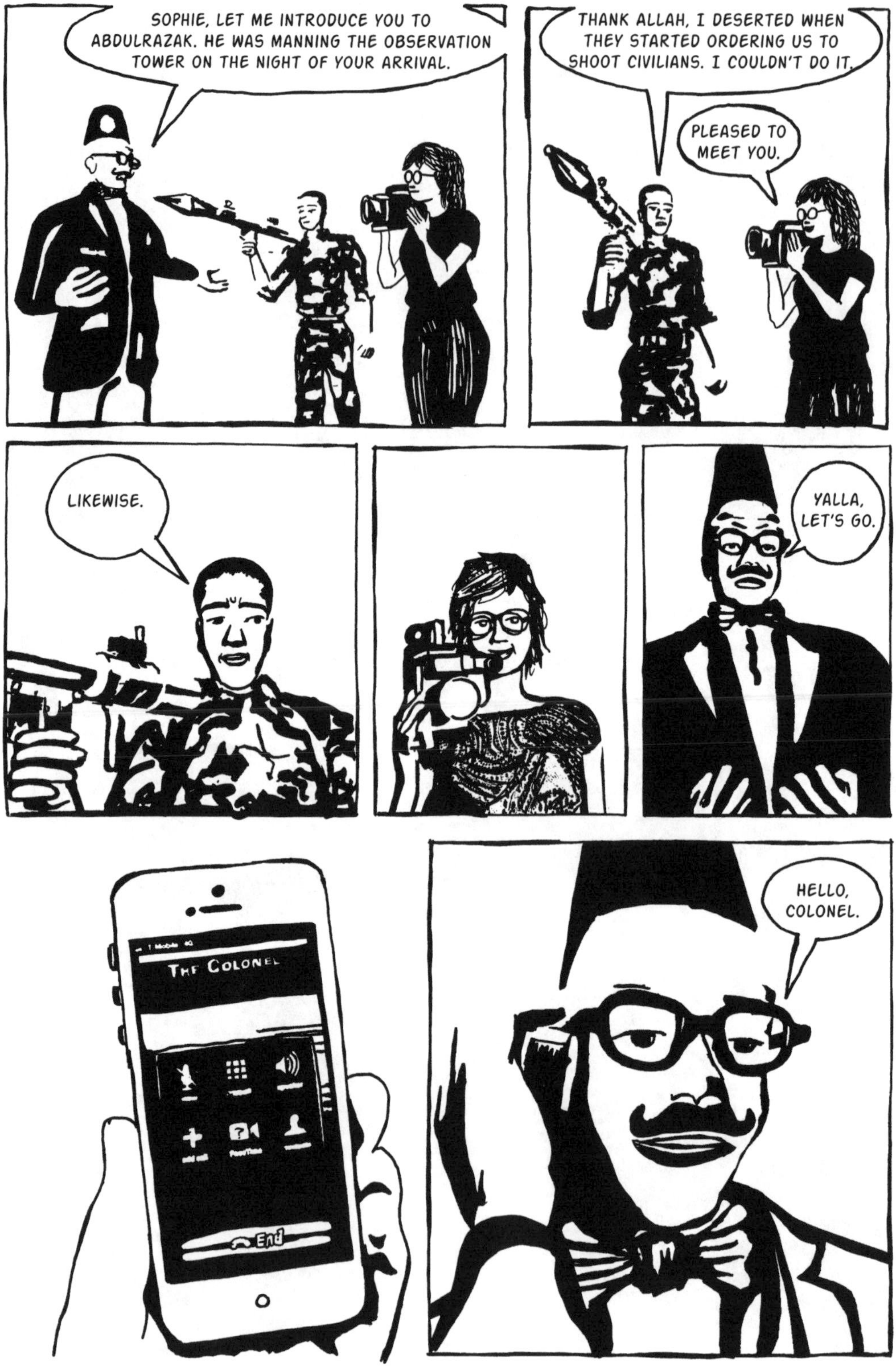
SOPHIE, LET ME INTRODUCE YOU TO ABDULRAZAK. HE WAS MANNING THE OBSERVATION TOWER ON THE NIGHT OF YOUR ARRIVAL.
THANK ALLAH, I DESERTED WHEN THEY STARTED ORDERING US TO SHOOT CIVILIANS. I COULDN'T DO IT.
PLEASED TO MEET YOU.
LIKEWISE.
YALLA, LET'S GO.
THE COLONEL
End
HELLO, COLONEL.

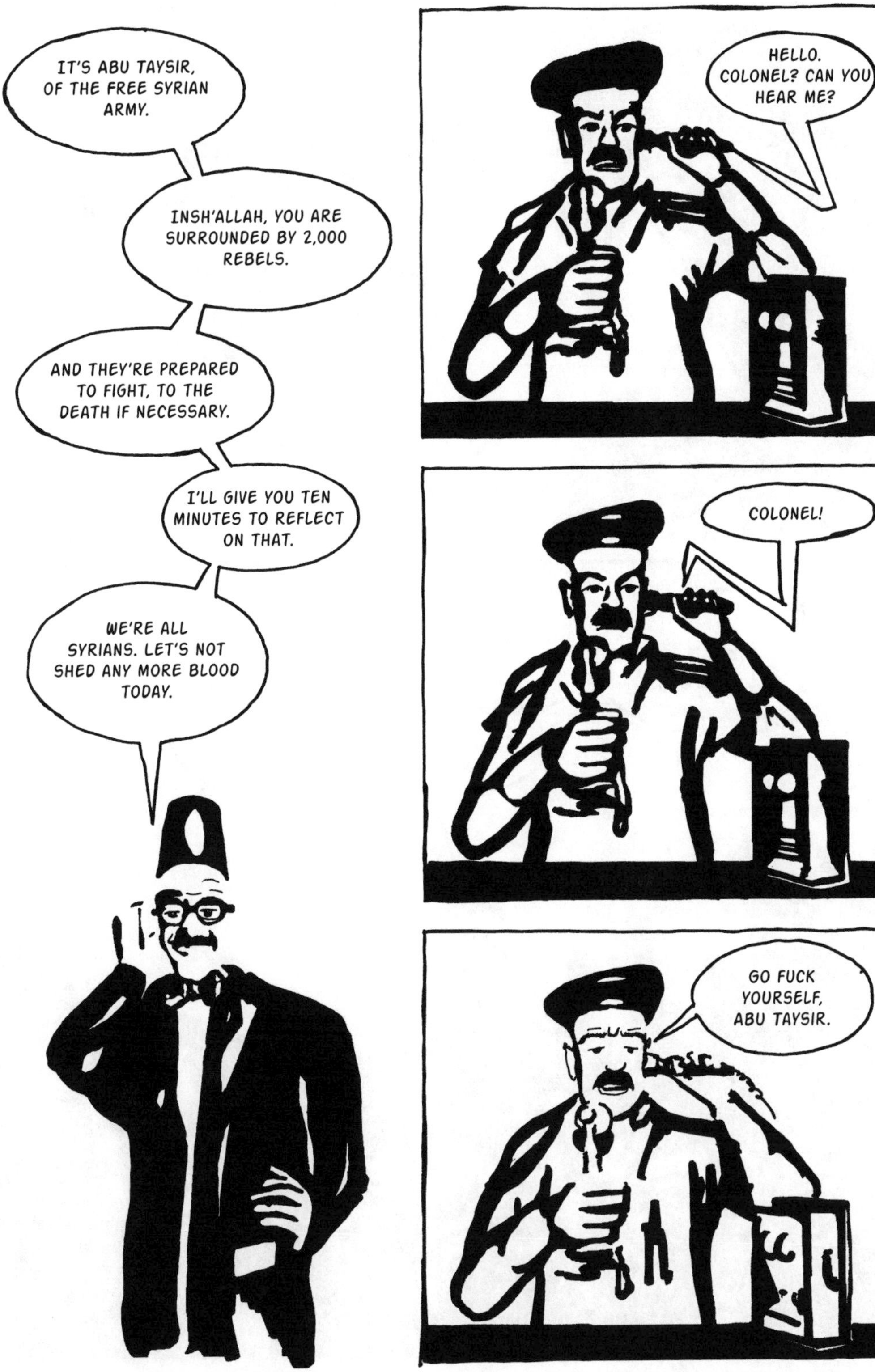
IT'S ABU TAYSIR, OF THE FREE SYRIAN ARMY.
INSH'ALLAH, YOU ARE SURROUNDED BY 2,000 REBELS.
AND THEY'RE PREPARED TO FIGHT, TO THE DEATH IF NECESSARY.
I'LL GIVE YOU TEN MINUTES TO REFLECT ON THAT.
WE'RE ALL SYRIANS. LET'S NOT SHED ANY MORE BLOOD TODAY.
HELLO. COLONEL? CAN YOU HEAR ME?
COLONEL!
GO FUCK YOURSELF, ABU TAYSIR.

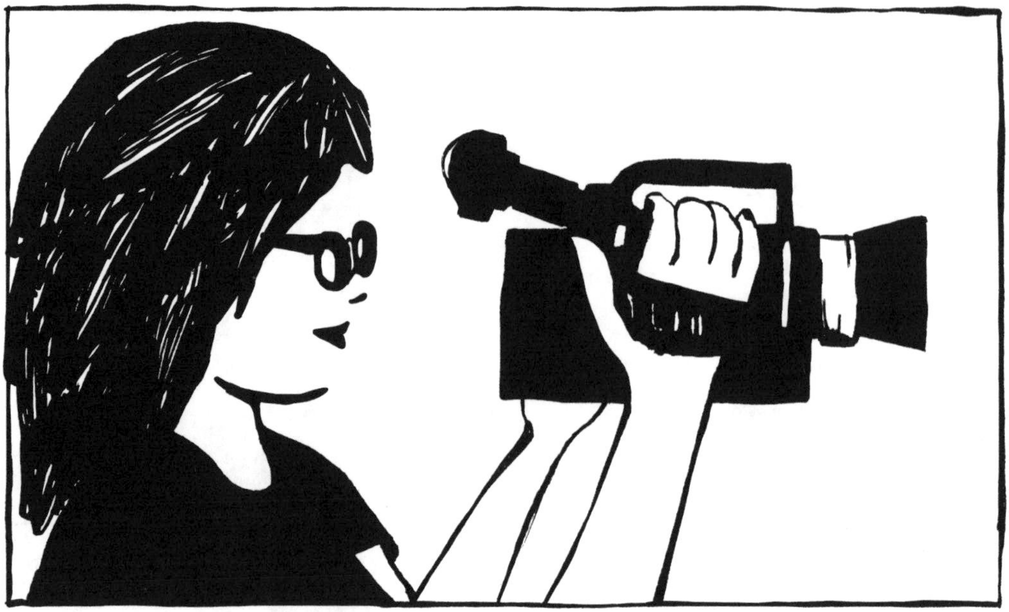

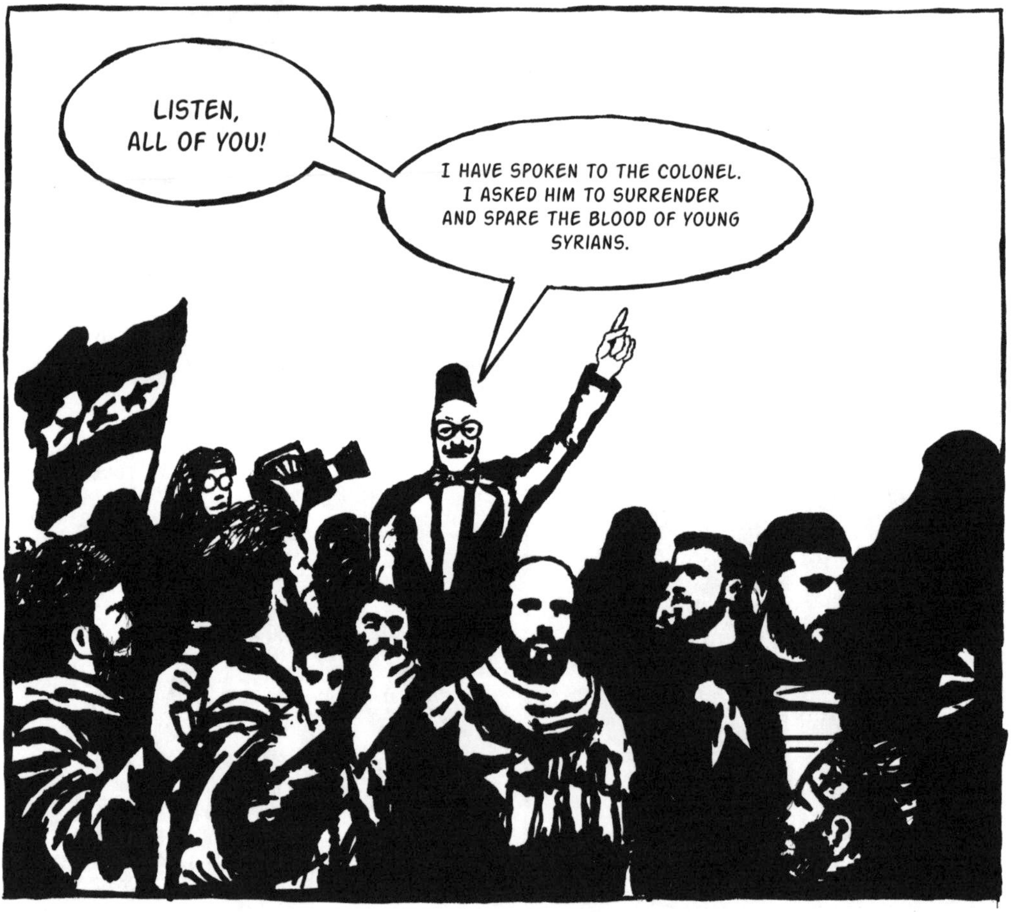
LISTEN, ALL OF YOU!
I HAVE SPOKEN TO THE COLONEL. I ASKED HIM TO SURRENDER AND SPARE THE BLOOD OF YOUNG SYRIANS.

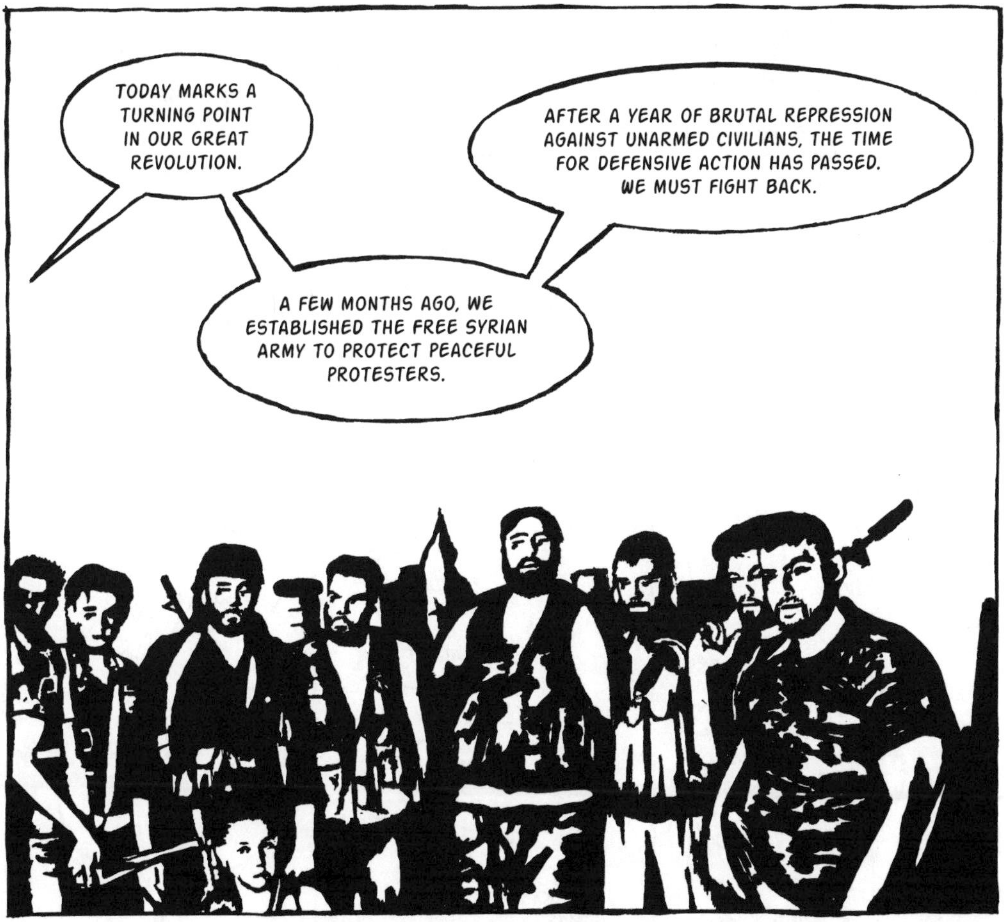
TODAY MARKS A TURNING POINT IN OUR GREAT REVOLUTION.
AFTER A YEAR OF BRUTAL REPRESSION AGAINST UNARMED CIVILIANS, THE TIME FOR DEFENSIVE ACTION HAS PASSED. WE MUST FIGHT BACK.
A FEW MONTHS AGO, WE ESTABLISHED THE FREE SYRIAN ARMY TO PROTECT PEACEFUL PROTESTERS.

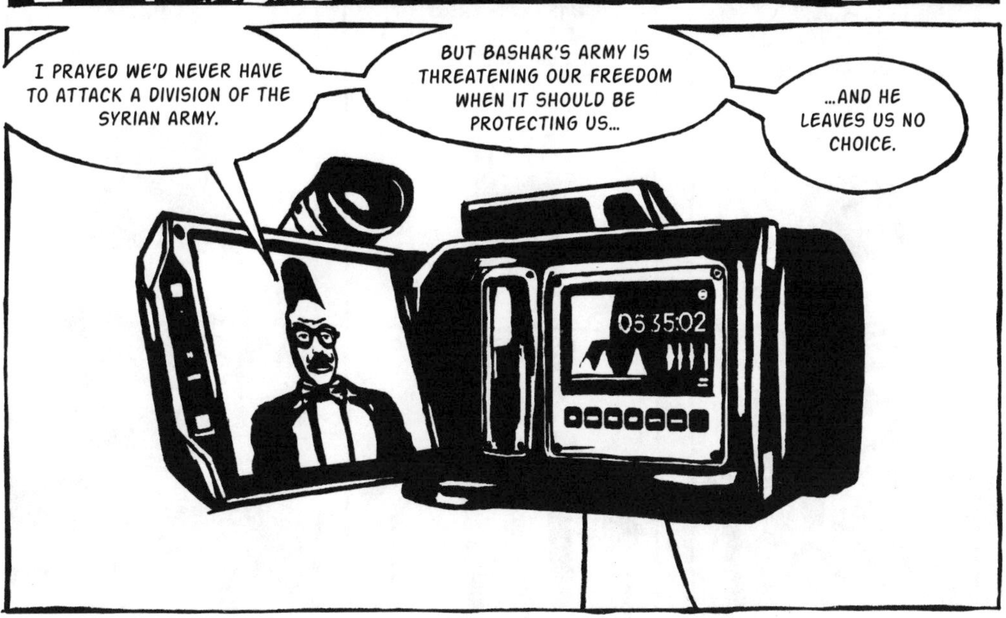
I PRAYED WE'D NEVER HAVE TO ATTACK A DIVISION OF THE SYRIAN ARMY.
BUT BASHAR'S ARMY IS THREATENING OUR FREEDOM WHEN IT SHOULD BE PROTECTING US...
...AND HE LEAVES US NO CHOICE.
05 35:02

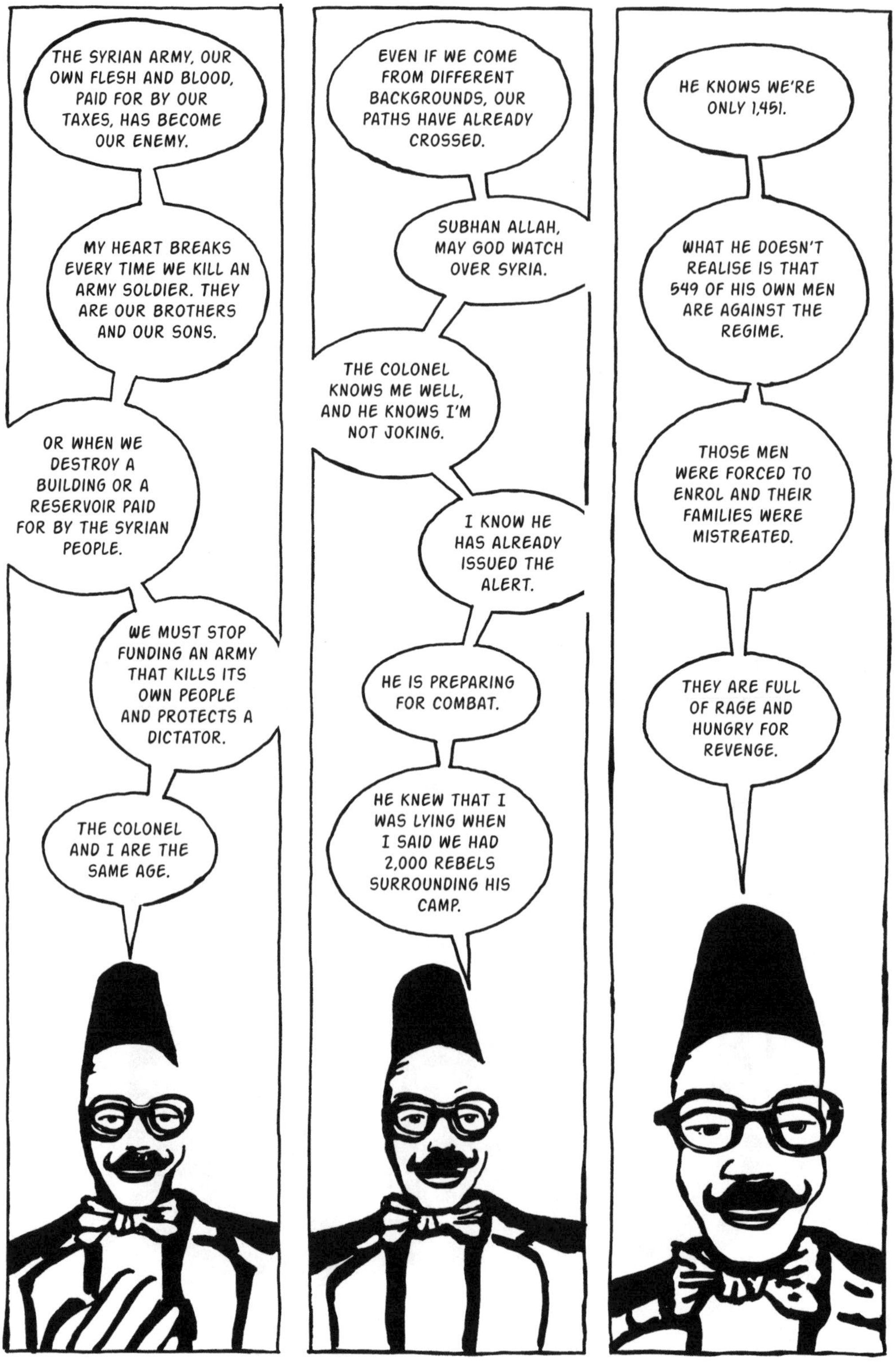
THE SYRIAN ARMY, OUR OWN FLESH AND BLOOD, PAID FOR BY OUR TAXES, HAS BECOME OUR ENEMY.
MY HEART BREAKS EVERY TIME WE KILL AN ARMY SOLDIER. THEY ARE OUR BROTHERS AND OUR SONS.
OR WHEN WE DESTROY A BUILDING OR A RESERVOIR PAID FOR BY THE SYRIAN PEOPLE.
WE MUST STOP FUNDING AN ARMY THAT KILLS ITS OWN PEOPLE AND PROTECTS A DICTATOR.
THE COLONEL AND I ARE THE SAME AGE.
EVEN IF WE COME FROM DIFFERENT BACKGROUNDS, OUR PATHS HAVE ALREADY CROSSED.
SUBHAN ALLAH, MAY GOD WATCH OVER SYRIA.
THE COLONEL KNOWS ME WELL, AND HE KNOWS I'M NOT JOKING.
I KNOW HE HAS ALREADY ISSUED THE ALERT.
HE IS PREPARING FOR COMBAT.
HE KNEW THAT I WAS LYING WHEN I SAID WE HAD 2,000 REBELS SURROUNDING HIS CAMP.
HE KNOWS WE'RE ONLY 1,451.
WHAT HE DOESN'T REALISE IS THAT 549 OF HIS OWN MEN ARE AGAINST THE REGIME.
THOSE MEN WERE FORCED TO ENROL AND THEIR FAMILIES WERE MISTREATED.
THEY ARE FULL OF RAGE AND HUNGRY FOR REVENGE.

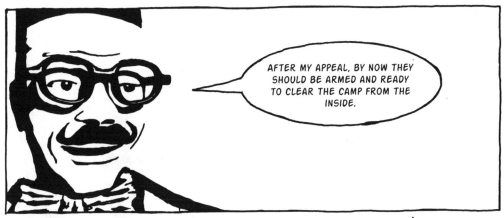

AFTER MY APPEAL, BY NOW THEY SHOULD BE ARMED AND READY TO CLEAR THE CAMP FROM THE INSIDE.

FIVE.

FOUR.

THREE.

TWO.

AND ONE.

GODDAMMIT!

MEANWHILE, AT THE HOSPITAL.

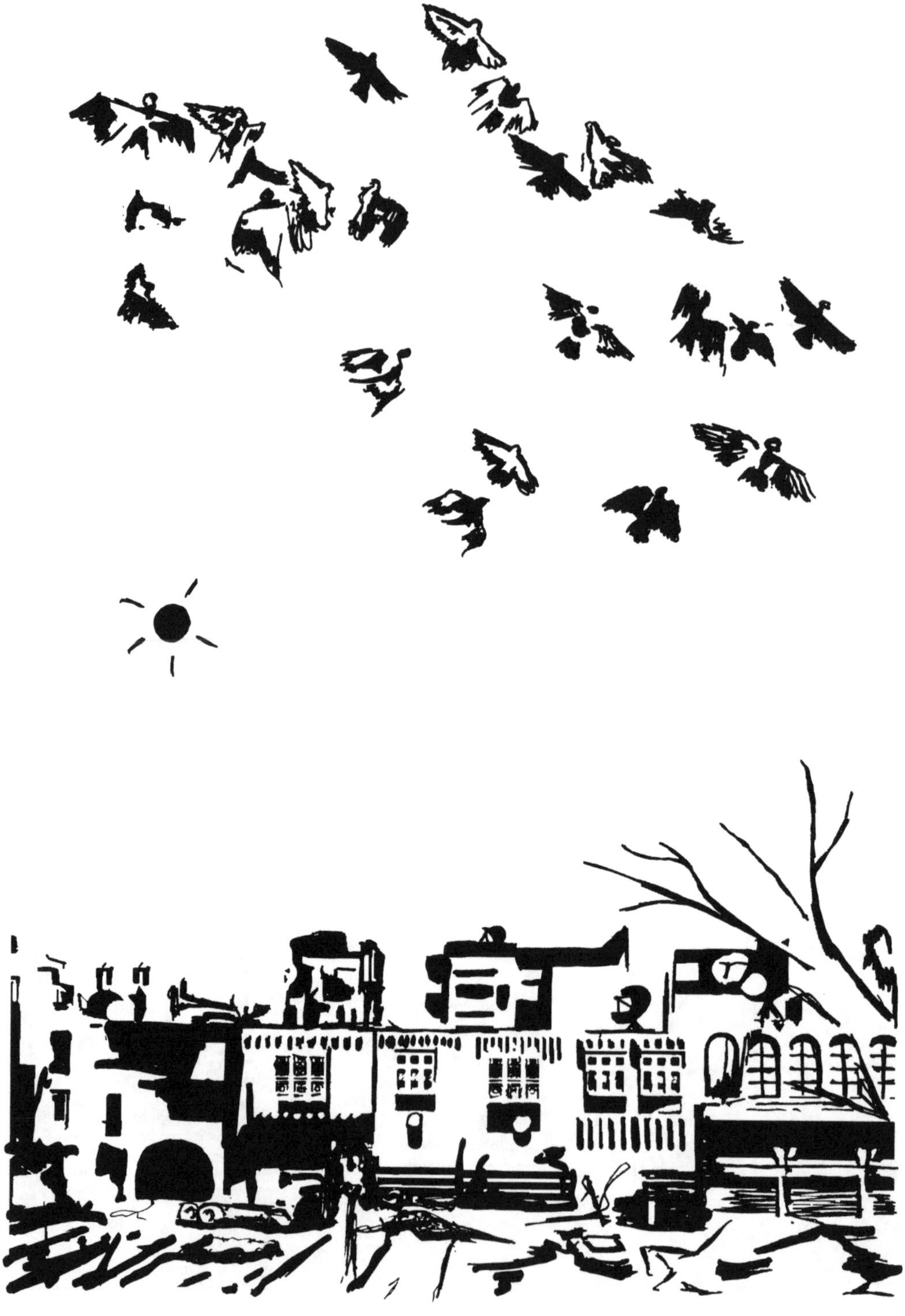

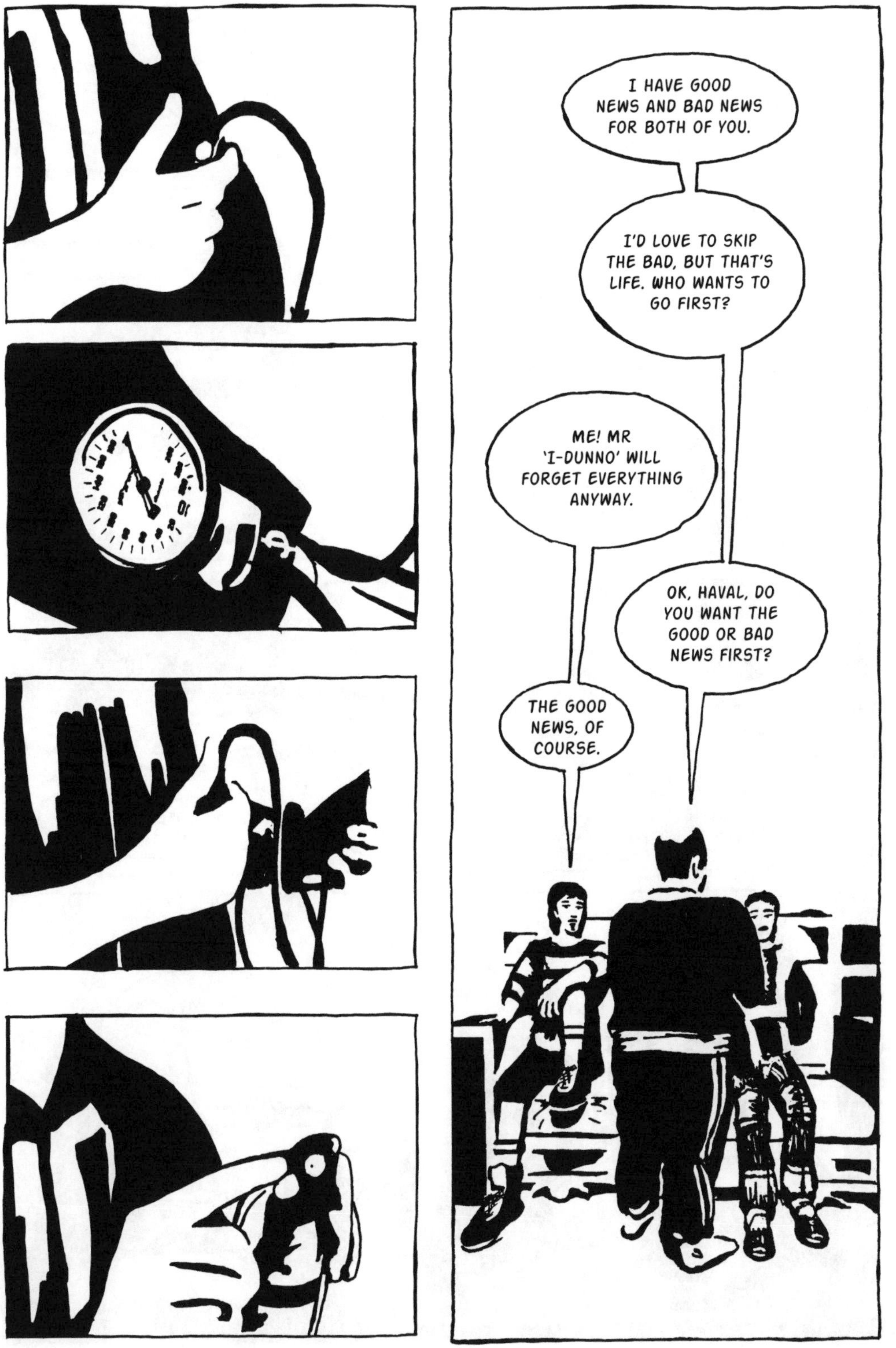
I HAVE GOOD NEWS AND BAD NEWS FOR BOTH OF YOU.
I'D LOVE TO SKIP THE BAD, BUT THAT'S LIFE. WHO WANTS TO GO FIRST?
ME! MR 'I-DUNNO' WILL FORGET EVERYTHING ANYWAY.
OK, HAVAL, DO YOU WANT THE GOOD OR BAD NEWS FIRST?
THE GOOD NEWS, OF COURSE.

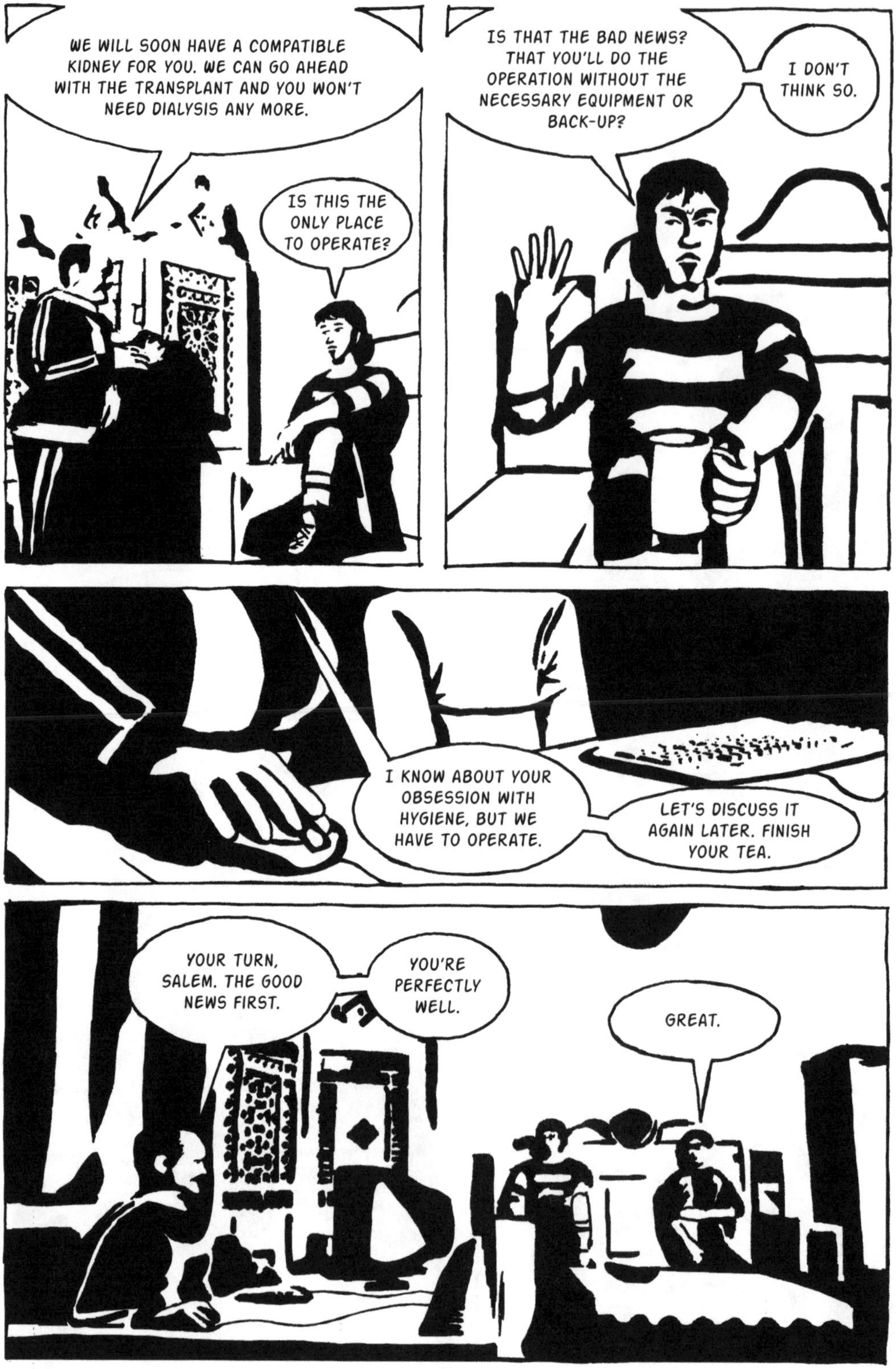
WE WILL SOON HAVE A COMPATIBLE KIDNEY FOR YOU. WE CAN GO AHEAD WITH THE TRANSPLANT AND YOU WON'T NEED DIALYSIS ANY MORE.
IS THIS THE ONLY PLACE TO OPERATE?
IS THAT THE BAD NEWS? THAT YOU'LL DO THE OPERATION WITHOUT THE NECESSARY EQUIPMENT OR BACK-UP?
I DON'T THINK SO.
I KNOW ABOUT YOUR OBSESSION WITH HYGIENE, BUT WE HAVE TO OPERATE.
LET'S DISCUSS IT AGAIN LATER. FINISH YOUR TEA.
YOUR TURN, SALEM. THE GOOD NEWS FIRST.
YOU'RE PERFECTLY WELL.
GREAT.

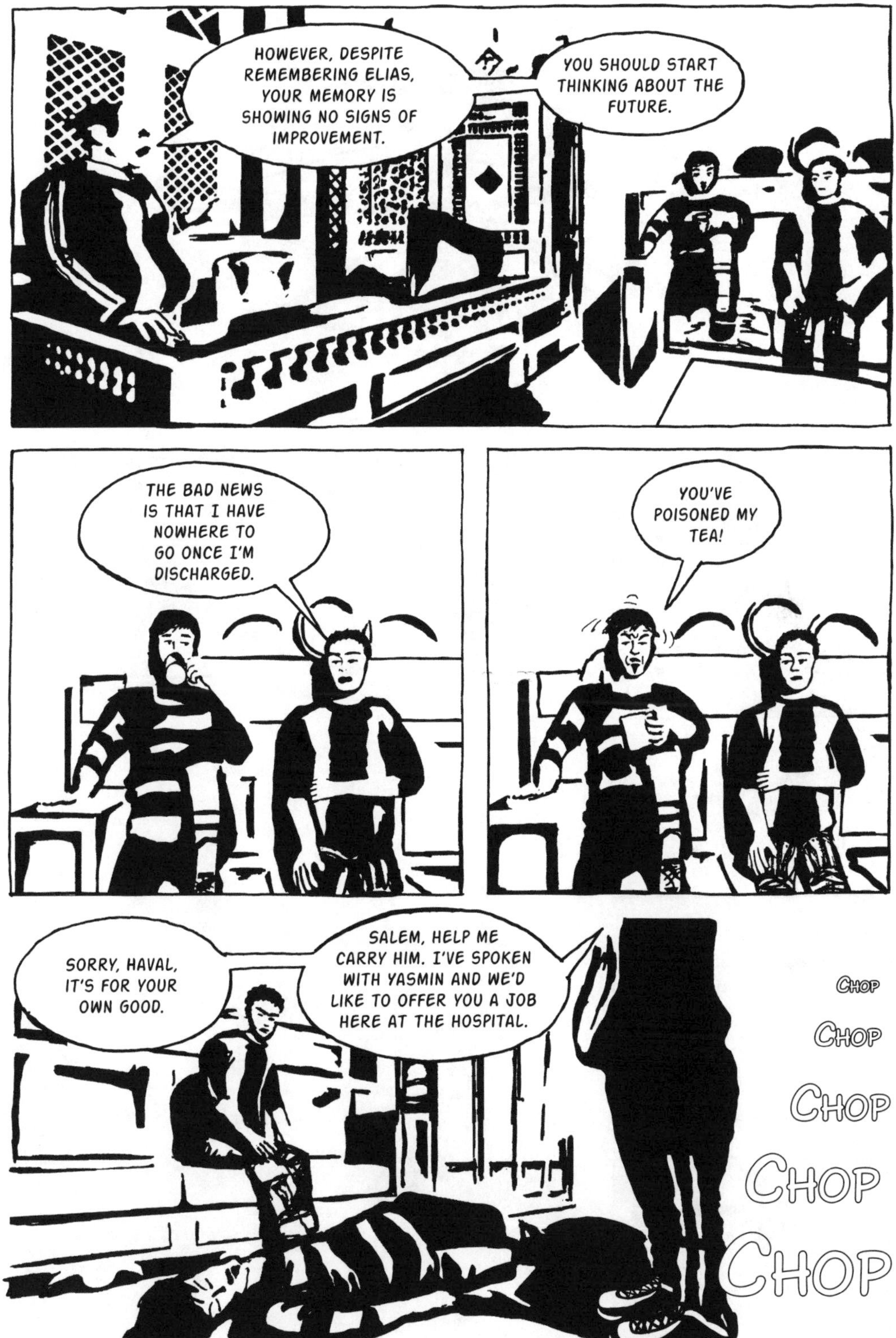
HOWEVER, DESPITE REMEMBERING ELIAS, YOUR MEMORY IS SHOWING NO SIGNS OF IMPROVEMENT.
YOU SHOULD START THINKING ABOUT THE FUTURE.
THE BAD NEWS IS THAT I HAVE NOWHERE TO GO ONCE I'M DISCHARGED.
YOU'VE POISONED MY TEA!
SORRY, HAVAL, IT'S FOR YOUR OWN GOOD.
SALEM, HELP ME CARRY HIM. I'VE SPOKEN WITH YASMIN AND WE'D LIKE TO OFFER YOU A JOB HERE AT THE HOSPITAL.
CHOP
CHOP
CHOP
CHOP
CHOP

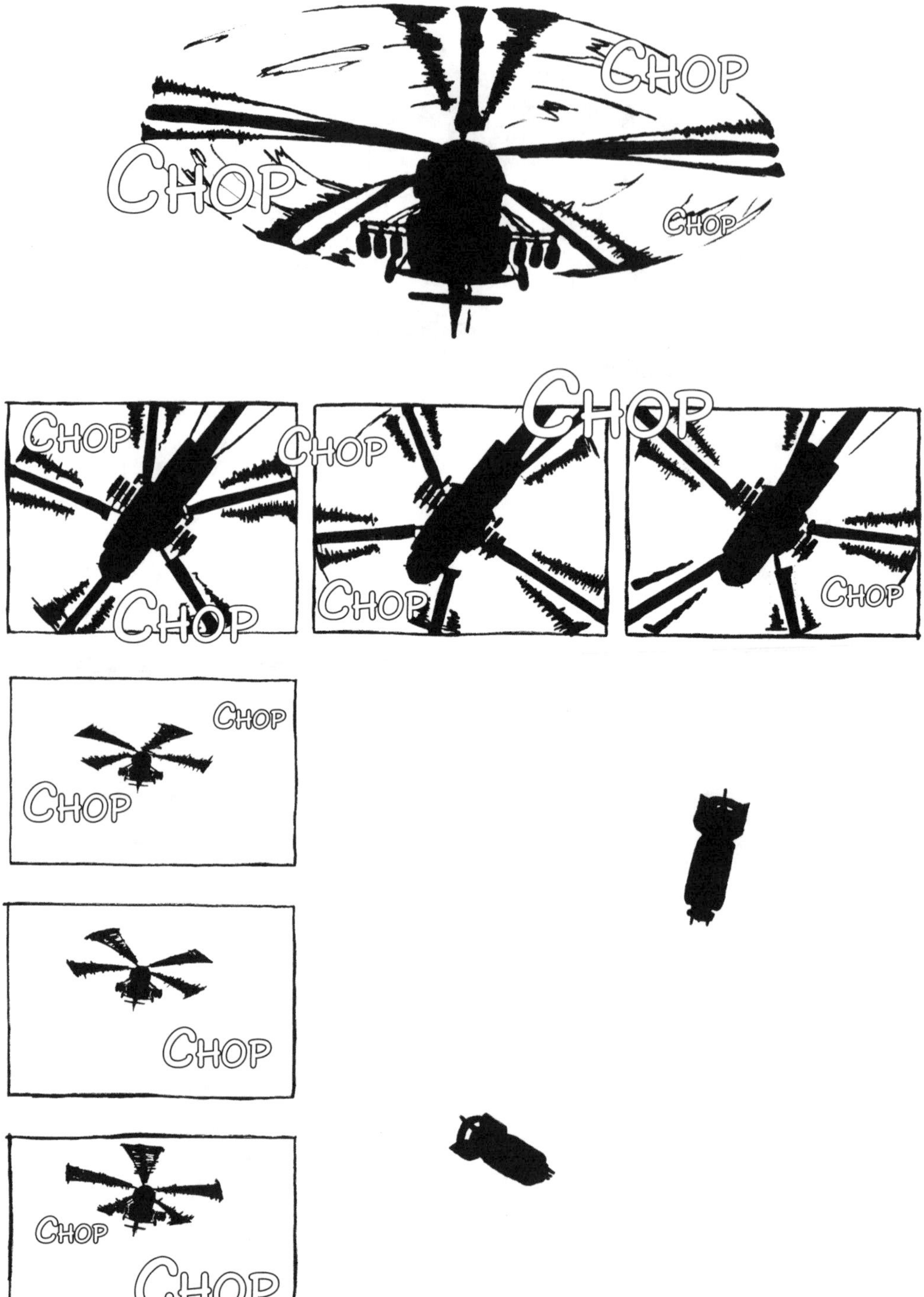
CHOP
CHOP
CHOP
CHOP
CHOP
CHOP
CHOP
CHOP
CHOP
CHOP
CHOP
CHOP
CHOP
CHOP

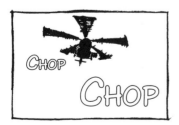

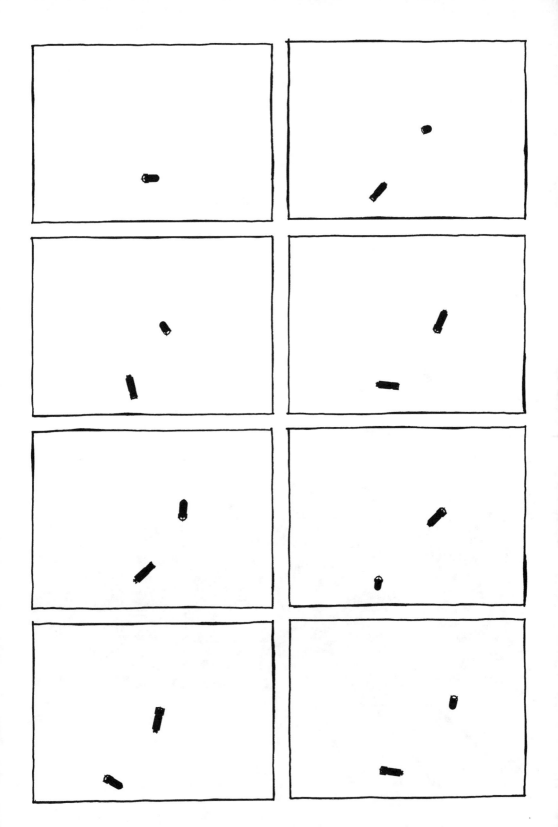

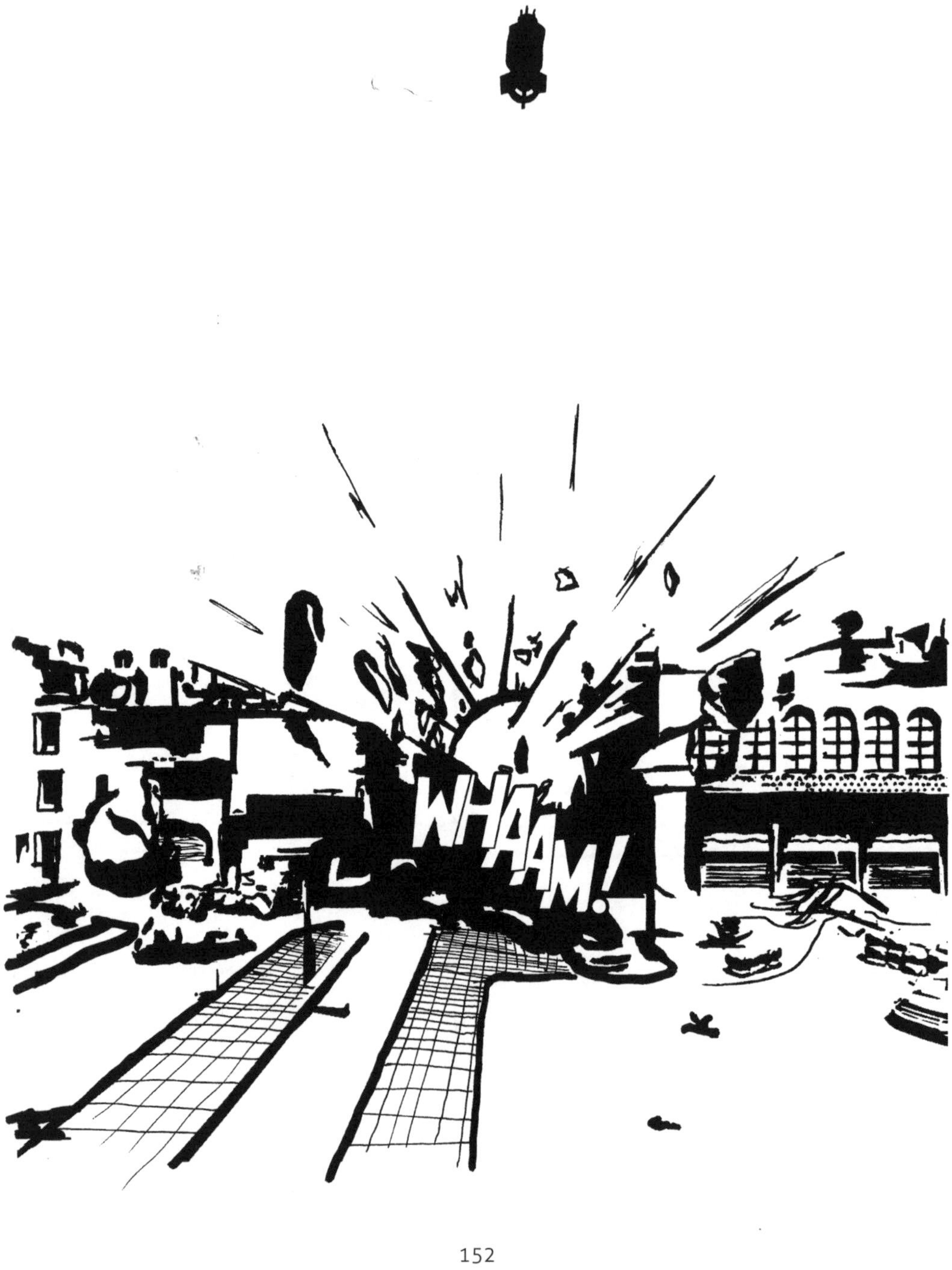
WHAAM!

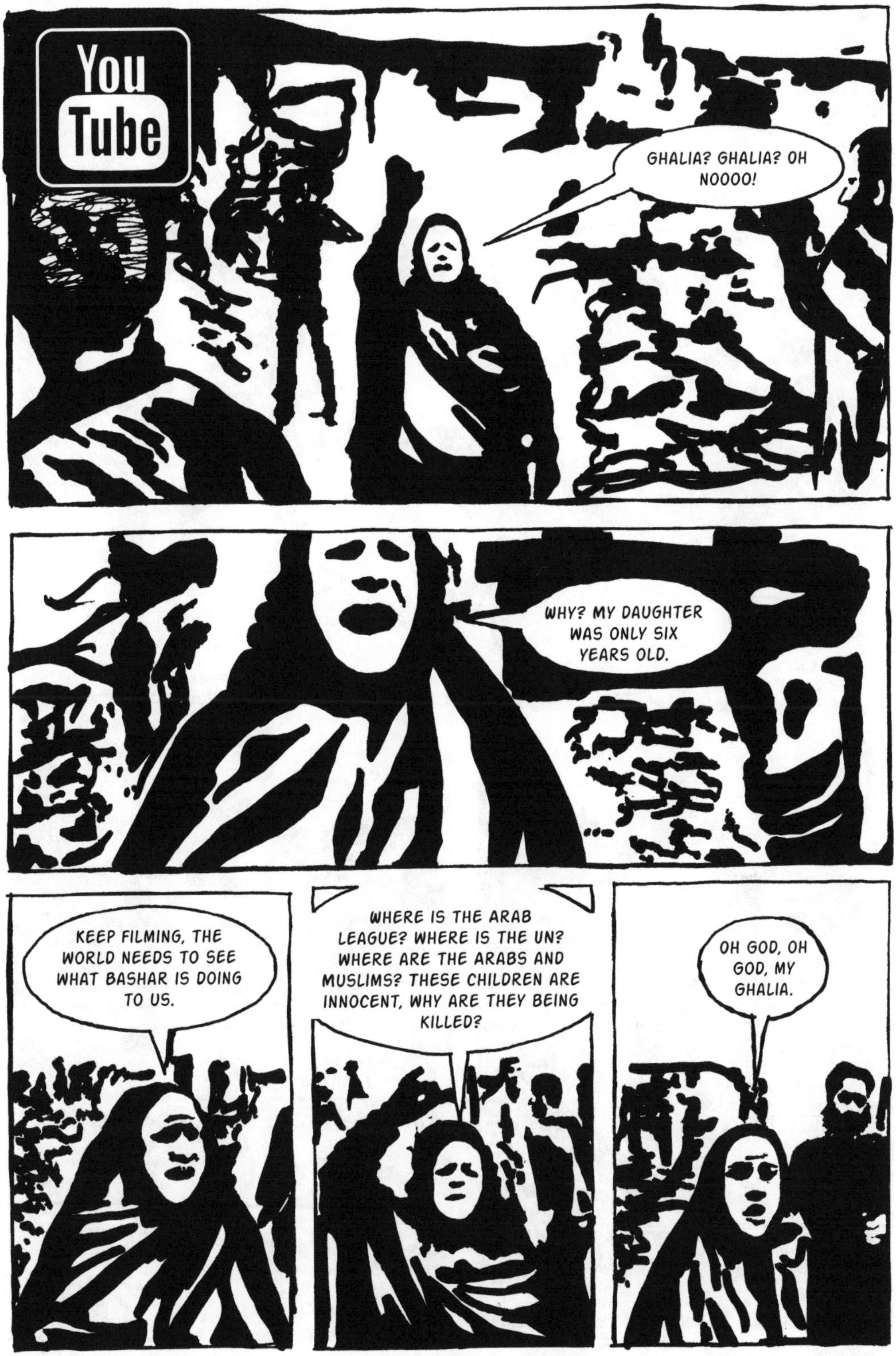
YouTube
GHALIA? GHALIA? OH NOOOO!
WHY? MY DAUGHTER WAS ONLY SIX YEARS OLD.
KEEP FILMING, THE WORLD NEEDS TO SEE WHAT BASHAR IS DOING TO US.
WHERE IS THE ARAB LEAGUE? WHERE IS THE UN? WHERE ARE THE ARABS AND MUSLIMS? THESE CHILDREN ARE INNOCENT, WHY ARE THEY BEING KILLED?
OH GOD, OH GOD, MY GHALIA.

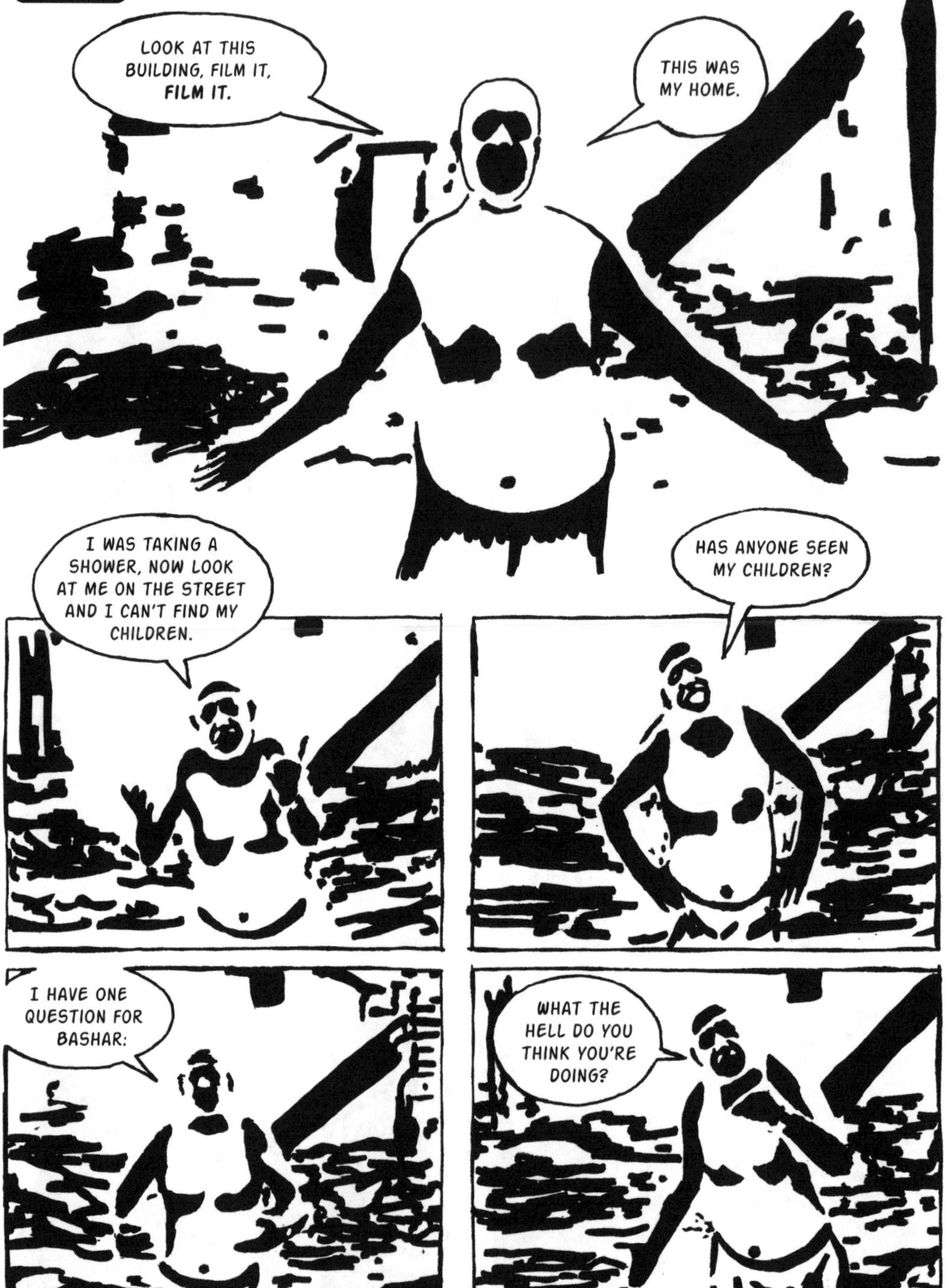
LOOK AT THIS BUILDING, FILM IT, FILM IT.
THIS WAS MY HOME.
I WAS TAKING A SHOWER, NOW LOOK AT ME ON THE STREET AND I CAN'T FIND MY CHILDREN.
HAS ANYONE SEEN MY CHILDREN?
I HAVE ONE QUESTION FOR BASHAR:
WHAT THE HELL DO YOU THINK YOU'RE DOING?

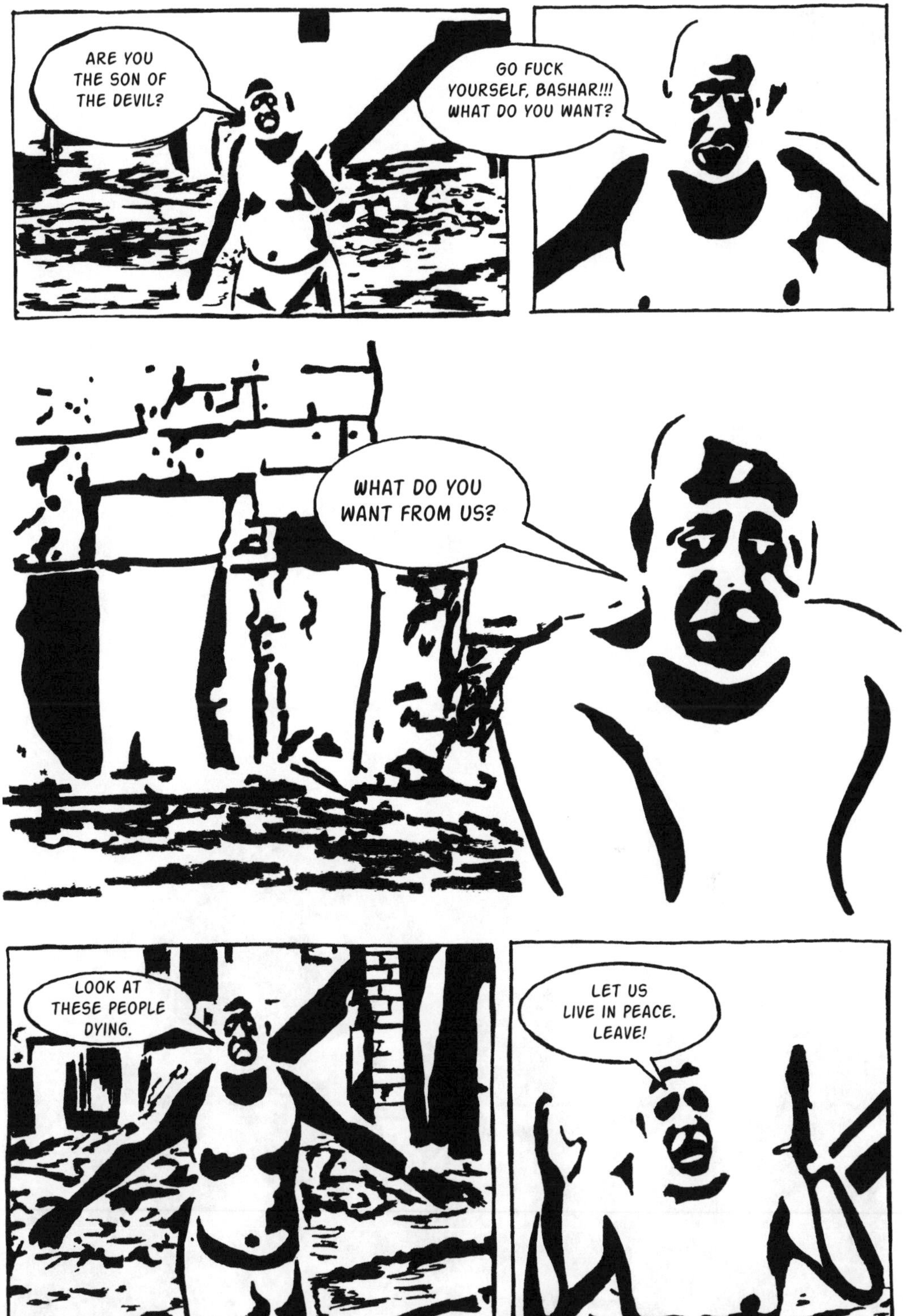
ARE YOU THE SON OF THE DEVIL?
GO FUCK YOURSELF, BASHAR!!! WHAT DO YOU WANT?
WHAT DO YOU WANT FROM US?
LOOK AT THESE PEOPLE DYING.
LET US LIVE IN PEACE. LEAVE!

YouTube

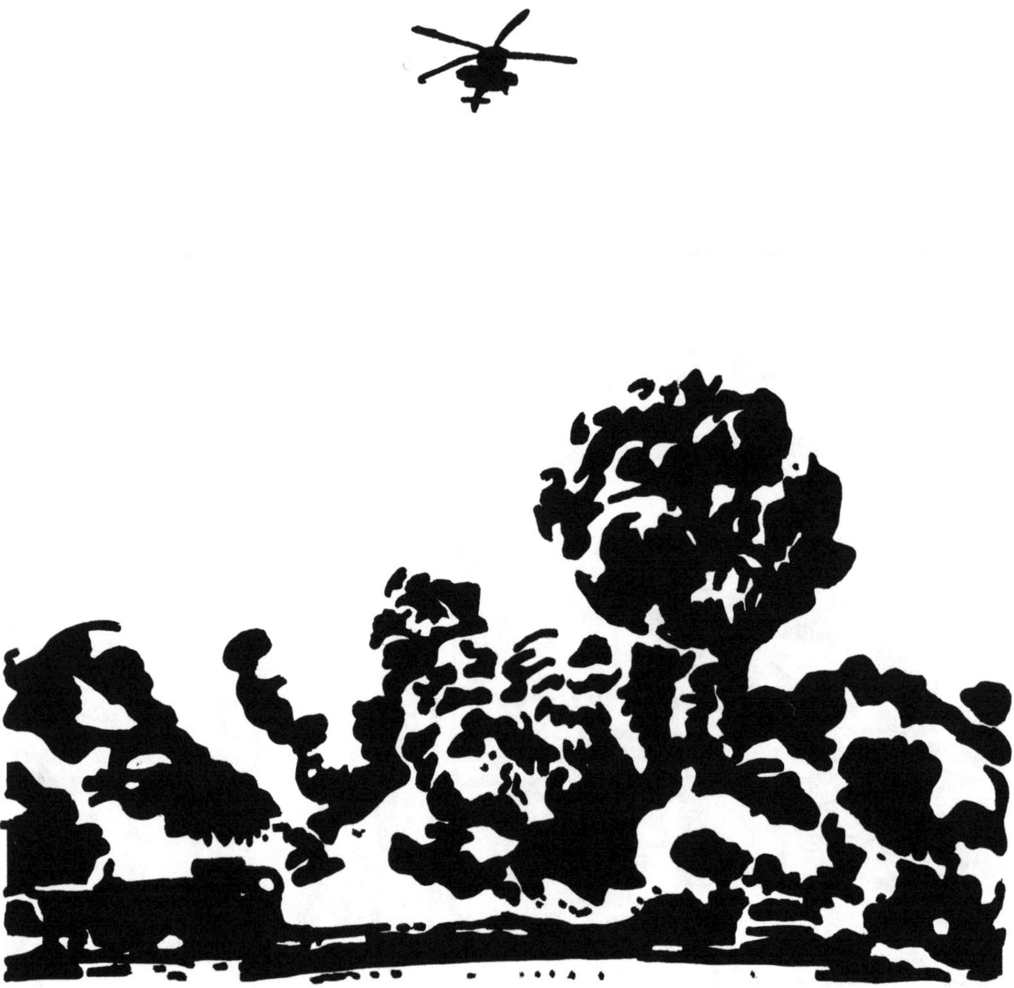

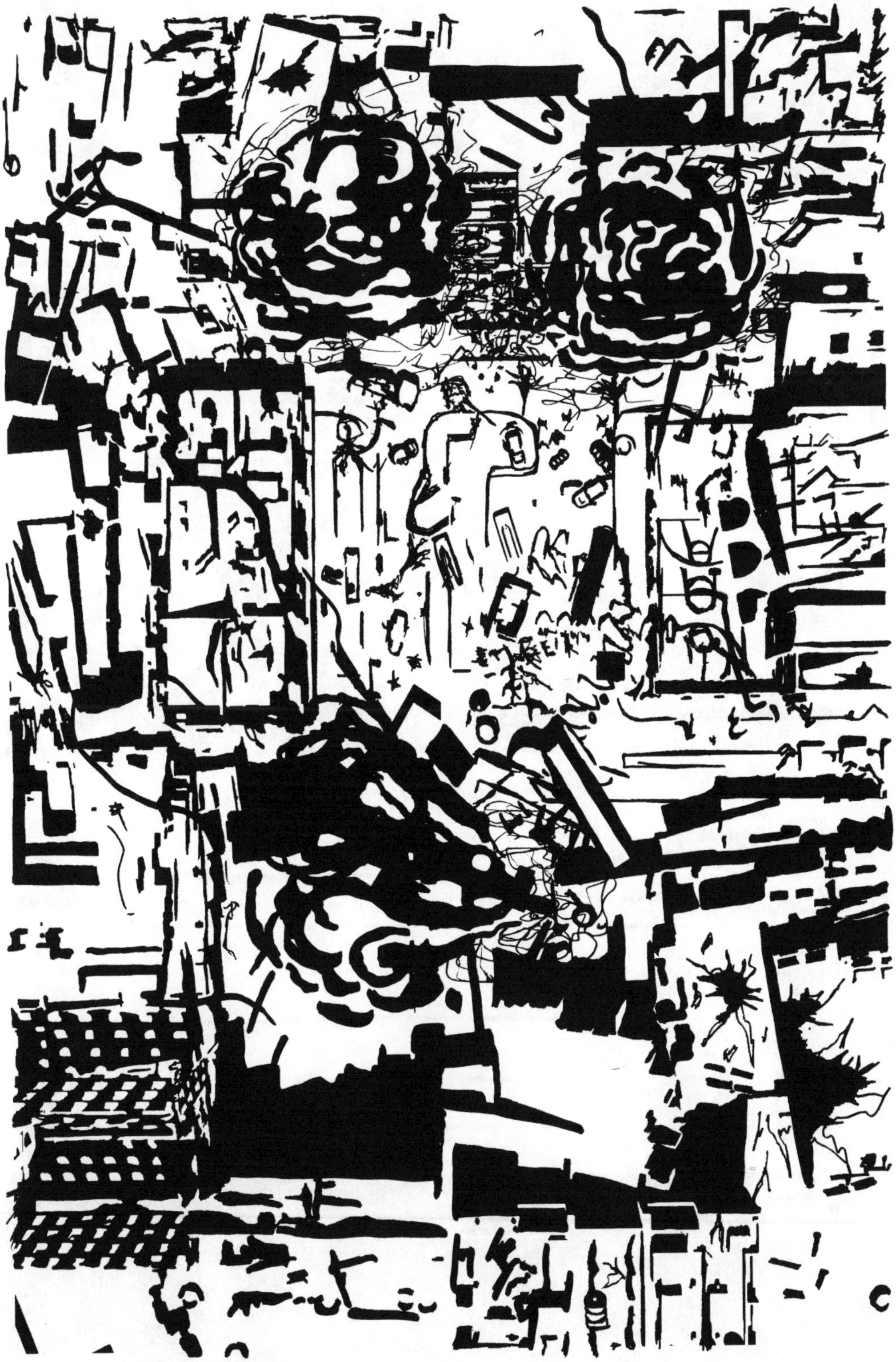

▶ ▶▌ ▌◀ ◀)) 2:17 / 2:15 ⚙ ▢ ⛶

سوريا : النظام يقصف مشفى الحرية بالبراميل المنفجرة

 427

3561

➕ Add to 👍 Shar ⋯ Plus   👍 168 👎 2

Published 16 March, 2013
Catalogue   People of blogs
License   License Youtube Plus

All Comments [4]

 Add a Comments

▼ •

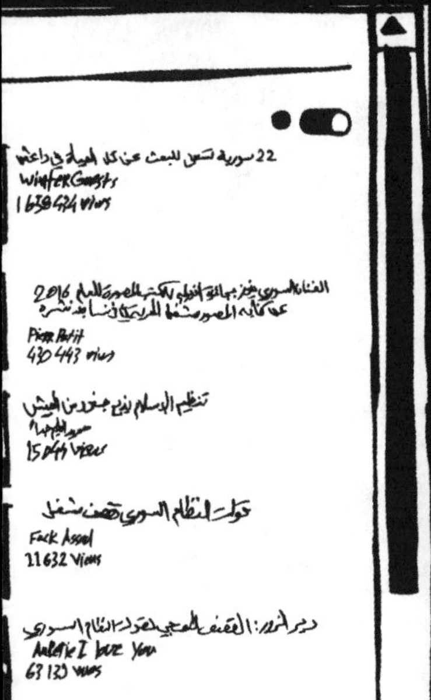

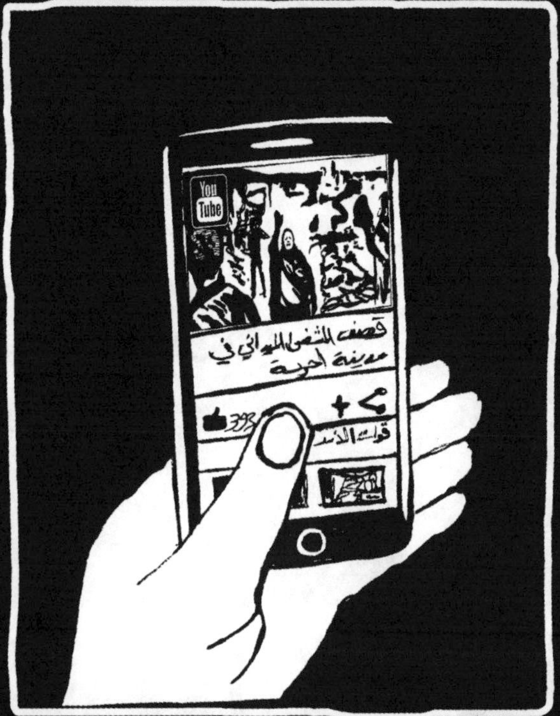

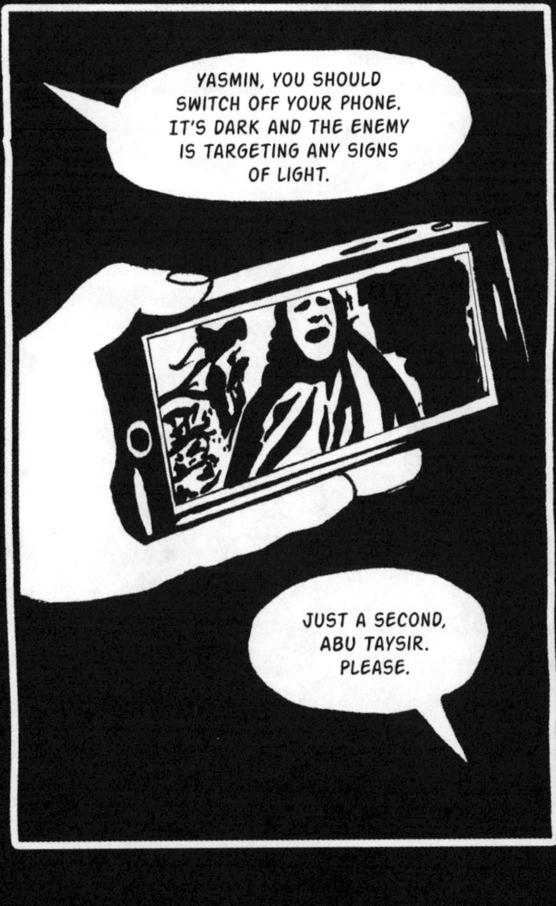
YASMIN, YOU SHOULD SWITCH OFF YOUR PHONE. IT'S DARK AND THE ENEMY IS TARGETING ANY SIGNS OF LIGHT.
JUST A SECOND, ABU TAYSIR. PLEASE.

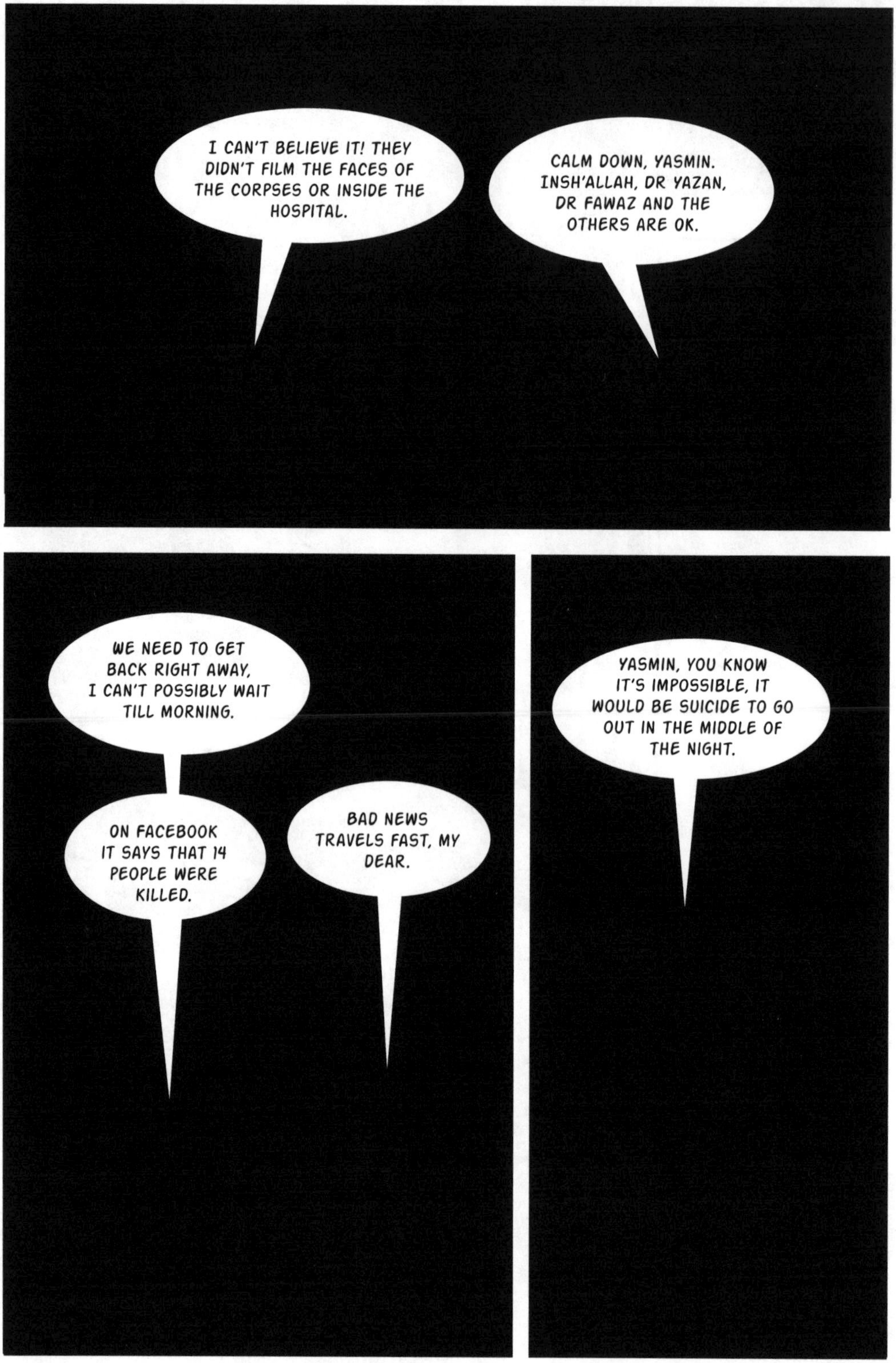
I CAN'T BELIEVE IT! THEY DIDN'T FILM THE FACES OF THE CORPSES OR INSIDE THE HOSPITAL.
CALM DOWN, YASMIN. INSH'ALLAH, DR YAZAN, DR FAWAZ AND THE OTHERS ARE OK.
WE NEED TO GET BACK RIGHT AWAY, I CAN'T POSSIBLY WAIT TILL MORNING.
ON FACEBOOK IT SAYS THAT 14 PEOPLE WERE KILLED.
BAD NEWS TRAVELS FAST, MY DEAR.
YASMIN, YOU KNOW IT'S IMPOSSIBLE, IT WOULD BE SUICIDE TO GO OUT IN THE MIDDLE OF THE NIGHT.

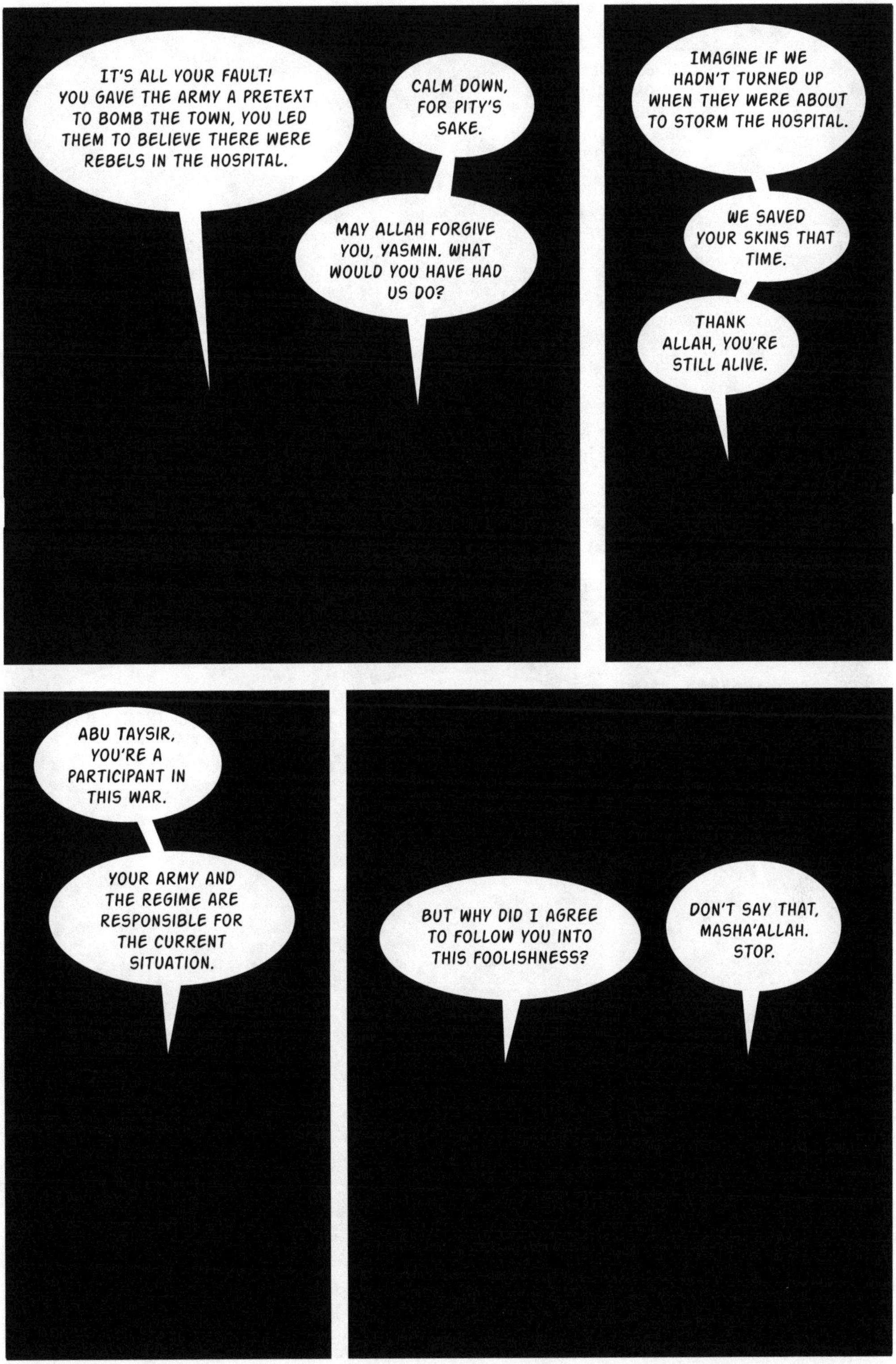
IT'S ALL YOUR FAULT! YOU GAVE THE ARMY A PRETEXT TO BOMB THE TOWN, YOU LED THEM TO BELIEVE THERE WERE REBELS IN THE HOSPITAL.
CALM DOWN, FOR PITY'S SAKE.
MAY ALLAH FORGIVE YOU, YASMIN. WHAT WOULD YOU HAVE HAD US DO?
IMAGINE IF WE HADN'T TURNED UP WHEN THEY WERE ABOUT TO STORM THE HOSPITAL.
WE SAVED YOUR SKINS THAT TIME.
THANK ALLAH, YOU'RE STILL ALIVE.
ABU TAYSIR, YOU'RE A PARTICIPANT IN THIS WAR.
YOUR ARMY AND THE REGIME ARE RESPONSIBLE FOR THE CURRENT SITUATION.
BUT WHY DID I AGREE TO FOLLOW YOU INTO THIS FOOLISHNESS?
DON'T SAY THAT, MASHA'ALLAH. STOP.

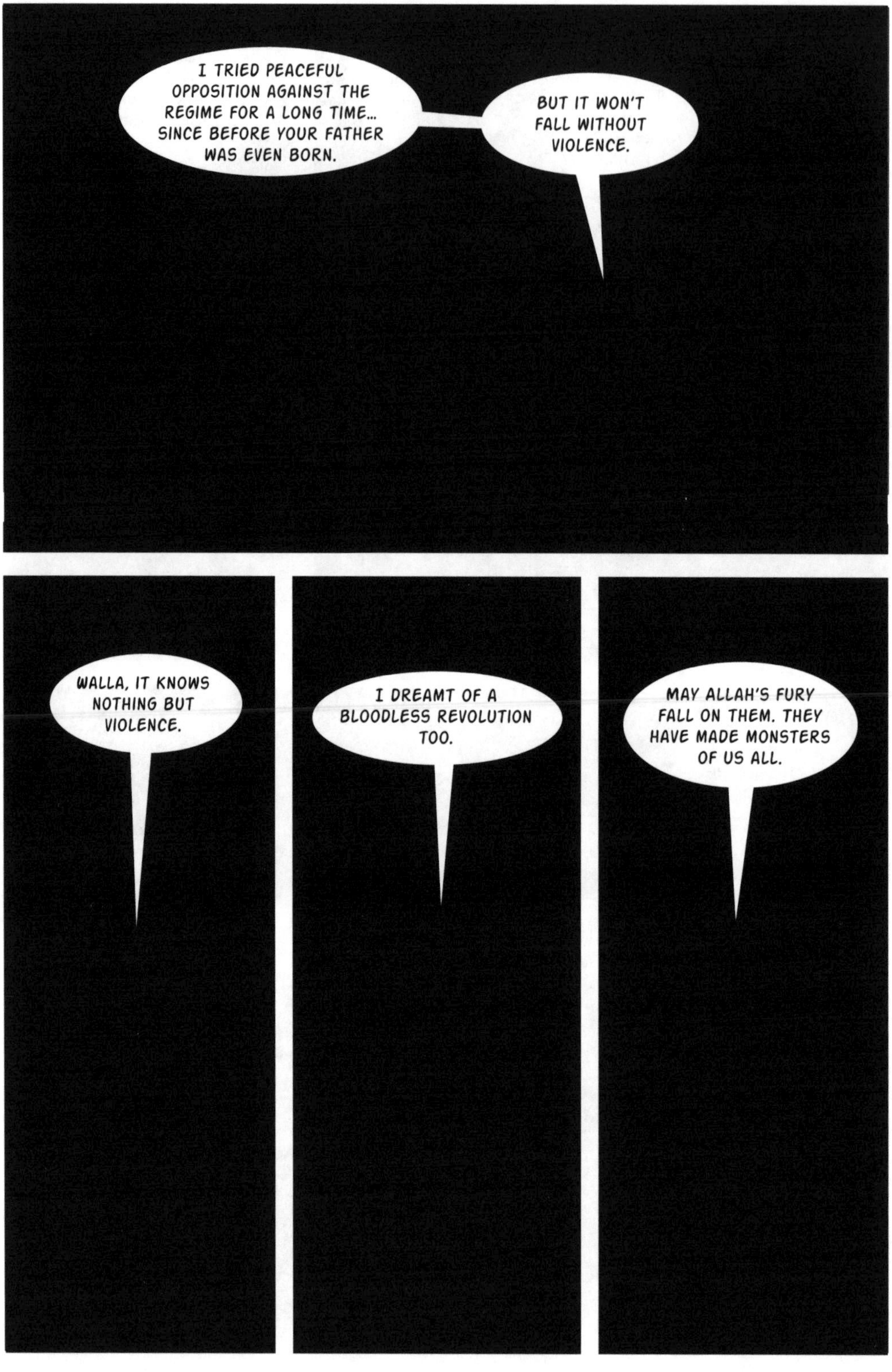
I TRIED PEACEFUL OPPOSITION AGAINST THE REGIME FOR A LONG TIME... SINCE BEFORE YOUR FATHER WAS EVEN BORN.
BUT IT WON'T FALL WITHOUT VIOLENCE.
WALLA, IT KNOWS NOTHING BUT VIOLENCE.
I DREAMT OF A BLOODLESS REVOLUTION TOO.
MAY ALLAH'S FURY FALL ON THEM. THEY HAVE MADE MONSTERS OF US ALL.

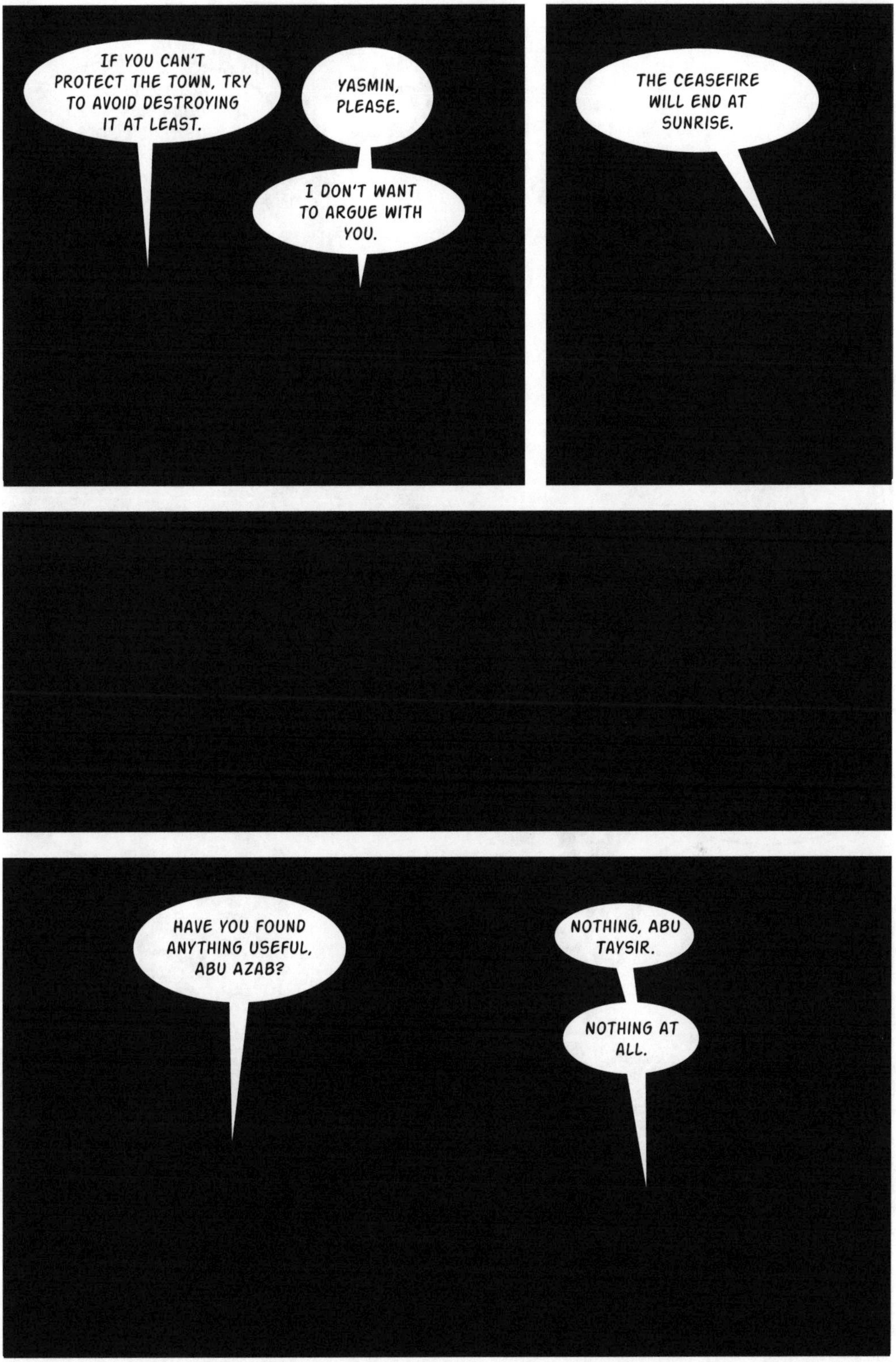
IF YOU CAN'T PROTECT THE TOWN, TRY TO AVOID DESTROYING IT AT LEAST.
YASMIN, PLEASE.
I DON'T WANT TO ARGUE WITH YOU.
THE CEASEFIRE WILL END AT SUNRISE.
HAVE YOU FOUND ANYTHING USEFUL, ABU AZAB?
NOTHING, ABU TAYSIR.
NOTHING AT ALL.

THE NEXT DAY: ANOTHER 219 PEOPLE KILLED.

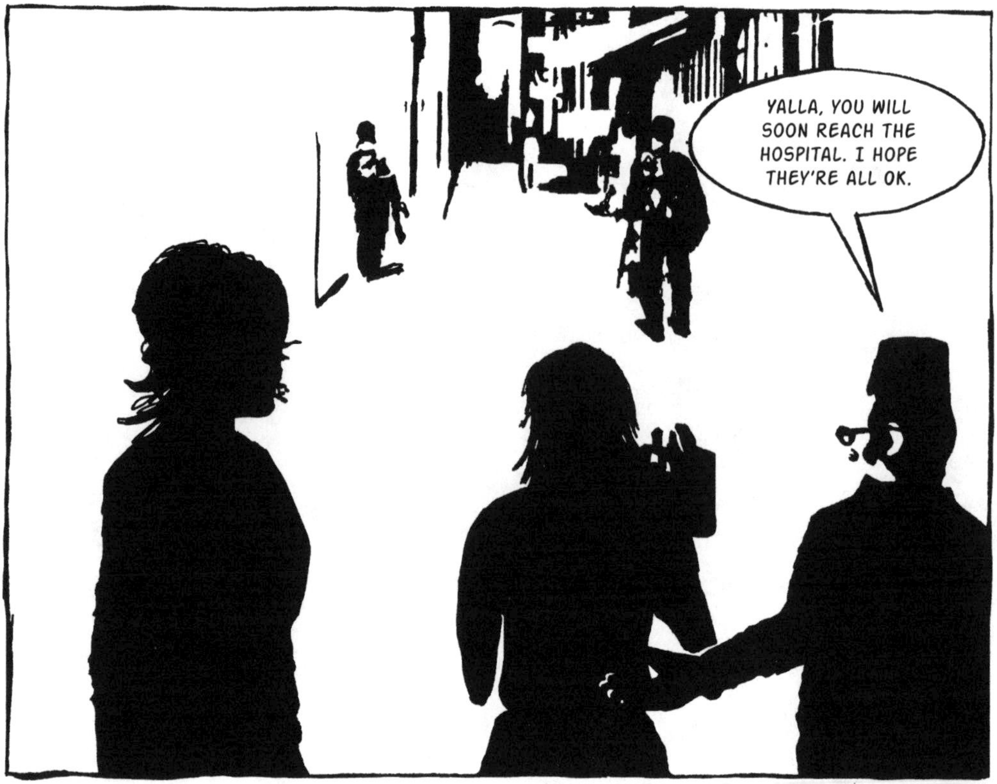
YALLA, YOU WILL SOON REACH THE HOSPITAL. I HOPE THEY'RE ALL OK.

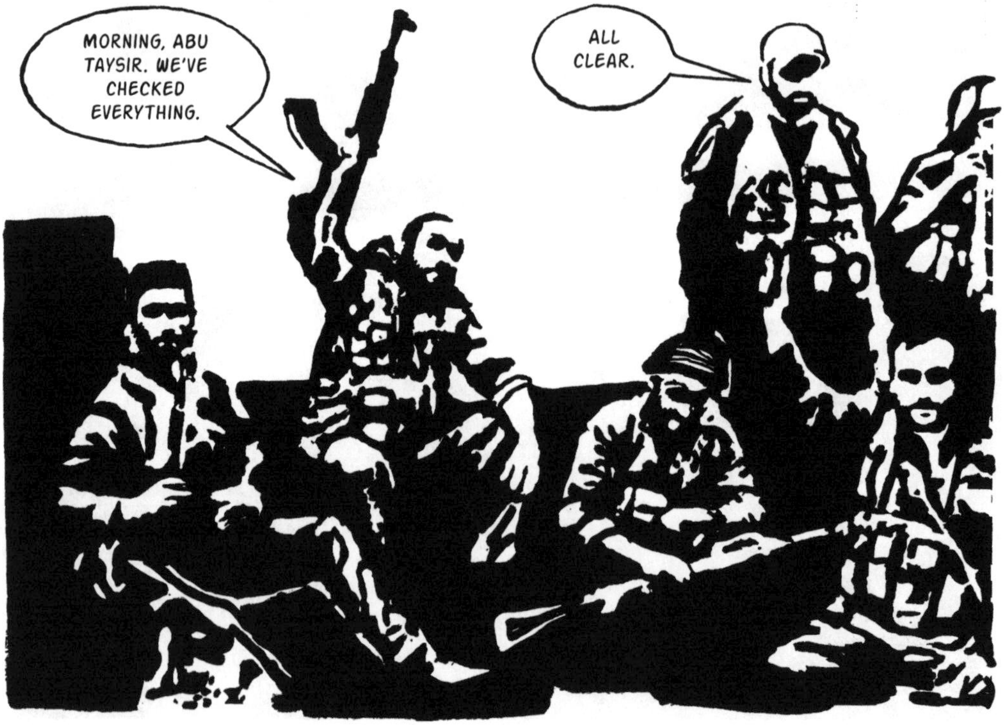
MORNING, ABU TAYSIR. WE'VE CHECKED EVERYTHING.
ALL CLEAR.

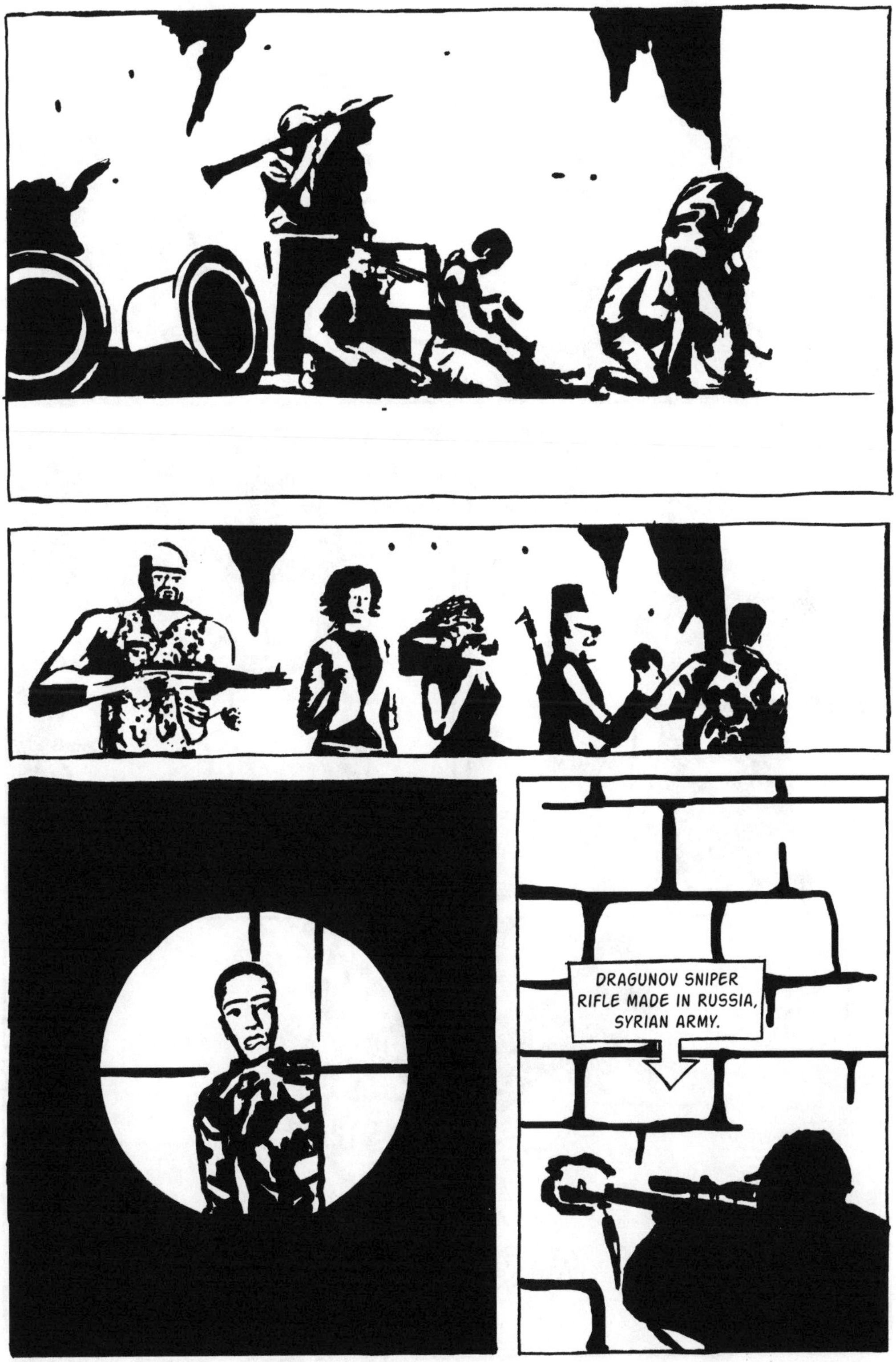
DRAGUNOV SNIPER
RIFLE MADE IN RUSSIA,
SYRIAN ARMY.

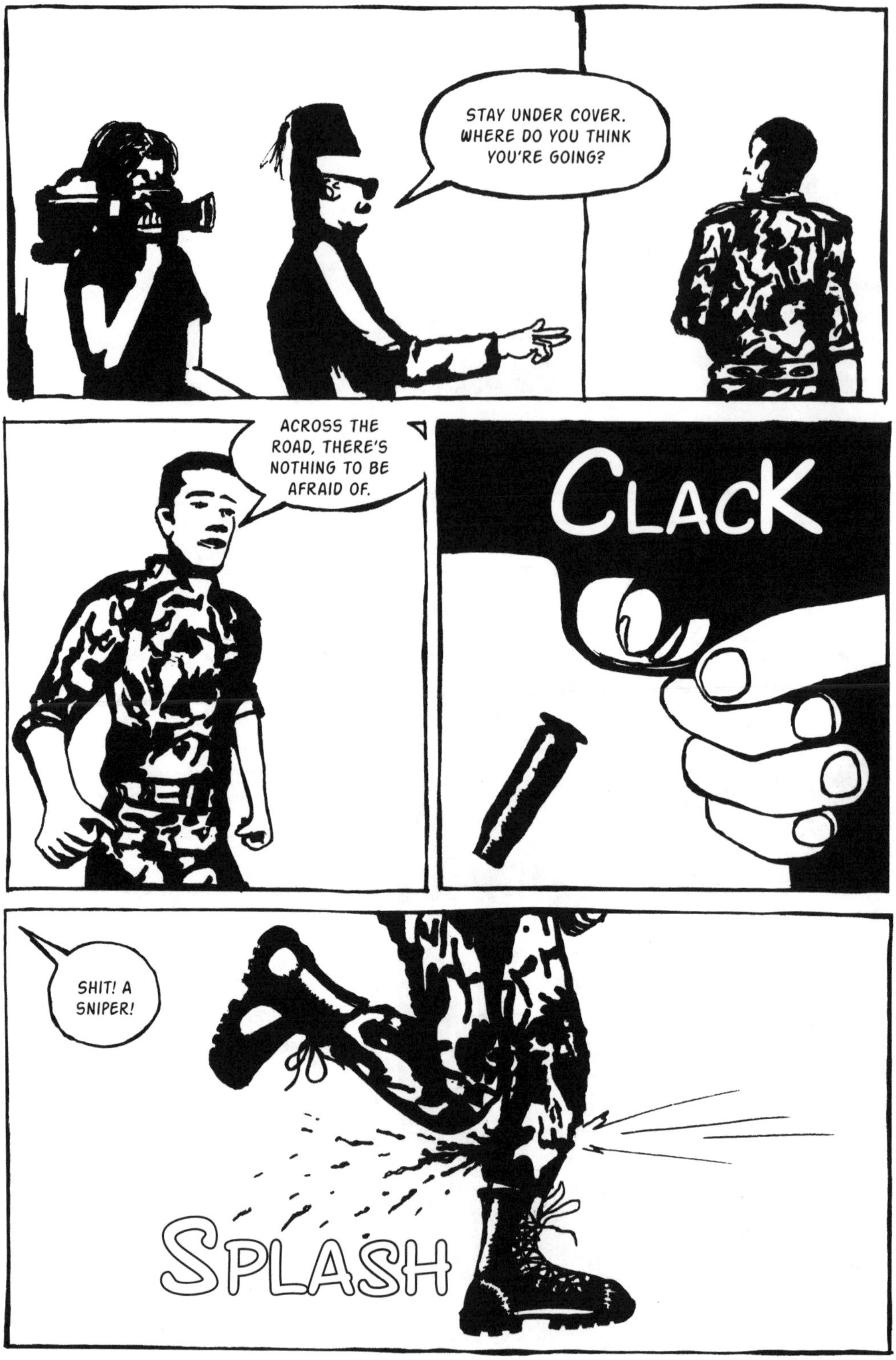
STAY UNDER COVER. WHERE DO YOU THINK YOU'RE GOING?
ACROSS THE ROAD, THERE'S NOTHING TO BE AFRAID OF.
CLACK
SHIT! A SNIPER!
SPLASH

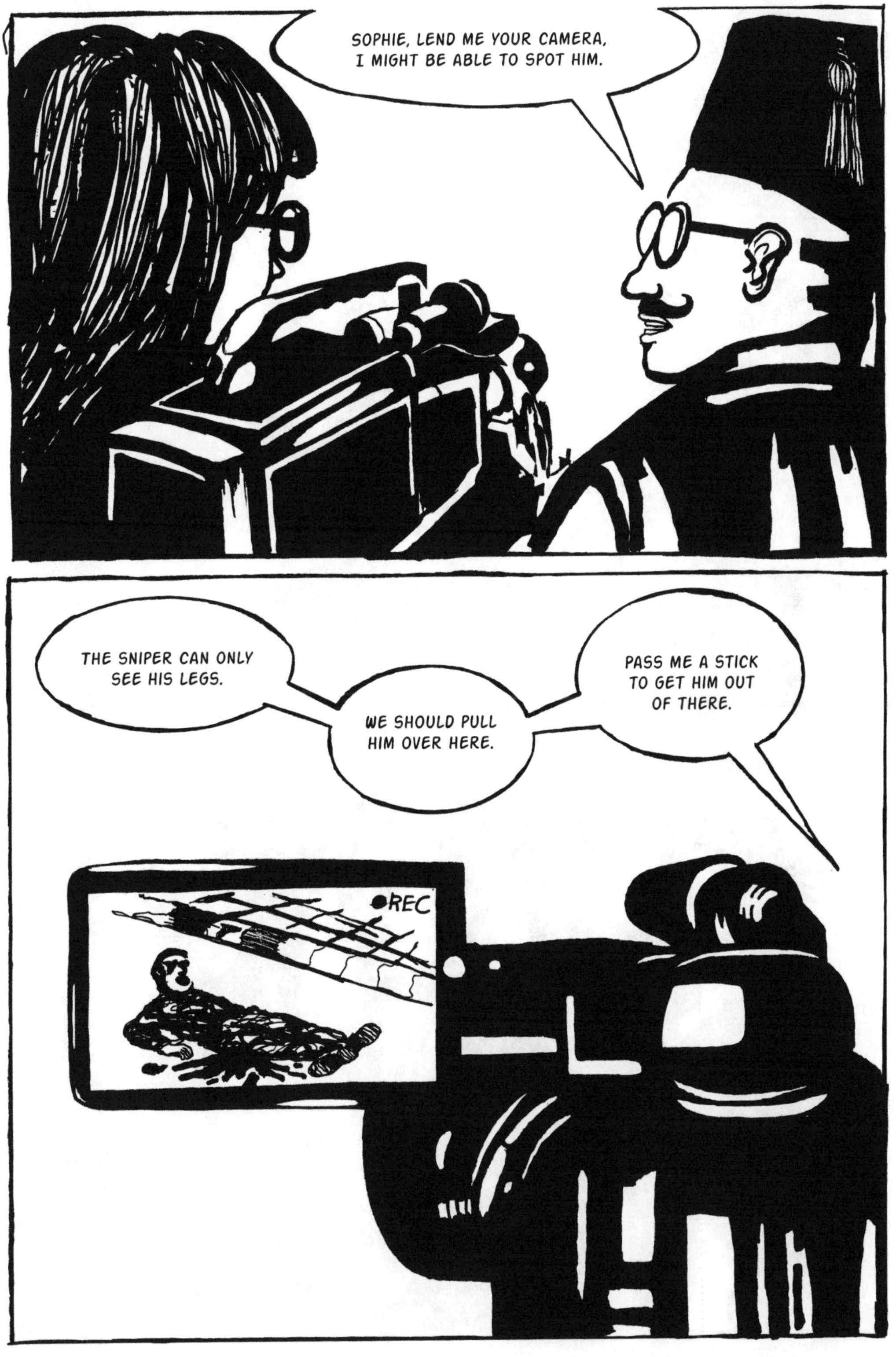
SOPHIE, LEND ME YOUR CAMERA, I MIGHT BE ABLE TO SPOT HIM.
THE SNIPER CAN ONLY SEE HIS LEGS.
WE SHOULD PULL HIM OVER HERE.
PASS ME A STICK TO GET HIM OUT OF THERE.
REC

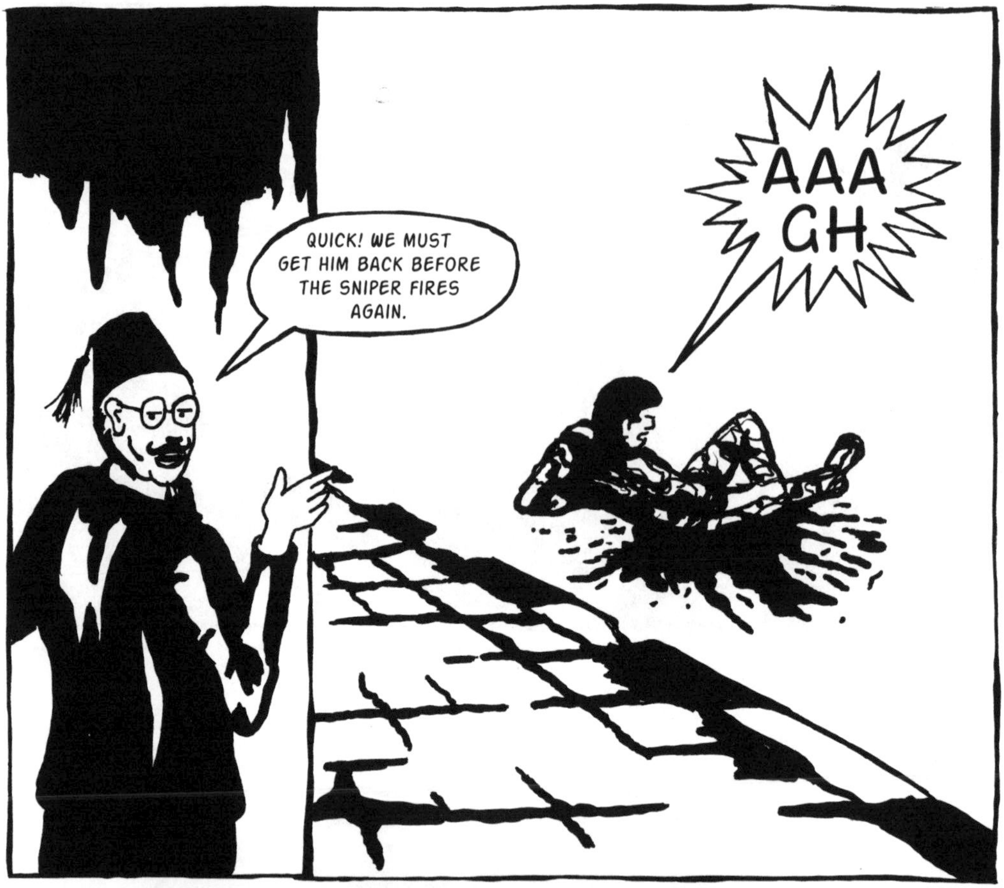
QUICK! WE MUST GET HIM BACK BEFORE THE SNIPER FIRES AGAIN.
AAA GH

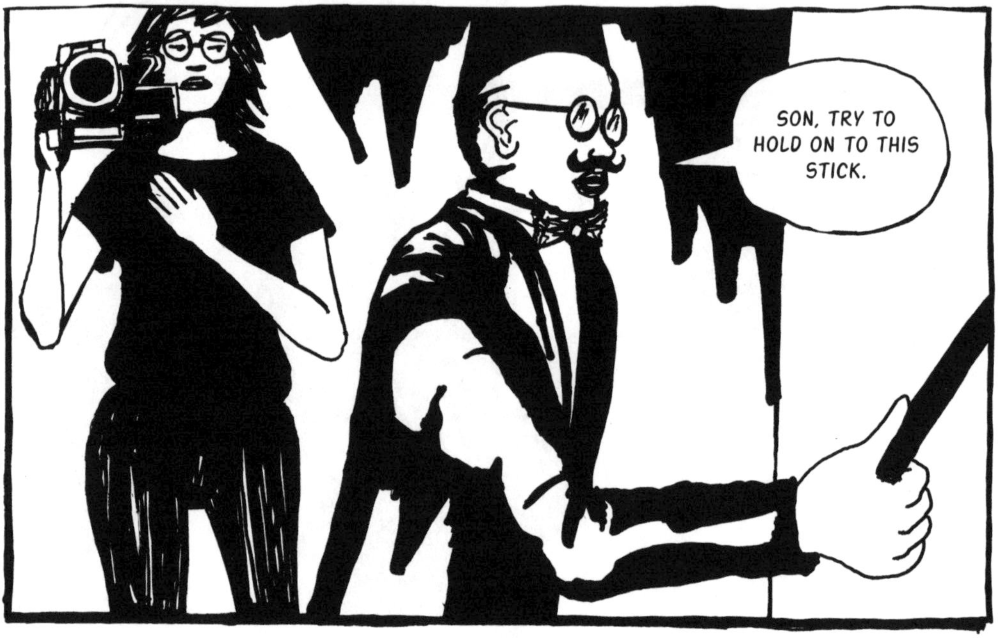
SON, TRY TO HOLD ON TO THIS STICK.

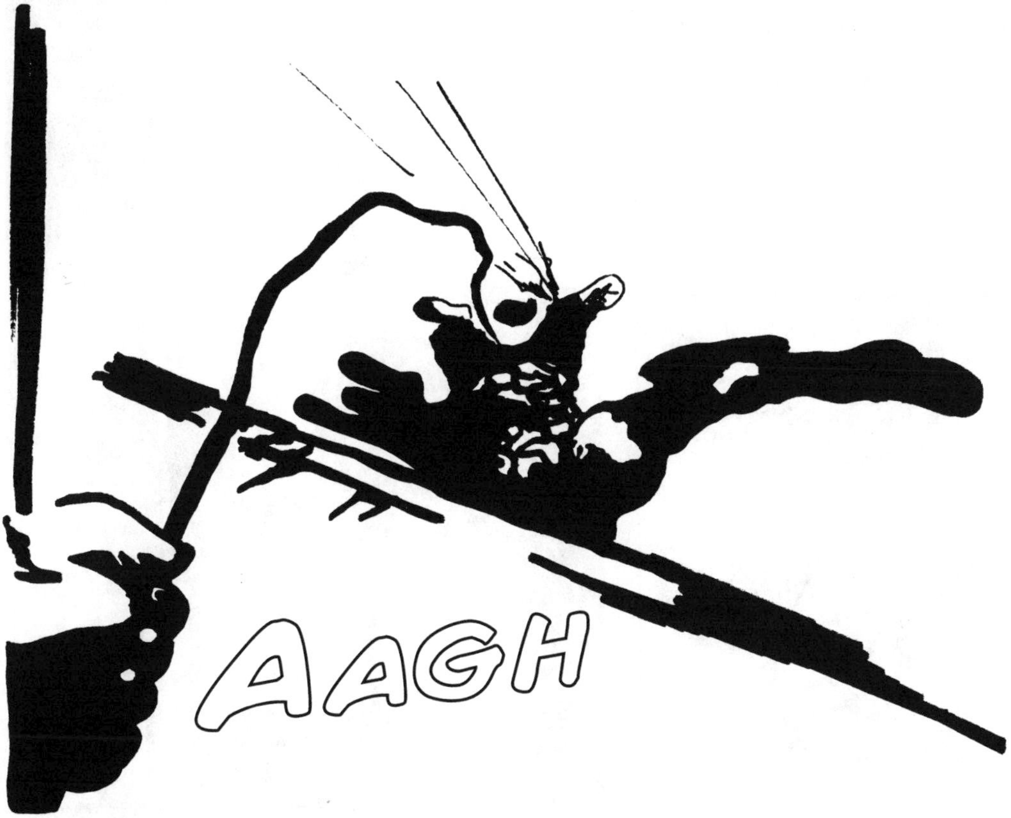
AAGH

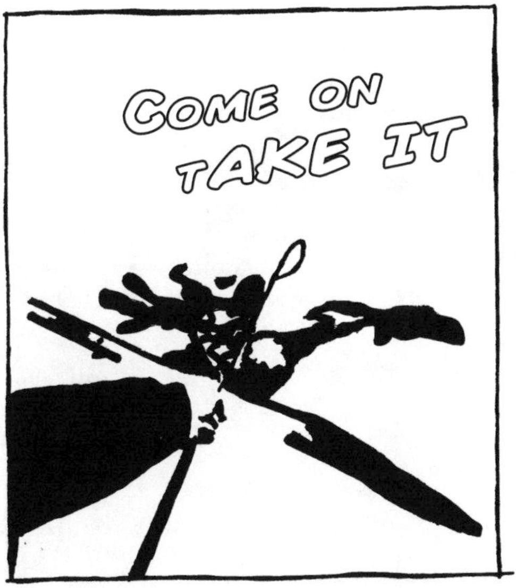
COME ON
TAKE IT

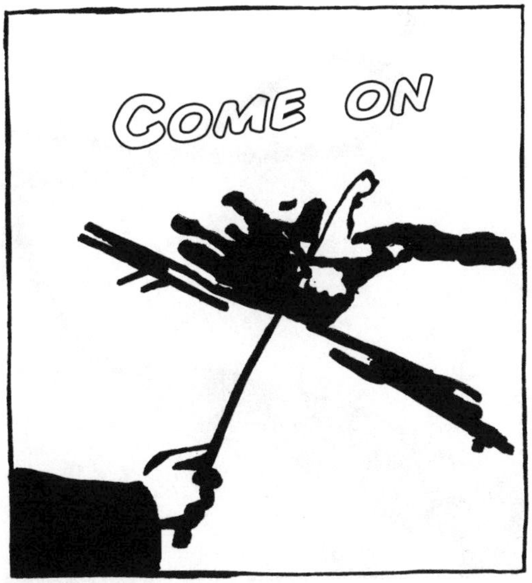
COME ON

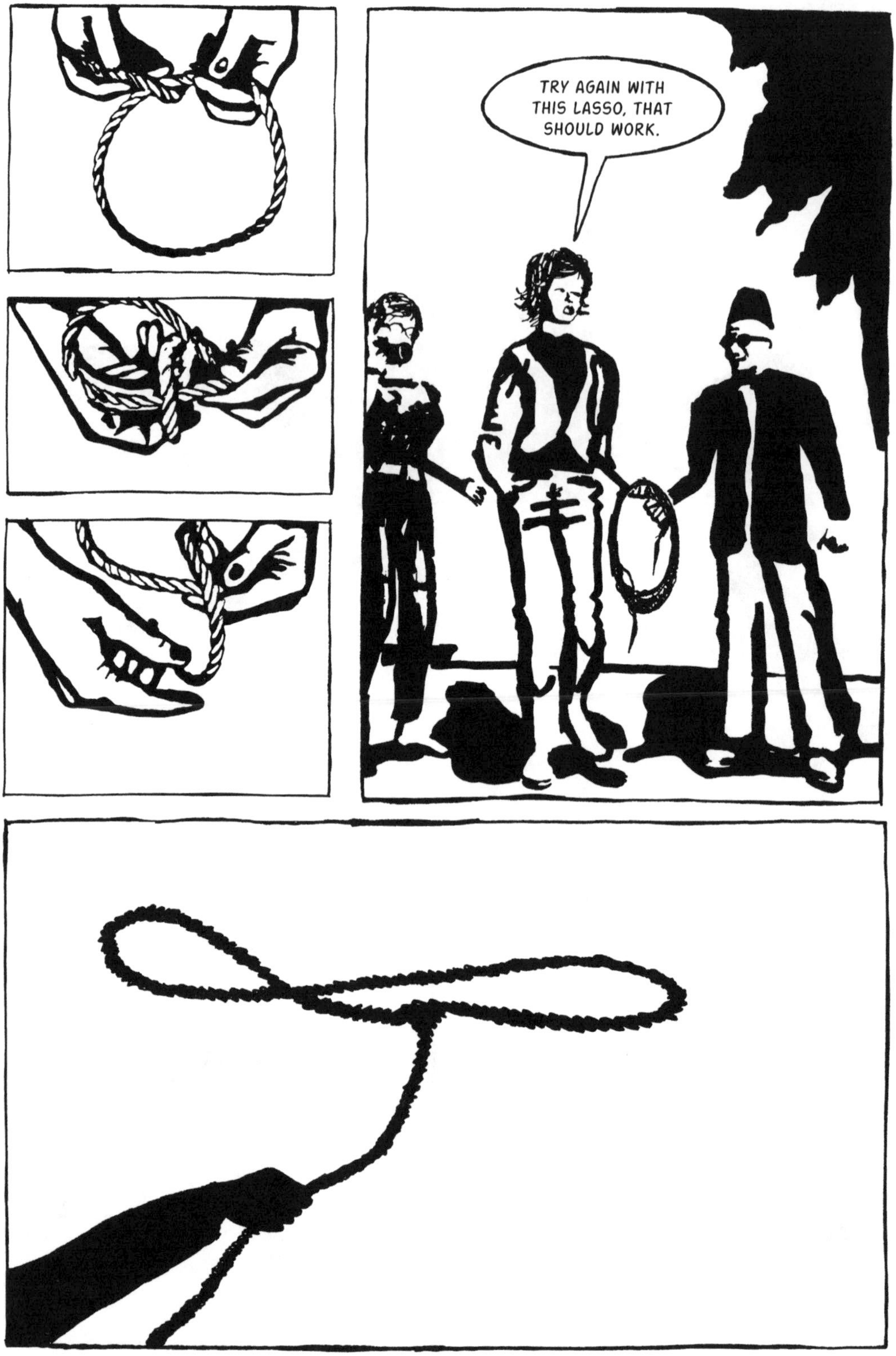
TRY AGAIN WITH
THIS LASSO, THAT
SHOULD WORK.

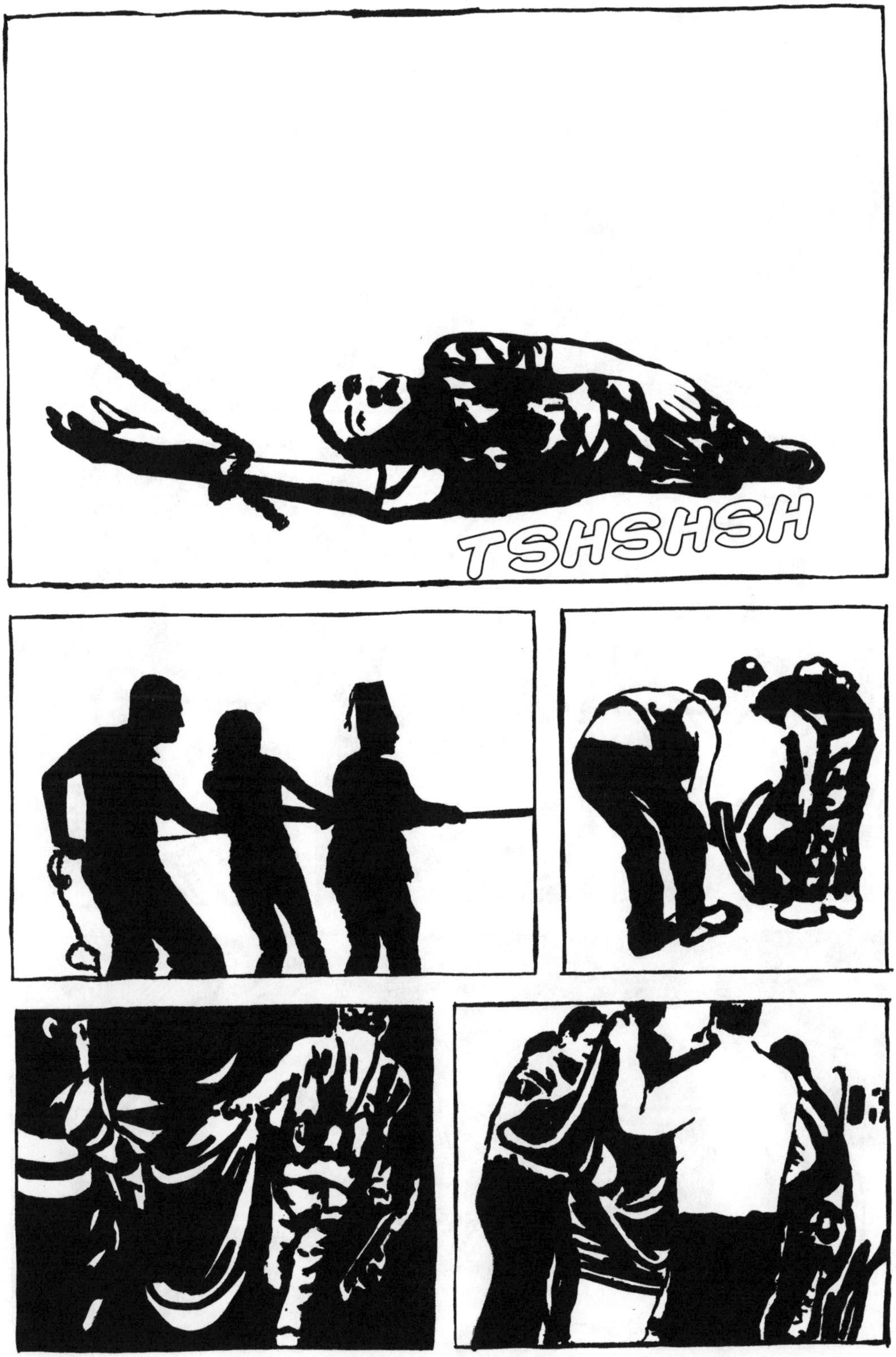
TSHSHSH

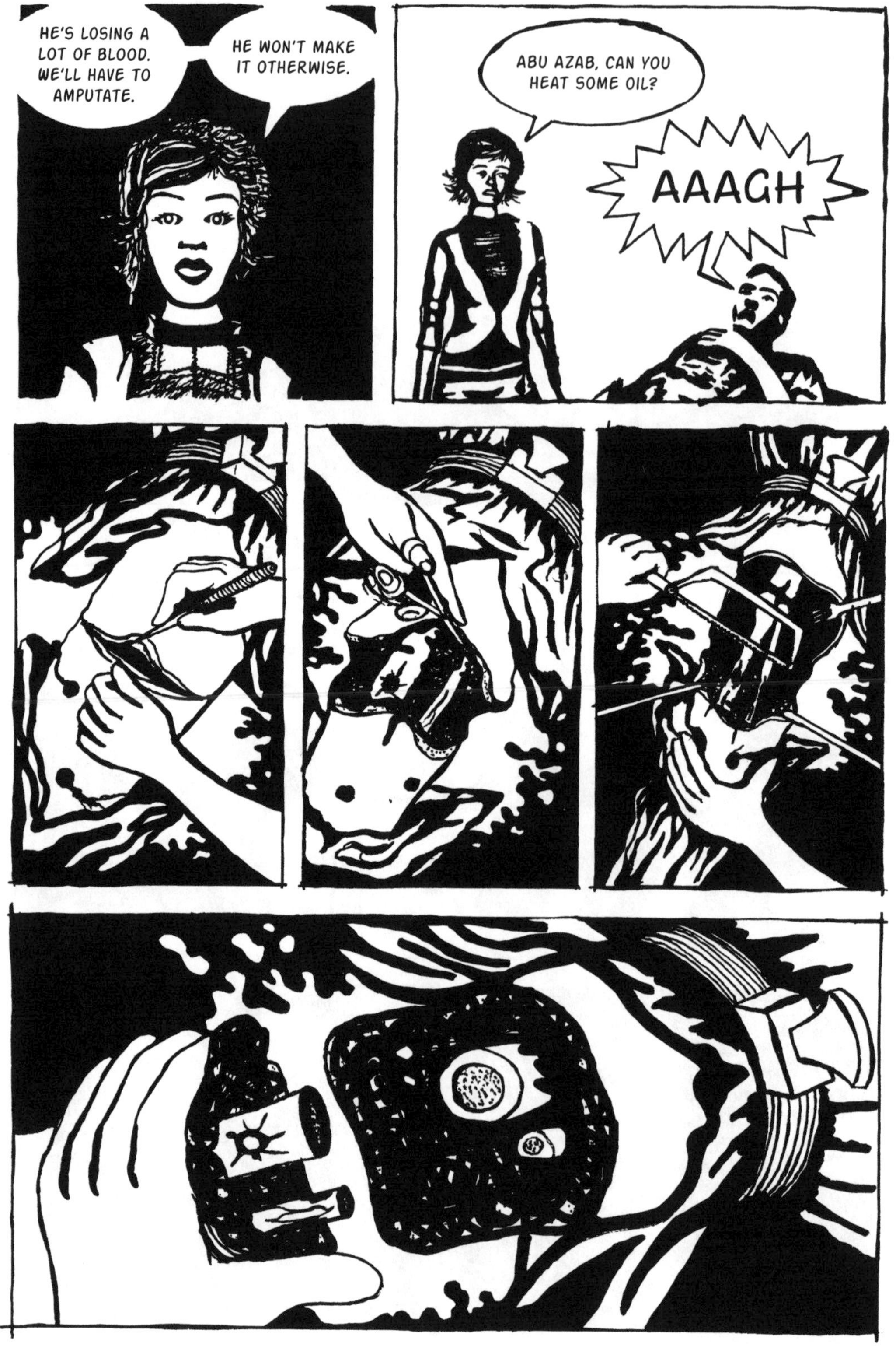
HE'S LOSING A LOT OF BLOOD. WE'LL HAVE TO AMPUTATE.
HE WON'T MAKE IT OTHERWISE.
ABU AZAB, CAN YOU HEAT SOME OIL?
AAAGH

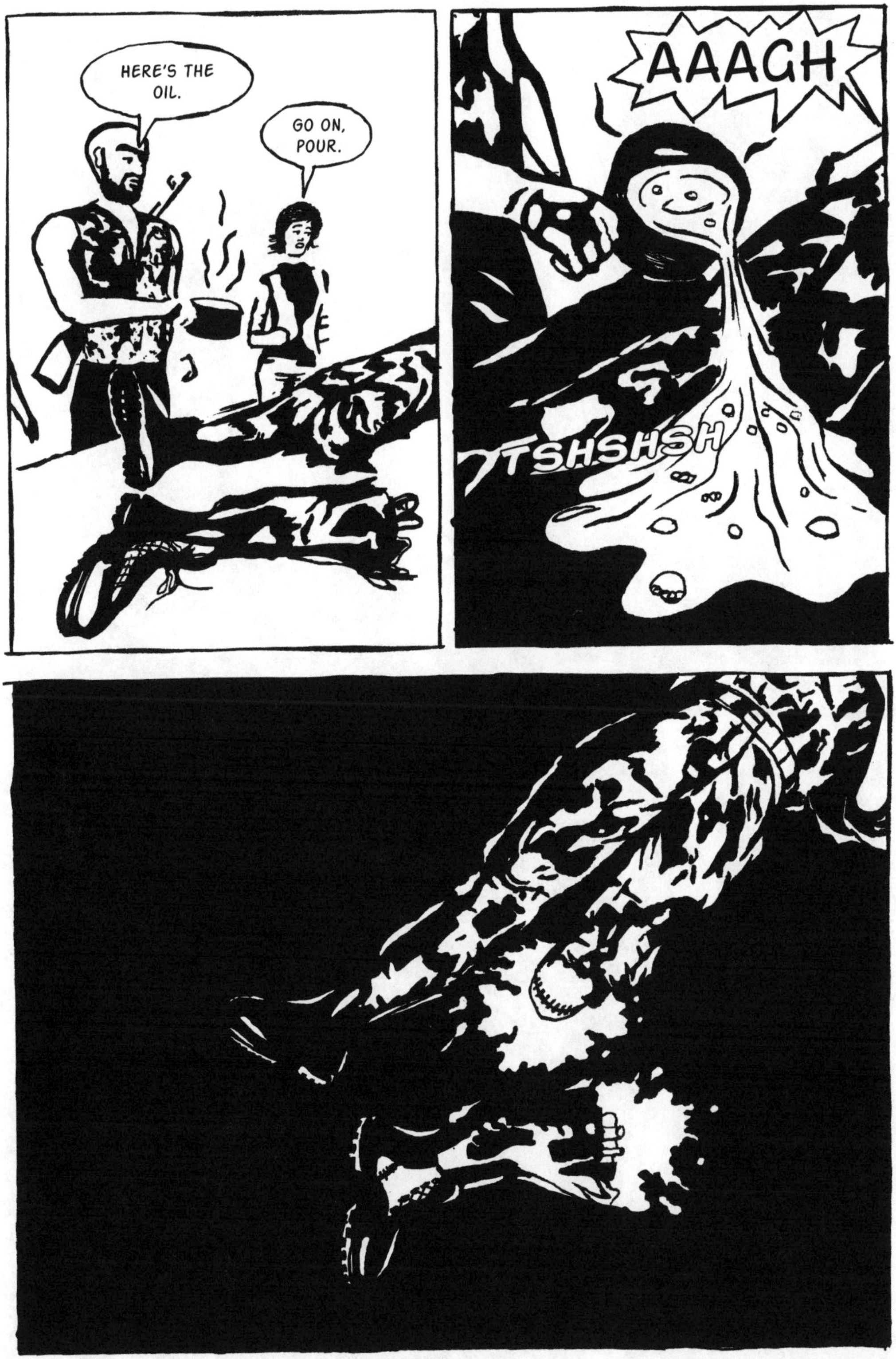
HERE'S THE OIL.
GO ON, POUR.
AAAGH
TSHSHSHSH

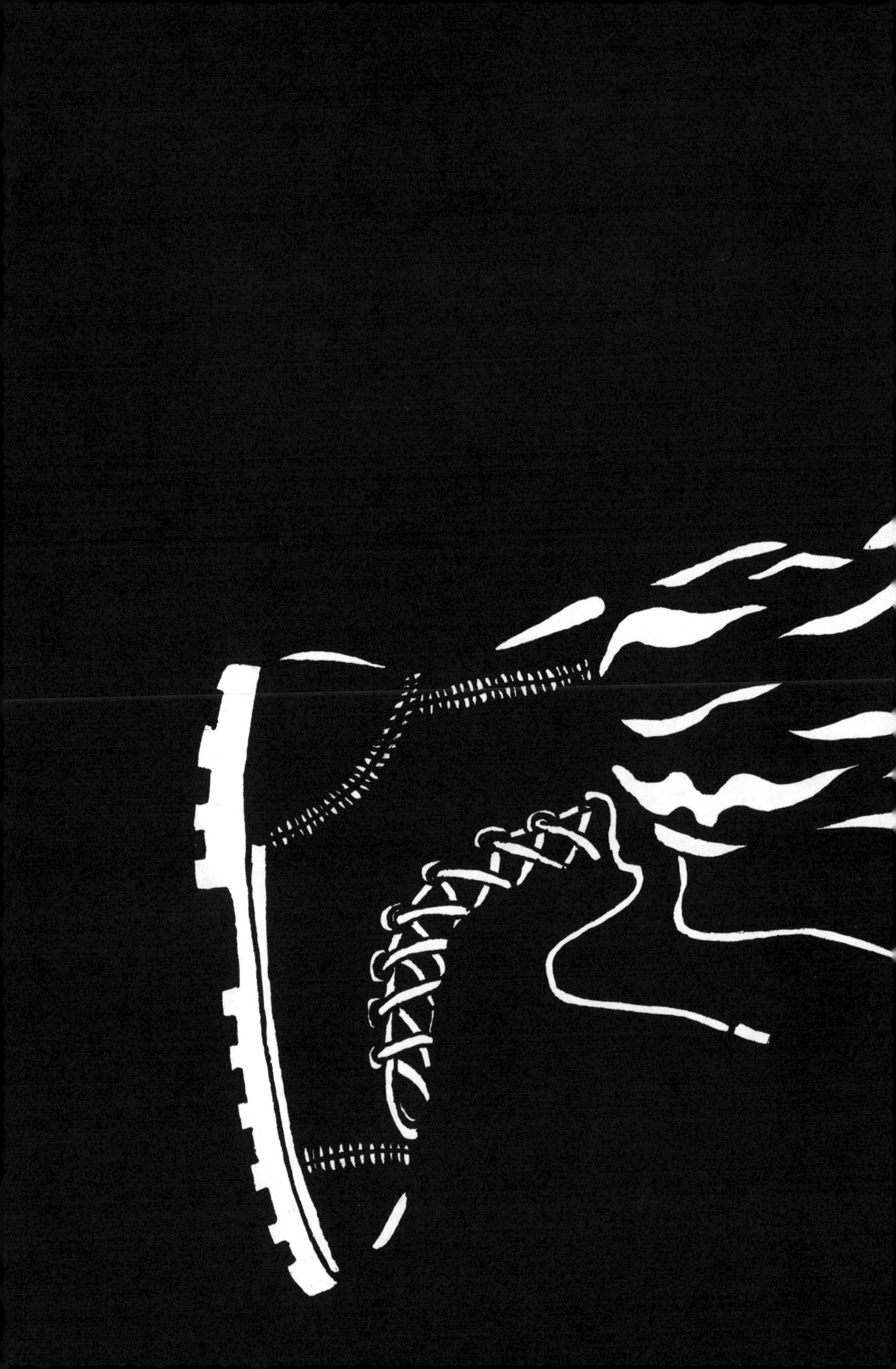

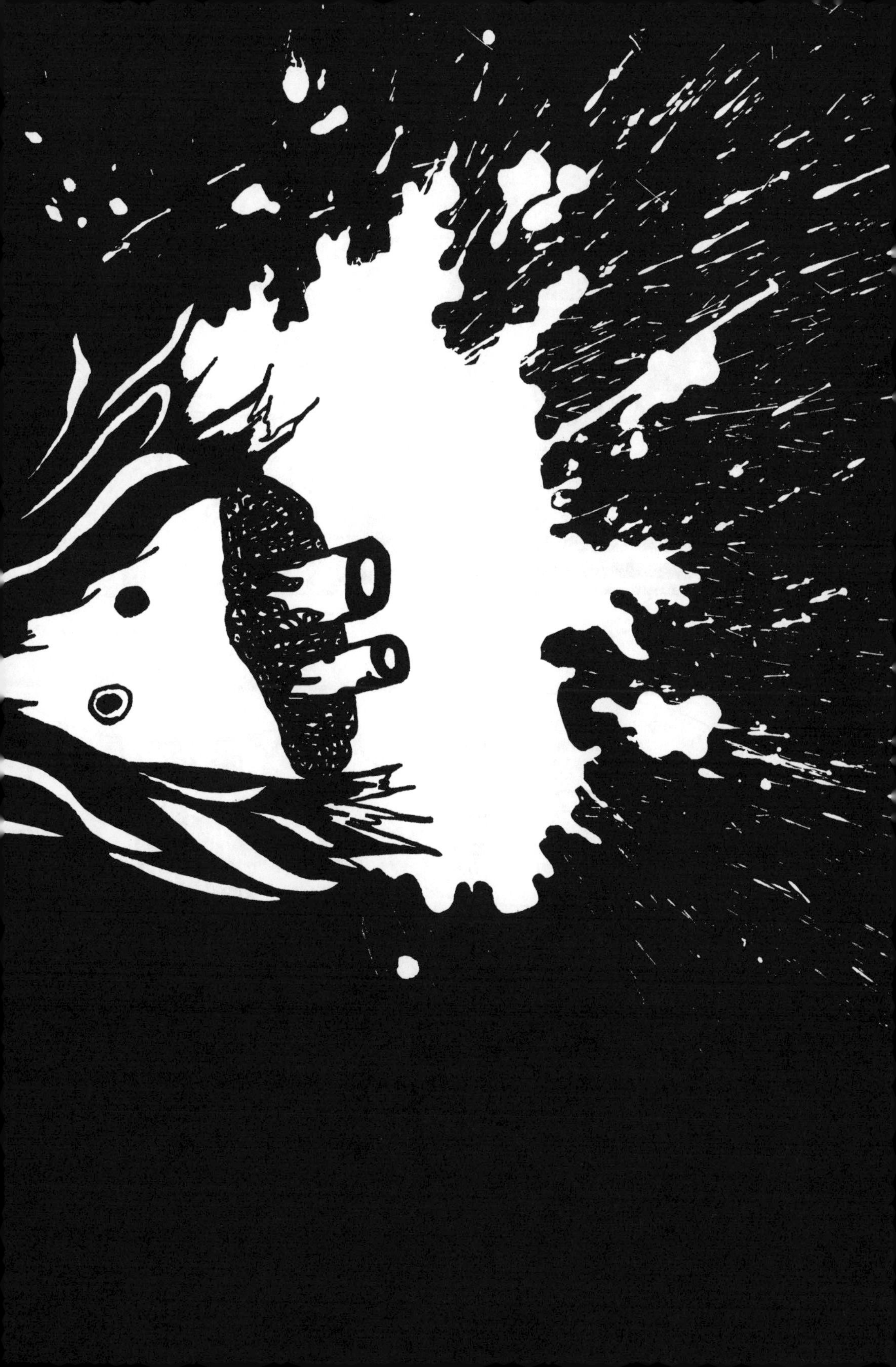

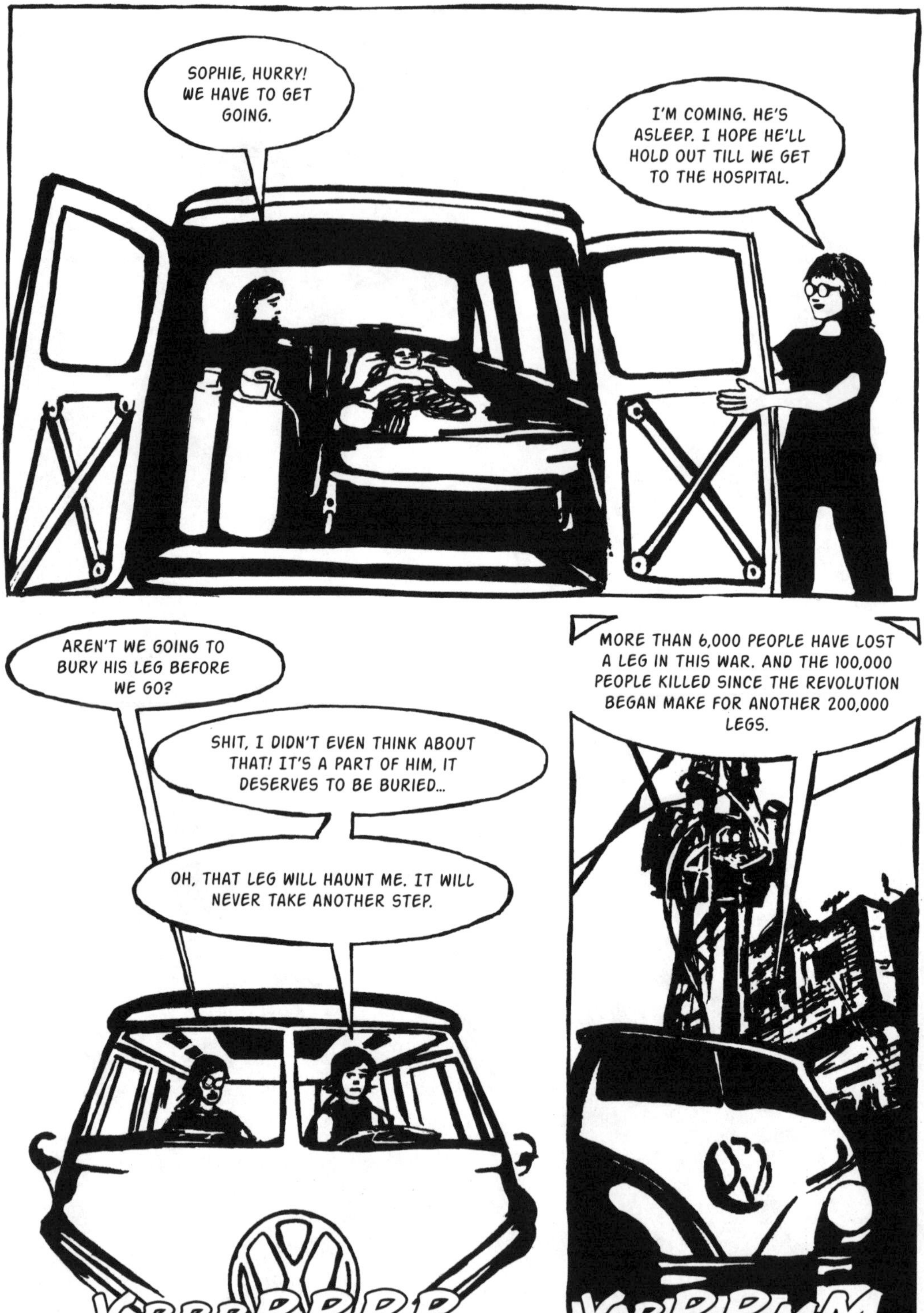
SOPHIE, HURRY! WE HAVE TO GET GOING.
I'M COMING. HE'S ASLEEP. I HOPE HE'LL HOLD OUT TILL WE GET TO THE HOSPITAL.
AREN'T WE GOING TO BURY HIS LEG BEFORE WE GO?
SHIT, I DIDN'T EVEN THINK ABOUT THAT! IT'S A PART OF HIM, IT DESERVES TO BE BURIED...
OH, THAT LEG WILL HAUNT ME. IT WILL NEVER TAKE ANOTHER STEP.
VRRRRRRR
MORE THAN 6,000 PEOPLE HAVE LOST A LEG IN THIS WAR. AND THE 100,000 PEOPLE KILLED SINCE THE REVOLUTION BEGAN MAKE FOR ANOTHER 200,000 LEGS.
VRRRRMM

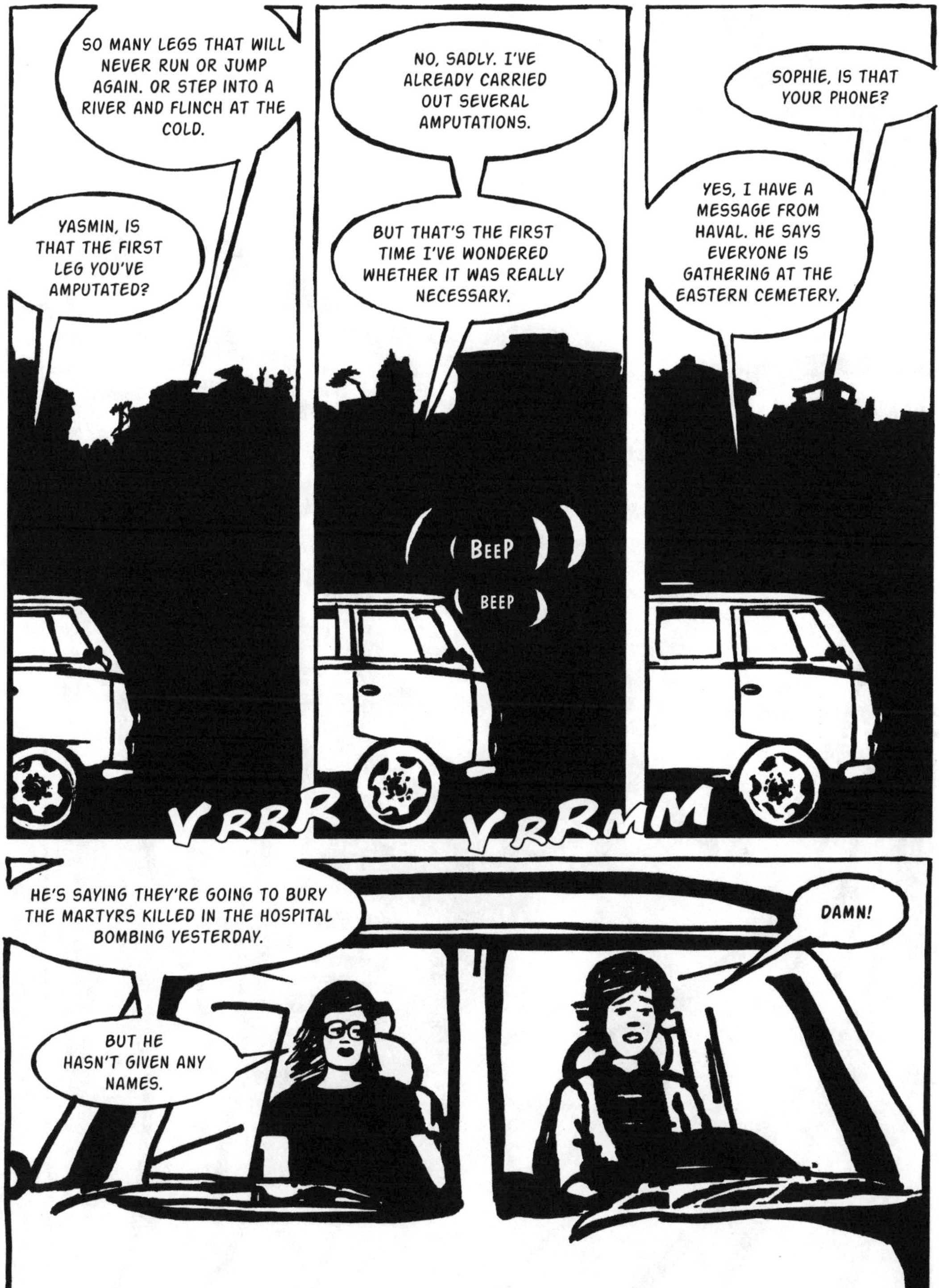
SO MANY LEGS THAT WILL NEVER RUN OR JUMP AGAIN. OR STEP INTO A RIVER AND FLINCH AT THE COLD.
YASMIN, IS THAT THE FIRST LEG YOU'VE AMPUTATED?
NO, SADLY. I'VE ALREADY CARRIED OUT SEVERAL AMPUTATIONS.
BUT THAT'S THE FIRST TIME I'VE WONDERED WHETHER IT WAS REALLY NECESSARY.
BEEP
BEEP
SOPHIE, IS THAT YOUR PHONE?
YES, I HAVE A MESSAGE FROM HAVAL. HE SAYS EVERYONE IS GATHERING AT THE EASTERN CEMETERY.
VRRR
VRRMM
HE'S SAYING THEY'RE GOING TO BURY THE MARTYRS KILLED IN THE HOSPITAL BOMBING YESTERDAY.
BUT HE HASN'T GIVEN ANY NAMES.
DAMN!

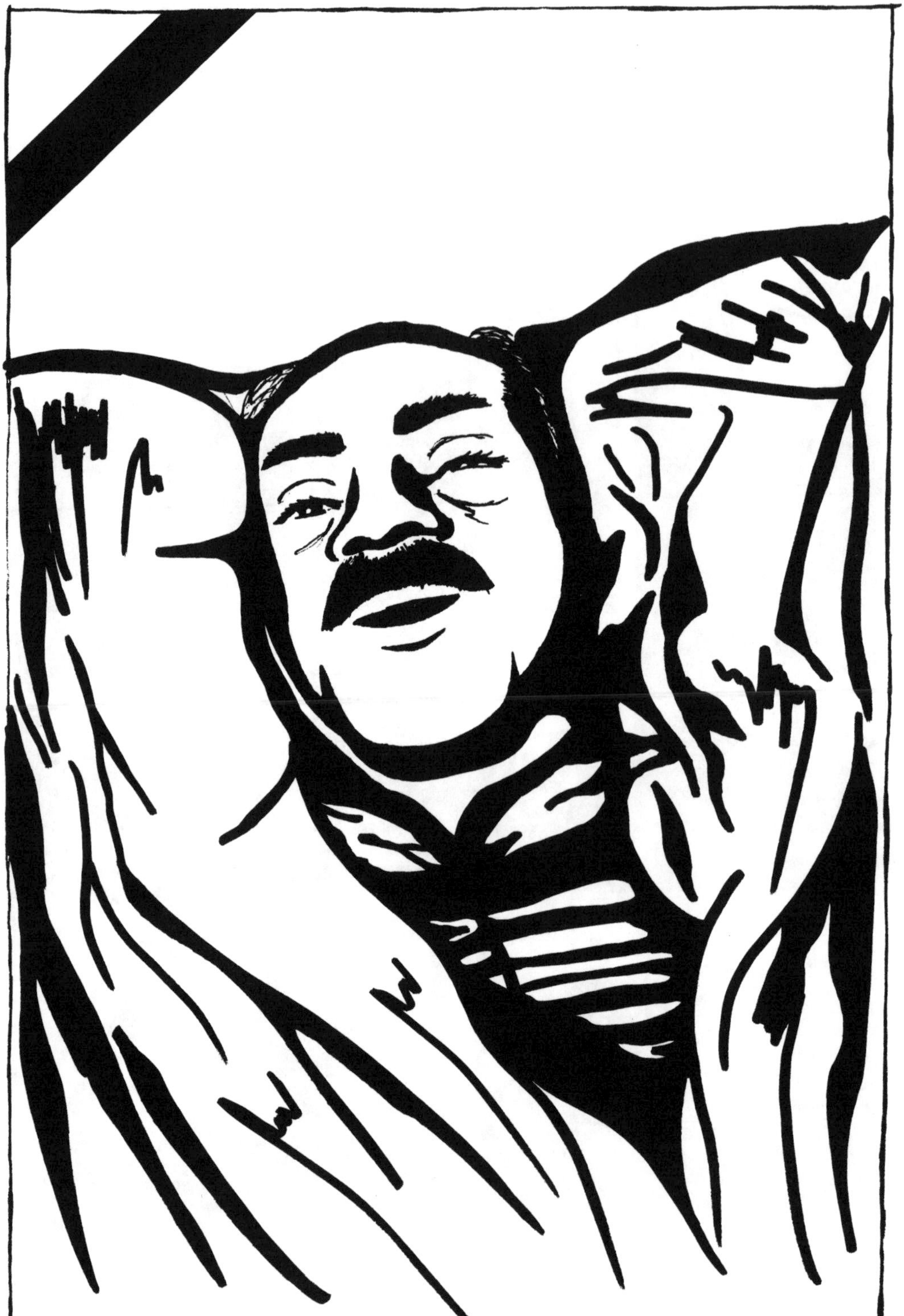

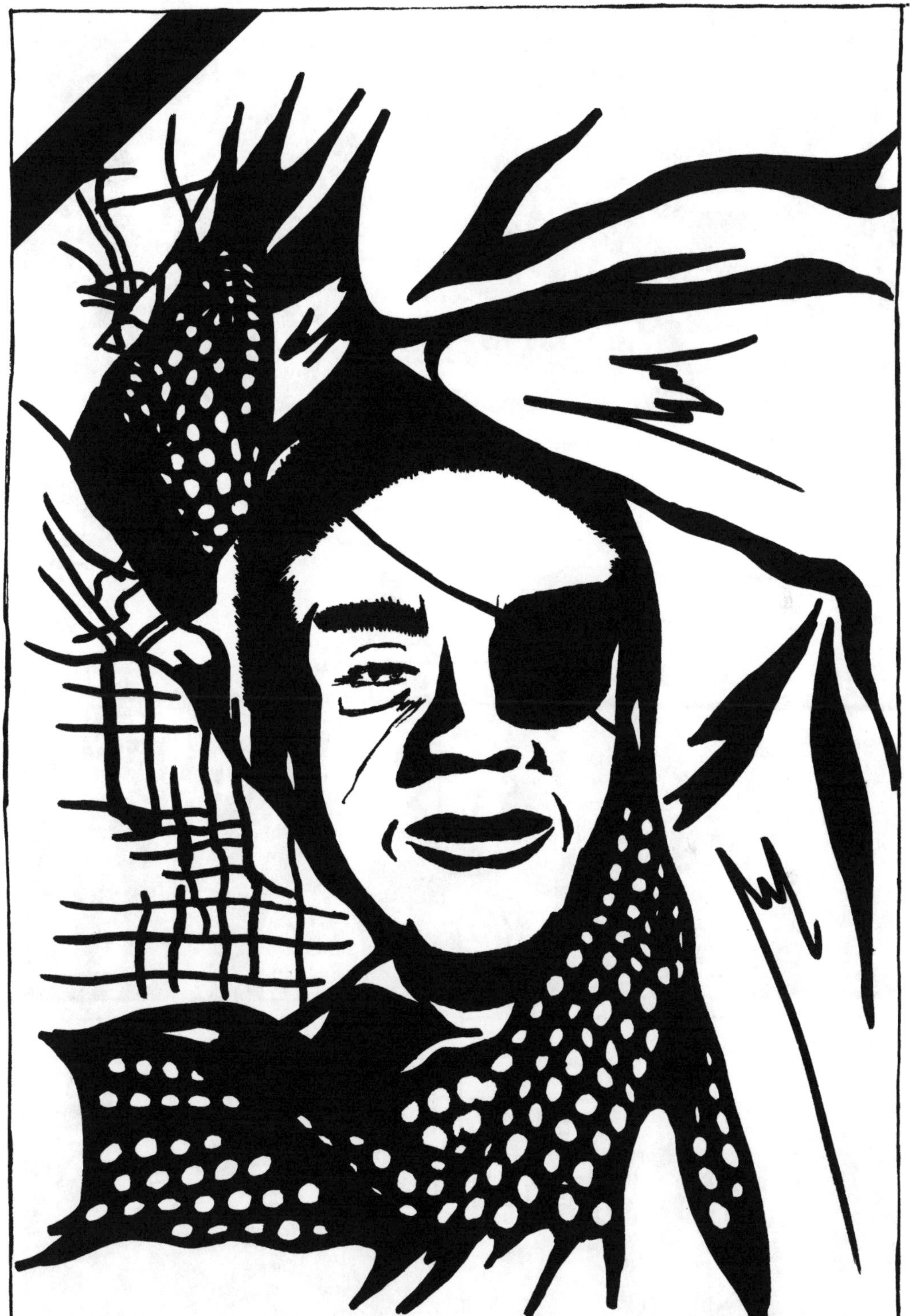

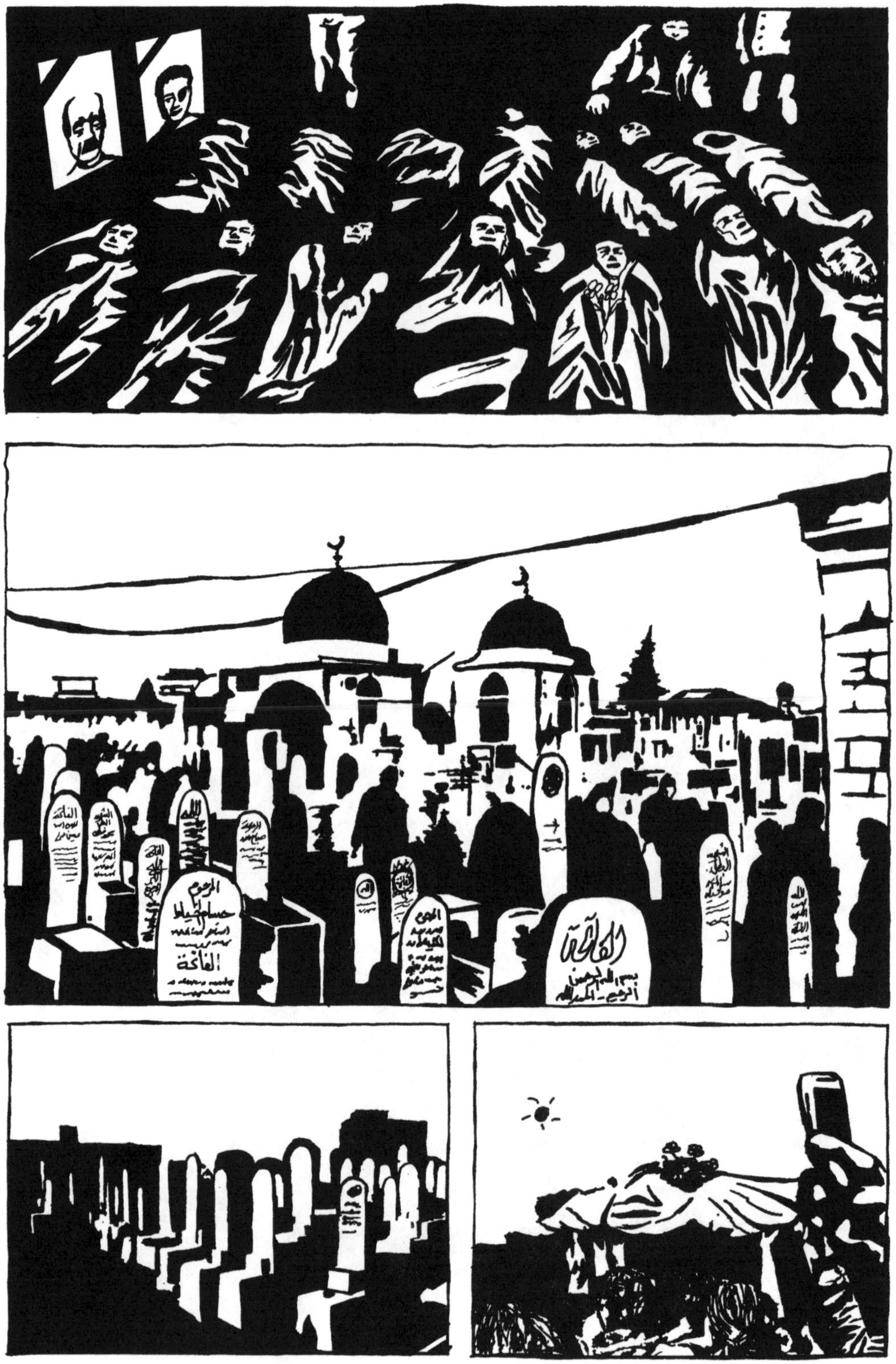
الفاتحة

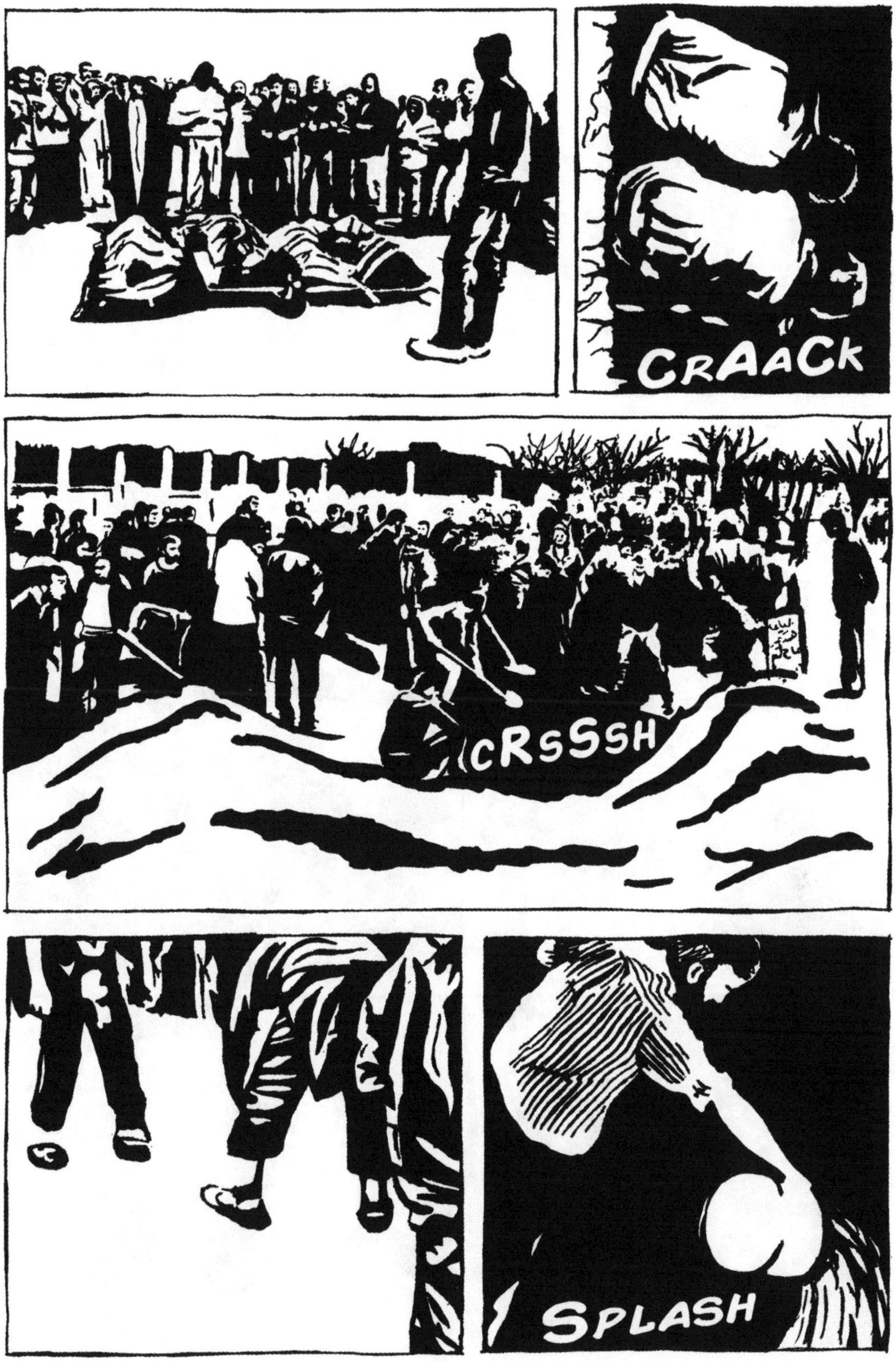
CRAACK
CRSSSH
SPLASH

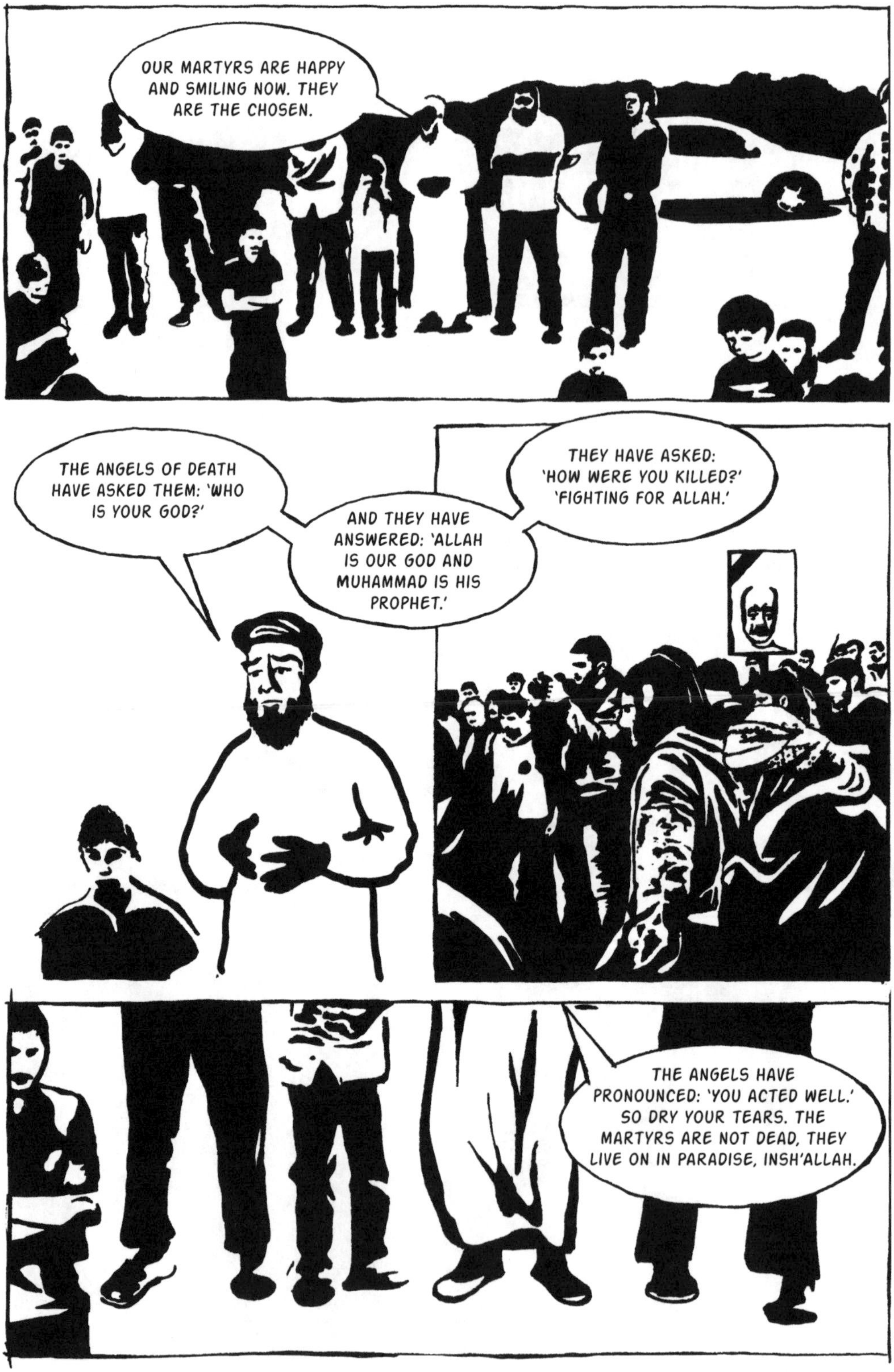
OUR MARTYRS ARE HAPPY AND SMILING NOW. THEY ARE THE CHOSEN.
THE ANGELS OF DEATH HAVE ASKED THEM: 'WHO IS YOUR GOD?'
AND THEY HAVE ANSWERED: 'ALLAH IS OUR GOD AND MUHAMMAD IS HIS PROPHET.'
THEY HAVE ASKED: 'HOW WERE YOU KILLED?' 'FIGHTING FOR ALLAH.'
THE ANGELS HAVE PRONOUNCED: 'YOU ACTED WELL.' SO DRY YOUR TEARS. THE MARTYRS ARE NOT DEAD, THEY LIVE ON IN PARADISE, INSH'ALLAH.

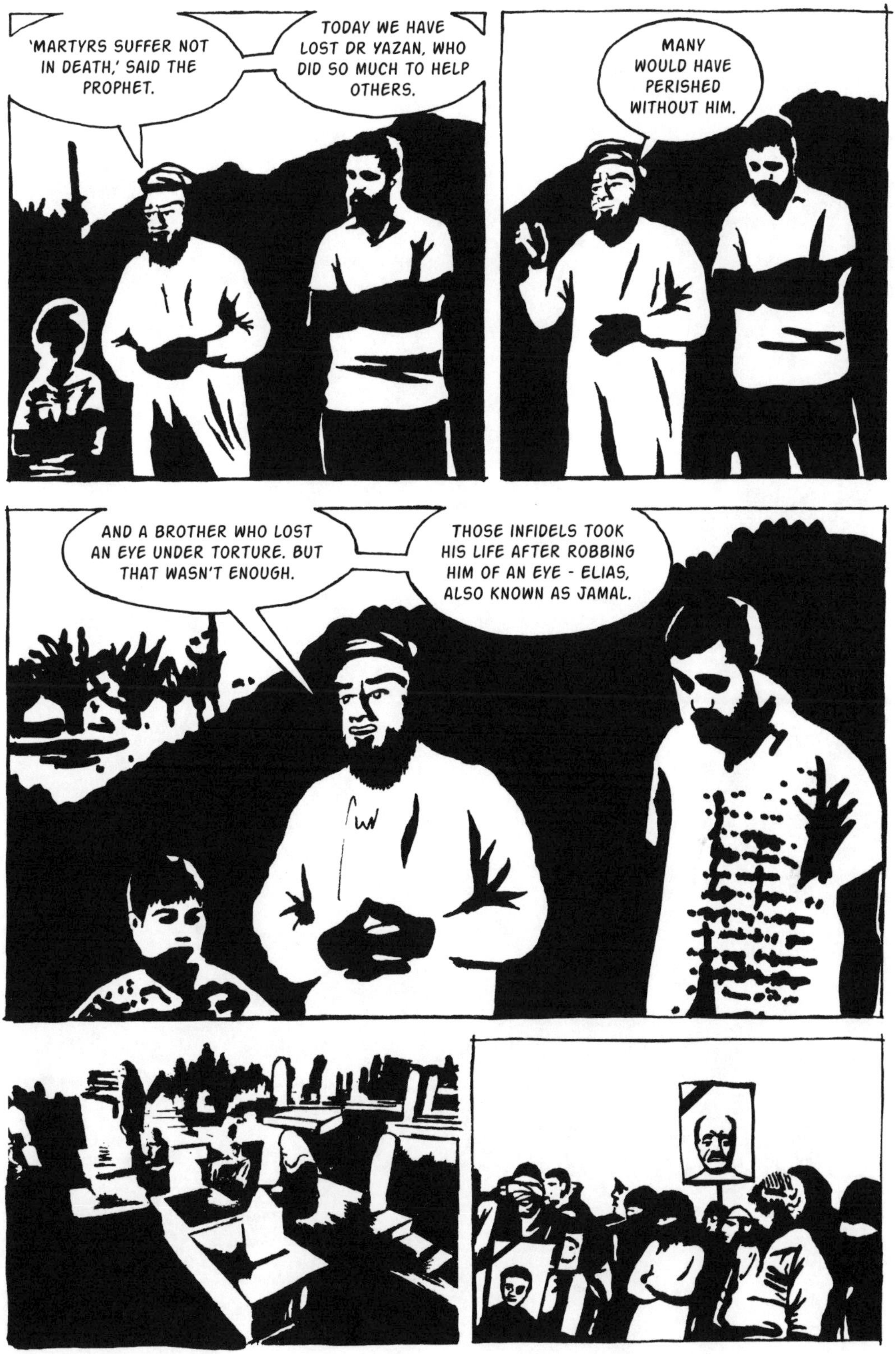
'MARTYRS SUFFER NOT IN DEATH,' SAID THE PROPHET.
TODAY WE HAVE LOST DR YAZAN, WHO DID SO MUCH TO HELP OTHERS.
MANY WOULD HAVE PERISHED WITHOUT HIM.
AND A BROTHER WHO LOST AN EYE UNDER TORTURE. BUT THAT WASN'T ENOUGH.
THOSE INFIDELS TOOK HIS LIFE AFTER ROBBING HIM OF AN EYE - ELIAS, ALSO KNOWN AS JAMAL.

Chapter 3

AUTUMN

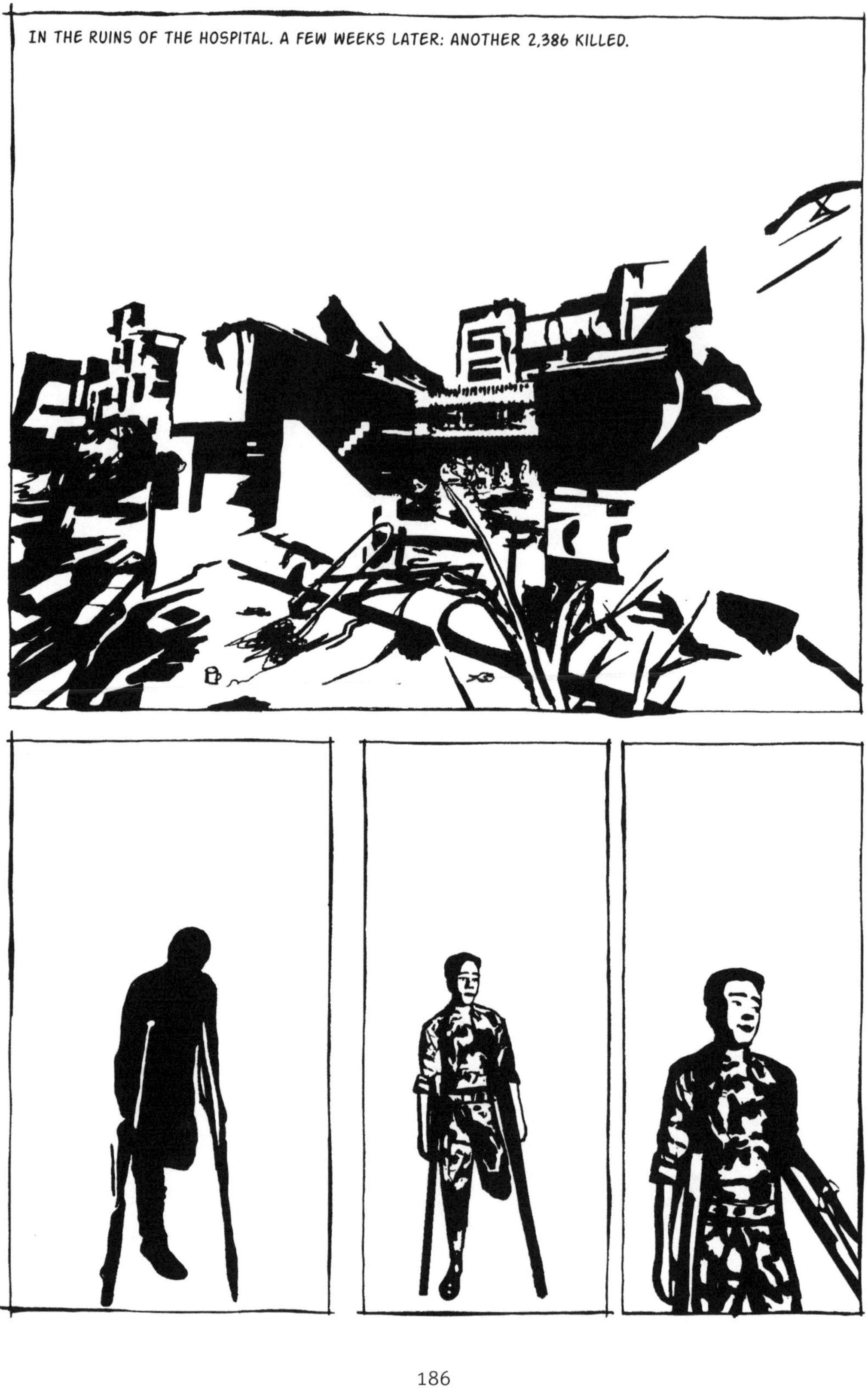
IN THE RUINS OF THE HOSPITAL. A FEW WEEKS LATER: ANOTHER 2,386 KILLED.

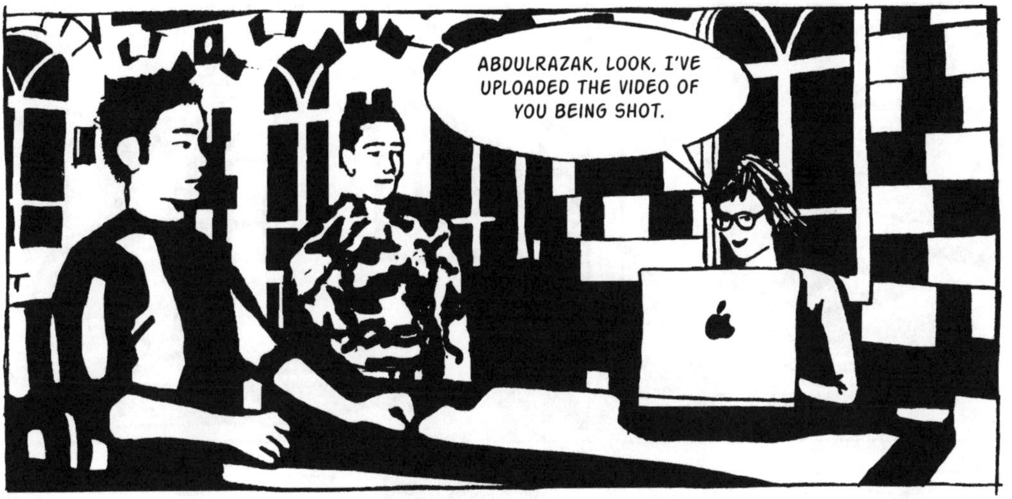
ABDULRAZAK, LOOK, I'VE UPLOADED THE VIDEO OF YOU BEING SHOT.

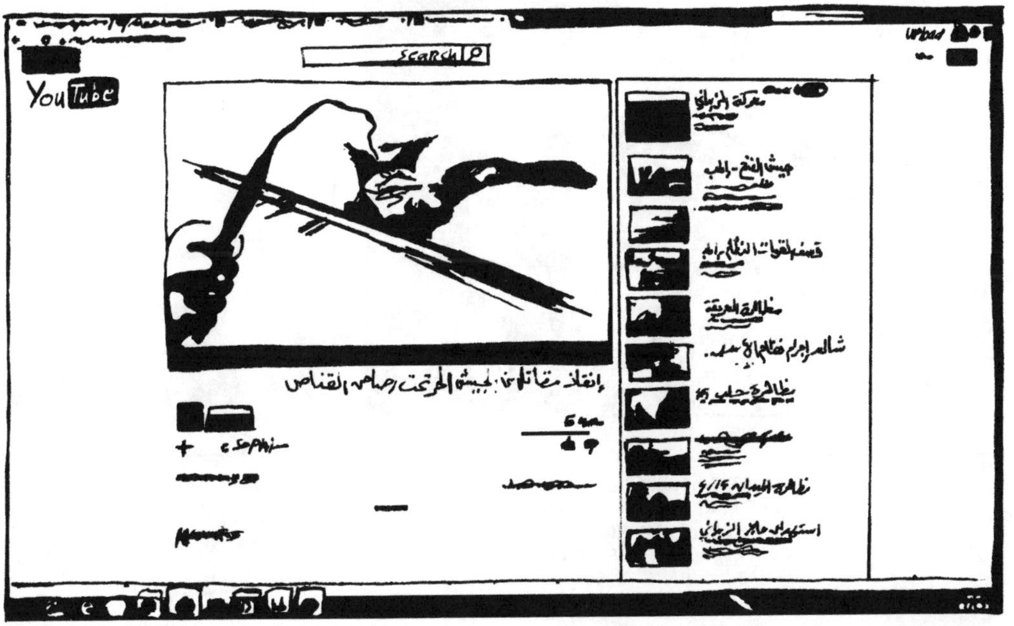
YouTube
SEARCH
إنقاذ مقاتل من الجيش الحر تحت رصاص القناص

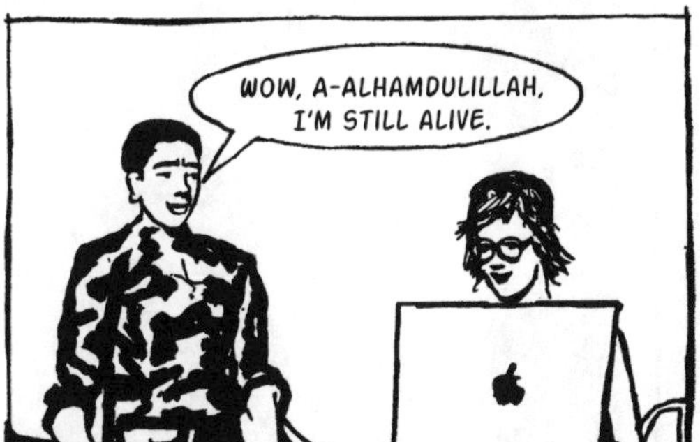
WOW, A-ALHAMDULILLAH, I'M STILL ALIVE.

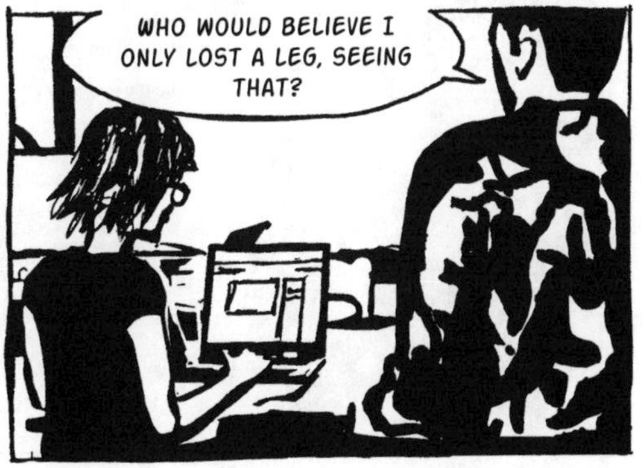
WHO WOULD BELIEVE I ONLY LOST A LEG, SEEING THAT?

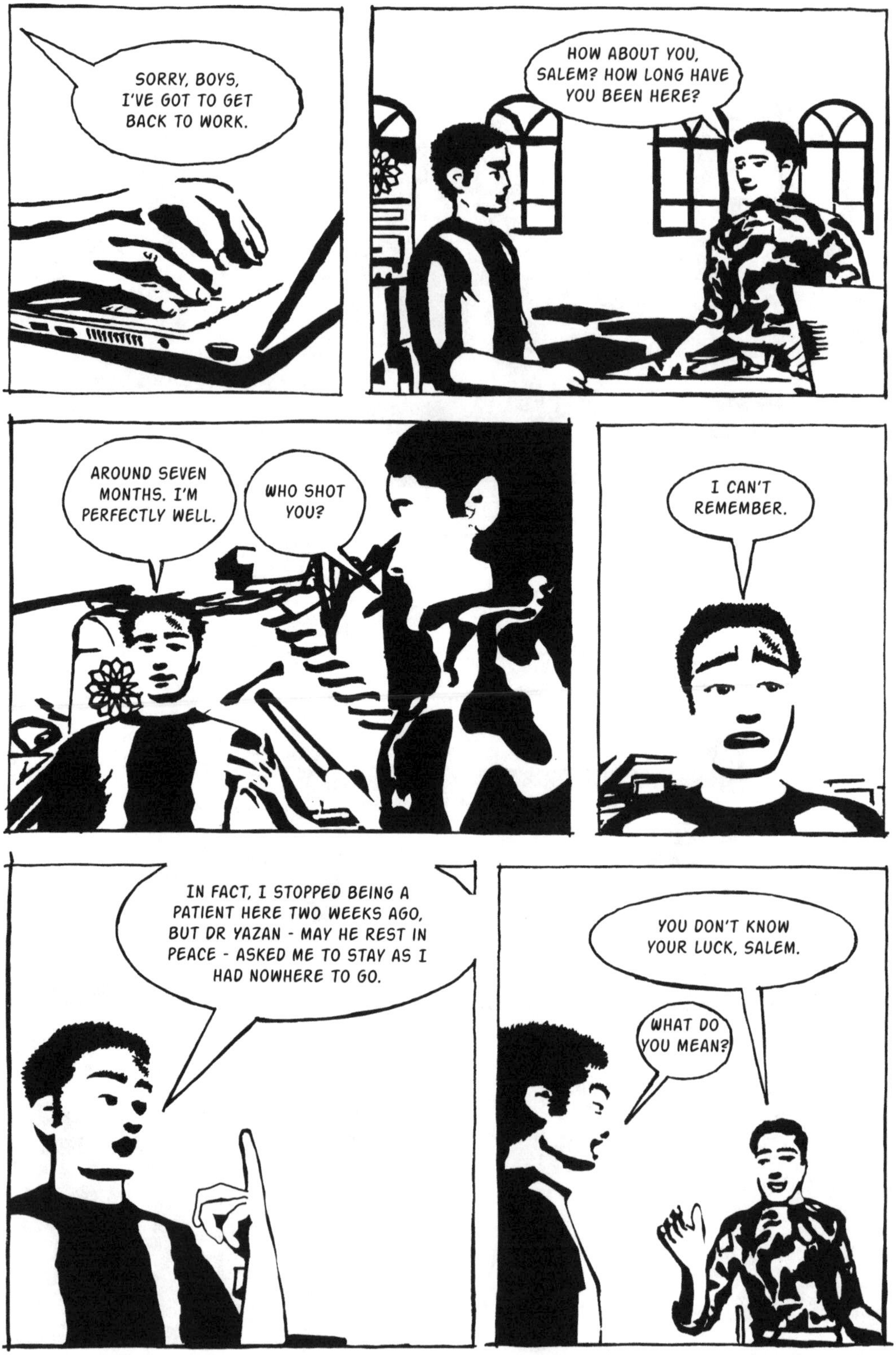
SORRY, BOYS, I'VE GOT TO GET BACK TO WORK.
HOW ABOUT YOU, SALEM? HOW LONG HAVE YOU BEEN HERE?
AROUND SEVEN MONTHS. I'M PERFECTLY WELL.
WHO SHOT YOU?
I CAN'T REMEMBER.
IN FACT, I STOPPED BEING A PATIENT HERE TWO WEEKS AGO, BUT DR YAZAN - MAY HE REST IN PEACE - ASKED ME TO STAY AS I HAD NOWHERE TO GO.
YOU DON'T KNOW YOUR LUCK, SALEM.
WHAT DO YOU MEAN?

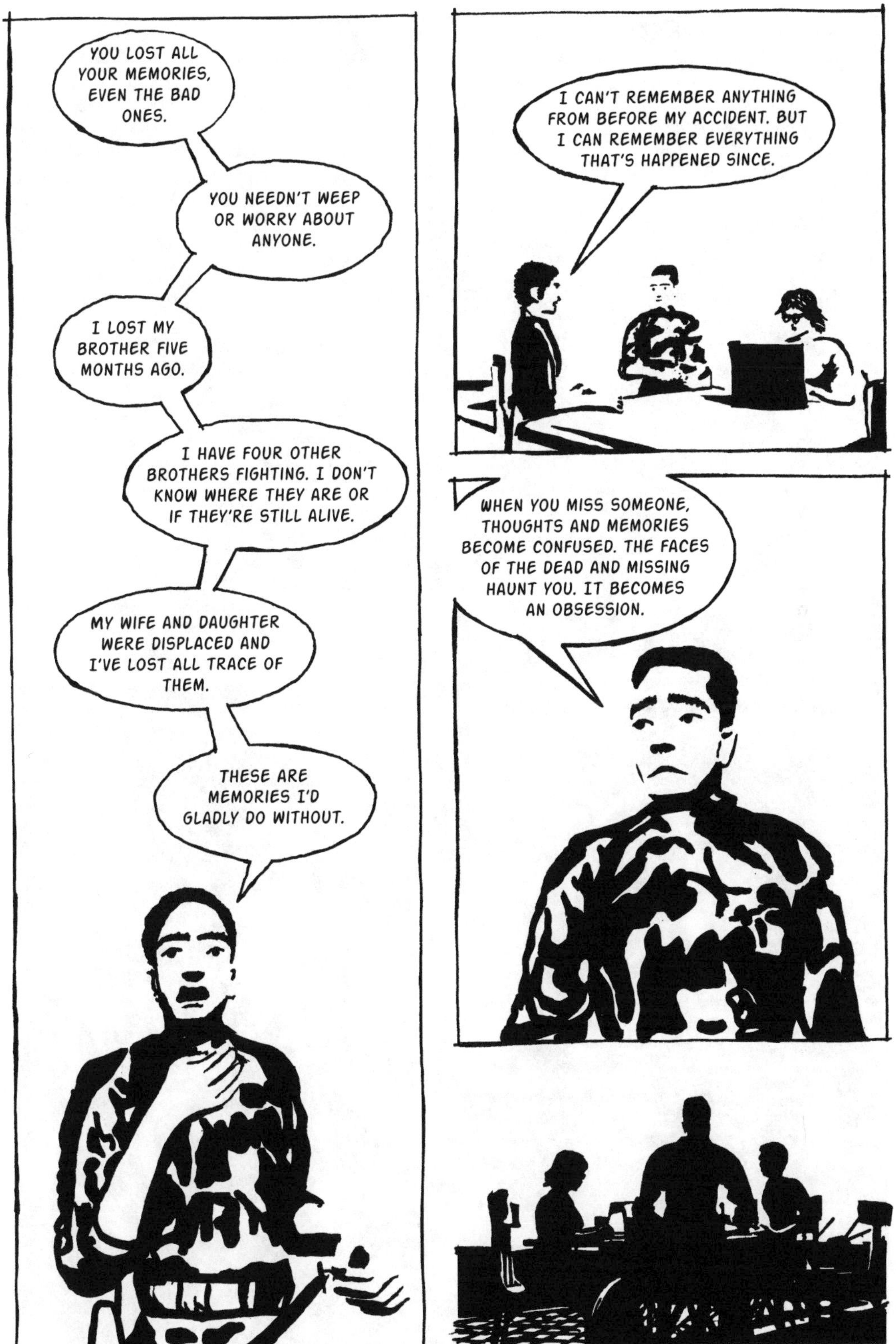
YOU LOST ALL YOUR MEMORIES, EVEN THE BAD ONES.
YOU NEEDN'T WEEP OR WORRY ABOUT ANYONE.
I LOST MY BROTHER FIVE MONTHS AGO.
I HAVE FOUR OTHER BROTHERS FIGHTING. I DON'T KNOW WHERE THEY ARE OR IF THEY'RE STILL ALIVE.
MY WIFE AND DAUGHTER WERE DISPLACED AND I'VE LOST ALL TRACE OF THEM.
THESE ARE MEMORIES I'D GLADLY DO WITHOUT.
I CAN'T REMEMBER ANYTHING FROM BEFORE MY ACCIDENT. BUT I CAN REMEMBER EVERYTHING THAT'S HAPPENED SINCE.
WHEN YOU MISS SOMEONE, THOUGHTS AND MEMORIES BECOME CONFUSED. THE FACES OF THE DEAD AND MISSING HAUNT YOU. IT BECOMES AN OBSESSION.

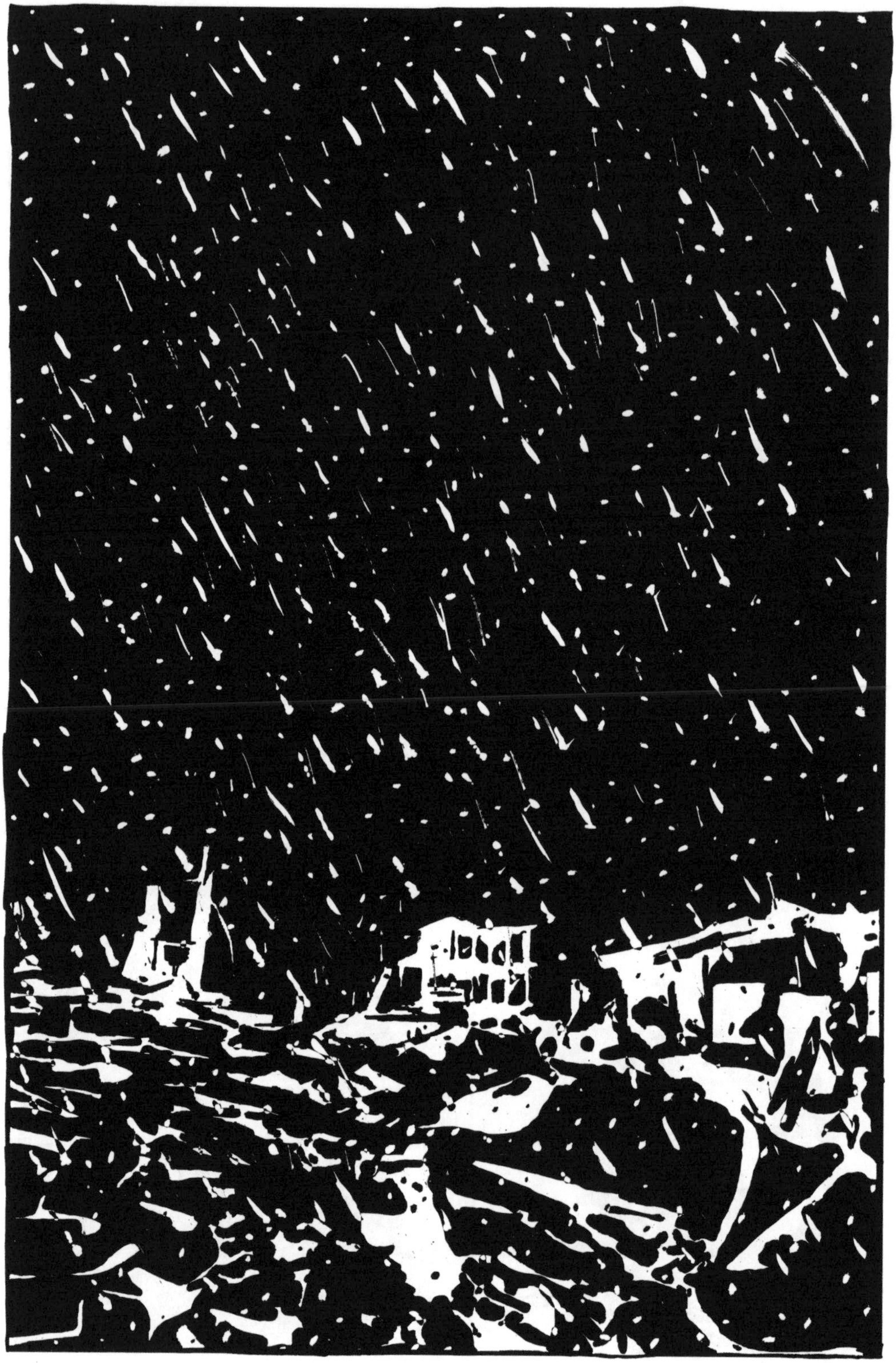

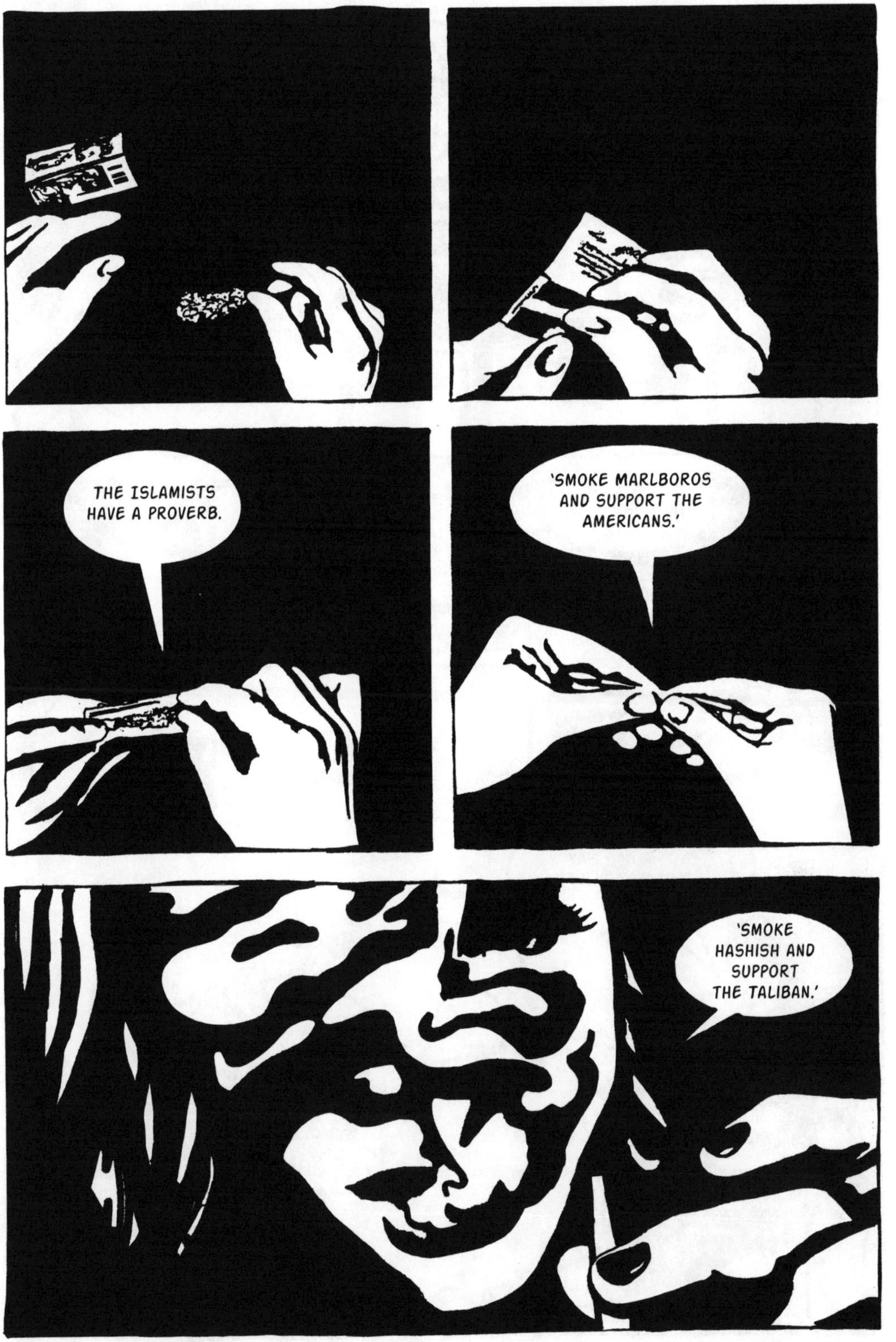
THE ISLAMISTS HAVE A PROVERB.
'SMOKE MARLBOROS AND SUPPORT THE AMERICANS.'
'SMOKE HASHISH AND SUPPORT THE TALIBAN.'

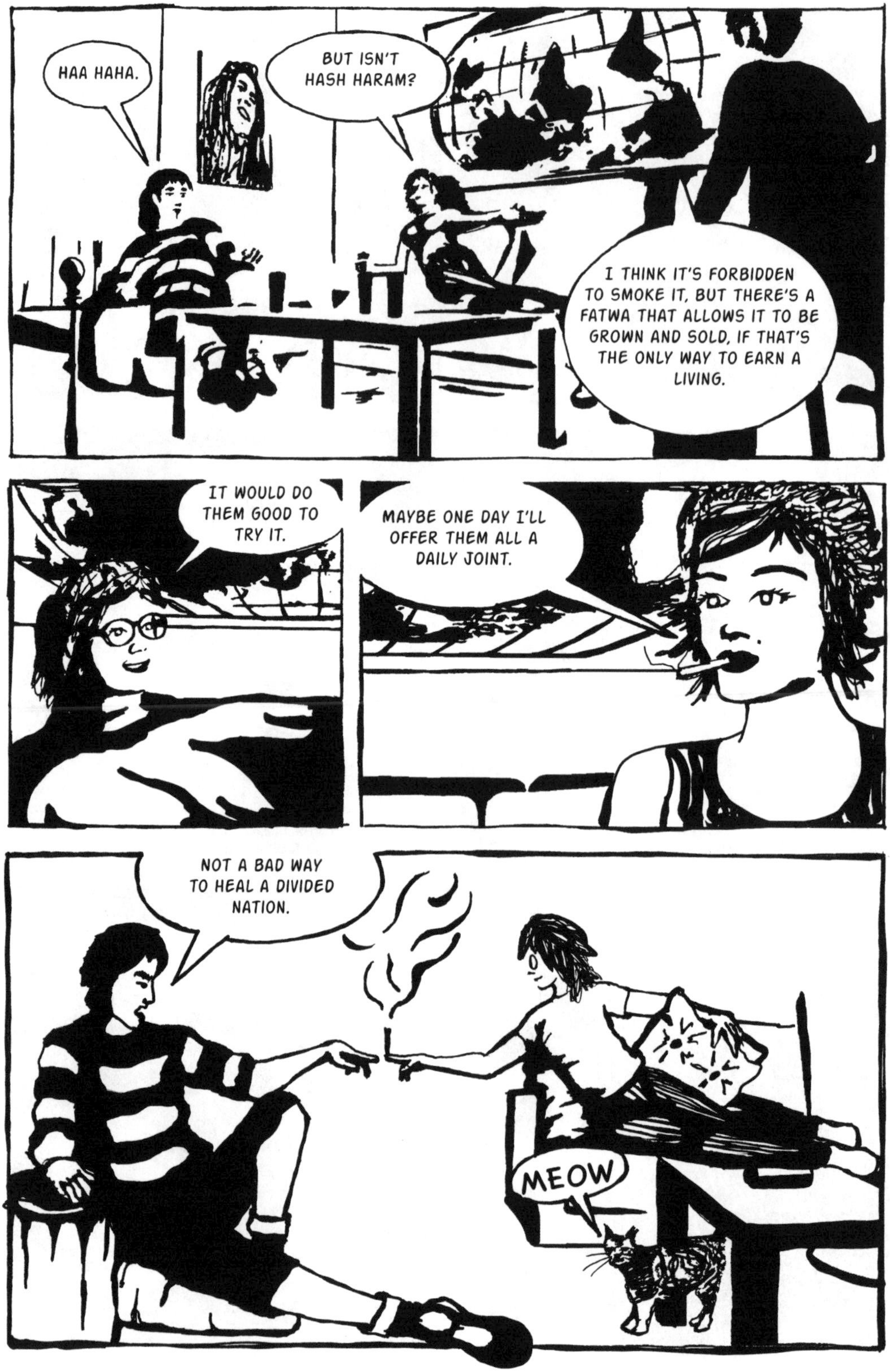
HAA HAHA.
BUT ISN'T HASH HARAM?
I THINK IT'S FORBIDDEN TO SMOKE IT, BUT THERE'S A FATWA THAT ALLOWS IT TO BE GROWN AND SOLD, IF THAT'S THE ONLY WAY TO EARN A LIVING.
IT WOULD DO THEM GOOD TO TRY IT.
MAYBE ONE DAY I'LL OFFER THEM ALL A DAILY JOINT.
NOT A BAD WAY TO HEAL A DIVIDED NATION.
MEOW

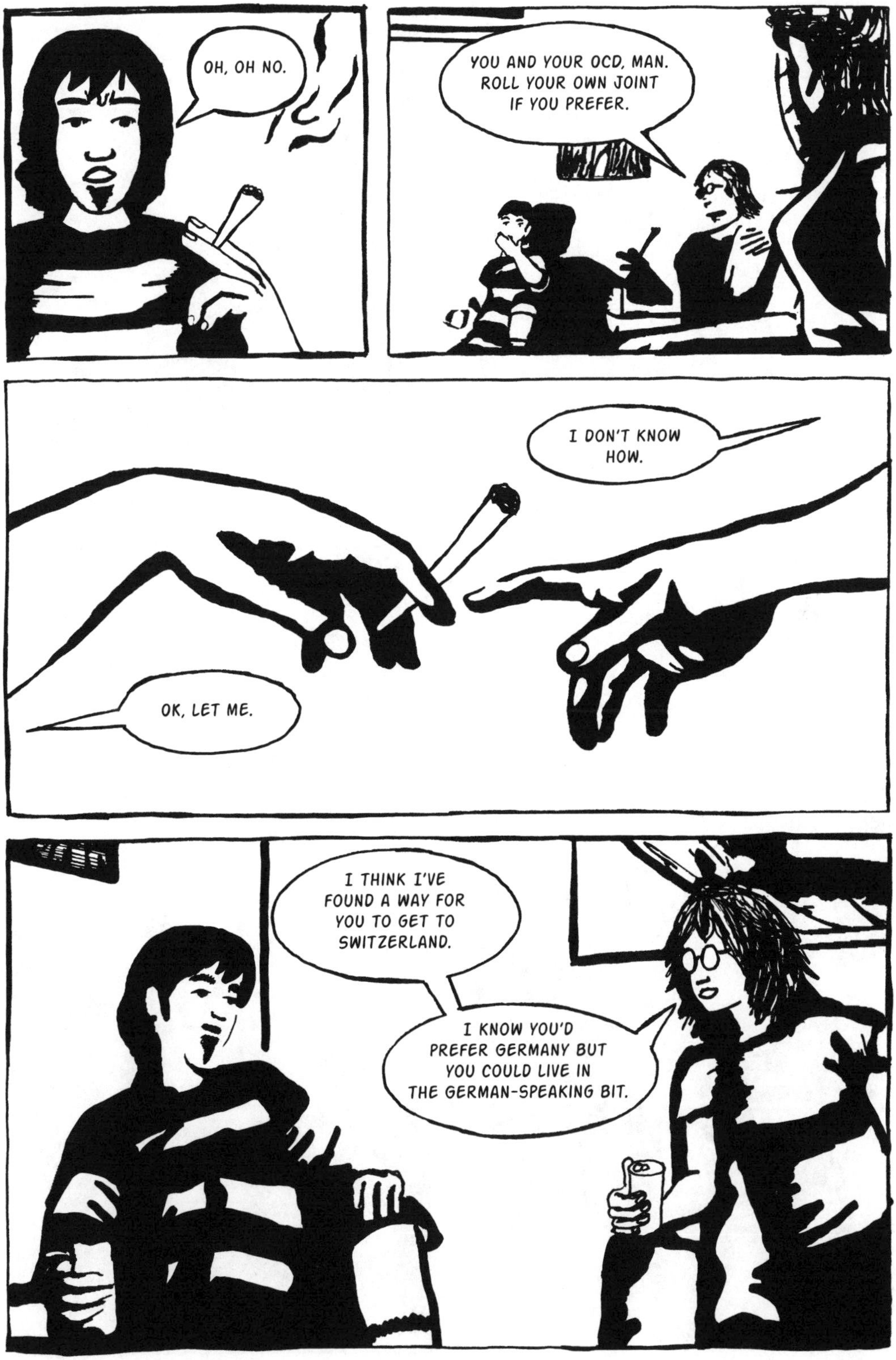
OH, OH NO.
YOU AND YOUR OCD, MAN. ROLL YOUR OWN JOINT IF YOU PREFER.
I DON'T KNOW HOW.
OK, LET ME.
I THINK I'VE FOUND A WAY FOR YOU TO GET TO SWITZERLAND.
I KNOW YOU'D PREFER GERMANY BUT YOU COULD LIVE IN THE GERMAN-SPEAKING BIT.

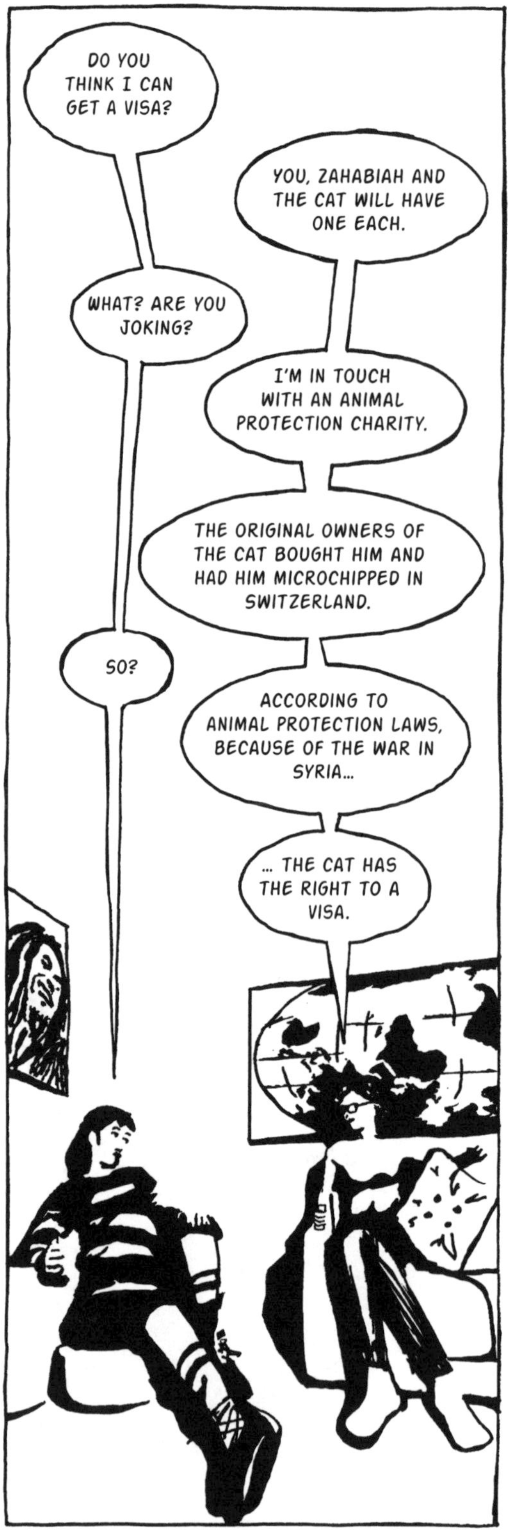
DO YOU THINK I CAN GET A VISA?
YOU, ZAHABIAH AND THE CAT WILL HAVE ONE EACH.
WHAT? ARE YOU JOKING?
I'M IN TOUCH WITH AN ANIMAL PROTECTION CHARITY.
THE ORIGINAL OWNERS OF THE CAT BOUGHT HIM AND HAD HIM MICROCHIPPED IN SWITZERLAND.
SO?
ACCORDING TO ANIMAL PROTECTION LAWS, BECAUSE OF THE WAR IN SYRIA...
... THE CAT HAS THE RIGHT TO A VISA.

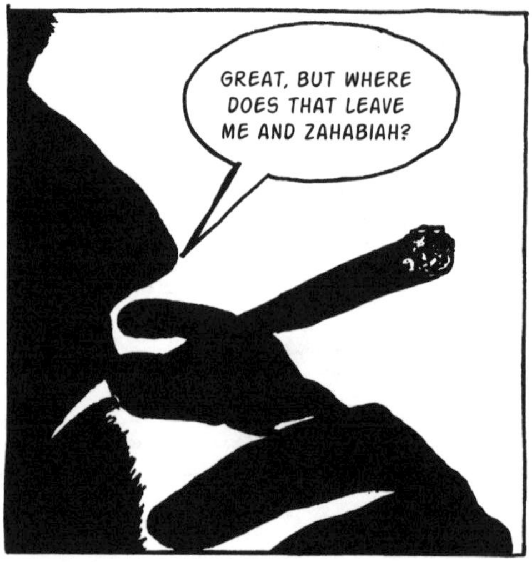
GREAT, BUT WHERE DOES THAT LEAVE ME AND ZAHABIAH?

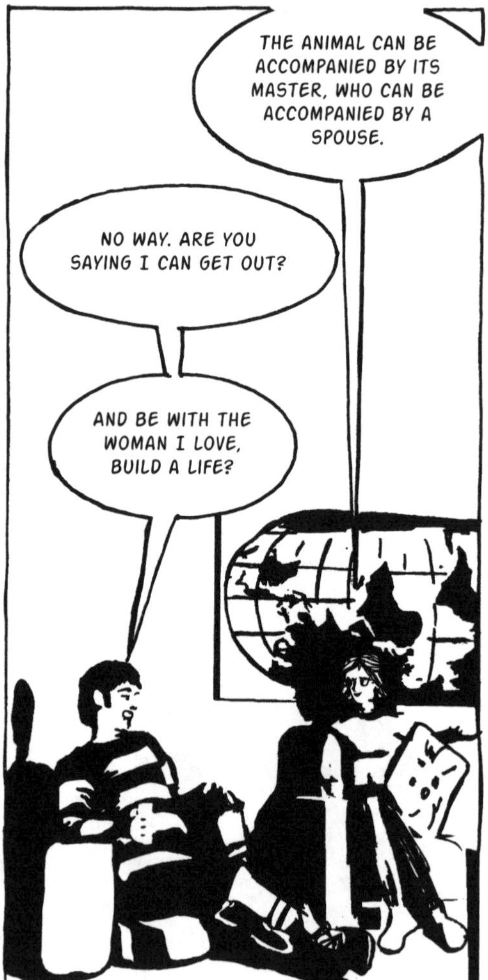
THE ANIMAL CAN BE ACCOMPANIED BY ITS MASTER, WHO CAN BE ACCOMPANIED BY A SPOUSE.
NO WAY. ARE YOU SAYING I CAN GET OUT?
AND BE WITH THE WOMAN I LOVE, BUILD A LIFE?

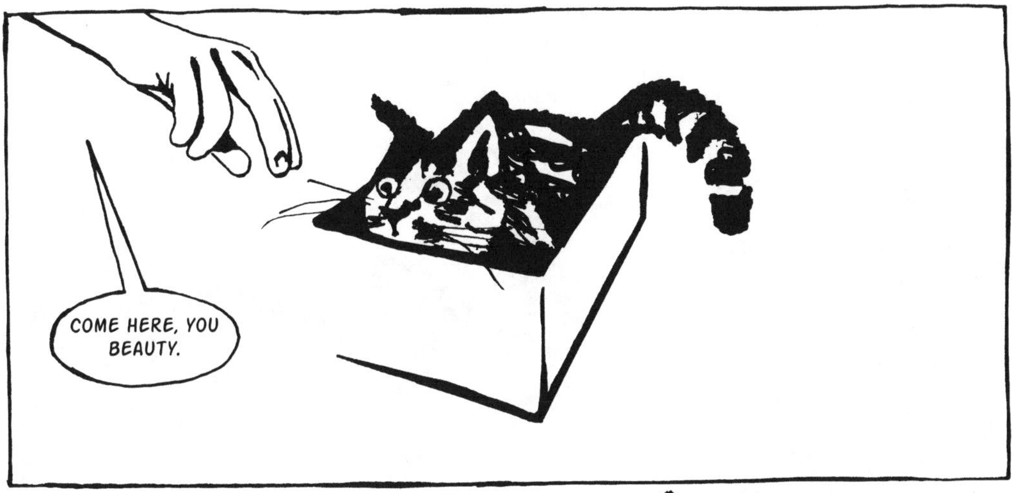
COME HERE, YOU BEAUTY.

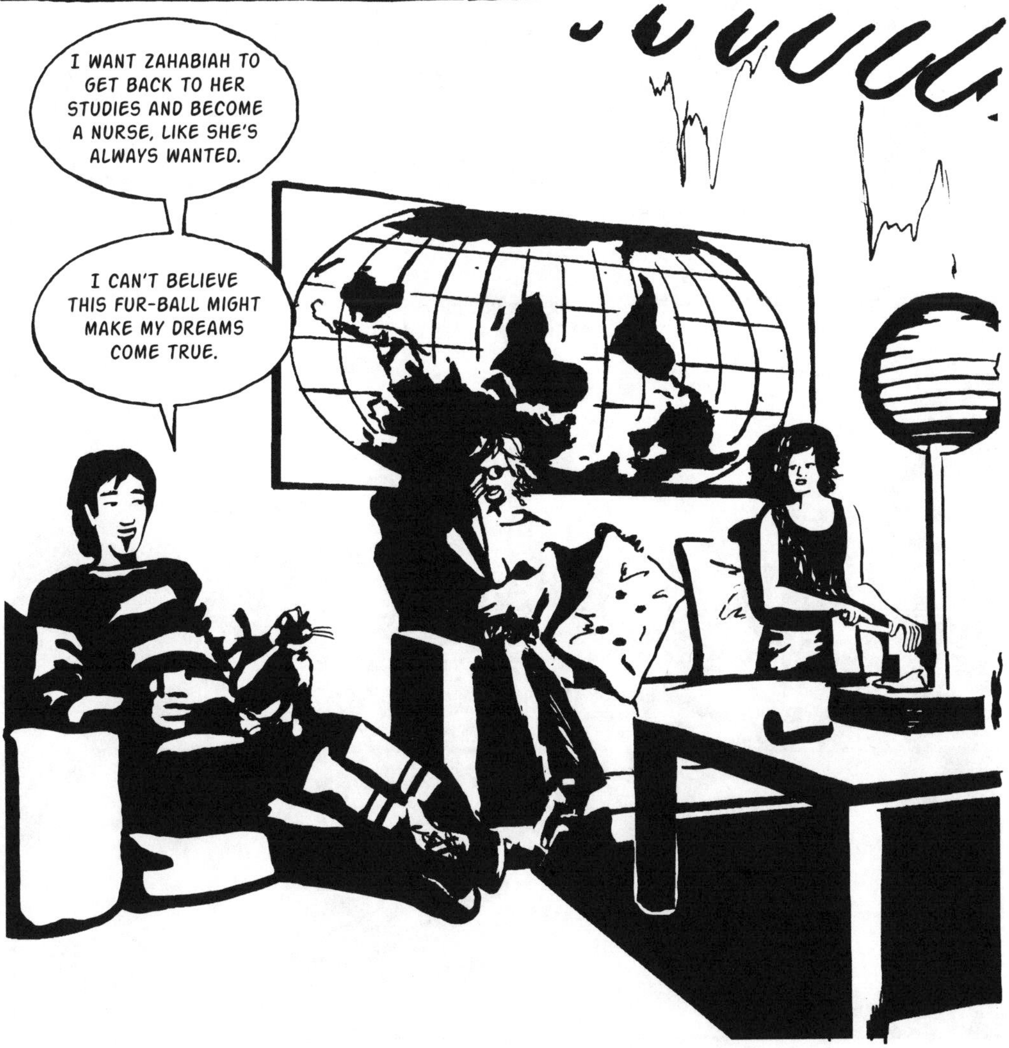
I WANT ZAHABIAH TO GET BACK TO HER STUDIES AND BECOME A NURSE, LIKE SHE'S ALWAYS WANTED.
I CAN'T BELIEVE THIS FUR-BALL MIGHT MAKE MY DREAMS COME TRUE.

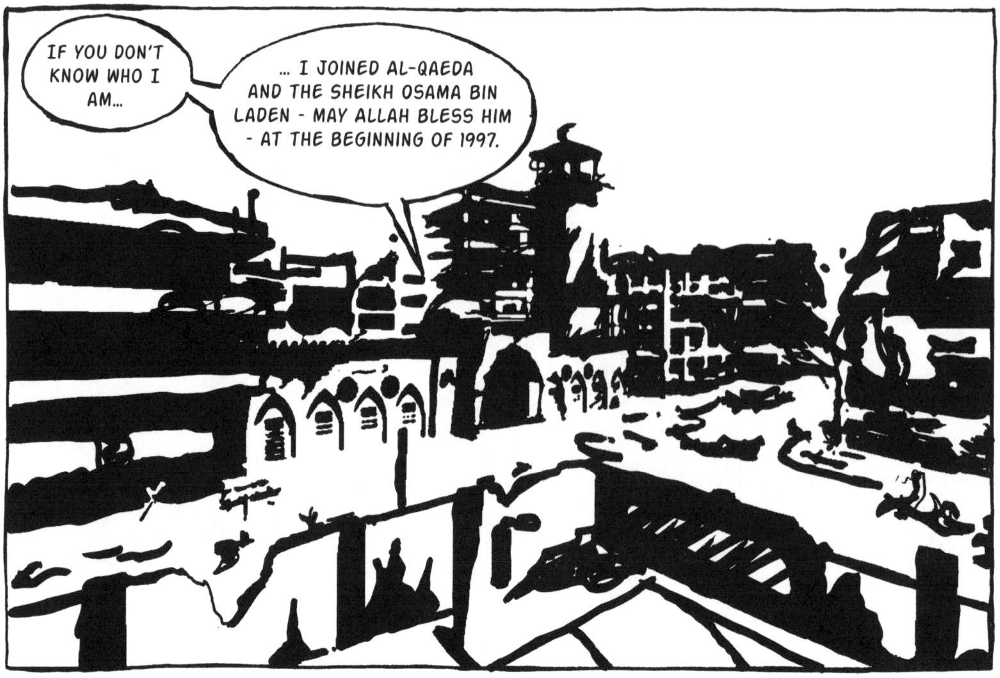
IF YOU DON'T KNOW WHO I AM...
... I JOINED AL-QAEDA AND THE SHEIKH OSAMA BIN LADEN - MAY ALLAH BLESS HIM - AT THE BEGINNING OF 1997.

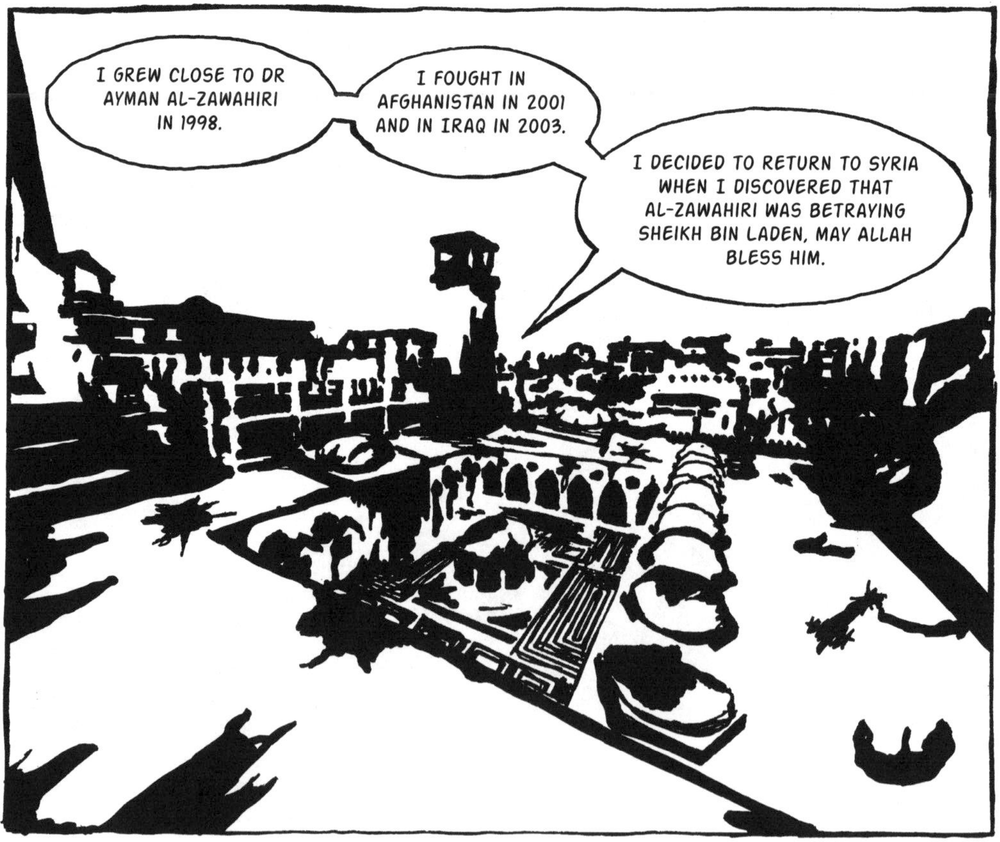
I GREW CLOSE TO DR AYMAN AL-ZAWAHIRI IN 1998.
I FOUGHT IN AFGHANISTAN IN 2001 AND IN IRAQ IN 2003.
I DECIDED TO RETURN TO SYRIA WHEN I DISCOVERED THAT AL-ZAWAHIRI WAS BETRAYING SHEIKH BIN LADEN, MAY ALLAH BLESS HIM.

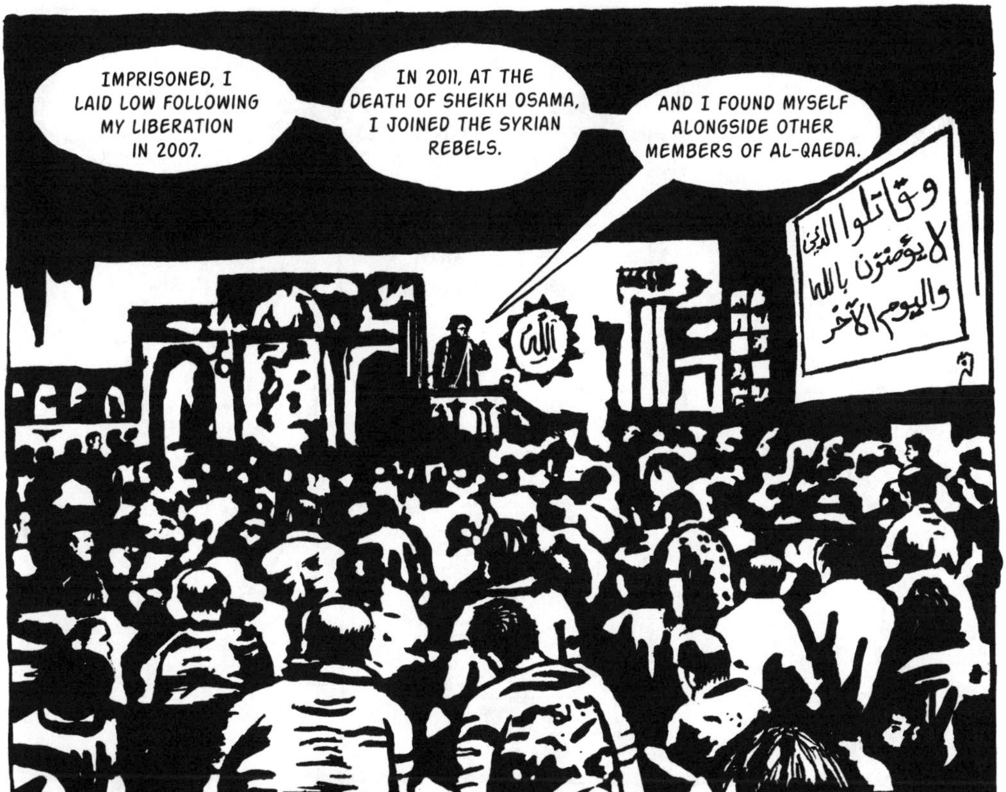
IMPRISONED, I LAID LOW FOLLOWING MY LIBERATION IN 2007.
IN 2011, AT THE DEATH OF SHEIKH OSAMA, I JOINED THE SYRIAN REBELS.
AND I FOUND MYSELF ALONGSIDE OTHER MEMBERS OF AL-QAEDA.
وقاتلوا الذين لا يؤمنون بالله واليوم الآخر

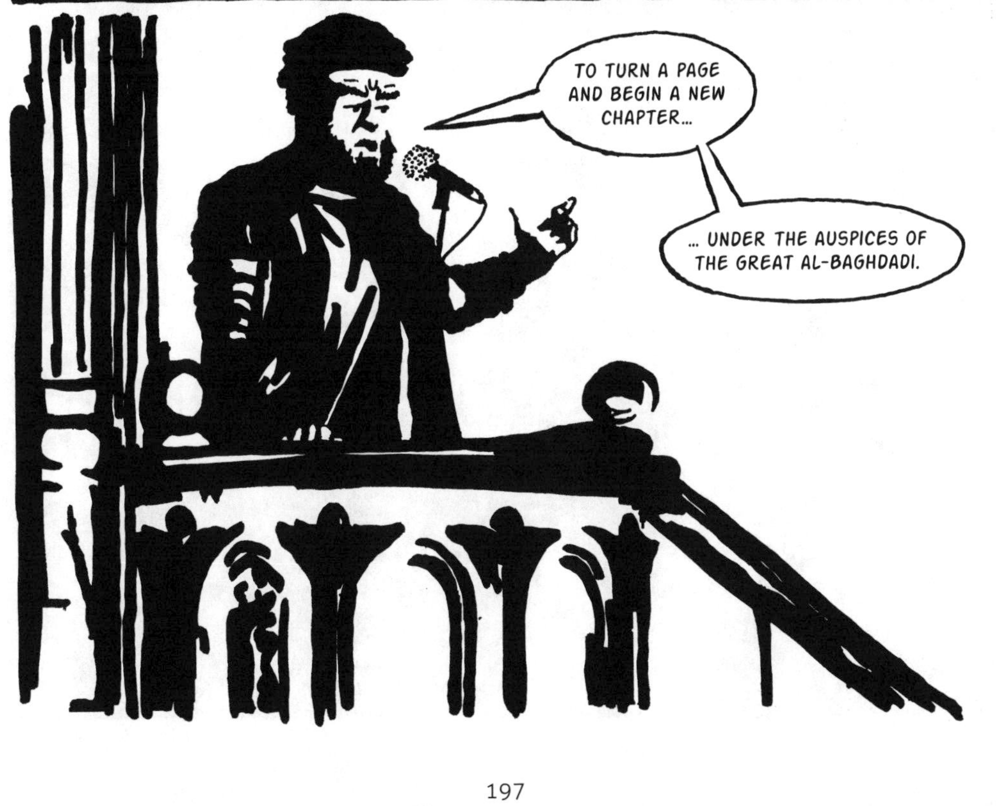
TO TURN A PAGE AND BEGIN A NEW CHAPTER...
... UNDER THE AUSPICES OF THE GREAT AL-BAGHDADI.

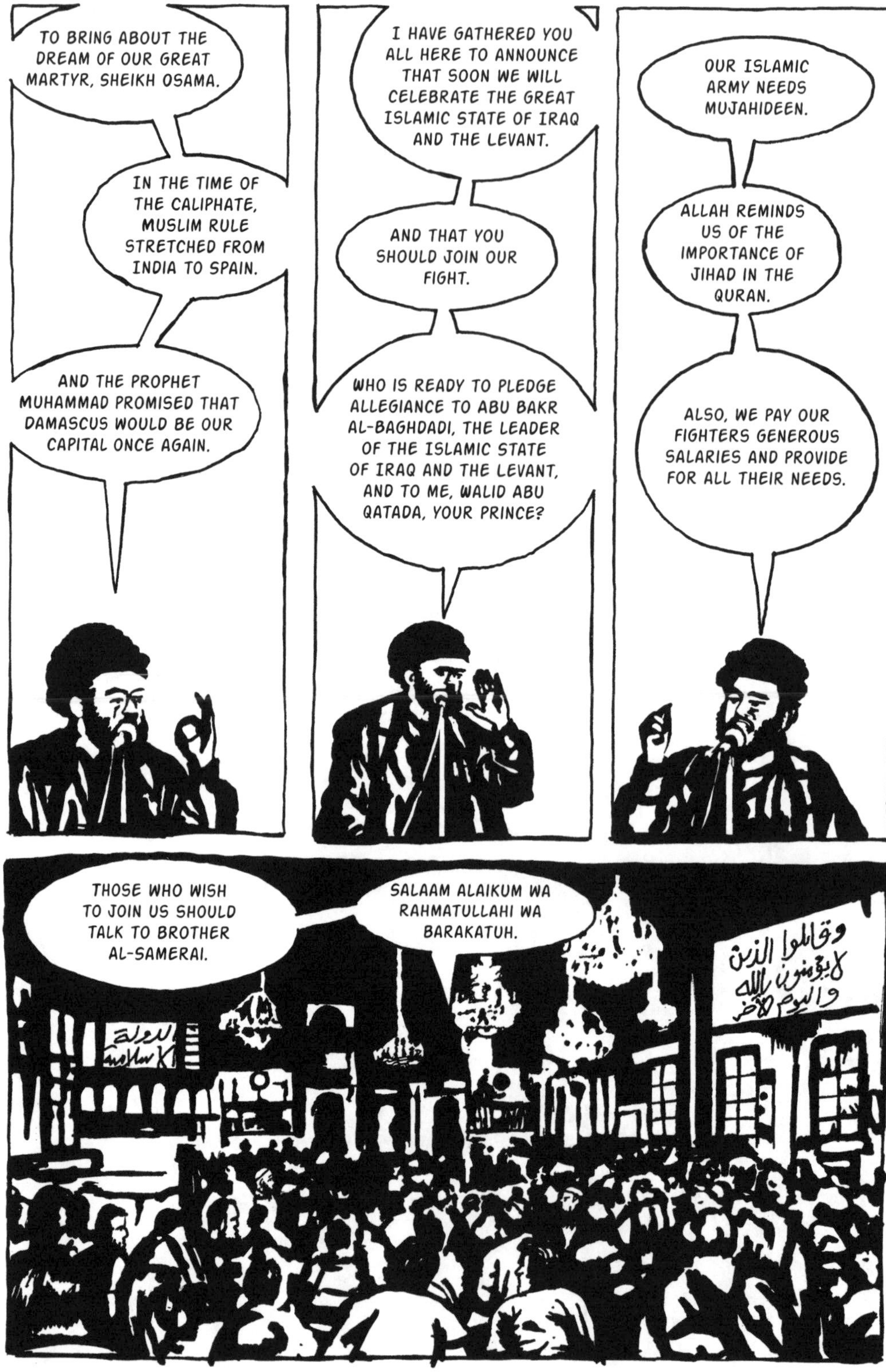

TO BRING ABOUT THE DREAM OF OUR GREAT MARTYR, SHEIKH OSAMA.
IN THE TIME OF THE CALIPHATE, MUSLIM RULE STRETCHED FROM INDIA TO SPAIN.
AND THE PROPHET MUHAMMAD PROMISED THAT DAMASCUS WOULD BE OUR CAPITAL ONCE AGAIN.
I HAVE GATHERED YOU ALL HERE TO ANNOUNCE THAT SOON WE WILL CELEBRATE THE GREAT ISLAMIC STATE OF IRAQ AND THE LEVANT.
AND THAT YOU SHOULD JOIN OUR FIGHT.
WHO IS READY TO PLEDGE ALLEGIANCE TO ABU BAKR AL-BAGHDADI, THE LEADER OF THE ISLAMIC STATE OF IRAQ AND THE LEVANT, AND TO ME, WALID ABU QATADA, YOUR PRINCE?
OUR ISLAMIC ARMY NEEDS MUJAHIDEEN.
ALLAH REMINDS US OF THE IMPORTANCE OF JIHAD IN THE QURAN.
ALSO, WE PAY OUR FIGHTERS GENEROUS SALARIES AND PROVIDE FOR ALL THEIR NEEDS.
THOSE WHO WISH TO JOIN US SHOULD TALK TO BROTHER AL-SAMERAI.
SALAAM ALAIKUM WA RAHMATULLAHI WA BARAKATUH.
وقاتلوا الذين لا يؤمنون بالله واليوم الآخر

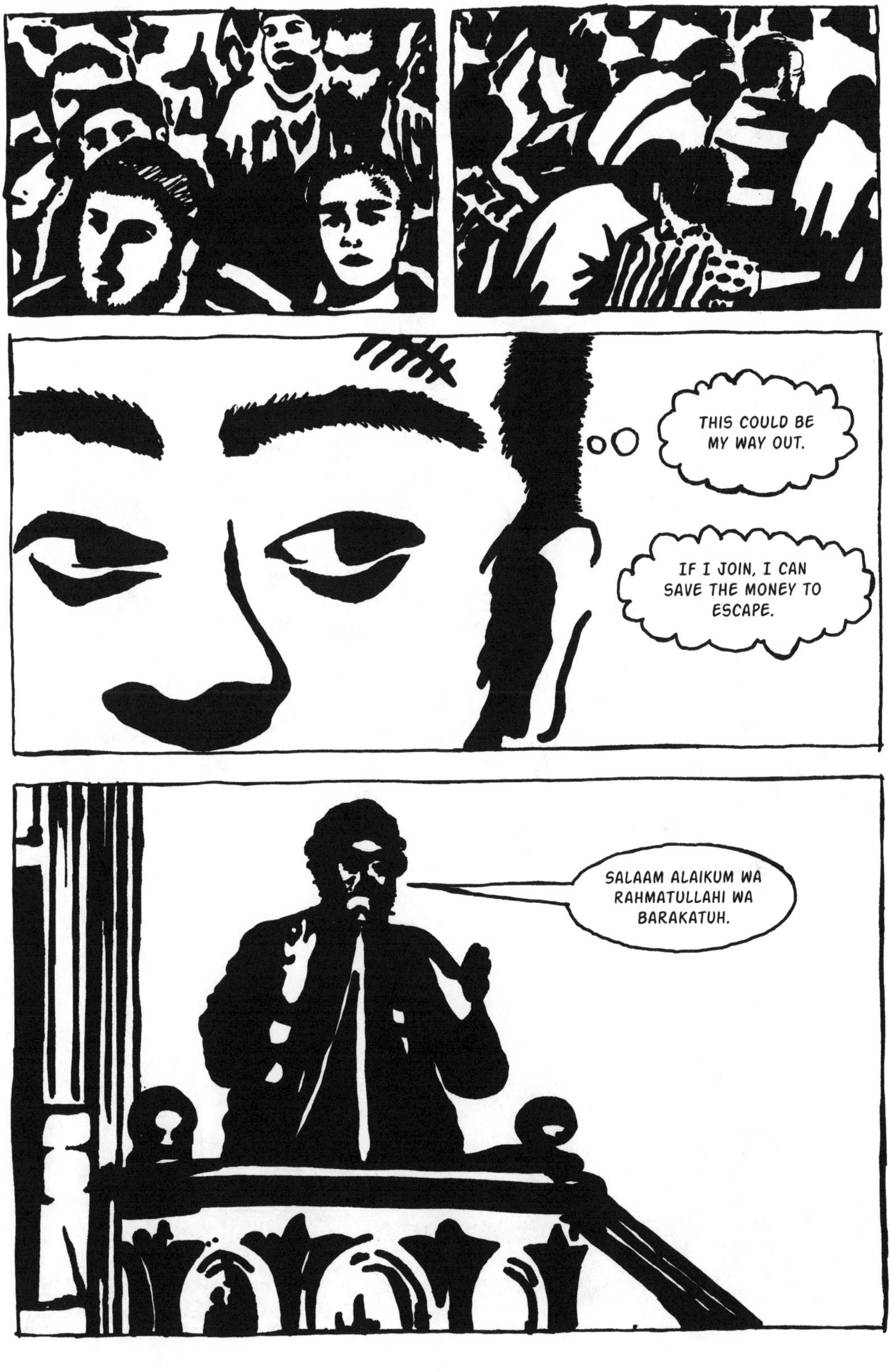
THIS COULD BE MY WAY OUT.
IF I JOIN, I CAN SAVE THE MONEY TO ESCAPE.
SALAAM ALAIKUM WA RAHMATULLAHI WA BARAKATUH.

TWELVE DAYS LATER: ANOTHER 1,698 KILLED.

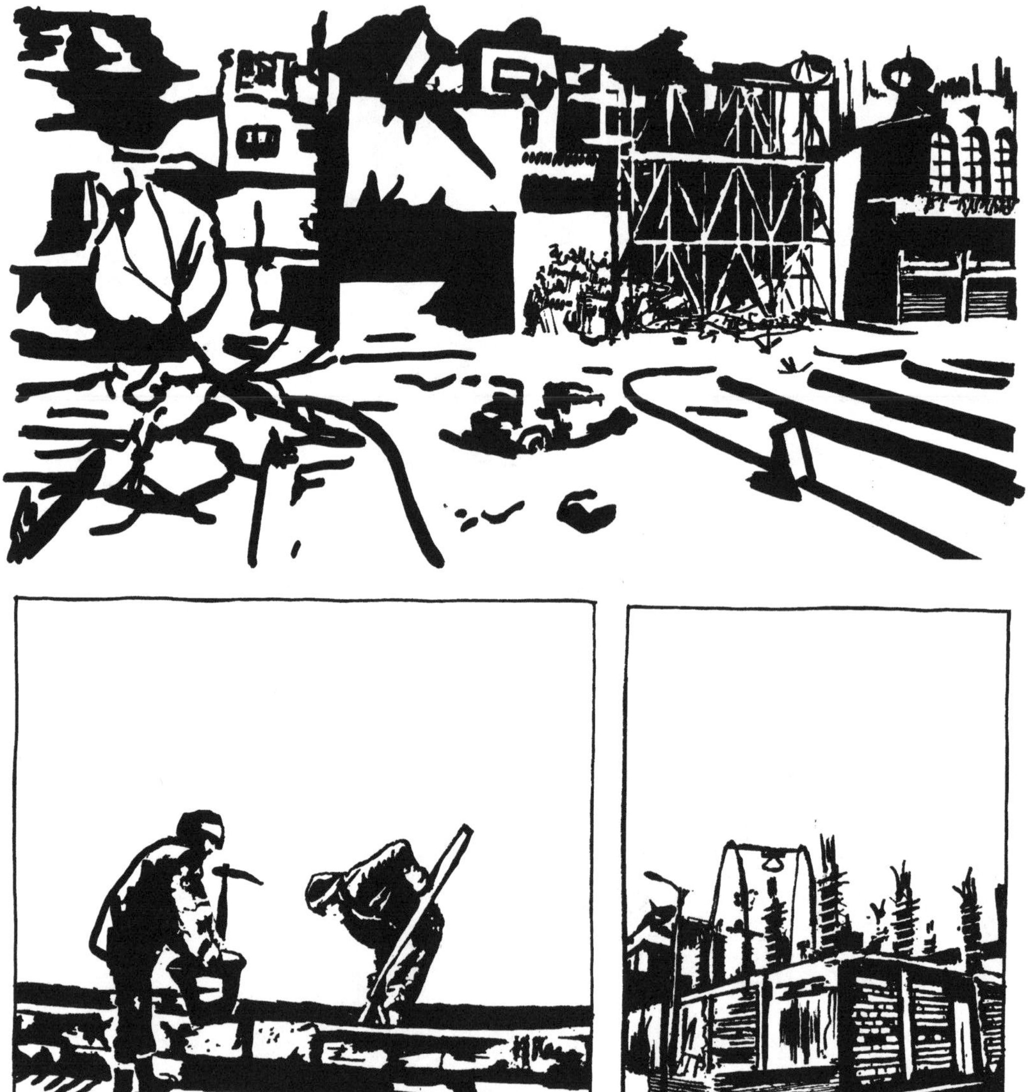

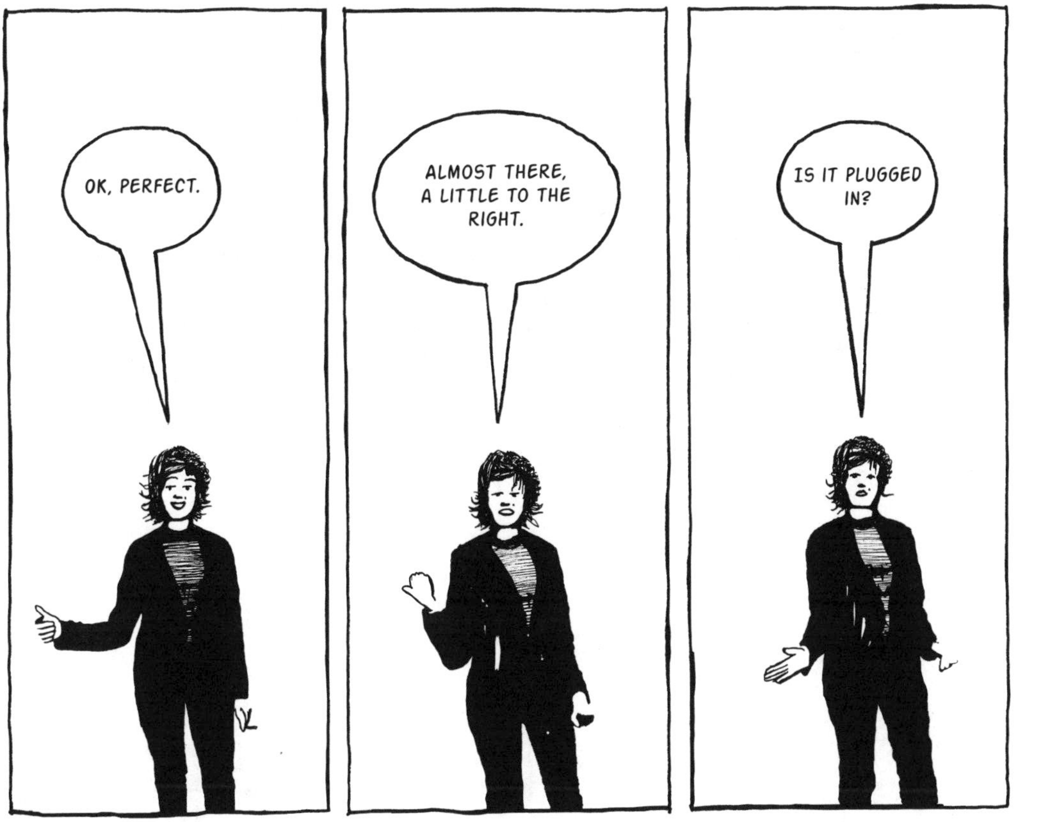
OK, PERFECT.
ALMOST THERE, A LITTLE TO THE RIGHT.
IS IT PLUGGED IN?

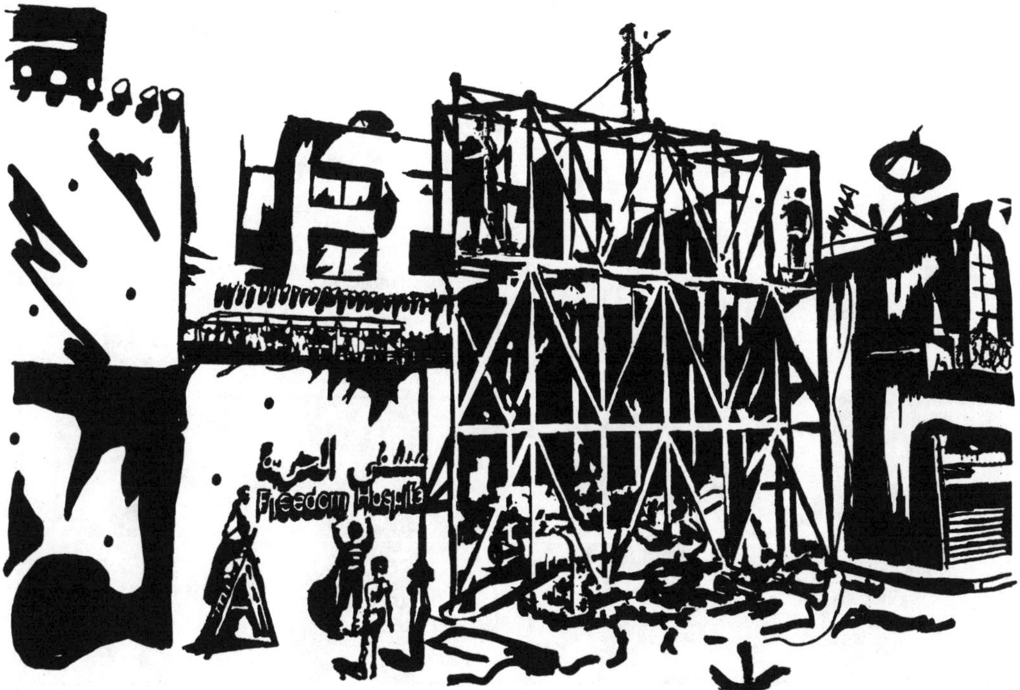

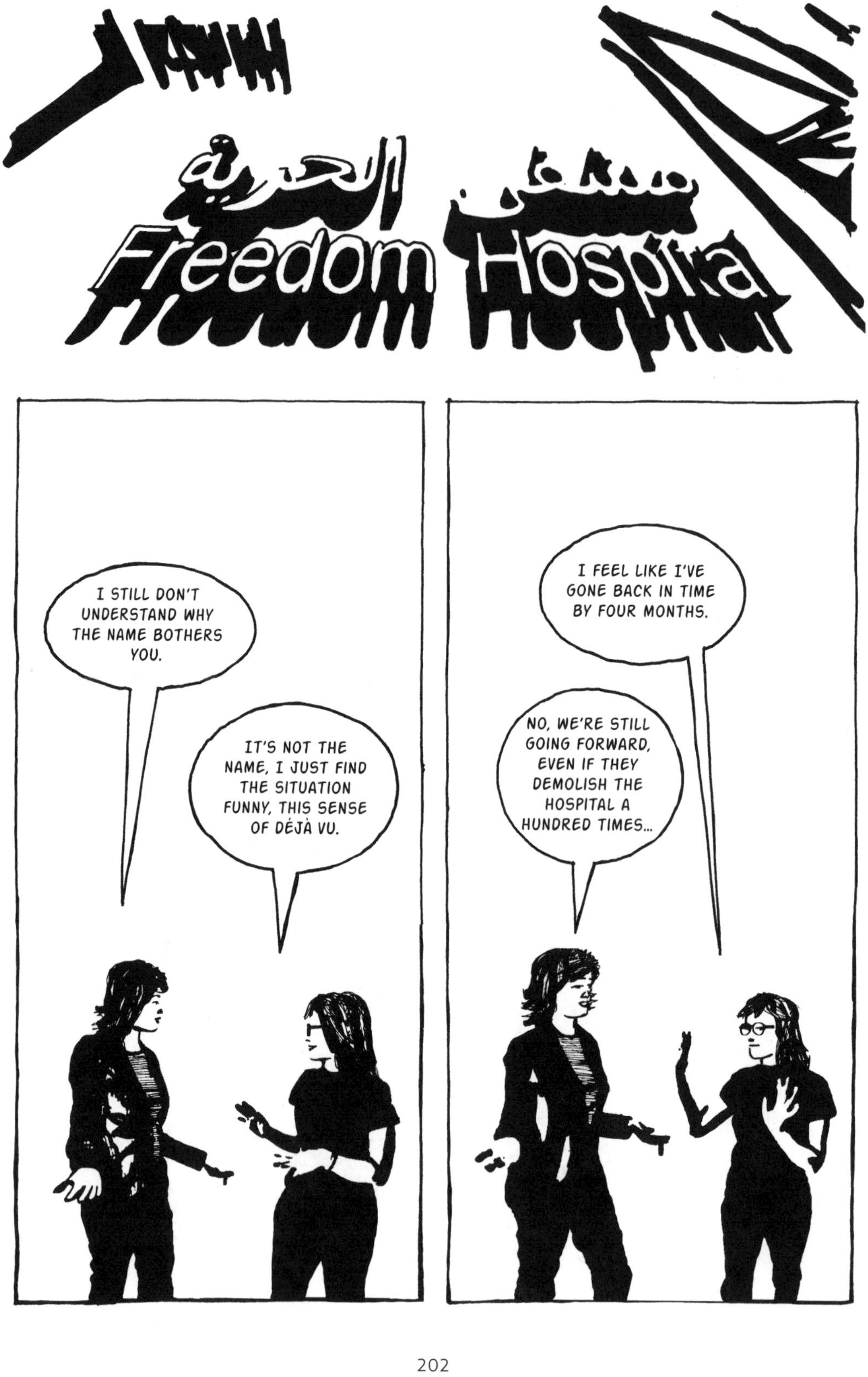

الحرية
Freedom Hospita
I STILL DON'T UNDERSTAND WHY THE NAME BOTHERS YOU.
IT'S NOT THE NAME, I JUST FIND THE SITUATION FUNNY, THIS SENSE OF DÉJÀ VU.
I FEEL LIKE I'VE GONE BACK IN TIME BY FOUR MONTHS.
NO, WE'RE STILL GOING FORWARD, EVEN IF THEY DEMOLISH THE HOSPITAL A HUNDRED TIMES...

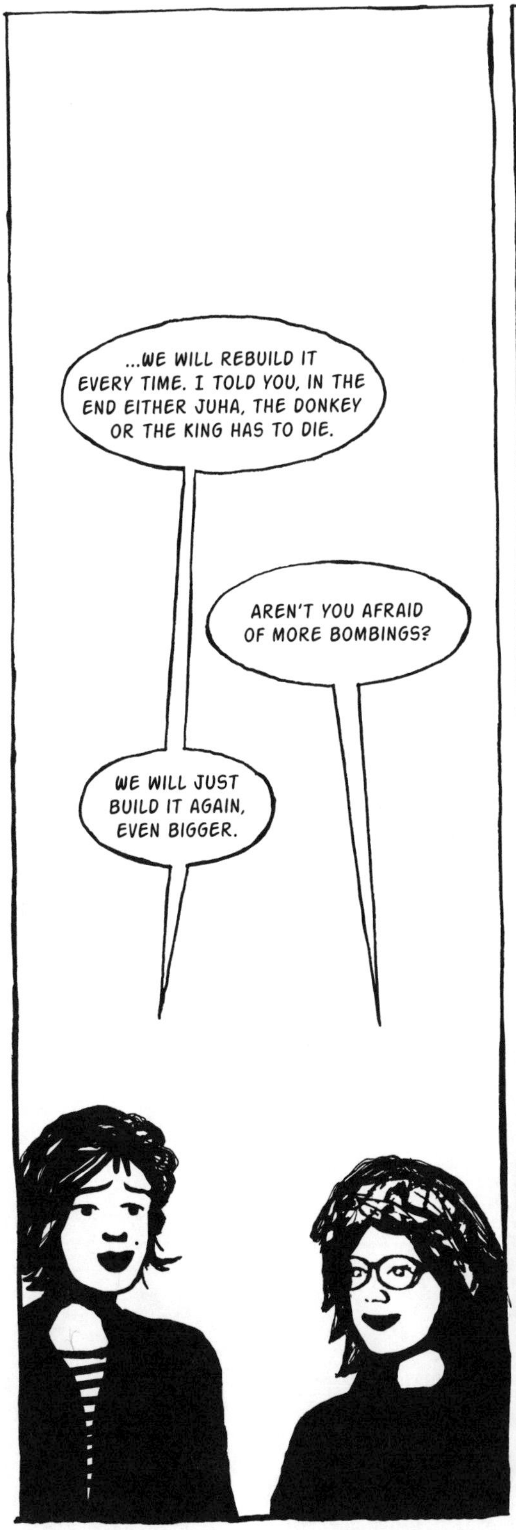
...WE WILL REBUILD IT EVERY TIME. I TOLD YOU, IN THE END EITHER JUHA, THE DONKEY OR THE KING HAS TO DIE.
AREN'T YOU AFRAID OF MORE BOMBINGS?
WE WILL JUST BUILD IT AGAIN, EVEN BIGGER.

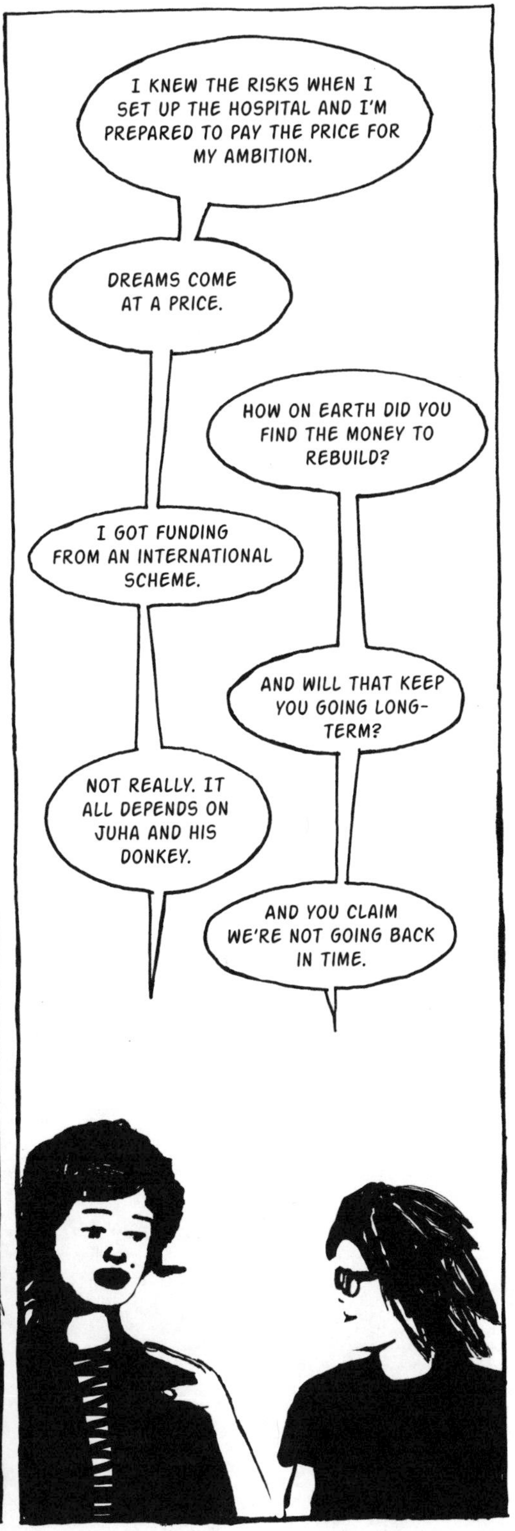
I KNEW THE RISKS WHEN I SET UP THE HOSPITAL AND I'M PREPARED TO PAY THE PRICE FOR MY AMBITION.
DREAMS COME AT A PRICE.
HOW ON EARTH DID YOU FIND THE MONEY TO REBUILD?
I GOT FUNDING FROM AN INTERNATIONAL SCHEME.
AND WILL THAT KEEP YOU GOING LONG-TERM?
NOT REALLY. IT ALL DEPENDS ON JUHA AND HIS DONKEY.
AND YOU CLAIM WE'RE NOT GOING BACK IN TIME.

Chapter 4

WINTER

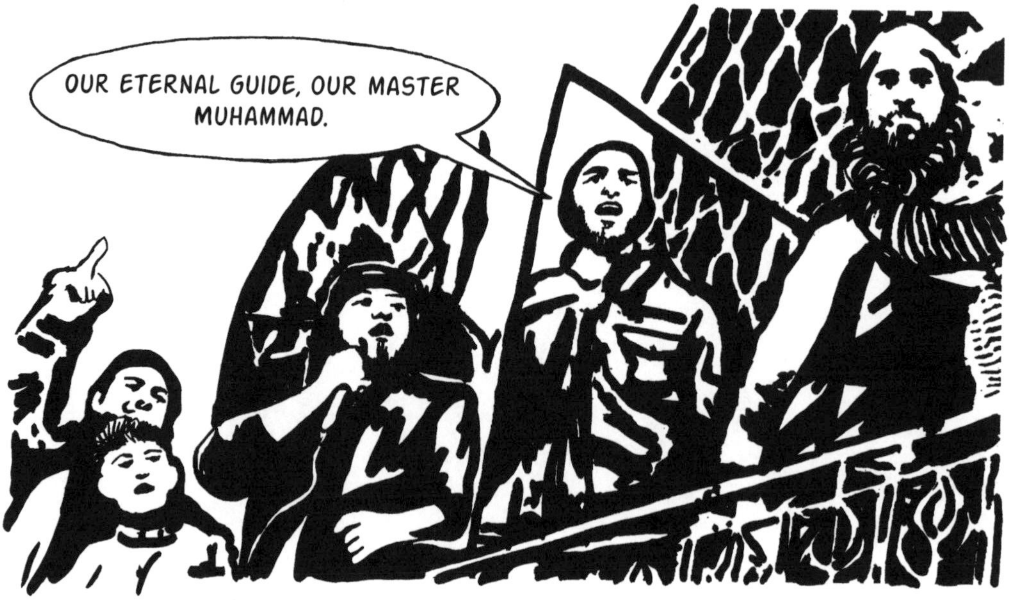
OUR ETERNAL GUIDE, OUR MASTER MUHAMMAD.

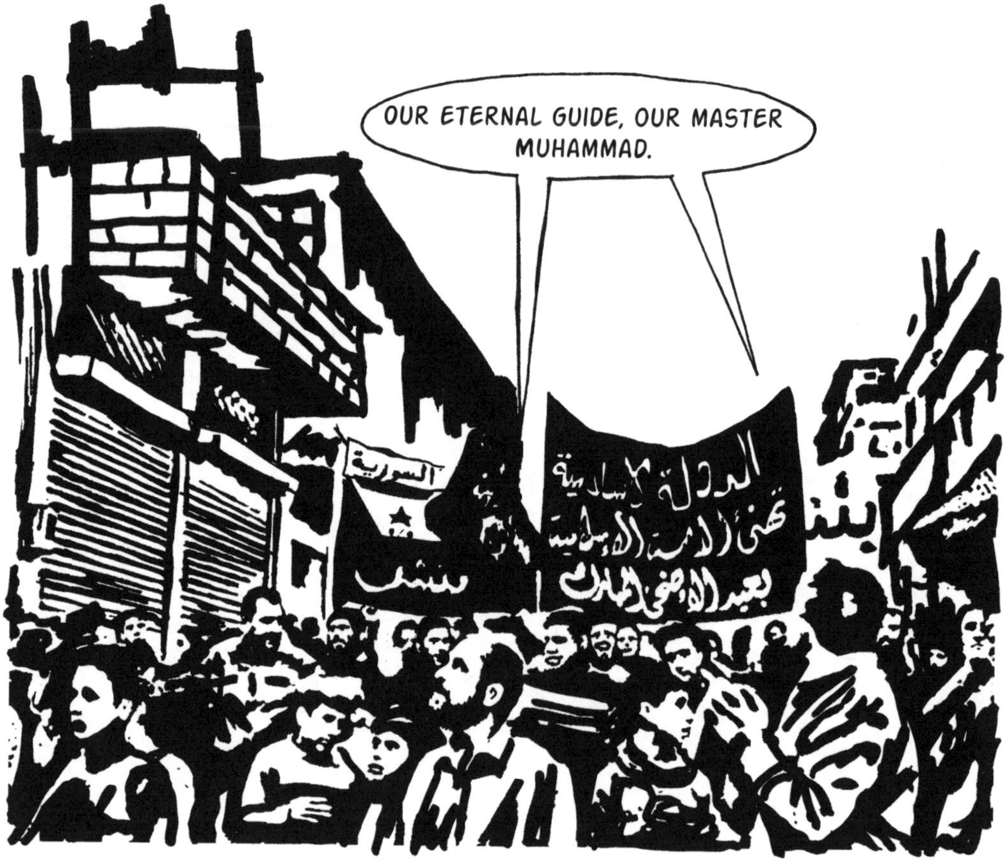
OUR ETERNAL GUIDE, OUR MASTER MUHAMMAD.

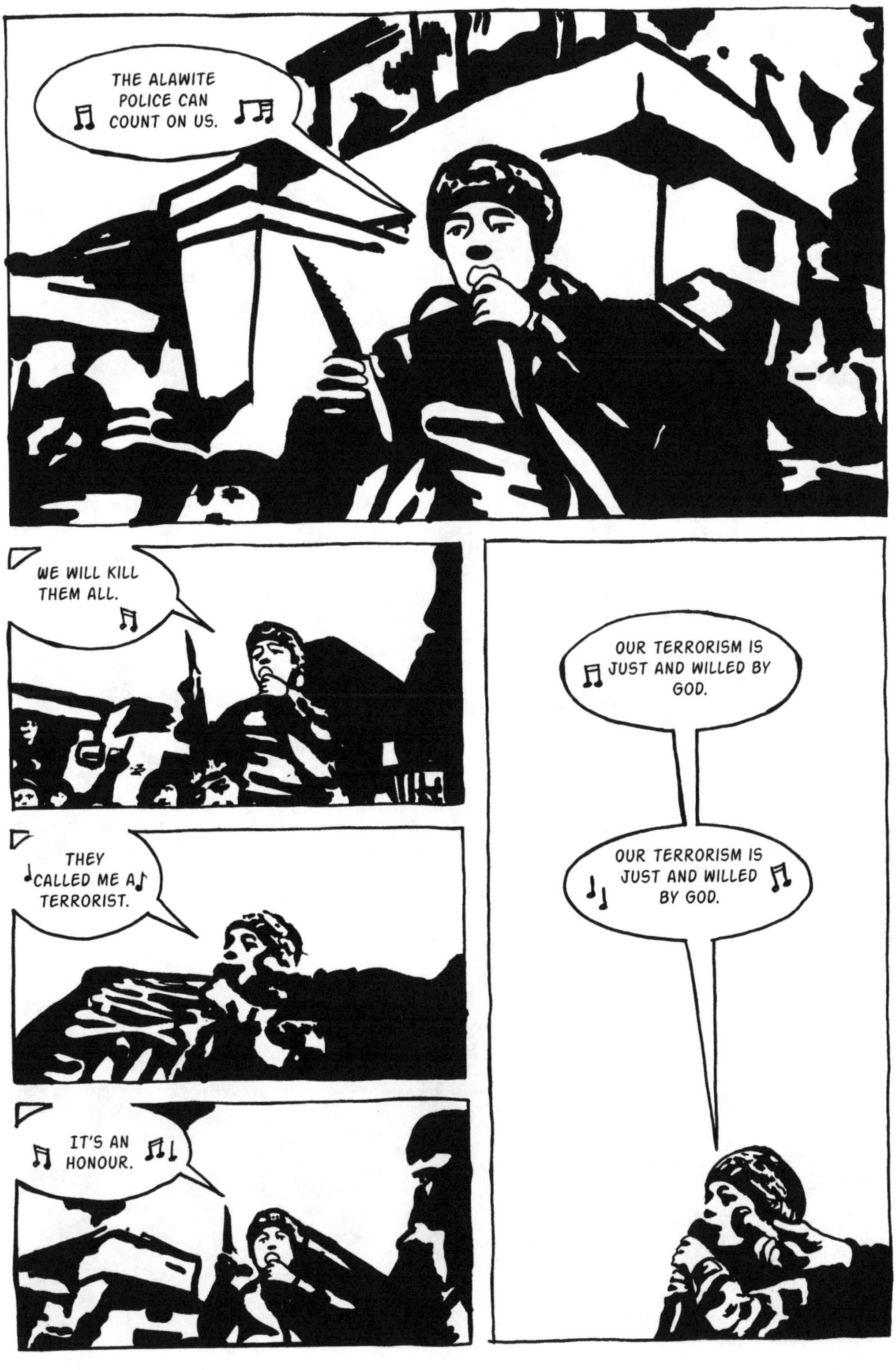
THE ALAWITE POLICE CAN COUNT ON US.
WE WILL KILL THEM ALL.
THEY CALLED ME A TERRORIST.
IT'S AN HONOUR.
OUR TERRORISM IS JUST AND WILLED BY GOD.
OUR TERRORISM IS JUST AND WILLED BY GOD.

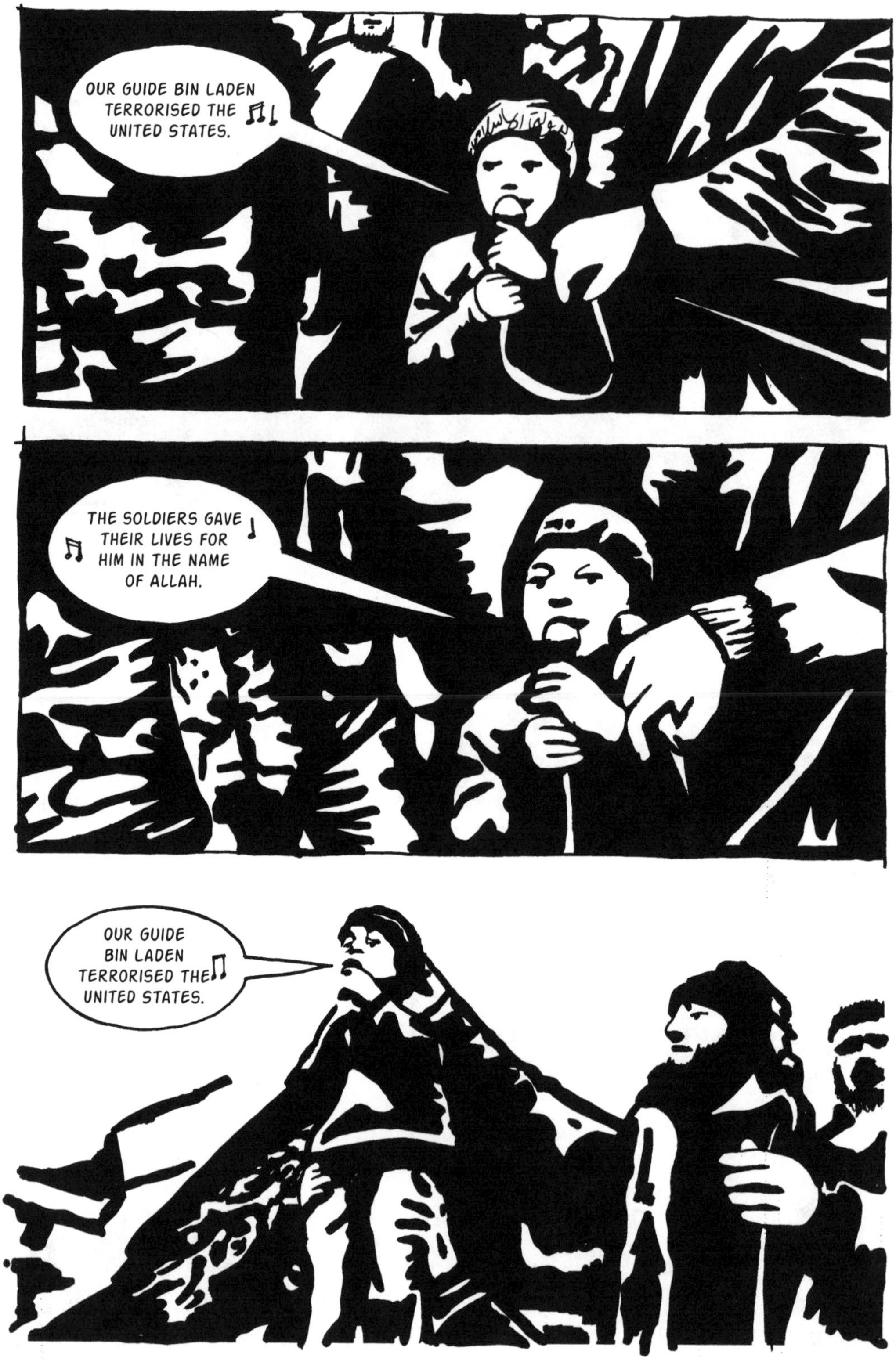
OUR GUIDE BIN LADEN TERRORISED THE UNITED STATES.
THE SOLDIERS GAVE THEIR LIVES FOR HIM IN THE NAME OF ALLAH.
OUR GUIDE BIN LADEN TERRORISED THE UNITED STATES.

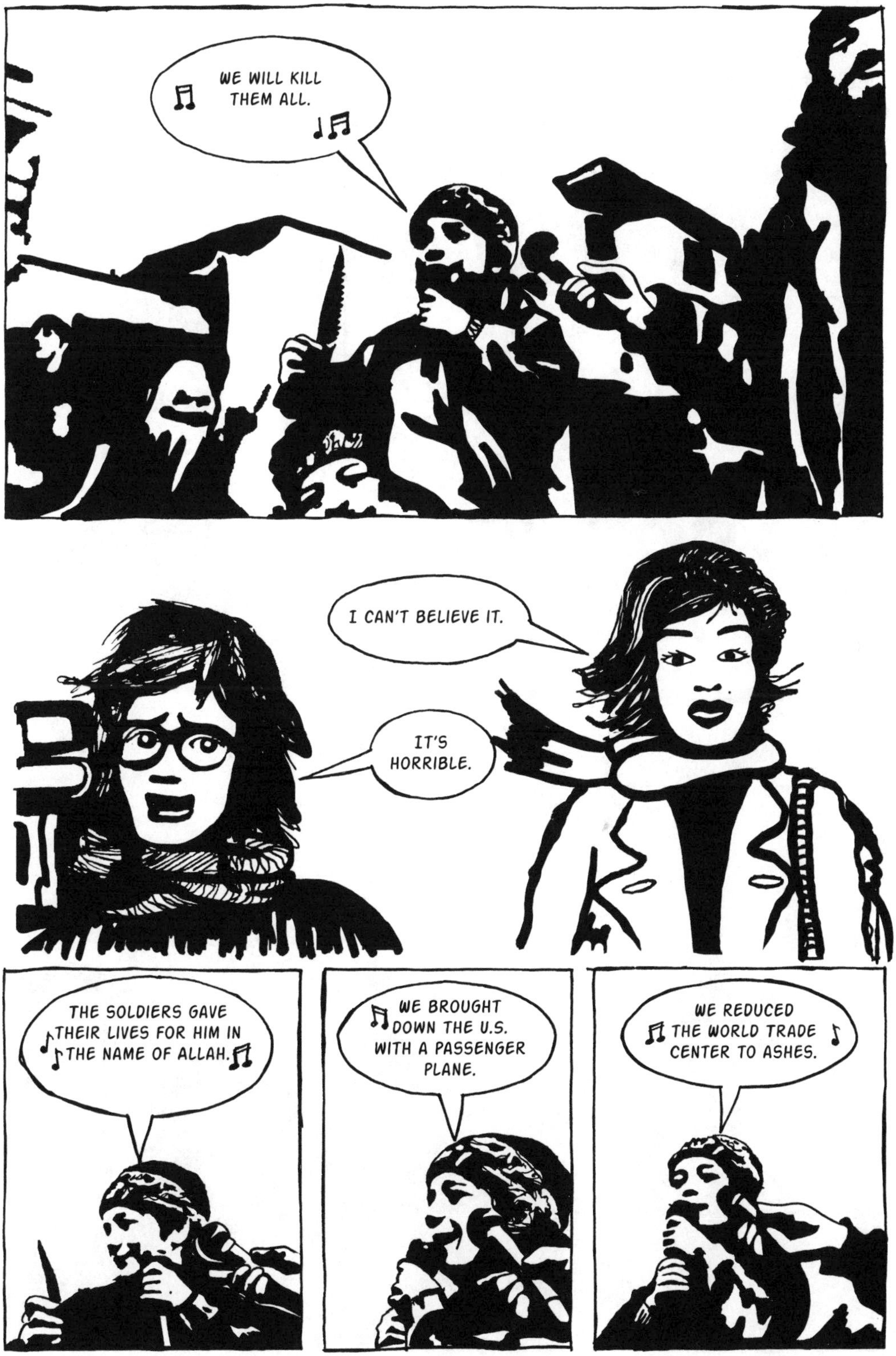
WE WILL KILL THEM ALL.
I CAN'T BELIEVE IT.
IT'S HORRIBLE.
THE SOLDIERS GAVE THEIR LIVES FOR HIM IN THE NAME OF ALLAH.
WE BROUGHT DOWN THE U.S. WITH A PASSENGER PLANE.
WE REDUCED THE WORLD TRADE CENTER TO ASHES.

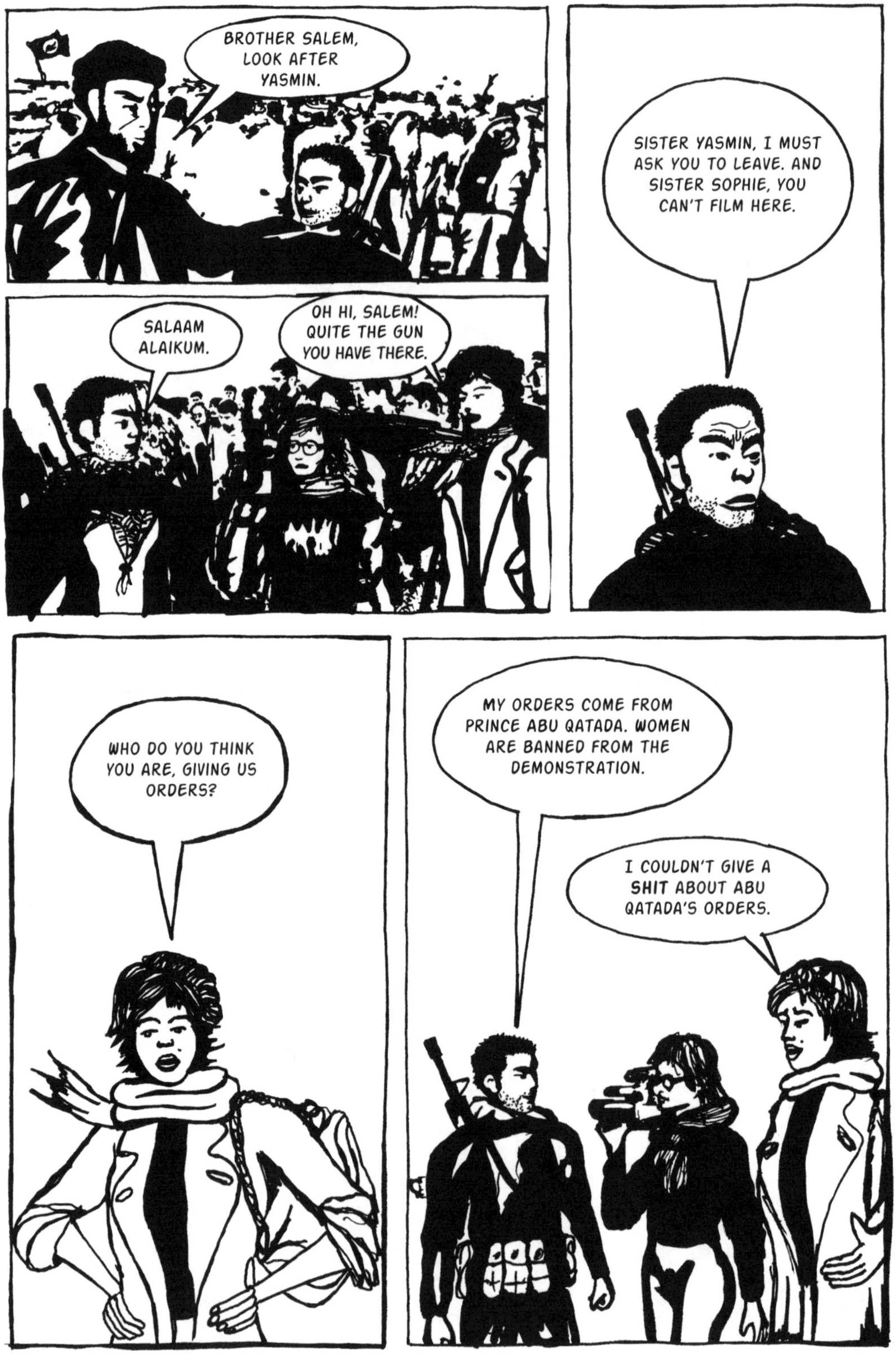
BROTHER SALEM, LOOK AFTER YASMIN.
SALAAM ALAIKUM.
OH HI, SALEM! QUITE THE GUN YOU HAVE THERE.
SISTER YASMIN, I MUST ASK YOU TO LEAVE. AND SISTER SOPHIE, YOU CAN'T FILM HERE.
WHO DO YOU THINK YOU ARE, GIVING US ORDERS?
MY ORDERS COME FROM PRINCE ABU QATADA. WOMEN ARE BANNED FROM THE DEMONSTRATION.
I COULDN'T GIVE A **SHIT** ABOUT ABU QATADA'S ORDERS.

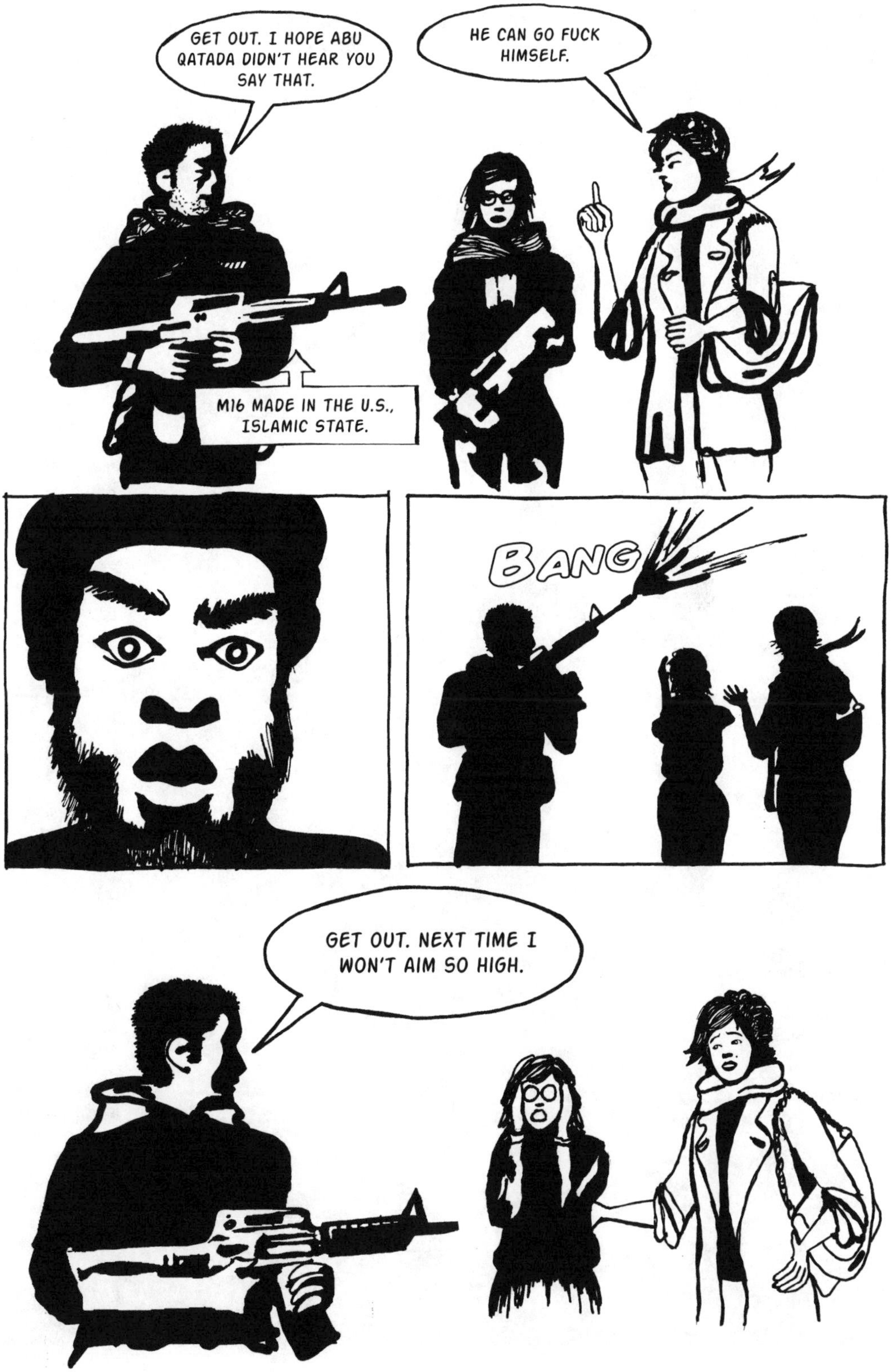
GET OUT. I HOPE ABU QATADA DIDN'T HEAR YOU SAY THAT.
HE CAN GO FUCK HIMSELF.
M16 MADE IN THE U.S., ISLAMIC STATE.
BANG
GET OUT. NEXT TIME I WON'T AIM SO HIGH.

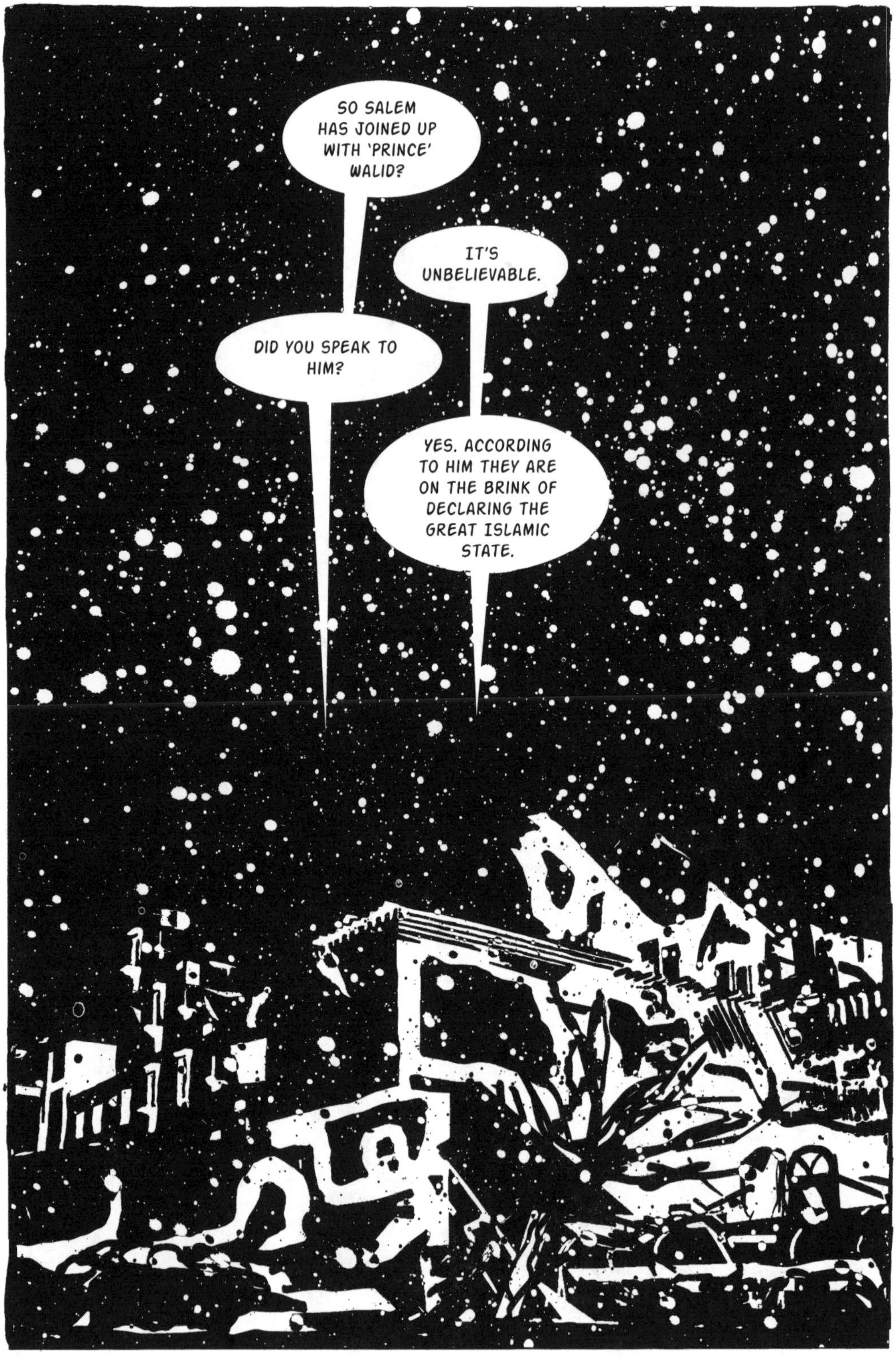
SO SALEM HAS JOINED UP WITH 'PRINCE' WALID?
IT'S UNBELIEVABLE.
DID YOU SPEAK TO HIM?
YES. ACCORDING TO HIM THEY ARE ON THE BRINK OF DECLARING THE GREAT ISLAMIC STATE.

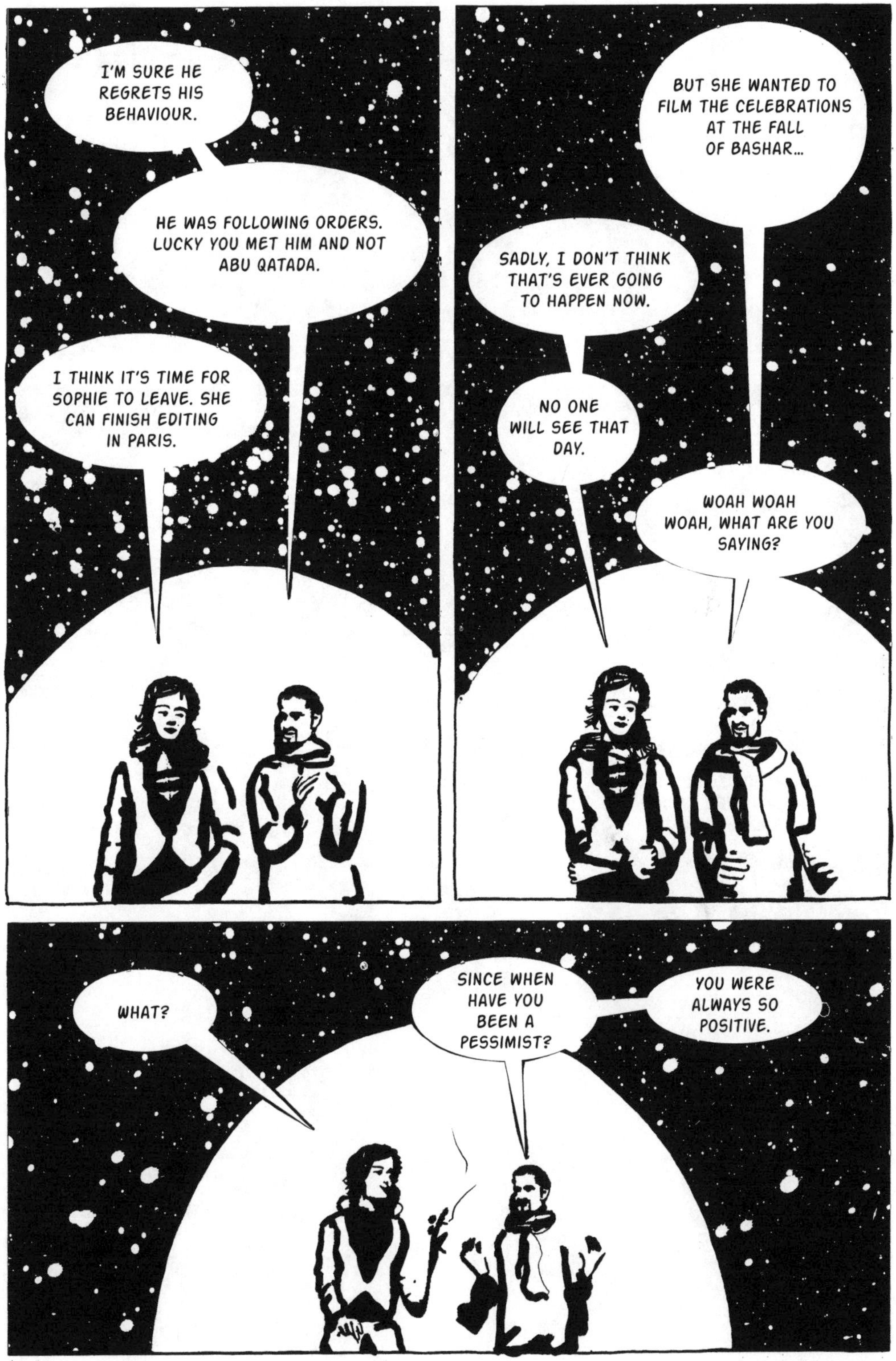
I'M SURE HE REGRETS HIS BEHAVIOUR.
HE WAS FOLLOWING ORDERS. LUCKY YOU MET HIM AND NOT ABU QATADA.
I THINK IT'S TIME FOR SOPHIE TO LEAVE. SHE CAN FINISH EDITING IN PARIS.
BUT SHE WANTED TO FILM THE CELEBRATIONS AT THE FALL OF BASHAR...
SADLY, I DON'T THINK THAT'S EVER GOING TO HAPPEN NOW.
NO ONE WILL SEE THAT DAY.
WOAH WOAH WOAH, WHAT ARE YOU SAYING?
WHAT?
SINCE WHEN HAVE YOU BEEN A PESSIMIST?
YOU WERE ALWAYS SO POSITIVE.

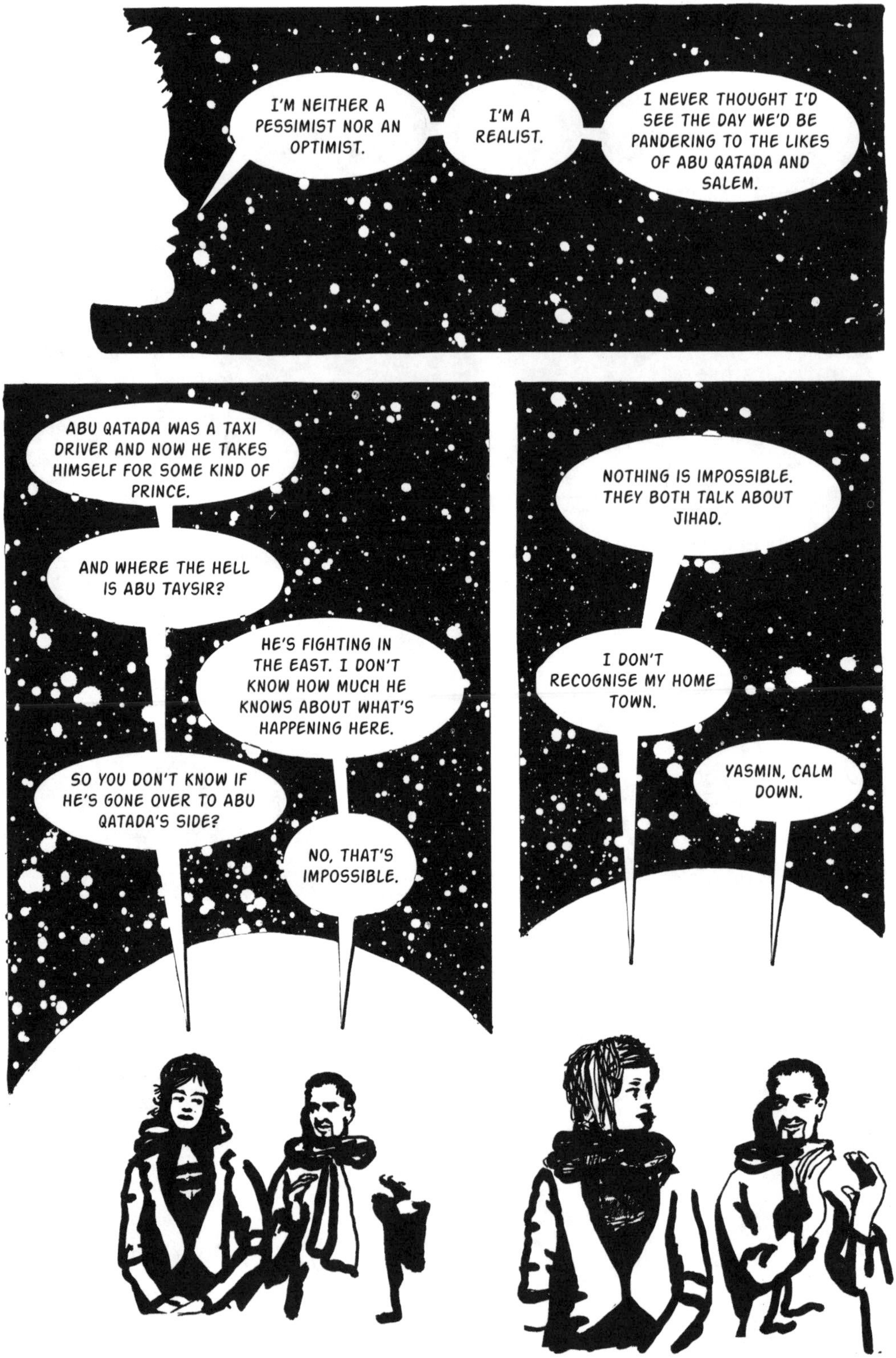
I'M NEITHER A PESSIMIST NOR AN OPTIMIST.
I'M A REALIST.
I NEVER THOUGHT I'D SEE THE DAY WE'D BE PANDERING TO THE LIKES OF ABU QATADA AND SALEM.
ABU QATADA WAS A TAXI DRIVER AND NOW HE TAKES HIMSELF FOR SOME KIND OF PRINCE.
AND WHERE THE HELL IS ABU TAYSIR?
HE'S FIGHTING IN THE EAST. I DON'T KNOW HOW MUCH HE KNOWS ABOUT WHAT'S HAPPENING HERE.
SO YOU DON'T KNOW IF HE'S GONE OVER TO ABU QATADA'S SIDE?
NO, THAT'S IMPOSSIBLE.
NOTHING IS IMPOSSIBLE. THEY BOTH TALK ABOUT JIHAD.
I DON'T RECOGNISE MY HOME TOWN.
YASMIN, CALM DOWN.

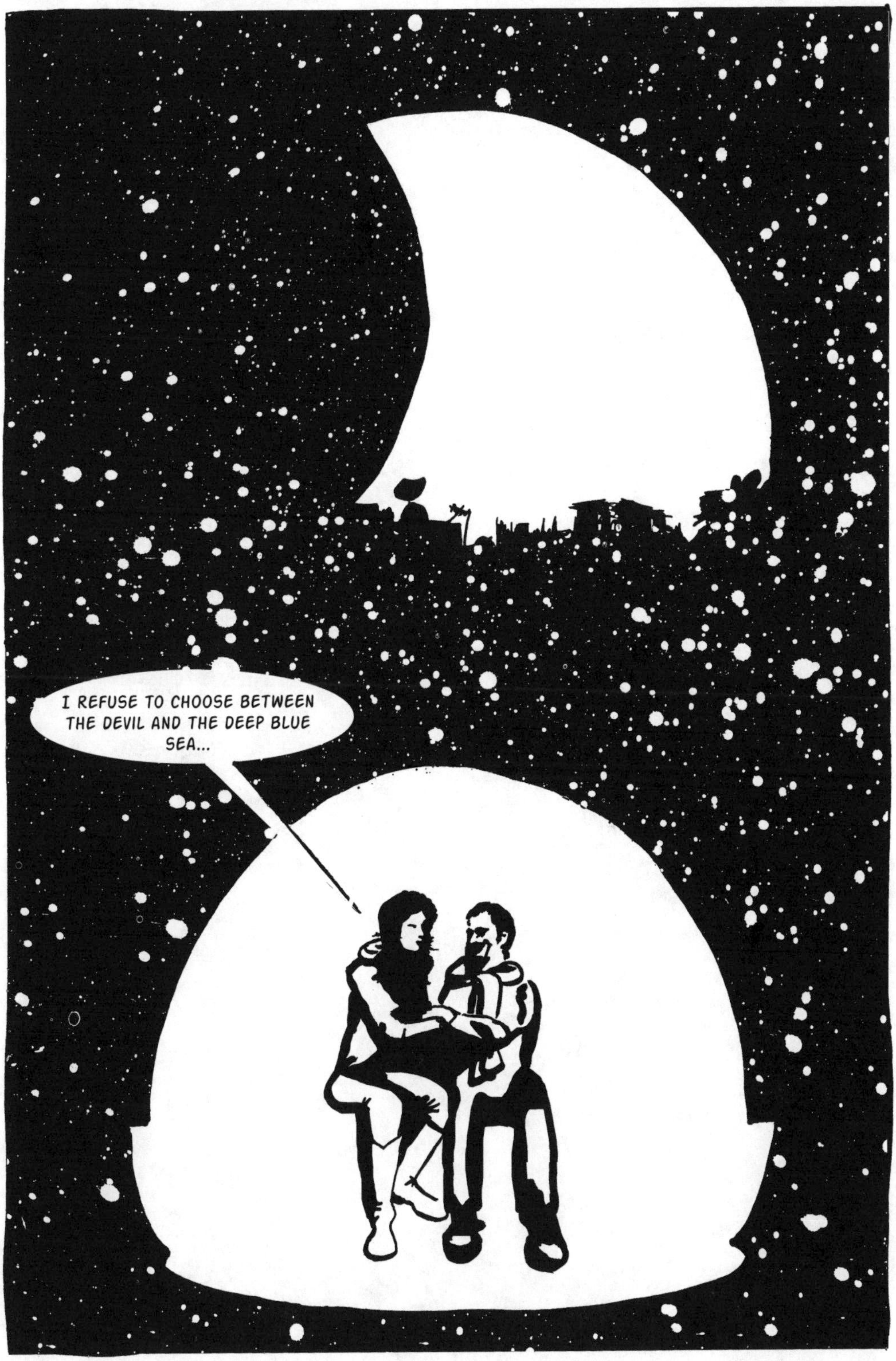
I REFUSE TO CHOOSE BETWEEN THE DEVIL AND THE DEEP BLUE SEA...

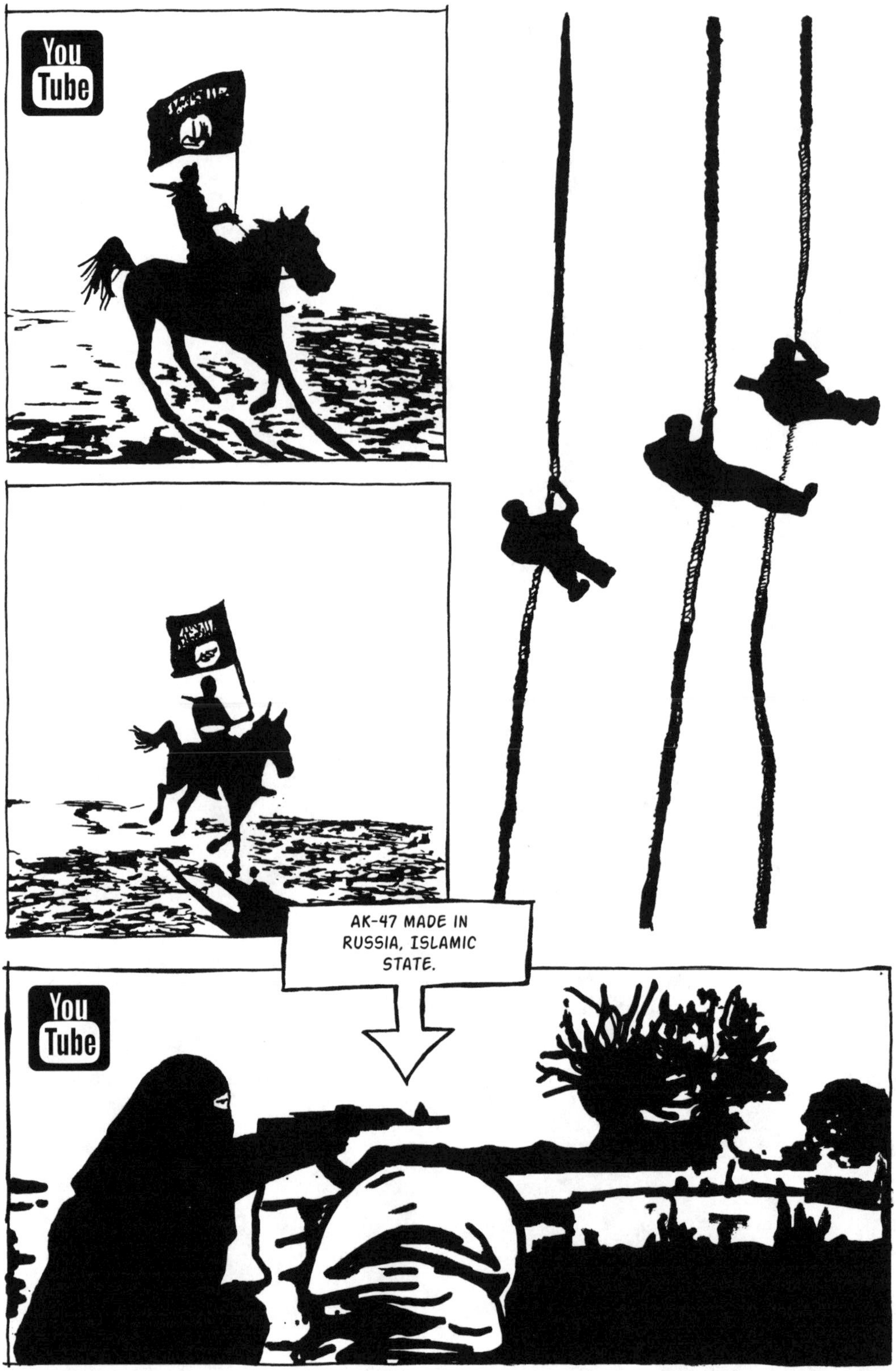
You Tube
AK-47 MADE IN RUSSIA, ISLAMIC STATE.
You Tube

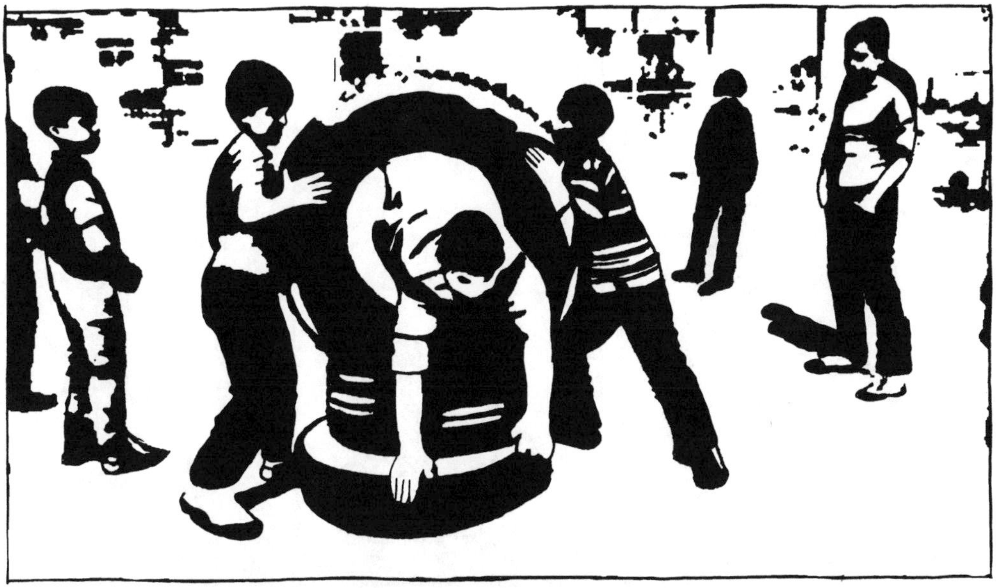

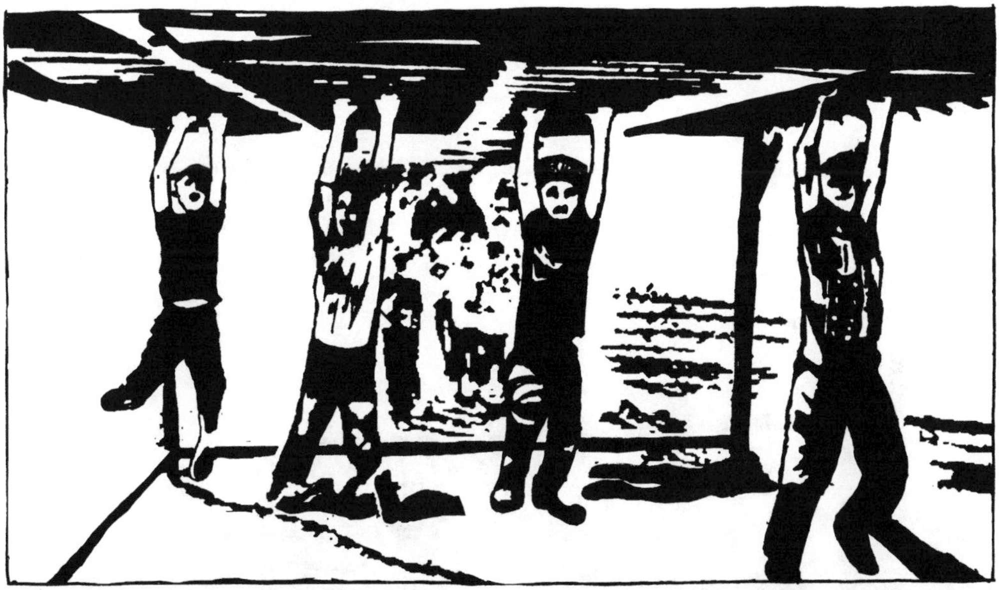

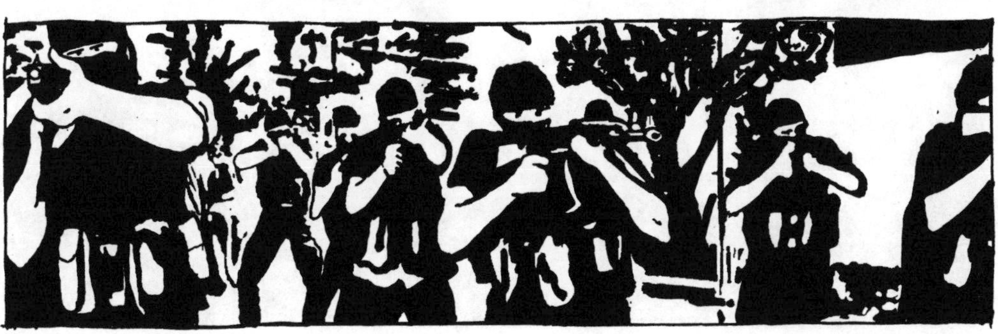

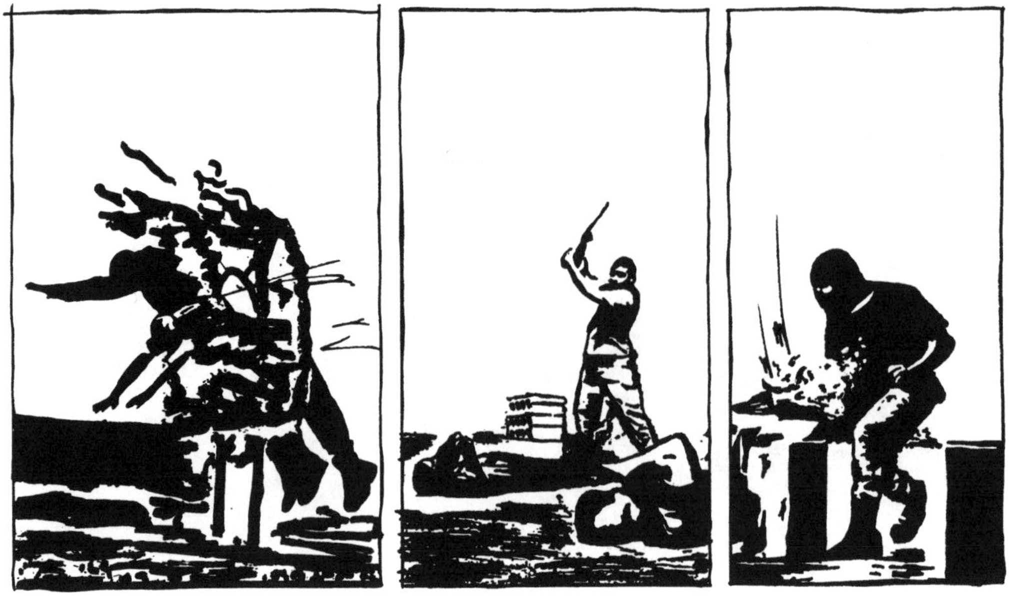

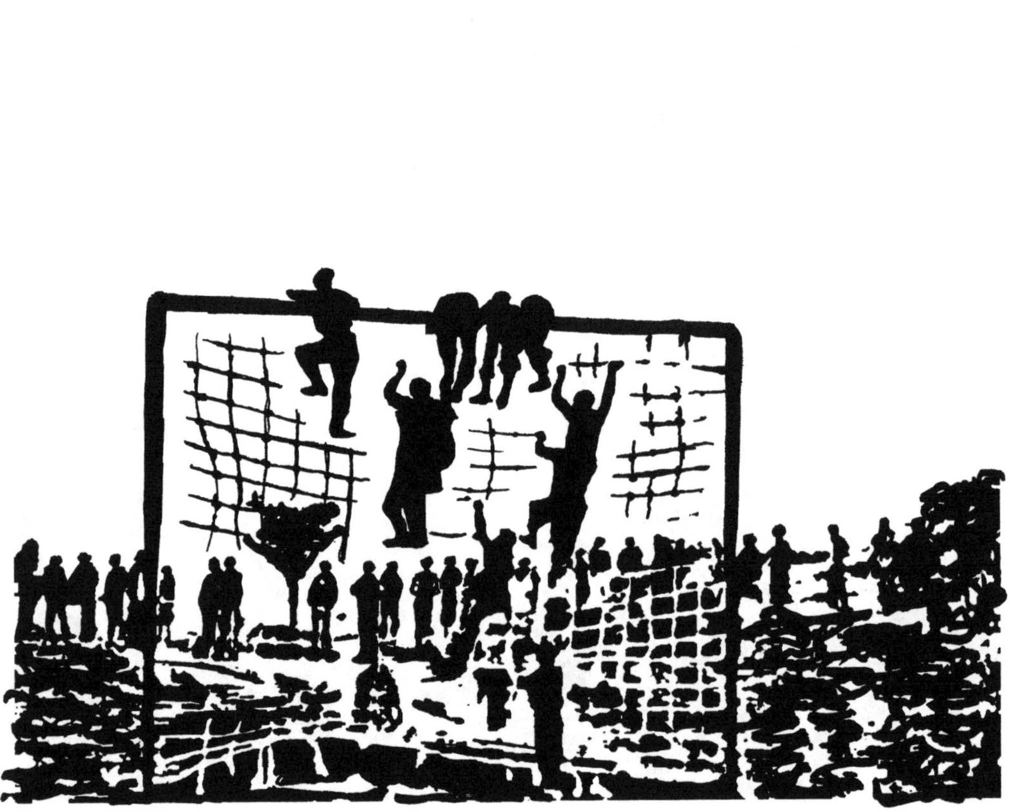

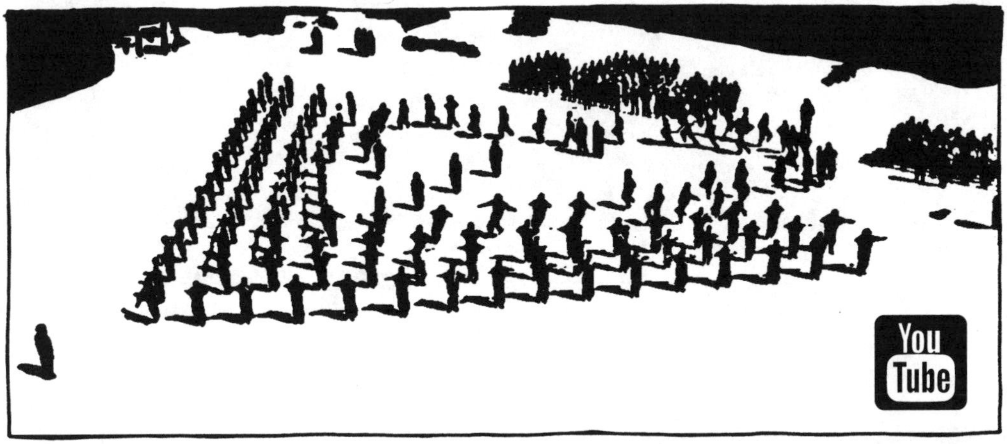
You
Tube

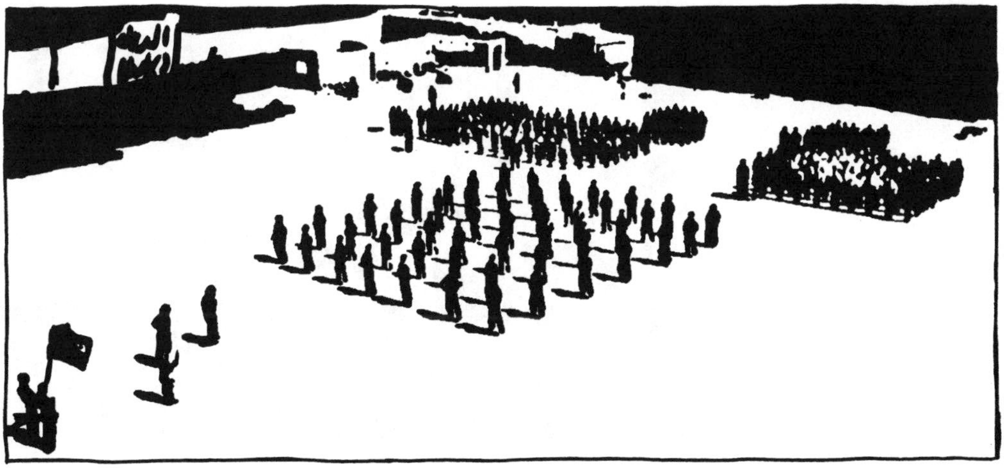

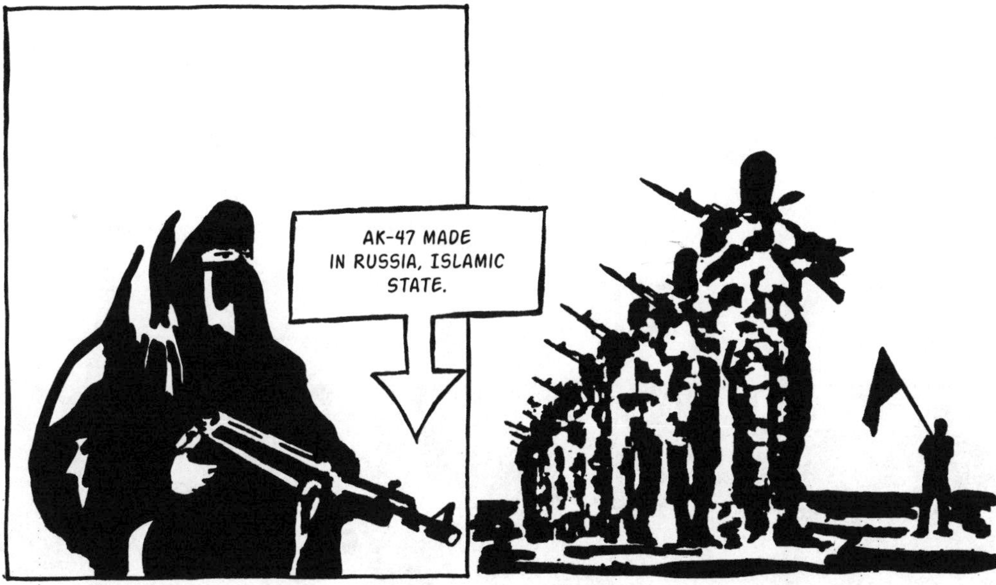
AK-47 MADE IN RUSSIA, ISLAMIC STATE.

← → C 🔒 https://www.youtube.com/watch?v=...

APPS ★ Favorites

≡ YouTube   الدولة الإسلامية 🔍

► ►► ◄◄ ◀) 2:07 / 2:15

سوريا: تدريبات الدولة الإسلامية العسكرية

TV ISIS   532

✚ Add to   ➤ Share   ••• Plus

Published 3 April 2013
Catalogue   people of blogs
Liaison   License YouTube ...

All comments 151

Add a comment

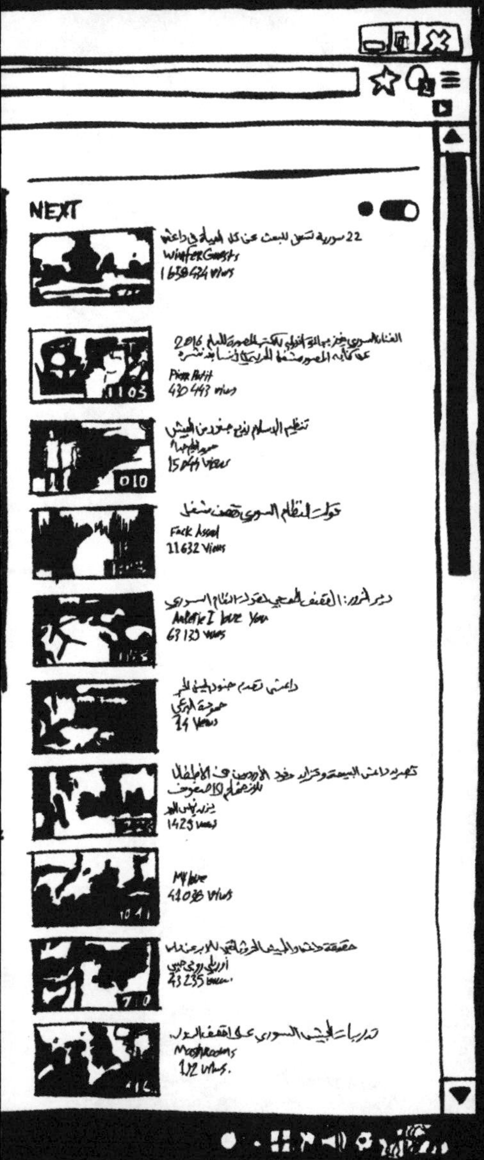
NEXT

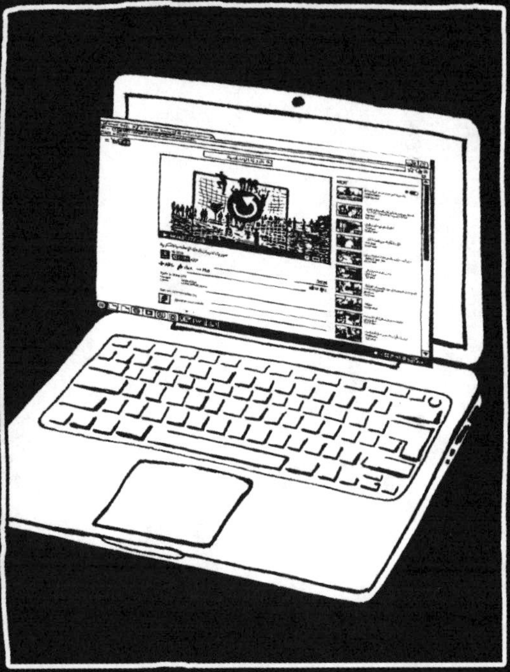

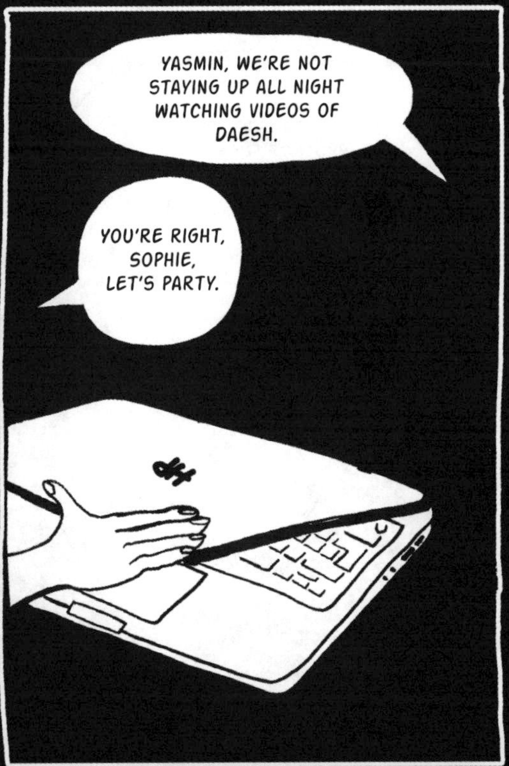
YASMIN, WE'RE NOT STAYING UP ALL NIGHT WATCHING VIDEOS OF DAESH.
YOU'RE RIGHT, SOPHIE, LET'S PARTY.

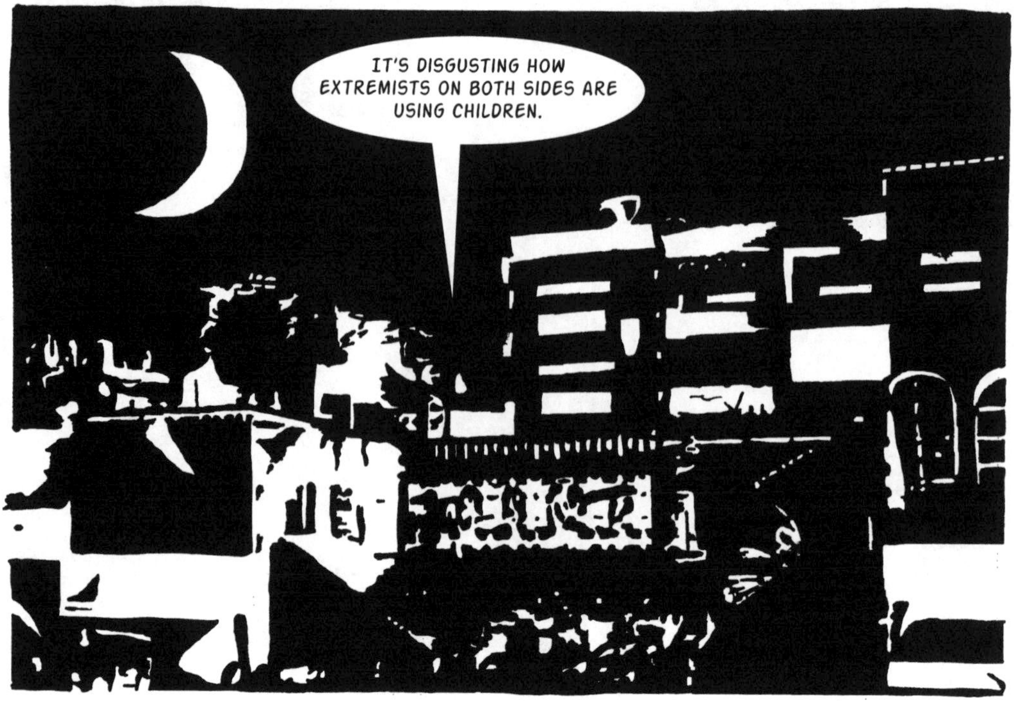
IT'S DISGUSTING HOW EXTREMISTS ON BOTH SIDES ARE USING CHILDREN.

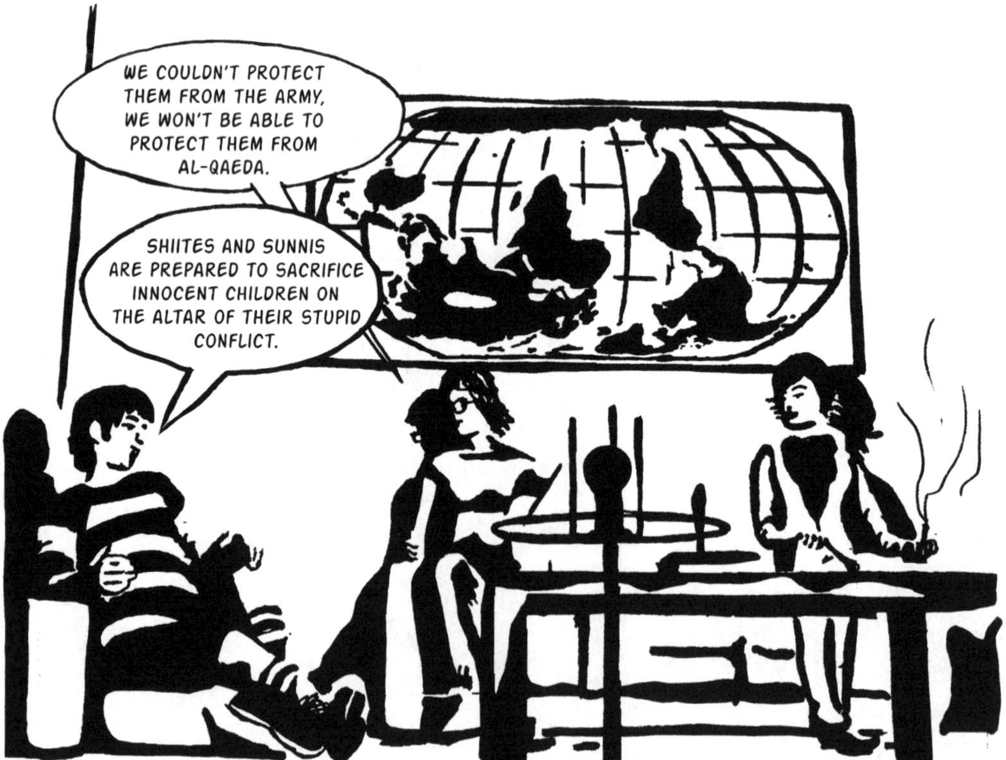
WE COULDN'T PROTECT THEM FROM THE ARMY, WE WON'T BE ABLE TO PROTECT THEM FROM AL-QAEDA.
SHIITES AND SUNNIS ARE PREPARED TO SACRIFICE INNOCENT CHILDREN ON THE ALTAR OF THEIR STUPID CONFLICT.

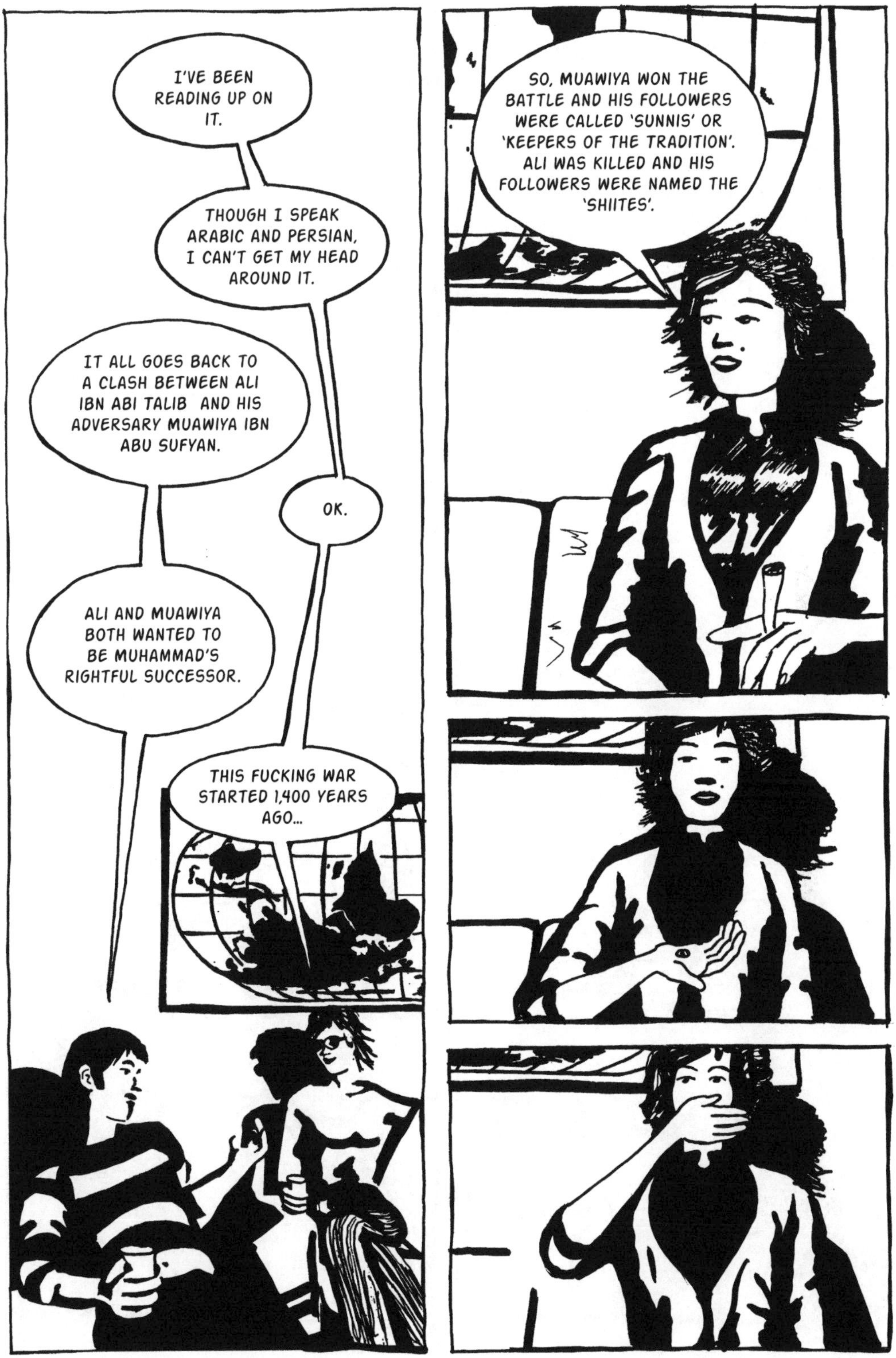
I'VE BEEN READING UP ON IT.
THOUGH I SPEAK ARABIC AND PERSIAN, I CAN'T GET MY HEAD AROUND IT.
IT ALL GOES BACK TO A CLASH BETWEEN ALI IBN ABI TALIB AND HIS ADVERSARY MUAWIYA IBN ABU SUFYAN.
OK.
ALI AND MUAWIYA BOTH WANTED TO BE MUHAMMAD'S RIGHTFUL SUCCESSOR.
THIS FUCKING WAR STARTED 1,400 YEARS AGO...
SO, MUAWIYA WON THE BATTLE AND HIS FOLLOWERS WERE CALLED 'SUNNIS' OR 'KEEPERS OF THE TRADITION'. ALI WAS KILLED AND HIS FOLLOWERS WERE NAMED THE 'SHIITES'.

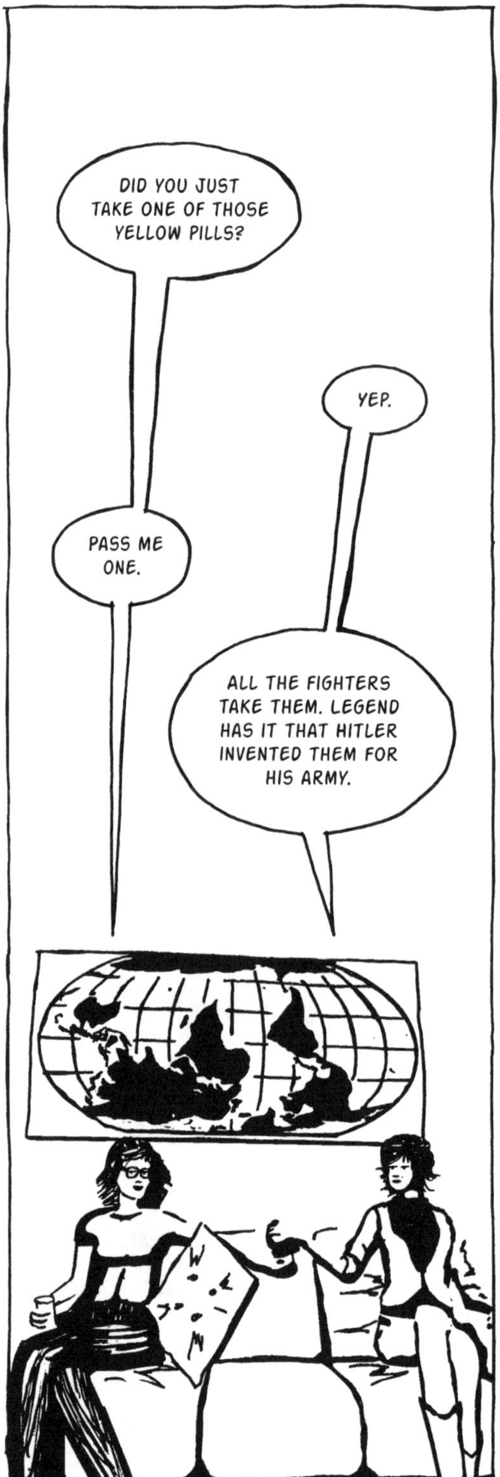
DID YOU JUST TAKE ONE OF THOSE YELLOW PILLS?
YEP.
PASS ME ONE.
ALL THE FIGHTERS TAKE THEM. LEGEND HAS IT THAT HITLER INVENTED THEM FOR HIS ARMY.

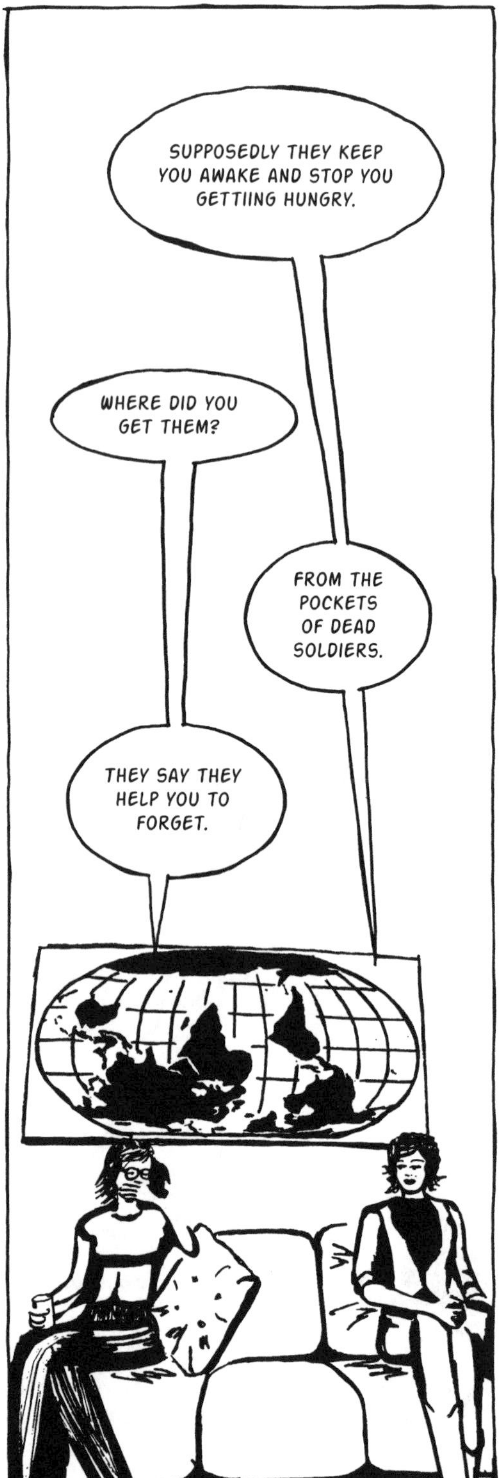
SUPPOSEDLY THEY KEEP YOU AWAKE AND STOP YOU GETTIING HUNGRY.
WHERE DID YOU GET THEM?
FROM THE POCKETS OF DEAD SOLDIERS.
THEY SAY THEY HELP YOU TO FORGET.

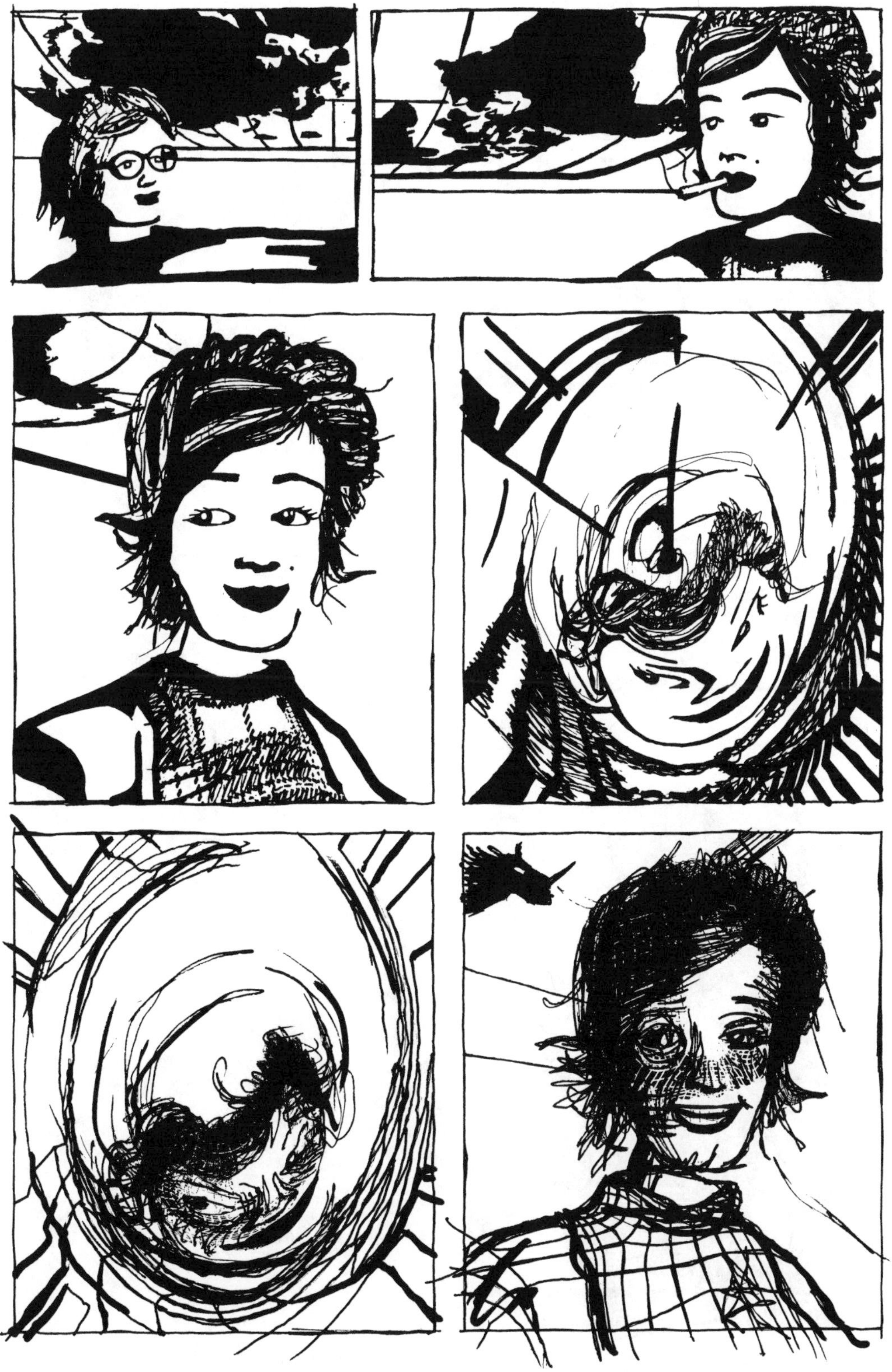

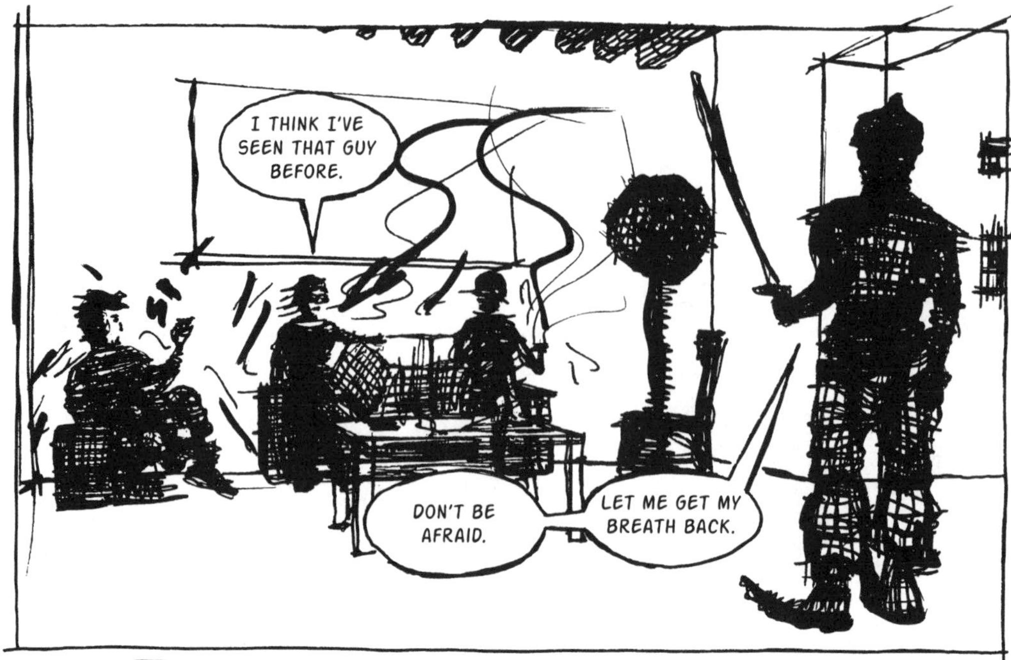
I THINK I'VE SEEN THAT GUY BEFORE.
DON'T BE AFRAID.
LET ME GET MY BREATH BACK.

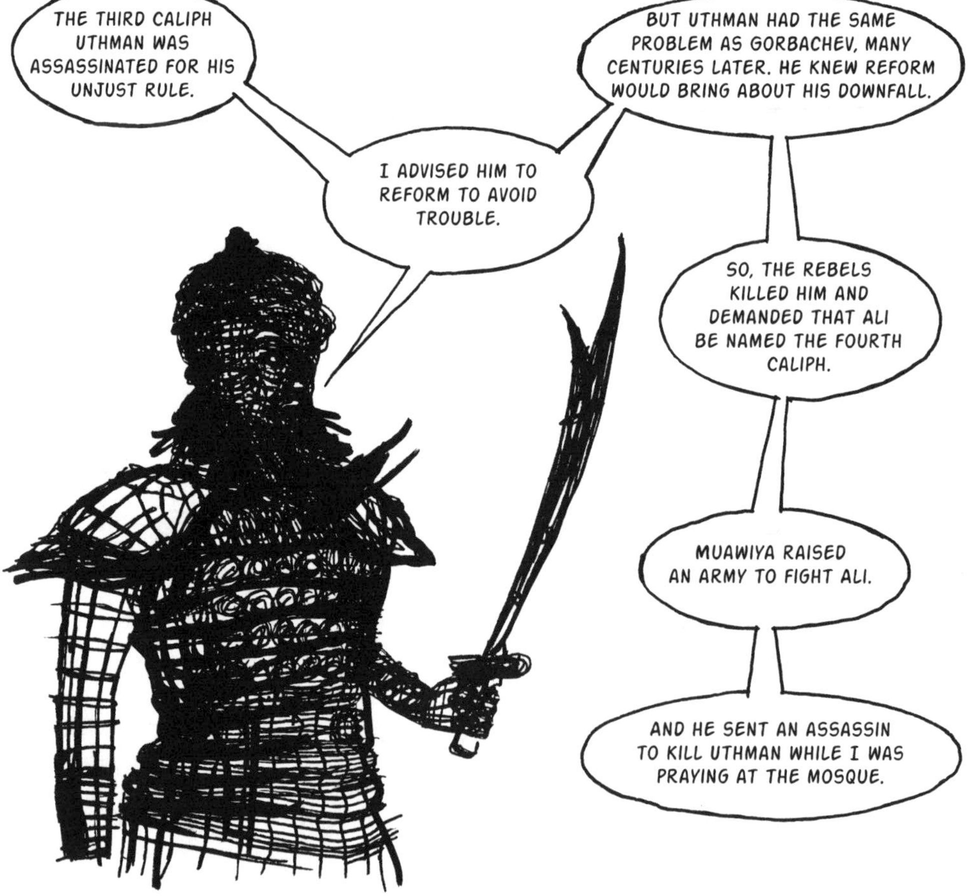
THE THIRD CALIPH UTHMAN WAS ASSASSINATED FOR HIS UNJUST RULE.
I ADVISED HIM TO REFORM TO AVOID TROUBLE.
BUT UTHMAN HAD THE SAME PROBLEM AS GORBACHEV, MANY CENTURIES LATER. HE KNEW REFORM WOULD BRING ABOUT HIS DOWNFALL.
SO, THE REBELS KILLED HIM AND DEMANDED THAT ALI BE NAMED THE FOURTH CALIPH.
MUAWIYA RAISED AN ARMY TO FIGHT ALI.
AND HE SENT AN ASSASSIN TO KILL UTHMAN WHILE I WAS PRAYING AT THE MOSQUE.

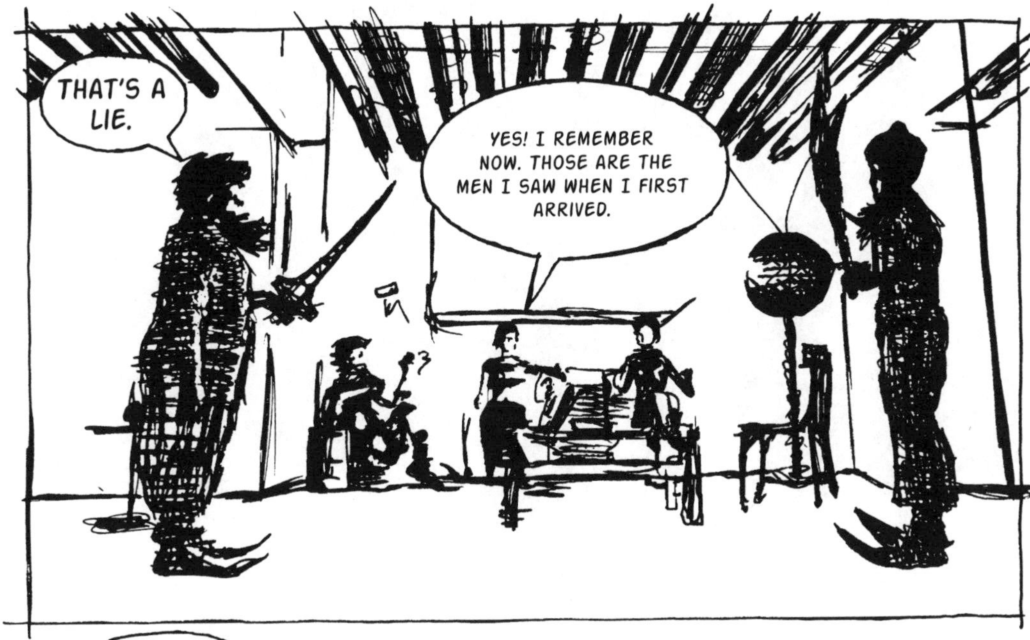
THAT'S A LIE.
YES! I REMEMBER NOW. THOSE ARE THE MEN I SAW WHEN I FIRST ARRIVED.

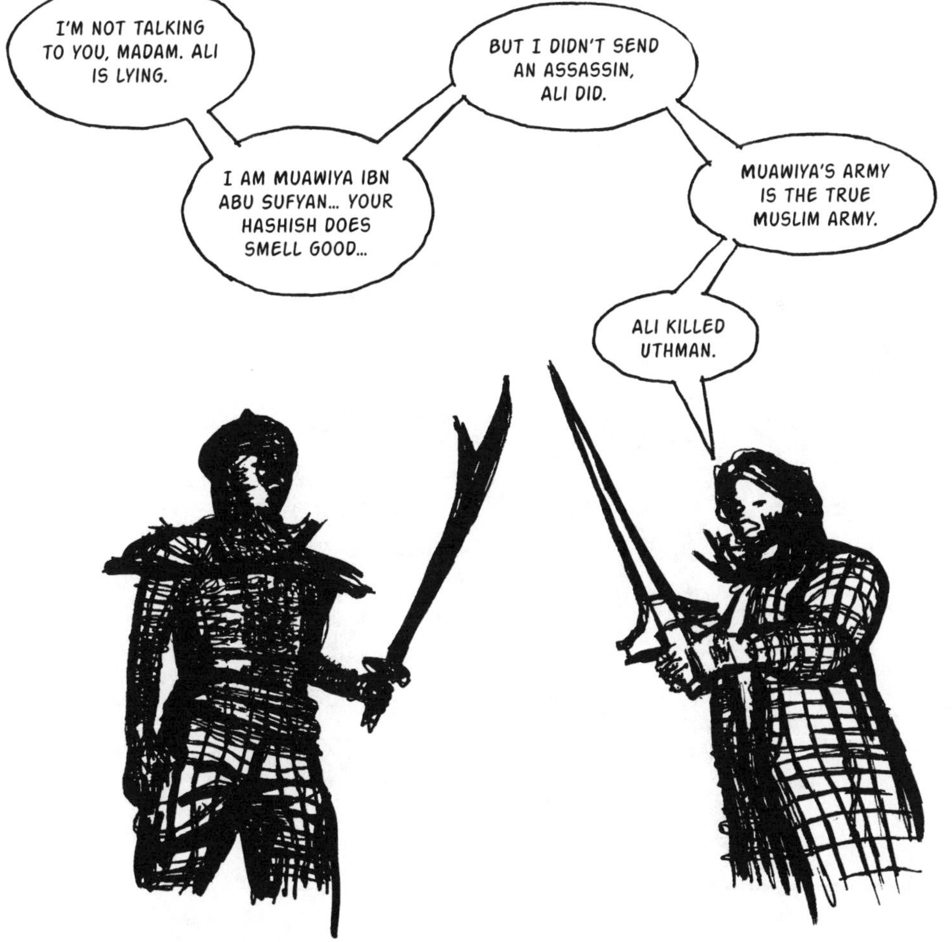
I'M NOT TALKING TO YOU, MADAM. ALI IS LYING.
I AM MUAWIYA IBN ABU SUFYAN... YOUR HASHISH DOES SMELL GOOD...
BUT I DIDN'T SEND AN ASSASSIN, ALI DID.
MUAWIYA'S ARMY IS THE TRUE MUSLIM ARMY.
ALI KILLED UTHMAN.

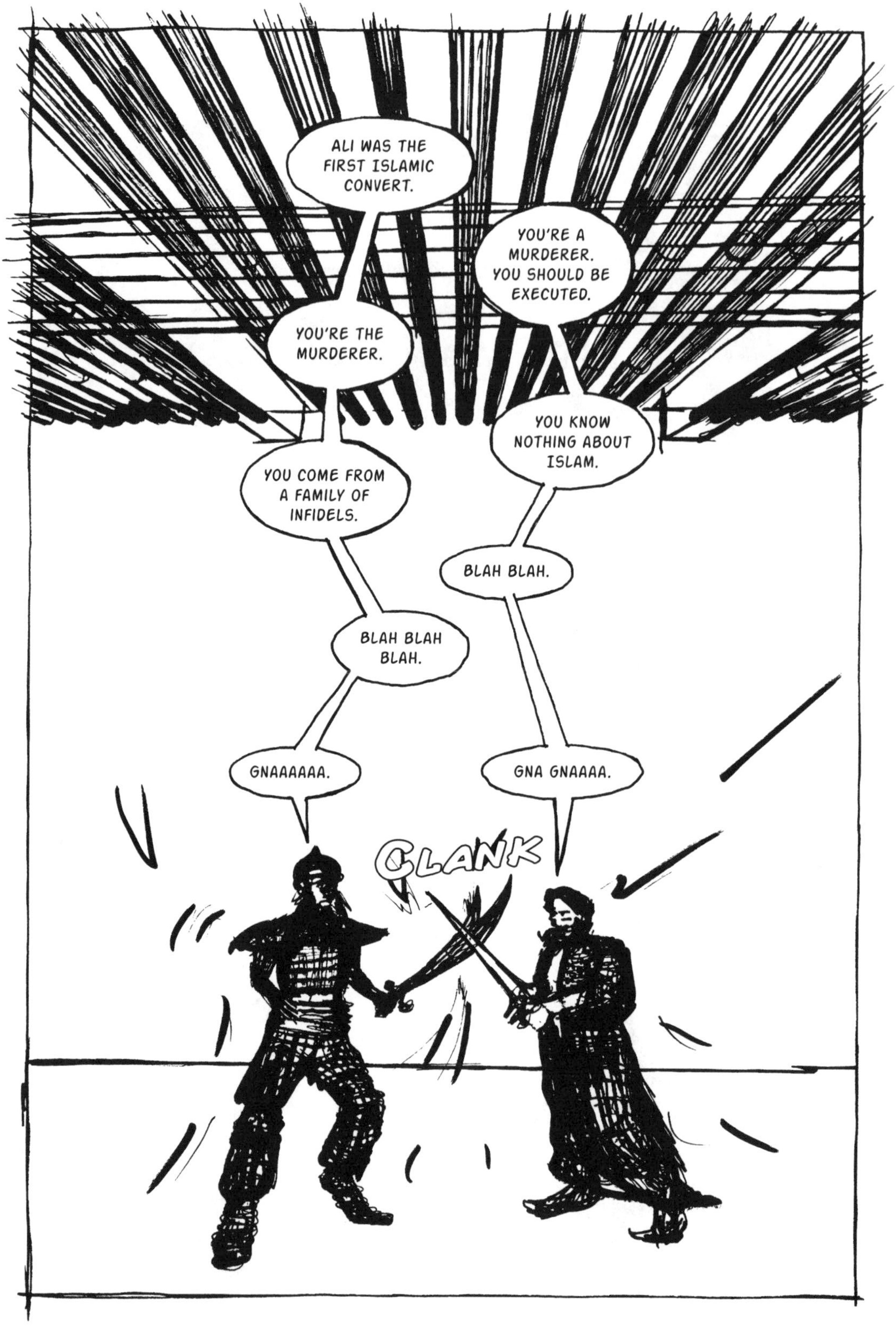
ALI WAS THE FIRST ISLAMIC CONVERT.
YOU'RE A MURDERER. YOU SHOULD BE EXECUTED.
YOU'RE THE MURDERER.
YOU KNOW NOTHING ABOUT ISLAM.
YOU COME FROM A FAMILY OF INFIDELS.
BLAH BLAH.
BLAH BLAH BLAH.
GNAAAAAA.
GNA GNAAAA.
CLANK

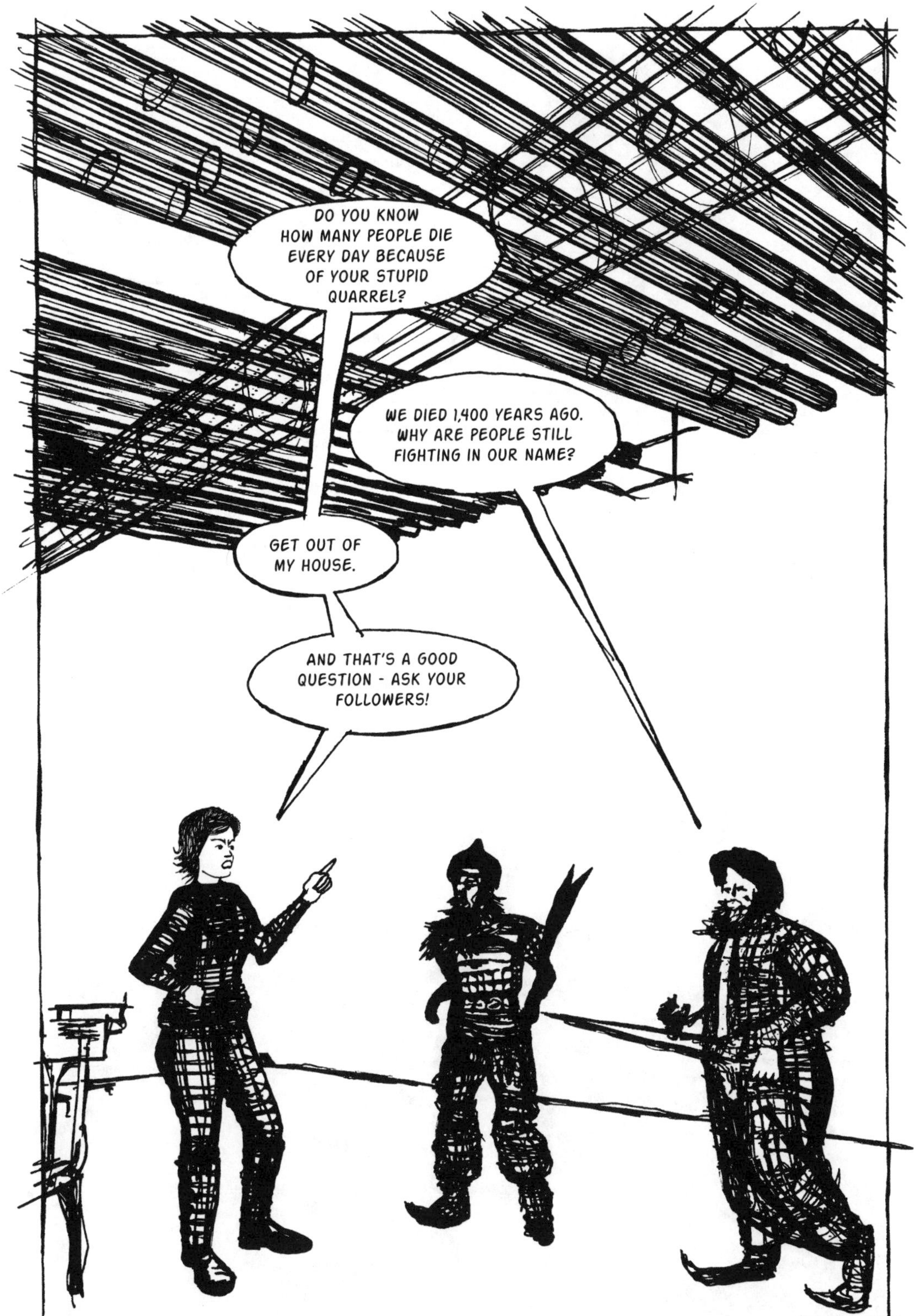
DO YOU KNOW HOW MANY PEOPLE DIE EVERY DAY BECAUSE OF YOUR STUPID QUARREL?
WE DIED 1,400 YEARS AGO. WHY ARE PEOPLE STILL FIGHTING IN OUR NAME?
GET OUT OF MY HOUSE.
AND THAT'S A GOOD QUESTION - ASK YOUR FOLLOWERS!

ONE DAY LATER: ANOTHER 503 KILLED.

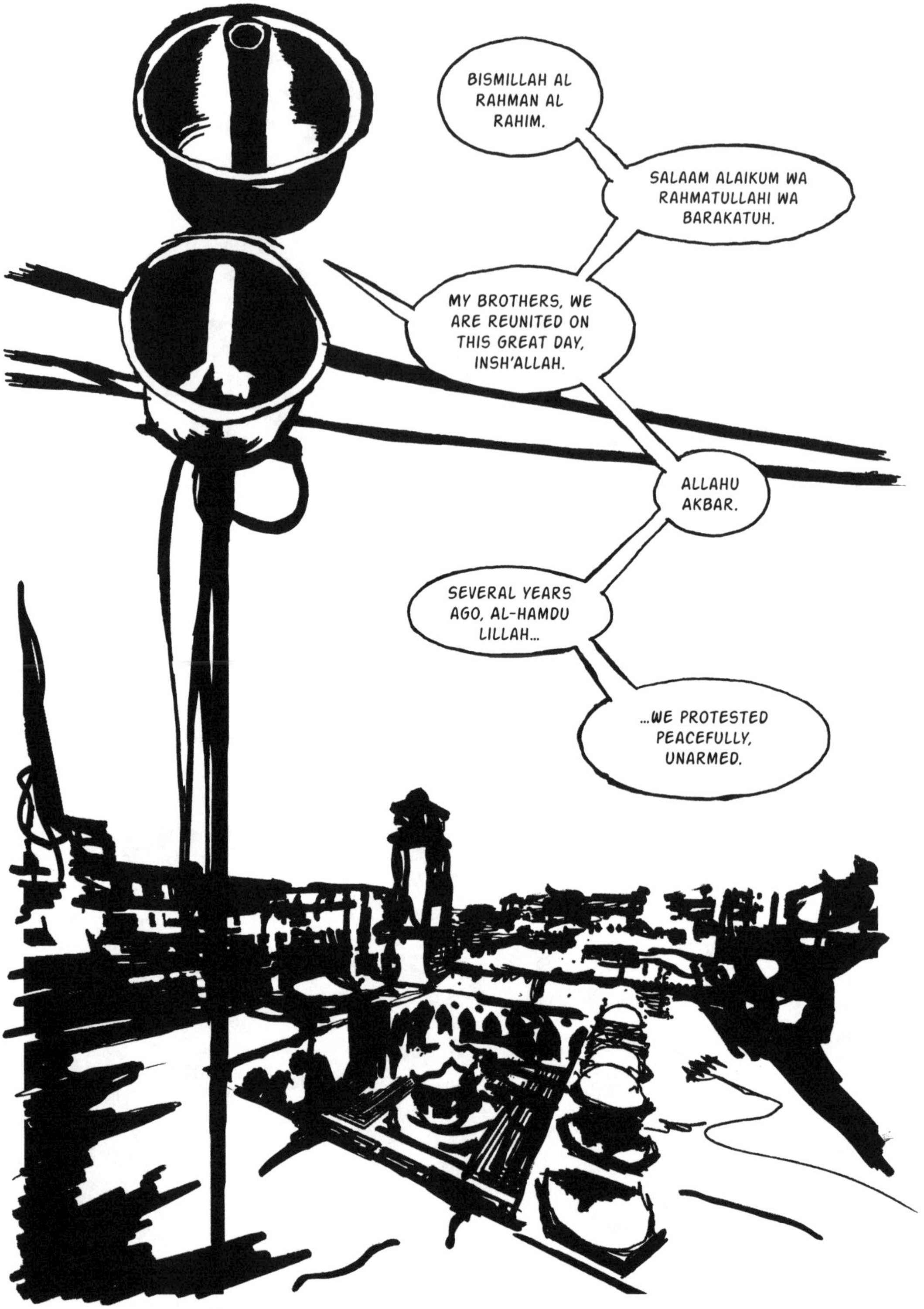
BISMILLAH AL RAHMAN AL RAHIM.
SALAAM ALAIKUM WA RAHMATULLAHI WA BARAKATUH.
MY BROTHERS, WE ARE REUNITED ON THIS GREAT DAY, INSH'ALLAH.
ALLAHU AKBAR.
SEVERAL YEARS AGO, AL-HAMDU LILLAH...
...WE PROTESTED PEACEFULLY, UNARMED.

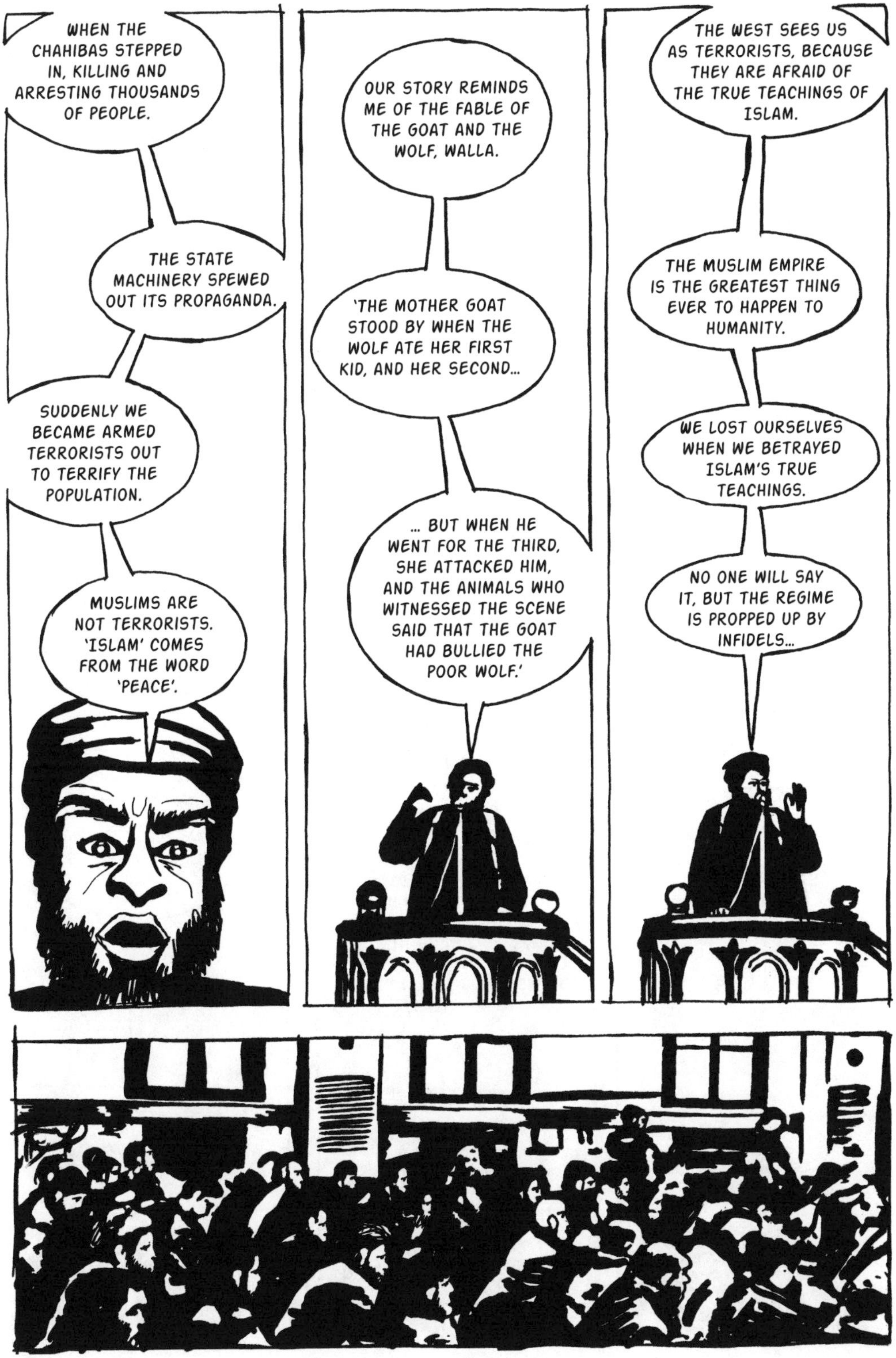
WHEN THE CHAHIBAS STEPPED IN, KILLING AND ARRESTING THOUSANDS OF PEOPLE.
THE STATE MACHINERY SPEWED OUT ITS PROPAGANDA.
SUDDENLY WE BECAME ARMED TERRORISTS OUT TO TERRIFY THE POPULATION.
MUSLIMS ARE NOT TERRORISTS. 'ISLAM' COMES FROM THE WORD 'PEACE'.
OUR STORY REMINDS ME OF THE FABLE OF THE GOAT AND THE WOLF, WALLA.
'THE MOTHER GOAT STOOD BY WHEN THE WOLF ATE HER FIRST KID, AND HER SECOND...
... BUT WHEN HE WENT FOR THE THIRD, SHE ATTACKED HIM, AND THE ANIMALS WHO WITNESSED THE SCENE SAID THAT THE GOAT HAD BULLIED THE POOR WOLF.'
THE WEST SEES US AS TERRORISTS, BECAUSE THEY ARE AFRAID OF THE TRUE TEACHINGS OF ISLAM.
THE MUSLIM EMPIRE IS THE GREATEST THING EVER TO HAPPEN TO HUMANITY.
WE LOST OURSELVES WHEN WE BETRAYED ISLAM'S TRUE TEACHINGS.
NO ONE WILL SAY IT, BUT THE REGIME IS PROPPED UP BY INFIDELS...

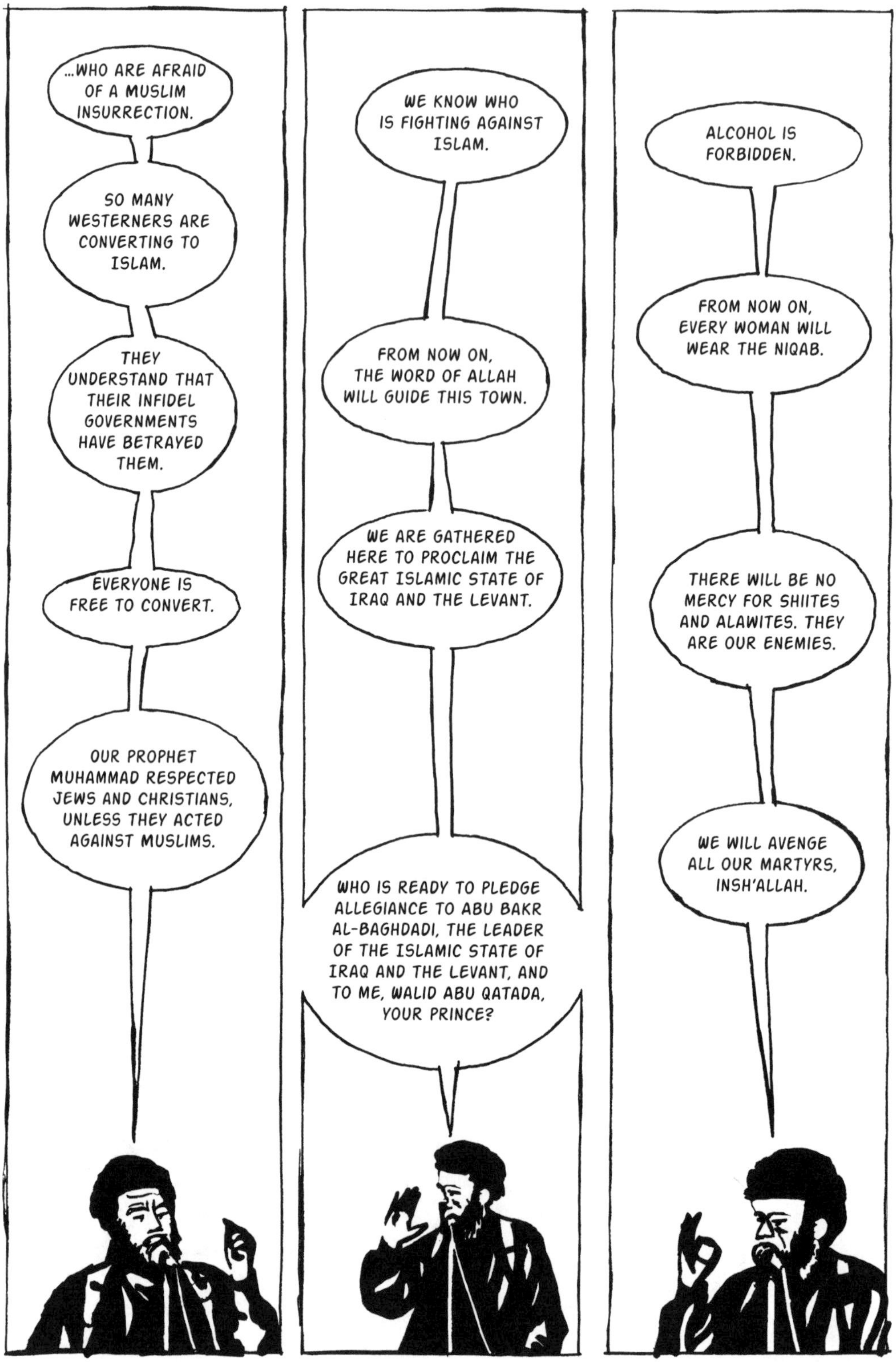
...WHO ARE AFRAID OF A MUSLIM INSURRECTION.
SO MANY WESTERNERS ARE CONVERTING TO ISLAM.
THEY UNDERSTAND THAT THEIR INFIDEL GOVERNMENTS HAVE BETRAYED THEM.
EVERYONE IS FREE TO CONVERT.
OUR PROPHET MUHAMMAD RESPECTED JEWS AND CHRISTIANS, UNLESS THEY ACTED AGAINST MUSLIMS.
WE KNOW WHO IS FIGHTING AGAINST ISLAM.
FROM NOW ON, THE WORD OF ALLAH WILL GUIDE THIS TOWN.
WE ARE GATHERED HERE TO PROCLAIM THE GREAT ISLAMIC STATE OF IRAQ AND THE LEVANT.
WHO IS READY TO PLEDGE ALLEGIANCE TO ABU BAKR AL-BAGHDADI, THE LEADER OF THE ISLAMIC STATE OF IRAQ AND THE LEVANT, AND TO ME, WALID ABU QATADA, YOUR PRINCE?
ALCOHOL IS FORBIDDEN.
FROM NOW ON, EVERY WOMAN WILL WEAR THE NIQAB.
THERE WILL BE NO MERCY FOR SHIITES AND ALAWITES. THEY ARE OUR ENEMIES.
WE WILL AVENGE ALL OUR MARTYRS, INSH'ALLAH.

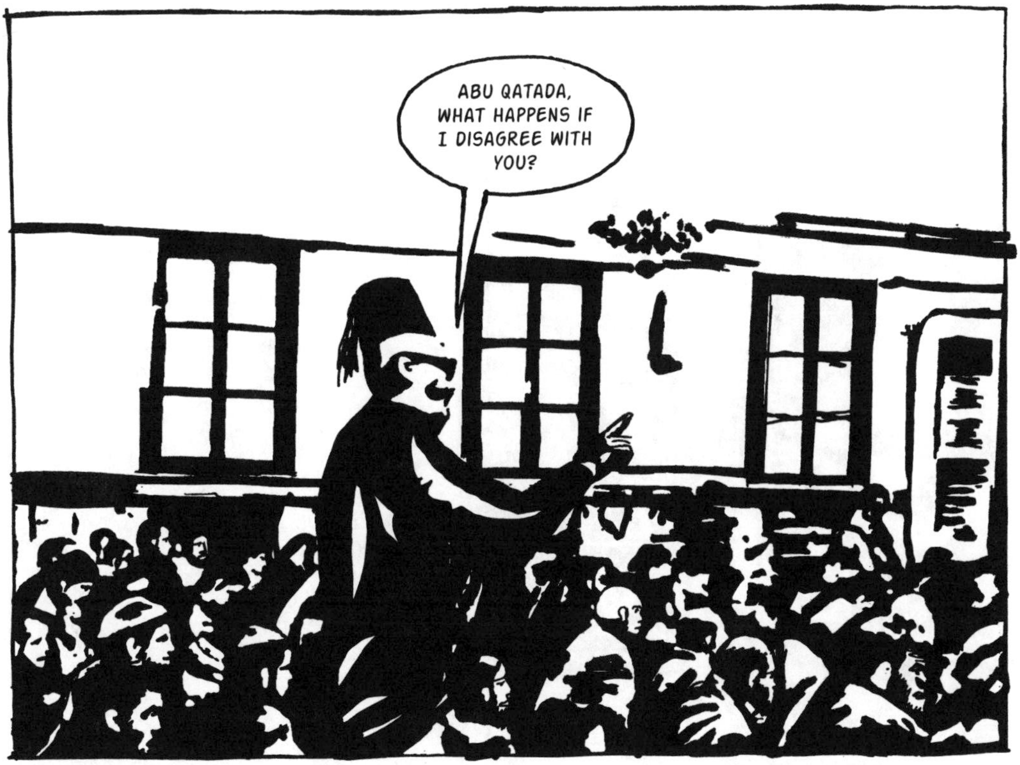
ABU QATADA, WHAT HAPPENS IF I DISAGREE WITH YOU?

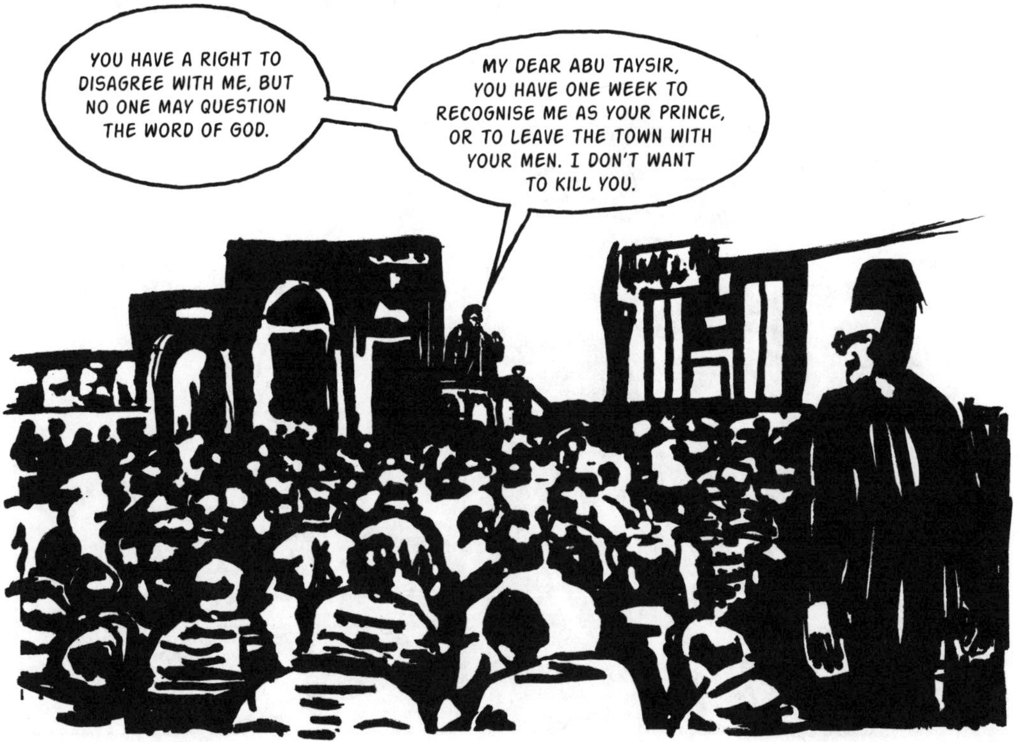
YOU HAVE A RIGHT TO DISAGREE WITH ME, BUT NO ONE MAY QUESTION THE WORD OF GOD.
MY DEAR ABU TAYSIR, YOU HAVE ONE WEEK TO RECOGNISE ME AS YOUR PRINCE, OR TO LEAVE THE TOWN WITH YOUR MEN. I DON'T WANT TO KILL YOU.

A FEW HOURS, AND SEVERAL KILLINGS, LATER.

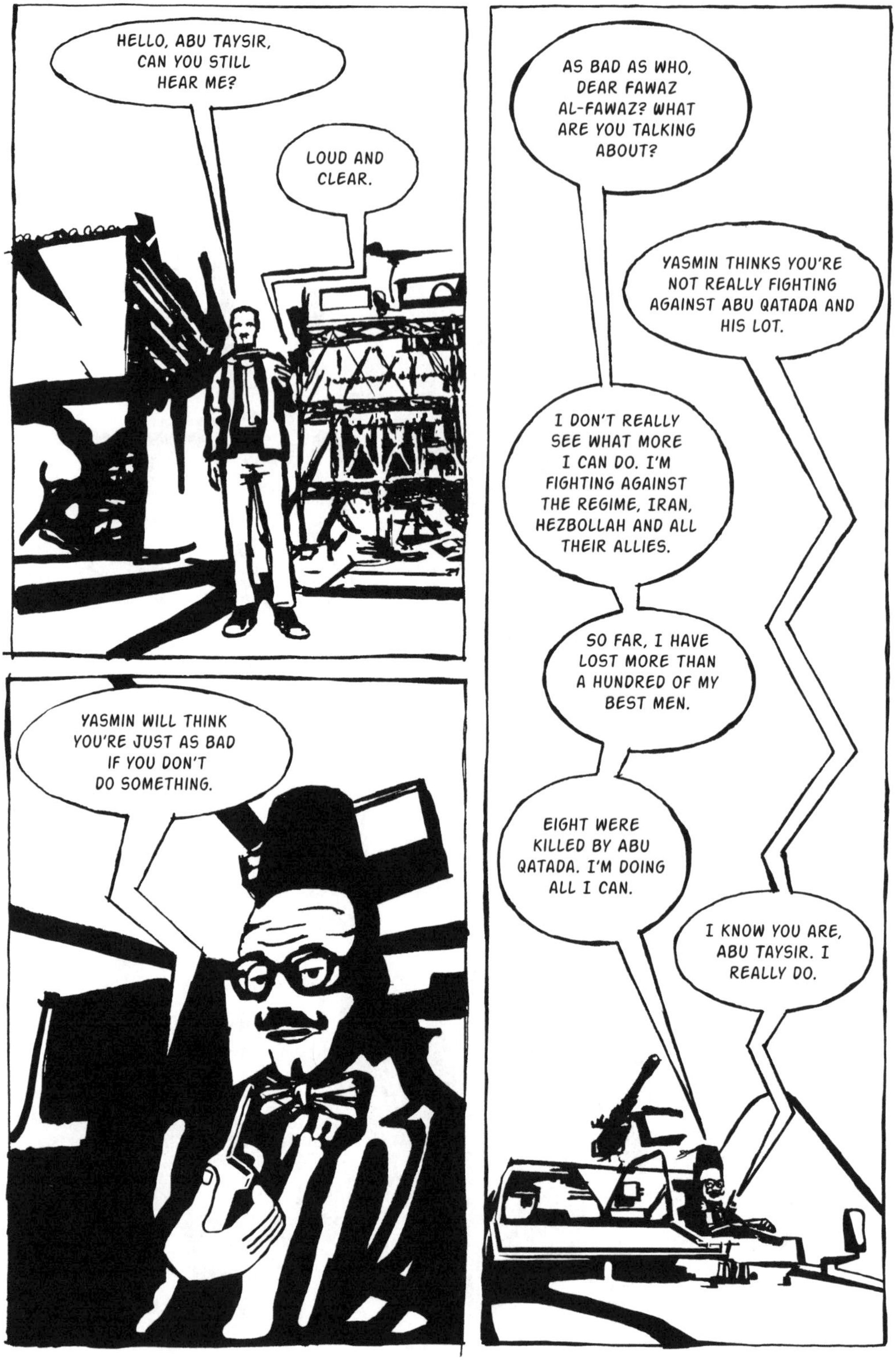
HELLO, ABU TAYSIR, CAN YOU STILL HEAR ME?
LOUD AND CLEAR.
YASMIN WILL THINK YOU'RE JUST AS BAD IF YOU DON'T DO SOMETHING.
AS BAD AS WHO, DEAR FAWAZ AL-FAWAZ? WHAT ARE YOU TALKING ABOUT?
YASMIN THINKS YOU'RE NOT REALLY FIGHTING AGAINST ABU QATADA AND HIS LOT.
I DON'T REALLY SEE WHAT MORE I CAN DO. I'M FIGHTING AGAINST THE REGIME, IRAN, HEZBOLLAH AND ALL THEIR ALLIES.
SO FAR, I HAVE LOST MORE THAN A HUNDRED OF MY BEST MEN.
EIGHT WERE KILLED BY ABU QATADA. I'M DOING ALL I CAN.
I KNOW YOU ARE, ABU TAYSIR. I REALLY DO.

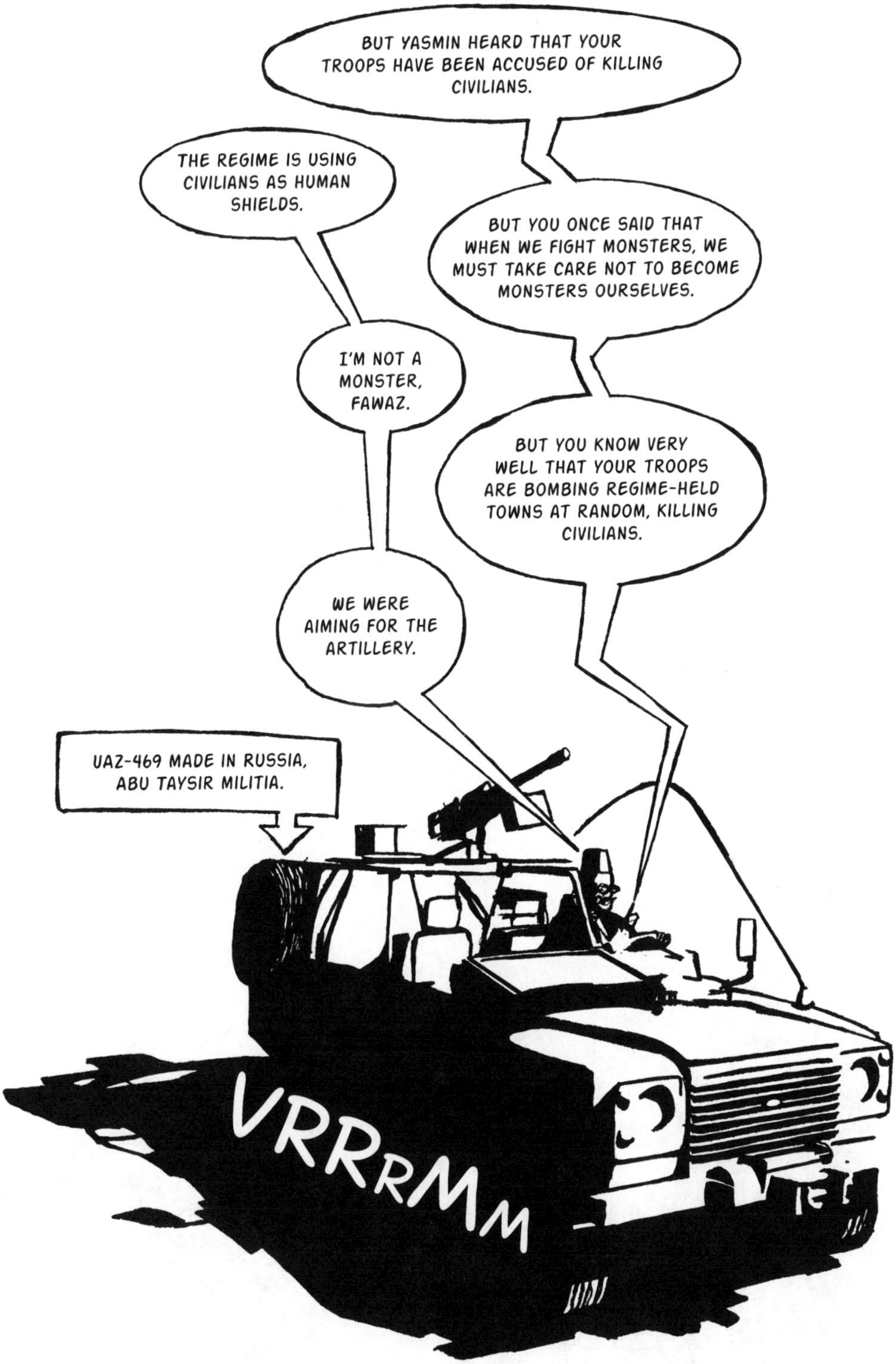
BUT YASMIN HEARD THAT YOUR TROOPS HAVE BEEN ACCUSED OF KILLING CIVILIANS.
THE REGIME IS USING CIVILIANS AS HUMAN SHIELDS.
BUT YOU ONCE SAID THAT WHEN WE FIGHT MONSTERS, WE MUST TAKE CARE NOT TO BECOME MONSTERS OURSELVES.
I'M NOT A MONSTER, FAWAZ.
BUT YOU KNOW VERY WELL THAT YOUR TROOPS ARE BOMBING REGIME-HELD TOWNS AT RANDOM, KILLING CIVILIANS.
WE WERE AIMING FOR THE ARTILLERY.
UAZ-469 MADE IN RUSSIA, ABU TAYSIR MILITIA.
VRRrMm

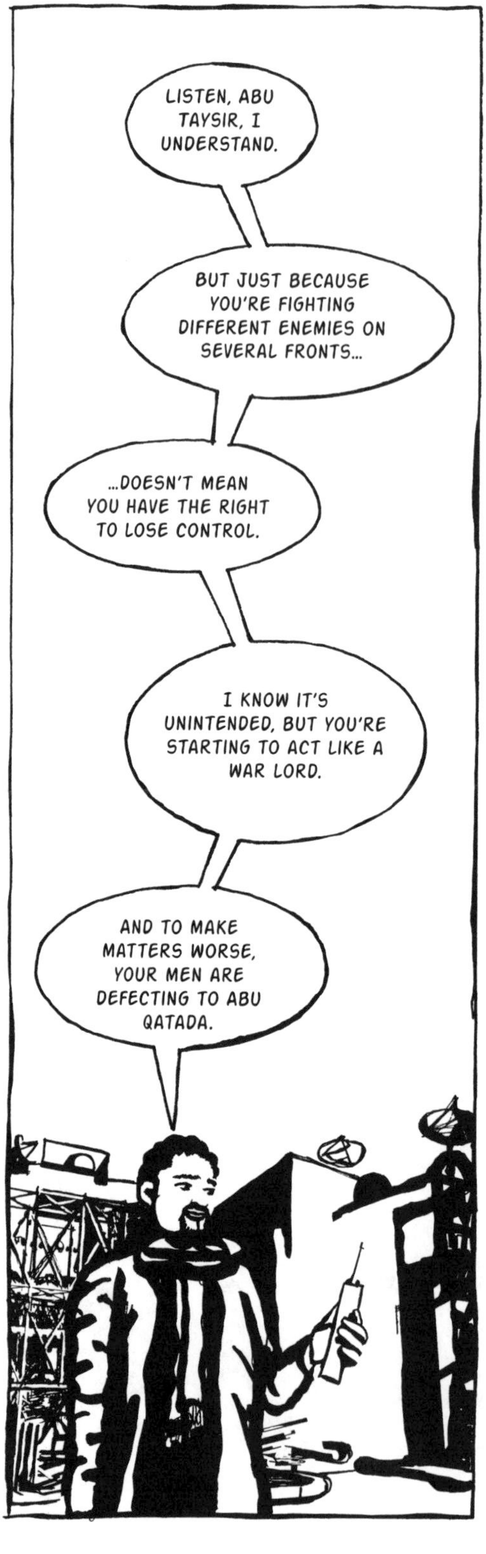
LISTEN, ABU TAYSIR, I UNDERSTAND.
BUT JUST BECAUSE YOU'RE FIGHTING DIFFERENT ENEMIES ON SEVERAL FRONTS...
...DOESN'T MEAN YOU HAVE THE RIGHT TO LOSE CONTROL.
I KNOW IT'S UNINTENDED, BUT YOU'RE STARTING TO ACT LIKE A WAR LORD.
AND TO MAKE MATTERS WORSE, YOUR MEN ARE DEFECTING TO ABU QATADA.

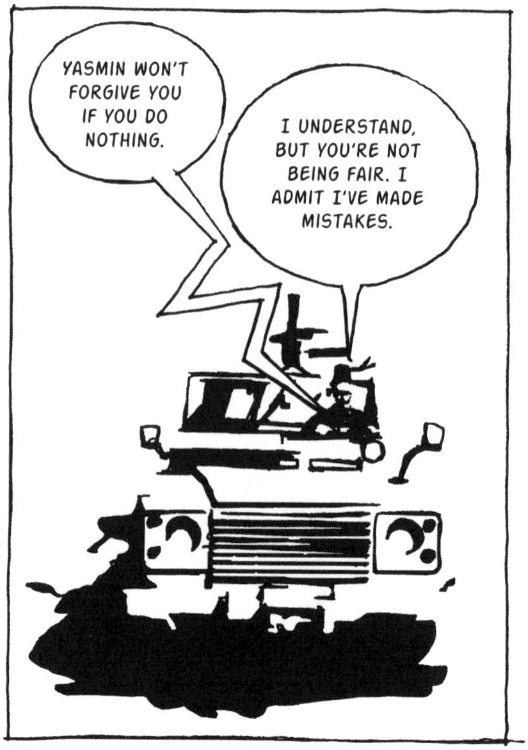
YASMIN WON'T FORGIVE YOU IF YOU DO NOTHING.
I UNDERSTAND, BUT YOU'RE NOT BEING FAIR. I ADMIT I'VE MADE MISTAKES.

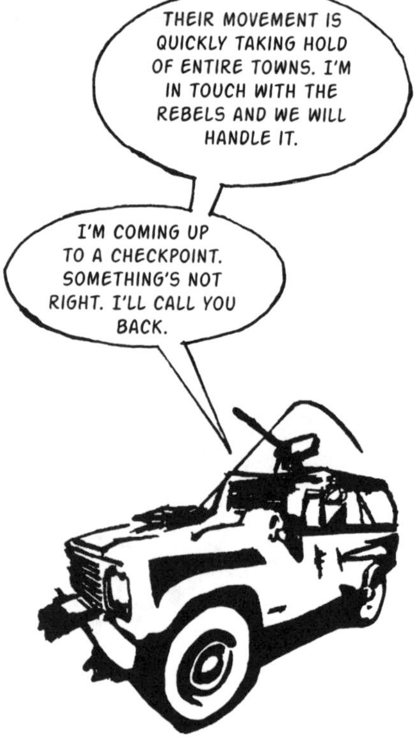
THEIR MOVEMENT IS QUICKLY TAKING HOLD OF ENTIRE TOWNS. I'M IN TOUCH WITH THE REBELS AND WE WILL HANDLE IT.
I'M COMING UP TO A CHECKPOINT. SOMETHING'S NOT RIGHT. I'LL CALL YOU BACK.

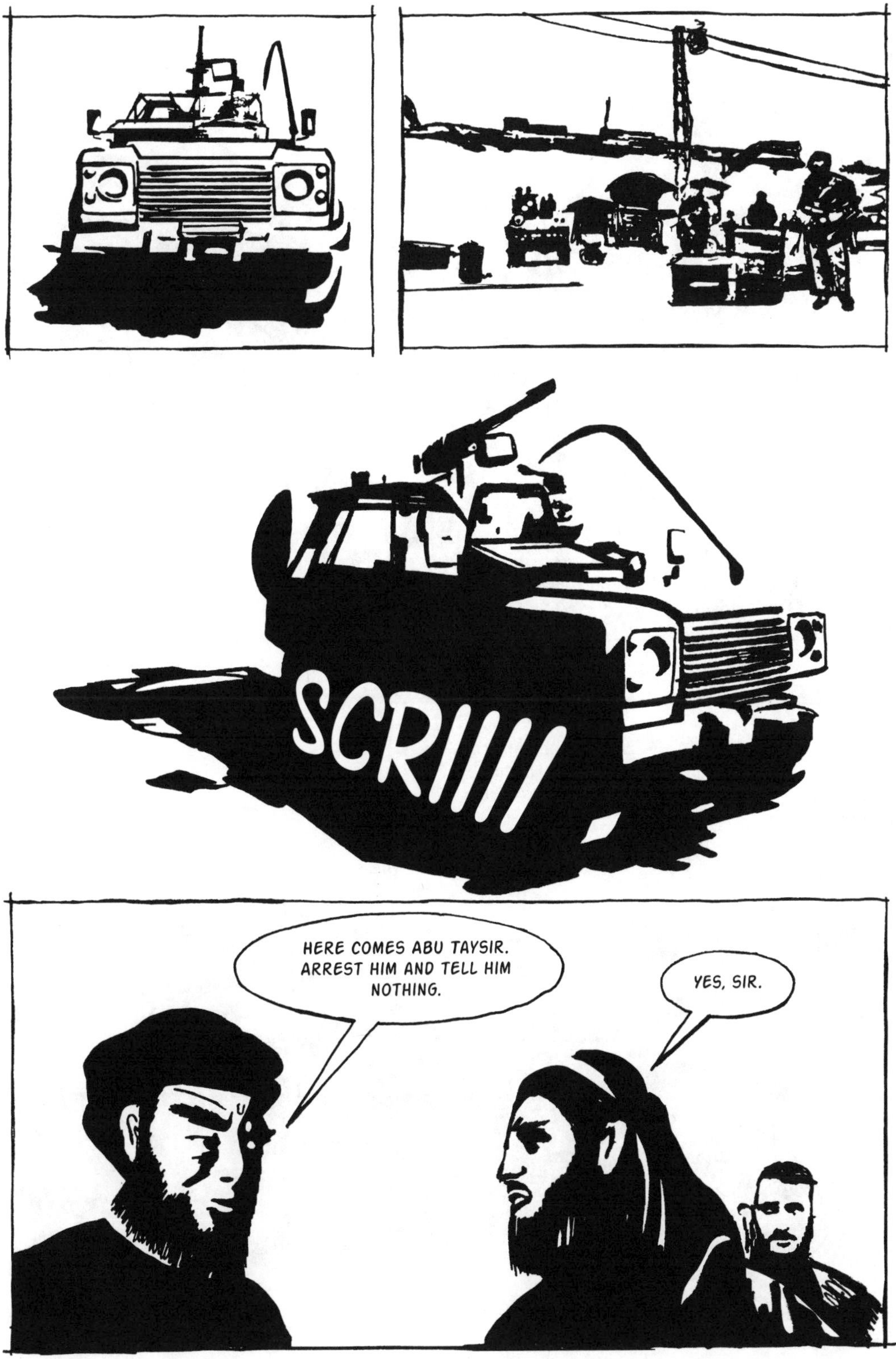
SCRIIIII
HERE COMES ABU TAYSIR. ARREST HIM AND TELL HIM NOTHING.
YES, SIR.

THREE DAYS LATER: ANOTHER 436 KILLED.

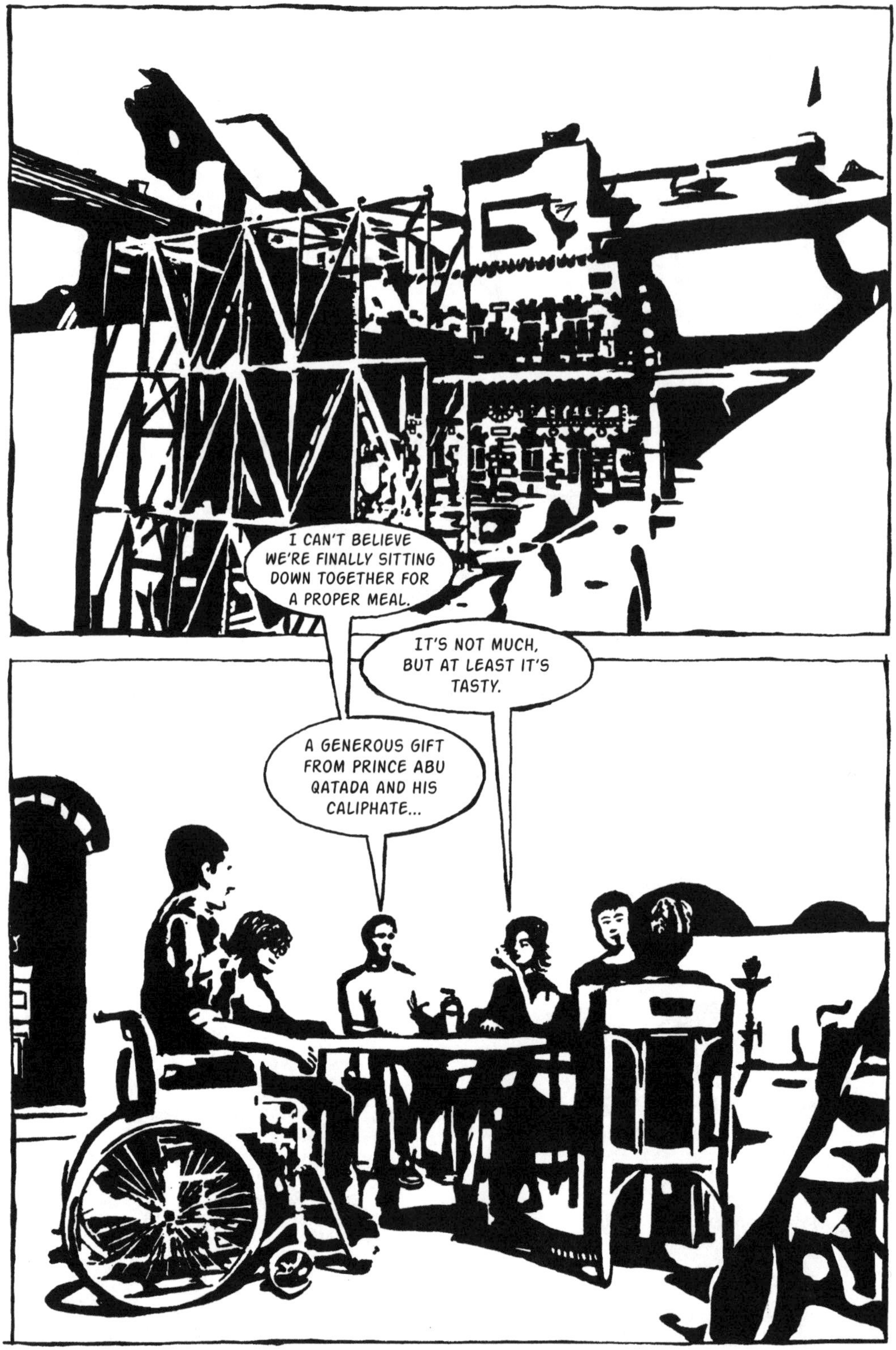
I CAN'T BELIEVE WE'RE FINALLY SITTING DOWN TOGETHER FOR A PROPER MEAL.
IT'S NOT MUCH, BUT AT LEAST IT'S TASTY.
A GENEROUS GIFT FROM PRINCE ABU QATADA AND HIS CALIPHATE...

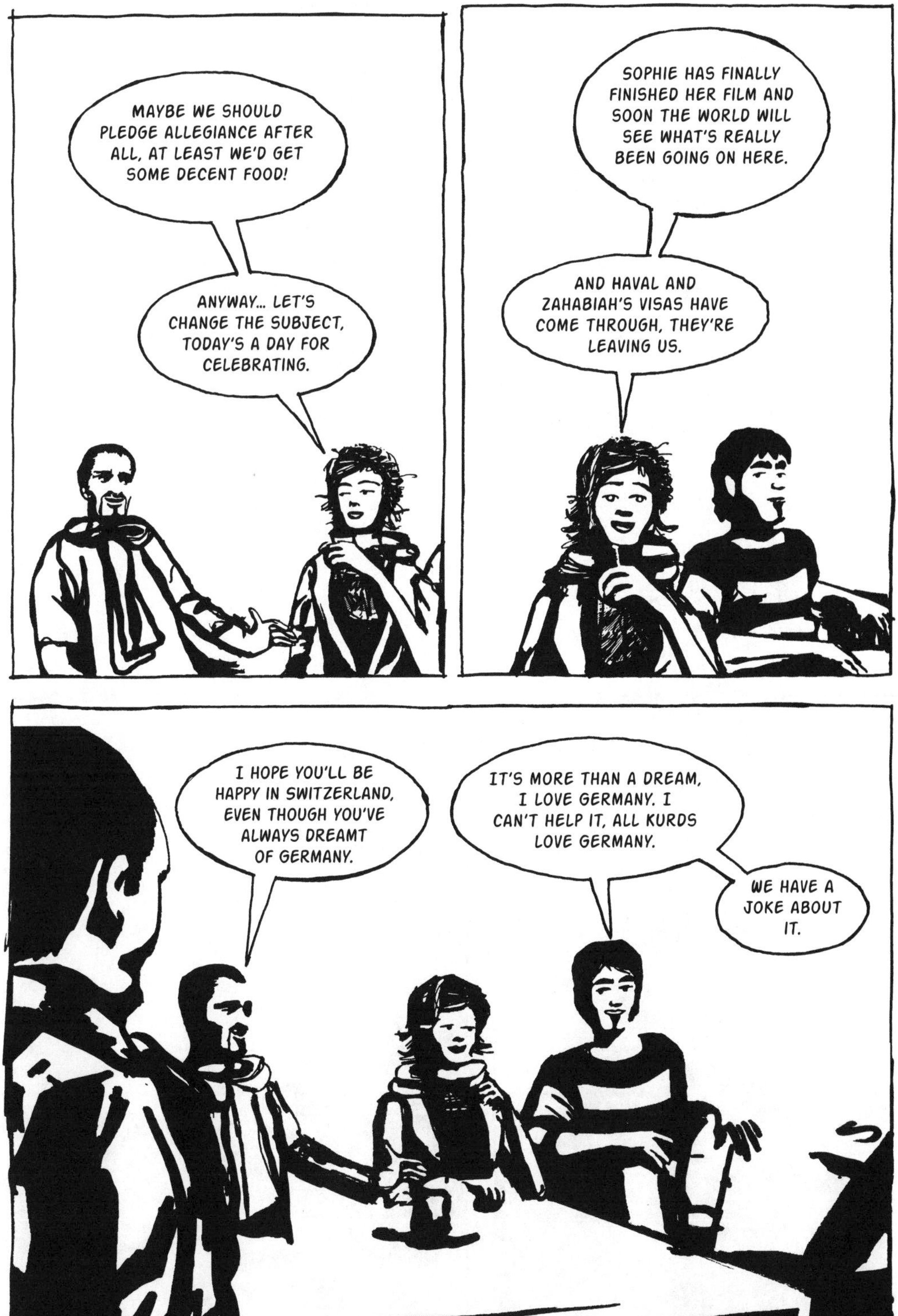
MAYBE WE SHOULD PLEDGE ALLEGIANCE AFTER ALL, AT LEAST WE'D GET SOME DECENT FOOD!
ANYWAY... LET'S CHANGE THE SUBJECT, TODAY'S A DAY FOR CELEBRATING.
SOPHIE HAS FINALLY FINISHED HER FILM AND SOON THE WORLD WILL SEE WHAT'S REALLY BEEN GOING ON HERE.
AND HAVAL AND ZAHABIAH'S VISAS HAVE COME THROUGH, THEY'RE LEAVING US.
I HOPE YOU'LL BE HAPPY IN SWITZERLAND, EVEN THOUGH YOU'VE ALWAYS DREAMT OF GERMANY.
IT'S MORE THAN A DREAM, I LOVE GERMANY. I CAN'T HELP IT, ALL KURDS LOVE GERMANY.
WE HAVE A JOKE ABOUT IT.

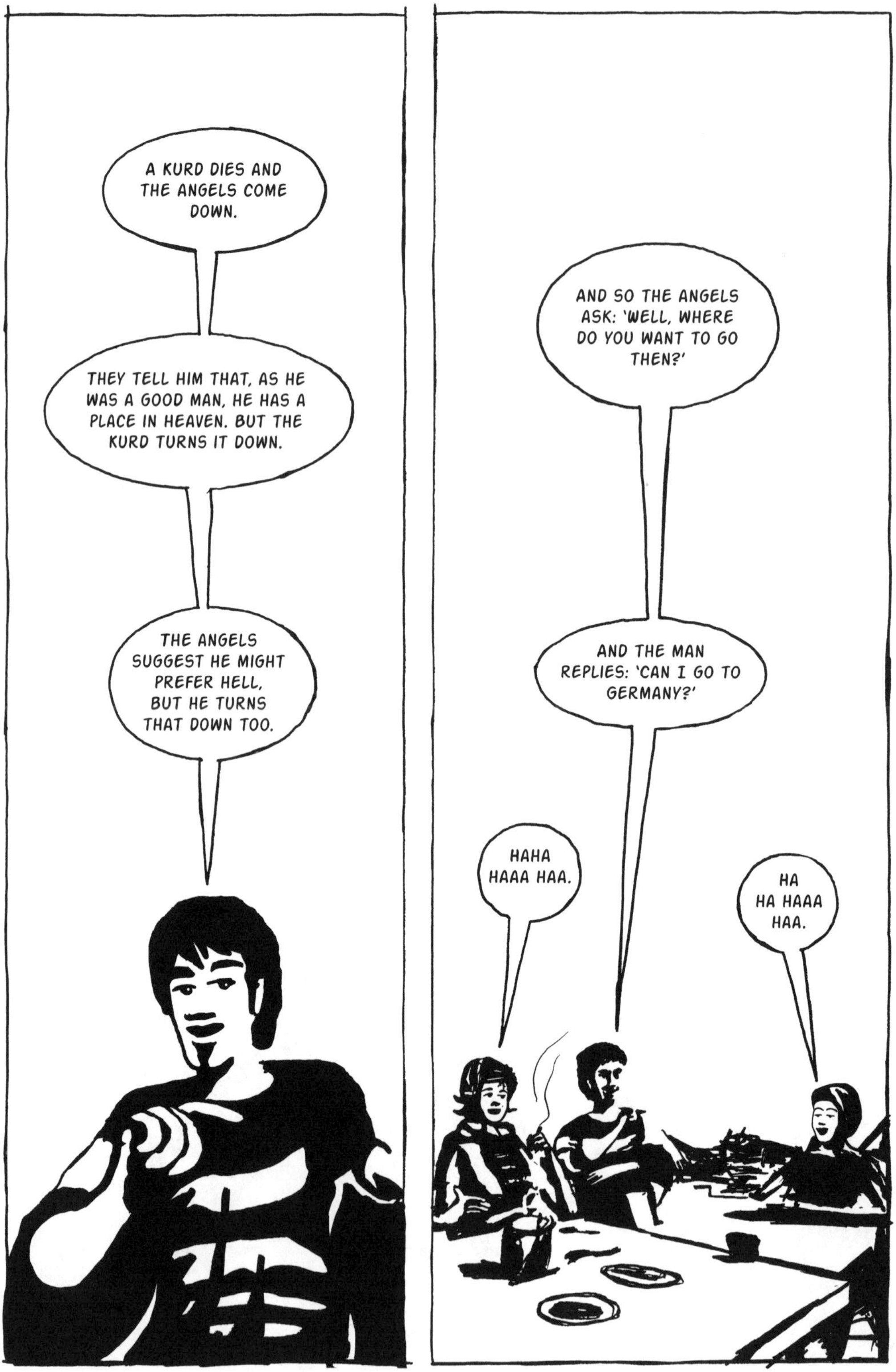
A KURD DIES AND THE ANGELS COME DOWN.
THEY TELL HIM THAT, AS HE WAS A GOOD MAN, HE HAS A PLACE IN HEAVEN. BUT THE KURD TURNS IT DOWN.
THE ANGELS SUGGEST HE MIGHT PREFER HELL, BUT HE TURNS THAT DOWN TOO.
AND SO THE ANGELS ASK: 'WELL, WHERE DO YOU WANT TO GO THEN?'
AND THE MAN REPLIES: 'CAN I GO TO GERMANY?'
HAHA HAAA HAA.
HA HA HAAA HAA.

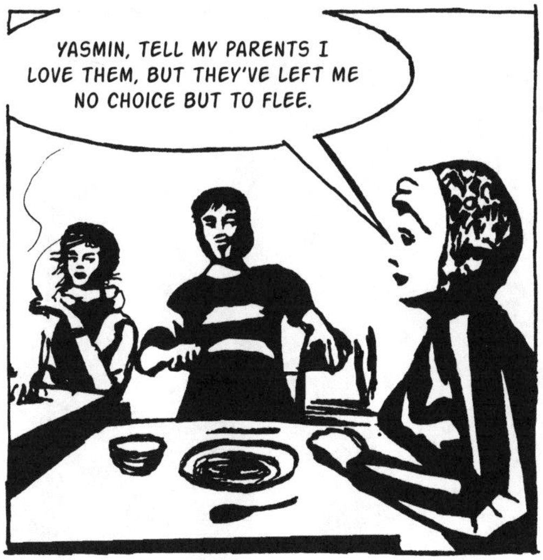
YASMIN, TELL MY PARENTS I LOVE THEM, BUT THEY'VE LEFT ME NO CHOICE BUT TO FLEE.

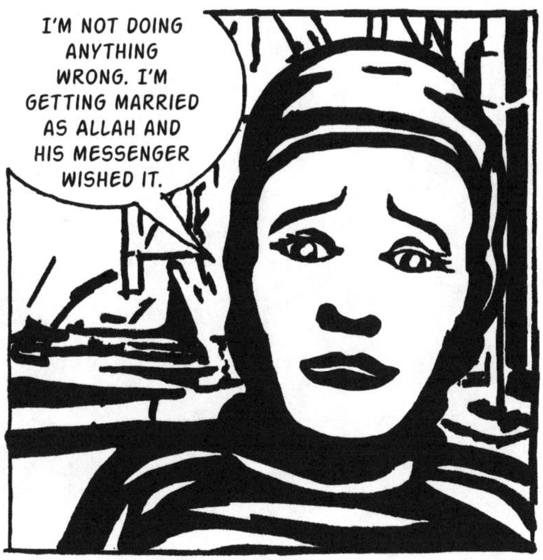
I'M NOT DOING ANYTHING WRONG. I'M GETTING MARRIED AS ALLAH AND HIS MESSENGER WISHED IT.

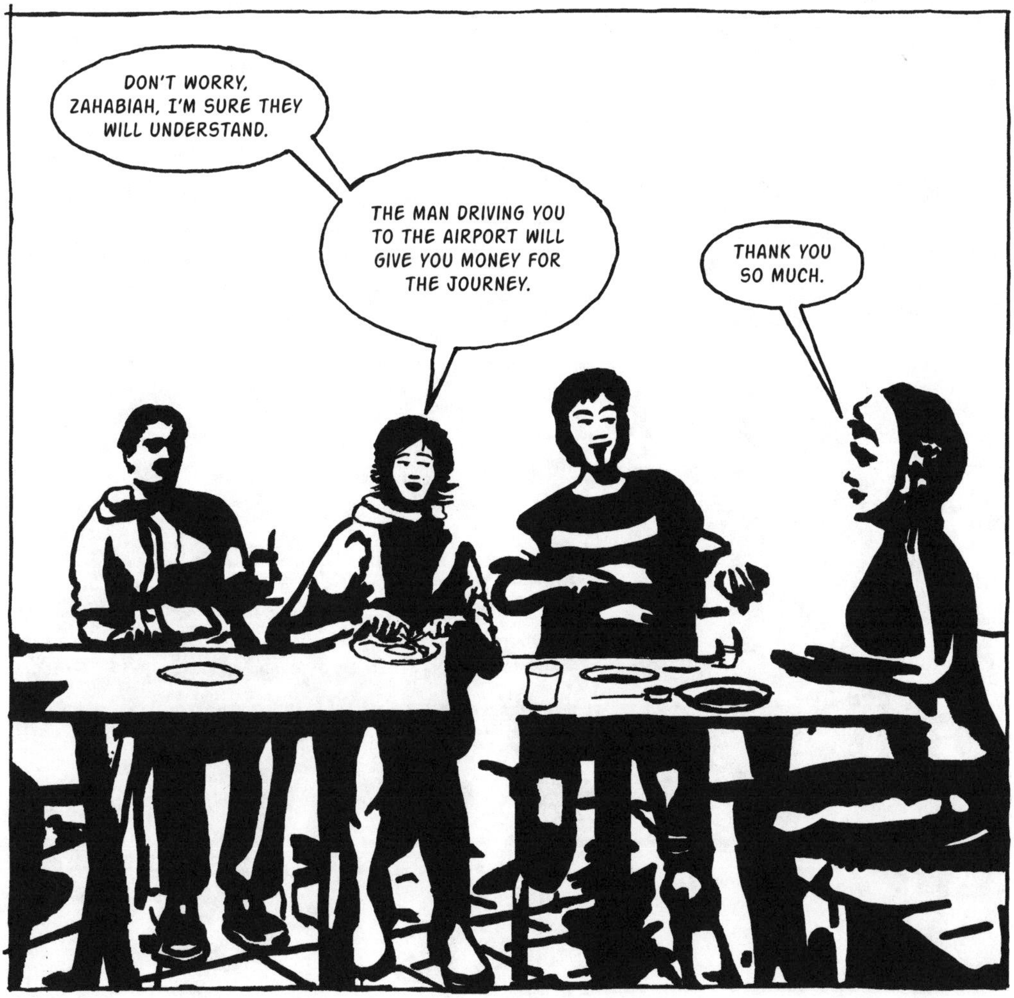
DON'T WORRY, ZAHABIAH, I'M SURE THEY WILL UNDERSTAND.
THE MAN DRIVING YOU TO THE AIRPORT WILL GIVE YOU MONEY FOR THE JOURNEY.
THANK YOU SO MUCH.

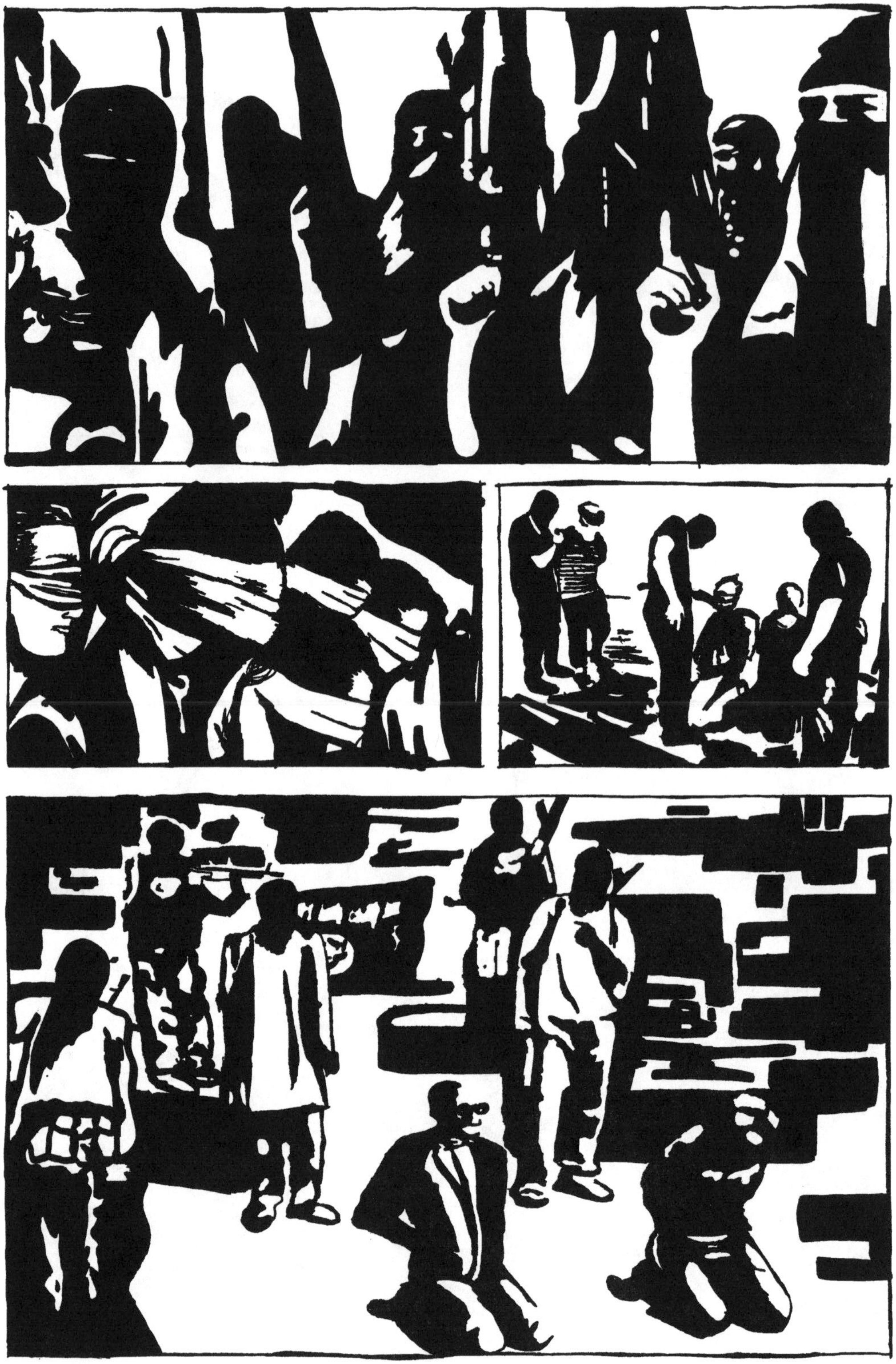

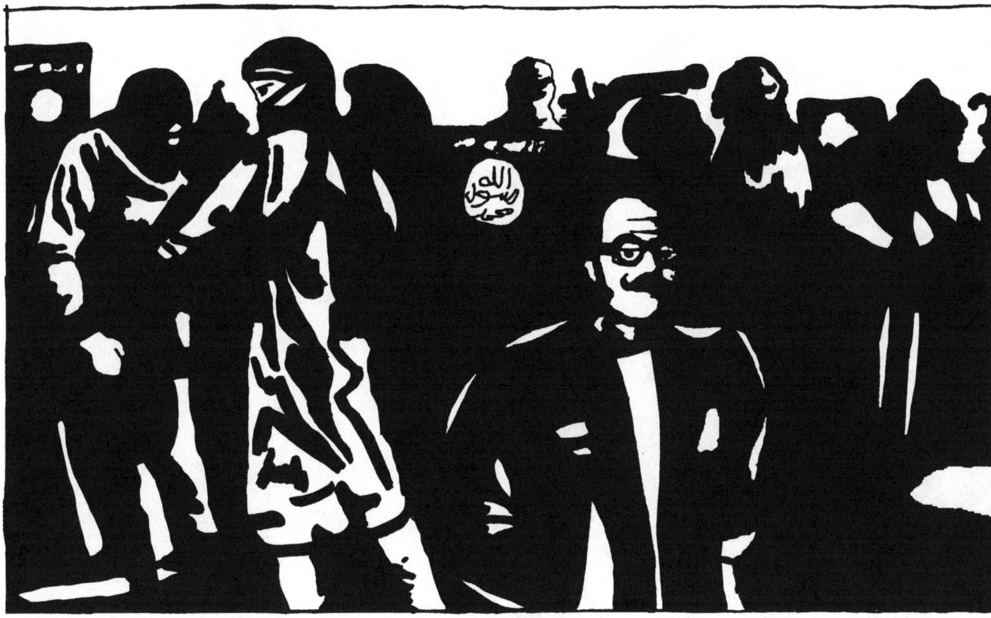

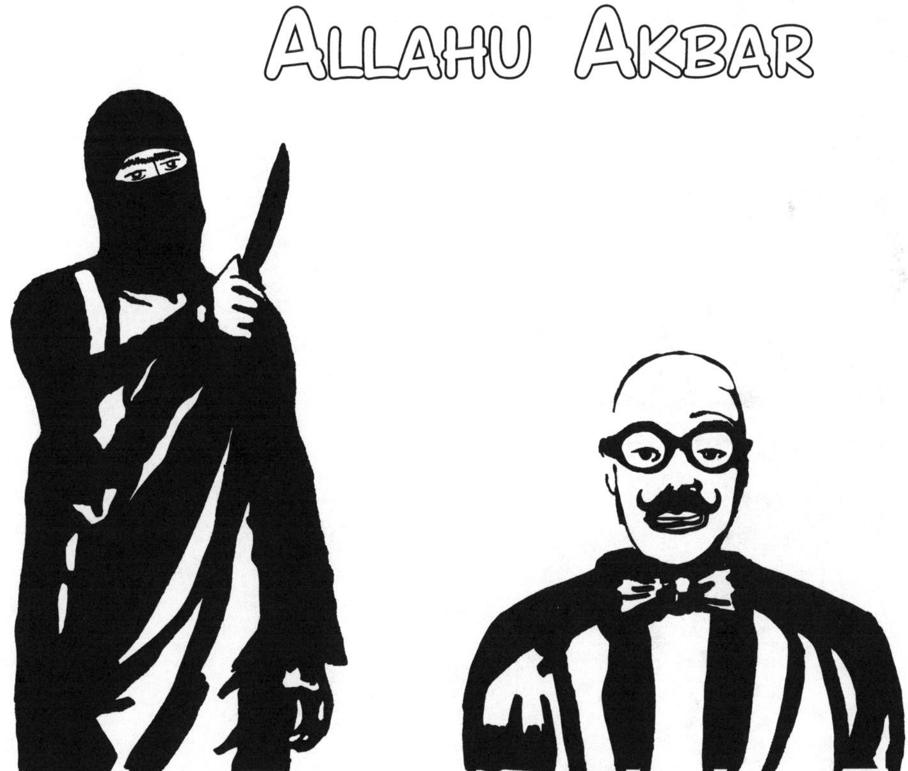
Allahu Akbar

عذاب

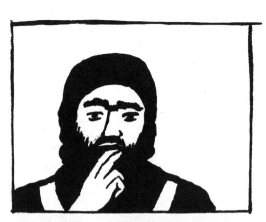

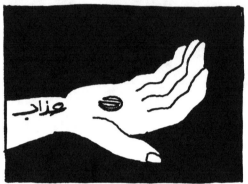

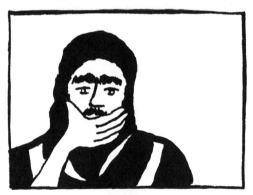

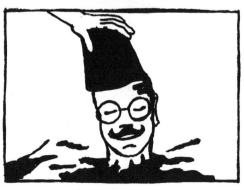

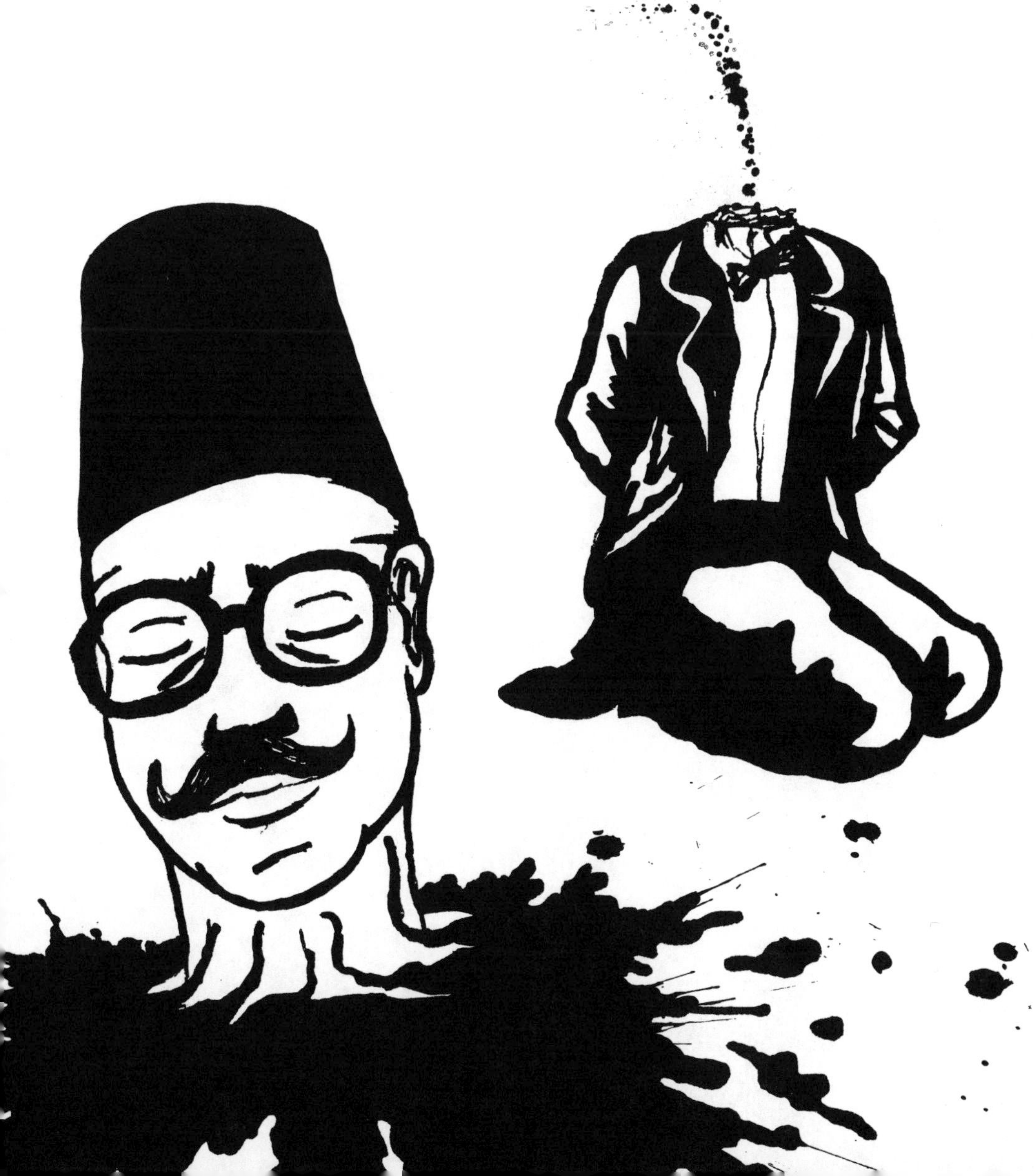

ONE DAY LATER: ANOTHER 329 KILLED.

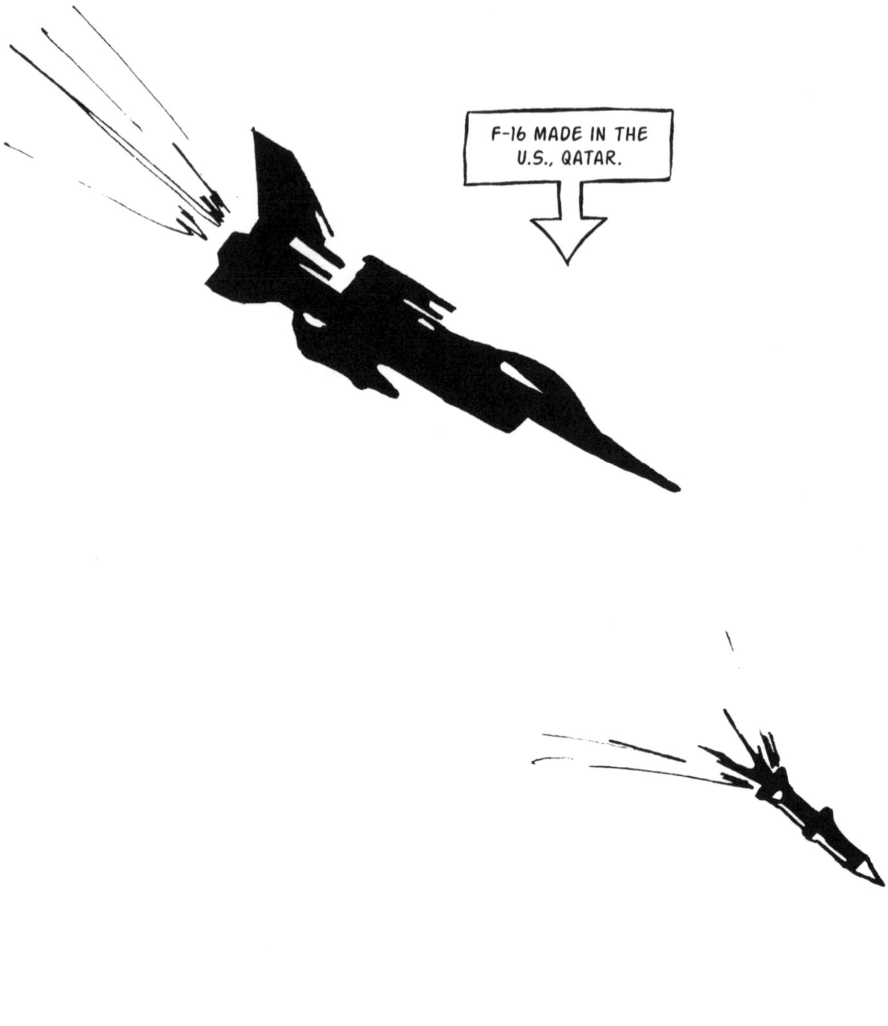
F-16 MADE IN THE U.S., QATAR.

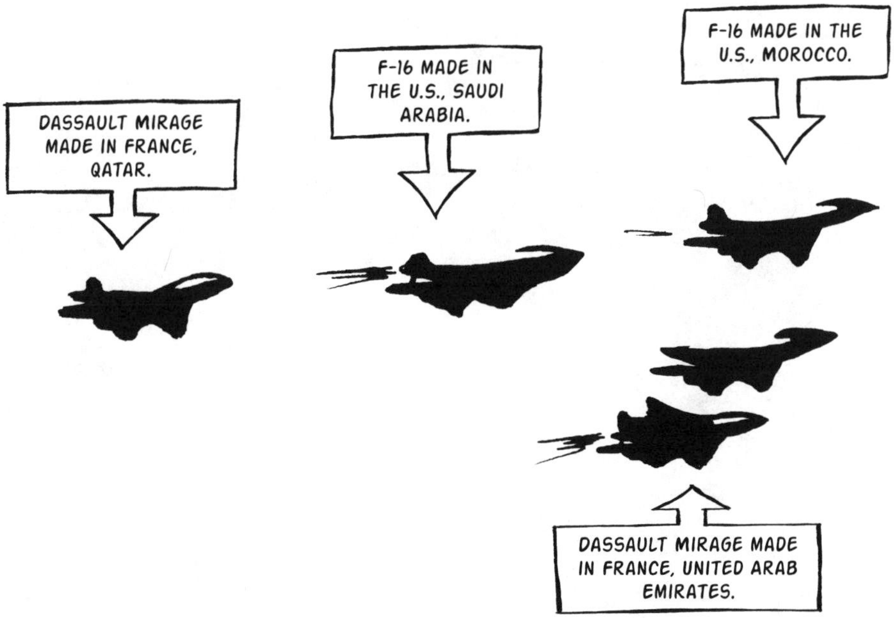
DASSAULT MIRAGE MADE IN FRANCE, QATAR.
F-16 MADE IN THE U.S., SAUDI ARABIA.
F-16 MADE IN THE U.S., MOROCCO.
DASSAULT MIRAGE MADE IN FRANCE, UNITED ARAB EMIRATES.

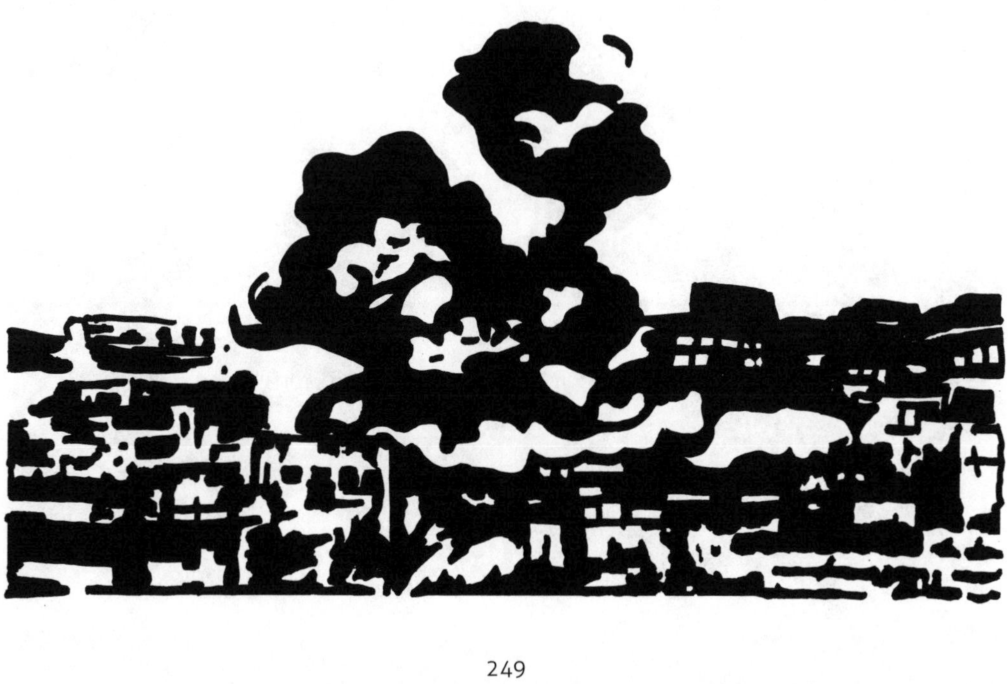

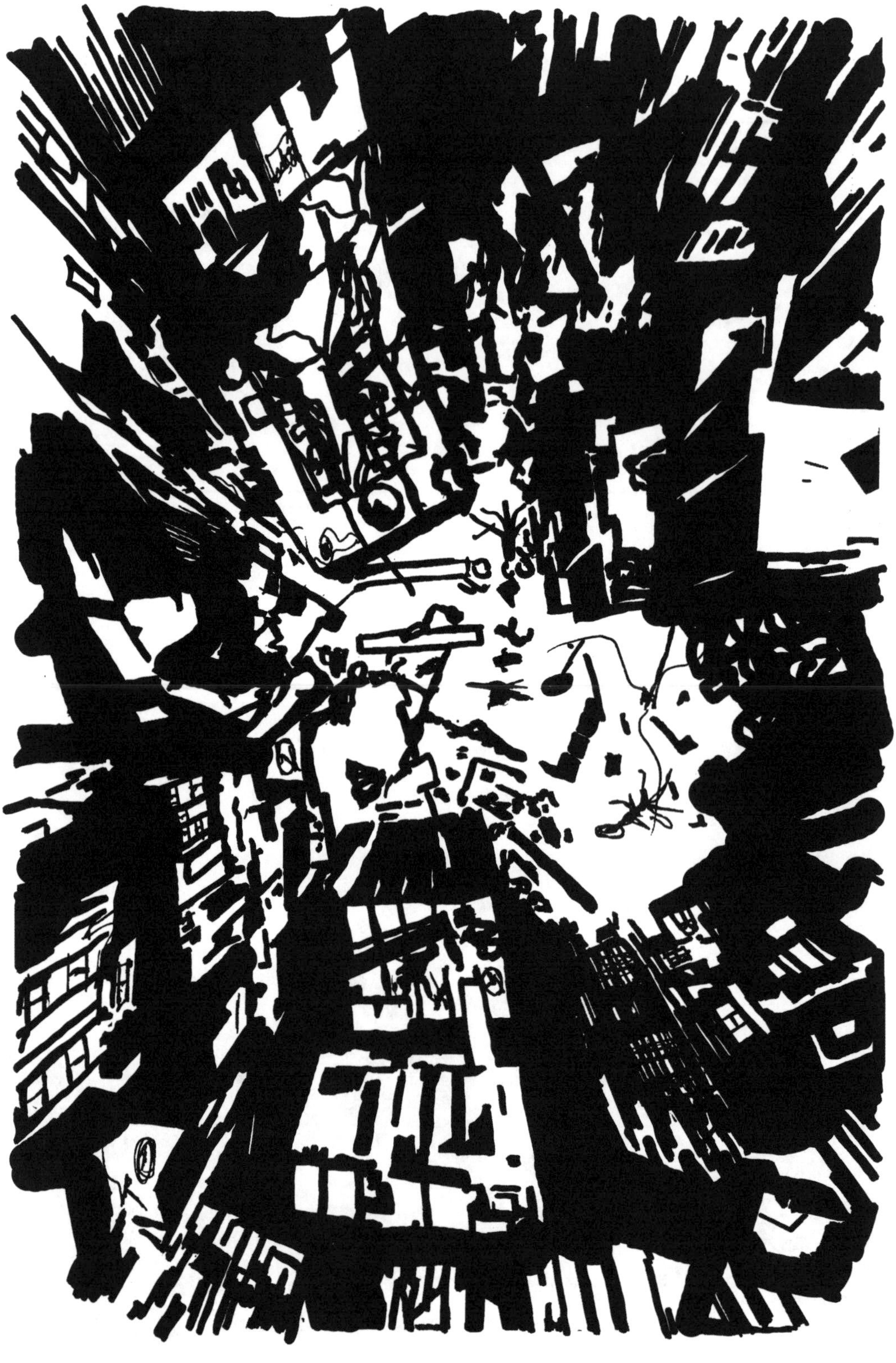

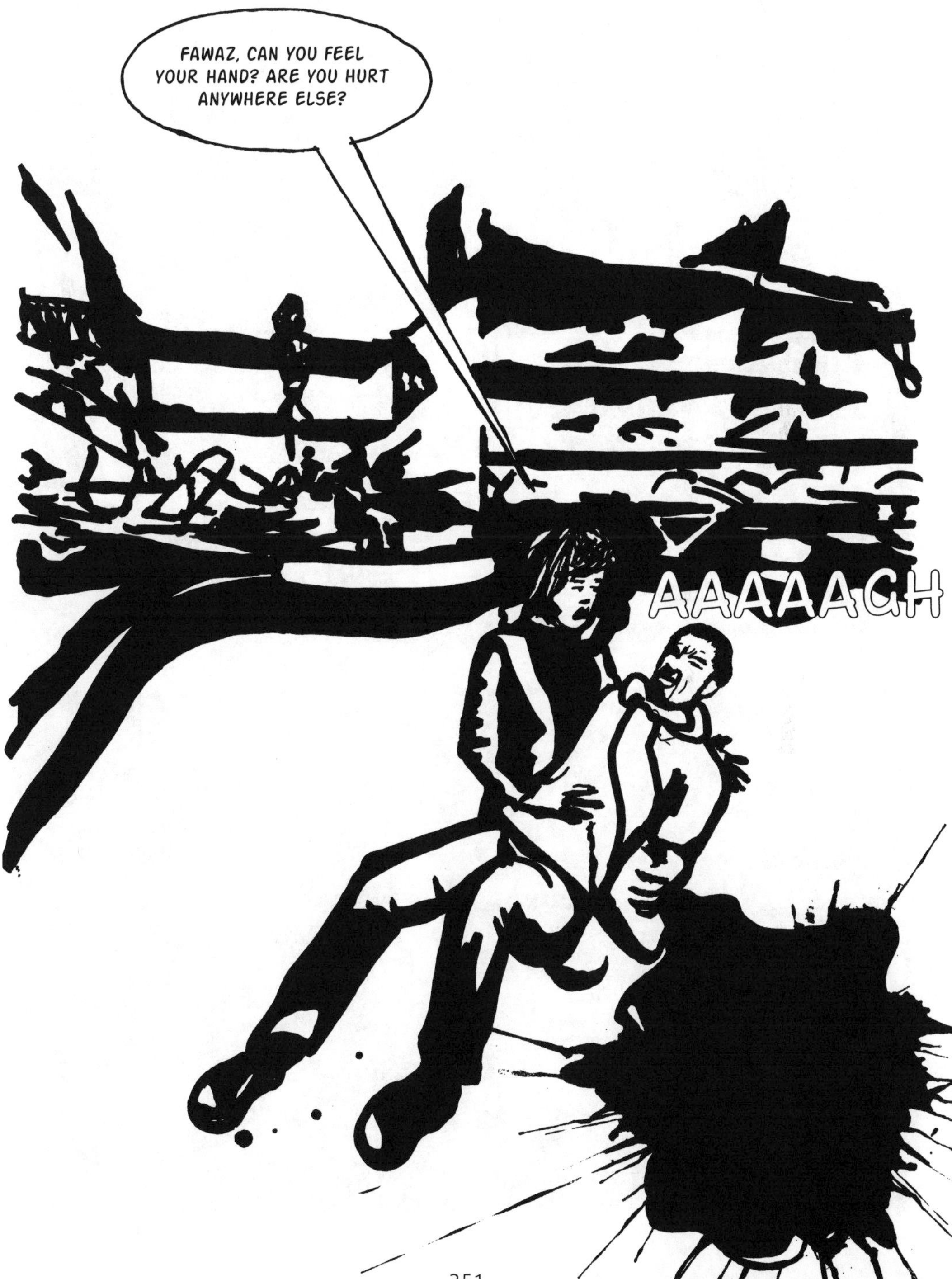

FAWAZ, CAN YOU FEEL YOUR HAND? ARE YOU HURT ANYWHERE ELSE?
AAAAAGH

THAT NIGHT IN PARIS: ANOTHER 68 KILLED.

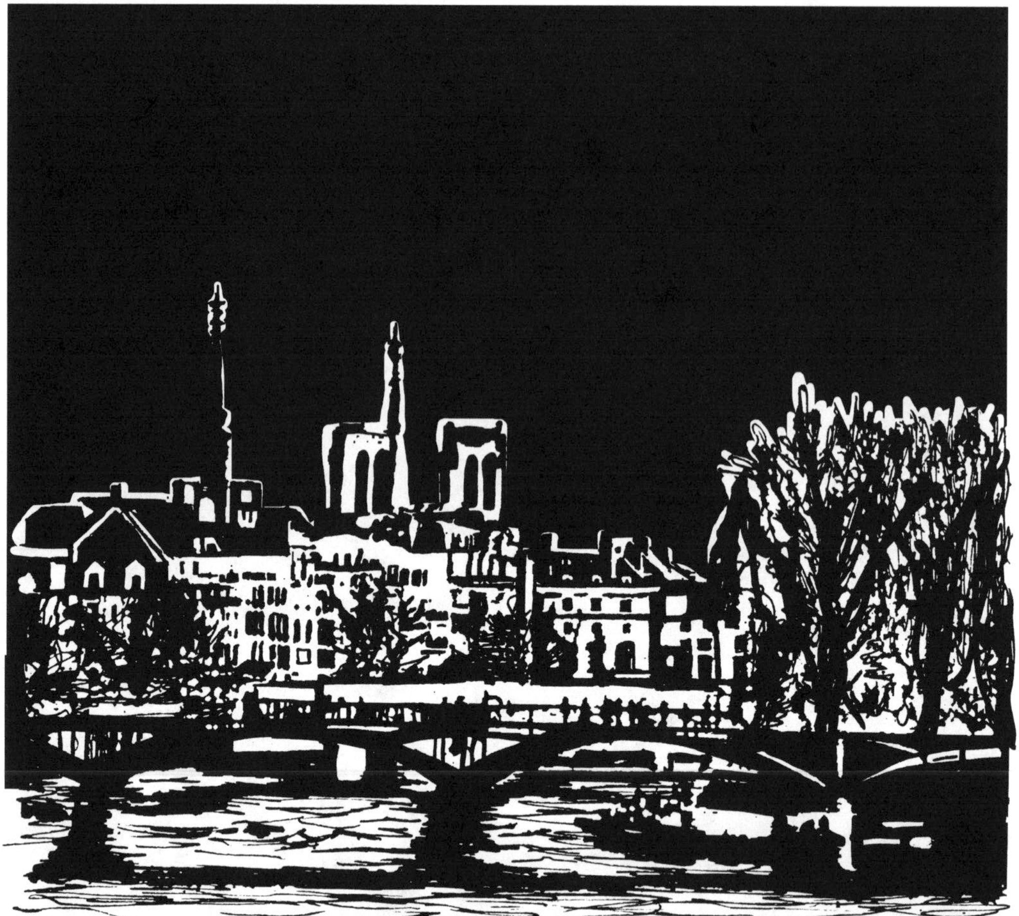

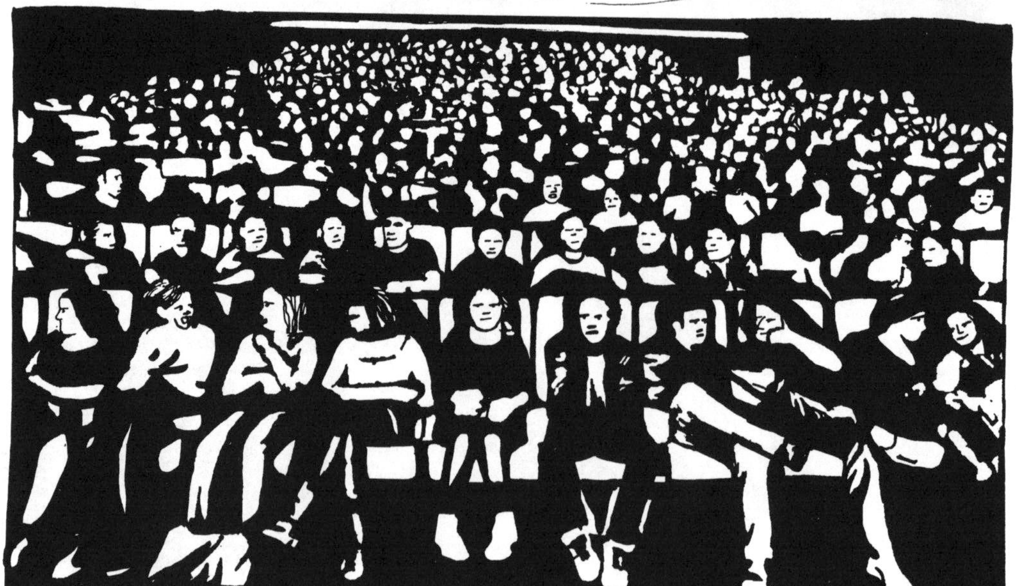

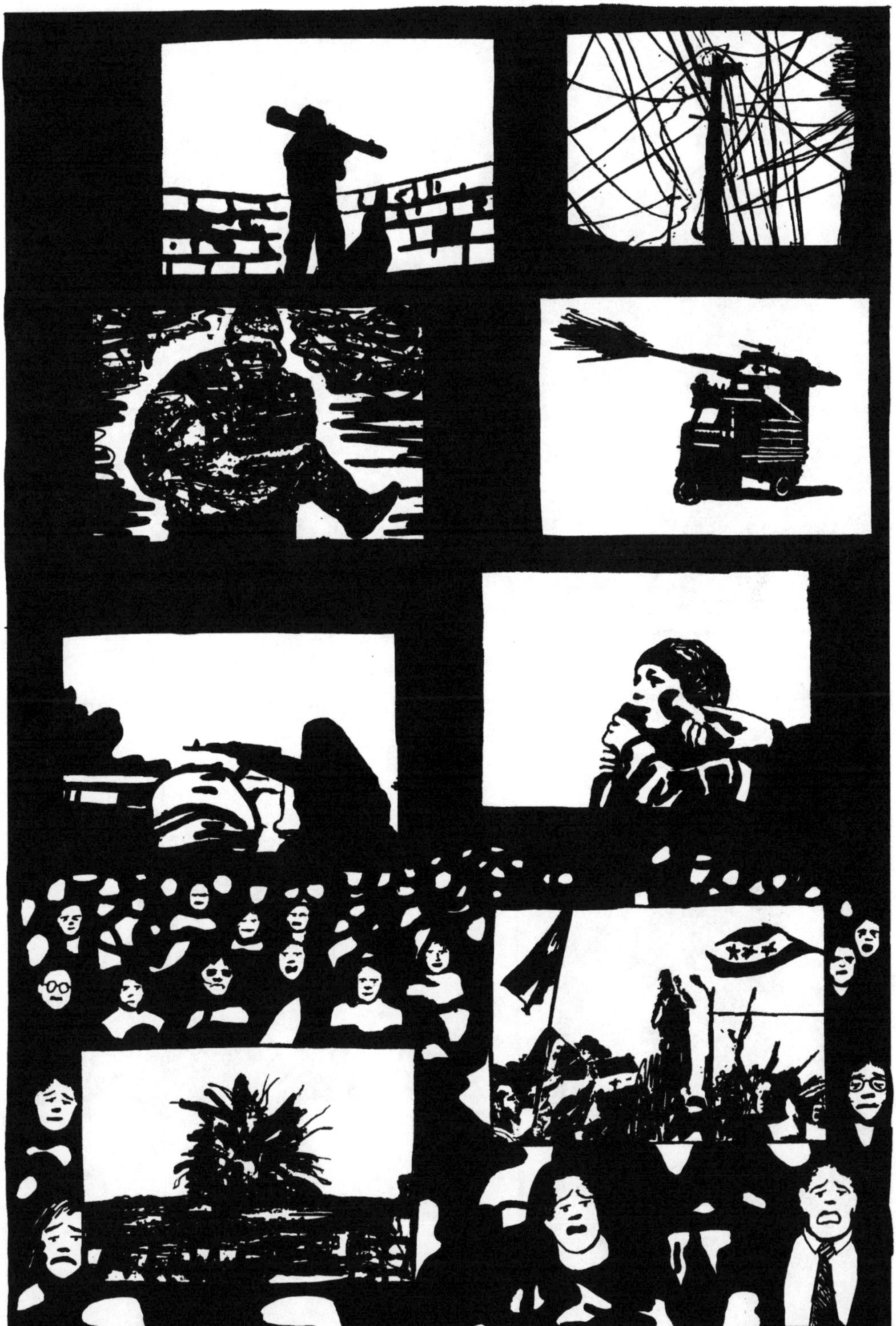

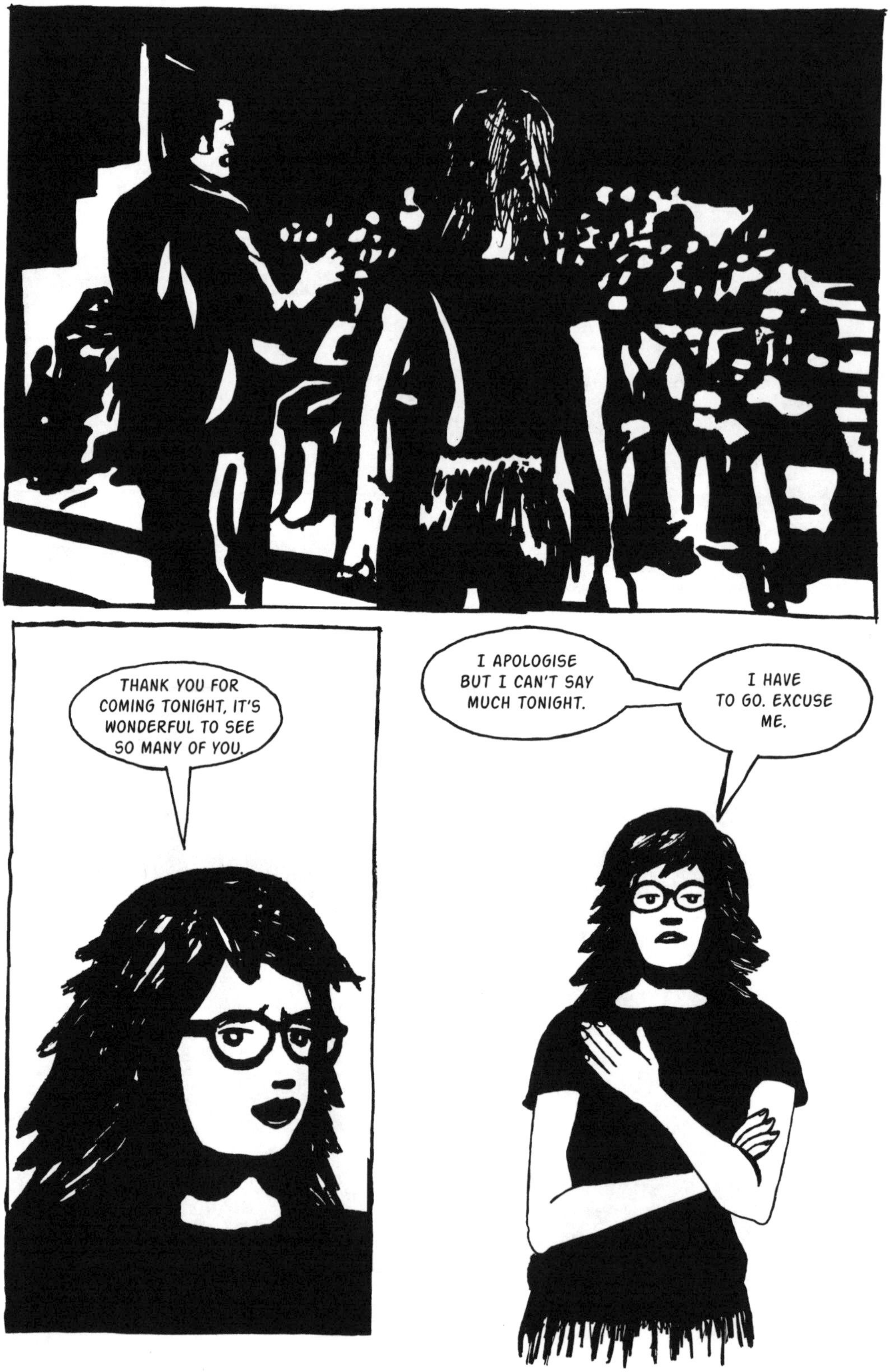
THANK YOU FOR COMING TONIGHT, IT'S WONDERFUL TO SEE SO MANY OF YOU.
I APOLOGISE BUT I CAN'T SAY MUCH TONIGHT.
I HAVE TO GO. EXCUSE ME.

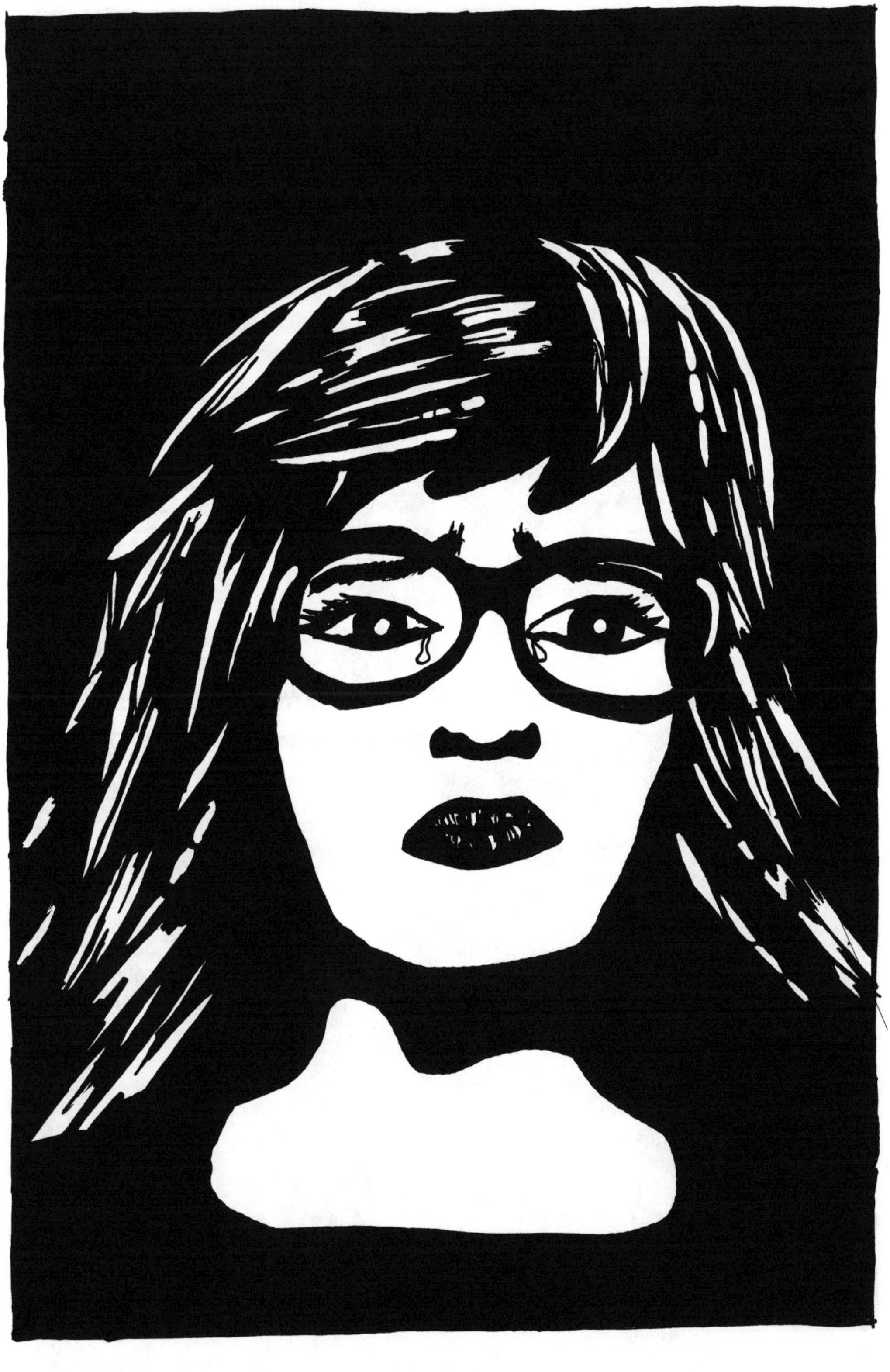

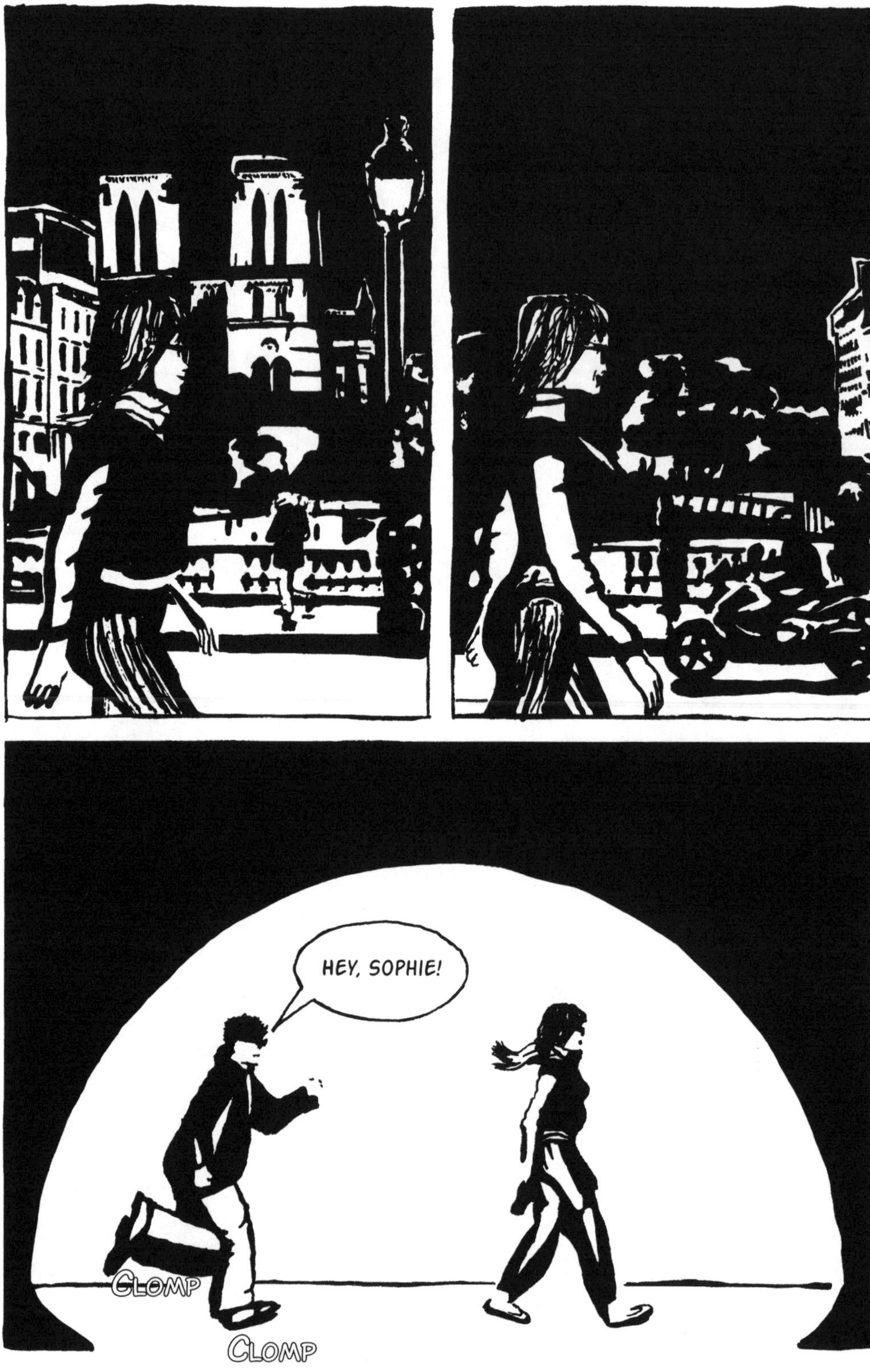
HEY, SOPHIE!
CLOMP
CLOMP

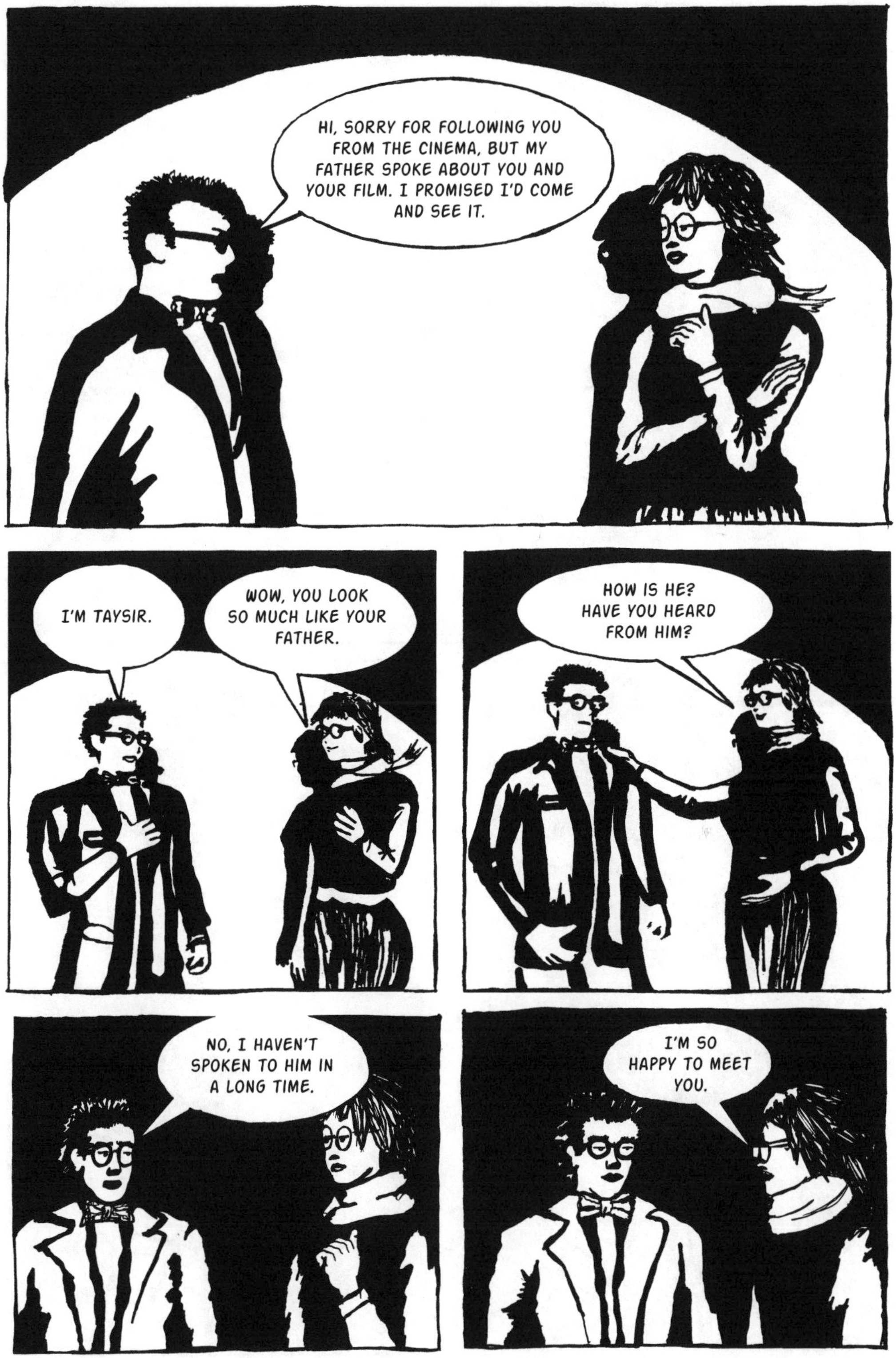
HI, SORRY FOR FOLLOWING YOU FROM THE CINEMA, BUT MY FATHER SPOKE ABOUT YOU AND YOUR FILM. I PROMISED I'D COME AND SEE IT.
I'M TAYSIR.
WOW, YOU LOOK SO MUCH LIKE YOUR FATHER.
HOW IS HE? HAVE YOU HEARD FROM HIM?
NO, I HAVEN'T SPOKEN TO HIM IN A LONG TIME.
I'M SO HAPPY TO MEET YOU.

TEN HOURS LATER: ANOTHER 37 KILLED.

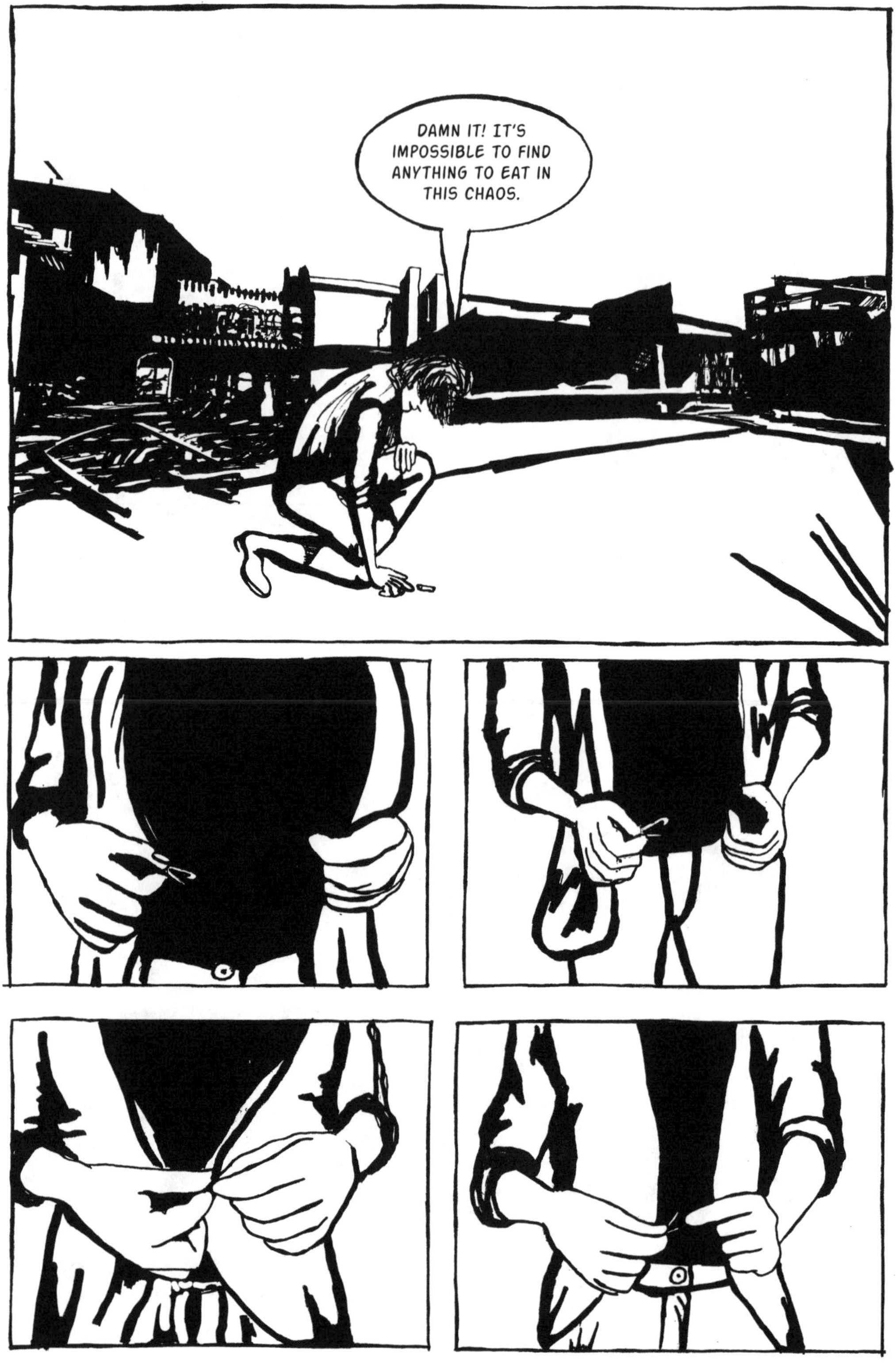
DAMN IT! IT'S IMPOSSIBLE TO FIND ANYTHING TO EAT IN THIS CHAOS.

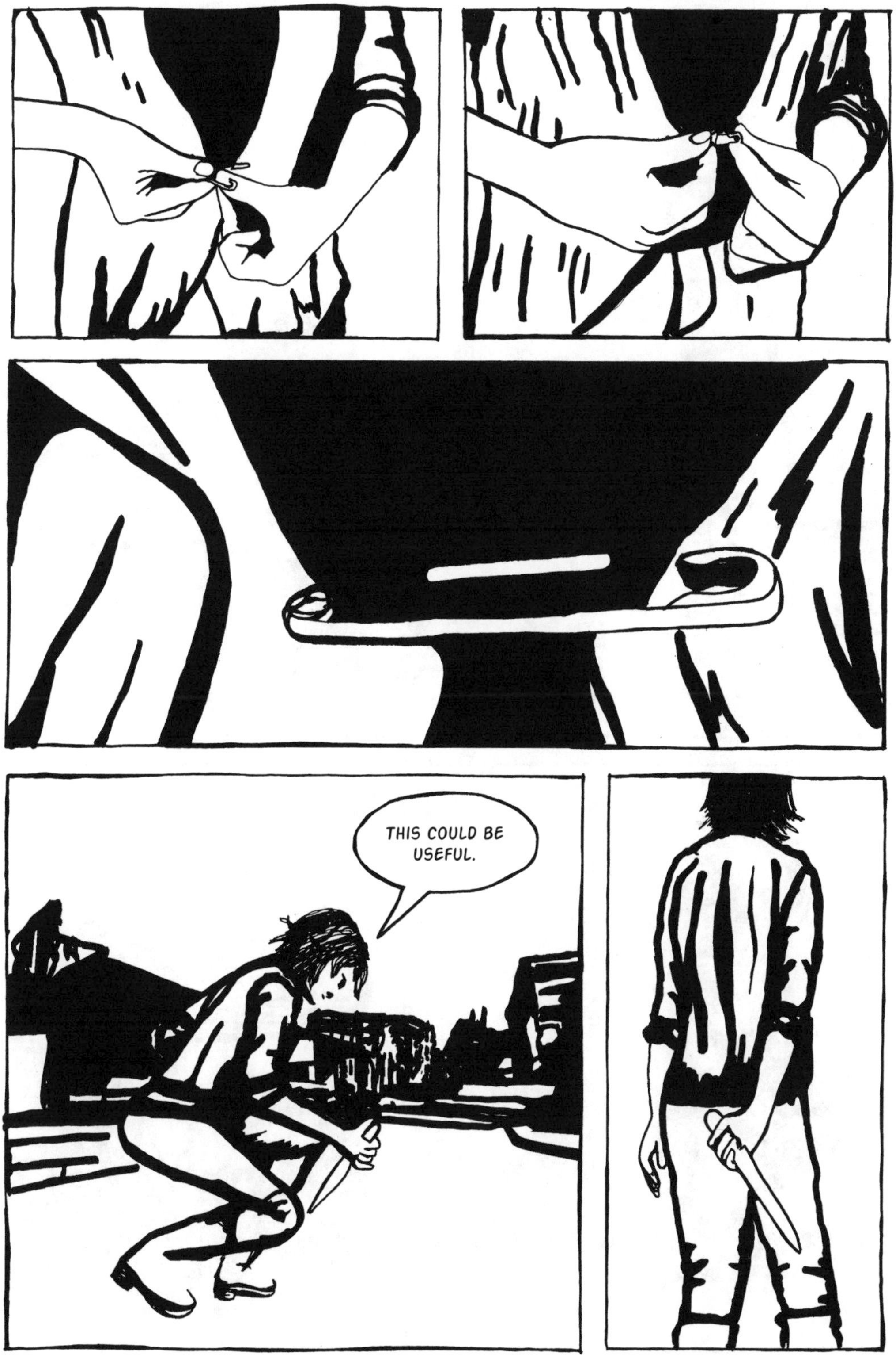
THIS COULD BE
USEFUL.

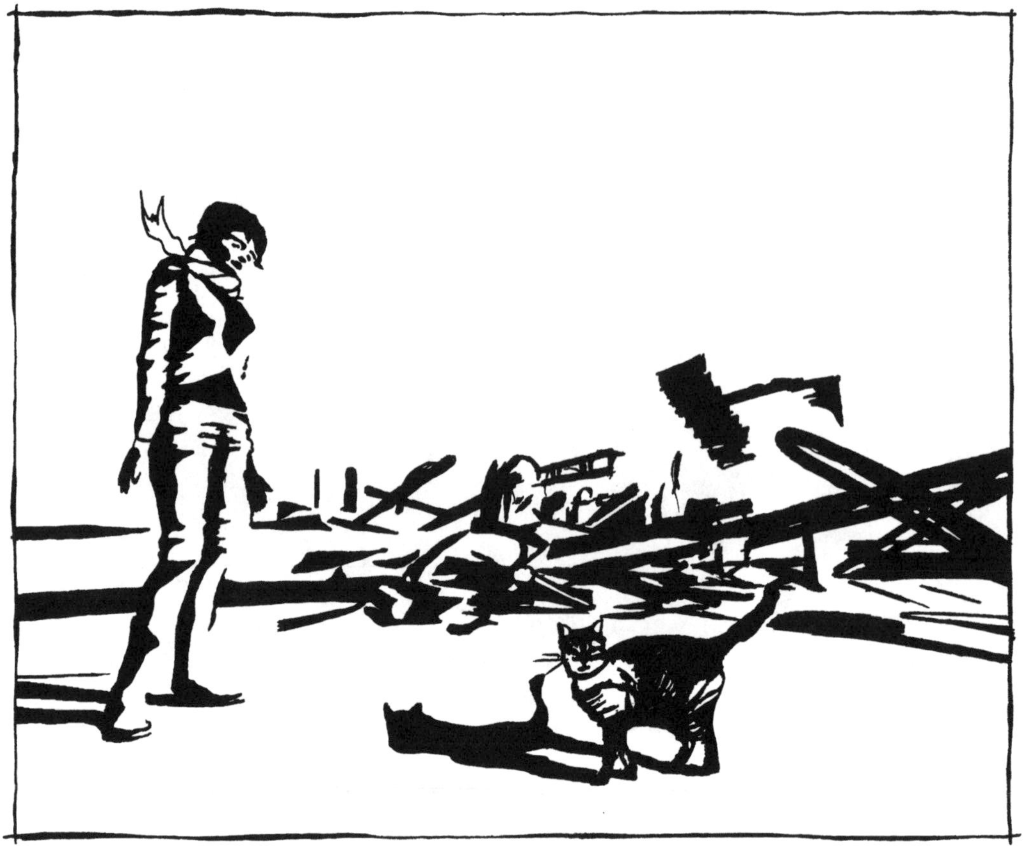

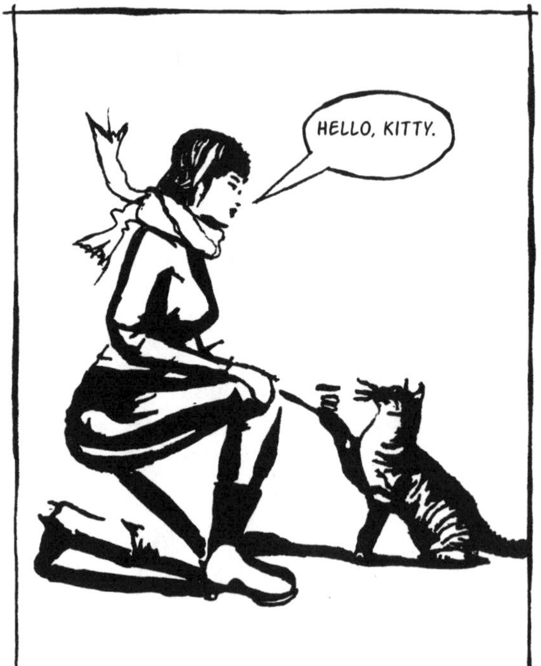
HELLO, KITTY.

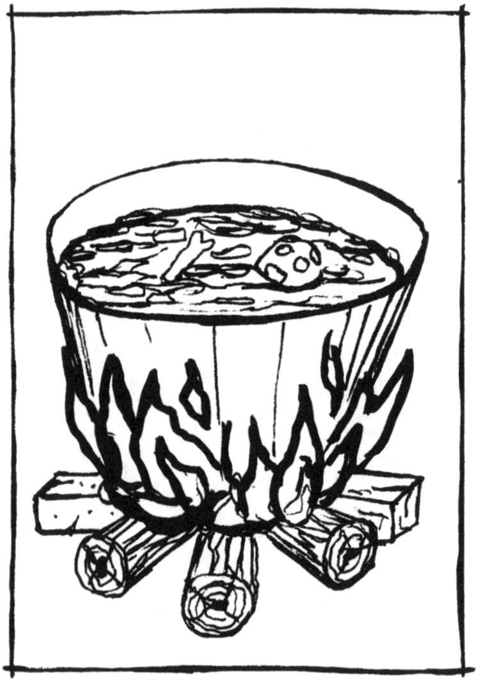

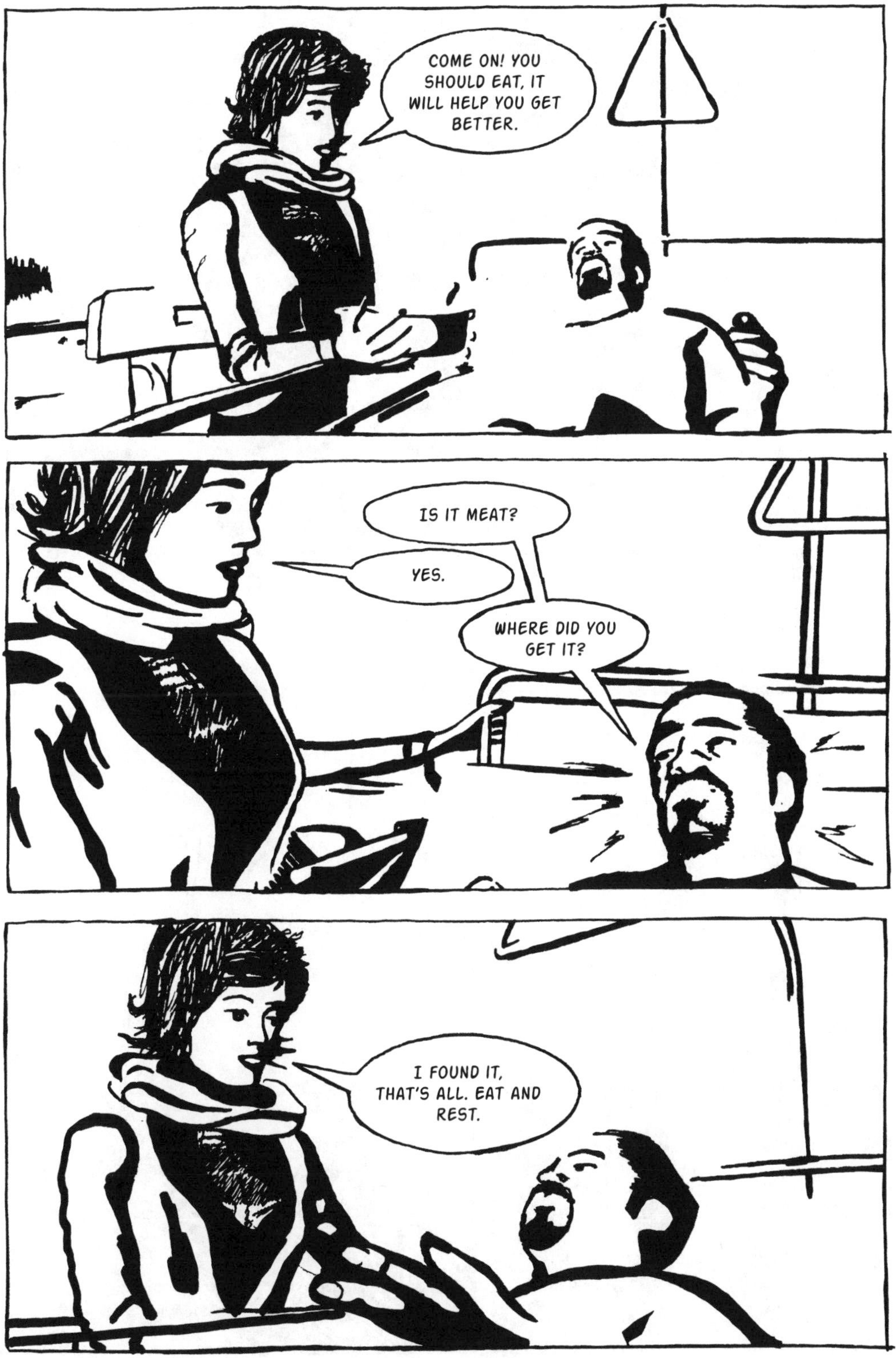
COME ON! YOU SHOULD EAT, IT WILL HELP YOU GET BETTER.
IS IT MEAT?
YES.
WHERE DID YOU GET IT?
I FOUND IT, THAT'S ALL. EAT AND REST.

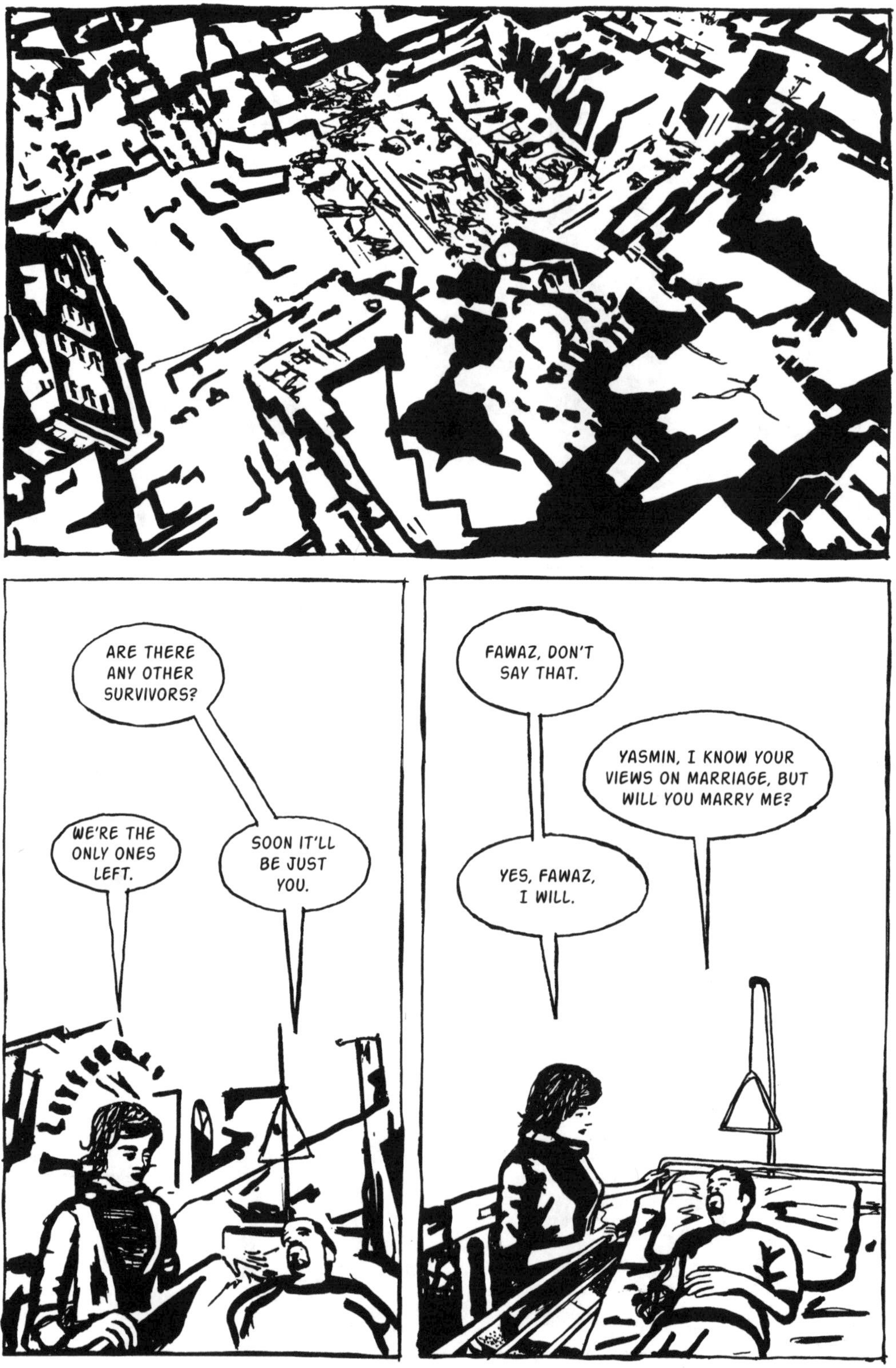
ARE THERE ANY OTHER SURVIVORS?
WE'RE THE ONLY ONES LEFT.
SOON IT'LL BE JUST YOU.
FAWAZ, DON'T SAY THAT.
YASMIN, I KNOW YOUR VIEWS ON MARRIAGE, BUT WILL YOU MARRY ME?
YES, FAWAZ, I WILL.

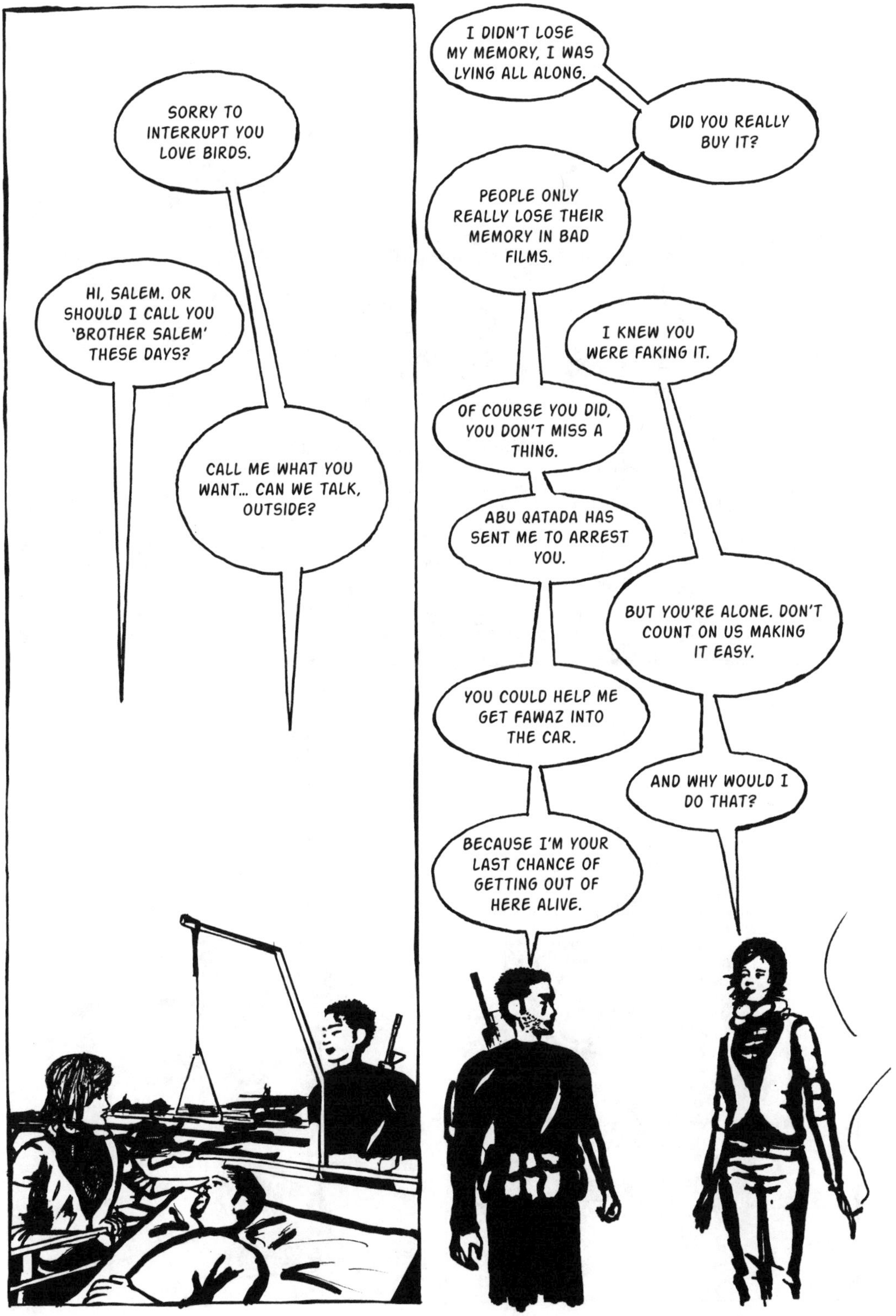
SORRY TO INTERRUPT YOU LOVE BIRDS.
HI, SALEM. OR SHOULD I CALL YOU 'BROTHER SALEM' THESE DAYS?
CALL ME WHAT YOU WANT... CAN WE TALK, OUTSIDE?
I DIDN'T LOSE MY MEMORY, I WAS LYING ALL ALONG.
DID YOU REALLY BUY IT?
PEOPLE ONLY REALLY LOSE THEIR MEMORY IN BAD FILMS.
I KNEW YOU WERE FAKING IT.
OF COURSE YOU DID, YOU DON'T MISS A THING.
ABU QATADA HAS SENT ME TO ARREST YOU.
BUT YOU'RE ALONE. DON'T COUNT ON US MAKING IT EASY.
YOU COULD HELP ME GET FAWAZ INTO THE CAR.
AND WHY WOULD I DO THAT?
BECAUSE I'M YOUR LAST CHANCE OF GETTING OUT OF HERE ALIVE.

MEANWHILE, IN ZURICH.

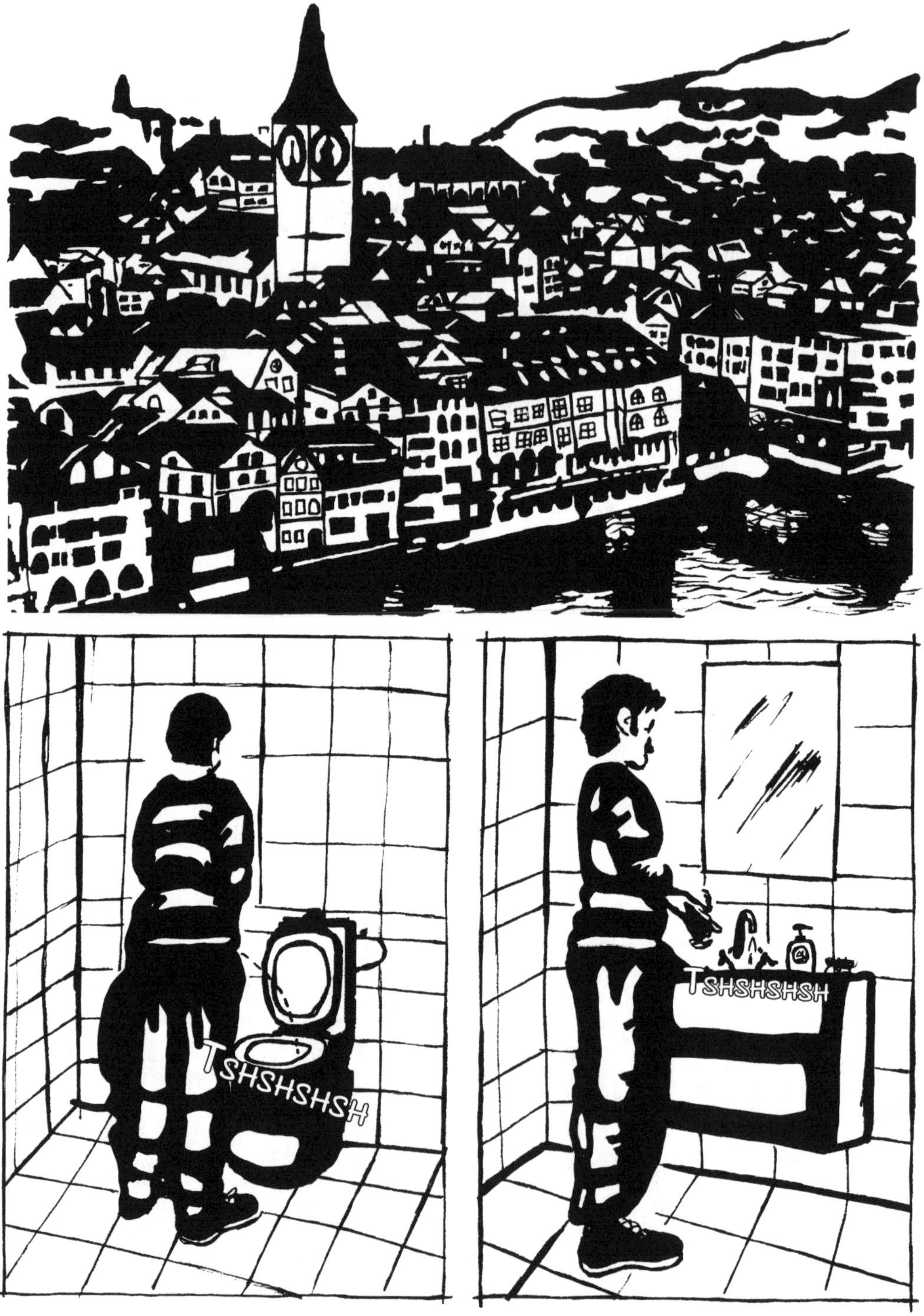
TSHSHSHSH
TSHSHSHSH

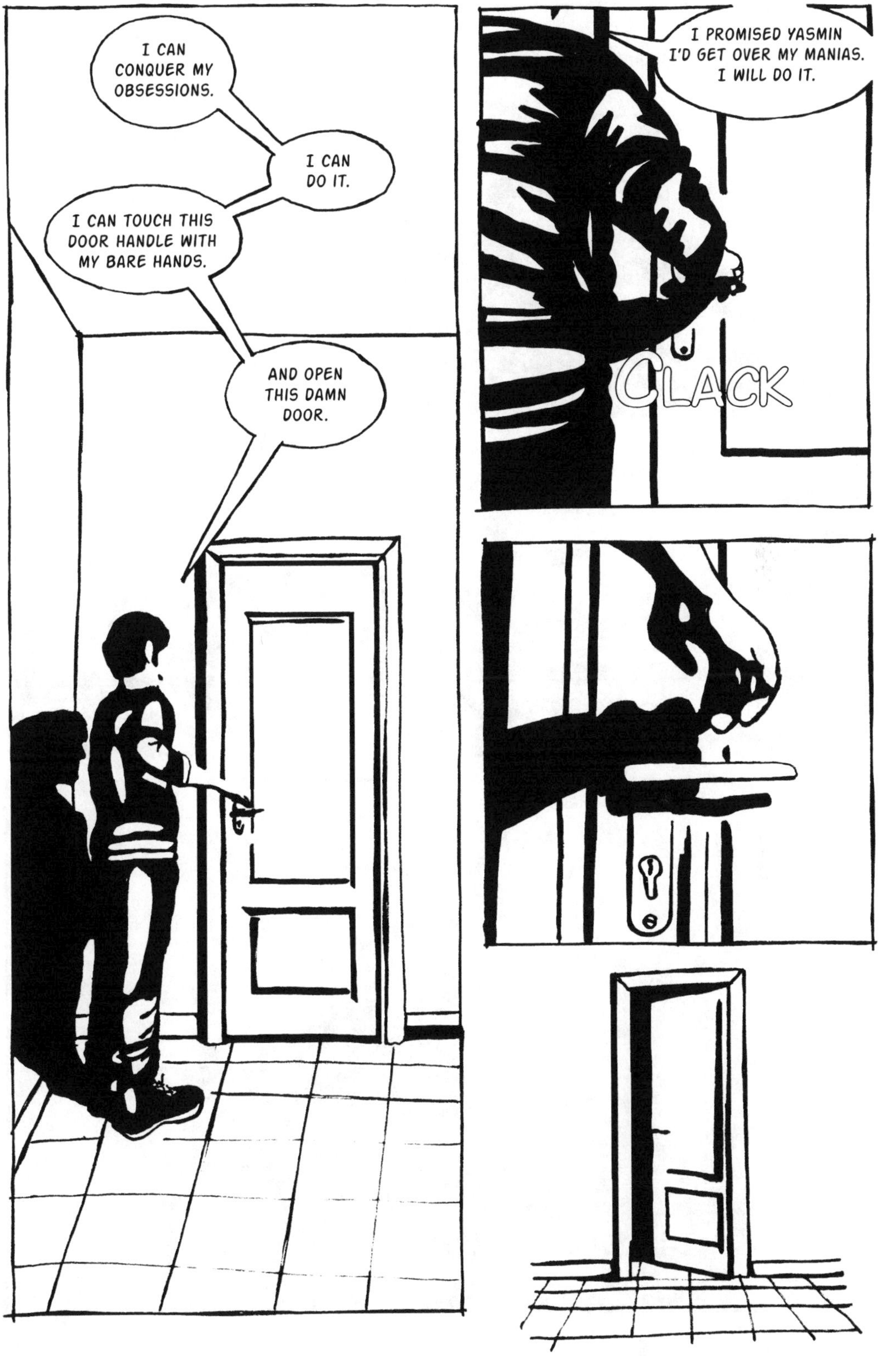
I CAN CONQUER MY OBSESSIONS.
I CAN DO IT.
I CAN TOUCH THIS DOOR HANDLE WITH MY BARE HANDS.
AND OPEN THIS DAMN DOOR.
I PROMISED YASMIN I'D GET OVER MY MANIAS. I WILL DO IT.
CLACK

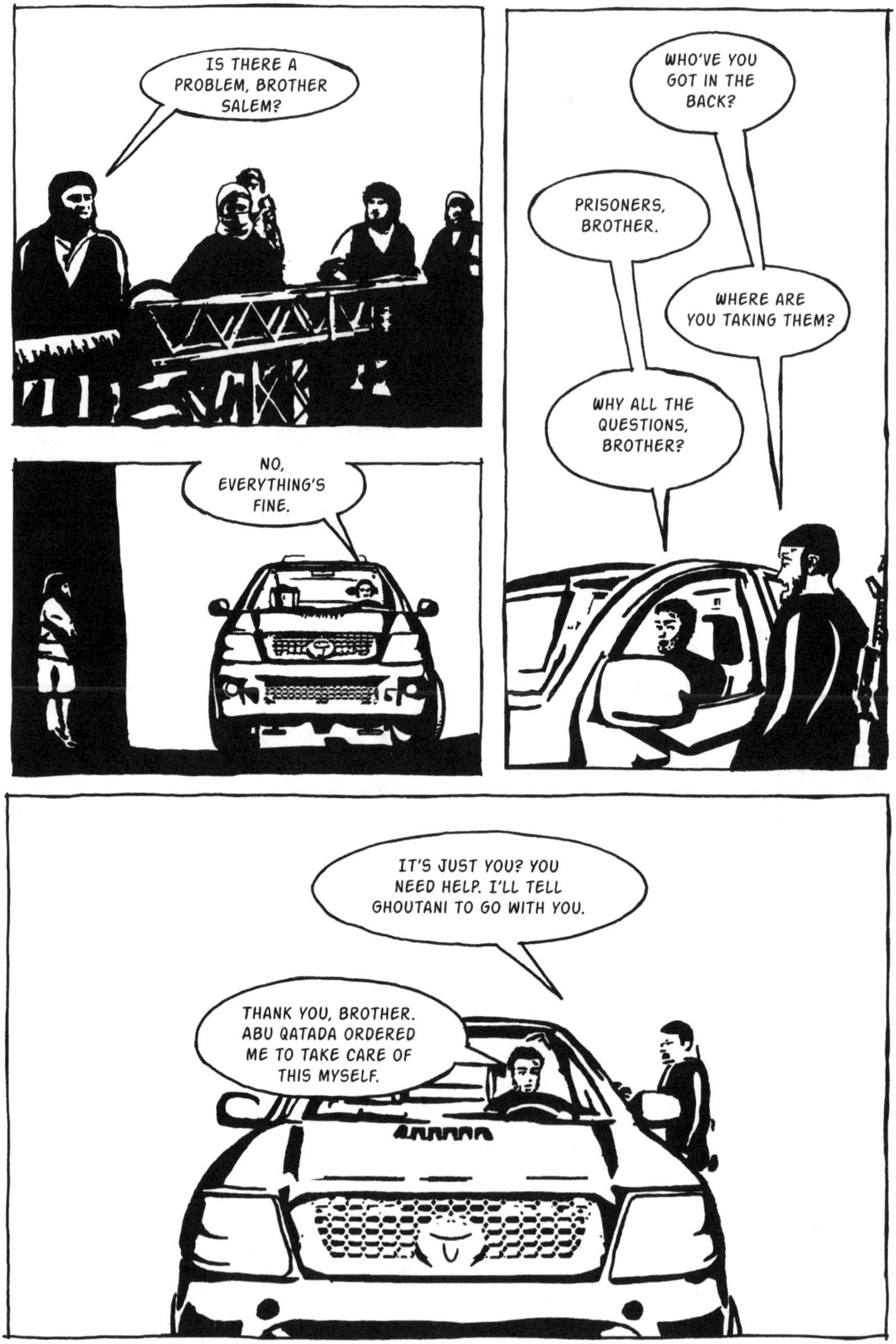
IS THERE A PROBLEM, BROTHER SALEM?
WHO'VE YOU GOT IN THE BACK?
PRISONERS, BROTHER.
WHERE ARE YOU TAKING THEM?
WHY ALL THE QUESTIONS, BROTHER?
NO, EVERYTHING'S FINE.
IT'S JUST YOU? YOU NEED HELP. I'LL TELL GHOUTANI TO GO WITH YOU.
THANK YOU, BROTHER. ABU QATADA ORDERED ME TO TAKE CARE OF THIS MYSELF.

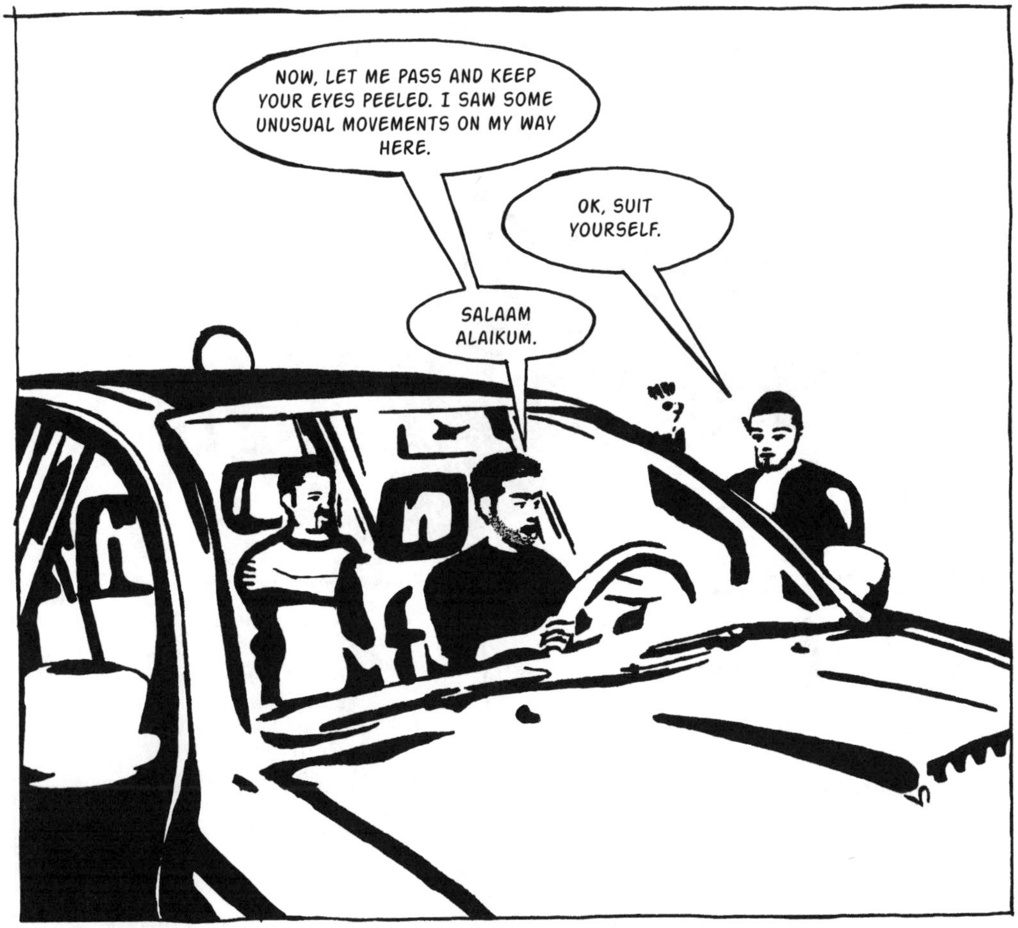
SALAAM ALAIKUM.
NOW, LET ME PASS AND KEEP YOUR EYES PEELED. I SAW SOME UNUSUAL MOVEMENTS ON MY WAY HERE.
OK, SUIT YOURSELF.

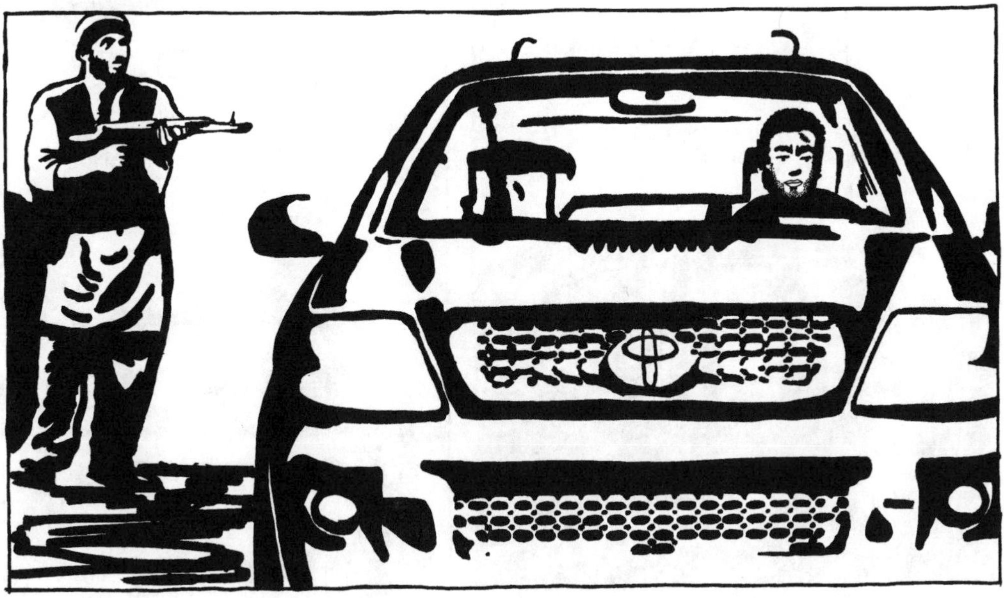

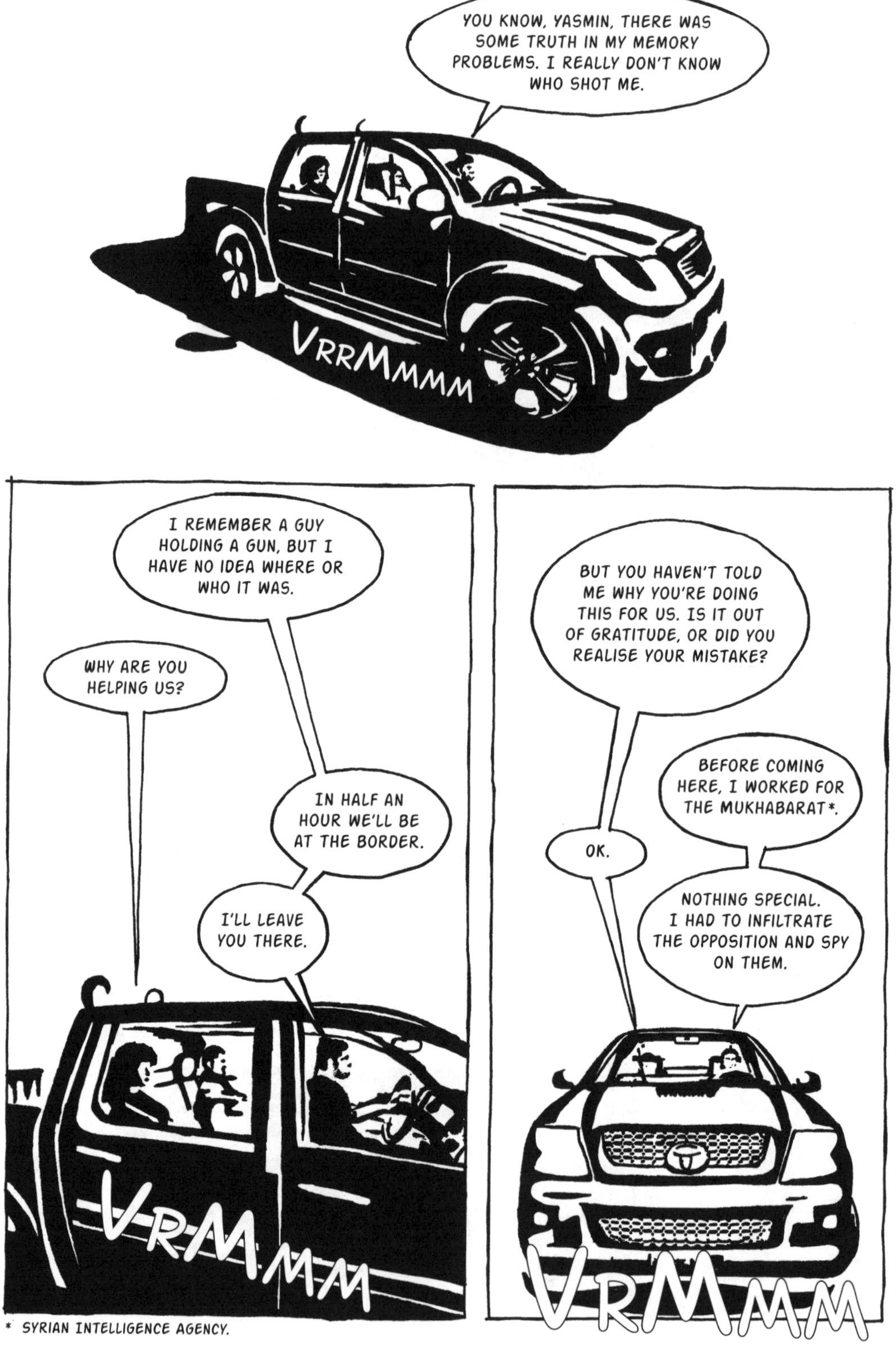
YOU KNOW, YASMIN, THERE WAS SOME TRUTH IN MY MEMORY PROBLEMS. I REALLY DON'T KNOW WHO SHOT ME.
VRRMMMM
WHY ARE YOU HELPING US?
I REMEMBER A GUY HOLDING A GUN, BUT I HAVE NO IDEA WHERE OR WHO IT WAS.
IN HALF AN HOUR WE'LL BE AT THE BORDER.
I'LL LEAVE YOU THERE.
VRMMM
BUT YOU HAVEN'T TOLD ME WHY YOU'RE DOING THIS FOR US. IS IT OUT OF GRATITUDE, OR DID YOU REALISE YOUR MISTAKE?
OK.
BEFORE COMING HERE, I WORKED FOR THE MUKHABARAT*.
NOTHING SPECIAL. I HAD TO INFILTRATE THE OPPOSITION AND SPY ON THEM.
VRMMM

* SYRIAN INTELLIGENCE AGENCY.

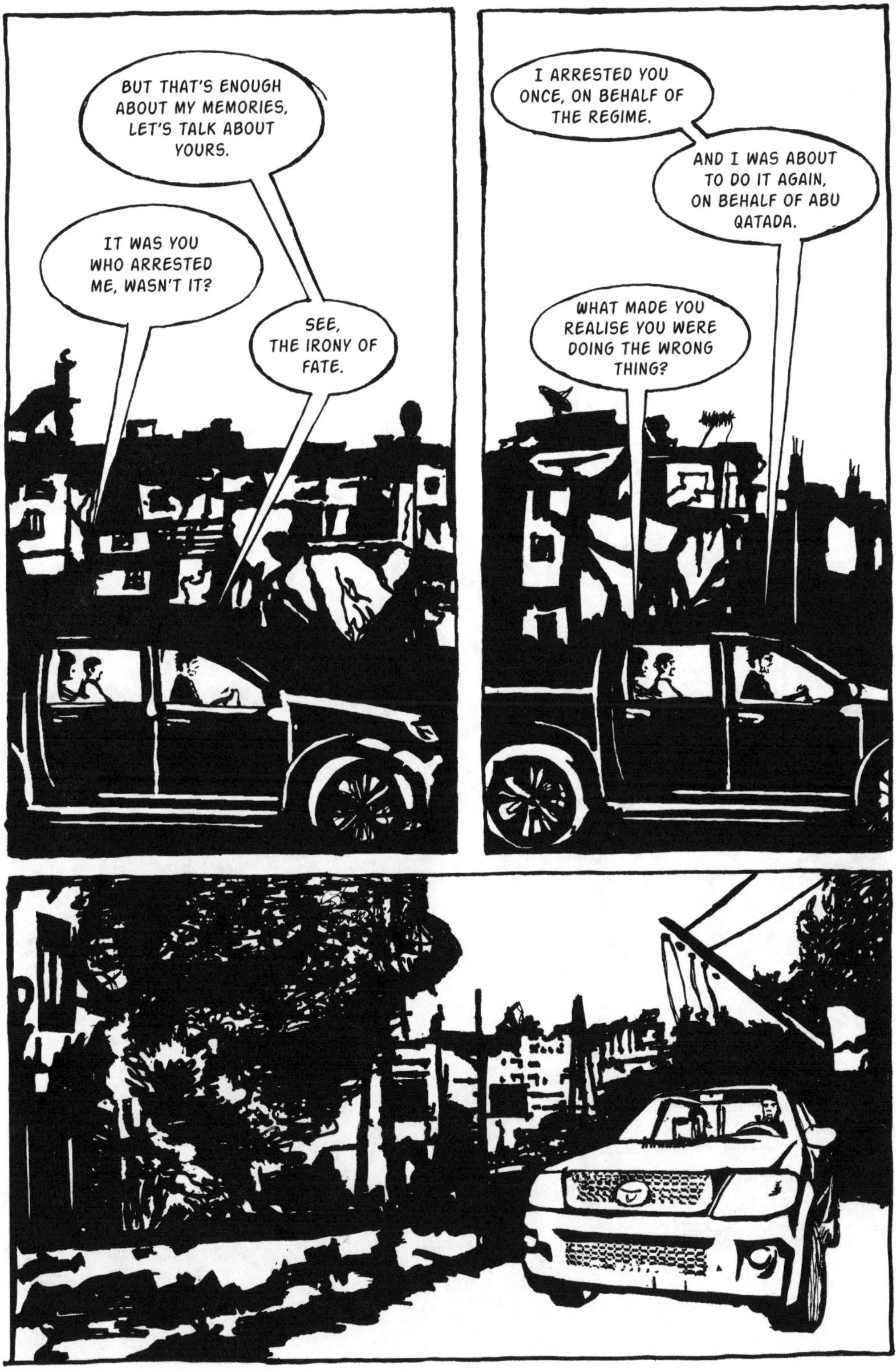
BUT THAT'S ENOUGH ABOUT MY MEMORIES, LET'S TALK ABOUT YOURS.
IT WAS YOU WHO ARRESTED ME, WASN'T IT?
SEE, THE IRONY OF FATE.
I ARRESTED YOU ONCE, ON BEHALF OF THE REGIME.
AND I WAS ABOUT TO DO IT AGAIN, ON BEHALF OF ABU QATADA.
WHAT MADE YOU REALISE YOU WERE DOING THE WRONG THING?

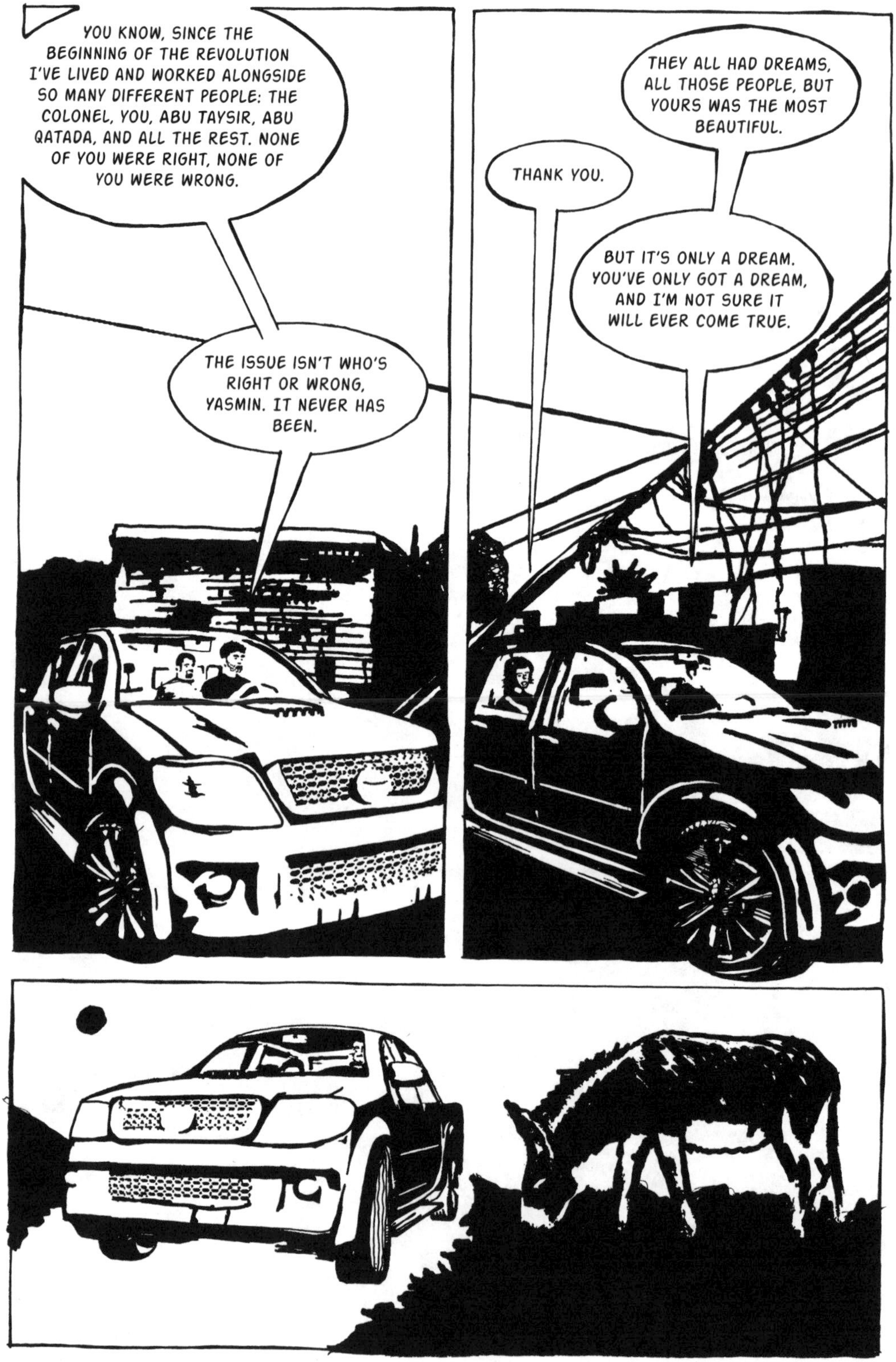
YOU KNOW, SINCE THE BEGINNING OF THE REVOLUTION I'VE LIVED AND WORKED ALONGSIDE SO MANY DIFFERENT PEOPLE: THE COLONEL, YOU, ABU TAYSIR, ABU QATADA, AND ALL THE REST. NONE OF YOU WERE RIGHT, NONE OF YOU WERE WRONG.
THE ISSUE ISN'T WHO'S RIGHT OR WRONG, YASMIN. IT NEVER HAS BEEN.
THEY ALL HAD DREAMS, ALL THOSE PEOPLE, BUT YOURS WAS THE MOST BEAUTIFUL.
THANK YOU.
BUT IT'S ONLY A DREAM. YOU'VE ONLY GOT A DREAM, AND I'M NOT SURE IT WILL EVER COME TRUE.

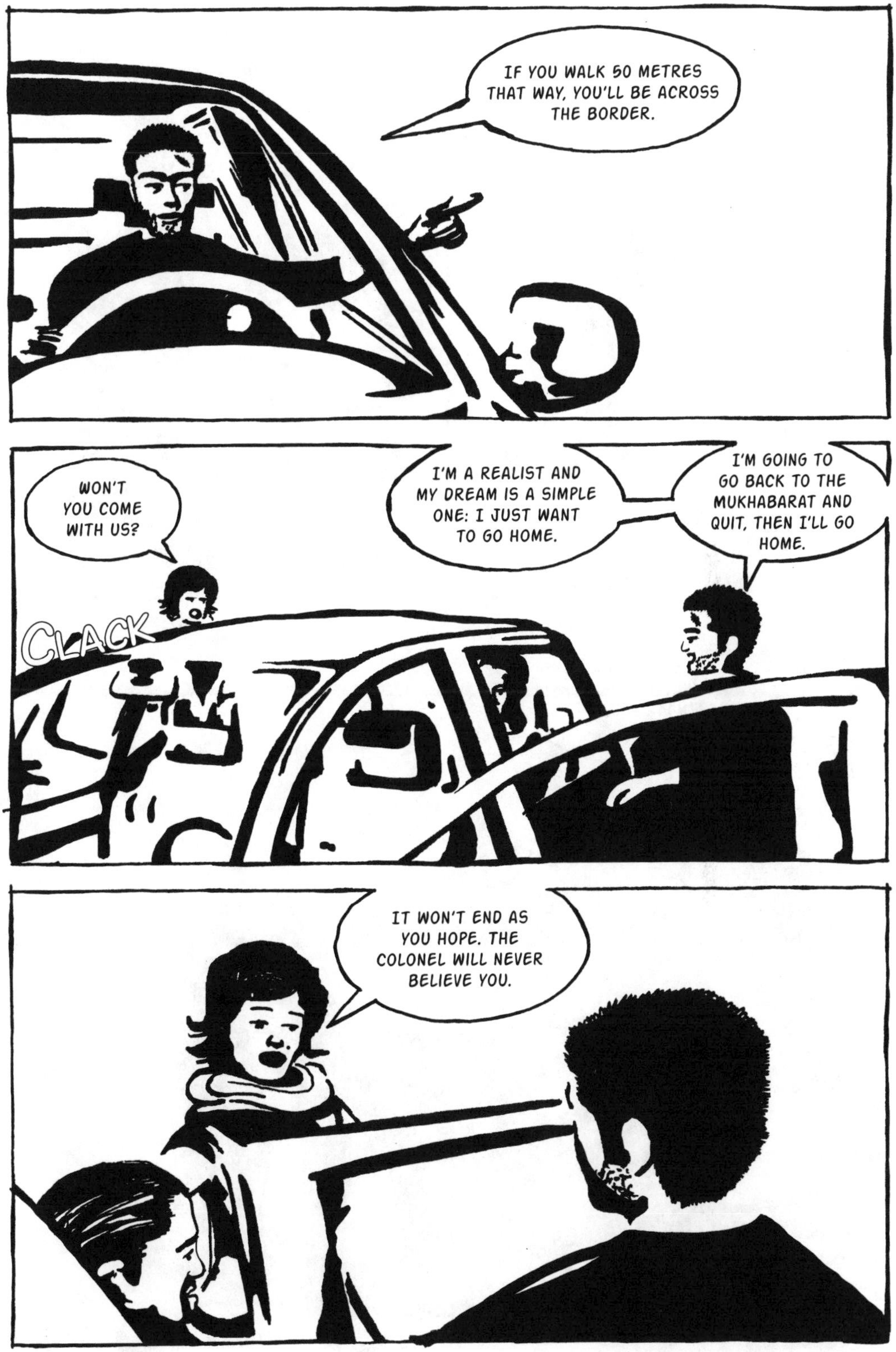
IF YOU WALK 50 METRES THAT WAY, YOU'LL BE ACROSS THE BORDER.
WON'T YOU COME WITH US?
CLACK
I'M A REALIST AND MY DREAM IS A SIMPLE ONE: I JUST WANT TO GO HOME.
I'M GOING TO GO BACK TO THE MUKHABARAT AND QUIT, THEN I'LL GO HOME.
IT WON'T END AS YOU HOPE. THE COLONEL WILL NEVER BELIEVE YOU.

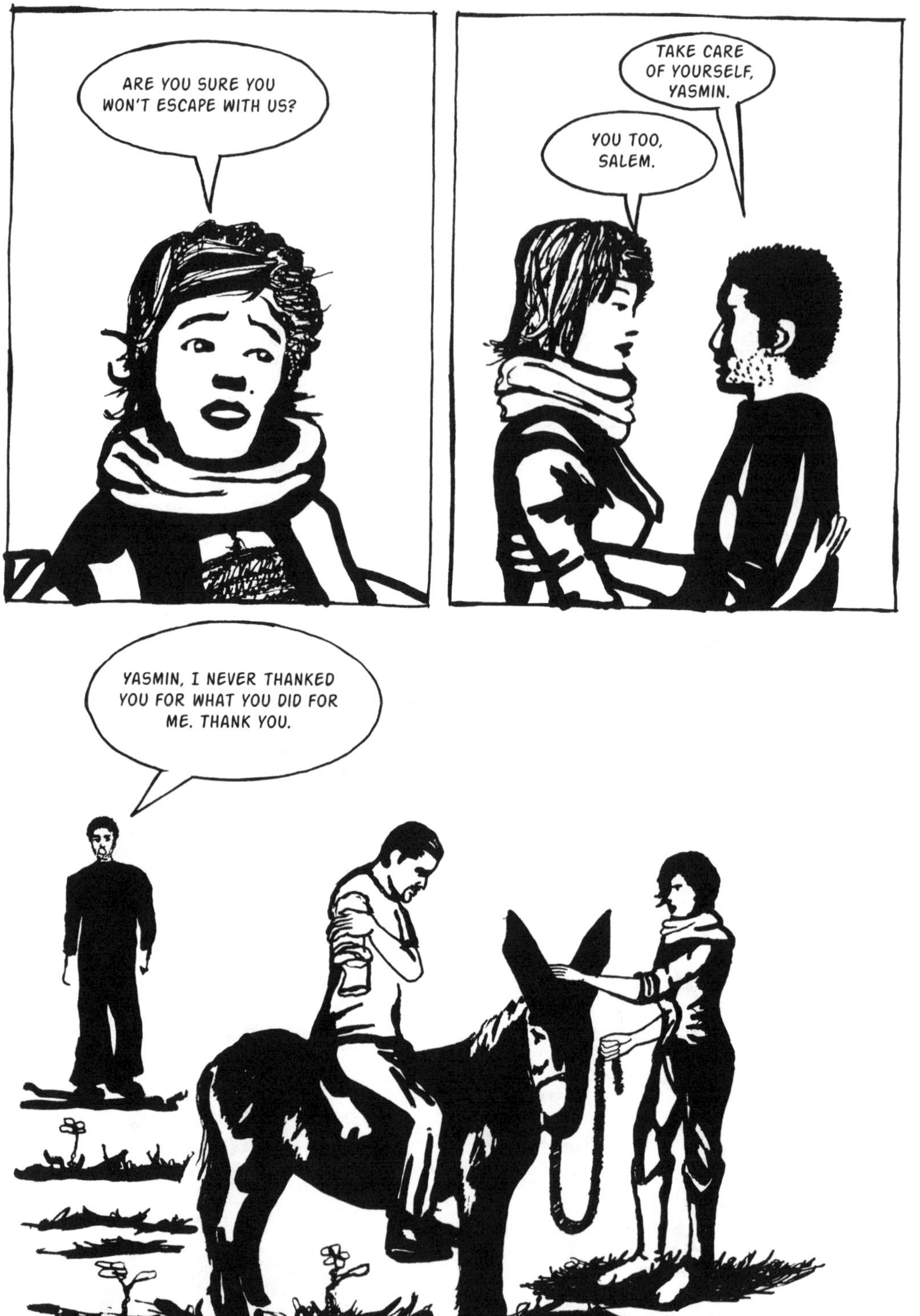
ARE YOU SURE YOU WON'T ESCAPE WITH US?
TAKE CARE OF YOURSELF, YASMIN.
YOU TOO, SALEM.
YASMIN, I NEVER THANKED YOU FOR WHAT YOU DID FOR ME. THANK YOU.

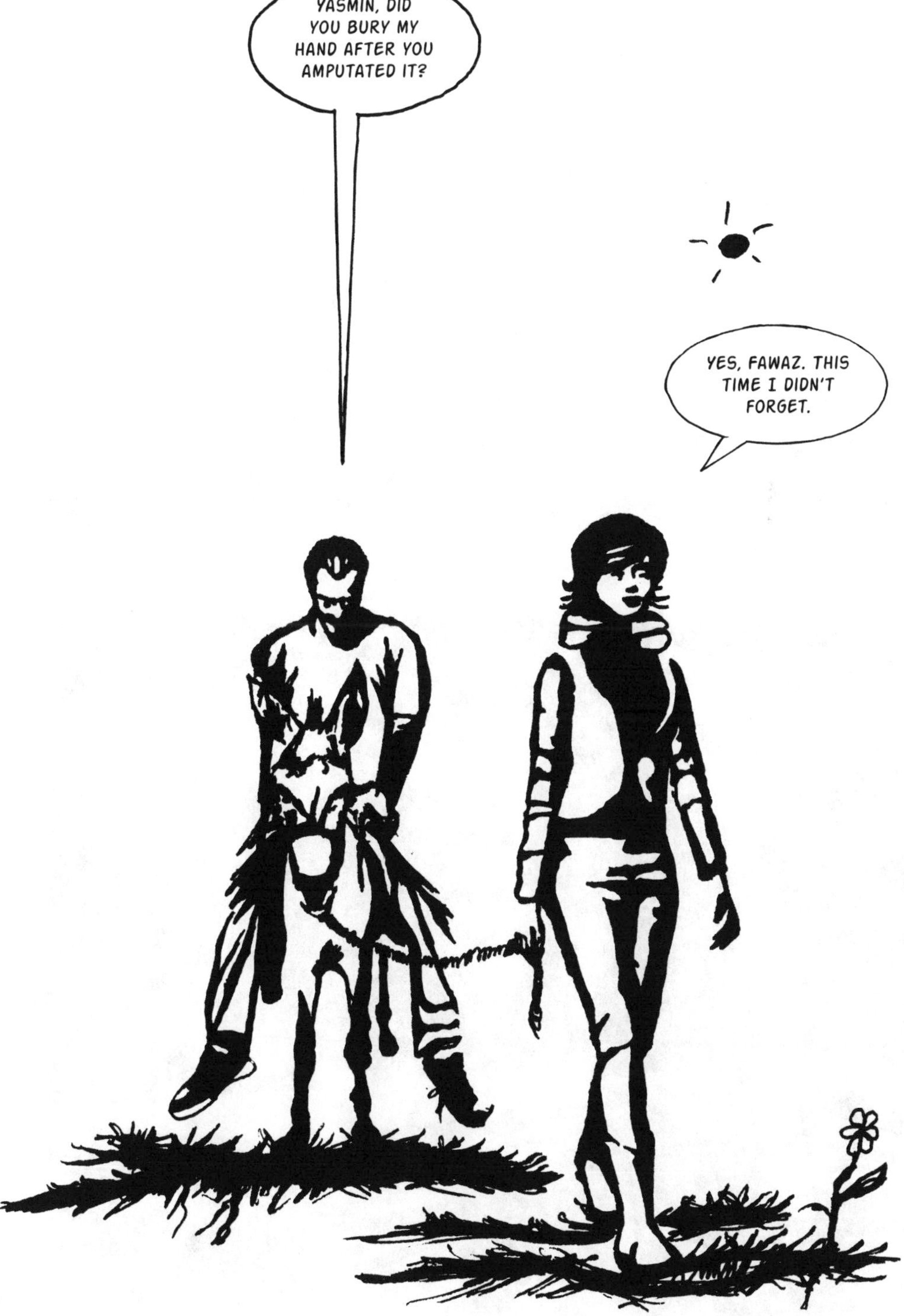
YASMIN, DID YOU BURY MY HAND AFTER YOU AMPUTATED IT?
YES, FAWAZ. THIS TIME I DIDN'T FORGET.

ONE DAY LATER: ANOTHER 291 KILLED.

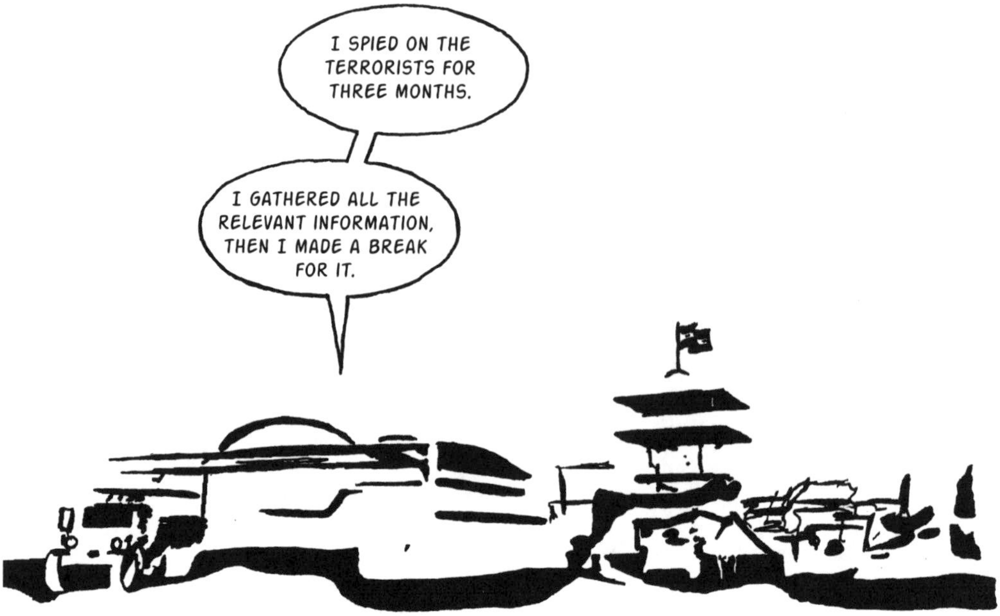

I SPIED ON THE TERRORISTS FOR THREE MONTHS.
I GATHERED ALL THE RELEVANT INFORMATION, THEN I MADE A BREAK FOR IT.

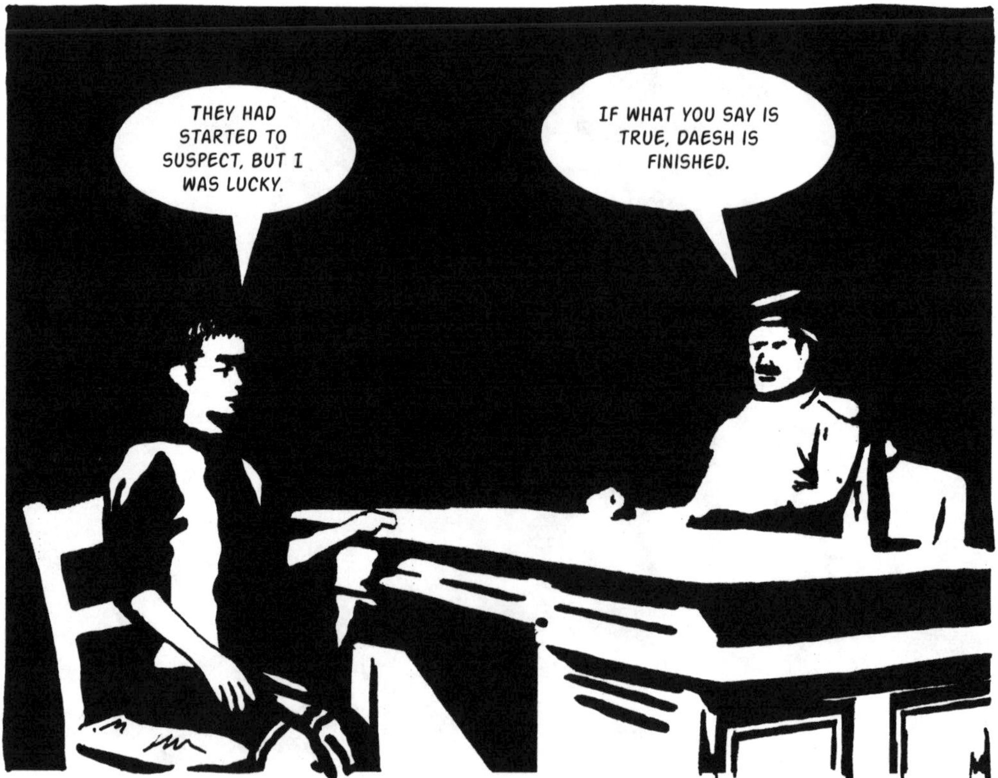

THEY HAD STARTED TO SUSPECT, BUT I WAS LUCKY.
IF WHAT YOU SAY IS TRUE, DAESH IS FINISHED.

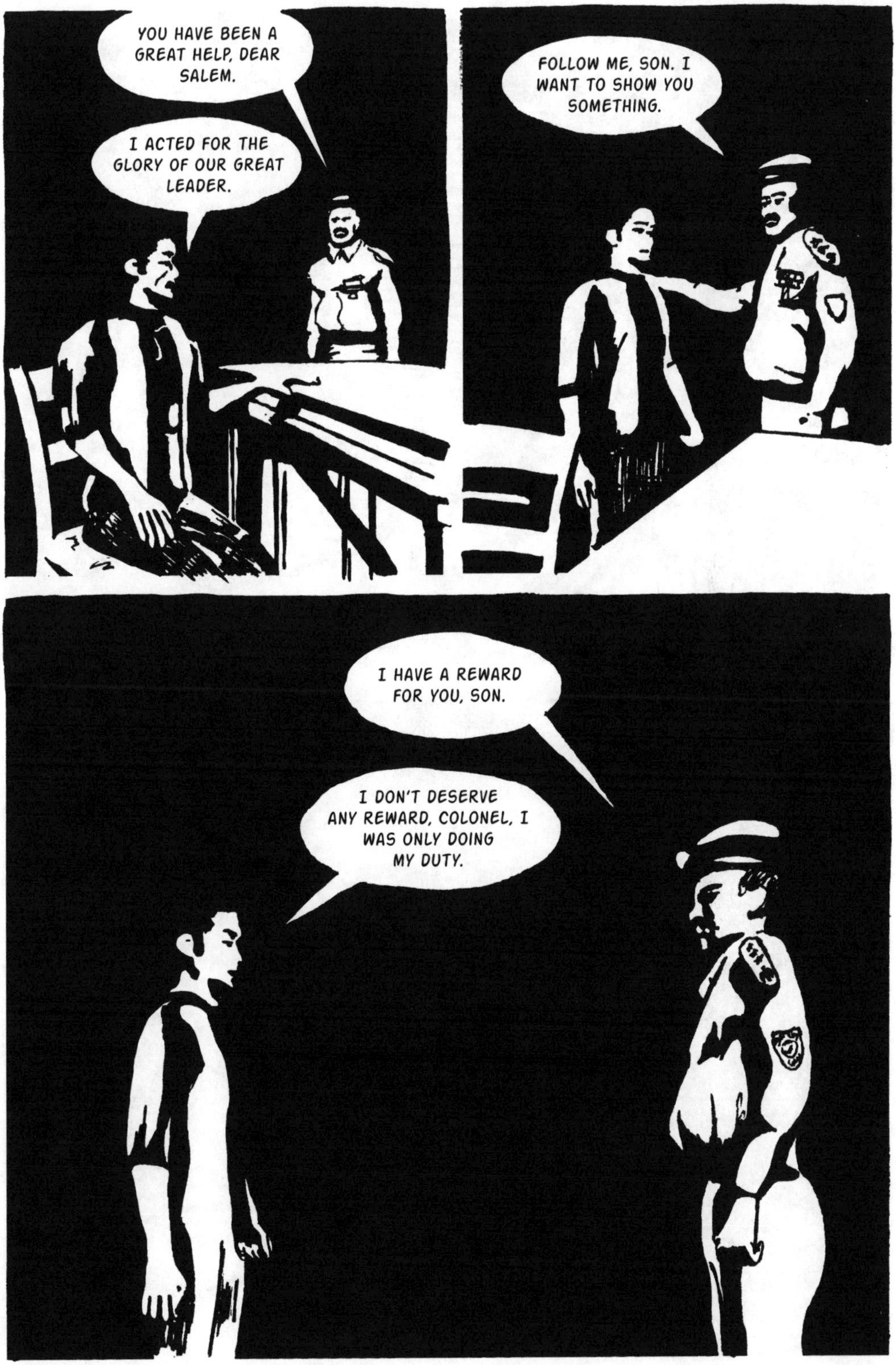
YOU HAVE BEEN A GREAT HELP, DEAR SALEM.
I ACTED FOR THE GLORY OF OUR GREAT LEADER.
FOLLOW ME, SON. I WANT TO SHOW YOU SOMETHING.
I HAVE A REWARD FOR YOU, SON.
I DON'T DESERVE ANY REWARD, COLONEL, I WAS ONLY DOING MY DUTY.

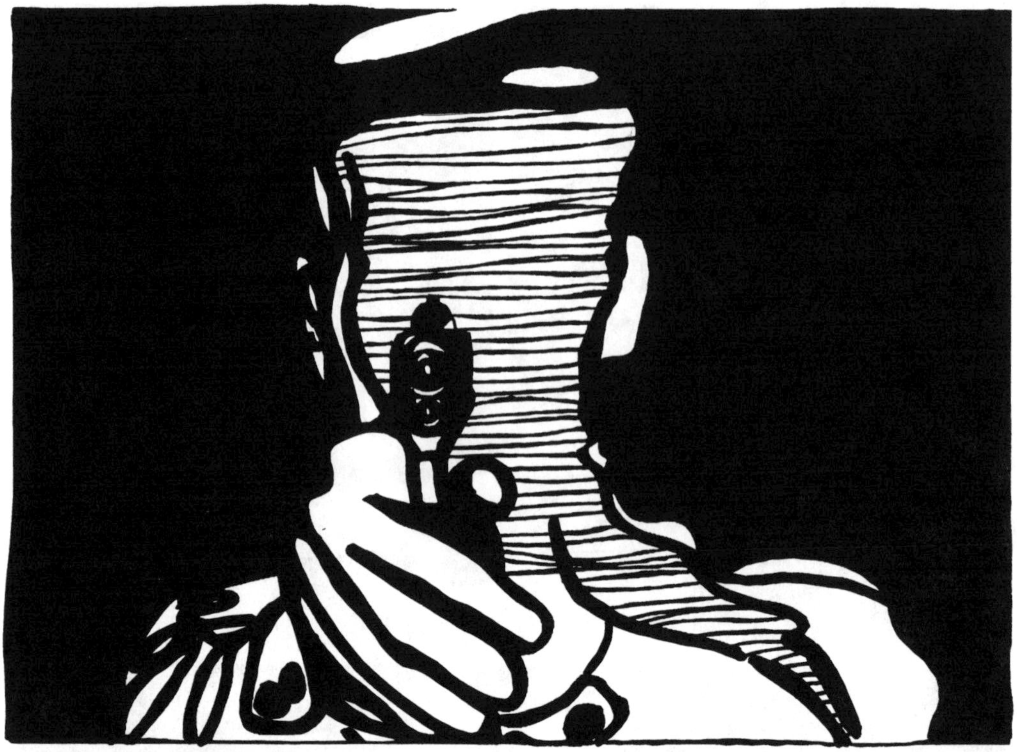

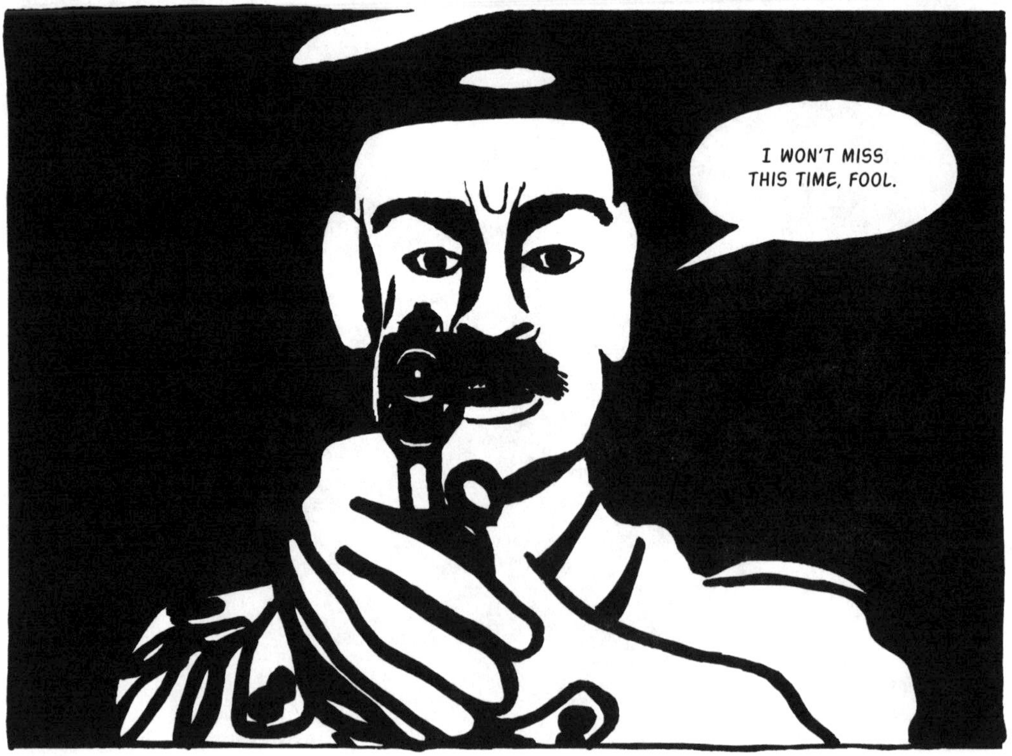
I WON'T MISS THIS TIME, FOOL.

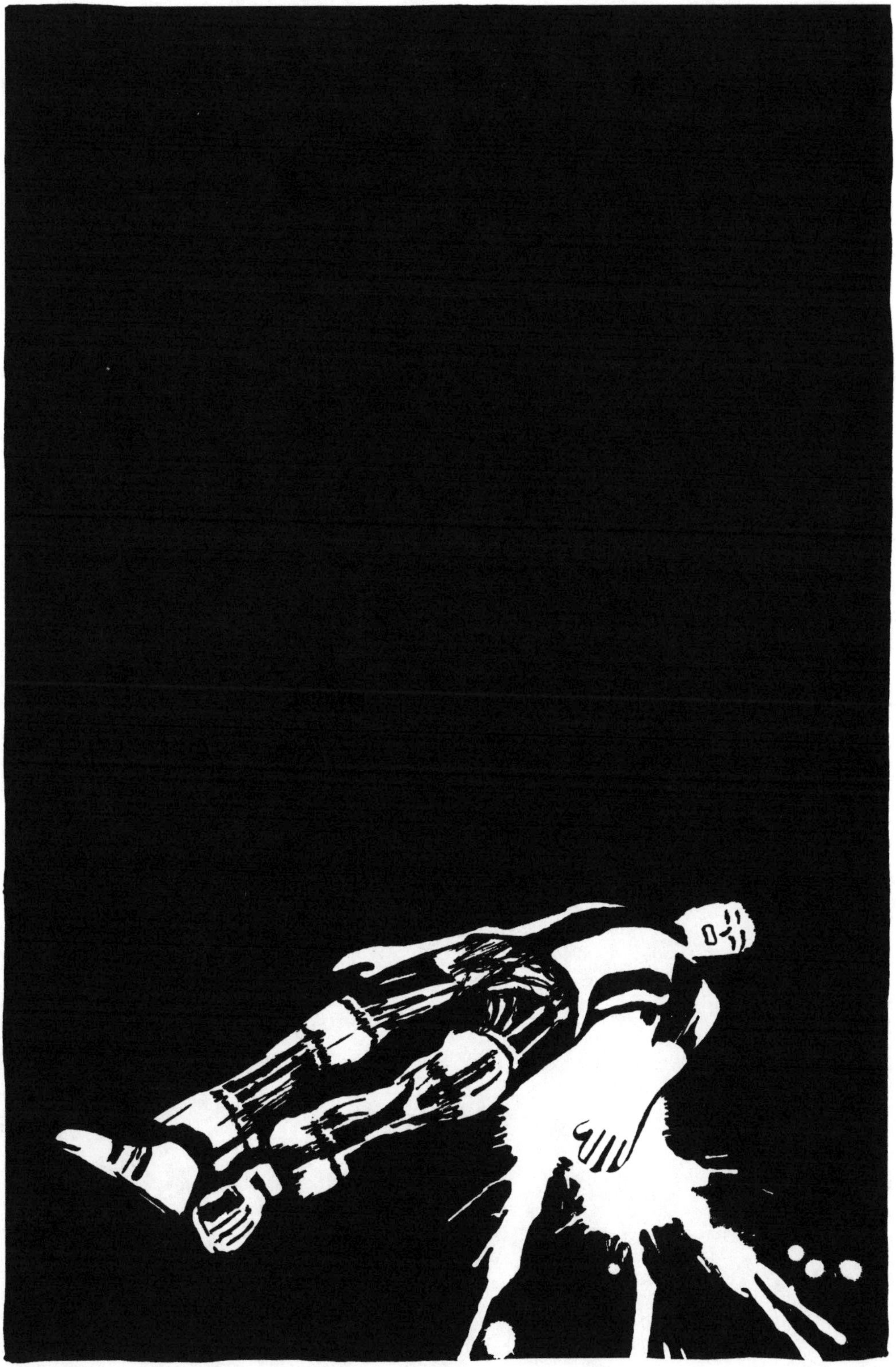

Chapter 5

SPRING, AGAIN

REFUGEE CAMP, SYRIAN-TURKISH BORDER.
THREE MONTHS LATER: ANOTHER 12,569 PEOPLE KILLED.

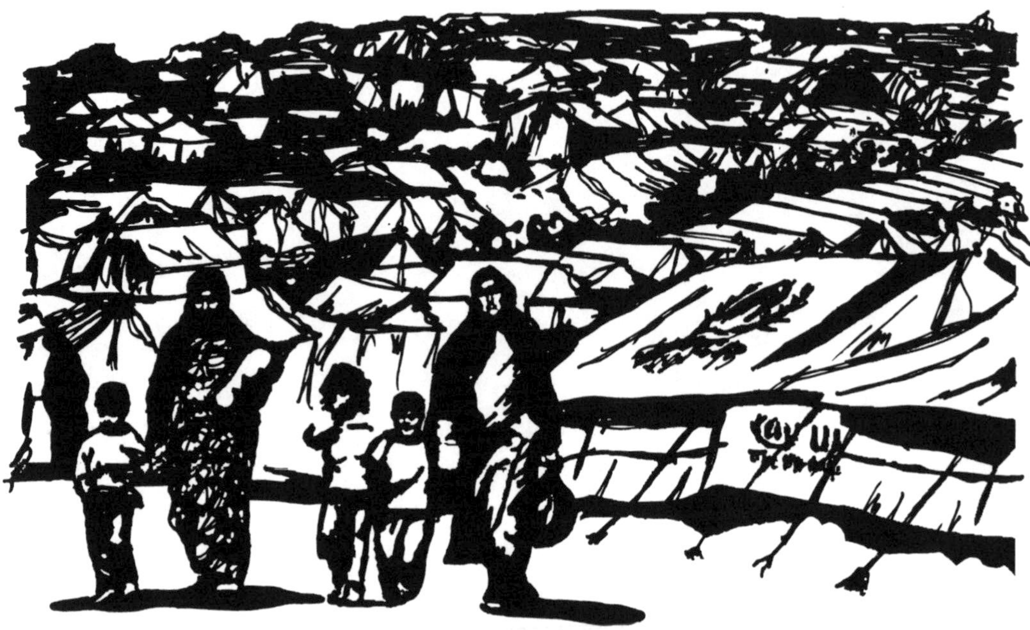

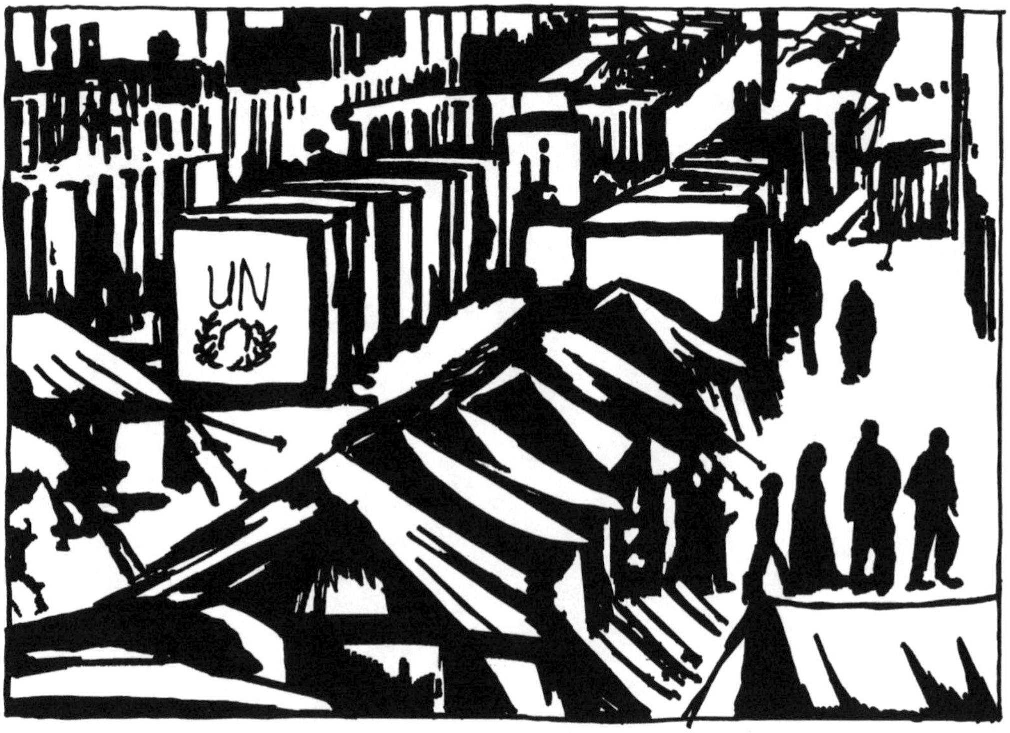
UN

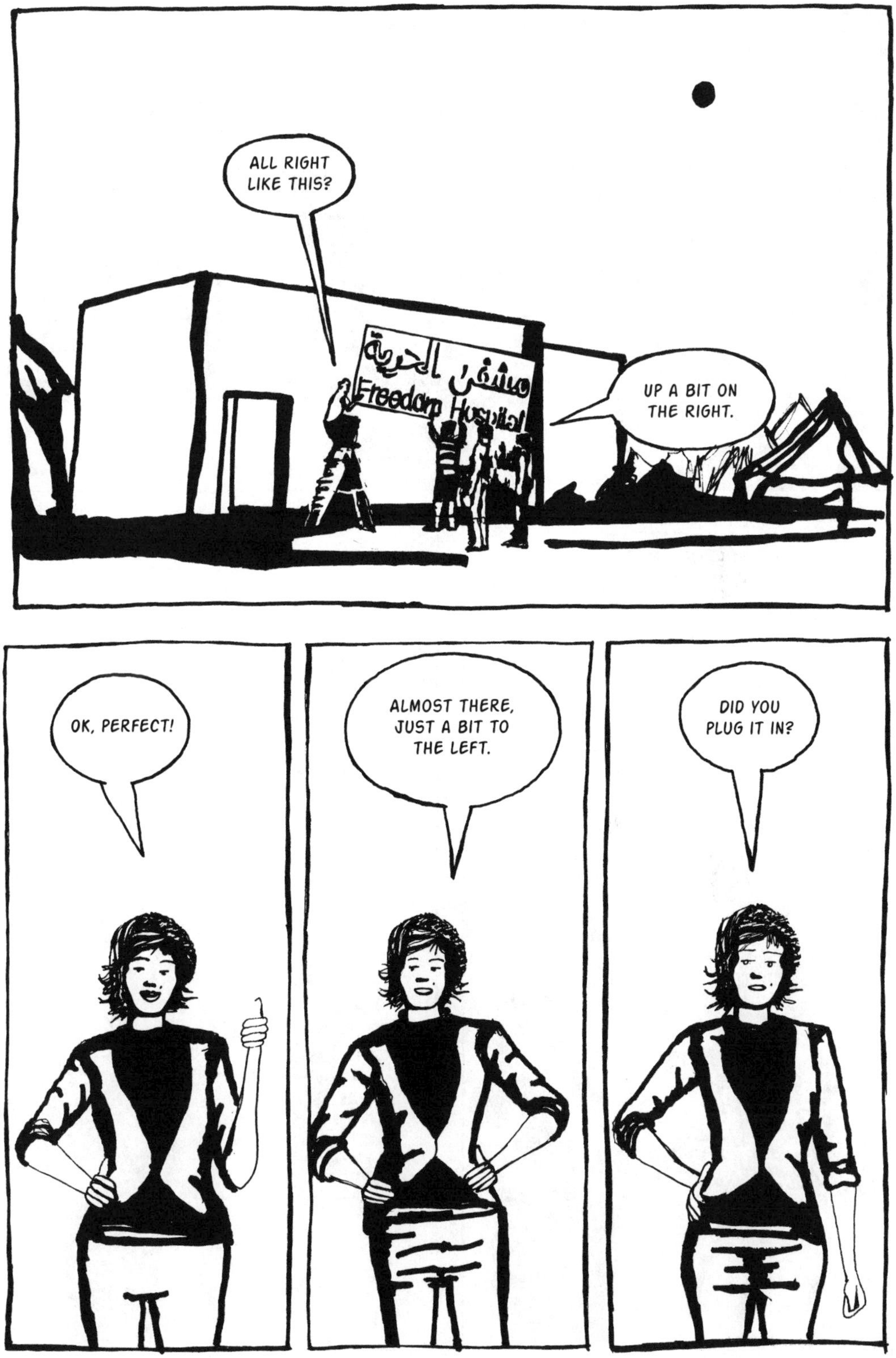
ALL RIGHT LIKE THIS?
Freedom Hospital
UP A BIT ON THE RIGHT.
OK, PERFECT!
ALMOST THERE, JUST A BIT TO THE LEFT.
DID YOU PLUG IT IN?

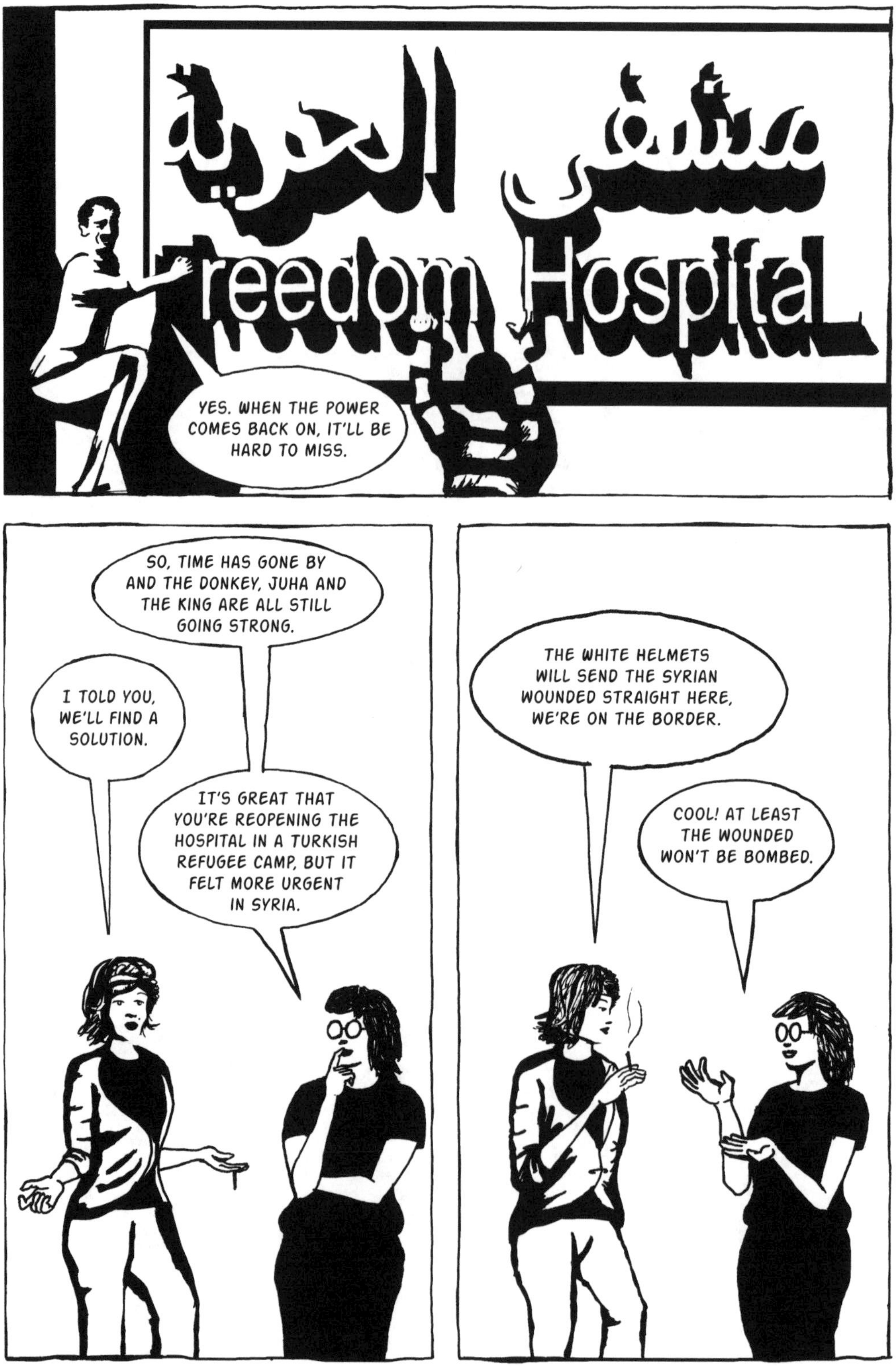
مشفى الحرية
reedom Hospital
YES. WHEN THE POWER COMES BACK ON, IT'LL BE HARD TO MISS.
SO, TIME HAS GONE BY AND THE DONKEY, JUHA AND THE KING ARE ALL STILL GOING STRONG.
I TOLD YOU, WE'LL FIND A SOLUTION.
IT'S GREAT THAT YOU'RE REOPENING THE HOSPITAL IN A TURKISH REFUGEE CAMP, BUT IT FELT MORE URGENT IN SYRIA.
THE WHITE HELMETS WILL SEND THE SYRIAN WOUNDED STRAIGHT HERE, WE'RE ON THE BORDER.
COOL! AT LEAST THE WOUNDED WON'T BE BOMBED.

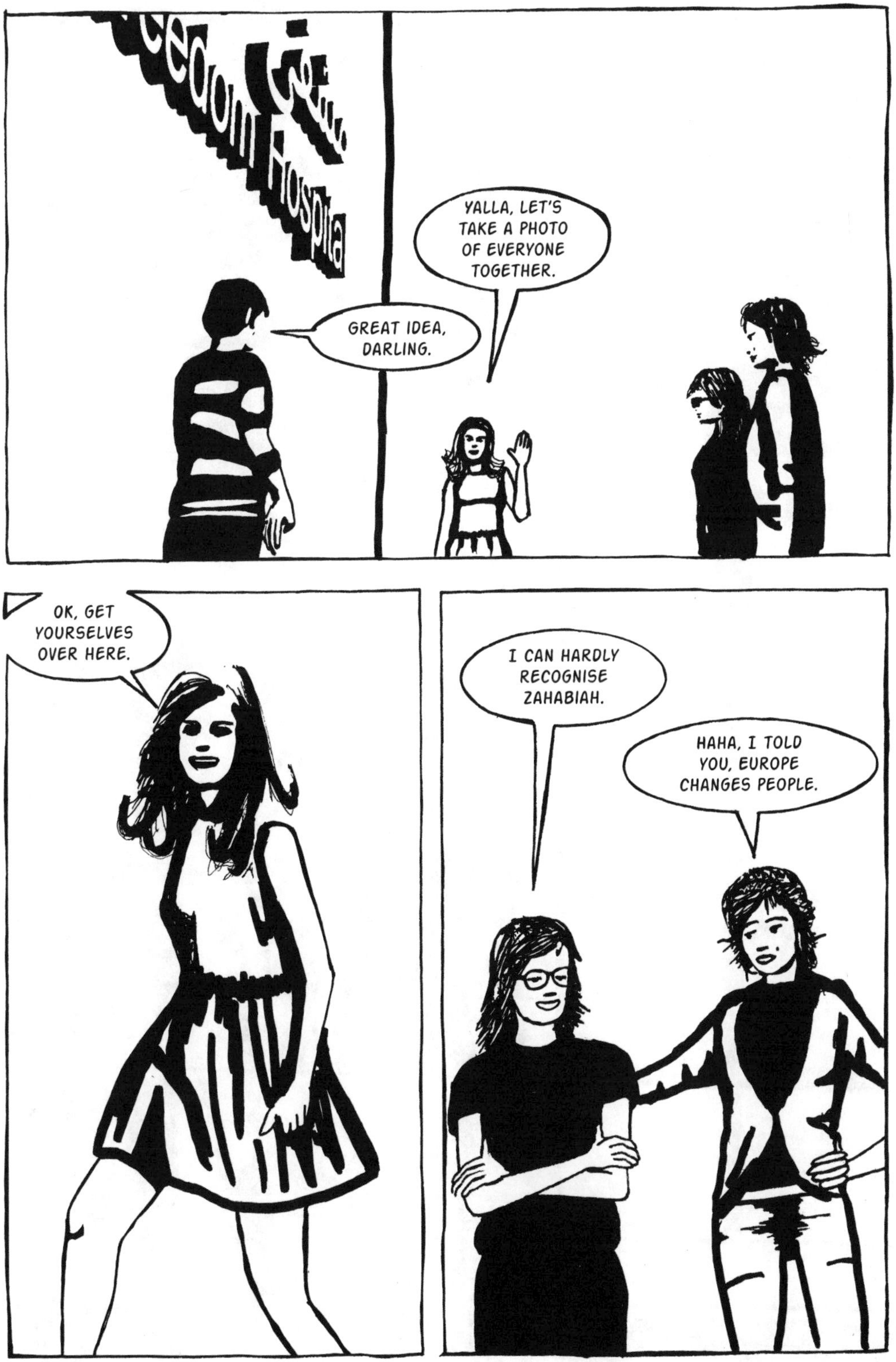
YALLA, LET'S TAKE A PHOTO OF EVERYONE TOGETHER.
GREAT IDEA, DARLING.
OK, GET YOURSELVES OVER HERE.
I CAN HARDLY RECOGNISE ZAHABIAH.
HAHA, I TOLD YOU, EUROPE CHANGES PEOPLE.

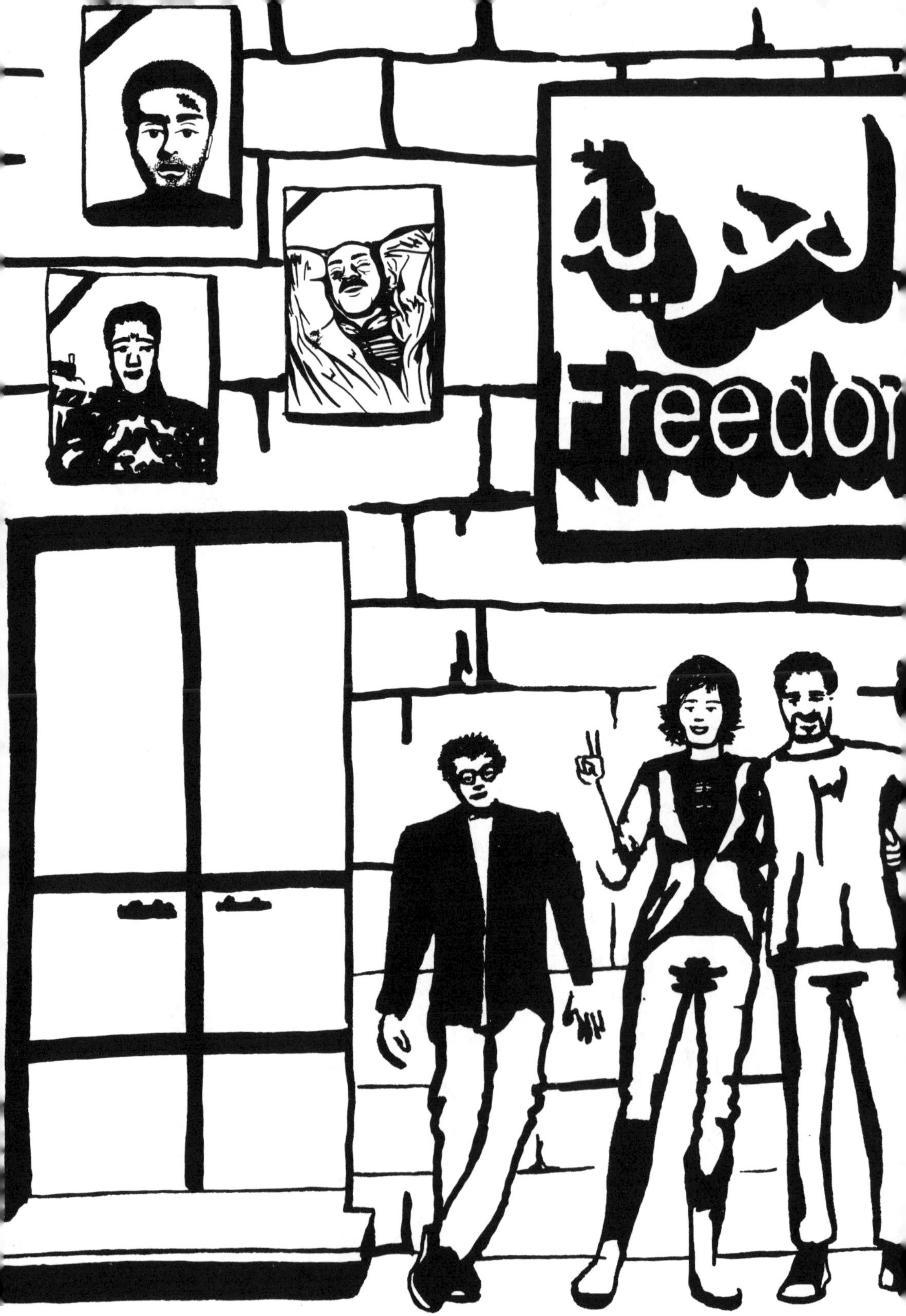
Freedo

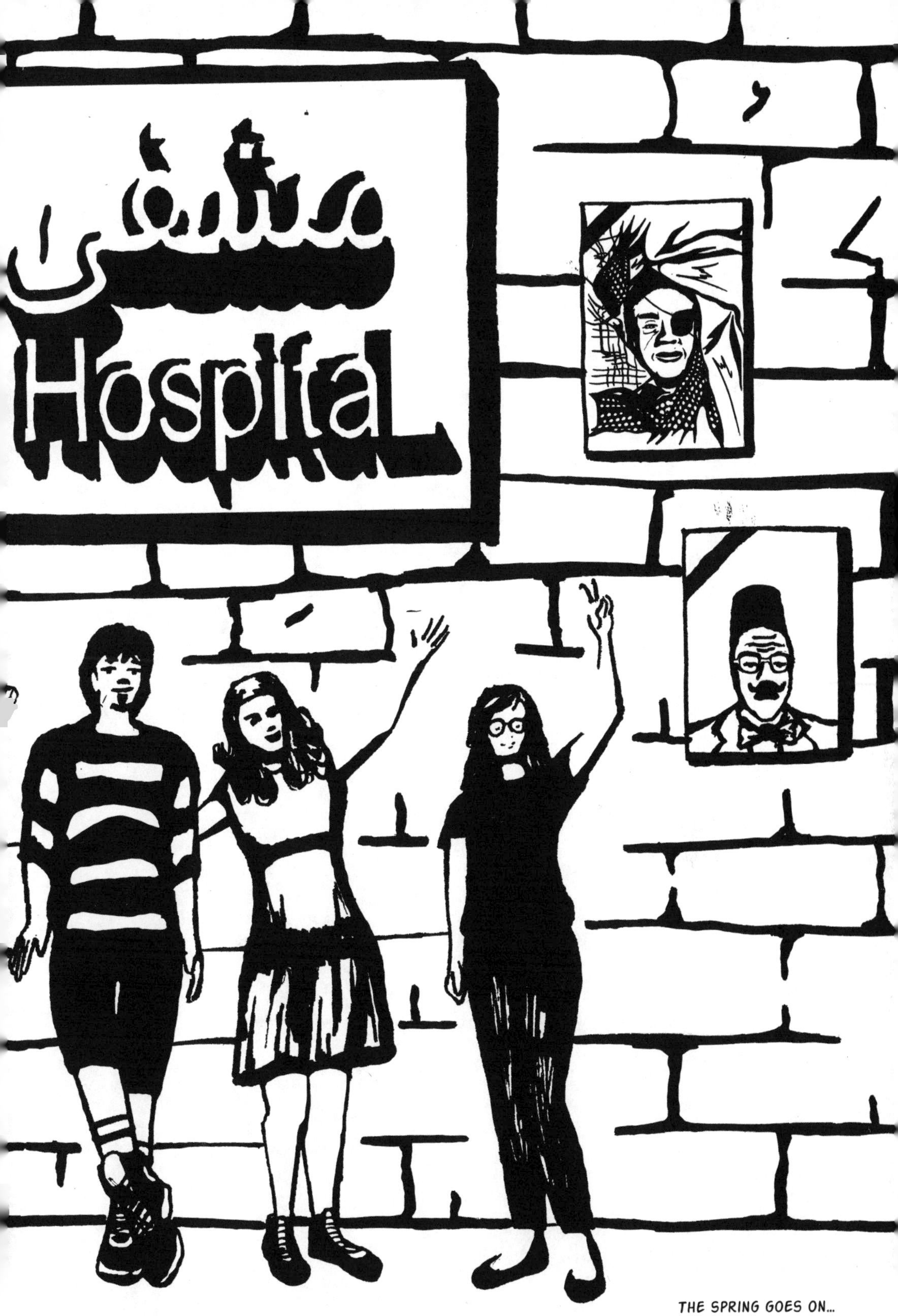
مستشفى
Hospital

THE SPRING GOES ON...

POSTSCRIPT

When I fled Syria, on 17 August 2011, my first destination was Egypt. A few months in, I was in a taxi and the driver started asking me questions about Syria. He didn't understand the first thing about what was happening, and he even asked me if Bashar al-Assad was on the side of the Free Syrian Army... I realised that the absence of a free press in Syria had led to a massive lack of understanding, and while official Syrian media outfits were transmitting nothing but pro-Assad propaganda, pro-rebel media were no less guilty of churning out propaganda of their own. When I arrived in France in 2012, I saw that people's confusion about the situation in Syria was even greater.

I don't think anyone can capture exactly what is happening in Syria, even those on the ground right now. I decided to write *Freedom Hospital* to reflect the situation as I see it, not to explain it. I haven't tried to be neutral, and I can't claim to be depicting an exact reality, but I needed to give voice to everything that had been stuck in my throat since the beginning of the revolution.

I began this project in 2012 and it has taken nearly four years to complete. I chose to blend fiction and fact to avoid having to explain what was true or false. I'm interested in showing how events unfolded in a personal way. To tell Yasmin's story, and the stories of the other protagonists, I drew on real events that I witnessed with my own eyes before leaving Syria, and on the lived experiences of people I know. Some of my friends and acquaintances have stayed in Syria, others have since left, like me, and are now living in exile, in Europe or the United States.

For the purposes of the book, I invented a small rural town, Houria, which is an amalgam of many towns in the north of Syria, with a mosque presiding over the central square. It is on this square that Yasmin set up her clandestine hospital. The layout of the roads and buildings that I've drawn can be found in most towns and villages in Syria. Finally, I integrated images and text taken directly from the news into the story. For instance, the sequence on pages 154–5 is taken from a YouTube video streamed after a bombardment. I also used photos taken during demonstrations, extracts from speeches, and the propaganda slogans used by different factions in the course of the conflict.

Hamid Sulaiman
February 2016

ACKNOWLEDGEMENTS

This book has been selected to receive financial assistance from English PEN's Writers in Translation programme supported by Bloomberg and Arts Council England. English PEN exists to promote literature and its understanding, uphold writers' freedoms around the world, campaign against the persecution and imprisonment of writers for stating their views, and promote the friendly co-operation of writers and free exchange of ideas.

Each year, a dedicated committee of professionals selects books that are translated into English from a wide variety of foreign languages. We award grants to UK publishers to help translate, promote, market and champion these titles. Our aim is to celebrate books of outstanding literary quality, which have a clear link to the PEN charter and promote free speech and intercultural understanding.

In 2011, Writers in Translation's outstanding work and contribution to diversity in the UK literary scene was recognised by Arts Council England. English PEN was awarded a threefold increase in funding to develop its support for world writing in translation.

www.englishpen.org